UNITED STATES HOLOCAUST MEMORIAL MUSEUM

PUBLISHED IN ASSOCIATION WITH
THE UNITED STATES HOLOCAUST MEMORIAL MUSEUM

JEWISH HONOR COURTS

Revenge, Retribution, and Reconciliation in Europe and Israel after the Holocaust

EDITED BY
LAURA JOCKUSCH
GABRIEL N. FINDER

WAYNE STATE UNIVERSITY PRESS
DETROIT

© 2015 by Wayne State University Press, Detroit, Michigan 48201.
All rights reserved. No part of this book may be reproduced
without formal permission. Manufactured in the United States of America.

ISBN 978-0-8143-3877-3 (paperback)
ISBN 978-0-8143-3878-0 (e-book)

Library of Congress Control Number: 2014951468

The assertions, arguments, and conclusions contained herein are those
of the author or other contributors. They do not necessarily reflect the
opinions of the United States Holocaust Memorial Museum.

Designed and typeset by Bryce Schimanski
Composed in Adobe Caslon Pro

CONTENTS

Acknowledgments   vii

Introduction: Revenge, Retribution, and Reconciliation in the Postwar Jewish World   1
LAURA JOCKUSCH AND GABRIEL N. FINDER

1. Why Punish Collaborators?   29
DAVID ENGEL

2. Rehabilitating the Past? Jewish Honor Courts in Allied-Occupied Germany   49
LAURA JOCKUSCH

3. Judenrat on Trial: Postwar Polish Jewry Sits in Judgment of Its Wartime Leadership   83
GABRIEL N. FINDER

4. An Unresolved Controversy: The Jewish Honor Court in the Netherlands, 1946–1950   107
IDO DE HAAN

5. *Jurys d'honneur*: The Stakes and Limits of Purges Among Jews in France After Liberation   137
SIMON PEREGO

6. Viennese Jewish Functionaries on Trial: Accusations, Defense Strategies, and Hidden Agendas   165
HELGA EMBACHER

CONTENTS

7. "The Lesser Evil" of Jewish Collaboration? The Absence of a Jewish Honor Court in Postwar Belgium   197
   VEERLE VANDEN DAELEN AND NICO WOUTERS

8. Jews Accusing Jews: Denunciations of Alleged Collaborators in Jewish Honor Courts   225
   KATARZYNA PERSON

9. "I'm Going to the Oven Because I Wouldn't Give Myself to Him": The Role of Gender in the Polish Jewish Civic Court   247
   EWA KOŹMIŃSKA-FREJLAK

10. Revenge and Reconciliation: Early Israeli Literature and the Dilemma of Jewish Collaborators with the Nazis   279
    GALI DRUCKER BAR-AM

11. Changing Legal Perceptions of "Nazi Collaborators" in Israel, 1950–1972   303
    DAN PORAT

12. The Gray Zone of Collaboration and the Israeli Courtroom   327
    RIVKA BROT

    Contributors   361
    Index   367

ACKNOWLEDGMENTS

The idea for this book crystallized at a summer research workshop on Jews and the law in modern Europe that was held at the United States Holocaust Memorial Museum in Washington, D.C., in August 2011. The workshop was sponsored by the Museum's Jack, Joseph and Morton Mandel Center for Advanced Holocaust Studies. We wish to thank the organizers of the workshop, Professors Warren Rosenblum and Devin Pendas, and all of the workshop's participants, who fostered a memorable and stimulating environment for intellectual exchange. We also wish to thank the Mandel Center for hosting this event and especially Krista Hegburg, the Mandel Center's Program Officer for University Programs, who worked behind the scenes to make the workshop a success. We would also like to thank Steven Feldman, Book Publications Officer at the Museum, for his support and helpful comments on our book proposal. We are grateful to the Mandel Center for its institutional support of our own research and writing on Jewish honor courts. Gabriel Finder was the recipient of a Center for Advanced Holocaust Studies Fellowship during the 2000–2001 academic year, and Laura Jockusch was a Ben and Zelda Cohen Fellow in the summers of 2012 and 2013.

We want to thank our colleagues Michael Berkowitz, Lisa Leff, Tamar Lewinsky, Douglas Morris, Avinoam Patt, and Shimon Redlich, who all read first drafts of chapters appearing in this volume. Our book has benefited from

ACKNOWLEDGMENTS

the superlative skills of copyeditors Merav Levkowitz, Amy Hackett, and especially Mimi Braverman and of translators Avner Greenberg, Lenn Schramm, and Katarzyna Maciejczyk. We wish to thank the anonymous readers who reviewed our book for their helpful comments.

When this book was in its infancy, Steven Feldman encouraged us to approach Wayne State University Press. It was an excellent piece of advice. Kathryn Wildfong, editor-in-chief of Wayne State University Press, and her talented staff, Carrie Downes Teefey, Kristina Elizabeth Stonehill, and Bryce Schimanski, deftly and sensitively shepherded the manuscript from its initial editorial stages to the finished product. It has been a pleasure to work with them.

We owe a deep debt of gratitude to our respective spouses, Omer Offen and Frances Park, for their love, encouragement, and patience. Finally, we would be remiss if we failed to thank one another. This book has been a joint endeavor between two equal partners from beginning to end.

Laura Jockusch and Gabriel N. Finder

JEWISH
HONOR
COURTS

INTRODUCTION

Revenge, Retribution, and Reconciliation in the Postwar Jewish World

LAURA JOCKUSCH AND GABRIEL N. FINDER

At the various Conferences something very tragic has been revealed: There have been, as it seems, hundreds of Jewish collaborationists in the various concentration camps and even in the various crematoriums. While it is painful to speak about it, it seems that representative Jewish bodies ought to be aware of it. It is important to know this fact because it may make it possible for us to understand developments in Jewish life which are bound to occur against such collaborationists. The various Jewish partisan groups and especially the specific Jewish fighting units will make an attempt to punish many of those surviving collaborationists, a list of whom is in the possession of the leaders of the Jewish fighting units. Nobody knows how these things will develop. There is a hope that the processes of punishment will be conducted through organized responsible channels but there is also a great fear that small groups may constitute themselves as high courts meting out such punishment. Mr. Zuckerman thinks that organized Jewish bodies must intervene in order to give those Jewish groups who have participated in the general partisan movements and especially those groups who were organized as Jewish units, an opportunity to bring their cases before a proper tribunal which should mete out punishment if punishment is deserved.

> While such occurrences of collaboration to our sorrow have been quite numerous; while one party formulated collaboration as a policy for its members believing that, when Hitlerism and Fascism will be destroyed, this party will assume power and will need its manpower, giving for that reason instructions to its members to save their lives at any cost—these occurrences have been much overshadowed by occurrences of heroism in the various concentration camps, cremation establishments and ghetto tortures. We must pay attention to both, the heroism and the occurrences I mentioned before. We must try to find the sources which led to the possibility even of Jewish collaboration. This problem cannot be dealt with in a passing remark. We will have to devote to it much of our thought in the years to come. What is important at the moment is to realize that these spiritual wounds must find their cure as speedily as possible and that the only place which gives the greatest hope of cure for these people is Eretz Israel. Mr. Zuckerman also expresses his opinion that delegations of world Jewry to the various European countries could bring the Jewish survivors some moral comfort and spiritual cure.[1]

These comments, articulated by the American Labor Zionist leader Baruch Zuckerman (1887–1970) at a meeting of the Executive Committee of the World Jewish Congress in New York shortly after the end of World War II, reflect a strong sentiment in the Jewish world, be it in Western, Central, or Eastern Europe or later in Israel, that something had to be done about Jews who exhibited questionable behavior during the war and who were perceived by their Jewish peers as collaborators with the Nazi regime. Zuckerman acknowledged that the issue of Jewish collaboration was controversial, vexing, and, as he himself put it, painful, but it could not be swept under the rug. As he alludes, certain Jews, especially those from partisan units, had already taken justice into their own hands during the war by targeting collaborators for assassination. He expressed the fear that vigilante justice would continue after the war, unless the search for vengeance could be channeled into an institutional framework, in particular, tribunals. It should be made clear that Zuckerman had in mind Jewish tribunals, because only Jews should be responsible for judging other Jews. The reason for tribunals was not just to contain violence in Jewish society. There was a deeper reason: Jewish collaboration had caused a deep rift in Jewish communities across Europe; it had caused what Zuckerman called spiritual wounds. Just as it was necessary for moral regeneration to commemorate heroes, it was also necessary to heal wounds from within the Jewish body politic caused by collaboration. Although Jewish Palestine and later the State of Israel seemed like the natural place to begin this institutionalized healing process, it was also imperative in formerly Nazi-occupied Europe.

The overarching theme of *Jewish Honor Courts: Revenge, Retribution, and Reconciliation in Europe and Israel After the Holocaust* is the actual postwar confrontation, which Zuckerman contemplated, between Jewish individuals and communities on the one hand and putative Jewish collaborators with Nazism on the other. Among the latter were former members of the Jewish councils (the *Judenräte*) and the ghetto police, and informants and prisoner functionaries in Nazi concentration, labor, and death camps. Although the subject of Jewish collaboration became taboo in Jewish circles in the 1960s, it mesmerized both Jewish leaders and ordinary Jews during the Holocaust and for the first quarter of a century after the catastrophe. Already during the Holocaust, Jews pondered the causes of collaboration and wrought vengeance on suspected collaborators from within their midst. After the war, reemerging Jewish communities across Europe abandoned the strategy of revenge and pursued one of justice and retribution, creating ad hoc internal Jewish courts to investigate and, if accusations proved credible, put on trial suspected Jewish collaborators in Jewish communal tribunals.

Commonly known as a court of honor or an honor court (*Ehrengericht* in German, *ern-gerikht* in Yiddish, *jury d'honneur* or *tribunal de l'honneur* in French, and *ereraad* in Dutch), these judicial bodies also went by various other names, such as arbitral court (*Schiedsgericht* in German), social court (*sąd społeczny* in Polish or *gezelshaftlekh gerikht* in Yiddish), and civic court (*sąd obywatelski* in Polish or *birger-gerikht* in Yiddish). In general terms, an honor court was an unofficial or semi-official nongovernmental tribunal set up by a professional, social, cultural, or communal organization to arbitrate conflicts between two or more of its members. Offenses brought to justice mainly involved matters of honor, that is, insults, breeches of honor, breeches of social or professional protocol, breeches of etiquette, or the abuse of rights and privileges. Although these courts had the purpose of repairing such breeches of honor by disciplining the guilty, their disciplinary measures (such as moral rebuke, professional ban, fines, or the exclusion from membership) were of limited punitive power, because the court's decisions were not binding on nonmembers and had no legal relevance outside the respective body.

The Jewish honor courts set up by Jewish communities and survivor organizations after World War II clearly echo the tradition of legal autonomy that Jewish communities had enjoyed in premodern times when Jews handled their religious and civil matters in their own court system. Yet there was one important difference: Whereas premodern Jewish courts were religious courts, the Jewish honor courts after 1945 were purely secular initiatives that existed independent of the rabbinic courts that the reemerging Jewish communities in Europe also maintained for consultation in religious matters.² However, inquiring into the wartime past of certain Jewish survivors and, if facts warranted, censuring the immoral behavior of a Jewish individual were not subject to religious authority. It should also be noted that Jewish honor courts dealt not only with the issue of collaboration with the Nazis but also investigated and adjudicated various other conflicts among Jews; often, honor courts maintained a special department designated as a rehabilitation commission (*rehabilitatsye komisye* in Yiddish), a purge commission, or a purge committee (*commission d'épuration* or *comité d'épuration* in French), which had the special task of inquiring into the wartime conduct of an individual. For Jewish communities in postwar Europe the legal autonomy embodied by the honor courts was an important ingredient in the process of rehabilitation and the reclaiming of agency after years of persecution.

To be sure, among tens of thousands of cases, state prosecutors and state courts in several Western and Eastern European countries, including Greece, Belgium, the Netherlands, Austria, Poland, Czechoslovakia, Hungary, and the Soviet Union investigated and passed judgment on a modest number of suspected Jewish collaborators. In some of these countries Jewish honor courts coexisted with state legal institutions that had jurisdiction over collaboration cases, including those in which the defendants were Jews. But Jewish honor courts emerged in several countries precisely because Jewish communal leaders wished to wrest control of the cases of putative Jewish collaborators from state prosecutors and state courts, as they believed that it was the business of Jews to sit in judgment of fellow Jews and that only a Jewish court could render justice on internal foes. Thus in the Netherlands the Jewish community reluctantly established an honor court and competed with state prosecutors and courts to adjudicate cases of suspected collaborators because it was loath to see others wash its dirty linen in public. But in Poland the Jewish leadership erected its honor court when it no longer trusted the state courts to find accused Jewish collaborators guilty, especially those who were public figures.³

By the same token, the nascent State of Israel tried dozens of putative collaborators with the Nazis on the basis of a law it passed just two years after its foundation, the Nazis and Nazi Collaborators (Punishment) Law of 1950, which was designed primarily to identify and punish Jewish collaborators among the immigrants. The courts in which the Israeli trials were held were duly constituted state courts, in which criminal charges were filed by state prosecutors and the rules of criminal law and procedure applied. In contrast, the honor courts applied rather open-ended moral standards in determining the guilt or innocence of a defendant. Moreover, unlike the Israeli courts, honor courts in Europe lacked the state-sanctioned authority to compel suspected collaborators to appear before them. Putative collaborators stood trial in honor courts either because they sought to clear their names and wanted a clean bill of political health or because they succumbed to the pressure of opinion on the Jewish street to defend their claims to have clean hands. Despite these differences, in essence both the honor courts in Europe and the Israeli courts adjudicated the same issue: whether the defendant in the dock had betrayed the trust of the Jewish people, whether he— the percentage of female defendants was relatively low—should be deemed "a traitor to the Jewish nation."

What is noteworthy in this context is that, rather than take justice into their own hands, Jews were strongly inclined after the liberation of Nazi-occupied Europe and the cessation of hostilities to pursue in a courtlike setting their grievances against fellow Jews whose behavior during the war had been questionable. During the war armed Jewish underground organizations targeted suspected Jewish collaborators for assassination, and Jewish inmates in camps occasionally killed Jewish kapos when the opportunity arose. Even after the war was over, survivors here and there harassed, hounded, and even killed putative Jewish collaborators. With the establishment of the honor courts, however, vigilante justice in Jewish communities came to a virtual halt. Indeed, the creation of the honor courts was largely a conscious effort on the part of postwar Jewish leaders to counteract tendencies to engage in vigilante justice and for these leaders to parlay the desire for vengeance into a quasi-judicial, institutional forum for the expression of this sentiment. And to their credit, the honor courts—and for that matter, the Israeli courts in trials authorized by the 1950 law—made it their business, while eschewing revenge, to exact retribution when the facts of an individual case warranted it.[4] With time the pursuit of justice yielded in part to sentiments to seek reconciliation with suspected collaborators and to take a broad, and thereby more forgiving, view of the circumstances in which they were compelled to cooperate with the Nazis to the detriment of their fellow Jews, circumstances over which they exercised minimal control.

As is widely known, in ghettos and camps the Nazis intentionally turned their victims into abettors and accomplices. This enforced "collaboration" constituted a central component of the Nazi regime's mass murder machinery and was a profound expression of the unprecedented perfidy of its genocidal designs.

Jews in Nazi-dominated Europe colluded in various forms: Members of the Jewish councils and ghetto police forcibly supplied the Germans with Jewish laborers and were instrumental in selections for deportations; and kapos and other prisoner functionaries implemented the will of their German superiors when managing their fellow camp inmates. Some individuals cooperated to save their own lives in the face of persecution and mass murder. Most, however, did not act for their own benefit but rather operated under the assumption that by cooperating to a degree, they could mitigate Nazi oppression, retain a measure of Jewish autonomy and agency, or enhance chances for the survival of their fellow Jews. Not only did this division of labor that the Nazis forced upon their victims undermine group solidarity by creating a violent hierarchy and gruesome pecking order among the persecuted, but it also played a central role in weakening and dehumanizing the victims. Although they were well aware of the Nazis' efforts to turn victims against one another, this did not prevent Jewish leaders and their constituencies from decrying a handful of their fellow Jews' cooperation with the oppressor—conduct that caused profound rupture and resentment in Jewish communities and resistance groups both during and after the Holocaust.

Even during the war but more so after it, Jews across Europe felt compelled to settle scores with those among them who were suspected of aiding the Nazis in carrying out anti-Jewish actions. The vehement discourse about collaboration often distorted the historical realities of the recent catastrophe, placing the blame for the genocide largely on those perceived as collaborators as well as—and occasionally rather than—on the Nazi perpetrators, disregarding that members of Jewish councils and ghetto police as well as kapos had also been victims. In the early years after the Holocaust, Jews sought to rebuild their lives by excluding those with dirty hands and by preventing them from assuming leadership roles in the community and representing it to others. Just as important is that precisely when postwar Jewish leaders were emphasizing the high moral conduct of Jews in the face of the Nazis' assault on their lives and dignity, Jewish self-respect was being undermined by the reminder of collaboration from within. To many contemporaries, purging collaborators from the international Jewish body politic appeared to be a precondition of sustainable communal life and the moral and ethical rehabilitation of Holocaust survivors in both the Diaspora and Israel.

Although essential to understanding the political and emotional reconstruction of Jewish life in the postwar era, retribution in the postwar Jewish world has remained an underexplored topic. In this volume contributors approach the subject from various disciplinary perspectives—Jewish studies, political, social and cultural history, law, literature, and memory studies—while drawing from a broad variety of sources such as trial records, published and unpublished testimonies, and the contemporary press in addition to memoirs, diaries, and scholarly literature. This book is also the first study to explore the transnational dimension of Jewish retribution.

Historiographical Background: Jewish Collaborators and Postwar Emotions

Until now, there has been no broad historical treatment of Jewish honor courts. But ever since the war, Jewish commentators have tried to come to grips with Jewish collaboration, creating a contentious and ongoing debate. The first to engage in historical research on the wartime Jewish leadership and its compromises under Nazism were historians who were themselves survivors and who engaged in the numerous Jewish historical commissions and documentation centers that emerged across Europe in the latter half of the 1940s.[5] The most prominent scholar who called for a thorough and critical yet balanced historical study of Jewish collaboration was the Polish Jewish historian Philip Friedman. In a number of articles on individual Jewish council members and on broader methodological problems of studying the Holocaust from a Jewish perspective, published in the first half of the 1950s, Friedman demanded that in-depth historical inquiries into the social history of Jews under Nazism focus on the histories of individual Jewish leaders and their ambitions, choices, and mistakes rather than merely condemn Jewish leadership collectively.[6] He further envisioned that historians should analyze social conflicts in Jewish society and address the negative phenomenon of Jewish collaboration in the same nuanced and scholarly fashion as they did positive aspects, such as Jewish resistance.[7] Even though Friedman was highly critical of the actions of Jewish council members, whom he called "ghetto dictators" and "pseudo-saviors" of the Jewish people, he did not believe that there was anything inherently Jewish about those leaders or that there was a historical continuity with previous forms of Jewish self-government. Rather, many leaders of Jewish councils were a tragic by-product of the Nazi genocide of European Jews. "Despite their historical shortsightedness and their incomprehension of the spirit of Israel's destiny," Friedman maintained, "these were not simple brutes or tyrants, nor were they traitors in the ordinary sense of the word. Their struggles were a dramatic new phenomenon in the history of the Jewish people."[8] It was up to the historians to fathom the "profound complex of internal and external contradictions" bound to their actions.[9] Friedman's own research proved visionary, yet his untimely death in 1960 prevented him from reaching a wider audience beyond the survivors' own circles.

The debate on Jewish collaboration was cast into sharp relief by two books published in the first half of the 1960s. In his pathbreaking 1961 book, *The Destruction of the European Jews*, Raul Hilberg set for himself the primary goal of understanding the Nazi "destruction process," advancing step by step and leading to the annihilation of the Jews, and the "machinery of destruction," the decentralized apparatus in charge of the destruction process.[10] In this context Hilberg felt driven to explain "the role of the Jews in their own destruction."[11] According to Hilberg, it was not enough to explain the destruction of Europe's Jews by analyzing how Germans overcame their administrative and psychological obstacles and how they dealt with the internal administrative machine: "In a destruction process, the perpetrators do not play the only role; the process is shaped by the victims, too. It is the *interaction* of perpetrators and victims that is 'fate.'"[12] In Hilberg's view the scale of the destruction of European Jews was precipitated by traditional patterns of Jewish political behavior. Over centuries of persecution and expulsion European Jews had preserved the survival of the Jewish community by compliance, acquiescence, and negotiations with their oppressors, persuading them that there was value in having a Jewish community rather than obliterating it. Hilberg stresses that this pattern of Jewish leadership proved self-destructive, because the Nazis were not interested in preserving Jews but wanted to kill them.

> When the Nazis took over in 1933, the old Jewish reaction pattern set in again, but this time the results were catastrophic. The German bureaucracy was not slowed by Jewish pleading; it was not stopped by Jewish indispensability. Without regard to cost, the bureaucratic machine, operating with accelerating speed and ever-widening destructive effect, proceeded to annihilate the European Jews. The Jewish community, unable to switch to resistance, increased its co-operation with the tempo of the German measures, thus hastening its own destruction.[13]

In her controversial coverage of the Eichmann trial and her 1963 book *Eichmann in Jerusalem: A Report on the Banality of Evil*, Hannah Arendt castigated the wartime Jewish leadership, whose behavior she found "pathetic and sordid," from a different angle. "To a Jew," Arendt wrote, "this role of the Jewish leaders in the destruction of their own people is undoubtedly the darkest chapter of the whole dark story."[14] In her view, their behavior can be explained only in the context of the "totality of the moral collapse the Nazis caused in respectable European society ... not only among the persecutors but also among the victims."[15] In other words, what made this chapter so dark was the Germans' utter success in having victims turn on one another. Nevertheless, Arendt still allotted special blame to Jewish leaders for direct responsibility for the deaths of millions of Jews: "The whole truth was that if the Jewish people had really been unorganized and leaderless, there would have been chaos and plenty of misery, but the total number of victims would hardly have been between four and a half and six million people."[16]

Deborah E. Lipstadt's pointed criticism of Arendt's argument is largely on the mark. The Nazis' mobile killing units, the Einsatzgruppen, murdered a million and a half Jews during the first phase of the German invasion of the Soviet Union and Soviet-controlled territories in the absence of an organized Jewish leadership, and Arendt, moreover, attributed to Jewish councils more power than they had.[17] The same is true for Hilberg's argument. That said, Hilberg and Arendt's view of the complicity of Jewish leaders in the destruction of European Jewry remained regnant throughout the 1960s. There was one major difference between them: Hilberg ascribed the role of the Jews in their own destruction to a historical pattern of behavior, whereas Arendt considered it part and parcel of the moral collapse induced by the Nazi totalitarian state from which its Jewish victims were not immune. But whatever their distinctive viewpoints, both writers ultimately blamed Jewish leaders for becoming, in Arendt's provocative phrase, "instruments of murder."[18]

A watershed in the debate over Jewish collaboration occurred in the 1970s; it was reflected in Isaiah Trunk's seminal 1972 study *Judenrat: The Jewish Councils in Eastern Europe Under Nazi Occupation*. Unlike Hilberg and Arendt, Trunk used internal Jewish sources. Like Hilberg, he saw analytical value in comparing the Jewish councils to historical forms of corporate Jewish leadership operating under extreme conditions, but Trunk drew a basic distinction between them: "For the first time in Jewish history a Jewish organ was forced to help a foreign, criminal regime destroy coreligionists."[19] Unlike Arendt, Trunk viewed the Jewish councils and their individual members with appreciation for the enormous pressure placed on them by the Nazi regime to cooperate with its demands. Trunk pointed not only to Jewish leaders who acted contemptuously and with an iron fist (and whose prime concern was saving their own skin) but also to numerous Jewish council officials who acted honorably, labored tirelessly to preserve lives, refused to obey or attempted to subvert Nazi commands, and even cooperated with the armed Jewish underground. Thus, because of the wide divergence of behavior among them, Trunk argues that the cooperation of each Jewish council and its members with the Nazi regime has to be evaluated on its own merits.

In many ways Trunk's magisterial study implemented the agenda for studying Jewish collaboration for which Philip Friedman had created a blueprint a decade and a half earlier; Trunk, who, like Friedman, was a historian and a survivor, had known Friedman from prewar Poland and followed his path of studying the social and cultural history of Jewish society under Nazism.[20] By 1975, Lucy Dawidowicz, in her then popular book *The War Against the Jews*, would feel confident enough to clear the names of wartime Jewish leaders: "The officials of the Judenräte were coerced by German terror to submit and comply. To say that they 'cooperated' or 'collaborated' with the Germans is semantic confusion and historical misrepresentation."[21]

Eventually even Hilberg came to adopt a more charitable view of the behavior of Jewish leaders. As Christopher Browning has noted recently, the second edition of Hilberg's *Destruction of the European Jews*, published in 1985 "with much softer language, also sought to capture the tragic paradox of the Jewish Councils."[22] Thus Hilberg would write:

> Members of the Jewish councils were genuine if not always representative Jewish leaders who strove to protect the Jewish community from the most severe exactions and impositions and who tried to normalize life under the most adverse circumstances. Paradoxically, these very attributes were being exploited by the Germans against the Jewish victims....
>
> The councils could not subvert the continuing process of constriction and annihilation. The ghetto as a whole was a German creation. Everything that was designed to maintain its viability was simultaneously promoting a German goal.... In short, the Jewish councils were assisting the Germans with their good qualities as well as their bad, and the very best accomplishments of a Jewish bureaucracy were ultimately appropriated by the Germans for the all-consuming destruction process.[23]

These passages did not appear in the original 1961 version of Hilberg's book. Then, in his influential book *Perpetrators, Victims, Bystanders*, published in 1992, Hilberg further revised his analysis of Jewish leaders.

> The Jewish leaders were in the cauldron themselves. They too were victims.... They believed that their service was an obligation, and they were convinced with absolute certainty that they carried the entire burden of caring for the Jewish population.... The Jewish leaders were, in short,

remarkably similar in their self-perception to rulers all over the world, but their role was not normal and for most of them neither was their fate.[24]

In other words, Jewish leaders, themselves victims, were not to blame for the destruction of European Jews.[25]

Younger historians are following the same path. Doron Rabinovici has examined the Jewish council in Vienna. He often takes its members to task for being duped into facilitating the destruction of the Jewish community, but he does not blame Jews for their role in their own destruction. Rabinovici does not paint with a broad brush but examines the behavior of each council member on an individual basis: "The study of the attitudes of Jewish victims under the destructive regime is always in danger of turning into a complacently moralizing reproach, shifting the blame for the crimes to the victims."[26] We agree with this approach. What is interesting, however, is that during the war and the first decade and a half thereafter, large segments of the Jewish world, survivors and nonsurvivors, did condemn Jews for playing a significant role in the Holocaust and perceived them as collaborators.

An illustrative example can be taken from the trial of Shepsl Rotholc in the Polish Jewish honor court in November 1946. Rotholc was accused of being a brutal Jewish policeman in the Warsaw ghetto and was eventually convicted. A pivotal moment during the trial was the testimony of a witness who described how she had turned to Rotholc for help during a roundup in the Warsaw ghetto, but he had turned a deaf ear to her appeal. During the same roundup another Jewish policeman had pursued a Jewish woman and her child up the stairs, where he wrested the child from its mother's grasp and threw him out the window to his death. She punctuated her testimony with the invective that the Jewish police in the ghetto "were worse than the Germans."[27]

Why did Jews feel this way? Why did they cast blame on fellow Jews, who were of course themselves victims, for the destruction? There are two possible explanations. The first is that the wound, as Baruch Zuckerman said, was so painful that Jews could not fathom how their brethren could help the Nazi enemy persecute and even kill them. Whereas Jews expected the Germans to do evil to them, the fact that some fellow Jews followed the Germans in their footsteps came as a shock and was perceived as a betrayal to the Jewish people. Thus across Europe they were often called "traitors to the Jewish nation." Because so little time had passed for reflection, the atmosphere was still so charged, and the wound was still so raw, many Jews were unable to make a distinction between the actual perpetrators (the Nazi Germans and their non-Jewish accomplices) and the few Jewish victims who aided them for whatever reason, between those with power and the Jewish powerless. The second reason for this Jewish response is that there was no mechanism for Jews to demand retribution from the actual perpetrators. At least before the creation of the State of Israel in 1948, Jews had no political representation that would have allowed them to participate in international efforts to address Nazi atrocities and human rights issues. In the same vein Jews had no access to any legal mechanism to put Nazis on trial for their crimes against Jews. Even after the State of Israel was created, Jews had no expectation that a Nazi German would be tried in an Israeli court; the Eichmann trial would be the exception to the rule. Moreover, the survivors and Jews worldwide were deeply disappointed by the Allies' postwar proceedings, which marginalized the crimes of the Holocaust.[28] This is not to say that the Allies did not address the Holocaust, but it was far down the list of the prosecution's concerns, as exemplified by the Nuremberg trials. One result of the inclination of the victims to blame other victims was the creation of Jewish honor courts across Europe in the immediate postwar period and the creation of Israeli courts to try three dozen cases pursuant to the 1950 law on collaborators.

Thus, contrary to common wisdom, the topic of Jewish collaboration was *not* taboo in the Jewish world for at least a decade after the war; rather, it became taboo only later, in the 1960s and 1970s.[29] Ironically, this was an aftereffect of the Eichmann trial, the first real Holocaust trial. With its focus on Jewish victimhood and "crimes against the Jewish people"—the main charge leveled against Adolf Eichmann at his trial—we suggest that the classification of victims and perpetrators and their public evaluation became frozen into two inflexible categories: Jewish victims and Nazi perpetrators. As a result, it became widely unacceptable in Jewish society to discuss any questionable behavior by some Jewish victims.

In several respects both prosecutors and judges at the Eichmann trial sought to keep the issue of Jewish collaboration at bay, because the trial of Rudolph Kasztner in 1954 and his murder in March 1957 had shown Israeli society's extreme sensitivity on the topic of Jewish collaboration.[30] In his opening speech at the Eichmann trial, Attorney General Gideon Hausner made it clear that the controversy over the behavior of Jews in the face of Nazism had "no place in the present trial," which was not about judging the Jewish leadership but establishing the guilt or innocence of a major Nazi perpetrator. Nor did this trial seek to "establish a book of rules for the proper behaviour of a victim in his relations with the beast of prey"; rather, this form of judgment was to be banned from the courtroom and left "to the historian of the Holocaust."[31]

INTRODUCTION

Although it proved impossible to shut the issue of collaboration entirely out of the trial, something changed in the way the topic was addressed and the relative weight it received in relation to other issues, most important, the various forms of Jewish victimhood at the hands of the Nazis. To be sure, the testimony of Pinchas Freudinger, who was a former functionary of the Orthodox community in Budapest and was involved in the negotiations with Eichmann over saving Hungarian Jews in exchange for goods, elicited catcalls from the public in attendance.[32] And Judge Benjamin Halevi, who had presided at the Kasztner trial, pointedly asked Hansi Brand whether the Jewish committee in Hungary—she had been one of its leaders—had contemplated assassinating Eichmann.[33] As Deborah Lipstadt writes, "Implicit in his question was the accusation that those at the top, the leaders who knew precisely what faced their fellow Jews, had failed to take actions that might have stopped the process."[34] Yet at the same time it was also possible to put on the witness stand Vera Alexander, a female Jewish kapo at Auschwitz, to testify for the prosecution and convey an image of a kapo who had helped fellow Jews.[35] Moreover, in the wake of the trial, the vehement attack against Arendt's *Eichmann in Jerusalem*—wrongheaded though the conclusion of her book may have been—indicates that the issue of Jewish collaboration was becoming a forbidden topic.[36] By that time, Israeli court cases against alleged collaborators had waned, and they ultimately stopped entirely a few years later. In Europe, most Jewish honor courts had already ceased to exist or had stopped adjudicating cases involving Jewish collaboration. In some cases, as, for example, in Germany, Jewish communities apparently even destroyed the records of those court cases, and we can only speculate that this was a conscious effort to end the inconvenient and transitional chapter of Jews' painful reckoning with the problem of collaboration.

With the passage of time, this electrified atmosphere in which any legal, historical, or literary treatment of collaboration was unbecoming began to change in the Jewish world and in public discourse more generally. One watershed event was the English-language publication of Primo Levi's acclaimed book *The Drowned and the Saved* in 1988 and especially one essay in it, "The Gray Zone," in which Levi openly discusses Jewish collaboration and shows that victims could also be collaborators but still be victims.[37] Levi's essay has given scholars and others a green light to once more plumb the depth of this extremely sensitive topic without the feeling that they are going to be under attack for doing so.

An illustrative example of the fact that the issue of Jewish collaboration is becoming less taboo and finding increased public interest is the recently released film *The Last of the Unjust* by the acclaimed director Claude Lanzmann, the creator of the epic 1985 film *Shoah*. *The Last of the Unjust* features Lanzmann's lengthy interviews with Benjamin Murmelstein, the last leading "elder" of the Jews in the Theresienstadt model ghetto and camp and an important functionary in the Viennese Jewish council. Lanzmann interviewed Murmelstein in 1975 with the intention of including this footage in *Shoah*, but he did not. The question is why not. In Lanzmann's own words in a recent interview in the *New York Times*: "He impressed me. He was the first protagonist I filmed for 'Shoah,' but I didn't know how to fit him into the film. I was fascinated by the Jewish Council because it was vital to understand what it was, who they were. Despite what others thought, I never thought they were collaborators."[38] What is interesting is that *Shoah* does not include any interview with any member of a Jewish council. As Lanzmann acknowledges, he knew that after the war, fellow Jews accused Murmelstein of being a collaborator. It is noteworthy that it took Lanzmann almost thirty-five years to find a place for Murmelstein's story in a separate movie.[39]

Another example of the proposition that Jewish collaboration is becoming less of a taboo topic is the English-language translation and broad reception of two books by foreign independent scholars: Doron Rabinovici's *Eichmann's Jews*, which was assessed by renowned historian Christopher Browning in the *New York Review of Books*; and Agata Tuszyńska's account of the life of the singer Wiera Gran, who was tried and acquitted by the Polish Jewish honor court on charges of being a Gestapo informer in the Warsaw ghetto.[40] Proof of popular interest in Tuszyńska's book was reflected in an online audio program created by *Tablet Magazine*.[41]

That said, there has been no synthetic study, in the form of either a monograph or an edited volume, of European Jewish communities' postwar attempts to confront their own collaborators. To be sure, the past decade has witnessed burgeoning interest in the postwar efforts of European governments to come to grips with citizens who collaborated with the Nazi occupation of their countries.[42] But studies of this topic do not deal with responses of postwar European governments to Jewish collaboration. Nor do they examine Jewish responses to Jewish collaboration. Apart from one thin and rather schematic Dutch book on the proceedings against Jewish council members in Holland,[43] the only sustained scholarly undertaking of this subject has been on the Polish case.[44] A handful of monographs on Jews in postwar Germany and Austria, some of them published recently, include short chapters on Jewish honor courts.[45] A few articles and a couple of monographs investigate Israeli collaborator trials in the first decade and a half after the founding of the State of Israel. However, these studies make no attempt to link those trials to similar proceedings in Jewish communities in the Diaspora.[46] Thus our book meets the need for a volume on Jewish honor courts; the contributors examine from a transnational perspective intramural Jewish revenge, retribution, and reconciliation from across the European Jewish Diaspora and in Israel.

We can offer several plausible explanations for the delay in the appearance of much scholarly literature on this topic. The records of Jewish honor courts have in some cases been made available by archives only during the past decade. Proper study of this topic requires deep familiarity with Jewish life in several countries and regions, not to mention knowledge of Hebrew and several European languages, including Yiddish. The underlying reason for this gap, however, is emotional. For decades the subject of Jewish collaboration and the postwar encounter with it has struck a raw nerve in the Jewish world, and the sensitivity of the topic has inhibited scholars from exploring it properly in their writings. The greater temporal and emotional distance of today enables scholars to ask historical questions about how Jewish societies in various places and points in time dealt with putative collaborators in their midst. Rather than feeling the need to engage in moral questions of attributing blame or valor, the scholarly discourse has now moved from a moral to a historical plane.

The Scope and Structure of This Volume

The contributors to *Jewish Honor Courts* argue that, notwithstanding deep-seated Jewish resentment against collaborators from within, Jews in the postwar world—be it in the Diaspora or in Israel—were disinclined to pursue unfounded accusations of collaboration and engage in vigilante justice. Rather, postwar Jews undertook the agonizing and serious task of identifying and punishing suspected collaborators with a great deal of caution and integrity. The contributors to this volume also demonstrate that although the same basic mechanisms and impulses motivated retribution in the Jewish communities across Europe and in Israel, there nevertheless were significant differences among the distinct court cases. At the same time, there were considerable areas of convergence between them, including Jews' desire for the recuperation of agency and the quest to keep retribution in Jewish hands because non-Jews could not be trusted to do a proper job. Not least, the contributors show that, even though retroactive justice elicited satisfaction and relief among many survivors in the early postwar years, this feeling increasingly exhausted itself, as victimhood became empowering on the eve of what French historian Annette Wieviorka describes as "the era of the witness."[47]

"Why Punish Collaborators?" is the title of this volume's first chapter. In it David Engel asks why postwar Jewish communities sought to punish some of their members for their wartime behavior and to purge them from their ranks. The wartime example of the Jewish Fighting Organization (Żydowski Organizacja Bojowa; ŻOB) in the Warsaw ghetto, which assassinated at least thirteen perceived Jewish collaborators, demonstrates that the ŻOB's quest to punish collaborators was motivated by tactical, deterrent, political, or psychological reasons as much as by the desire for retribution. Following the war, ŻOB veterans in Poland, along with former members of the communist underground, continued to pursue accused collaborators—now in the Polish Jewish honor court—primarily for political reasons. By contrast, Engel finds that the honor courts in displaced persons (DP) camps, the rehabilitation commission run by Jewish displaced persons, and the Israeli courts hearing cases brought under the 1950 Nazis and Nazi Collaborators (Punishment) Law concerned themselves less with the political question of whether an individual obeyed a legitimate or an illegitimate authority during the war than with the strictly legal question of whether that individual had beaten, extorted, or otherwise harmed the persons or property of others with criminal intent. Engel suggests that the Jewish honor court in Poland could afford to promote a political criterion for judgment because the Polish Jewish leadership was not responsible for governing, as opposed to DP legal mechanisms and the Israeli courts, which were sources for the maintenance of social cohesion in DP camps and Israeli society, respectively.

In "Rehabilitating the Past? Jewish Honor Courts in Allied-Occupied Germany," Laura Jockusch analyzes the so-called rehabilitation cases of putative collaborators among the quarter of a million Jewish survivors who lived in Allied-occupied Germany in the first five years after the war. Focusing on the Jewish honor courts in Munich and Berlin, two pivotal centers of Jewish life, she compares the parallel but distinct tribunals created by surviving German Jews and Jewish displaced persons of predominantly Eastern European backgrounds who temporarily stayed in Germany under Allied protection waiting to rebuild their lives overseas. She demonstrates that although the communities of Jewish displaced persons and German Jews were culturally and socially remote from each other, their approach to putative collaborators was nevertheless similar, and in both communities the court cases provided a vital tool for the moral rehabilitation of survivors after years of persecution and the deprivation of rights.

Among the Jews most vilified in Poland by their fellow Jews during and after the war were the chairmen of Jewish councils, followed closely by other prominent council members. In "Judenrat on Trial: Postwar Polish Jewry Sits in Judgment of Its Wartime Leadership," Gabriel N. Finder examines how surviving Jewish council members fared in the Jewish honor court in postwar Poland, which operated from 1946 to 1950. In general, the legal staff and judges assigned to the Polish Jewish honor court acted with circumspection, frustrating strong sentiments in both the Jewish leadership and the remaining remnant of Jews in Poland to punish collaborators in the community, including reviled Jewish council members who were still alive after the war. However, Jewish lawyers investigated only twenty cases of Jewish council members. They terminated six investigations because of a lack of incriminating evidence and eventually brought only four cases to trial in the honor court. Of these, only one defendant was found guilty. Finder analyzes the acquittal of Alfred Merbaum, the chairman of the Jewish council in Horodenka. Basing its verdict on Merbaum's actions to preserve Horodenka's Jewish community, the honor court concluded that not all Jewish councils were cut from the same cloth. This case in particular illustrates that the Polish Jewish honor court resisted the temptation to condemn all Jewish councils and their members and took seriously the agonizing task of drawing distinctions between questionable and truly execrable behavior by fellow Jews—in this case, wartime Jewish leaders—suspected of collaboration.

In "An Unresolved Controversy: The Jewish Honor Court in the Netherlands, 1946–1950," Ido de Haan examines the Jewish honor court in the Netherlands, with its single-minded pursuit of the Amsterdam Jewish council's wartime leadership, in particular, two former Jewish council members, Abraham Asscher and David Cohen, who were prominent figures in the Jewish community before the German invasion. Their conviction in November 1947 for demonstrating "reprehensible" behavior under the Nazi occupation, with particular emphasis on their role in the deportations of Jews, became entangled with their arrest by postwar Dutch authorities before the disposition in their case in the honor court. The sudden haste with which the honor court reached a verdict, prompted by Asscher and Cohen's arrest, provoked the ire of many Dutch Jews and confirmed their suspicion, formed when the court was established, that the honor court was detrimental to the fragile position of Jews in Dutch society. The Dutch prosecutor ultimately dropped the cases against Asscher and Cohen, but the reputation of the honor court, which enjoyed only minimal support in the Jewish community, had become tainted beyond repair. In January 1950 the Jewish establishment demanded that Cohen and two others convicted by the honor court—Asscher had died in the meantime—be reinstated by the court as members of the community in good standing. This meant de facto the abolishment of the Jewish honor court. As de Haan shows, the dismantlement of the honor court left unresolved the question of what roles the Jewish council, prominent members of the Jewish community, and Jewish collaborators played in the destruction of Dutch Jewry, constituting a source of friction within the Jewish community for years to come.

In *"Jurys d'honneur:* The Stakes and Limits of Purges Among Jews in France After Liberation," Simon Perego examines the approach of the French Jewish community to putative collaborators within its midst. He looks at a number of trials brought before the honor courts and purge committees set up by various Jewish organizations for the purpose of intramural purges, discussing the controversies and structural weaknesses that surrounded these cases. Perego places the issue of Jewish retribution within the context of France's more widespread and frequently violent purges of putative Nazi collaborators, seeing in both an attempt by all Frenchmen, Jew and non-Jew alike, to come to terms with the country's dark wartime past. He also sees it as an attempt at the autonomous rebuilding of a persecuted and traumatized minority seeking to come to grips with its recent past.

The starting point for "Viennese Jewish Functionaries on Trial: Accusations, Defense Strategies, and Hidden Agendas," by Helga Embacher, is the intense purge in Austria of former Jewish council members. Looking at three case studies—Josef Löwenherz, Emil Tuchmann, and Ernst Feldsberg—Embacher highlights the controversies that surrounded the treatment of these individuals by Allied occupying forces, the Austrian government, and the newly reestablished Jewish community (*Israelitische Kultusgemeinde*) in Vienna. Even though the Viennese Jewish community relentlessly scrutinized the wartime roles played by these three individuals, it nevertheless never organized an honor court; such a body would crystallize only among Austrian Jewish émigrés in London. Embacher also analyzes the strategies used by the accused to defend themselves against accusations of collaboration.

In "'The Lesser Evil' of Jewish Collaboration? The Absence of a Jewish Honor Court in Postwar Belgium," Veerle Vanden Daelen and Nico Wouters investigate the Belgian Jewish community's postwar treatment of the surviving leaders of the Association of Jews in Belgium, the German-established Jewish council. They demonstrate that Belgium provides an instructive countercase to other European countries, because although individual survivors filed complaints against former Jewish council members with Belgian military courts, Belgian authorities did not make the prosecution of Jewish collaboration a priority and investigations never led to an actual court case. Nor did the Jewish community establish autonomous courts to try alleged collaborators in their midst, mainly because they sought to avoid bringing public attention to an inconvenient issue. Ultimately, Jewish functionaries, some of whom played influential roles in the Belgian Jewish community after the war, used the same arguments to justify their wartime behavior as the members of the Belgian political elite, namely, that their actions had not contravened Belgian interests.

Cases in Jewish honor courts, especially of defendants who were former mid- and low-level Jewish functionaries, were generally initiated by denunciations made by one or more survivors, frequently in letters. In "Jews Accusing Jews: Denunciations of Alleged Collaborators in Jewish Honor Courts," Katarzyna Person explores letters of denunciation sent to the honor court in Poland and to DP honor courts in Allied-occupied Germany. The motivation for most denunciations was vengeance for the wrongs allegedly perpetrated by the accused against the letter writers and their families in ghettos and camps. But some letters were clearly motivated by personal grudges that exaggerated or distorted the wartime behavior of the accused, who, in turn, felt obliged to write their own letters to the court. These accused attempted to refute the allegations or, if a trial ensued, to find witnesses who would testify on their behalf. Because virtually no wartime documents attested to the behavior of ordinary people, the honor court system relied almost exclusively on oral statements, including denunciations. But this circumstance created a dilemma for the honor courts, because they had to determine the veracity of denunciations without the help of corroborating documentation. This dilemma aside, Person suggests that the large number of denunciations that survivors sent to the honor courts demonstrates their reclamation of agency and their growing confidence in the rehabilitation of Jewish communal institutions after the war.

The treatment of women in honor courts is explored in a case study of the modus operandi of one honor court. Ewa Koźmińska-Frejlak's chapter, "'I'm Going to the Oven Because I Wouldn't Give Myself to Him': The Role of Gender in the Polish Jewish Civic Court," identifies a close link between prewar Jewish views of women, including their "proper" place in society, and the Polish honor court's handling of such cases. Only a small number of Jewish women were investigated by the lawyers attached to this honor court, and an even smaller number stood trial before it. Almost all of them were accused of being prison functionaries or kapos in concentration camps. The reason for this is simple: As a consequence of prewar attitudes, which discouraged the employment of women in positions of responsibility, virtually no women became officials in Jewish councils. Yet several women were held responsible for the actions of their husbands who served on Jewish councils, in the Jewish police, or as kapos. Moreover, the role of gender in the Polish Jewish honor court was subject to a double standard that was largely dictated by traditional views of the female body. Some female defendants were suspected, both in overt terms and in insinuations, of exchanging their bodies in return for favors from Germans and others, including Jewish kapos. But when women were the victims of sexual abuse by Jewish men, the Jewish lawyers and judges, almost all of them men, were, with rare exceptions, loath to make it the basis for an indictment, let alone a conviction. Koźmińska-Frejlak concludes that the Polish Jewish honor court, reflecting the sentiment and norms of the postwar Jewish community in whose name it acted, in large part validated and reinforced the prewar conception of gender roles.

In the last three chapters the geographic focus of this book moves from Europe to Israel. In "Revenge and Reconciliation: Early Israeli Literature and the Dilemma of Jewish Collaborators with the Nazis," Gali Drucker Bar-Am explores the theme of Jewish collaboration as reflected in Hebrew and Yiddish literature published in Israel in the 1950s. Drucker Bar-Am analyzes literary creations by Nathan Alterman and Yitskhok Perlov, the central theme of which is postwar encounters between Jewish collaborators and their victims in the nascent State of Israel. She scrutinizes the literary treatment of the emotional oscillation of immigrants from among the surviving remnant of European Jews, whose feelings ranged from seeking revenge to a need for reconciliation when they confronted putative collaborators in their new homeland.

In "Changing Legal Perceptions of 'Nazi Collaborators' in Israel, 1950–1972," Dan Porat examines public attitudes and political debates that surrounded the legislation of Israel's Nazis and Nazi Collaborators (Punishment) Law of 1950 and traces a number of cases that illustrate how Israeli courts applied the law in the 1950s and 1960s. Porat points to changes in the application of the law over the course of time, from a harsh and restrictive reading in the early years of Israeli statehood to a more lenient approach to collaboration in the wake of the Eichmann trial, leading to an end to collaborator trials in Israeli courts by the early 1970s.

In "The Gray Zone of Collaboration and the Israeli Courtroom," Rivka Brot analyzes two Israeli collaborator trials that were conducted in the early 1950s. Moshe Puczyc and Mordechai Goldstein were Jewish residents of the Polish town of Ostrowiec. Puczyc was an officer in the ghetto police, and Goldstein was a rank-and-file policeman. Their differing levels of authority were reflected in their prewar and postwar lives: Puczyc was a lawyer before the war and an activist in the DP camps before settling in Israel; Goldstein was a simple man throughout his entire life. Both Puczyc and Goldstein beat fellow Jews. But although Puczyc wielded power in the ghetto, he was acquitted of all charges, whereas Goldstein was found guilty on some charges. The difference in their verdicts is explained by Puczyc's success in persuading the court that his beatings were mild, performed "in the line of duty," and meant to prevent the Germans from doing worse to Ostrowiec's Jews, whereas, for his part, Goldstein was unable to present a narrative

INTRODUCTION

with any redeeming qualities to counter the prosecution's harsh reduction of him to a policeman who administered cruel and gratuitous beatings. Ironically, in Puczyc's case the judges did not believe the witnesses for the prosecution, whereas in Goldstein's case, they did not believe the witnesses for the defense. Brot argues that the judges were unable to imagine the gray zone—a term she borrows from Primo Levi—that reigned in the ghetto, that they were unable to imagine the Nazi-created, inverted moral system from which the defendants and the witnesses came, a system in which a Jewish police officer's compliance with German directives to maintain order in the ghetto was inextricably bound with abuse on his part. However, in an obiter dictum, an incidental expression of opinion unessential to the decision, one judge acknowledged the inadequacy of the law, created in normal times, to judge the behavior of Jews forced to negotiate daily life in ghettos and camps. This judge seems to suggest that if the law were able to comprehend the world from which the defendants and the witnesses came, perhaps the verdict in Goldstein's case would have been different. Israeli courts were increasingly caught on the horns of this dilemma, a dilemma explored in this chapter.

Thus, taken both individually and collectively, the essays in this volume pose a number of key questions. What were Jewish opinions of fellow Jews whose wartime behavior was questionable or worse? Who was perceived as a Jewish collaborator? On what grounds?

Which factors occasioned a transition among Jews from vigilante justice against putative Jewish collaborators to retributive justice in honor courts and the Israeli courts? Did Jews involved in establishing the honor courts or the Israeli court system make any reference to or cooperate with non-Jewish courts or Allied occupation forces? How did Jews justify the need for their own courts when they had recourse to state courts?

What sorts of sanctions or penalties did honor courts and Israeli courts impose? Were there any aftereffects of being deemed a collaborator or being tried in an honor court or in the Israeli courts? Was a defendant (even if acquitted!) thereafter permanently branded with a mark of Cain and ostracized in Jewish society?

What were the functions of the honor courts and the Israeli courts apart from criminalizing collaborative behavior? Did their architects intend them to serve educational, psychological, historical, or moral purposes, related to restoring dignity and inculcating "civic behavior" for the future as well as imposing sanctions upon reproachable conduct?

Did the most widely held Jewish attitudes toward collaborators evolve (soften or harden) with time? Was there movement toward reconciliation and forgiveness?

As the contributors demonstrate in this volume, Zuckerman's fears that vigilante justice would rule the Jewish street if the remnant of European Jews and their brethren in North America, Israel, and elsewhere did not have the courage to address the issue of collaboration with honesty ultimately proved unwarranted. In fact, Jews, of their own communal accord, did channel their emotions into organized tribunals. One might argue that the Jewish honor courts and the Israeli collaborator trials had no legal relevance or moral reverberation in Jewish communities beyond the immediate postwar years. But, to their credit, the Jewish honor courts and, to a lesser extent, the Israeli collaborator trials not only restored prewar patterns of Jewish autonomy but also allowed survivors, through their creation of a legal mechanism, to bring to justice fellow Jews with bloody hands, to reclaim agency and reassert their dignity, and, through their testimony, to work through their traumatic pasts on the witness stand.[48]

Notes

1. "Minutes of Executive Committee Meeting of World Jewish Congress," September 11, 1945, American Jewish Archives, Papers of the World Jewish Congress, file A 80/16, pp. 4–5.

2. One may wonder whether the honor courts drew inspiration, either explicitly or implicitly, from Jewish law (Halakha). They did not. In fact, they were separated from any Jewish theological principles. According to Jewish law, Jews may not hand over a fellow Jew, if unnamed or unspecified, to government authorities responsible for their systematic persecution, even if the entire community is threatened with obliteration. Jewish law only permits surrender of a named fellow Jew to an oppressive regime when an uncompromising stand might endanger the survival of the community if the authorities want him for an offense reasonably punishable by death. According to the rabbis, the demand for a named person, even if his probable fate is death, is probably not entirely arbitrary, for the named person had in all likelihood done something to draw the wrath of the government on himself. See David Daube, *Collaboration with Tyranny in Rabbinic Law* (London: Oxford University Press, 1965). Indeed, under this strict standard, which was far from any used by any of the postwar Jewish honor courts, all but a handful of putative collaborators standing trial would have been convicted. This was, however, not the case.

3. For the Polish case, see Gabriel N. Finder and Alexander V. Prusin, "Jewish Collaborators on Trial in Poland, 1944–1956," *Polin: Studies in Polish Jewry* 20 (2008): 122–48.

4. There is often a fine line between revenge and retribution. According to the Israel Supreme Court's interpretation of the Nazis and Nazi Collaborators (Punishment)

Law in one of the first collaborator cases tried under it, the intent of the law was "to seek revenge on the enemies and haters of Israel." Berel Lang notes that this interpretation "seems quite consciously to conflate revenge and the institution of justice." Berel Lang, "Holocaust-Memory and -Revenge: The Presence of the Past," in Berel Lang, *The Future of the Holocaust: Between History and Memory* (Ithaca, NY: Cornell University Press, 1999), 150. Simply put, when the victims of a perceived injury punish the perpetrators with their own hands and seek to inflict harm and suffering on the perpetrators, it is revenge. When the perpetrators are made to answer for their actions in a court of law, it is retribution. Punishment inspired by vengeance is unconstrained; retribution requires calibrating the punishment to fit the crime. In general, survivors exhausted their desire for revenge fairly soon after liberation and made their peace with the pursuit of retributive justice through the honor courts. Even so, it is not always easy to draw a distinction between revenge and retribution in the operation of the honor courts in specific cases, because both impulses seem sometimes to coexist. Hannah Arendt's censure of Attorney General Gideon Hausner's didactic approach to the prosecution of Adolf Eichmann, in which he put scores of witnesses on the stand not to establish the defendant's guilt but to shine a glaring light on Jewish suffering (not to mention Hausner's opening address at the trial, in which he invoked "six million prosecutors" whose "blood rises to heaven, but their voice cannot be heard"), might arguably be applicable to select proceedings in honor courts. It could appear, to borrow from Arendt's criticism of the Eichmann trial, that they were conducted "not in order to satisfy the demands of justice but to still the victims' desire for and, perhaps, right to revenge." Hannah Arendt, *Eichmann in Jerusalem: A Report on the Banality of Evil* (New York: Penguin, 1994 [1963]), 260–61. In two important articles, Berel Lang discusses the activities of the short-lived and mostly ineffectual attempts by a group of survivors led by Abba Kovner to wreak revenge on Germans after the war and the displaced revenge among Jews in political relations between Israel and Germany, in Jewish boycotts of German products, in the Israeli Philharmonic Orchestra's long-standing boycott of Richard Wagner's music, and in other modest forms. It is interesting to note that, aside from the one fleeting reference to the 1950 Israeli law, there is no reference in Lang's essays to the desire of many survivors to settle scores with suspected Jewish collaborators or to the honor courts. In addition to Lang's article "Holocaust-Memory and -Revenge," see Berel Lang, "Forgiveness, Revenge, and the Limits of Holocaust Justice," in Berel Lang, *Post-Holocaust: Interpretation, Misinterpretation, and the Claims of History* (Bloomington: Indiana University Press, 2005), 17–31. As Ulrike Weckel and Mark Roseman have recently shown, the idea of Jewish revenge was largely a construct in the minds of non-Jews, especially the Germans. See Ulrike Weckel, "Jüdische Rache? Wahrnemungen des Nürnberger Hauptkriegsverbrecherprozesses durch Angeklagte, Verteidiger und die deutsche Bevölkerung 1945/46," *Jahrbuch für Antisemitismusforschung* 22 (2013): 57–78; and Mark Roseman, "'But of Revenge, not a Sign': Germans' Fear of Jewish Revenge After World War II," *Jahrbuch für Antisemitismusforschung* 22 (2013): 79–95.

5. On the history of these Jewish historical commissions and documentation centers, see Laura Jockusch, *Collect and Record! Jewish Holocaust Documentation in Early Postwar Europe* (New York: Oxford University Press, 2012).

6. See the following Philip Friedman essays published in his *Roads to Extinction: Essays on the Holocaust* (New York: Jewish Publication Society, 1980): "Pseudo-Saviors in the Polish Ghettos: Mordechai Chaim Rumkowski of Lodz" (originally published in 1954), 333–52; "The Messianic Complex of a Nazi Collaborator in a Ghetto: Moses Merin of Sosnowiec" (originally published in 1953), 353–64; and "Jacob Gens: 'Commandant' of the Vilna Ghetto" (originally published in 1954), 365–80.

7. See Philip Friedman, "Outline of Program for Holocaust Research" (which Friedman had first published in 1950), in Friedman, *Roads to Extinction*, 571–76, esp. 574; and Philip Friedman, "Problems of Research on the Holocaust: An Overview," in Friedman, *Roads to Extinction*, 554–67, esp. 564–65.

8. Friedman, "Pseudo-Saviors," 334.

9. Friedman, "Pseudo-Saviors," 334.

10. Raul Hilberg, *The Destruction of the European Jews* (Chicago: Quadrangle Books, 1961), 31–32.

11. Hilberg, *Destruction of the European Jews* (1961), 206.

12. Hilberg, *Destruction of the European Jews* (1961), 662 (emphasis in original).

13. Hilberg, *Destruction of the European Jews* (1961), 17.

14. Arendt, *Eichmann in Jerusalem*, 117, 118. In the same breath, Arendt acknowledges the contribution of Hilberg's *Destruction of the European Jews* to exposing the role of Jewish leaders in the destruction process.

15. Arendt, *Eichmann in Jerusalem*, 125–26.

16. Arendt, *Eichmann in Jerusalem*, 125.

17. Deborah E. Lipstadt, *The Eichmann Trial* (New York: Schocken, 2011), 156–57.

18. Arendt, *Eichmann in Jerusalem*, 118.

19. Isaiah Trunk, *Judenrat: The Jewish Councils in Eastern Europe Under Nazi Occupation* (New York: Macmillan, 1972), 574.

20. See Jockusch, *Collect and Record*, 84–120.

21. Lucy S. Dawidowicz, *The War Against the Jews, 1933–1945* (New York: Holt, Rinehart & Winston, 1975), 348.

22. Christopher R. Browning, "In the Cauldron," *New York Review of Books* (August 16, 2012): 70.

23. Raul Hilberg, *The Destruction of the European Jews* (New York: Holmes & Meier, 1985), 1037–38.

24. Raul Hilberg, *Perpetrators, Victims, Bystanders: The Jewish Catastrophe, 1933–1945* (New York: Harper Collins, 1992), 116.

INTRODUCTION

25. The same sentiment had already been adumbrated in 1979 in the assessment of Adam Czerniaków, the head of the Jewish council in Warsaw, that Hilberg coauthored with Stanislaw Staron in their introduction to the English translation of Czerniaków's diary. See Raul Hilberg and Stanislaw Staron, introduction to *The Warsaw Diary of Adam Czerniaków*, ed. Raul Hilberg, Stanislaw Staron, and Josef Kermisz, trans. Stanislaw Staron and the Staff of Yad Vashem (Chicago: Ivan R. Dee in association with the United States Holocaust Memorial Museum, 1999 [1979]), 25–70.
26. Doron Rabinovici, *Eichmann's Jews: The Jewish Administration of Holocaust Vienna, 1938–1945*, trans. Nick Somers (Cambridge, MA: Polity Press, 2011), 11.
27. Gabriel N. Finder, "The Trial of Shepsl Rotholc and the Politics of Retribution in the Aftermath of the Holocaust," *Gal-Ed* 20 (2006): 80 (English section).
28. Laura Jockusch, "Justice at Nuremberg? Jewish Responses to Nazi War-Crime Trials in Allied-Occupied Germany," *Jewish Social Studies* 19.1 (2012): 107–47.
29. Thus Hannah Arendt could claim in *Eichmann in Jerusalem* that the prosecution avoided the issue of Jewish collaboration like the plague because it was the diametric opposite of what Israeli leaders wished to emphasize: Jewish resistance, which they claimed was Zionist in spirit. See Arendt, *Eichmann in Jerusalem*, 119–22.
30. On the attempt by the Eichmann trial prosecution and judges to avoid the pitfalls of the Kasztner trial, see Lawrence Douglas, *The Memory of Judgment: Making Law and History in the Trials of the Holocaust* (New Haven, CT: Yale University Press, 2001), 155–56; and Leora Bilsky, *Transformative Justice: Israeli Identity on Trial* (Ann Arbor: University of Michigan Press, 2004), 87–93.
31. State of Israel, Ministry of Justice, *The Trial of Adolf Eichmann* (Jerusalem: The Trust for the Publication of the Proceedings of the Eichmann Trial, in cooperation with the Israel State Archives and Yad Vashem—The Holocaust Martyrs' and Heroes' Remembrance Authority, 1994), 1: 71.
32. State of Israel, Ministry of Justice, *Trial of Adolf Eichmann*, 3: 946.
33. State of Israel, Ministry of Justice, *Trial of Adolf Eichmann*, 3: 1059.
34. Lipstadt, *Eichmann Trial*, 97.
35. State of Israel, Ministry of Justice, *Trial of Adolf Eichmann*, 3: 1286–91.
36. It is interesting to note that, in response to Eichmann's statement during his interrogation by the Israeli police, in which he said that he was responsible for loading the freight cars that took Jews to their death to their maximum capacity, the court ruled that "the legal and moral responsibility of the person who delivers the victim to his death is ... no less, and maybe even greater than the liability of the one who does the victim to death." State of Israel, Ministry of Justice, *Trial of Adolf Eichmann*, 5: 2160. Of course, the court was referring to Eichmann, but because he, like suspected Jewish collaborators, was tried under the Nazis and Nazi Collaborators (Punishment) Law, the same reasoning should have been applicable to Jewish collaborators.
37. Primo Levi, *The Drowned and the Saved* (New York: Summit, 1988), 36–69.

38. "Claude Lanzmann's Postscript to 'Shoah,'" *New York Times* (May 17, 2013), www.nytimes.com/2013/05/18/arts/18iht-dupont18.html?_r=0 (accessed October 14, 2014). Murmelstein gave several interviews to newspapers after the war (e.g., in 1963 to the *Neue Zürcher Zeitung*), which indicates that he could have appeared in Lanzmann's film had Lanzmann been able to find a place for him. See Rabinovici, *Eichmann's Jews*, ch. 11.

39. A recent book inspired by the 1975 outtake of Lanzmann's interview with Murmelstein but published before the release of *The Last of the Unjust* is Ronny Loewy and Katharina Rauschenberger, eds., *"Der Letzte der Ungerechten": Der "Judenälteste": Benjamin Murmelstein in Filmen 1942–1975* (Frankfurt: Campus, 2011). Several of the essays in this volume examine the interview, but none ask why Lanzmann omitted it from *Shoah*.

40. Browning, "In the Cauldron," 70–75; Agata Tuszyńska, *Vera Gran: The Accused* (New York: Knopf, 2013) (originally published in Polish in 2010).

41. www.tabletmag.com/tag/agata-tuszynska (accessed October 14, 2013).

42. Treatment of this subject has expanded in the last decade and a half. See István Deák, Jan T. Gross, and Tony Judt, eds., *The Politics of Retribution in Europe: World War II and Its Aftermath* (Princeton, NJ: Princeton University Press, 2001); and Alice Kaplan, *The Collaborator: The Trial and Execution of Robert Brasillach* (Chicago: University of Chicago Press, 2000). For the trials of Nazi collaborators in Czechoslovakia, see Benjamin Frommer, *National Cleansing: Retribution Against Nazi Collaborators in Postwar Czechoslovakia* (Cambridge, UK: Cambridge University Press, 2004). In his well-received and widely read magnum opus *Postwar: A History of Europe Since 1945* (New York: Penguin, 2006), Tony Judt devotes the second chapter to trials of collaborators throughout Europe in the late 1940s. Before 2000 the most significant book on this topic was Peter Novick, *The Resistance Versus Vichy: The Purge of Collaborators in Liberated France* (New York: Columbia University Press, 1968).

43. N. K. C. A. in't Veld, *De joodse ereraad* (The Hague: SDU Uitgeverji, 1989).

44. David Engel, "Who Is a Collaborator? The Trial of Michał Weichert," in Sławomir Kapralski, ed., *The Jews in Poland* (Krakow: Judaica Foundation, Center for Jewish Culture, 1999), 2: 339–70; Gabriel N. Finder, "Honor Courts," in *The YIVO Encyclopedia of Jews in Eastern Europe*, ed. Gershon David Hundert (New Haven, CT: Yale University Press, 2008), 751–53 (available online at www.yivoencyclopedia.org); Finder, "Trial of Shepsl Rotholc"; Finder and Prusin, "Jewish Collaborators"; and Hans-Jürgen Bömelburg, "Der Kollaborationsvorwurf in der polnischen und jüdischen Öffentlichkeit," in Joachim Tauber, ed., *"Kollaboration" in Nordosteuropa: Erscheinungsformen und Deutungen im 20. Jahrhundert* (Wiesbaden, Germany: Veröffentlichungen des Nordost-Instituts, 2006), 250–88.

45. Evelyn Adunka, *Die Vierte Gemeinde: Die Wiener Juden in der Zeit von 1945 bis heute* (Berlin: Philo, 2000); Jael Geis, *Übrig sein, Leben "danach": Juden deutscher Herkunft in der britischen und amerikanischen Zone Deutschlands 1945–1949* (Berlin: Philo, 2000); Angelika Königseder and Juliane Wetzel, *Waiting for Hope: Jewish Displaced Persons in Post–World War II Germany* (Evanston, IL: Northwestern University Press, 2001);

Zeev Mankowitz, *Life Between Memory and Hope: The Survivors of the Holocaust in Occupied Germany* (Cambridge, UK: Cambridge University Press, 2002); Susanne Rolinek, *Jüdische Lebenswelten 1945–1955: Flüchtlinge in der amerikanischen Zone Österreichs* (Vienna: Studienverlag, 2007); Margarete Meyers Feinstein, *Holocaust Survivors in Postwar Germany, 1945–1957* (New York: Cambridge University Press, 2010). One chapter in Isaiah Trunk's pioneering treatment of the Jewish councils also addresses the postwar treatment of their surviving leaders (Trunk, *Judenrat)*.

46. Yehiam Weitz, *The Man Who Was Murdered Twice: The Life, Trial, and Death of Dr. Israel Kastner* (Jerusalem: Keter, 1995) (Hebrew); Yehiam Weitz, "The Law for the Punishment of Nazis and Their Collaborators and the Relationship of Israeli Society in the 1950s to the Holocaust and Survivors," *Kathedra* (1996): 153–64 (Hebrew); Hanna Yablonka, "The Development of Holocaust Consciousness in Israel: The Nuremberg, Kapos, Kastner, and Eichmann Trials," *Israel Studies* 8.3 (2003): 1–24; Orna Ben-Naftali and Yogev Tuval, "Punishing International Crimes Committed by the Persecuted: The Kapo Trials in Israel (1950s and 1960s)," *Journal of International Criminal Justice* 4 (March 2006): 128–78; Tuvia Friling, *Who Are You, Leon Berger? The Story of a Kapo in Auschwitz: History, Politics, and Memory* (Jerusalem: Yad Vashem, 2009) (Hebrew) (translated into English as *A Jewish Kapo in Auschwitz: History, Memory, and the Politics of Survival*, trans. Haim Watzman (Waltham, MA: Brandeis University Press, 2014); Rivka Brot, "Julius Siegel: A 'Kapo' in Four (Judicial) Acts," *Dapim: Studies on the Shoah* 25 (2011): 65–127.

47. Annette Wieviorka, *The Era of the Witness* (Ithaca, NY: Cornell University Press, 2006) (originally published in French in 1998).

48. The transformation of testimony into legal evidence and thus into a judicially potent act, with its potential to restore closure and normative coherence to a survivor's world, itself interrupted by traumatic memory, is discussed in Douglas, *Memory of Judgment*, ch. 6; and in Shoshana Felman, *The Juridical Unconscious: Trials and Traumas in the Twentieth Century* (Cambridge, MA: Harvard University Press, 2002), chaps. 3 and 4.

1

Why Punish Collaborators?

DAVID ENGEL

That many members of European communities recently liberated from Nazi occupation felt a powerful need to punish other members whom they suspected of having aided the occupiers in establishing or strengthening their oppressive regime is patent. Indeed, nearly every government that assumed power after 1945 in a territory formerly under Nazi rule quickly established instruments to identify purported collaborators and to call them to account for their alleged misdeeds.[1] In several countries those instruments were underwritten by widespread popular outrage, which expressed itself virtually from the moment of liberation in individual or mob acts of vengeance against fellow countrymen whose wartime conduct had aroused their neighbors' ire. In some cases, in fact, the instruments can even be viewed as an attempt to bring such violent emotion under state control.[2] The number of people against whom governmental and popular measures were directed across the continent has yet to be estimated, but in a few regions for which figures have been compiled, investigations of collaboration charges during the immediate postwar years appear to have encompassed perhaps as much as 5 percent of the total population.[3]

European Jews who survived the Holocaust had no governmental apparatus of their own. Hence they could not wield the power of the state on their own behalf to prosecute those of their number who they thought had done them wrong under Nazi rule. Still, both Jews who returned to their former countries of residence and refugees in displaced persons (DP) camps in Italy and in the Allied occupation zones of Germany and Austria took action to settle accounts with those who they believed had transgressed the boundaries of morally obligatory communal solidarity. So-called honor courts, citizens' tribunals, or rehabilitation commissions became significant features of efforts by Jews to reorganize their communities in the wake of catastrophe. International Jewish political organizations used ad hoc disciplinary mechanisms to consider charges within their ranks against members whose actions during the Nazi years may not have comported with their expectations.[4] Even in countries beyond the former Nazi orbit to which survivors emigrated following the war, Jewish communal institutions occasionally pronounced judgment on recent arrivals accused by others of wartime misbehavior.[5] And in Israel, where state power could be invoked in the name of the Jewish people as a whole, a 1950 law imposed criminal penalties against anyone, Jew or non-Jew, who, "during the period of the Nazi regime, committed in an enemy country an act by which, had he committed it in Israel[i] territory, he would have been guilty of" a range of offenses, including murder, rape, robbery, kidnapping, grievous harm, or extortion against "a persecuted person as a persecuted person."[6] The proportion of Jews who became targets for prosecution by other Jews was surely far less than the norm among other European communities that had been part of the Nazi orbit;[7] after all, the Third Reich had left virtually no room for Jewish collaboration on the ideological or political levels, and of the relatively small number of Jews who played a role in the administration of Jewish communities or other aggregations of Jews under Nazi rule—officials of the Judenräte, members of ghetto police forces, camp functionaries (kapos)—only a minority lived long enough to be called on to answer for their deeds. Nevertheless, in many parts of the postwar Jewish world, judging such purported malefactors occupied a significant measure of communal attention.

It is hardly self-evident that it should have done so. The European states that sought out collaborators and put them on trial were concerned largely with obviating the prospect that people who viewed the Third Reich sympathetically might continue to occupy positions of public influence under regimes whose legitimacy depended on repudiation of the Nazi legacy. Jews hardly needed to worry about similar influence in their own communities: Unlike other populations emerging from Nazi hegemony, European Jewry did not come away from World War II with a significant body of former Nazi fellow travelers in its midst. Nor did others reproach it for having accepted or believed in the Nazis' vision for its future. Its motivation to undertake a collective moral reckoning with respect to its actions and attitudes toward the Nazi regime ought, then, at first glance, to have been far less acutely felt than among populations where noticeable numbers had thought that regime a good thing. But if so, why did postwar Jewish communities seek to punish some of their members for their wartime behavior and to purge them from their ranks?

The punishment of collaborators has often been figured as a form of retribution—literally, payback for actions supposed to have introduced a debit in a community's moral balance. The concept is familiar to ethicists and to legal theorists alike. It has figured prominently in intellectual debates concerning proper maintenance of a just social order, especially since 1797, when Immanuel Kant famously postulated it as both the sole legitimate basis for punishment and an essential foundation of a just regime.

> Judicial punishment (*poena forensis*) ... must never be applied simply as a means to some other good, whether for the criminal himself or for civil society. Instead it must be imposed upon [the criminal] solely because he has committed a crime, for a person must never be treated simply as a means to another's ends.... He must first be found deserving of punishment before any thought can be given to whether his punishment will bring any advantage to himself or to his fellow citizens. The law of punishment is a categorical imperative, and woe be to anyone who meanders through the twists and turns of happiness theory [*Schlangenwindungen der Glückseligkeitslehre*] in order to locate the advantage that punishment, or even a measure of release from it, promises to bestow upon someone, according to the pharisaic precept that "it is better for one person to die than for the entire people to be destroyed."[8] For if justice perishes, then there is no more value to human life on earth.[9]

By terming punishment a categorical imperative, Kant raised it to the status of an unconditional commandment of human reason, to be undertaken as an end in itself, not on condition that it fulfill any specific goal. He based his determination on what was for him the intuitive notion that social life is possible only in a state of moral equilibrium.[10] Individuals who, of their own volition, take the property of other members of their community or harm their persons jeopardize the security of all property and of every person, and if they are permitted to do so with impunity, no secure existence is possible. Hence, Kant inferred, all individuals are bound by an absolute moral duty to refrain from doing so, and communities are bound by a parallel moral duty to punish transgressors in proportion to the injury their actions have caused. For Kant, justice can obtain only when communities obey this retributive obligation.

Yet Jews who lived through the Nazi occupation hardly inhabited a Kantian judicial universe—one in which the duties of individuals toward one another and toward their larger communities were clearly defined, in which individuals could choose freely whether to fulfill their duties or to transgress them, and in which communities agreed regarding the severity with which particular transgressions ought to be punished. Small wonder, then, that classical theoretical conceptions of justice and punishment were severely strained when those Jews tried to apply them under Nazi impact. Indeed, as a description of how Jews who pondered the matter actually spoke about how to deal with suspected collaborators in their midst, retribution hardly exhausts the range of justifications for punishment that they advanced. In fact, in some instances it misses the mark altogether.

Consider, for example, what was perhaps the first instance in which a group of Jews took organized punitive action against some of their fellows who they believed to have abetted the Nazi regime: the death sentences imposed by the Jewish Fighting Organization (Żydowska Organizacja Bojowa; ŻOB) in Warsaw, shortly after the organization's establishment in late July 1942, on members of the Judenrat and the Jewish police in the Warsaw ghetto and on others suspected of being Gestapo informants.[11] No contemporary document is extant that details the process by which ŻOB decided to undertake such actions or the reasons advanced for them. However, several later representations, both by ŻOB activists and by observers at close range, offer a broad assortment of explanations for why punishment was sought.

Emmanuel Ringelblum, keeper of the Warsaw ghetto's clandestine archive—who, although not a member of a ŻOB combat unit, had been keen since the organization's founding to assist it and to record its activities[12]—put forth an early explanation, in December 1942, when executions remained the only armed actions in which ŻOB actively engaged.

> [After the mass deportations from the ghetto to Treblinka in summer 1942] people think about who was guilty of the mass slaughter, and they come to the conclusion that much guilt falls on the Jewish police. Many even claim that the Jewish police were the only guilty ones. So now people are taking revenge. The police are reminded of their sin at every opportunity.... The time for a moral accounting [*kheshbon hanefesh*] has come, for reflection on what had transpired. People seek revenge against

> the guilty. A secret hand put away [Jakób] Lejkin [deputy commandant of the Warsaw Jewish ghetto police], who was the principal culprit in the resettlement.¹³ At every step the Jewish police are reminded of their guilt for the resettlement. The Jewish police are pursued wherever it is possible to do so.¹⁴

Ringelblum went on to record a series of heinous actions in which the police had allegedly engaged during the deportations, which began on July 22, 1942, and sent 265,000 Warsaw Jews to their deaths over the next seven weeks: kidnapping Jews on the street or in their dwellings and carrying them by force to the deportation trains, beating recalcitrant Jews to death, extorting payment in cash or kind (including sex) from potential deportees in return for release, and in general behaving like wild beasts.¹⁵ Such deeds, he indicated, were habitually recounted when policemen and former policemen were chased down and ostracized from ghetto society.¹⁶ Ringelblum's text thus strongly suggests that the "secret hand" that had recently dispatched police commandant Lejkin (a hand that, he was surely aware, belonged to ŻOB) executed a broad public demand for retributive justice in precisely the Kantian sense: as an intuitive response to a perceived deficit in the community's moral ledger, no more, no less.

ŻOB itself also used the language of moral restoration in its own retrospective description of Lejkin's assassination. In a March 1944 report to Jewish representatives in London that summarized the organization's activities since inception, the report's author (probably Icchak Cukierman, the organization's commander following the ghetto revolt of April 1943) indicated that ŻOB had undertaken from the earliest moments of its existence "to purify the atmosphere in the ghetto by liquidating the most demoralized elements, the criminals who had sold out to the Germans."¹⁷ Another ŻOB member, Cywia Lubetkin (who married Cukierman in 1946), also stressed the theme of resetting a moral balance in her recollection of the assassination of Lejkin's predecessor as police commandant, Józef Szeryński.

> We determined that our first armed action ... would begin with the killing of a resident of the ghetto. And as strange as it may seem, we could not behave differently. By killing the commandant of the police, we wanted to expunge the stain of Jews leading their brothers to the slaughter with their own hands. We knew that this detestable band understood no language except that of the gun. [We also knew] that

if we hoped to achieve anything at all, we need first to purify the atmosphere.[18]

Nevertheless, these same texts also adduced additional justifications for punishing those who would eventually be branded collaborators, justifications that not only depart from the model of Kantian retributive justice but also actually contradict it. The ŻOB report of March 1944, for instance, made it clear that the expenditure of valuable ammunition for the purpose of killing *Jews* before Germans was not only a moral demand but an instrumental, tactical necessity.

> Because the people of the Ordnungsdienst [the Jewish police] ... and the Judenrat are carrying out the German demands together with the Ukrainians and the Letts, it is necessary actively to oppose their collective deeds. ... [By killing those who have sold out to the Germans] we will throw fear into the Judenrat and its institutions. The death of the commandant of the Order Police, Jakób Lejkin ... was a warning to his colleagues in the police, and the death sentence upon Izrael Fürst[19] ... served as a warning to the degenerate Judenrat.[20]

Cukierman spoke in later documents as well about actions against Judenrat and police members as a way to retard the killing of Jews, reproaching himself in hindsight for not having sent more collaborators to their deaths sooner. "We needed to execute not only Józef Szeryński,"[21] he declared in an oral history recorded in the 1970s. Retrospectively, he ventured that "before Szeryński we needed to execute a few policemen so that [others] would be afraid to enter a Jewish courtyard." Had he and his colleagues done so, he estimated, the destruction of Warsaw Jewry would not have been stopped altogether, but "we could have made it difficult for the Germans, we could have forced them to deploy 10,000 Germans to do the job that was done by 2,000–3,000 Jews."[22] In this representation, then, executions of Jewish policemen and Judenrat officials were justified less for their retributive than for their deterrent and preventive values. Indeed, Cukierman suggested that the reason ŻOB had not acted sooner was that, even though its moral disapproval of collaboration was clear from the start, its sense that collaborators merited violent punishment did not become so until their vital role in the deportation process was revealed.[23] And in fact, it was only following the failed attempt on Szeryński's life on August 20, 1942, after the mass deportations had already sent 180,000 Warsaw Jews to their deaths, that ŻOB declared *all* members of the Jewish police outlaws, subjecting them potentially to punishment not necessarily for any specific acts already committed but for acts they *might* commit as a result of their positions.[24]

Lubetkin also stressed the preventive aim of assassination, but she added a further defense as well: "The most important thing was to make the Jews feel that there was a ruling authority in the ghetto other than the Judenrat and the Jewish police."[25] The ŻOB leadership was aware virtually from the outset that its activities constituted a challenge to the ability of the Judenrat to determine how Warsaw Jews should behave in the face of the German deportation of the bulk of the ghetto's population, and it expressed dismay that ghetto residents appeared to prefer their official leaders' advice against active resistance to that of the fighters.[26] In Lubetkin's words, ŻOB sought "to take into [its] own hands the rudder of communal life . . . , to elevate [itself] to the rank of the element that determined the Jews' life and fate."[27] From the largely hostile public reception it initially received, ŻOB learned that it would need to take power in the ghetto by force. Such use of force against other Jews could be justified most easily by branding its targets as traitors to the Jewish people and by representing their assassination as punishment for their crime. It was, however, actually no less an instrumental act than a retributive one, one aimed at least as much at a political end as at a judicial one.

Ringelblum mentioned yet another justification for killing, one that he sensed not so much within the ŻOB leadership as among the broader community. He suggested that although few ghetto residents behaved as ŻOB desired, they largely approved of actions against the Jewish police as a way to atone for their own passivity.

> As long as the deportations were going on . . . everyone remained silent. People let themselves be led like sheep to the slaughterhouse. . . . This can be said about the majority of the men and women who were taken to the *Umschlagplatz*[28] during the deportations. This will remain a permanent riddle, this passivity of the Jewish population, even toward their own police. Now that people have calmed down a bit and are summing up what has transpired, a feeling of shame has arisen over the fact that Jews did not resist even their own police.[29]

It was in this context, Ringelblum proposed, that the ghetto police became objects of popular revulsion.[30] Ringelblum's implication was that, even though the Jews of the ghetto themselves had failed to challenge the police's authority during the deportations, they later rhetorically excluded it from their community in order to transfer onto others what they actually believed to be their own responsibility for their fate.[31] Punishing a few members of the police thus became a way of releasing many more who had survived the 1942 deportation from the moral stigma that, Ringelblum hinted, may rightly have been attached to them.[32]

Turning the police into rhetorical others also appears to have provided an additional justification for demanding punishment on the basis of membership in the police force instead of on the basis of specific crimes that individual members allegedly committed. Ringelblum explained that although every policeman remaining after the great deportations claimed either to have played no active role in them or to have used his position to assist Jews, in fact it was "the crude and common characters among the police who remained among the 300 officers maintaining order in the ghetto today, while the less brazen, who didn't have enough money for bribes, were sent away either to Treblinka or to various camps like Smolensk or Lublin."[33] In other words, policemen who survived could be assumed to have done so precisely because they had committed criminal acts. Here was yet an additional basis for inculpating *all* policemen on the basis of membership instead of specific action.

Retributive theories of justice in the Kantian mode categorically invalidate punishment for tactical, deterrent, political, or psychological reasons. The ethics that guided ŻOB in its quest to punish those whom it regarded as collaborators thus appears to have relied implicitly on notions that extended well beyond retribution.

Following the war ŻOB veterans in Poland, along with former members of the communist underground, continued to pursue accused collaborators for reasons that displayed both retributive and instrumental motives. To be sure, the tactical and deterrent grounds for punishment had lost their relevance with the end of occupation, but political and psychological justifications continued to figure prominently in the language of those who demanded most vociferously that Jews whose wartime conduct had been improper in their eyes be called to account for their behavior.

The persistence of such motifs, adjusted to fit the postwar environment, is evident in the pronouncements of the Civic Tribunal for Former Collaborators with the Germans, established by the Central Committee of Polish Jews in October 1946, and in public discussions of the tribunal's activities.[34] In descriptions of the Civic Tribunal's purpose the notion of purification figured prominently.[35] However, such purification was presented more often than not as an instrumental good more than as an absolute moral imperative. Two such goods were articulated most frequently. One was stated most clearly in the Central Committee's summary report for 1947, which described the Civic Tribunal's work during its initial months as follows: Along with "cleansing Jewish society of people who for one reason or another collaborated with the Nazi authorities during the occupation," the quasi-judicial body was charged with "unmasking traitors to the Jewish nation, who have tens and hundreds of victims on their conscience and still pass or want to pass for respectable people or want to play a certain role in the life of our society."[36] Indeed, it appears that the Civic Tribunal's most immediate task in the eyes of its architects was to control access to positions of prominence and influence in the postwar Polish Jewish community or in Polish social and cultural life more broadly.[37] In all probability it was for this reason that its initial targets were Jews who had held such positions before the war and sought to reclaim them after the war ended.

The chain of events that resulted in the Civic Tribunal's creation was set in motion first of all by the postwar Polish government's appointment of renowned theater director and Jewish communal activist Michał Weichert, who during most of the occupation period directed a Jewish social welfare agency that the German authorities permitted to operate legally as its liaison to the surviving Jewish population in Kraków and vicinity—a prospect that ŻOB activists affiliated with the Central Committee could not abide.[38] The Civic Tribunal brought its first cases against a Jewish sports hero turned Warsaw ghetto policeman, Shepsl Rotholc, when he sought to resume his boxing career.[39] Also prominently mentioned as a person to be prosecuted was popular Jewish singer and actress Wiera Gran, who was suspected of having provided information to the German secret police in return for permission to perform outside the Warsaw ghetto.[40] In all cases the principal punishment that threatened those convicted was disqualification from serving as a governor, official, or employee of a Jewish community, on the grounds that the offender had failed during the war to "behave in a manner befitting a Jewish citizen."[41]

The manner in which the Civic Tribunal determined what constituted "behavior befitting a Jewish citizen" pointed to the political aspect of its mission. For the most part, the Civic Tribunal appears to have held that once the German authorities began deporting Jews to their deaths, no path other than complete refusal to cooperate with the regime on any level was acceptable. Hence anyone who, like Rotholc, continued to serve in the Jewish police after the summer of 1942 was to be considered culpable by virtue of that fact alone, no matter whether he played an active role in leading Jews to the deportation transports, used his position to shelter Jews, or simply remained behind a desk filing papers and answering the telephone while the deportations were proceeding.[42]

But police service was not the only form of collaboration the Civic

Tribunal condemned. Weichert, for example, headed an organization whose sole purpose, from his point of view and from that of his many prominent Jewish public supporters, was to provide food, clothing, and medicine to thousands of Jews who remained alive in labor camps after the mass deportations of 1942—sustenance to which many survivors of the Holocaust owed their survival. Yet the Civic Tribunal found that "no matter how much [Weichert's agency] might have actually assisted [Jews in] the camps . . . , it must be asserted that [it] was a collaborationist organization by virtue of its very existence."[43] What made it such, in the Civic Tribunal's mind, was not only that it continued to exist after mass deportations had begun but also that in October 1943 Weichert had refused a direct order from ŻOB and from the underground political parties to which it reported to close the organization and to turn its store of supplies over to a ŻOB-supported underground relief group.[44] Such insubordination at a time when all Jews were expected actively to resist the Nazi regime at all levels provided the Civic Tribunal with the clearest indication that Weichert had not behaved in a manner "befitting a Jewish citizen."

> Dr. Weichert's cooperation with the Hitlerite occupier occurred at a time when the community in Poland was mustering its forces to fight the enemy, when . . . the Jewish Fighting Organization in the Warsaw ghetto set the benchmark for struggle with the enemy through heroic and steadfast resistance, when in virtually every camp a resistance movement was organized. . . . Dr. Weichert's behavior must be censured all the more severely because it deviated so greatly from the behavior of the community in arms.[45]

The Civic Tribunal's verdict against Weichert thus echoed the political justification advanced for ŻOB's wartime assassinations: It underwrote ŻOB's claim to sole legitimate authority against the pretensions of Jewish bodies sanctioned by the Nazi regime. In addition, by invoking "the community in arms" as the proper source for Jewish behavioral norms, it recalled the psychological difficulty Ringelblum had called to mind in his description of Jewish attitudes toward the ghetto police: Attributing their fate to the treachery of collaborators permitted them to avoid confronting their own lack of active resistance. Offering an escape from that difficulty was the second instrumental good commonly attributed to the Civic Tribunal, a good that was articulated explicitly at the time of the Civic Tribunal's creation.

> Throughout the world, wherever the Hitlerite plague reached, wherever Nazi "morality" devoured the spirits and souls of people who were unable to resist the temptation, a purge is being conducted. Everywhere—in Poland, France, Czechoslovakia, Yugoslavia, Norway, Denmark, Holland, and Belgium—special tribunals have been established, with the task of investigating the guilt of those citizens who cooperated with the Hitlerite authority and its agents. . . . A self-respecting people cannot allow itself to ignore this matter. . . . We will be committing a sin toward future Jewish generations if we falsify the historical truth by covering it up. . . . We must have the courage to state that our people does not consist entirely of innocent martyrs. Our standing will be no less in the eyes of the world if we brand and try our own turncoats and traitors.[46]

In fact, the Civic Tribunal aimed at elevating Polish Jewry's standing not only in the eyes of the world but also in its own eyes. It did so by underwriting a version of history according to which, after 1942, Jews were able to survive in Poland only through collaboration or through resistance. Accordingly, it rejected the arguments of Jewish policemen, like Rotholc, who claimed in effect that collaboration (through police membership) and resistance (through using the privileges that collaboration provided to rescue Jews) were compatible behaviors,[47] along with Weichert's contention that he had maintained a middle ground between the two poles by operating a nonpolitical agency that assisted Jews in a manner that the Germans tolerated.[48] Doing so allowed all Jews, except for the small number branded collaborators, to claim the mantle of resisters, thereby representing themselves to others and to themselves not as craven victims complicit in their own fate but as heroes who, though hopelessly outgunned by their enemies, fought the good fight to the end.

Weichert had earlier stood trial before a Polish criminal court, which found, in stark contrast to the Jewish Civic Tribunal, that "neither the manner in which the accused behaved nor his personal deportment lead to the conclusion that the accused intended to collaborate with the occupier."[49] In demanding that the Jewish Civic Tribunal take up Weichert's case nevertheless, his Jewish accusers indicated that "the criminal court examined the case on the level of violation of the law . . . , whereas the Civic Tribunal will examine the case exclusively on the ethical plane."[50] The distinction drawn between the two levels offers yet another indication that Jews who made use of the Civic Tribunal to dispense punishment to collaborators sought something more than simple retributive *poena forensis* in the Kantian sense.

In two other locations in which Jews undertook to identify and punish collaborators in their midst—in the DP camps and in the State of Israel—the balance of intrinsic and instrumental values ascribed to such undertakings appears to have tended more toward the intrinsic value than it did in wartime or in postwar Poland. Such a tendency is evidenced primarily by the insistence of the heads of the so-called rehabilitation commissions in the camps and of legislators and judges in Israel upon doing precisely what the Civic Tribunal in Poland was supposed not to do: to consider the problem of collaboration on a strictly legal instead of on a broadly "ethical" basis. They did so by undertaking to assign culpability only to specific acts normally regarded as criminal, not to broader patterns of conduct deemed not "befitting a Jewish citizen." The Israeli Nazis and Nazi Collaborators (Punishment) Law of 1950 enumerated such acts in detail.[51] It also provided for release from criminal responsibility under conditions that the Civic Tribunal in Poland often disallowed: where an offender "did or omitted to do the act in order to save himself from the threat of immediate death" or "with intent to avert consequences more serious than those which resulted from the act or omission."[52] Similarly, the Rehabilitation Commission of the Central Committee of Liberated Jews in the American Zone of Occupied in Germany dissented from the notion that once mass killings began, the only legitimate behavior for Jews was complete noncooperation with any instrument of the Nazi regime. Considering the case of Beinisz Tkacz, a policeman in the ghetto of Kaunas (where the police force and the Judenrat were established only after a quarter of the city's Jews had already been murdered), the Rehabilitation Commission noted that the police were composed of different individuals with various motives for service.

> Tkacz joined the police during the initial period, when the Judenrat introduced a civic element, generally from Zionist circles, with the aim of protecting the ghetto from the influence of irresponsible elements. ... [But] even in the initial period various individuals with criminal tendencies joined, and they used their positions to perform criminal acts, helping the German murderers to destroy the Jewish population. There were also those who lost their former moral balance and allowed themselves to be led away from the straight path by the poisonous atmosphere that the Germans created.... In general the police did not have a good name among ghetto inhabitants. But applying that opinion as a generalization about all members of the police without exception, without approaching each case individually, can lead to grave injustice.[53]

Hence, the Rehabilitation Commission noted, "In the absence of a definite statutory regulation or a decision by a higher legislative authority declaring mere membership in the ghetto police or a similar body to be a crime, the Rehabilitation Commission dealt with the matter ... according to general legal principles, basing itself upon concrete proofs of guilt of innocence."[54] In other words, the Rehabilitation Commission, like the Israeli courts, concerned itself less with the political question of whether an individual obeyed a legitimate or an illegitimate authority and more with the strictly legal question of whether that individual had beaten, extorted, or otherwise harmed the persons or property of others with criminal intent.

To be sure, when Jews in the DP camps and in Israel talked about the reasons why collaborators should be punished, instrumental considerations were invoked along with expressions of the need for retributive justice *strictu sensu*. In the camps the commissions that passed judgment on suspects were usually figured as vehicles for "rehabilitation"; as with their counterpart in Poland, their primary public task was the future-oriented one of determining who was fit or unfit to assume positions of authority in the displaced persons community.[55] Indeed, a significant number of the cases they heard were initiated by individuals seeking to clear their own names from suspicion so that they could play a communal role or avail themselves of communal services.[56] In Israel the Nazis and Nazi Collaborators (Punishment) Law appears to have been widely perceived as a vehicle for expressing public identification with the heroic legacy of ŻOB and other armed resistance groups together with rejection of the ignominy generally imputed at the time to the (ultimately unsuccessful) survival and rescue strategies that had been pursued by the Judenräte in Lodz, Wilno, Białystok, and other large Jewish communities.[57] Here, too, punishment of collaborators helped Holocaust survivors and other Jews who had lived through the period come to grips psychologically with the catastrophe that had recently befallen the Jewish people.

Nevertheless, the judicial instruments in the DP camps and in the State of Israel that were entrusted with the punishment of collaborators appear on the whole to have operated with somewhat less regard for the demands of a public pursuing largely instrumental ends and somewhat greater concern for a strictly proportional retribution as an end in itself than did their counterparts in Poland during and immediately following the Nazi occupation. This difference may have resulted because the former instruments bore greater responsibility for maintaining public order than the latter instruments did. The underground courts of the ghetto fighters that sentenced members of the Jewish police and other legal organizations to death were, according to their own self-conception, working actively to subvert the public order that the German occupiers had imposed. In postwar Poland the task of establishing and preserving public order was retained by the Polish state, which assigned to Jewish communal bodies no necessary role in its administration. By contrast, in the DP camps, at least in the American Occupation Zone in Germany beginning in late 1946, Jews were afforded a significant measure of autonomy, including an implicit charge to police their own.[58] And in Israel, of course, the state and the Jewish community were effectively united.

These differences became significant when, following the war, survivors, mainly in the DP camps but in other locations as well, began spontaneously to exact revenge on former ghetto policemen and especially on people identified as kapos or block elders in labor or concentration camps who allegedly beat Jews under their charge.[59] In Poland the question of how to deal with such instances of popular violence remained under the exclusive purview of state authorities. As a result, the Jewish Civic Tribunal that tried suspected collaborators and the Jewish communal agencies that supported it were freed from the fundamental judicial responsibility of making certain that individuals suffered no loss of life, limb, or property without due process of law. Consequently, they could devote their full attention to the communal consequences of their action; they were not required to take into account the individual reckoning that constitutes the heart of Kantian judicial retribution. The bodies in the DP camps and in the State of Israel that sought to punish collaborators did not enjoy comparable release. Unlike the Jewish Civic Tribunal in Poland, for example, they could not dismiss consideration of the cases brought before them "on the level of violation of the law" in favor of examining the actions of the accused exclusively "on the ethical plane," for they functioned not only as voices of their communities' attitudes toward the recent destruction of European Jewry but also as agents for upholding long-standing principles of jurisprudence designed to guarantee the peaceful interaction of their communities' individual members. Such situations appear to have provided more of an opening for strictly retributive measures than did situations in which the punishment of Jewish collaborators was detached from the criminal justice system.

In sum, retribution does not suffice universally as a description of the considerations that guided postwar Jewish communities confronting the presence of suspected collaborators in their midst. Jews sought to punish collaborators for a range of reasons, whose relative weight varied across time and place. Such variation might serve as a useful analytical framework for considering this important aspect of post-Holocaust Jewish life.

Notes

1. There is as yet no comprehensive monographic study of the phenomenon continent-wide. Several collections of articles on individual states have contributed to building a base for comparative analysis. Most noteworthy among them are Klaus-Dietmar Henke and Hans Woller, eds., *Politische Säuberung in Europa: Die Abrechnung mit Faschismus und Kollaboration nach dem Zweiten Weltkrieg* (Munich: Deutscher Taschenbuch, 1991); and István Deák, Jan T. Gross, and Tony Judt, eds., *The Politics of Retribution in Europe: World War II and Its Aftermath* (Princeton, NJ: Princeton University Press, 2000).

2. For descriptions, see Peter Novick, *The Resistance Versus Vichy: The Purge of Collaborators in Liberated France* (New York: Columbia University Press, 1968), 67–72; and Benjamin Frommer, *National Cleansing: Retribution Against Nazi Collaborators in Postwar Czechoslovakia* (Cambridge, UK: Cambridge University Press, 2005), 33–57.

3. Martin Conway notes that in Belgium there were 405,067 investigations of suspected collaborators (out of a population of 8.3 million) ("Justice in Postwar Belgium: Popular Passions and Political Realities," in Deák et al., *Politics of Retribution*, 134). Frommer (*National Cleansing*, 3–4) cites a June 1947 report indicating that 1.5 million people in the Czech portion of Czechoslovakia (out of a population of 10 million) were affected by three presidential decrees concerning "offenses against national honor." However, the figure includes not only suspected collaborators but also their dependents. Assuming an average of two dependents per suspect, the proportion of suspects would be 5 percent. These appear to be the only such figures that have been suggested for any country to date. They indicate numbers of individuals *investigated*, not numbers against whom charges were filed or upon whom sentence was imposed.

4. Perhaps the best-known of these proceedings was the hearing conducted during the twenty-second Zionist Congress in December 1946 concerning the wartime activities of Rezső Kasztner in Hungary. See Yechiam Weitz, *HaIsh sheNirtsah pe'amayim: Hayav, mishpato uMoto shel Dr. Yisrael Kasztner* (Jerusalem: Keter, 1995), 51–53.

5. For example, in October 1950 the American Jewish Congress convened a special *beit din* (rabbinic court) to consider an accusation brought by Benjamin Krieger that his Brooklyn neighbor, Majer Mittelman, had beaten Krieger's brother to death in April 1945 while serving as a German-appointed block clerk at Mühldorf, a satellite camp of Dachau. See Joel Silverman, "*Krieger v. Mittelman* and Jewish Perceptions of the Refugee in the Early Cold War," *Judaism* 55.1/2 (2006): 40–54.

6. Nazis and Nazi Collaborators (Punishment) Law, 5710/1950, *Laws of the State of Israel* 4 (5710–1949/50), no. 64, pp. 154–58. On the adoption and implementation of the law, see Hanna Yablonka, "HaHok leAsiyat din baNatsim uveOzereihem: Heibet nosaf lishe'elat haYisra'elim, haNitsolim vehaSho'ah," *Cathedra* 82 (1996–97): 135–52; and Yechiam Weitz, "HaHok leAsiyat din baNatsim uveOzereihem veYahasah shel haHevrah haYisra'elit biShenot haHamishim laSho'ah uleNitsoleiha," *Cathedra* 82 (1996–97): 153–64.

7. Lists prepared in 1947 by the Central Committee of Polish Jews identified about 2,000 suspected Jewish collaborators. Assuming that all who were named on the list were alive and present within Poland's new borders in mid-1946, the figure would constitute 0.7 percent of the number of Jews estimated to have been present on Polish soil at some time between liberation and the mass exodus of July–August 1946. For the lists, see Gabriel N. Finder, "The Trial of Shepsl Rotholc and the Politics of Retribution in the Aftermath of the Holocaust," *Gal-Ed* 20 (2006): 72. For the population estimate, see David Engel, *Bein shihrur liVerihah: Nitsolei haSho'ah bePolin vahaMa'avak al hanhagatam, 1944–1946* (Tel Aviv: Am Oved, 1996), 155.
8. Cf. John 11:50. The statement is attributed to the High Priest Caiaphas (hardly a Pharisee). It may represent an interpretation of the rabbinic rulings in *Genesis Rabbah* 94:9 concerning how to behave in a situation in which a group is ordered to turn over one of its members to be killed in order to prevent the killing of all, but no such statement actually appears in a rabbinic ("pharisaic") text.
9. Immanuel Kant, *Metaphysik der Sitten*, ed. J. H. von Kirchmann (Berlin: L. Heiman, 1870), 173–74.
10. Cf. Kant, *Metaphysik der Sitten*, 174: "Welche Art... und welcher Grad der Bestrafung ist es, welche die offentliche Gerechtigkeit sich zum Prinzip und Richtmasse macht? Kein anders, als das Prinzip der Gleichheit (im Stande des Zünglreins und der Wage der Gerechtigkeit), sich nicht mehr auf die eine, als auf die andere Seite hinzuneigen."
11. At least thirteen such sentences were carried out in 1942 and 1943. For a list, see Emmanuel Ringelblum, *Polish-Jewish Relations During the Second World War* (Jerusalem: Howard Fertig and Yad Vashem, 1976), 250–51.
12. On Ringelblum's relations with ŻOB, see Samuel D. Kassow, *Who Will Write Our History? Emanuel Ringelblum, the Warsaw Ghetto, and the Oyneg Shabes Archive* (Bloomington: Indiana University Press, 2007), 353–54.
13. Lejkin assumed command of the ghetto police following ŻOB's attempt on the life of commandant Józef Szeryński on August 20, 1942. He was assassinated two months later, on October 29.
14. Emmanuel Ringelblum, *Ksovim fun geto, band 2: Notitsn un ophandlungen (1942–1943)* (Warsaw: Yidish Bukh, 1963), 34–35.
15. Ringelblum, *Ksovim fun geto*, 36–37.
16. Ringelblum, *Ksovim fun geto*, 35.
17. "Di idishe kamf-organizatsie: Antshteyung un antviklung," in Melech Neustadt, *Khurbn un oyfshtand fun di idn in Varshe: Edus-bleter un azkores* (Tel Aviv: Histadrut, 1948), 147.
18. Cywia Lubetkin, *BiYmei kilayon uMered* (Lohamei haGeta'ot, Israel: Beit Lohamei haGeta'ot, 1979), 81.
19. Izrael Fürst was the head of the Economic Department in the Warsaw Judenrat who served as Judenrat liaison with the city's German administration. According to Ringelblum, he "showed brutality towards the employees of the Jewish Council"

(Ringelblum, *Polish-Jewish Relations*, 250). He was assassinated by a member of ŻOB on November 29, 1942.

20. "Di idishe kamf-organizatsie," 140, 147.
21. Szeryński served as commandant of the Jewish police in the Warsaw ghetto from its inception until the assassination attempt. The attempt failed when the assassin's bullet lodged in the victim's cheekbone. However, Szeryński did not return to service. During the armed ŻOB action in January 1943, he committed suicide. On his leadership of the police, see Aldona Podolska, *Służba porządkowa w getcie warszawskim w latach 1940–1943* (Warsaw: Historia pro Futuro, 1996), 25–28.
22. Yitshak Cukierman, *Sheva haShanim hahen* (Lohamei haGeta'ot, Israel: HaKibbutz haMe'uhad, [1990]), 178–79.
23. Cukierman, *Sheva haShanim hahen*, 178: "We could have gone against them with clubs and with knives, we could have strangled them, hanged them. . . . We needed to be cruel, to use violence. Unfortunately we didn't do this, even though our moral judgment of them was firm."
24. The ŻOB announcement of Szeryński's attempted assassination, distributed in the Warsaw ghetto on August 21, proclaimed that "the commanding officer and the officers *as well as the men* of the police force have been declared accused, and accordingly an attempt has been made on the life of Józef Szeryński. *Further repressive acts of the same kind will be carried out with the utmost severity*" (quoted in Ringelblum, *Polish Jewish Relations*, 161; emphasis mine). A diarist who read the announcement concluded that a "sentence of death has been passed on the *entire* police" (quoted in Ringelblum, *Polish Jewish Relations*, 161; (emphasis mine).
25. Lubetkin, *BiYmei kilayon*, 80.
26. See, for example, "Di idishe kamf-organizatsie," 140: "To our astonishment and embitterment, our proclamations [to the ghetto population for resistance] found no response at first." Cywia Lubetkin later described scenes in which "Jews grabbed [our young men and women] as they were distributing the proclamations and beat them brutally. . . . It hurt to see how the proclamations, which we printed with such effort and posted with such dedication, were now being torn down from the walls by Jews themselves" (quoted in "Di idishe kamf-organizatsie," 141; ellipsis in source).
27. Quoted in Yisrael Gutman, *BaAlatah uvaMa'avak: Pirkei iyun baSho'ah uvaHitnagdut haYehudit* (Tel Aviv: Sifriyat Po'alim, 1985), 208–9.
28. The departure point for the trains to Treblinka.
29. Ringelblum, *Ksovim fun geto*, 34.
30. The text, quoted earlier from Ringelblum, *Ksovim fun geto*, 34–35, begins immediately after the quotation referenced on p. 34.
31. A trace of this attitude can be found in the diary of Hillel Seidman, director of the Warsaw Judenrat archive. On October 12, 1942 (precisely when Ringelblum suggested that popular revulsion against the police was crystallizing), he wrote: "In exile, Jews in general are an *object* of *external* conditions. It was others, namely *the Germans*, who

created those conditions. Those conditions changed the moral and ethical foundations [of Jewish life].... Evil people became more evil, corrupt people became more corrupt, while people of a higher moral level raised themselves even higher! ... It should be noted that in the entire police force there was *not a single Orthodox Jew*.... It should be noted that I did not encounter a single known Zionist worker in the Warsaw ghetto police. The police consisted of alien [*folksfremde*] elements or even of elements who hated the people" (Hillel Seidman, *Tog-bukh fun varshever geto* [Buenos Aires: Dos Poylishe Yidntum, 1947], 152–53). Extant records do not provide sufficient data for evaluating Seidman's claim about the composition of the police force.

32. Ringelblum's text does not provide a clear indication of whether he himself affirmed this justification or not.
33. Ringelblum, *Ksovim fun geto*, 34–35.
34. On the establishment of the Civic Tribunal, see David Engel, "Who Is a Collaborator? The Trials of Michał Weichert," in Sławomir Kapralski, ed., *The Jews of Poland* (Kraków: Judaica Foundation, 1999), 2: 340–41; Finder, "Trial of Shepsl Rotholc," 68–73; and Gabriel N. Finder and Alexander V. Prusin, "Jewish Collaborators on Trial in Poland, 1944–1956," *Polin: Studies in Polish Jewry* 20 (2008): 136–37.
35. See the citations in Finder, "Trial of Shepsl Rotholc," 69.
36. Quoted in Finder, "Trial of Shepsl Rotholc," 69.
37. See Cukierman, *Sheva haShanim haHen*, 384.
38. Engel, "Who Is a Collaborator?" 355–56, 361–62. Weichert was also later employed by the Polish government as an investigator and expert witness in the trials of senior Nazi leaders. Weichert and ŻOB had a long history of strained relations, to the point where ŻOB placed Weichert under sentence of death in 1944. According to one account, Cukierman, who became a member of the Central Committee, had sought to have Weichert assassinated even after the end of the war but had been dissuaded from his demand by the realization that legally constituted state courts could be counted on to give traitors their due. Weichert was indeed tried in a Polish state court but was acquitted of wrongdoing; his acquittal catalyzed the establishment of the Jewish Civic Tribunal. Engel, "Who Is a Collaborator?" 341–43, 354.
39. Finder, "Trial of Shepsl Rotholc," 67.
40. "In'm prezidium fun yidishn Ts. K.," *Dos naje lebn* (October 18, 1946): 3. The Civic Tribunal acquitted Gran in January 1949 on grounds of insufficient evidence. See Agata Tuszyńska, *Vera Gran: The Accused* (New York: Knopf, 2013), 171–88.
41. The Civic Tribunal's charter empowered it to determine whether those brought before it had behaved in this fashion. Finder and Prusin, "Jewish Collaborators," 137.
42. Finder, "Trial of Shepsl Rotholc," 84–86.
43. "Wyrok [Sądu Społecznego przy Centralnym Komitecie Żydów w Polsce]," December 28, 1949, Yad Vashem Archives, Jerusalem, O21/7, quoted in Engel, "Who Is a Collaborator?" 366.
44. For details, see Engel, "Who Is a Collaborator?" 351–52.

45. "Wyrok," quoted in Engel, "Who Is a Collaborator?" 367. In taking this position, the Civic Tribunal affirmed an argument that had been brought unsuccessfully by the prosecution in Weichert's 1946 Polish criminal trial (in which he was acquitted of all criminal wrongdoing): "Since the Jewish supreme underground authorities ... recognized and stated clearly the harm done by the existence of [his organization] ..., the accused was obliged to conform to their instructions, no matter how he may have viewed the situation himself or what his personal convictions may have been.... The issue was instead a general, political one." "Do Najwyższego Trybunalu w Łodzi," n.d., Yad Vashem Archives, O21/7; quoted in Engel, "Who Is a Collaborator?" 360.

46. Cincinnatus, "Di natsionale fareter tsum folks-mishpet," *Dos naje lebn* (October 18, 1946): 3; quoted in Engel, "Who Is a Collaborator?" 340.

47. Its position with regard to Judenrat members who were not involved with the police force appears to have been more forgiving in cases where the accused could be shown to have assisted Jews. At times, this attitude placed it at odds with former underground fighters who condemned Judenrat members on the basis of membership alone. See Finder, "Trial of Shepsl Rotholc," 87–88.

48. For further explication of Weichert's position, see Engel, "Who Is a Collaborator?" 369–70.

49. "Wyrok [Specjalnego Sądu Karnego w Krokowie]," January 7, 1946, Jewish National Library, Jerusalem, Ms. Var. 371/45, p. 165b; quoted in Engel, "Who Is a Collaborator?" 342–43.

50. Rzecznik Oskarżenia Sądu Społecznego przy CKŻwP, "Akt oskarżenia," Yad Vashem Archives, O21/7; quoted in Engel, "Who Is a Collaborator?" 368–69.

51. Nazis and Nazi Collaborators (Punishment) Law, pars. 1, 2, 4. The law held membership in an "enemy organization" to be punishable. It defined an enemy organization as one that "existed in an enemy country and the object or one of the objects of which was to carry out or to assist in carrying out actions of an enemy administration directed against persecuted persons" (par. 3). Israeli courts refused to apply this provision to members of the Judenräte or ghetto police forces. See Isaiah Trunk, *Judenrat: The Jewish Councils in Eastern Europe Under Nazi Occupation* (New York: Macmillan, 1972), 565–69.

52. Nazis and Nazi Collaborators (Punishment) Law, par. 10. On the Civic Tribunal's rejection of the excuse of duress, see Finder, "Trial of Shepsl Rotholc," 86.

53. "Baszlus," EX-I 25/43, May 17, 1948, YIVO Archives, New York, RG483, folder 397a.

54. "Baszlus." Cf. Trunk, *Judenrat*, 549–50.

55. See Trunk, *Judenrat*, 551.

56. Trunk, *Judenrat*, 553. In Poland, Rotholc appears to have sought rehabilitation on his own initiative, but the Civic Tribunal had already identified him independently as a target for prosecution. Finder, "Trial of Shepsl Rotholc," 68.

57. See, in particular, Weitz, "HaHok leAsiyat din," 157–59; and Yablonka, "Hahok leAsiyat din," 144.

58. On the emergence of an autonomous displaced persons regime, see Zeev W. Mankowitz, *Life Between Memory and Hope: The Survivors of the Holocaust in Occupied Germany* (Cambridge, UK: Cambridge University Press, 2002), 265–68.
59. On such instances see, for example, Trunk, *Judenrat*, 552; Silverman, "*Krieger v. Mittelman*," 40; Tuvia Friling, *Mi atah Leon Berger? Sipuro shel kapo beAuschwitz* (Tel Aviv: Resling, 2009), 141–42; and Tom Segev, *HaMilion haShevi'i: HaYisra'elim vehaSho'ah* (Jerusalem: Domino, 1991), 242–43. An estimate of the number and geographic distribution of such infrajudicial actions has yet to be undertaken.

2

Rehabilitating the Past?

Jewish Honor Courts in Allied-Occupied Germany

LAURA JOCKUSCH

In the years 1945–1949 defeated and occupied Germany became a central venue of Nazi war crimes trials and post-Holocaust justice. In accordance with the Moscow Declaration of November 1943, the four victorious Allies placed all so-called major war criminals, that is, central figures of the Nazi regime whose crimes had no specific location, under the jurisdiction of the International Military Tribunal (IMT) at Nuremberg. In addition, in their respective occupation zones they held hundreds of separate trials of so-called minor war criminals who committed war crimes at specific locations, mainly concentration, labor, and death camps.

Although the Allied prosecutors dedicated considerable attention to crimes against Jews, none of their trials focused on the Holocaust. The specific fate of European Jewry at the hands of the Nazis remained marginal, and Jews hardly appeared as active participants in these trials. The IMT trial, which concentrated on the Nazi leadership, allowed for only three Jewish witnesses, because the suffering of individual Jews at the periphery of the Third Reich could hardly be linked to the crimes of the defendants from the power center of the regime. Moreover, the prosecutorial philosophy that guided the trial focused on documentary evidence of the Nazis' own making rather than on testimonial evidence.[1] Holocaust survivors were a greater presence on the witness stand at the separate zonal trials that focused on crimes committed in concentration camps. Their accounts often called attention to a distinct Jewish fate at the hands of the Nazis, although the Allied prosecutors and judges did not build their cases against the defendants around the Nazi genocide of European Jewry per se.[2] Because Allied military tribunals primarily dealt with war crimes committed by Axis nationals against Allied nationals, the issue of collaboration of non-Germans, let alone of Jews, with Nazi authorities was hardly addressed in these proceedings. Nor did the Allies have a clear sense that some collaborators with the Nazis clearly needed to be classified as perpetrators, whereas others remained primarily the Nazis' own victims.

Two of these zonal trials, one British, the other Soviet, adjudicated alleged Jewish collaborators with the Nazis. In mid-September 1945 the British military court in the northern German town of Lüneburg opened the two-month trial of former SS-Hauptsturmführer Josef Kramer, the last commandant of the Bergen-Belsen concentration camp, and forty-four other camp personnel. Although it soon became known as the Belsen trial, it was in fact also the first Auschwitz trial, because Kramer and almost all the other defendants had earlier committed crimes at Auschwitz-Birkenau before their deployment to Bergen-Belsen in late 1944 and early 1945. The British tried sixteen SS men, sixteen female camp guards, and eleven prisoner functionaries for war crimes committed against Allied nationals at Bergen-Belsen and Auschwitz-Birkenau. Among the prisoner functionaries in the dock was the Austrian Jewish political prisoner Ignatz Schlomowicz, who was charged with war crimes he had allegedly committed as a kapo at Bergen-Belsen. Born in 1918 in Vienna, the former salesman escaped Austria after the so-called *Anschluss*; he was arrested in Holland and incarcerated at Oranienburg and Gross-Rosen until he was sent to Auschwitz in September 1942. From mid-1943 until September 1944, he worked as a kapo and foreman at the IG Farben factory in Auschwitz-Monowitz. After imprisonment at Laurahütte and Mauthausen, Schlomowicz arrived in Bergen-Belsen in early April 1945, where he was made block elder (*Blockältester*); in that capacity he was responsible for the maintenance of order and the distribution of food among the 1,300 prisoners of the block under his authority. After liberating the camp on April 14, the British military arrested Schlomowicz on the grounds that two former prisoners accused him of having beaten prisoners with a stick.[3] The inclusion of both SS officers and prisoner functionaries in the dock shows how little the British prosecutors at Lüneburg understood the inner workings of the German camp system. Schlomowicz and two other prisoner functionaries were acquitted because charges against them could not be proven; moreover, the accusations against them paled in comparison to other crimes committed at both Bergen-Belsen and Auschwitz-Birkenau.[4]

The second trial of an alleged Jewish collaborator with the Nazis was the proceeding against Stella Goldschlag (also known as Stella Kübler or Stella Isaaksohn) before a Soviet military court in Berlin in May 1946. Born in Berlin in 1922 to a secular Jewish family of journalists and musicians, Goldschlag was arrested and interned at the Gestapo-run assembly camp at Grosse Hamburger Strasse 26 in Berlin in August 1943. After an unsuccessful attempt to escape from the camp, Goldschlag was tortured and eventually recruited as a Gestapo informant by SS-Hauptsturmführer Walter Dobberke. Seeking to avoid further physical suffering and to prevent the deportation of her family (her husband Manfred Kübler had already been deported to Auschwitz), she became a feared and infamous snatcher (*Greiferin*) of Jews in hiding; she allegedly delivered several hundred Berlin Jews to the Gestapo. In the final weeks of the war, in April 1945, she went into hiding outside the German capital. A few months after the liberation of the city, fellow survivors discovered her when she registered as a Victim of Fascism (*Opfer des Faschismus*) to collect social benefits from the Soviet military authorities. A Soviet military tribunal in Berlin tried her in May of the following year for crimes against humanity (i.e., the betrayal of Jews to the Gestapo) and sentenced her to ten years in the prison camps at Torgau, Sachsenhausen, Hoheneck, and Waldheim. In January 1956, after serving her sentence, she settled in West Berlin. Her release stirred up emotions inside the Jewish community, leading to a new court case before the Moabit District Court in Berlin in 1957. Several dozen witnesses from the Jewish community came forward to testify, thus rendering the trial a cause célèbre in Jewish circles and beyond. The West Berlin court found Goldschlag guilty of "accessory to murder" and sentenced her to ten years in prison; yet because she had already served ten years for the same offenses, she was allowed to go free.[5]

In addition, between December 1945 and the reorganization of the German justice system upon the formation of two German states in the summer of 1949, the Allies allowed local German courts (*Schwurgerichte*) to adjudicate "crimes against humanity," that is, crimes committed by Germans against other Germans or stateless persons. The thousands of court cases held at local German courts under Allied Control Council Law No. 10 involved hundreds of offenses that non-Jewish Germans had committed against German and stateless Jews in Germany, mainly denunciations, violence, and arson in the context of the Crystal Night pogrom; yet a small number of cases also involved defendants of Jewish backgrounds accused of having committed crimes against other Jews as snatchers and kapos. Even if members of the German Jewish communities welcomed the punishment of these individuals, whether or not their fate should be decided by German courts remained a contentious issue in German Jewish circles.[6]

That non-Jewish courts in Germany tried alleged Jewish collaborators with the Nazis remained the exception to the rule. Most cases of suspected collaboration were adjudicated inside the Jewish communities, where they were brought before unofficial tribunals. These tribunals, which formed outside the Allied military governments and were entirely independent of the German justice system, were established on the initiative of the survivor communities themselves. Not intended as permanent institutions, they quickly arose in the months following the end of the war and almost as quickly disappeared after having operated for a number of years. They evolved from the sense shared by many survivors that non-Jewish courts could not be trusted to adjudicate crimes committed by Jews against other Jews and from the strong belief—indeed, the sense of urgency—that Jews not only had the right but also the duty to deal with these internal matters themselves.

In the first five years after the war, the Jewish population in Germany consisted of two largely separate communities. The first community consisted of 15,000–30,000 German Jews who had survived the war in Germany—in hiding and thanks to their mixed marriages with non-Jews—or who had returned to Germany from camps or exile abroad.[7] The second community was composed of 250,000–300,000 mostly Eastern European Jewish displaced persons who temporarily resided in the western zones of occupation in the years 1945–1949.[8] They had either been liberated by Allied forces from concentration camps on German soil, which they had reached through the notorious death marches in the final months of the war, or they had survived in Eastern Europe but had escaped violent anti-Semitism and economic and political instability by moving westward and finding refuge in Allied-occupied Germany. Accommodated in so-called displaced persons (DP) camps—former concentration camps, requisitioned army barracks, and civilian buildings—for the most part these Jewish displaced persons had no intention of staying in Germany permanently but rather hoped to rebuild their lives overseas. Their numbers rapidly diminished after the founding of the State of Israel and passage of the American Displaced Persons Acts of 1948 and 1950. Although the interaction of the two groups of survivors was often characterized by social and cultural distance, prejudice, and even conflict, they nevertheless shared the impulse to cleanse their communities of those who supposedly had harmed other Jews by collaborating with the Nazis.[9]

This sense of urgency with which the postwar Jewish communities in Germany (as in Europe more generally) dealt with the problem of collaboration in their midst is particularly striking. Unlike most non-Jewish collaborators in German-occupied Europe, Jews did not engage in ideological collusion with Nazism or hope for a German victory and its promise of a new European order. Also, other nations under the Nazi yoke received material benefits and varying degrees of autonomy in return for playing along with the Germans, although as Jan T. Gross rightly observed, the terms of this collusion were never fully clear and changed drastically over the course of the war.[10] For Jews inside the Nazi orbit, collaboration could not change the fact that the Germans had sentenced *all* Jews to death; those individuals who had forcibly or voluntarily assumed leadership roles in the ghettos and camps had no ability to avert or even mitigate the genocide that the Nazis designed for European Jewry as a whole.[11] Yet in the eyes of many survivors these Jews had committed an even greater crime than the Nazi perpetrators themselves, because they had undermined communal solidarity and gravely violated the ethical standards of Jewish society. A profound sense of moral offense led many survivors to greatly exaggerate the roles of alleged Jewish collaborators and misjudge their power inside the Nazi terror system. Clearly, survivors thirsted for the punishment of Nazi war criminals and even at times took active revenge on individual Germans.[12] But because they could not, for the most part, lay their hands on German war criminals or participate in bringing them to justice in military or state courts, purging their own ranks of putative collaborators appeared as an urgent precondition for the rebuilding of Jewish life. Remarkably, they largely chose to carry out this purge by establishing courts, not by resorting to raw violence.

For what reason and under what conditions did survivors establish autonomous courts that were chiefly dedicated to trying alleged collaborators? What juridical purpose and which educational and historical functions did the internal Jewish courts serve in bringing cases against putative collaborators? What roles did these court cases play in survivors' moral rehabilitation, the formation of their historical consciousness, and their self-understanding as members of a Jewish nation with a need for community?

In this chapter I provide preliminary answers to these questions by exploring the functioning and significance of two major courts dedicated to trials of alleged Jewish collaborators in the years 1946–1951: the honor court of the Jewish community in Berlin set up by German Jews and the central Jewish honor court in Munich founded by Jewish displaced persons. Both Berlin and Munich played important roles for the German Jews and Jewish displaced persons. With a population of about 8,000 German Jews—just 5 percent of the city's prewar Jewish community—and at least an equal number of Jewish displaced persons,

Berlin nonetheless emerged as a center of Jewish life in the latter half of the 1940s.[13] In the fall of 1947 most of the 157,000 Jewish displaced persons living in the western occupation zones of Germany in the first postwar years were concentrated in the U.S. zone, with about 7,000 of them in Munich.[14] Hence the courts in both cities provide important insights into the ways in which German Jews and Jewish displaced persons in Germany dealt with putative collaborators in their midst.[15]

The Emergence of an Autonomous Jewish Court System

On November 12, 1945, U.S. Army major Irving Heymont, the 27-year-old commander of the DP camp Landsberg in Bavaria, informed the camp's more than 5,000 Jewish survivors of several recent incidents in which residents had attacked and in some cases seriously injured survivors who supposedly had served as kapos or other prisoner functionaries in the Nazi camp system.[16] Speaking as the American army commander of the camp and also in the name of the Central Committee of Liberated Jews, the political representation of the Jewish survivors in the American zone of occupation, Heymont exhorted the camp population:

> No self-respecting community can allow such mob-rule to exist. Very often innocent people suffer from such action. An excited mass of people cannot hear witnesses and find out the truth. Respect [is] due us and you [and] demands that such incidents do not occur again. We appear [*sic*] to you not to participate in such mass attacks. Persons under suspicion must be turned over to the police and not beaten. All individuals who participate in such attacks will in the future be turned over to the proper authorities.[17]

This appeal exemplifies the great urgency with which local representatives of the American occupation authorities and the Jewish displaced persons leadership sought to let survivors handle cases involving alleged Nazi collaborators in a civilized manner rather than by raw violence. Acting on their own initiative, both German Jews and the Jewish displaced persons formed internal Jewish courts to investigate cases of alleged wartime collaboration.

In mid-December 1945 the leadership of the Jewish community at Oranienburgerstrasse in Berlin's Soviet sector decided to form an honor court (*Ehrengericht*) within one month. This decision of the board of directors and the board of representatives responded to popular pressure in the face of frequent cases in which members of the community accused others of having cooperated with the Gestapo or having otherwise behaved indecently toward their fellow Jews during the Nazi regime. According to its statutes, the honor court had the "task to determine whether and to what extent a member of the Jewish community in Berlin harmed the Jewish collective through dishonorable and ignoble behavior."[18] But whether or not an honor court case was adjudicated depended on whether the person against whom accusations were leveled with the community requested that the honor court convene on his or her behalf.[19] The accused were allowed to bring their own lawyers, either lawyers who were also members of the Jewish community or German lawyers accredited to work in any German court.[20] Every year the members of the Jewish community elected seven to fifteen members of the honor court who would serve alternately as tribunal chairmen and assessors. Chairmen were required to have training in law, but the assessors could also be laypeople. Each honor court case was staffed with three chairmen and two assessors. At least one of the assessors had to be a member of the office of the Victims of the Nuremberg Laws (Opfer der Nürnberger Gesetzgebung), a subsection of the Main Committee for the Victims of Fascism (Hauptausschuss Opfer des Faschismus), which the new Berlin municipality in the Soviet sector had founded at the end of May 1945 to care for those persecuted by the Nazi regime.[21] The court publicized all its decisions in the Jewish press and sent them to the Main Committee for the Victims of Fascism and to the Office of Religious Affairs in the Berlin Senate.[22] Between 1946 and 1951 the Jewish honor court in Berlin conducted sixty-five court cases involving matters in the recent past.[23]

Among the Jewish displaced persons population in the American zone, local camp courts (*lager-gerikht* or *ern-gerikht*) emerged in the fall of 1945 in the Deggendorf, Landsberg, and Föhrenwald DP camps. Although these courts prosecuted all kinds of offenses that Jews had committed against other Jews *since* the liberation, such as various forms of insult, slander, abuse of material goods, theft, corruption, violence, and moral infractions, they also included so-called rehabilitation cases against survivors suspected of having collaborated with the Nazis before the liberation.[24] Local initiatives soon gave rise to a zonewide court system. At the end of January 1946 the U.S. zonewide congress of liberated Jews resolved that the survivor community must purge all those who had supposedly aided the Nazis in their genocide and that putative collaborators should be banned from holding office in the survivor community.[25] In the following month the Central Committee of Liberated Jews established a legal department to handle various legal matters and to collect evidence against Nazi perpetrators and their alleged Jewish collaborators.[26] By June 1946 the Central Committee established the Central Jewish Honor Court in Munich to supervise the local camp courts that had emerged in all major Jewish DP camps throughout the U.S. zone.[27] Like other representative bodies of the Jewish displaced persons, camp courts were elected by the camp inhabitants; the Central Jewish Honor Court in Munich was first appointed by the Central Committee and later elected by the delegates attending the U.S. zone-wide survivor congresses in 1947 and 1948. With the exception of the presiding judge, the three to five judges adjudicating each case were not required to have training in law, but they often had training or prewar careers in law.[28] Although the Central Jewish Honor Court handled so-called rehabilitation cases from the beginning—along with a much larger caseload involving various other offenses that had occurred in the DP camps after the liberation—as of June 1947 a separate "rehabilitation commission" within the court focused exclusively on cases involving alleged collaborators with the Nazis.[29]

The Jewish displaced persons were able to establish their own courts only on the sufferance of the American occupying forces. Jewish displaced persons were under the jurisdiction of the U.S. military government for all criminal offenses; however, they initially fell under German courts in all civil matters.[30] This changed under the impact of the Harrison Report of August 1945, an inquiry into the living conditions of Holocaust survivors in American occupation zones in Germany and Austria commissioned by President Harry S. Truman. As a consequence, separate camps were established for Jewish displaced persons, and these camps were granted a considerable measure of self-government.[31] Because exposure to the German justice system would have been untenable for Holocaust survivors, the military government also let Jewish displaced persons handle civil cases in their own court system. The American military authorities were initially apprehensive about allowing the Jewish courts to adjudicate criminal offenses that predated the liberation.[32] Thus the military government generally tolerated the camp courts but repeatedly sought to curb their activity. In October 1946 General Horace L. McBride, the commander of the U.S. Army's 9th Infantry Division, issued a formal prohibition of displaced persons courts' handling of cases involving putative collaborators during wartime, yet the order was not enforced and the camp courts continued to hold hearings. In the summer of 1948 the military authorities began to enforce stricter control, but court cases continued into 1949, when most DP camps closed down and the majority of Jewish displaced persons had emigrated.[33] It is hard to determine the exact caseload of these courts, but 100–150 cases involved survivors accused of collaborating with the Nazis in committing wartime offenses against other Jews.[34]

In both the German Jewish and the Jewish displaced persons communities, trials of alleged collaborators occurred in response to popular demands for the punishment of those who had supposedly raised their hands against other Jews. Fearing that public unrest or even vigilante justice might create disunity, disrupt the fragile public order, and confirm negative stereotypes of Jewish survivors in the eyes of the occupying forces and the German public, the communal leadership pursued an educational agenda to further survivors' moral and ethical rehabilitation after years of brutalization and lawlessness.[35] Thus the courts were created with an eye to prevent assaults but also to reeducate the survivor population in "civilized" forms of conflict resolution. Bringing alleged collaborators to court—rather than making their lives miserable by denunciations, pillorying, and violence—was an exercise in the value of a fair trial; the outcome of the proceedings was not predetermined and defendants remained innocent until proven guilty. Just as in other retribution trials across Europe, there was a danger that individuals might try to settle personal scores. For this reason, charges needed to be made in writing and an accusation by one individual was insufficient to open an investigation unless several witnesses could be heard. In most cases the defendants themselves initiated investigations in an effort to clear their names of accusations that they had acted against the Jewish community.[36]

Both among the Jewish displaced persons and the German Jews justice was done in the name of an imagined "Jewish collective" that supposedly had been harmed by the defendants' actions. As discussed in more detail later, punishments were socially construed and, for those found guilty, affected social relations with other members of the Jewish community and the Jewish displaced persons population. In the worst cases they led to the defendant's excommunication; more often they had material or financial repercussions.

Yet the honor courts suffered from a number of functional ambiguities. They had limited legal capacities, because they could adjudicate only civil cases involving offenses committed by Jews against other Jews and had no legal relevance beyond the Jewish communities. They lacked formalized procedure, and the legal basis on which they operated was highly improvised and usually limited to the statutes of the tribunals and a vague reliance on general standards of jurisprudence, for example, the axiom that a defendant is innocent until proven guilty. Because the courts could not rely on any existing legal codifications that would have defined transgressions related to the collaboration of Jews with Nazism and specified possible measures of punishment, the cases against alleged collaborators were essentially more about morality than the law. Consequently, the proceedings were less concerned with determining guilt or innocence on the basis of the law than with determining moral or immoral Jewish behavior in times of persecution and mass murder. Therefore the court cases in Berlin and

Munich mainly reflect the dire struggles of defendants, witnesses, and judges to evaluate Jews' excruciating choices of the recent past and balance diverging views of morality.

The Jewish honor courts were legitimate institutions, not because of any constitutional origins (i.e., through the acceptance by an outside authority) but because they largely enjoyed social acceptance in the Jewish community. The judges, not all of whom had legal training and a prewar career in law, mainly based their authority on their election by the residents of a certain DP camp or by the members of the Jewish community in a German city. Nevertheless, the courts, which laid claim to representing a Jewish collective, also faced criticism from inside the survivor community. For example, some factions of the community demanded harsher sentences than those imposed.[37] Others, mainly those affected by the courts' coercive measures, challenged their authority by such measures as failing to appear at a proceedings or arguing that it was immoral for a Jewish court to expel a Jew from Jewish society.[38] Another source of contention was the dependence on survivors' recollections of the recent past as the only form of evidence used in the proceedings; thus one account stood against another, because forensic evidence and documents related to the alleged misdeeds of Jewish council members, the Jewish police, kapos, or other prisoner functionaries were not available to complement witness testimony. Although the courts generally enjoyed wide support in the respective communities, they faced expressions of disrespect as time went on, especially in the DP camps, whose population diminished rapidly after 1948. Accordingly, dozens of cases were closed because witnesses and even defendants had left Germany to rebuild their lives overseas, undermining the efficiency and authority of the courts.

Although the honor courts in Berlin and Munich share many similarities in their adjudication of collaborator cases, there were fundamental differences in the kinds of crimes they dealt with and in the geographic scope where these episodes from the past had taken place. The Berlin honor court dealt exclusively with cases involving the city's Jewish community. Because 5,000–7,000 Berlin Jews had gone underground—of whom only some 1,400 survived[39]—most cases brought before the court involved Jews who, like Stella Goldschlag and her husband Rolf Isaaksohn, supposedly had served the Gestapo by finding these so-called "submarines" (*U-Boote*) and delivering them for deportation; other cases involved misconduct against Jews detained in the predeportation assembly camps at the Jewish cemetery and home for the elderly at Grosse Hamburger Strasse 26 and the Jewish Hospital at Schulstrasse 78.[40] Because in mid-1946 5,500 of the 8,000 German Jews in Berlin lived in mixed marriages, a large number of honor court cases involved the non-Jewish or converted spouse.[41] By contrast, the displaced persons courts heard cases that involved ghettos and camps from all across Nazi-occupied Eastern Europe; defendants were former Jewish council members, ghetto policemen, and privileged prisoners in German labor and concentration camps whose misdeeds mainly involved the use of violence against other Jews.

Conceptualizing Wrongdoing: Accusations and Offenses Adjudicated by the Honor Courts

What kinds of offenses were judged in Jewish honor courts and rehabilitation commission proceedings in Germany? How did the courts conceptualize wrongdoing, given that the defendants most likely had not voluntarily chosen to cooperate with the Germans but instead had been forced into their functions in one way or another? The cases adjudicated in both Munich and Berlin reveal considerable awareness of the Nazis' duplicity in turning their victims into accomplices. Jews under the Nazi regime were forced to make what Lawrence Langer termed "choiceless choices," that is, decisions that "did not reflect options between life and death, but between one form of abnormal response and another, both imposed by a situation that was in no way of the victim's own choosing."[42] Thus the honor court proceedings did not ascribe culpability based on the mere fact that an individual had (voluntarily or forcibly) been a member of a Jewish council or the ghetto police or had held the post of a kapo or block elder. In that respect the honor courts' prosecutorial logic differed from that applied by the Allied courts against Nazi war criminals. The IMT classified certain bodies, such as the Gestapo, the SS, or the Nazi Party, as criminal organizations; in the Nuremberg successor trials membership in a criminal organization in and of itself constituted a count of indictment. This allowed prosecutors to hold individuals responsible for having conspired to commit the regime's crimes even if they did not commit any of its crimes with their own hands.[43] Similarly, the Belsen trial and other British trials applied the concept of concerted action, by which defendants were held collectively responsible for the crimes committed at a certain camp by dint of having belonged to the personnel that had administered the camp.[44]

Although the precise rationale that led to the honor courts in the first place was the general sense among survivors that members of the Jewish councils and ghetto police were to be *collectively* regarded as criminals and ejected from the Jewish community, it was the courts' task to conduct a more nuanced examination of the defendants' wartime behavior and discern *individual* guilt or innocence.

The trial of Beinisz Tkacz before the rehabilitation commission in Munich is a case in point. As a candidate for election to the Central Committee of Liberated Jews in the American Zone in March 1948, Tkacz's political career was challenged by an accusation from fellow survivor Alter Berger that the former secretary of the Jewish police in the Kovno ghetto in 1941–1943 had mistreated Jews; in particular, he had beaten Alter's wife. Wishing to clear his name, Tkacz petitioned the Central Jewish Honor Court in Munich to hear his case. Berger's testimony during the trial revealed that he had little factual evidence against Tkacz and that the motivation behind his accusation was his revulsion at the thought that a former member of the ghetto police might run for office and assume a role in the Jewish displaced persons leadership: "A policeman could not possibly be a good person—they supplied the Germans with girls [and] drank with them. . . . The policemen were like the SS and they were feared just like the Germans. It happened that the policemen assisted in shooting men in order to lay hands on their wives. . . . The police were bad because they went hand in hand with the Germans." Berger finally admitted: "I oppose Tkacz because I deem it my civic duty to oppose all those with higher functions in the surviving remnant of European Jewry who worked together with the Germans during the occupation."[45] After several witnesses confirmed that Tkacz had fulfilled his post with decency and had not shown brutality toward any individuals in the ghetto, the court rehabilitated Tkacz from Berger's accusations. Nonetheless, in its ruling the court observed that the Kovno ghetto police

> included certain individuals with criminal leanings, who abused their posts for criminal activities assisting the German murderers in their work of killing the Jewish population. There were some who lost their moral balance and were led astray from the straight path by the poisoned atmosphere created by the Germans. Their strength of moral resistance ceased to function and they sacrificed other Jewish human lives with indifference in order to improve their own fate.

The court further remarked:

> The ghetto police in general did not have a good name among the ghetto population. However, generalizing this opinion for all policemen without treating each case individually, may lead to harmful injustices. In the absence of definite regulations . . . that would define the mere belonging to the ghetto police or a similar body as a criminal act, the

rehabilitation commission sat in judgment over this case in the same way as over all other cases: namely, in agreement with general principles of jurisprudence, basing judgment on concrete evidence of guilt or innocence.[46]

The concern of Jewish honor court proceedings in Germany thus was not the mere fact that someone had fulfilled a certain function. Rather, their purpose was to determine whether or not the individual defendant had crossed the fine line between acceptable and unacceptable, moral and immoral behavior. If an individual had crossed that line, the court tried to assess how much damage he or she had thereby done to the Jewish collective.

Curt Naumann was one of more than a dozen Berlin Jews who stood trial for having worked as a snatcher. In 1943 he was a trustee (*Kalfaktor*) at the Grosse Hamburger Strasse assembly camp. One day the deputy camp commandant SS-Oberscharführer Felix Lachmuth ordered Naumann to accompany him to an apartment in Berlin's Weissensee neighborhood, where a Jewish woman living there illegally had been arrested earlier that day. When arresting the woman, Lachmuth discovered that it was her birthday. Expecting that friends who had also gone underground would pass by the apartment in the evening to congratulate her, Lachmuth hoped that posting himself at the apartment would yield a number of arrests. Naumann protested that his job in the camp was not that of a snatcher, and he begged Lachmuth not to make him go, but to no avail. Several Jews did appear, and Lachmuth locked them in the kitchen until a Gestapo officer with a car arrived and took them to the Grosse Hamburger Strasse camp. Another Gestapo officer replaced Lachmuth, but Naumann was forced to wait for more well-wishers. Posted by the door, he tried to warn those who arrived and encouraged them to leave immediately, but without success. At the end of the day, twelve Jews were arrested, of whom nine would later perish during the Holocaust. One of the arrested Jewish men succumbed to the Gestapo's pressure and gave up the location of his family and other Jews in hiding, who were also arrested. The man's wife, who survived the war, accused Naumann of betrayal and claimed that he had voluntarily stayed in the apartment to catch more Jews even after the Gestapo had left the premises. However, one witness exculpated Naumann by saying that the Gestapo never left Jews to themselves for the purpose of catching other Jews and that the second officer must have remained with Naumann. "For someone who is familiar with the circumstances back then," the witness explained, "this means that Naumann did not stay in the apartment voluntarily, but only followed an order from the Gestapo. He cannot be reproached for abiding by this order."

Other witnesses attested that Naumann was essentially good-natured and concerned with the well-being of other Jews. One woman reported that while she was in hiding, Naumann had warned her of impending Gestapo roundups and saved her from deportation through a phone call to the apartment where she was hiding. Another woman attested to similar warnings and even deliveries of food, and a male witness claimed that Naumann had saved his life by talking a Gestapo officer out of shooting him. The Berlin honor court rejected any possibility that Naumann had gained any benefit from working with the Gestapo and in its acquittal stated that he "cannot be accused of having complied with Lachmuth's order"; indeed, despite having involuntarily served as a snatcher, Naumann did not display "malicious behavior intended to harm Jews."[47] Ultimately, it was a defendant's *intent* to harm Jews that counted rather than the fact that he or she had served the Nazis in one or another function.

Accordingly, the courts generally judged harshly those individuals who raised suspicion that, after their recruitment by the Nazis, they had not reluctantly carried out their assigned tasks but rather had exhibited undue enthusiasm or even ambition. Their moral wrongdoing was not that they performed tasks they had been ordered to complete but that they apparently showed some measure of personal engagement and intention in acting against other Jews. For example, Martha Raphael, who worked as an office aide and stenotypist for the Gestapo at the Grosse Hamburger Strasse assembly camp, stood trial before the Berlin honor court in May 1947 for allegedly having assisted in selections and, by showing unseemly ambition in her task, having harmed other Jews. The testimony of nineteen witnesses did not substantiate the claim that Raphael had selected individuals for deportation. One witness reported that the notorious Stella Goldschlag (who was currently serving a ten-year sentence as a snatcher) had accused Raphael of having employed her own snatcher of Jews; however, the court rejected this charge, given Goldschlag's own reputation. Indeed, several witnesses confirmed that Raphael had helped them, warned about deportations, and even rescued a Jewish foster child.

Regarding the accusation of Raphael's demonstration of zeal at her job, the court showed a nuanced understanding of the conflict forced on Jews working for Germans. It was not these Jews' individual choice to fulfill their assigned tasks; rather, they confronted a dilemma that resulted from the Jewish community's general policy of cooperation with the authorities: "This brought those Jewish employees who had to comply with this demand into a severe conflict between their Jewish consciousness and the task they were given. It required a great deal of strength of character from Jews [*jüdische Charakterstärke*] to be able to manage this double performance." The court also pointed out the obvious mismatch between the powers that the internees at the assembly camp ascribed to Raphael owing to her position versus her actual influence on the decisions and actions of the Gestapo, for whom Raphael remained "merely an executive organ." Nonetheless, the court found Raphael guilty of several transgressions. In addition to precipitating the deportation of one person—about whom she had apparently complained to her superiors—she had addressed Jews in an unfriendly and dismissive manner and displayed callousness regarding the fate of other Jews. In a situation that called for special sensitivity when talking to Jews who feared for their lives, the court ruled that her behavior "signified an extraordinary emotional brutality, which was not officially required and which must be severely condemned from the perspective of a Jewish human being." Thus, even taking into account that Raphael had involuntarily been brought into a conflict between her "professional activity and [her] loyalty to her Jewish convictions," she had not used her "difficult position at the Gestapo" as she might have to help other Jews "but instead sometimes placed her professional tasks higher than her Jewish conscience."[48]

Thus, because the honor courts did not investigate defendants' respective functions in the Nazi regime but rather the manner in which they had fulfilled them and whether or not they had intended to cause any harm to other Jews, court proceedings focused on the motivations and rationale of the accused and on the moral and physical constraints they faced.

Rationalizing Choiceless Choices: Defense Strategies in the Courtroom

In general, the Jewish honor court cases under review display a high level of awareness that Jews in privileged positions under the Nazi regime had not chosen these functions out of their own free will but rather had accepted them out of fear that noncompliance would endanger their own lives or those of their families. Often the courts acknowledged that retaining one's decency in such cases required special strength of character from Jews, or, rather, they maintained that defendants' weakness of character or being ill-suited to withstand the pressures of being placed between the Nazis and the Jewish community had prevented them from maintaining their moral integrity and human decency when working for the Nazis. For example, Arnold Rosenberg, who worked as a guard of a work commando at the Schulstrasse camp in Berlin in 1944 and 1945, stood trial in Berlin in April 1949 for allegedly treating his workers harshly and occasionally beating them and threatening to hand them over to the Gestapo. In his defense Rosenberg testified that he had never intended to deliver inmates to the Gestapo; however, he had been confronted with "awkward exigencies" in which the Gestapo had pressured him to increase the productivity of his workers. The court acquitted Rosenberg "with reservations" because he had sometimes behaved in an unseemly manner, but it acknowledged "the circumstances of the time, the fact that he had to work under the eyes of the Gestapo . . . and that he was personally ill-suited for the task he was to fulfill and that he found himself under constant pressure and demands."[49]

Age and immaturity often worked in favor of the accused, as it did in the case of Siegfried Goldstein, who was arrested and tortured by the Gestapo for supplying falsified identity cards to Jews but who had been able to save his life by betraying another Jew. The court in Berlin acquitted Goldstein on the basis of his youthful lack of maturity.

> Even if this betrayal which Goldstein, a so-called *Geltungsjude*—he is a Jewish-educated *Mischling*[50]—committed against a co-religionist, constitutes a severe offense from a Jewish point of view, even if his own plight is taken into account, then his guilt is considerably mitigated by the circumstance that Goldstein was only in the seventeenth year of his life when he committed the offense. From such a young and inexperienced person in such a precarious and perilous situation one cannot expect the same courage and consideration that would be expected of an adult matured man.[51]

Still, neither the recognition that most Jews had involuntarily been conscripted for tasks that they carried out under duress nor consideration for defendants' ages always meant that they would be exonerated. Even if the courts generally recognized that the assumption of posts such as a Judenrat member, ghetto policeman, or kapo was not a matter of choice, they nevertheless regarded the way in which individuals fulfilled their tasks as a matter of choice for which they could be held accountable. Thus in November 1948 Ruth Rosenzweig, a former camp elder of the women's section of the Burgau concentration camp in Bavaria, stood trial before the Rehabilitation Commission of the Central Jewish Honor Court in Munich for having beaten female Jewish inmates, in one case allegedly inflicting permanent damage to her victim's hearing. The defendant justified her actions by saying that she had not chosen her post and that the Germans had appointed her against her will. Moreover, in her capacity as camp elder she *had* to ensure that camp regulations were followed, and the women whom she admitted beating had violated those rules. Rejecting this logic, the Rehabilitation Commission ruled that Rosenzweig "must have known upon taking up the position of camp elder that this function would bring her into conflict with the Jewish inmates. Because the accused did not refuse her role—for the sake of being in a privileged position—she has to bear the consequences of her deeds."[52] Without acknowledging that fear for her life might have prevented Rosenzweig from refusing her assigned task, the court ruled that even for a camp elder, beating was a matter of individual choice.[53]

Accused individuals could get away with acts of violence if they were not systematic and caused no serious harm to anyone. In May 1948 the Berlin honor court acquitted Samuel Zuckermann of charges that he mistreated other Jews as a kapo in the Reichenbach concentration camp. Several witnesses confirmed that Zuckermann, like other kapos, regularly carried and occasionally used a whip, and he was reported to have said that he would "rather beat others to death than relinquish his whip." The court accepted Zuckermann's claim that he had neither meant this literally nor truly hurt anyone, ruling that "hits by kapos could sometimes avert more severe measures of punishment by the guards. In any case, the plaintiff did not avail himself of his right [to use the whip] in an inhumane manner." Although Zuckermann "wanted to be a kapo, in fact a good kapo, in order to save himself," because his occasional strikes had done no real harm to inmates, the court ruled further that Zuckermann was "not innocent, but he is not burdened with such a grave guilt that would require a sentence. Rather, the general situation [of the persecution], in which [saving] one's own life became of uppermost concern, must be taken into account in his favor."[54]

In a similar vein the Rehabilitation Commission in Munich opined in October 1948 that although Szmul Zbik, a former block elder and kapo in the Dachau-Kaufering concentration camp, had in some cases beaten Jewish fellow prisoners, "the beating was not of a systematic nature and was not an expression of the usual level of brutality that came with an exposed position of bloc elders and camp kapos." Thus the judges showed some understanding of the extraordinary circumstances that the Nazis had created for their victims, such that in some instances the camp authorities "had forced the defendant into beating other Jews." Yet the court did not relieve Zbik of all responsibility for his actions. The court found that "because the accused did not have to accept his position and could have refused his functions, there is no reason to justify the deeds of the defendant as having been perpetrated under duress."[55]

Like the actual Nazi perpetrators tried elsewhere, many defendants in Jewish honor courts tried to minimize their agency, claiming that they had acted on the orders of others. Although the honor courts in Munich and Berlin generally recognized the mortal danger posed by the refusal of orders, even for Jews in privileged positions within the power structure of Nazi ghettos and camps, the courts did not accept the claim that merely following orders diminished the responsibility of an individual defendant. For example, in November 1947 the Munich Rehabilitation Commission heard the case of Chaim Aleksandrowicz, a high-ranking police official in the Kovno ghetto from 1941 to 1944 and a block elder and kapo responsible for clothing distribution in the Dachau-Kaufering concentration camp in 1944–1945. Accused of violent and sadistic acts against Jews, Aleksandrowicz sought to justify his acts by arguing that he had been forced into his job as a police official against his will. He based his defense not only on following an order from the Germans but also on his duty as a loyal member of the Zionist underground, at whose behest he had taken upon himself the onerous job of high-ranking police official, under direct supervision by the SS, thus suggesting that by fulfilling this assignment he had done a service to the Jewish community. The court rejected this line of defense, which "relieves the accused from any responsibility for his individual deeds and even legitimizes a priori any wrongdoing committed against another Jew."[56] The court rejected Aleksandrowicz's assertion of an order from below, given that the underground had formed after he assumed his post. And although his prewar membership in a Zionist youth movement might have influenced his decision, joining the ghetto police was Aleksandrowicz's "private affair," even as harming other Jews was a personal choice.[57] The court further questioned the idea of an order to take the job of bloc elder and kapo at Dachau-Kaufering; rather, having witnessed the horrifying liquidation of the Kovno ghetto in fall 1943, it was "no wonder that upon arriving at the camp [the accused] had only one goal: saving his own life at any cost. The accused was a bloc elder because he had wanted to and succeeded." Finally, having accepted these camp positions to improve his chances of survival, Aleksandrowicz "must have foreseen that this would bring him into conflict with other Jews,"[58] especially given his previous experiences in the Kovno ghetto police.

The courts generally rejected attempts by defendants to justify their mistreatment of fellow prisoners or their betrayal of Jews in hiding for fear of their own lives, given that the circumstances of persecution had placed everyone's life at a greater risk. This was especially the case if their story failed to ring true. For example, in February 1951 the Berlin honor court found a Jewish man married to a non-Jewish woman guilty of having betrayed two Jews to the Gestapo, which led to their deportation and the death of one of them. The court rejected his explanation that he was trying to avert the persecution of his wife and two children because it reasoned that the Gestapo would not have acted against his non-Jewish wife and *Mischling* children. It ruled that the defendant was "culpable because he knew the consequences of the arrest of Jews who lived in illegality" and because his act "led to the death of one illegal Jew and caused great danger for other Jews and non-Jews. Such behavior cannot be stigmatized severely enough. Therefore, it must be noted that the defendant violated his duties toward the Jewish community in the sincerest way."[59]

The Berlin court was more accepting of the argument that a defendant had acted against fellow Jews to protect them from a worse fate, most likely because—unlike the justification out of fear—it had a collective rationale and showed a sense of social solidarity. For example, Selmar Neumann, a former supervisor of the Jewish Hospital at Schulstrasse in Berlin, successfully defended himself against accusations that he had beaten Jews by arguing that any such beatings were intended to prevent worse; by keeping order and punishing minor offenses with "small" punishments, such as slaps in the face, he had largely prevented the Gestapo from administering more severe punishments to prisoners alleged to have broken the rules of this hospital turned detention facility. The honor court acquitted Neumann in July 1947.[60]

In dozens of cases the rehabilitation process not only acquitted the defendants but also validated their wartime behavior as examples of good conduct in times of oppression and persecution. For example, Henryk Gliksman, from 1942 to 1945 both a foreman overseeing the Jewish workers employed by the German Ostbahn company in Częstochowa and a camp elder of the Częstochowa-Raków labor camp, was accused of harmful acts against Jews. However, the testimonies of nine witnesses "spoke only of good deeds"; in particular, Gliksman had been in close contact with the ghetto underground and had assisted in acts of sabotage against the Germans, for which he suffered severe corporal punishment. Dismissing a single witness who claimed that Gliksman had brutally assaulted Jews, the court acquitted him in August 1949.[61]

Similarly, in January 1948 Hermann Rothschild, who at the time sought to run for a position on the board of delegates of the Berlin Jewish community, requested a trial to clear his name of accusations that he had collaborated with the Gestapo. As a functionary of the Reich Association of Jews in Germany (Reichsvereinigung der Juden in Deutschland) in 1942, Rothschild worked as a security guard (*Ordner*) at the Grosse Hamburger Strasse assembly camp from

February to December 1943. In that capacity he assisted a Gestapo officer named Wenzel in fetching people for deportation, moving their luggage, and assisting in other deportation-related tasks. The honor court proceedings clarified that Rothschild neither voluntarily filled this position nor acted independently. Eight witnesses testified to his good character.

> Within the limits of his subordinate position he endeavored to help those struck by misfortune. He offered support, not just by means of encouragement and good words; he dispatched letters for the inmates of the camp and abundantly cared for them with packages. It was well known that he had a warm heart for his co-religionists and acted accordingly.... It is also to be regarded as proven that he suffered physically and psychologically from his work, that he called in sick, and at the end of 1943 [he] volunteered for forced labor [*Arbeitseinsatz*] regardless of the dangers it entailed.

Moreover, Rothschild warned people of dangers and helped them escape from the camp. In its acquittal the court ruled that "the mere circumstance that he was forced to work as a security guard, pressured by the Gestapo, does not incriminate him. He served only under severe psychological pressure and most reluctantly, and in the framework of his job, he assiduously endeavored to mitigate the lot of those struck by the catastrophe."[62]

Similarly, in January 1947 Samuel Eisenmann put himself on trial in Berlin for the purpose of clearing his name of the allegation that he had mistreated Jews while serving as a Jewish policeman in the Lodz ghetto. Three witnesses testified that after a short time he asked to be released from this position, after which he resumed economic work in the ghetto. They also related that Eisenmann saved forty-seven Jews from deportation shortly before the liquidation of the ghetto by assigning them to work in the cemetery. These facts led to Eisenmann's unanimous acquittal.[63]

Measuring Guilt, Meting Out Punishment

If evidence warranted the accusations, the courts presented defendants' guilt in terms of their acts against an imagined and rather elusive Jewish collective that had suffered both moral and physical injury. In committing such acts, the defendants severed their ties with the Jewish collective, indeed voluntarily placed themselves outside it. The punishments handed down by the honor courts in the name of the Jewish collective reenacted that very separation; anyone who had acted against the Jewish collective during times of persecution did not deserve to be a part of it in times of peace.

The lightest sentence came in the form of a moral reprimand that effectively shamed the guilty and put them on notice that their behavior was unacceptable. Cuts in social welfare benefits, or even their suspension, constituted the next level of punishment, even though they also often involved moral rebukes. In the DP camps this punishment meant the denial of supplies from the American Jewish Joint Distribution Committee, whereas for German Jews it involved not only the loss of welfare from the Jewish community but also the loss of Victim of Fascism status, which entailed social welfare benefits and preferential treatment by city authorities in finding housing and work.[64] In more serious cases sentences might include "lustration," that is, the loss of active and passive voting rights in community elections along with a ban on holding public office in the Jewish community or the DP camp structure. In the worst-case scenario defendants were banished from the Jewish community: the punishment for flouting standards of behavior deemed obligatory for members of the Jewish community, namely, violating the bonds of group solidarity.[65] Essentially, then, these punishments were as much about regulating the governance of the postwar Jewish community (who was to fulfill leadership roles) as they were about determining its character (who was a proper member of the Jewish collective).

On the scale of offenses adjudicated in the Jewish honor courts, harming Jewish interests in a moral sense was deemed the lightest offense. Such cases included *verbal* abuse, insults, acts intended to demoralize, and exerting psychological pressure on individuals in existential distress. For example, in June 1946 the Jewish community in Berlin received accusations against one of its members, Wilhelm Tobias, who allegedly mistreated the Jewish workers he supervised as a foreman in a German firm. Because the community suspended its welfare allowance until the accusations were investigated, Tobias requested an honor court proceeding, hoping to settle his case. However, five witnesses testified that he had "harassed his Jewish co-workers in the harshest manner, insulted them and Jews in general and . . . even repeatedly declared that Jews should be delivered to the Gestapo," in addition to verbally attacking a pious Jew working under his command. One witness even claimed that on one occasion Tobias had beaten a co-worker for no reason and told another one, "Shut your Jewish snout." The judges ruled that "in the horrific time of Nazi persecution, Mr. Tobias did not behave toward his Jewish co-workers as must be expected and demanded of a decent human being and, in addition, of a Jew, that is, of a co-religionist and fellow-persecuted." Therefore he was found guilty and his wartime behavior was "frowned upon,"[66] earning him a moral rebuke from the court.

Worse than verbal insult was the neglect of communal duty, which often involved failing to show solidarity with Jews and to help ameliorate their fate. For example, the Jewish couple Emil and Marie Baer were wrongly accused of the betrayal of a group of Jews who worked illegally in the workshop of a Mrs. Brucks on Rosenthalerstrasse in the Berlin neighborhood of Mitte, leading to their arrest and subsequent deportation and death. At their honor court trial in September 1947, the couple managed to convince the court that they were not responsible for the betrayal and that they themselves had been arrested and threatened by the Gestapo. The court believed in the innocence of Emil, who had been kept in Gestapo captivity longer than his wife, a non-Jew who had converted to Judaism upon marriage. It maintained, however, that Marie, who had been released before the Jews' arrest, bore some responsibility for their fate, because she indicated during her interrogation at the trial that she knew of the Gestapo's interest in Mrs. Brucks's workshop but had failed to warn her immediately after her release. "Herewith," the court ruled, "Mrs. Baer became an accessory to the fact that the Jews whom Mrs. Brucks employed for altruistic reasons could be fetched by the Gestapo." Ultimately, Mrs. Baer had "failed to fulfill those duties which she had inherited through her belonging to the Jewish collective."[67]

The courts judged Jews who, in one way or another, had sided with the Nazi perpetrators and had thereby placed themselves outside the Jewish community, far more harshly than those who had neglected their duty toward the community. One such case involved Ferdinand Abraham Kranefeld, who jointly with his son Werner ran a wartime business that manufactured goods for the Wehrmacht. In 1948 Kranefeld stood trial in Berlin on charges of mistreating Jewish forced laborers. Kranefeld had converted to Judaism in 1919 after his marriage to a Jewish woman, and the couple had raised their two sons in the Jewish religion. In 1936 Kranefeld canceled his membership in Berlin's Jewish community but renewed it in 1945. In his defense Ferdinand claimed that he had tried to alleviate the fate of his Jewish workers and had helped them on various occasions; for example, he employed a Jew who posed as an Aryan and helped him escape once his identity was discovered. Twelve witnesses largely confirmed that Ferdinand treated his Jewish workers fairly, except for one instance when he called a worker with whom he had a conflict a "stinking Jew" and threatened to deliver him to the Gestapo. Other witnesses testified that the true villains were Ferdinand's son Werner and the non-Jewish operations manager, who insulted Jewish workers, threatened them with the Gestapo to make them work harder, and prohibited their going to the aerial shelter during bombings. Because neither the son nor the manager stood trial—the son was apparently no longer in Germany and the manager could not be tried by the honor court since he was not Jewish—Ferdinand was held responsible for his son's treatment of Jewish forced laborers, which the court found "inhumane and reminiscent of National Socialist methods," thus associating him with the Nazis even though he was born Jewish and raised in the Jewish faith. Although the verdict recognized that, with one exception, Ferdinand had treated his employees well, he was nevertheless chastised morally because he had condoned the behavior of his son and the operations manager toward the Jewish workers in his employ. In finding that Ferdinand had acted against the Jewish collective, the court argued that, by converting, he had become subject to the same moral standards as those who belonged to the Jewish community by birth.

Implicitly, however, the court seems to have applied harsher moral standards to Kranefeld as a convert, especially one who had voluntarily dissociated himself from the Jewish community in the years 1936–1945, because as an "Aryan" he had not faced the same mortal dangers as had those who were Jews "by race." The court ruled that as a converted Jew, married to a Jew and the father of two *Mischling* children, Kranefeld "should have demonstrated more understanding for the situation of the Jewish forced laborers and [that] as a matter of principle he should have refrained from any harshness, let alone threats and insults." Further, by insulting one of his employees, Ferdinand Kranefeld had violated "Jewish honor and sense of decency" and had "confessed to the terminology and mind-set inherent in the Nazi system." His threat to turn a worker over to the Gestapo, even if only a threat, was not to be forgiven: "Merely the fact that someone who claims to adhere to Judaism even utters such a threat toward Jews is an unforgivable breach of Jewish and general human decency. Ferdinand Kranefeld, in particular, should have known what psychological martyrdom [i.e., the mortal fear] such a threat meant for those concerned and their families." In at least one case Kranefeld was found guilty of failing to treat Jewish forced laborers "as would have been mandatory from the point of view of the Jewish collective."[68] By his immoral wartime behavior, Kranefeld had thus gambled away his reacceptance by and active membership in the Jewish community.

Actually betraying Jews to the authorities and thus indirectly contributing to the Nazi deportation and murder of Jews was, not surprisingly, an even more severe offense. Thus in November 1946 the Jewish honor court in Berlin found Selma Bier, a Jew by "religion, not race"—she had converted to Judaism—guilty of having "grossly violated her duties toward the Jewish community." In 1941 she reported her Jewish landlord and subtenant to the police because they had bought coal outside the shopping hours designated for Jews. Initially, the landlord was merely fined 50 reichsmarks, but Selma Bier's complaint to the police established a "criminal record," which led to his detention at the Sachsenhausen concentration camp in May 1942, where he died in the following months. After hearing three witnesses, the court ruled that Mrs. Bier should have known the full consequences of her action.

> Every Jew, who in 1941 reported another Jew to the authorities over a negligible offense, must have been aware that this must have aggravating and severe consequences for those concerned. Therefore, every pressing of charges by a Jew against another Jew at that time is a serious violation of the obligations of belonging to the Jewish community. Awareness of the consequences as such is less important than the fact that in 1941 the Jewish conscience of every Jew must have prohibited reporting a co-religionist to Nazi authorities.[69]

Mrs. Bier thus lost her membership in the Jewish community, although any further punishment she received remains unknown.

The most severe offense in the eyes of the courts was using physical violence to harm a fellow Jew, in particular, severe beating or other forms of torture as well as the deprivation of food. Those accused in such cases were most often former inmates of camps, in particular, kapos, block elders, and other prisoner functionaries. The judgment of individual guilt in these cases led to the defendant's condemnation as a "traitor to the Jewish people" or, as often happened, in the case of Jewish displaced persons as a "traitor to the surviving remnant [*sheyris hapleyte*]" or among German Jews as someone who had "failed the Jewish community." Such acts were punished with excommunication, that is, denial of the right to belong to the Jewish community, to maintain contacts with Jewish organizations, or to live among other Jews. At least in principle, excommunication meant total isolation from the defendants' Jewish peers.

In April 1948 the Rehabilitation Commission in Munich held one of its most prominent trials, against Regina Szenberg (Kupiec), a Polish Jewish woman in her thirties who was accused of brutally assaulting fellow Jews as a prisoner functionary at Auschwitz-Birkenau. Her case had earlier come to the court's attention in May 1946, when former Auschwitz inmates who recognized Szenberg attacked her at a soccer match at the Neu-Freimann DP Camp near Munich. She subsequently requested that her case be transferred to the Central

Committee in Munich so that it could inquire into her wartime behavior, clear her name from the accusation, and prevent similar attacks in the future.[70] After hearing several witnesses, however, the Rehabilitation Commission resolved that

> the accused, Regina Szenberg (Kupiec), born September 15, 1916 in Warsaw, . . . while holding [the] position of house-senior during the years 1943–1944 in KZ Birkenau in Auschwitz, block 25 A, is declared guilty of sadistic treatment of Jewish women and children, of beating without reason Jewish women, of making their lives miserable, selling food which she stole from rations that belonged to children and women, and has therefore committed a crime against the Jewish people. For the above-mentioned deeds, the accused Regina Szenberg (Kupiec) will be punished by being publicly declared traitor of [*sic*] the Jewish people.[71]

The charge that Szenberg had participated in selections could not be substantiated and was dismissed. The final verdict was published in the Jewish press and sent to various Jewish institutions in Germany and abroad, including the Jewish Agency, the American Jewish Joint Distribution Committee, and the Hebrew Immigrant Aid Society. Szenberg used her right of appeal with the help of a Jewish defense attorney who doubted the legitimacy of excluding a Jew from Jewish society, which he deemed a practice so "archaic" that it was "unknown even at the time of the Inquisition." Moreover, he questioned the court's authority because it used an improvised, indeed "non-existent procedure."[72] The court rejected Szenberg's appeal in July 1948, ruling that it used "prescribed procedure based on the example of European procedures, which in a good many countries are also unwritten."[73] Although various Jewish organizations were informed that Szenberg was blacklisted as a "traitor to the Jewish people," whose emigration from Germany should be prevented under all circumstances, she managed to immigrate to the United States in December 1948.

The American military government required that in cases where Jews were found guilty of causing the deaths of others, the internal Jewish courts transfer those cases to the military courts.[74] This procedure was followed in the case involving Josef Wlodawski, a member of the Warsaw ghetto police and a prisoner functionary in the Radom labor camp and the Hessental concentration camp. On February 25, 1949, the Munich honor court tried Wlodawski on charges of brutal acts and sadism, after twenty-one witnesses related gruesome details of how he had beaten Jewish inmates, aiming for their head and genitals, deprived them of food rations, subjected them to severe corporal punishment for random "offenses," removed the gold teeth of inmates, and incited other kapos to act against Jews. In light of such evidence, the court held that Wlodawski had "found enjoyment in seeing Jewish blood spilled and had behaved worse than the men of the SS."[75] Because his actions directly led to the deaths of at least two prisoners, his case was transferred to the military authorities; however, its outcome remains unknown.[76]

Individuals convicted and sentenced by the Jewish honor courts in Munich and Berlin had the right of appeal. Although appeals often led to a reformulation of the verdict, they did not necessarily affect the punishment. In December 1946 the Berlin Jewish honor court found Rosa Blond, a security guard at the Gestapo camp at Schulstrasse in the Berlin neighborhood of Wedding, guilty of mistreating and insulting prisoners and of pressuring prisoners to betray the hiding places of other Jews, indeed, of having said that Jewish inmates deserved to be murdered. The court ruled that Blond be excluded from the Jewish community because her behavior "deserved decisive condemnation because of not only her harsh attack on innocent persecuted and tormented co-religionists but also her crude incitement against them, which showed an agreement and equality of mind-set with Nazi criminals and Gestapo members, those deadly enemies of Judaism and civilized humanity." The court further opined:

> It would have been the human and religious duty of every member of our community of faith to do everything possible to assist the persecuted brothers and sisters in their misery and to alleviate their hardship, as some members of the camp personnel attempted in a very laudable manner to the best of their ability and at great personal risk. [Therefore] Mrs. Blond's behavior must be seen as even more condemnable and degrading.[77]

Five years later, Blond appealed to the honor court to clear her name of the accusation and possibly even resume her membership in the Berlin congregation. Although she brought in a new witness who testified to her good and humane behavior, the court rejected the appeal, maintaining that this one case did not change the fact that in many other cases Blond had "glaringly violated her duties toward the Jewish community."[78]

Another case in point is the verdict of the Rehabilitation Commission in Munich in the case of Dawid Najman, a policeman in the Ostrowiec-Świętokrzyski ghetto. In May 1948 that court found Najman guilty of having caused the deaths of more than twenty Jews shot by the SS during the third *Aktion* of the SS in January 1943 (when 2,000 ghetto inhabitants were rounded up and deported to Treblinka), because he had revealed the location of a bunker in which the Jews had been hiding. Accordingly, he was declared a "traitor to the Jewish people" and denied the right both to participate in Jewish public life and to hold office in the Jewish community. Najman appealed two days after the verdict, leading to a second round of hearings in January 1949. This time the court found him guilty of *indirectly* contributing to the murder of the Jews after new witnesses testified that Najman had not betrayed the bunker's location but rather that his appearance at the bunker had caused a panic in which people fled the hiding place and were found and shot by the SS. The court argued that Najman's appearance at the bunker proved to those in hiding that the Jewish police knew about their hideout and that Najman "must have been aware of how people in the bunker would react to his appearance in such a critical moment. Because he accepted this possible eventuality [*dolus eventualis*] he must now bear the consequences of his deed."[79] Although the court revised its verdict, it did not lessen Najman's earlier punishment.

In some cases appeal did lead to a lighter sentence. Such was the case of Ruchela Bursztajn, whom the Rehabilitation Commission in November 1948 declared a "traitor to the Jewish people" because of her actions as a kapo in the "potato commando" at the Stutthof concentration camp in early 1945. In particular, Bursztajn "behaved in a sadistic manner toward the starving and weakened Jewish women, beating them like a murderer and betraying them to the Germans and ordering a dog to attack the women, who suffered serious bites. Moreover, during the camp evacuation she assisted the German kapo in finding and driving out Jewish women from their hideouts."[80] In March 1949 a new witness claimed that Bursztajn was not responsible for ordering the nearly fatal dog attack because the dog had been trained to attack only on the command of its genuine handler, the German kapo, and would never have acted on Bursztajn's command. Whereas the court had at first sentenced Bursztajn to banishment from the Jewish community, the revised verdict reduced the sentence to a prohibition to hold office in the Jewish community.[81]

Conclusion

In sum, although the Berlin Jewish community and the Munich DP camp courts formally served to maintain order, facilitate communal life, and prevent vigilante justice against putative collaborators, their essential significance lay elsewhere. Hannah Arendt's observation that the "right to have rights"[82] is the most fundamental right of any human being and a precondition for human dignity and survival is in some sense echoed in the context of the Jewish honor courts. These courts were perhaps the most fundamental expression of survivors' urge to restore their rights and reappropriate the rule of law after experiencing the traumatic total loss of their rights as citizens and human beings and after having seen the travesty of justice under the Nazis, when laws, rather than protecting individuals, became instruments of terror and ultimately of genocide. By establishing their own courts, Jews sought not only to restore their participation in the rule of law and morality but also to avert the danger that vindictiveness against those who supposedly had harmed the Jewish collective by aiding the Nazis in their genocide would promote extra-legal modes of dealing with collaborators; indeed, they were an attempt to grant the accused a forum in which they, too, were legal persons rather than fair game. Following years of rightlessness and persecution, Jews were no longer merely the objects of the laws and courts of others. They had returned to being legal persons; they were again active participants in legal frameworks, which they would shape by and for themselves. This experience might also explain the urgency with which survivor communities in the years following the liberation adjudicated collaboration in their own ranks, subjecting to judicial procedures fellow survivors who had also been victims rather than focusing on the actual Nazi perpetrators and their non-Jewish collaborators.

Likewise, the court cases also reflect the deep urge to mend the profound moral rifts that the enforced collaboration with the Nazis had left in Jewish society. By working through the moral dilemmas of the choiceless choices of the recent past, the courts sought to set ethical standards for the present and future while also determining who could belong to and lead the Jewish collective in the postwar years. It is striking but perhaps understandable, given that Nazism had defined Jews out of humanity, that the Jewish honor courts were not concerned with universal terms of morality but rather with sorting out the moral dilemmas that Jews came up against when interacting with other Jews in the face of genocide. In seeking to restore the bonds of group solidarity among Jews, not among Jews and non-Jews, what was at stake in the honor court proceedings was whether or not a Jew had failed against other Jews, not against a non-Jewish fellow persecuted.

In that sense honor courts were instrumental in enabling survivors' moral rehabilitation, because they provided them with a means to restore self-respect and agency. These honor courts also contributed to the forging of a collective identity and helped to enforce the autonomy of the Jewish community from both the German society that surrounded it and the Allied occupying forces.

Given their distrust of the Allies and the Germans, the DP camp courts gave survivors the opportunity to institute their own principles of justice. Moreover, the honor courts served the educational purpose of reestablishing social norms and ethical values among Jews after years of persecution. The rehabilitation cases also served as a prism through which survivors with diverse backgrounds, wartime experiences, and ideological outlooks could begin to process the traumatic events of the recent catastrophe. This contributed to forging a community with a clearly defined ethical and behavioral code. In distinguishing between moral and immoral, acceptable and unacceptable behavior in the recent past and by ejecting those who had acted against the collective, the Jewish community, in whose name justice was meted out, defined the terms of belonging for its members.

The symbolic significance of trying Jews in separate Jewish courts in Allied-occupied Germany and its impact on the formation of a national consciousness and group cohesion among the surviving remnant should not be underestimated. At a time when prominent Nazi war crimes trials held by the Allies in Nuremberg, Dachau, Lüneburg, Berlin, and elsewhere largely marginalized the distinct Jewish fate and excluded the active participation of Jews (who as a nonstate entity had no means of participating in international criminal justice and military tribunals), these courts were also an attempt to establish an autonomous Jewish judicial sphere, even if it was limited to Jewish communities. Here, crimes against the Jewish people rather than crimes against humanity stood at the center, and justice was done in the name of a Jewish collective.

Notes

I wish to thank Elisabeth Gallas, Douglas Morris, and Amy Hackett for their insightful comments on this manuscript.

1. See, for example, Lawrence Douglas, *The Memory of Judgment: Making Law and History in the Trials of the Holocaust* (New Haven, CT: Yale University Press, 2001), 11–94. I have discussed the role of Jews at Nuremberg elsewhere in more detail; see Laura Jockusch, "Justice at Nuremberg? Jewish Responses to Nazi War Crimes Trials in Allied Occupied Germany," *Jewish Social Studies* 19.1 (2012): 107–47.
2. See, for example, Tomaz Jardim, *The Mauthausen Trial: American Military Justice in Germany* (Cambridge, MA: Harvard University Press, 2012).
3. Raymond Phillips, ed., *The Trial of Josef Kramer and 44 Others: The Belsen Trial* (London: HMSO, 1947), 367–69.
4. On the Belsen trial, see John Cramer, *Belsen Trial 1945: Der Lüneburger Prozess gegen Wachpersonal der Konzentrationslager Auschwitz und Bergen-Belsen* (Göttingen, Germany: Wallstein, 2011).

5. In 1973 Goldschlag's case was reopened on appeal; the trial confirmed the guilty verdict, but her ill health kept her out of prison. She committed suicide in 1994. See Andreas Hilger, Mike Schmeitzner, and Ute Schmidt, eds., *Die Sowjetische Militärtribunale: Verurteilung deutscher Zivilisten, 1945–1955* (Vienna: Böhlau, 2003), 2: 172–73; Christian Dirks, "Snatchers: The Berlin Gestapo's Jewish Informants," in Beate Meyer, Hermann Simon, and Chana Schütz, eds., *Jews in Nazi Berlin: From Kristallnacht to Liberation* (Chicago: University of Chicago Press, 2009), 249–73; and Peter Wyden, *Stella: One Woman's True Tale of Evil, Betrayal, and Survival in Hitler's Germany* (New York: Simon & Shuster, 1992).

6. On these German court cases, which compared to Allied war crime trials have received little attention in scholarly literature, see Devin O. Pendas, "Retroactive Law and Proactive Justice: Debating Crimes Against Humanity in Germany, 1945–1950," *Central European History* 43 (August 2010): 428–63. On cases involving alleged Jewish collaborators with the Nazis, see Jael Geis, *Übrig sein—Leben "danach": Juden deutscher Herkunft in der britischen und amerikanischen Zone Deutschlands, 1945–1949* (Berlin: Philo, 1999), 274–75.

7. Hagit Lavsky, *New Beginnings: Holocaust Survivors in Bergen-Belsen and the British Zone in Germany, 1945–1949* (Detroit: Wayne State University Press, 2002), 28–29; and Michael Brenner, *After the Holocaust: Rebuilding Jewish Lives in Postwar Germany* (Princeton, NJ: Princeton University Press, 1997), 138.

8. Margarete Myers Feinstein, *Holocaust Survivors in Postwar Germany, 1945–1957* (New York: Cambridge University Press, 2010), 1.

9. On the relations between Jewish displaced persons and German Jews in Germany, see Michael Brenner, "East European and German Jews in Postwar Germany, 1945–1950," in Y. Michal Bodemann, ed., *Jews, Germans, Memory: Reconstruction of Jewish Life in Germany* (Ann Arbor: University of Michigan Press, 1996), 49–63.

10. Jan T. Gross, "Themes for a Social History of War Experience and Collaboration," in István Deák, Jan T. Gross, and Tony Judt, eds., *The Politics of Retribution in Europe: World War II and Its Aftermath* (Princeton, NJ: Princeton University Press, 2000), 29.

11. István Deák, "Introduction," in Deák et al., eds., *Politics of Retribution*, 8.

12. See, for example, Jim G. Tobias and Peter Zinke, *Nakam: Jüdische Rache an NS-Tätern* (Hamburg: Konkret Literatur, 2000); Geis, *Übrig sein*, 239–87; and Jael Geis, "'Ja man muss seinen Feinden verzeihen, aber nicht früher als bis sie gehenkt werden': Gedenken an Rache für die Vernichtung der Juden im unmittelbaren Nachkriegsdeutschland," *Menora: Jahrbuch für deutsch-jüdische Geschichte* 9 (1998): 155–80.

13. Atina Grossmann, *Jews, Germans, and Allies: Close Encounters in Occupied Germany* (Princeton, NJ: Princeton University Press, 2007), 95, 97, 123.

14. Malcolm Proudfoot, *European Refugees, 1939–1952: A Study in Forced Population Movement* (London: Faber & Faber, 1957), 339 and 341; on the number of Jewish displaced persons in Munich, see Brenner, *After the Holocaust*, 16.

15. The reemerging German Jewish communities established arbitral courts (*Schiedsgerichte*) or honor courts (*Ehrengerichte*) that dealt with conflicts involving two or more of their registered members. Although many Jewish communities had such courts, I was able to locate the records of only the Berlin Jewish community. The archival records of trials

against putative collaborators with the Nazis are mainly found in the Berlin State Archives (Landesarchiv Berlin), because the Jewish honor court supplied summaries of its cases to the Berlin Senate. The archives of the Berlin Jewish community house only a small fraction of the case records, possibly indicating that the files were subsequently destroyed because of the sensitive issue of collaboration. This might also be the case with other Jewish community archives. I have so far been unable to locate honor court records of other German Jewish communities beyond Berlin. It should be further noted that the existing material is often incomplete, rendering the full reconstruction of the case histories difficult.

16. Heymont himself was of Jewish background, a fact that he did not make public for fear of subverting military discipline, but his Jewish background made him particularly receptive to the problems, needs, and concerns of the Jewish displaced persons under his supervision. See Patricia Sullivan, "Officer Ran Displaced Persons Camp After WWII," *Washington Post* (April 2009).

17. "Appeal to Residents of the Landsberg Jewish Center," *Landsberger Lager Cajtung* (November 12, 1945), English in original.

18. Statutes of the Jewish honor court, n.d., Archives of the Centrum Judaicum Berlin (hereafter ACJ), Bestand 5A1, Nr. 7.

19. "An die Repräsentantenversammlung," December 14, 1945, ACJ, Bestand 5A1, Nr. 7.

20. Statutes of the Jewish honor court, ACJ, Bestand 5A1, Nr. 7.

21. Letter from Vorstand to the Repräsentantenversammlung, January 25, 1946, ACJ, Bestand 5A1, Nr. 7. On the history of the Main Committee for the Victims of Fascism, see the finding aid to the collection of the Landesarchiv Berlin, C Rep. 118–01, http://www.landesarchiv-berlin.de/php-bestand/crep118-01-pdf/CRep118-01.pdf.

22. Letter from Vorstand to the Repräsentantenversammlung, January 21, 1946, ACJ, Bestand 5A1, Nr. 7.

23. A handful of additional cases involved disputes between members of the community that had occurred after the war and mainly involved business relations.

24. See Angelika Eder, *Flüchtige Heimat: Jüdische Displaced Persons in Landsberg am Lech 1945 bis 1950* (Munich: Kommissionsverlag UNI-Druck, 1998), 168; Feinstein, *Holocaust Survivors*, 239; and Angelika Königseder and Juliane Wetzel, *Waiting for Hope: Jewish Displaced Persons in Post–World War II Germany* (Evanston, IL: Northwestern University Press, 2001), 136–37.

25. See, for example, "Bericht über den Münchener Kongress," *Deggendorf Center Review* (February 15, 1946): 4; and "Die Konferenz beschliesst," n.d. [January 1946], Archives of the YIVO Institute for Jewish Research, Displaced Persons Camps and Centers in Germany (hereafter YIVO, DPG), reel 4, file 44.

26. Feinstein, *Holocaust Survivors*, 240. See the statutes of the legal department, "Organizacjoneler statut fun der Juridiszer Optejlung bajm C.K.," December 2, 1947, YIVO, DPG, reel 4, file 44.

27. See "Tätigkeitsbericht der Juridischen Abteilung beim Zentralkomitee," June 9, 1946, YIVO, DPG, reel 4, file 44.

28. See the honor court regulations, "Regulamin," n.d., YIVO, DPG, reel 4, file 44.

29. See the protocol of the Central Committee meeting of June 23–24, 1947, YIVO, Leo W. Schwarz Papers, reel 14, folder 130.

30. Feinstein, *Holocaust Survivors*, 240.

31. See the Harrison Report, quoted in Leonard Dinnerstein, *America and the Survivors of the Holocaust* (New York: Columbia University Press, 1982), 290–305.

32. See Wolfgang Jacobmeyer, "Jüdische Überlebende als 'Displaced Persons': Untersuchungen zur Besatzungspolitik in den deutschen Westzonen und zur Zuwanderung osteuropäischer Juden, 1945–1947," *Geschichte und Gesellschaft* 9.3 (1983): 442–43.

33. Feinstein, *Holocaust Survivors*, 246–47; and Königseder and Wetzel, *Waiting for Hope*, 139.

34. Leo W. Schwarz, director of the American Jewish Joint Distribution Committee in the U.S. zone in this period, mentioned 397 cases against putative collaborators. To date, however, the archival files in the YIVO and Yad Vashem archives have not substantiated these numbers. See Leo W. Schwarz, *The Redeemers: A Saga of the Years 1945–1952* (New York: Farrar, Straus & Young, 1953), 342. In his encyclopedia article on Jewish honor courts in Poland and Germany, Gabriel Finder states that honor court cases in the DP camps in Germany "probably exceeded 100 and may have approached 200." See Gabriel N. Finder, "Honor Courts," in *YIVO Encyclopedia of Jews in Eastern Europe*, ed. Gershon David Hundert (New Haven, CT: Yale University Press), 752.

35. According to Isaiah Trunk, it was common for survivors to settle accounts with individual collaborators before a legal framework was established; thus deep-seated anger at ghetto policemen led to acts of revenge after liberation. See Isaiah Trunk, *Judenrat: The Jewish Councils in Eastern Europe Under Nazi Occupation* (New York: Macmillan, 1972), 552–53. On lynching and acts of violence in the DP camps, see Jon Bridgman, *The End of the Holocaust: The Liberation of the Camps* (Portland, OR: Areopagitica, 1990), 13–14; Irving Heymont, *Among the Survivors of the Holocaust, 1945: The Landsberg DP Camp Letters of Major Irving Heymont, United States Army* (Cincinnati, OH: American Jewish Archives, 1982), letter of October 31, 1945; Abraham S. Hyman, *The Undefeated* (Jerusalem: Gefen, 1993), 339; and Schwarz, *Redeemers*, 68–69.

36. Trunk, *Judenrat*, 555.

37. "Harbere sztrofn far kapos!" *Landsberg Lager Cajtung* (November 12, 1945): 6; and Königseder and Wetzel, *Waiting for Hope*, 140.

38. See, for example, the Regina Szenberg case discussed later in this chapter.

39. Grossmann, *Jews, Germans, and Allies*, 88 and 303n4.

40. On Jewish life in illegality and Jewish snatchers, see, for example, Doris Tausendfreund, "'Jüdische Fahnder': Verfolgte, Verfolger und Retter in einer Person," in Wolfgang Benz, ed., *Überleben im Dritten Reich: Juden im Untergrund und ihre Helfer* (Munich: C. H. Beck, 2003), 239–56; and Moshe Zimmermann, *Deutsche gegen Deutsche: Das Schicksal der Juden 1938–1945* (Berlin: Aufbau, 2008), 165–88.

41. Grossmann, *Jews, Germans, and Allies*, 97.

42. Lawrence L. Langer, *Versions of Survival: The Holocaust and the Human Spirit* (Albany: State University of New York Press, 1982), 72.

43. See, for example, the charter of the International Military Tribunal: International Military Tribunal, ed., *Trial of the Major War Criminals Before the International Military Tribunal, Nuremberg 14 November 1945–1 October 1946*, 42 vols. (Nuremberg: International Military Tribunal, 1947), 1: 10–16; and "Order of the Tribunal Regarding Notice to Members of Groups and Organizations," in International Military Tribunal, ed., *Trial of the Major War Criminals*, 1: 97–101. See also Kim C. Priemel and Alexa Stiller, eds., *NMT: Die Nürnberger Militärtribunale zwischen Geschichte, Gerechtigkeit und Rechtsschöpfung* (Hamburg: Hamburger Edition, 2013), 69, 503.

44. Raymond Phillips, ed., *The Trial of Josef Kramer and Forty-Four Others: The Belsen Trial* (London: Hodge, 1949), 650.

45. Honor court case of Beinisz Tkacz, protocol, March 29, 1948, Alter Berger's testimony, YIVO, DPG, reel 20, file 221, p. 2.

46. Honor court case of Beinisz Tkacz, "Baszlus," May 17, 1948, YIVO, DPG, reel 20, file 221, pp. 1–2.

47. Honor court case of Curt Naumann, October 28, 1946, Landesarchiv Berlin (hereafter LAB), B Rep 002, Nr. 4860–4861.

48. Honor court case of Martha Raphael, May 7, 1947, LAB, B Rep 002, Nr. 4860–4861.

49. Honor court case of Elly and Arnold Rosenberg, April 7, 1949, LAB, B Rep 002, Nr. 4860–4861.

50. That is, Goldstein was a so-called racial half-Jew, with only one Jewish parent, but he was raised as a Jew.

51. Honor court case of Siegfried Goldstein, January 6, 1948, LAB, B Rep 002, Nr. 4860–4861.

52. Honor court case of Ruth Rosenzweig, "Baszlus," November 28, 1948, Yad Vashem Archives, Jerusalem (hereafter YV), M.21.2, file 41, p. 2.

53. Honor court case of Ruth Rosenzweig, p. 2.

54. Honor court case of Samuel Zuckermann, May 19, 1948, LAB, B Rep 002, Nr. 4860–4861.

55. Honor court case of Szmul Zbik, "Baszlus," October 31, 1948, YV, M.21.2, file 52.

56. Honor court case of Chaim Aleksandrowicz, "Baszlus," July 22, 1948, YV, M.21.2, file 32, p. 4.

57. Honor court case of Chaim Aleksandrowicz, p. 6.

58. Honor court case of Chaim Aleksandrowicz, p. 8.

59. Honor court case of Rudolf Schwersensky, February 21, 1951, LAB, B Rep 002, Nr. 4860–4861.

60. Honor court case of Selmar and Rosalie Neumann, July 16, 1947, LAB, B Rep 002, Nr. 4860–4861.

61. Honor court case of Henryk Gliksman, "Baszlus," August 7, 1949, YV, M. 21. 2, folder 51. See also the case of Jochanan Goldkranc, "Baszlus," August 29, 1948, YV, M.21.2, file 36.
62. Honor court case of Hermann Rothschild, March 22, 1948, LAB, B Rep 002, Nr. 4860–4861.
63. Honor court case of Samuel Eisenmann, January 22, 1947, LAB, B Rep 002, Nr. 4860–4861.
64. Protocol of the Repräsentantenversammlung, June 24, 1947, LAB, B Rep 002, Nr. 4860–4861.
65. See the honor court regulations, "Regulamin," n.d., YIVO, DPG, reel 4, file 44.
66. Honor court case of Wilhelm Tobias, September 30, 1946, LAB, B Rep 002, Nr. 4860–4861.
67. Honor court case of Emil and Marie Baer, September 18, 1947, LAB, B Rep 002, Nr. 4860–4861.
68. Honor court case of Ferdinand Kranefeld and Werner Kranefeld, December 1, 1948, LAB, B Rep 002, Nr. 4860–4861.
69. Honor court case of Eduard and Selma Bier, November 6, 1946, LAB, B Rep 002, Nr. 4860–4861.
70. Hayman Wachtel, "To Whom It May Concern: Incident at Neu-Freiman, May 1946," May 27, 1948, YIVO, DPG, reel 20, folder 222.
71. Honor court case of Regina Szenberg (Kupiec), "Verdict," April 19, 1948, YIVO, DPG, reel 20, file 222. English in original.
72. Attorney David Julian Holcman to the Rehabilitation Commission, June 17, 1948, YIVO, DPG, reel 20, file 222. English in original.
73. Honor court case of Regina Szenberg (Kupiec), "Resolve," July 2, 1948, YIVO, DPG, reel 20, file 222. English in original.
74. See the letter of the Juridical Department of the Central Committee of Liberated Jews to the Rehabilitation Commission in Munich, December 27, 1948, YV, M.21.2, file 41.
75. Letter of the Juridical Department of the Central Committee of Liberated Jews to the Rehabilitation Commission in Munich, December 27, 1948.
76. Honor court case of Josef Wlodawski, "Baricht," July 22, 1948, YV, M. 21.2, folder 54.
77. Honor court case of Rosa Blond, December 11, 1946, LAB, B Rep 002, Nr. 4860–4861.
78. Rejection of Rosa Blond's appeal, January 23, 1951, LAB, B Rep 002, Nr. 4860–4861.
79. Honor court case of Dawid Najman, "Baszlus," January 6, 1949, YV, M. 21.2, file 145.
80. Honor court case of Ruchela Bursztajn, "Baszlus," November 7, 1948, YV, M.21.2, file 72.
81. Honor court case of Ruchela Bursztajn, "Baszlus," March 13, 1949, YV, M.21.2, file 72.
82. Hannah Arendt, *The Origins of Totalitarianism* (Cleveland: Meridian, 1958 [1951]), 296.

3

Judenrat on Trial

Postwar Polish Jewry Sits in Judgment of Its Wartime Leadership

GABRIEL N. FINDER

On October 18, 1946, an article with the title "Traitors to the Nation—to the People's Court" (*Di natsionale fareter—tsum folks-mishpet*) appeared in the newspaper *Dos naje lebn*, the Yiddish-language organ of the Central Committee of Polish Jews (Centralny Komitet Żydów w Polsce; CKŻP) (also known as the Central Committee of Jews in Poland). From its establishment in 1945 even before the end of World War II until its dismantlement in 1950, the CKŻP was the principal body of Polish Jewry, representing the interests of Polish Jews both to the Polish government, which bestowed official recognition on it, and in the public arena, to the Jewish world. Writing under the pseudonym Cincinnatus, the author of the article appealed to his fellow Polish Jews to demonstrate their opposition to the social disintegration of Polish Jewry wrought by the Holocaust, symptomatic of which was the emergence of a limited number of collaborators with Nazi rule in occupied Poland from within the Jewish community. By rejecting the presence of collaborators in their midst, Polish Jews would demonstrate their commitment to universal justice, thereby reclaiming their mantle to civic virtue and signaling their successful integration into the postwar Polish state. Because peoples of all nations from the French to the Poles had put their own traitors on trial, so should the Jews establish their own tribunal and sit in judgment of fellow Jews suspected of collaboration, no matter how painful and embarrassing the process might be. The article by Cincinnatus appeared alongside an official announcement by the CKŻP's standing executive committee, or presidium, of its establishment on October 8, 1946, of a civic court. Of course, the simultaneous appearance of Cincinnatus's article and the CKŻP's announcement in the pages of *Dos naje lebn* was not mere happenstance. Cincinnatus was close to the inner circle of the CKŻP's leadership and had taken his cue from it when he advocated support for the selfsame institution, which CKŻP's lawyers had been developing since the summer of the same year.[1]

The members of the CKŻP presidium consisted primarily of former Jewish partisans, mostly Zionists, from the Jewish Fighting Organization (Żydowska Organizacja Bojowa; ŻOB) in the Warsaw ghetto and other Jewish underground movements and Jewish communists. They enthusiastically supported the creation of a civic court or honor court, which was known by various designations in both Polish (*sąd społeczny* or *sąd obywatelski*) and Yiddish (*birger-gerikht, folks-gerikht, gezelshaftlikh-gerikht*, and *ern-gerikht*). According to the CKŻP's second annual report, the goals of the civic court were the "cleansing [*oczyszczenie* in the Polish version, *optsuraynikn* in the Yiddish] of Jewish society of people who for one reason or another collaborated with Nazi authorities during the occupation" and the "unmasking [*demaskowanie* in Polish, *oyfdekn dos ponim* in Yiddish] of traitors to the Jewish nation, who have tens and hundreds of victims on their conscience and still pass or want to pass for respectable people or want to play a certain role in the life of our society."[2] In this statement one discerns an amalgam of moral, utilitarian, and political motives for the establishment of the civic court: a communal censure of the questionable conduct of the small fraction of Jews suspected of collaboration with the Nazi regime, the desire to prevent such Jews tainted by collaboration from holding positions of influence in the reconstituted postwar Jewish community, and an assertion of the mantle of political authority in the community by those who had, be it accurate or not, heroically resisted the Nazis.

Despite deep differences between them, the Zionists and communists in the CKŻP agreed that suspected Jewish collaborators ought to be held accountable for their actions. Their consensus reflected the mood of the average Polish Jewish man and woman on the street, who, even if they had not engaged the Nazi enemy in armed combat, drew a sharp distinction between themselves and collaborators from within the Jewish community. To be sure, they wished to settle scores with collaborators, but they also subscribed to the regnant myth woven by postwar Jewish leaders that, with the exception of a small minority, all Polish Jews had exhibited high moral standards during the Nazi occupation of Poland. This self-image, which was critical to the construction of a Jewish civic culture in postwar Poland, elsewhere in the Jewish Diaspora, or in Palestine, later Israel, let alone immunizing Jews from malicious anti-Semitic assertions of Jewish passivity during the Holocaust, was tarnished by the existence of putative collaborators, however small their number, among the surviving remnant. Ostracizing them would clear the ground and create a path to future Jewish reconstruction, be it in Poland or beyond its borders.

The Jewish population of prewar Poland numbered about 3.5 million. But only a remnant of this largest Jewish population in Europe survived the Holocaust. The total number of Polish Jewish survivors probably never exceeded 350,000 to 400,000. This rate of mortality—in Poland, about 90 percent—was higher only in the Baltic states. The majority of Poland's Jewish population died on Polish soil. The Germans and their accomplices killed Poland's Jews mainly in death camps and concentration camps, but a sizable proportion of the victims perished in ghettos, in hiding, in open fields and forests, and in numerous small labor camps.

Domicile in Poland proved unsustainable for the vast majority of returning Jews, whose numbers reached 220,000 by June 1946. Although the resumption of normal life for Jewish victims of the Holocaust was difficult everywhere, the difficulty was exacerbated in immediate postwar Poland by a variety of factors: Polish anti-Semitism and anti-Jewish violence, private and state-sanctioned expropriation of Jewish property, and the desire by most Jews to steer clear of communism. Moreover, most returnees, already traumatized, could not bear to remain in a country that they regarded as a vast Jewish cemetery of their murdered relatives and friends. Their lives under constant threat, unable to locate their relatives and friends, let alone any property, and drawn to the prospect of resettlement in various Western countries and the nascent State of Israel, most returnees saw no reason to stay in their hometowns and every reason to leave Poland forever. By 1950, when emigration from Poland became virtually impossible, the Jewish population had been reduced to roughly 60,000.

The burden of rebuilding a viable Jewish community in Poland in the immediate aftermath of the Holocaust fell to the CKŻP. The CKŻP had to assume responsibility for a wide array of communal activities: repatriation and resettlement of Polish Jews from the Soviet Union (mainly to the annexed territories in western Poland), vocational training, the health of the survivors, orphanages, self-defense units, cultural revival, legal disputes over property, historical documentation of the destruction of Polish Jewry, and commemoration of the victims of the Holocaust. However, regardless of whether Polish Jewish survivors stayed in Poland or left it, they wanted to see justice done to the perpetrators of the Holocaust.

The survivors were stunned by the enormity of both their personal loss and the devastation of their community, and many sought to make sense out of what had befallen them. Of course, first and foremost, they held the Germans responsible for the genocide and supported trials of Nazi criminals conducted in Poland and elsewhere. But the Germans did not act alone. Survivors did not hesitate to blame Poles under German occupation for general indifference to their suffering, if not approval of the Germans' mass murder of Jews, or even much worse, that is, collaboration. In the case of Poles, collaboration entailed several forms: blackmailing and extorting Jews in hiding, accompanied by the threat to turn them in to the Germans if they didn't pay; handing over to the Germans Jews whom they happened to run across; and, on innumerable occasions, as in Jedwabne, outright torturing and killing of Jews. The survivors held the Germans' ethnic accomplices accountable, especially Ukrainians, Latvians, and Lithuanians, who brutally took part in the liquidation of ghettos and the murder of Jews in camps. Accordingly, the survivors supported the Polish trials of Polish and Eastern European collaborators. Moreover, the survivors did not recoil, however painful an admission this was, from holding to account fellow Jews who aided the Nazis in various capacities: from serving on a Jewish council (Judenrat) or in the Jewish police in a ghetto to assuming the role of a kapo in a camp. Thus, they also backed the trials of putative Jewish collaborators, initially in Polish courts and then in the Polish Jewish honor court.[3]

Of the Jews who were reviled by the survivors for their alleged cooperation with the Germans, former members of the Jewish councils were high on the list. It is easy to see why. The Jewish councils (Judenräte), which the Germans established everywhere, were, in the words of historian Saul Friedländer, "the most effective instrument of German control of the Jewish population."[4] The function of the Jewish councils, which represented local Jewish communities in their relations with the occupation authorities, was to execute German orders and directives. Despite their veneer of independence, the Jewish councils worked under extreme pressure, distress, and threats of violence both to their members and to their communities. The prevailing opinion in most Jewish communities, in Western and Eastern Europe alike, of the Jewish councils and their personnel, especially their chairmen, was downright negative. Jewish councils' onerous and unfair tax policies, of which the poor bore the brunt, their conscription of overwhelmingly poor residents into forced labor contingents, and their tolerance of corruption within the ranks of the Jewish police forces, which the Germans ordered them to establish and which operated under their auspices, all elicited antipathy in Jewish circles. The disdain of Jewish communities was magnified by inflated and unrealistic expectations of the ability of Jewish councils to improve the lot of Jews under their domain when, in fact, their freedom of action was severely restricted by the Germans. Ordinary Jews' unfavorable encounters with Jewish council officials and personnel, whose reputation for their emotional distance from the Jewish masses went hand in hand with their perceived conciliatory approach to the Germans, only served to evoke contempt in Jewish communities.[5]

The disreputable behavior of the Jewish councils not only earned the enmity of Jewish populations but also provoked underground circles to charge them with collaboration. Exemplary of the underground's contempt for Jewish council officials in Warsaw is an article published in *Jutrznia* (Dawn), the underground paper of the Zionist organization Gordonia.

> Leaving aside the personal history and uprightness of a Judenrat man, the mere fact of belonging to this institution makes him objectively a Nazi agent, and so the most miserable traitor, who must in the future face his deserved punishment. The Jewish masses must be aware of this dispassionately viewed role of the Judenrat. They must approach it with profound, well-founded hatred and contempt, they must sabotage its decrees, they must at every turn unmask its role and remember well who collaborated with it, so that none escapes punishment.[6]

In the Warsaw ghetto ŻOB targeted Jewish council officials, along with other suspected collaborators, for assassination. ŻOB was motivated not only by vengeance but also by the tactical necessity of removing the mortal threat posed by a Jewish fifth column to the budding insurgency in the ghetto. In its founding statute, ŻOB proclaimed as one of its objectives, in anticipation of the Germans' intention to destroy the Jewish community, the protection of the Jewish community against internal "criminals and agents, collaborators with the occupier."[7] Three or four members of ŻOB's command staff passed death sentences on several putative collaborators, including officials from the Judenrat.[8] The Jewish Military Union (Związek Żydowski Wojskowy; ZŻW), founded by Revisionists and Betar, passed its own death sentences on collaborators. Between

August 1942 and the Warsaw Ghetto Uprising in April 1943, ŻOB targeted many individuals, including Izrael First, director of the Economics Department of the Judenrat who was a feared intermediary between the Germans and the Judenrat.⁹

Jewish vigilantism could be justified while the fighting raged. But ŻOB's surviving leaders began having a change of heart in the last months of the war. This shift in attitude is exemplified in a dramatic encounter in the offices of the CKŻP in January 1945, after the Soviet liberation of Warsaw. During a meeting of the CKŻP Executive Committee, ŻOB's legendary commander Yitzhak Zuckerman, who was popularly known by the nom de guerre Antek, requested the floor to denounce Michał Weichert, who was then leading efforts to provide relief to Jews returning to Kraków from the camps. ŻOB passed a death sentence on Weichert, accusing him of collaboration with the Germans on account of his leadership of the Jewish Social Assistance Society (Jüdische Soziale Selbsthilfe; JSS) in Kraków, which in the view of underground leaders played into German hands under Weichert. According to Leon (Arieh) Bauminger, whom the committee was dispatching to Kraków to oversee the reorganization of the Jewish community there, Zuckerman, after his denunciation of Weichert, turned to him and urged him to assassinate Weichert after his arrival in Kraków.

> "Lonek, take my pistol, and if you reach Kraków, put a bullet in his head." And Antek slid his pistol over the table to me. I answered: "Antek, I don't know Dr. Weichert and I don't know about his activities during the occupation because I was away for three-and-a-half years in the Kovno ghetto. In addition, now with the end of the war, I don't shoot Jews. There are courts now, and if he is a traitor, he will be punished." And I slid the pistol back to Antek.¹⁰

Zuckerman's own attitude seems to shift after this confrontation, for in either late January or early February 1945 Zuckerman rescued a former Jewish policeman in the Warsaw ghetto from an angry mob of fellow Jews and had him arrested by Polish Security Office militiamen, but somehow the arrested man was freed. Zuckerman then dispatched his own people to find him. They located him and alerted the Russian army to arrest him, but he was set free once again. Then one day in April the same former ghetto policeman entered Zuckerman's room while he was lying ill in his bed. The man could have killed Zuckerman then and there, but instead he said to him, "I came to you to judge me!" Zuckerman pulled his pistol out from under his pillow and listened to the man's story. He had agreed to become a Jewish policeman to save his mother, but it had been in vain. After the war he had come to hate himself, and now he was coming to Zuckerman's apartment to plead with him to end his life. When he finished telling his story, Zuckerman ordered him to leave. Although he had the opportunity, Zuckerman decided not to shoot the man, but not because he had forgiven him. "No, I didn't forgive him, absolutely not," relates Zuckerman. It seems that Zuckerman did not kill the man because Zuckerman was reexamining his view of vigilante justice.

> Beginning at that time, early January 1945, I decided I wouldn't issue any more death sentences. Objectively, it was right to execute that person, definitely—yes! But there's no end to that, once you start. So I wanted to try him, but he escaped that. Now he came because his conscience oppressed him and he wanted to commit suicide. Should I have killed him? In those days, I was becoming increasingly aware that we had to put an end to issuing sentences and their partisan execution.[11]

Thus it seems that there was a growing sentiment among the emerging leadership of what remained of Polish Jewry after the war that vengeance wreaked on putative Jewish collaborators needed to be pursued in a court rather than on the street.

At first, the Jewish leadership was content to see suspected Jewish collaborators stand trial in Polish criminal courts. Indeed, thirty of at least forty-four accused Jewish collaborators were ultimately convicted in Polish courts.[12] But, as David Engel shows, the postwar Jewish leadership decided by 1946 "to develop its own mechanism for holding Jews to account for their wartime behavior" because "there was a sense that the existing general Polish mechanisms had not proven sufficient for Jewish communal purposes."[13] The reason is that Polish courts acquitted some high-profile Jewish defendants, including Weichert, to the chagrin of Jewish leaders. As Engel argues, it was Weichert's acquittal in January 1946 that prompted the CKŻP to revise its policy of leaving the punishment of putative Jewish collaborators to the Polish legal system and, in turn, to establish, with the approval of the Polish government, a Jewish civic or honor court for this purpose.[14]

The CKŻP's official announcement of its creation of its civic court in *Dos naje lebn* stressed the court's intention to hear the cases of three people in particular: Shepsl Rotholc, accused of mistreating his fellow Jews while serving in the Jewish police in the Warsaw ghetto; Michał Weichert, a leading prewar Yiddish theatrical director accused of helping the Germans deceive world public opinion and of expropriating supplies intended for Jews for his own use; and Wiera Gran, a popular prewar cabaret singer suspected of being a Gestapo informant. Curiously, none of these three people targeted for prosecution in the CKŻP's honor court belonged to a Jewish council during the war, that is, to the leadership of Polish Jewry under Nazi occupation. In a similar vein, the article by Cincinnatus in *Dos naje lebn* mentioned several names of perceived collaborators. Moreover, Cincinnatus roundly condemned Jewish councils, together with the Jewish police in ghettos.

> It should be generally applicable [as a principle] that "Jewish councils" and the [Jewish] "order police" were formations that collaborated with the SS.... In 1941 it had already become clear to everyone that the so-called "autonomy" that the Nazi regime granted Polish Jews was intended to conceal the fiendish plan to destroy the entire Jewish population. In this new phase, from 1941, when total destruction commenced, the Jews who collaborated with the Jewish councils and the order police must have sooner or later reached the stage at which they were compelled to cross the line from "compromise" to crimes and national treason.[15]

But Cincinnatus did not mention the name of even one former member of a Jewish council. Why did neither the list in the CKŻP announcement nor Cincinnatus's article contain the names of Jewish council members?

An investigation conducted in 1947 by the Polish Central Jewish Historical Commission (Centralna Żydowska Komisja Historyczna; CŻKH), delegated by the CKŻP to reconstruct the fate of Polish Jewry during the Holocaust, uncovered the names of 2,000 Polish Jews suspected of collaboration with the Nazis. The overwhelming majority of the suspects in the CŻKH's lists were alleged members of a Jewish council or a Jewish ghetto police force. There were also many kapos. In all, close to 500 former members of Jewish councils appeared on the CŻKH's lists. The names of well-known chairmen of Jewish councils, such as Adam Czerniaków from Warsaw, Chaim Rumkowski from Lodz, and Jacob Gens from Wilno, are not listed, perhaps because they were known to be dead. Yet, by the same token, other slightly lesser-known former Jewish council members whose notoriety still preceded them did appear on the lists, for example, Izrael First from Warsaw, who was assassinated by ŻOB, and Moshe (Moniek) Merin and his brother Chaim Merin, who were killed by the Germans during the liquidation of the ghetto in Będzin. Indeed, the CŻKH's lists of former Jewish council members were neither exhaustive nor fully accurate. Rather, they resembled a laundry list of practically any known person who ever served on a Jewish council, regardless of what he did.[16]

Nevertheless, few Jewish council members survived the Holocaust. When the Germans had no further need for them upon the liquidation of a Jewish community, they either included them in the deportations or they shot them. A few Jewish council officials, such as Adam Czerniaków, took their own lives. Historian Barbara Engelking has compiled a list of thirty-one members of the Warsaw Jewish council. She has established that twenty-seven of them perished; the fate of the remaining four members is unknown.[17] There were no investigations of members of the Warsaw Jewish council by the CKŻP's lawyers for the simple fact that none apparently survived.

Indeed, among the 140 or so files on 158 putative Jewish collaborators opened by the CKŻP's lawyers (some files list multiple suspects), only 20 involve former Jewish council members. Of these, only four stood trial before the civic court. Three of the defendants were acquitted; one was convicted. A fifth individual was indicted, but there is no record of a trial in the archival file. The CKŻP's lawyers wanted to transfer the case of another individual to Polish state prosecutors because of the criminal nature of the offense, but the suspect was in Germany and beyond the reach of the Polish legal system. In fact, several files were closed because the suspected collaborators were abroad or dead. In addition, the CKŻP's lawyers terminated six files for lack of incriminating evidence.[18]

This is not to say that all Jewish council members under investigation who evaded indictment and trial had acted in an exemplary fashion. For example, female witnesses accused Naum Szenderowicz, a physician who was head of the Jewish council in Radom, of sexual harassment, a charge that, as Ewa Koźmińska-Frejlak shows, the CKŻP's lawyers and civic court's judges were loath to make the centerpiece of an official condemnation.[19] (Szenderowicz died during the investigation, bringing it to a halt.) What can be said is that when it came to the formal investigation of former Jewish council members, the CKŻP's lawyers and the judges on the civic court, itself an institution operating under the auspices of the CKŻP, do not appear to have been determined to obtain convictions under all circumstances. For example, they were reluctant to consider sexual assault charges. However, it appears that they generally took their responsibility seriously and were disinclined to rush to judgment.

The only former Jewish council member convicted by the honor court was Leon Czarny-Gidy, a member of the Central Office of the Jewish Communities in Eastern Upper Silesia (the region's Jewish council), with it headquarters in Sosnowiec. Moshe Merin was put in charge of it. Fani Czarna,

Czarny-Gidy's wife, was its secretary. Facing serious accusations that he collaborated with the Germans, Czarny-Gidy submitted an application for rehabilitation in January 1947. (He had also been investigated earlier by Polish state prosecutors.) One survivor after another leveled charges against him during the pretrial investigation. In urging the civic court to hear Czarny-Gidy's case, in the indictment the prosecutor, Ludwik Gutmacher, charged Czarny-Gidy, owing to his activities in the Central Office of the Jewish Communities and his holding of an office on its executive committee, with organizing the resettlement of Jews from Sosnowiec (to a smaller ghetto in nearby Środula), directing the collection of valuables from Jews for the German regime, and fraternizing with the Gestapo—all to "the harm of the Jewish people."[20] The court agreed to hear the case. A trial was held on August 5 and 6, 1947, but the trial transcript is missing from the case file. On August 6, the civic court found Czarny-Gidy guilty, though not on the basis of the individual offenses with which he was charged in the indictment, of which the judges acquitted him, but purely on the grounds that he collaborated with the Central Office of the Jewish Communities and its executive committee, "knowing that these institutions acted to the harm of the Jewish people."

The court sentenced Czarny-Gidy to a rebuke (*upomnienie*), the mildest form of sanction enumerated in its charter—the equivalent of a slap on the wrist. Apparently, the judges considered the evidence of Czarny-Gidy's personal infractions or his responsibility for the actions of the Central Office of the Jewish Communities insufficient to convict him, but, by the same token, they must have found the Jewish council's activities reprehensible enough to warrant convicting him, regardless of his role in it, for being a member of it. To be sure, the conduct of the Central Office of the Jewish Communities could be deemed questionable at best, especially given Moshe Merin's eagerness to cooperate with the Germans.[21] That said, Czarny-Gidy was found guilty by reason of his association with it all the same. This reasoning, I suggest, would change with time.

Of the three former Jewish council members who were acquitted, one was Szlama Lewkowicz, who worked for the Jewish council in Zawierz. Lewkowicz was accused of taking bribes to place Jews in better labor details, being responsible for sending Jews to labor camps, and throwing debauched bashes with other Jewish council members in the company of Gestapo officials. After a trial lasting one day in April 1947, the civic court, in a one-page verdict, found in favor of Lewkowicz, who in its opinion held a minor post in the Zawierz Jewish council, without the power or clout to do what he was accused of.[22]

Also acquitted was Eliasz Tabaksblatt, who was accused of treating teachers and students harshly, even sentencing students to hard physical labor, while he headed the school department in the Lodz ghetto. His trial in the civic court, conducted over two days, was held in Lodz in September 1948. The civic court did not find fault with his leadership of the school department and acquitted him.[23] In this case the court easily could have found Tabaksblatt guilty by association, because he was a confidant of the notorious Chaim Rumkowski, the dictatorial chairman of the Lodz ghetto, but it did not; Tabaksblatt's close association with "King Chaim" was not part of the verdict.

In neither Czarny-Gidy's nor Tabaksblatt's case did the civic court make any grand pronouncements, but it is interesting to compare the results of the two cases, which were separated by a year. Czarny-Gidy, tried in mid-1947 was, for all intents and purposes, found guilty by association with a notorious Jewish council; Tabaksblatt, tried in mid-1948, was not. It appears that the civic court's reflections on who ought to be deemed a collaborator became more mature and discerning over time.

The other defendant acquitted by the honor court was Alfred Merbaum, former chairman of the Jewish council in Horodenka. Merbaum's trial, which was conducted in 1949, in the last year of the civic court's existence, is particularly instructive because, unlike the trials of Lewkowicz and Tabaksblatt, it affords insight into not only the civic court's assessment of the conduct of Jewish councils but also how Polish Jews' attitudes toward the Jewish councils developed from the war years to the end of the immediate postwar period.

Horodenka (also spelled as Gorodenka, its name in Ukrainian) lies in eastern Galicia. In the interwar period it was part of Poland; in September 1939 it was occupied by the Red Army and incorporated into the annexation of eastern Poland by the Soviet Union. On the eve of World War II, Horodenka's Jewish population numbered roughly 3,500. Following the German invasion of the Soviet Union on June 22, 1941, units of the Hungarian army entered Horodenka on July 2. Local Ukrainians began to attack the Jews, but the Hungarians tried to restrain them. After the arrival of some 1,000 Jews deported from the Transcarpathian Ukraine, now occupied by Hungary, the number of Jews in Horodenka rose to about 4,500. A Jewish committee was formed, which the Hungarians, using threats and violence, required to make a contribution in cash and produce. Jews were also required to perform forced labor.

The town remained under Hungarian military administration until September, when authority was transferred to a German civil administration. The Germans immediately enacted anti-Jewish measures. They registered all Jews, confiscated most remaining Jewish property, imposed the requirement to wear a yellow Star of David, restricted free movement on the streets, prohibited Jews from leaving the town on pain of death, and instituted forced labor. In November the Germans ordered the Jews to move into a small Jewish quarter in the western part of town. The Germans further directed the town's Jews to form a Jewish council.

The systematic liquidation of the Jewish community commenced in December 1941. On December 4, Horodenka's Jews were ordered to assemble in the synagogue under the pretext of receiving vaccinations. On December 5, after the release of a few skilled laborers, the rest of the 2,500 Jews gathered there were marched to a forest outside the town and murdered by a detachment of the German security police from nearby Kołomyja. After this event the Germans ordered the remaining 1,500 Jews to move into a tiny ghetto. A new Jewish council was formed to assist with the transfer. The Germans sealed the overcrowded ghetto. Many people died of starvation and disease. Jewish forced labor was organized by the Jewish council under orders from the German authorities. On April 13, 1942, the Germans conducted a sweep of the ghetto, killing seventy-five people. From April through early September Jews from the vicinity were transferred into the ghetto, elevating its population to more than 2,000. At the same time, hunger, disease, and occasional roundups of younger Jews for labor camps reduced the ghetto's population.

On September 8, 1942, the final liquidation of the ghetto began. The Germans shot between 200 and 300 people on the spot and loaded about 2,000 people into freight cars. A few Jews fled to the nearby ghetto of Tłuste in search of temporary refuge, although most were killed there when that ghetto was liquidated. On September 10, most were transported to the Bełżec extermination camp, although a small group of Jews capable of work were sent to the Janowska Road labor camp outside Lvov. The Germans retained 120 Jewish laborers to help clear the ghetto area; several hundred Jews hid in bunkers. In late September the remaining Jewish laborers were transferred to Kołomyja. Only a few Jews managed to remain hidden until liberation; the Ukrainian police regularly captured Jews in hiding and immediately murdered them. Several dozen Jews managed to flee to the forests, and some joined Soviet partisan units. Many of those who reached the forest were killed by Ukrainian nationalists belonging to the Ukrainian Insurgent Army. The Red Army liberated Horodenka on March 27, 1944. The few Jewish survivors eventually left for Poland, most en route to the West.[24]

Although the Jewish council was forced to follow German orders, its members, according to survivor accounts, did what they could to alleviate the burden on the Jewish community. They established soup kitchens and offered bribes to German officials in an attempt to forestall their murderous acts. Thus the first chairman of the Jewish council tried to prevent the mass shooting of the town's Jews in December 1941 with a bribe; he was murdered along with all other members of the council.[25]

Alfred Merbaum was born in 1903 in Horodenka and lived there until the immediate postwar period. He was a lawyer by profession. The Germans forced him to assume the chairmanship of the Jewish council in Horodenka in December 1941, after the murder of the 2,500 Horodenka Jews outside the town, without asking his consent. It was the common practice of the Nazis to replace Jewish councils if they were dissatisfied with them or after ghetto-clearing operations. This was also the case in Horodenka.[26] Merbaum remained in Horodenka and witnessed its liberation by the Soviets in March 1944. I have yet to find even just one reference to Merbaum in a history book. I have located one reference to him in the Horodenka memorial book. A woman from Horodenka relates there that Merbaum procured a certificate that her husband was "productive"; permitted to work with this document in hand, the small number of Jews who obtained them hoped to prolong their survival and the survival of their families.[27]

Merbaum was not under investigation by the CKŻP's lawyers, but he submitted a petition to the civic court for rehabilitation in 1948 because of his desire to resume a normal life and become a member of the bar in Tarnów, where he settled after the war. Although the civic court's charter did not require former members of Jewish councils or the Jewish Order Service (the Jewish police) to submit petitions for rehabilitation to clear their names, the court publicly encouraged such rehabilitation applications in special announcements in the Jewish press.[28] When the CKŻP's lawyers began to investigate survivors from Horodenka, many testified in Merbaum's favor, but one witness in particular, Julian Kweczer, impugned his character and accused him of cooperating with the Germans during their killing spree in the ghetto on April 13, 1942. Owing to these charges, the CKŻP's prosecuting attorney, Marian Lasota, moved the civic court to hear the case.[29] The court granted the motion.

The civic court's charter dictated the standard by which Merbaum and all other defendants standing trial would be judged. The charter authorized the court to rule in cases of misconduct by a member of the Jewish community during the Hitlerite occupation [whether he acted] in a manner befitting a Jewish citizen, through his participation and harmful activity on "Jewish councils," in the [ghetto police], in the administration of concentration camps or any other type of collaboration with the occupier to the detriment of society.[30]

This was a deontological standard: The honor court was to ask whether a defendant met the obligations that were incumbent upon a Jewish citizen during the Nazi occupation of Poland. This essentially ethical standard, as opposed to a legal standard, exempted the court from determining whether the defendant's state of mind or intent was good or evil, whether his actions were inherently good or evil or the consequences of his actions were good or evil, or whether he possessed a good or evil character. What mattered was how the defendant acted or failed to act, measured by how a Jewish citizen was obligated to act under the circumstances. The open-endedness of this standard is self-evident. Moreover, according to the civic court's own interpretation of the applicable standard, a defendant's moral obligation encompassed acknowledgment, certainly by mid-1942, when German intentions were clear, of the one proper, legitimate, and constitutive authority from within the Jewish community, that is, the authority not of the Jewish councils but of the armed Jewish underground.[31] That said, an undated document apparently produced by the civic court for its own use, which from its placement in the file appears to originate near the end of 1948, shows a general presumption in favor of conviction: "Jews, who during the occupation, were employed either in the capacity of policeman, in the capacity of a member of the 'Judenrat,' as well as those who collaborated in various ways with the occupier to the detriment of society, did not act in a matter befitting a Jewish citizen."[32]

Merbaum's trial was held on January 25, 1949, in Wrocław.[33] Merbaum, the first witness to take the stand, testified in his own defense. By his own account, after the mass murder of the majority of Horodenka's Jews, including previous members of the Jewish council, two Jewish lawyers, including the head of the ghetto police, put forward his name to the Germans for chairman of the Jewish council without his knowledge or consent. He requested to have his appointment withdrawn, but the German officer in charge roundly rejected his request: "Whoever doesn't obey will be finished off." Merbaum put his reaction in these words: "With no possibility of withdrawing from the situation, in which I was placed against my will, I decided to bear the burden of my responsibility solely for the good of the Jewish people."[34] The rest of his testimony was devoted to his attempts to intervene with the German authorities and Ukrainian police officers in an effort to prevent anti-Jewish measures.

The main witness to testify against Merbaum was 47-year-old Julian Kweczer, a teacher by profession. Kweczer charged Merbaum with seeking the chairmanship of the Jewish council, enjoying material benefits as a result of his chairmanship of the Jewish council, neglecting the hunger of the Jewish population, knowing in advance of German intentions to sweep the ghetto on April 13, 1942, without informing its inhabitants, directing the roundup of Jews, and ordering the Jewish police to capture Jews on April 13, 1942. Kweczer further accused Merbaum of offenses of deep personal significance to him. According to Kweczer, Merbaum personally arrested him and placed him in prison, where he beat him, and Merbaum "selected" Kweczer's father for death during the German killing operation in the ghetto on April 13, 1942.[35]

Seven additional witnesses testified. Apart from Kweczer, none contradicted Merbaum's own testimony or cast Merbaum's actions in a bad light; nor did their testimony support Kweczer's litany of charges against Merbaum. A few testified in Merbaum's favor. For example, Marian Lubański, who was a member of a committee that offered help to those in need, testified that Merbaum did not want to become chairman of the Horodenka Jewish council, that he did not concentrate all power in his own hands, and that he informed the Jewish population that a German operation was planned for April 13, 1942.[36]

In its lengthy verdict, issued on the same day as the trial, the civic court acquitted Merbaum and gave him a clean bill of political health. The civic court laid the foundation for its ruling in Merbaum's favor by resisting any pressure to condemn all Jewish councils en masse. "The role of Jewish councils," the verdict notes, "is known to this court from previously held trials of member of Jewish ghetto administrations in various locales as well as from the rich literature and publications of the [Jewish Historical] Institute and the [Central Jewish] Historical Commission. On the whole, these institutions played a negative role. However, not all Jewish councils," the court opined, "are cut from the same cloth."[37] There were Jewish councils like the one in Upper Silesia—the judges must have had the Central Office of the Jewish Communities run by Merin in mind—"whose actions were outright criminal, that willfully served the occupier to the unequivocal detriment of the Jewish people," but there were Jewish councils, though implementing German orders, for which "the guiding principle of their work was characterized by the aim to lessen the burden of the wretched prisoners of that inhuman, colossal cell to which they were condemned—such was the Jewish ghetto."[38]

With regard to the Horodenka Jewish council, the court found no evidence that its actions were distinctly injurious to the Jewish population. According to the verdict, none of the witnesses, including Merbaum's main accuser, Kweczer, offered proof that the Jewish council was instrumental in the Nazis' registration of Jewish individuals, their physical transfer of Jews, or their extermination of the Jewish population, or that it took part in roundups. Rather, "The entire activity of the Jewish council went in the direction of relieving the burden of the Jews of Horodenka."[39] Because the judges could find no grounds for ruling that the Horodenka Jewish council was an institution that could be characterized as injurious to Jews, the court took the position that it was "not able to pass judgment on Alfred Merbaum by virtue of his membership in that institution."[40]

The civic court categorically rejected Kweczer's testimony. Contrary to Kweczer's testimony, Merbaum did not, in the court's opinion, seek his appointment to the chairmanship of the Jewish council. He was forced to assume the position. Indeed, he accepted it just days after the Germans had shot the prior chairman and members of the Jewish council. He did not conduct himself poorly in his relations with the Jewish population, eagerly support ghetto-clearing operations and the deportation of Jews, or participate in roundups. He did not loot Jewish property. He never took advantage of his leadership of the Jewish council for his own material gain. And he did not order Kweczer's arrest or personally arrest him, did not beat him, and—contrary to the most serious charge leveled by Kweczer—did not have his father selected during the German killing operation on April 13, 1942. Indeed, "Every witness, not excluding Kweczer, testified that the Jewish people were notified in advance of impending German [anti-Jewish] operations, which would not have occurred without the assistance to this degree from the side of the Jewish council and its chairman."[41]

It is clear that the civic court's acquittal of Merbaum was never in doubt, as Kweczer proved to be an unreliable and dubious witness. What is noteworthy is that the court took advantage of the fact that an admirable former Jewish council chairman was a defendant to make a larger point about evaluating Jewish councils and their former members. The court's ruling reflects a grasp of just how complex and varied the motives and conduct of Jewish councils and their members, especially their chairmen, were: Some men who accepted chairmanship of the Jewish councils were motivated by the best intentions and a feeling of responsibility for the local community; others were tempted by power and a privileged position; and still others tried to save their own skin through base collaboration. Some Jewish council chairmen briskly and avidly cooperated with the Germans; others sought to prevent harm to their fellow Jews by bribing

Germans; and then there were those who called on the community to offer resistance when the deportations began.[42]

One has to wonder how Adam Czerniaków, the head of the Warsaw Jewish council who took his own life when the Germans informed him of the imminent liquidation of the Warsaw ghetto in July 1942, would have fared if he had been summoned to the civic court to answer charges of collaboration. Like Merbaum, Czerniaków refused to exploit his privileged position for personal gain. Unlike Merbaum, Czerniaków failed to alert Jews to the Germans' deportation plans; instead, he committed suicide. Of course, Merbaum headed the Jewish council of a small town, and Czerniaków headed the Jewish council in Warsaw, the backbone of Polish Jewry. Moreover, working to Czerniaków's disadvantage would have been the identity of several members of his inner circle, such as Józef Szeryński, the head of the ghetto police, and Izrael First.[43] Szeryński and First were despised by ghetto inhabitants and targeted by ŻOB for assassination.

The trend in modern scholarship is to regard Czerniaków in a relatively positive light. His recent biographer, historian Marcin Urynowicz, paints a portrait of a man who tirelessly looked for allies among German officials in Warsaw in an effort to forestall or mitigate German measures intended to exploit, pauperize, starve, and ultimately liquidate the ghetto population. Urynowicz underscores Czerniaków's sense of responsibility for the welfare of the Jewish community in the ghetto, exemplified by his efforts to exempt 150,000 of the ghetto's poorest inhabitants from the tax on bread and to raise funds for the provision of orphans.[44] Even if a large number of notable Jews in the ghetto, including ŻOB's command staff, would have disagreed with Urynowicz's favorable assessment of his leadership, they did not see him, or other members of the Judenrat for that matter, in black and white. "We made certain distinctions in the Judenrat ... and considered who the person was," Yitzhak Zuckerman recalled. If a member of the Judenrat proved to be a collaborator or a sworn enemy of ŻOB, he "deserved to be killed." Not so Czerniaków. Although Zuckerman considered Czerniaków an inadequate leader, particularly because he acted to suppress the underground press, which warned of the impending danger, and failed to sound the alarm in the ghetto when the Germans' genocidal plans were unmistakable, he would not have demanded Czerniaków's execution. In Zuckerman's words, "I don't think we would have judged [Czerniaków] severely, although in the historical trial of him as a public leader, I'm one of the prosecutors."[45] In other words, Czerniaków may have been ill-suited to lead Warsaw's Jews in their darkest hour, but he was not a collaborator.

Zuckerman's measured opinion of Czerniaków did not represent the sentiments of ŻOB's rank and file, however. In Israel former fighters in the Warsaw Ghetto Uprising from left-wing Zionist movements considered him, together with all members of the Jewish council, a traitor to the Jewish people.[46] Their view was probably representative of most of the ghetto's survivors. Thus, had Czerniaków survived, it is difficult to imagine that the honor court would have been able, given his symbolic significance, to withstand the enormous pressure from the Jewish community to find him guilty and make him a scapegoat for the sins—actual and perceived—of the Jewish council and its members, especially under the malleable terms of the court's charter. In all likelihood, then, his conviction would have been a foregone conclusion precisely because of who he was, the head of the Warsaw Jewish council, irrespective of his actions.

But in less highly charged cases, certainly by the time of Merbaum's trial in January 1949, the honor court was inclined to make distinctions even among members of Jewish councils. The verdict in Merbaum's case reflects the celerity with which assessments by Polish Jews of the Jewish councils and their members developed within a compressed period of time. Szaje Szechatow was a judge on the civic court until he left Poland in 1948 (before Merbaum's trial). He eventually settled in Los Angeles in 1957. In 1955 Szechatow wrote an article titled "Kolaboratsye bay yidn" (Collaboration Among Jews) for a Yiddish periodical published in Mexico City. In it Szechatow relates the case of a member of the CKŻP's presidium who was accused in 1946 by his political party of having been a member of a Jewish council. Because the CKŻP's presidium included members from various Jewish political parties, it was decided to convene a seven-member intraparty judicial panel or court to determine whether the accused was actually guilty of collaboration with the Nazis. Szechatow was chosen to represent his party, the Bund, on the panel. Szechatow did not name names but referred to the accused by the Yiddish initial zayin ("Z"), and the minutes of the sessions of the CKŻP's presidium reveal that the accused was Mordechai Zonszajn, who represented the Ichud Party (General Zionists) on the presidium. It turned out that Zonszajn had served for a brief time in the ghetto administration of a small town in the province of Lodz and that his function had been to help Jews find an adequate roof over their heads, which was a thankless task in the overcrowded and crumbling ghetto. Szechatow described the deliberations of the judicial panel or court as follows:

> Some members of the court were of the opinion that Z cannot be condemned simply for belonging to the "Jewish council." ... Others argued

that since the "Jewish council," by its very nature, in collaborating [*mitarbetndik*] with the occupier had in any case helped the Germans kill the Jews, Z, therefore, by virtue of being a member of a "Jewish council" is responsible and deserves to be punished.[47]

The judicial panel was divided. Szechatow continued: "Legally speaking, the accused could find certain justifications and also extenuating circumstances in his favor, but from the standpoint of Jewish society he had to be convicted."[48] Ultimately, the panel split 4–3 in Zonszajn's favor. Although Szechatow does not mention this in his article, the minutes from the relevant meetings of the CKŻP's presidium show that Szechatow was one of the three members of the panel who voted against Zonszajn. The presidium's members decided to investigate the matter further. "One thing, however," writes Szechatow, "was clear to the court, that Z could no longer serve on the Jewish Central Committee." Zonszajn was removed from his party and forced to resign from the presidium.[49]

Although Szechatow voted to condemn Zonszajn, he seems to have softened his attitude with time. "There is . . . no uniform determination," he wrote in 1955, "of what actions may be considered collaboration [*kolaboratsye*]."[50] He then added:

> There is also no uniform opinion about "Jewish council members." To be sure, the Jews were *forced* to belong to the "Jewish councils." Without a doubt, there were those "Jewish council members" who truthfully and sincerely meant with their work in the "Jewish councils" to ameliorate the fate of Jews in the ghettos. . . . There remains only the question whether these "members of Jewish councils" drew the necessary conclusions concerning the possibility of collaborating [*mitarbetn*] further with the "Jewish councils" when the Germans' objective to destroy the Jews became clear. To be sure, for a long time people did not believe it.
>
> Can one make the argument that one should not be punished simply for belonging to a "Jewish council?" Is the issue simply one's actions, one's treatment of and relations with the Jews who were suffering?[51]

Szechatow did not answer his own question, but he seemed inclined in retrospect in 1955, unlike in 1946, to judge a former member of a Jewish council solely on the basis of his actions, at least until mid-1942, when the writing was on the wall for all to see that the Nazis intended to kill all Jews.

In mid-1949, the same year that the civic court passed judgment in Merbaum's case, the Jewish Historical Institute in Warsaw hosted an academic discussion about Jewish collaboration. Szymon Datner, one of the institute's most prominent researchers, tackled the behavior of the Jewish councils: "With regard to the collaboration of the Jewish councils, it is necessary to proceed very carefully and not to generalize." He urged his listeners to weigh the facts in each individual case. "It may be possible to level charges but simultaneously find justification" for certain actions. In this vein he raised the question of whether the Jewish council in Białystok should have surrendered 8,000 Jews to the Germans in order to preserve the lives of 32,000. Datner concluded: "It is necessary to consider all such incidents individually and with much caution." A Dr. Walewski spoke in a similar vein: "It is not possible to consider all institutions associated with the Jewish councils using one yardstick.... It is necessary to judge them separately, according to which functions they performed."[52]

In his reminiscences recorded several decades after the Holocaust, even Yitzhak Zuckerman, the commander of ŻOB who ordered the assassination of Jewish council members in the Warsaw ghetto, seemed reconciled to the tragic paradox of the Jewish councils, reflecting the sentiments of the lawyers and judges assigned to the honor court and of Polish Jewish scholars by the end of the 1940s. "The institution [of the Jewish council] was flawed," opined Zuckerman, "but that doesn't mean that everyone in it didn't try to do some good in his own way."[53]

In other words, the verdict in Merbaum's case reflected a mental shift that gradually took root among many Polish Jews—though certainly far from all, as much bitterness against Jewish councils lingered—inside and outside Poland from the late 1940s onward. Immediately after the war it seems that most Polish Jews wanted to see the heads of suspected Jewish collaborators, including members of the Jewish councils, roll. The CKŻP's creation of an honor court was in sync with this view. Notwithstanding the court's obligation to rule according to a deontological standard, its actual deliberations in Merbaum's case entailed exactly what a court should do: stand apart from popular sentiments and reach decisions on the basis of legal principles, sound reasoning, and notions of public policy (in this case, public policy meant forging a path to an emotionally sustainable Jewish future in which Jews were not endlessly pitting themselves against one another). Thus, unlike earlier when it was first established, the civic court, by the end of its mandate (it was dismantled in early 1950), eschewed any cynical or nonchalant expression of moral certainty when it came to the Jewish councils, echoing the maturing sentiments of Polish Jews.

Notes

1. See David Engel, "Who Is a Collaborator? The Trials of Michał Weichert," in Sławomir Kapralski, ed., *The Jews in Poland* (Kraków: Judaica Foundation Center for Jewish Culture, 1999), 2: 339–41; and Gabriel N. Finder, "The Trial of Shepsl Rotholc and the Politics of Retribution in the Aftermath of the Holocaust," *Gal-Ed: On the History and Culture of Polish Jewry* 20 (2006): 68–70 (English section).
2. Quoted in Finder, "Trial of Shepsl Rotholc," 69.
3. See Gabriel N. Finder and Alexander V. Prusin, "Jewish Collaborators on Trial in Poland, 1944–1956," *Polin: Studies in Polish Jewry* 20 (2008): 122–48.
4. Saul Friedländer, *The Years of Extermination: Nazi Germany and the Jews, 1939–1945* (New York: Harper Collins, 2007), 39.
5. The standard work on the Jewish councils in Eastern Europe is Isaiah Trunk, *Judenrat: The Jewish Councils in Eastern Europe Under Nazi Occupation* (Lincoln: University of Nebraska Press, 1996 [1972]). Utter disdain for the Jewish council in Warsaw permeates the pages of *Scroll of Agony: The Warsaw Diary of Chaim A. Kaplan,* trans. and ed. Abraham J. Katsh (Bloomington: Indiana University Press, published in association with the United States Holocaust Memorial Museum, 1999), one of the most acclaimed diaries from the Holocaust period.
6. Quoted in Barbara Engelking and Jacek Leociak, *The Warsaw Ghetto: Guide to the Perished City*, trans. Emma Harris (New Haven, CT: Yale University Press, 2009), 157.
7. Quoted in Bernard Mark, "Statut Żydowskiej Organizacji Bojowej," *Biuletyn Żydowskiego Instytutu Historycznego* 3.39 (1961): 59.
8. Yitzhak Zuckerman ("Antek"), *A Surplus of Memory: Chronicle of the Warsaw Ghetto Uprising*, trans. and ed. Barbara Harshav (Berkeley: University of California Press, 1993), 210–12, 246–47.
9. Israel Gutman, *Resistance: The Warsaw Ghetto Uprising* (Boston: Mariner Books, published in association with the United States Holocaust Memorial Museum, 1994), 170.
10. Arieh Bauminger, "Reshit darko shel 'ha-'ihud' be-polin: Pirkei zichronot," pt. 1, *Masu'ah* 19 (1991): 226; cited in part in Engel, "Who Is a Collaborator?" 340.
11. Zuckerman, *Surplus of Memory*, 636–37.
12. See Finder and Prusin, "Jewish Collaborators."
13. Engel, "Who Is a Collaborator?" 341.
14. Engel, "Who Is a Collaborator?" 361.
15. A. Cincinnatus, "Di natsionale fareter—tsum folks-mishpet," *Dos naje lebn* (October 18, 1946): 3.
16. The CŻKH's lists of putative Jewish collaborators, including suspected Jewish council members, can be found in Archiwum Żydowskiego Instytutu Historycznego (AŻIH), Warsaw, 313/152; available also at the archives of the United States Holocaust Memorial Museum (USHMM), Washington, DC, RG 15.189M. First's name appears on p. 73; Moshe Merin's name appears on p. 92; Chaim Merin's name appears on pp. 61 and

92. Chaim Merin is listed incorrectly as the chairman of the Będzin Jewish council, when, in fact, his brother Moshe was its chairman.

17. Engelking and Leociak, *Warsaw Ghetto*, 168–70.

18. Historian Piotr Wróbel intimates that the case against Michał Süss, a Communist Party activist after the war who was accused by a survivor of being a member of the Jewish council in Radziechów and of helping Ukrainian police organize a roundup of the town's Jews, was dropped on account of his political connections. Piotr Wróbel, "Hitler's Helpers? The *Judenräte* Controversy," in Larry V. Thompson, ed., *Lessons and Legacies IV: Reflections on Religion, Justice, Sexuality, and Genocide* (Evanston, IL: Northwestern University Press, 2003), 157–58. During the time of the investigation, however, Süss was active only in the Jewish religious community and in the executive committee of the Zionist party Ichud in Kraków. Because several survivors contradicted the statement of the survivor who accused Süss, the prosecutor moved the civic court to drop the case, which it did. "Wniosek o przeprowadzeniu rozprawy," n.d. [August 1948], file of Michał Süss (Zyss), Sąd Społeczny przy CKŻP, AŻIH, 313/114, pp. 59–60; available also at USHMM, RG 15.189M. The influence of political connections on Süss's case is not evident in the case file.

19. See Chapter 9 in this volume.

20. "Do Sądu Obywatelskiego przy CKŻP, Akt oskarzenia," July 7, 1947, file of Leon Czarny-Gidy, Sąd Społeczny przy CKŻP, AŻIH, 313/28, pp. 62–64; available also at USHMM, RG 15.189M.

21. Phillip Friedman, "The Messianic Complex of a Nazi Collaborator in a Ghetto: Moses Merin of Sosnowiec," in Phillip Friedman, *Roads to Extinction: Essays on the Holocaust*, ed. Ada June Friedman (New York: Conference on Jewish Social Studies; and Philadelphia: Jewish Publication Society of America, 1980), 353–64; Mary Fulbrook, *A Small Town near Auschwitz: Ordinary Nazis and the Holocaust* (Oxford, UK: Oxford University Press, 2012), 62–63, 159, 186–88, 222, 233.

22. "Urtayl [funem] birger gerikht baym tsentraln yidishn komitet," file of Szlama Lewkowicz, AŻIH, 313/66, p. 110; "Wyrok [Sądu Społecznego przy CKŻP]," [April 16, 1947], file of Szlama Lewkowicz, AŻIH, 313/66, p. 112; available also at USHMM, RG 15.189M.

23. "Wyrok Sądu Społecznego przy C.K.Ż.P. z dnia 19 września 1948 r.," file of Eliasz Tabaksblatt, Sąd Społeczny przy CKŻP, AŻIH, 313/126, pp. 196–98; available also at USHMM, RG 15.189M.

24. On Horodenka, see Aharon Weiss, "Gorodenka," in Israel Gutman, ed., *Encyclopedia of the Holocaust* (New York: Macmillan, 1990), 2: 598–99; Alexander Kruglov and Martin Dean, "Horodenka," trans. Ester-Basya Vaisman, in Geoffrey P. Megargee, general ed., *The United State Holocaust Memorial Museum Encyclopedia of Camps and Ghettos, 1933–1945* (Bloomington: Indiana University Press, 2012), vol. 2, pt. A, 780–81. The memorial or yizkor book published in Yiddish and Hebrew by survivors from Horodenka includes extensive survivor accounts of Horodenka during the Holocaust. See Shimon Meltzer, ed., *Seyfer Horodenke/Sefer Horodenka* (Tel Aviv: Farlag fun der

horodenker landsmanshaft in amerike un yisroel / Hotsa'at 'irgun yots'ey horodenka ve-hasevivah be-yisra'el u-ve'aratsot ha-brit, 1963), esp. 273–342 and 359–97.

25. Kruglov and Dean, "Horodenka," 780.
26. Trunk, *Judenrat*, 323, 325.
27. Etel Frifer, "In Horodenke un in Tluste," in Meltzer, ed., *Seyfer Horodenke*, 294. The identical account in Hebrew under the title "Be-horodenka uve-tlusta" appears on p. 382.
28. Article 13 of the civic court's charter empowered prosecutors from the legal bureau of the CKŻP who were attached to the civic court to move the court to consider petitions for rehabilitation. "Regulamin Sądu przy Centralnym Komitecie Żydów w Polsce," Sąd Społeczny przy CKŻP, AŻIH, 313/149, p. 129; available also at USHMM, RG 15.189M. An internal memorandum reflected the court's approach to this issue: "Every member of the [Jewish] community has the right to appeal to the court for rehabilitation." "Tezy wpisane do księgi zasad Sądu Obywatelskiego przy C.K.Ż.P.," Sąd Społeczny przy CKŻP, AŻIH, 313/149, p. 127; available also at USHMM, RG 15.189M.
29. "Rzecznik Oskarzenia Sądu Społecznego do Sądu Społecznego przy CKŻwP, w sprawie Alfreda Merbauma, Wniosek o wyznaczenie rozprawy po myśli art. 13 Regulaminu Sądu," n.d. [1948], file of Alfred Merbaum, Sąd Społeczny przy CKŻP, AŻIH, 313/78, pp. 63–67; available also at USHMM, RG 15.189M.
30. "Regulamin Sądu przy Centralnym Komitecie Żydów w Polsce," Sąd Społeczny przy CKŻP, AŻIH, 313/149, p. 129; available also at USHMM, RG 15.189M.
31. Engel, "Who Is a Collaborator," 367–69; Finder, "Trial of Shepsl Rotholc," 84–85.
32. "Tezy wpisane do księgi zasad Sądu Obywatelskiego przy C.K.Ż.P.," Sąd Społeczny przy CKŻP, AŻIH, 313/149, p. 127; available also at USHMM, RG 15.189M.
33. For the trial transcript, see file of Alfred Merbaum, Sąd Społeczny przy CKŻP, AŻIH, 313/78, pp. 89–172; available also at USHMM, RG 15.189M; Merbaum's testimony is on pp. 89–101.
34. File of Alfred Merbaum, 89.
35. Testimony of Julian Kweczer at the trial of Alfred Merbaum, file of Alfred Merbaum, Sąd Społeczny przy CKŻP, AŻIH, 313/78, pp. 101–31; available also at USHMM, RG 15.189M.
36. Testimony of Marian Lubański at the trial of Alfred Merbaum, file of Alfred Merbaum, Sąd Społeczny przy CKŻP, AŻIH, 313/78, pp. 141–55; available also at USHMM, RG 15.189M.
37. "Uzasadnienie wyroku," file of Alfred Merbaum, Sąd Społeczny przy CKŻP, AŻIH, 313/78, p. 174; available also at USHMM, RG 15.189M.
38. "Uzasadnienie wyroku," file of Alfred Merbaum, 174.
39. "Uzasadnienie wyroku," file of Alfred Merbaum, 175.
40. "Uzasadnienie wyroku," file of Alfred Merbaum, 175.
41. "Uzasadnienie wyroku," file of Alfred Merbaum, 176.

42. See Engelking and Leociak, *Warsaw Ghetto*, 138.
43. Marcin Urynowicz, *Adam Czerniaków, 1880–1942: Prezes ghetta warszawskiego* (Warsaw: Instytut Pamięci Narodowej, 2009), 259–77.
44. Urynowicz, *Adam Czerniaków*, esp. chaps. 9 and 10.
45. Zuckerman, *Surplus of Memory*, 272; see also, e.g., 194–95.
46. Roni Stauber, *The Holocaust in Israeli Public Debate in the 1950s*, trans. Elizabeth Yuval (London: Vallentine Mitchell, 2007), 12.
47. Szaje Szechatow, "Kolaboratsye bay yidn," *Foroys* (Mexico City) (September 1, 1955): 9; this essay was reprinted in Szaje Szechatow, *Yorn fun kamf un gerangl* (Ramat Gan, Israel: Lior, 1973), 72–86.
48. Szechatow, "Kolaboratsye bay yidn," 9.
49. Szechatow, "Kolaboratsye bay yidn," 9. For minutes of the relevant meetings of the CKŻP's presidium in November and December 1946, see "Prezydium CKŻP 1945–1949," AŻIH, 303/4, pp. 57–86; available also at USHMM, RG 15.088M.
50. Szechatow, "Kolaboratsye bay yidn," 8.
51. Szechatow, "Kolaboratsye bay yidn," 8 (emphasis in original).
52. All quotes from M[ichał] Mirski, "Der kharakter un rol fun der yidisher kolaboratsye," *Dos naje lebn* (September 12, 1949): 6.
53. Zuckerman, *Surplus of Memory*, 269.

4

An Unresolved Controversy

The Jewish Honor Court in the Netherlands, 1946–1950

IDO DE HAAN

One of the most painful and confusing issues in an already highly complicated history of the Holocaust is the collaboration of Jews in their own destruction. All over Europe the German authorities forced Jews, generally prominent men from prewar Jewish communities, to establish Jewish councils, variously named, that were made responsible for the compliance of their communities with German orders. To some extent, individual Jews, either willingly or under duress, also contributed to the persecution of other Jews. In these individual cases collaboration was inspired less by the responsibility, solicited or assigned, to act as the representative of the Jewish community and by the incentive to save as many Jewish lives as possible than by the immediate personal objective to survive. Although most of the leaders of the Jewish community perished together with the people they tried to protect, in general their acts were motivated by considerations that were both more ambitious, in the sense that they aimed at the community as a whole, and more abstract and pragmatic, in the sense that they weighed the loss of some lives against the survival of others. As a result, individual collaboration was often based on straightforward considerations of mortal danger and survival, but the collective and organized collaboration of the leadership of the Jewish councils was freighted with social and at times utilitarian considerations of relative relevance, worth, or usefulness as a way to distinguish between different categories of people in the Jewish community and, as many also suspected, influenced by financial, social, and political capital, that is, by corruption, favoritism, and nepotism. Also, in the Netherlands these issues played an important role in the post-Holocaust era. As elsewhere, a community that was already dramatically devastated by the murder of no less than 70 percent of its members was ripped apart by harsh and irreconcilable controversies among the small group of survivors. One of the platforms for these debates was the Joodse Ereraad (Jewish Honor Court), established in 1946 to inquire into the behavior of some members of the Jewish community who in the face of German persecution supposedly acted in a dishonorable manner.

The point of departure for understanding the establishment and workings of the Jewish Honor Court in the Netherlands is the attempt of the remnants of the community to come to terms with the problem of Jewish collaboration. Ever since Hannah Arendt's indictment of the Jewish councils in Nazi-dominated Europe in her 1961 *Eichmann in Jerusalem*, these bodies have often been considered a stain on the memory of the victims of the Holocaust and reference to them an attempt to blame the victims for their own suffering. Blaming the Jewish Council is even perceived as an extension of anti-Semitic attitudes and opinions. However, Jewish collaboration did exist also in the Netherlands. Examples are not just the acts of the Jewish Council; there are also a few high-profile individual cases of Jewish collaboration. A first such example is Ans van Dijk (1905–1948). After her arrest in the spring of 1943, she became a spy for the SS security service (Sicherheitsdienst). In 1947, a Dutch criminal court convicted her and sentenced her to death for the betrayal of 700 people, mainly Jews but also resistance members who had forged identity cards. Although she claimed in her appeal against the verdict that she had become insane from fear for her own life, Van Dijk was one of the 40 Dutch individuals who were actually executed, out of the 152 people who received a death sentence after the war, and the only woman who died before the firing squad.[1]

The second remarkable individual case is that of the economist and mystic Friedrich Weinreb (1910–1988), who was born in Lemberg but lived in the Netherlands beginning in 1916. He made Jews pay him to have themselves placed on a list of people exempt—so he claimed—from deportation because of obligations owed him by a fictitious German general. In fact, people on the list were still deported; yet when Weinreb himself was arrested by the

Germans, he was able to convince even them of the actual existence of a German general. For a while the German authorities encouraged him to continue his list, and although some people were temporarily exempt from deportation, he provided information on a substantial number of others who were deported to their deaths. In 1948 a Dutch court convicted and sentenced Weinreb to six years in prison, but he was released that very same year as part of a general pardon.[2]

Neither Van Dijk's case nor Weinreb's was discussed by the Jewish Honor Court, which might be indicative of the unorganized and arbitrary way in which this body functioned. Yet these two cases also illustrate the controversial context in which the honor court operated. All who were involved in the court were very much aware of the Jewish community's precarious position after the war and feared the negative effects that the public disclosure of Jewish complicity with the German occupying forces might have on the community as a whole. That is, the aborted history of the Jewish Honor Court also needs to be understood in the context of postwar relations between Jews and non-Jews. Considering the potentially damaging effects of unveiling the facts of Jewish collaboration to a wider audience, one might wonder why the Jewish Honor Court was established at all. Indeed, many people in the Jewish community were unhappy about the prospect of a Jewish honor court precisely because it would undoubtedly raise the issue of Jewish complicity and thereby make the community vulnerable to outside criticism. If it was deemed unacceptable that non-Jews would judge Jews for their attempts to avoid deportation, why did Jews give Gentiles the opportunity to do so by opening this can of worms, demanding accountability from their fellow Jews for the demise of the Jewish community and presenting evidence in support of this damning assertion? If a purge of alleged Jewish collaborators by outsiders was seen as unacceptable, why set up a body for the "self-purge" of the Jewish community?

To understand the workings and effects of the Jewish Honor Court in the Netherlands, the first question to address is why the institution came into being at all. Three contexts might help shed light on this issue: (1) the general characteristics of the postwar purge and self-purge in the Netherlands; (2) the long-term history of the Jewish community, characterized by a tradition of self-rule and political isolation; and (3) the complexities of the reconstruction of the postwar Jewish community. In the second part of this chapter I discuss the Jewish Honor Court's main focus on the Jewish Council's wartime leadership of Abraham Asscher and David Cohen, both of whom played prominent roles as representatives of the Jewish community before the German occupation. Their indictment by the Jewish Honor Court became entangled with their prosecution by postwar Dutch authorities. In response, the decimated Dutch Jewish community closed ranks against this tendency to blame the victim. As a result, the Jewish Honor Court left many issues unresolved, which continued to fuel antagonisms in the postwar Jewish community and to nurture recurrent debates over the Jewish Council, prominent members of the Jewish community, and Jewish collaborators in the Netherlands.

Purge, Self-Rule, and Reconstruction

The establishment of the Jewish Honor Court needs to be understood first and foremost in the context of the general legal purge of collaborators in postwar Europe. Compared to other countries, the purge in the Netherlands was ambitious.[3] Through a variety of means, a substantial number of cases of putative collaborators with the German occupying regime were reviewed, some of them in the context of prosecutions in criminal trials and many more by way of political and moral evaluations of specific sectors of society, such as the public administration, the liberal professions, the press, or the arts. The Jewish Honor Court can thus be seen as one of the many examples of purge bodies, all of which aimed to create a clean slate for the reconstruction of postwar society.[4]

The foundation for the postwar purge in the Netherlands was laid when the Dutch government-in-exile in London issued its Extraordinary Criminal Law Ruling (Besluit Buitengewoon Strafrecht) in December 1943, which made collaboration with the enemy punishable by law. Collaboration was defined as direct support, but it also included exposing others, or threatening to expose others, to enemy violence. Punishment varied from revocation of citizenship to life imprisonment and even the death penalty. On the basis of the Extraordinary Criminal Law Ruling and the regular criminal code, 14,562 Dutch citizens were convicted in postwar Dutch courts; almost 10 percent of them were convicted of betrayal, in many cases because they disclosed the whereabouts of Jews in hiding. Because almost without exception the betrayal and deportation of Jews led to their deaths in extermination camps, informing on Jews was punished more severely than informing on other people. In total, 152 people were sentenced to death. In the end, 39 men and 1 woman, Ans van Dijk, were executed.

Next to these criminal persecutions, the purge consisted of disciplinary measures against people who were found guilty of "political" offenses. The Tribunal Ruling (Tribunaalbesluit) of September 1944 led to the prosecution of a large number of Dutch citizens who had failed to demonstrate loyalty to the Dutch state. This included the members of the National Socialist Movement (Nationaal-Socialistische Beweging) and related organizations but also black marketers and others who had profited from the war economy. A lay tribunal could sentence those found guilty to confinement, revocation of citizenship rights, or the confiscation of property. Because every Dutch national was allowed to file a complaint against any other fellow citizen, complaints lodged in the tribunals led to the arrest of tens of thousands of people, who were held in the same concentration camps where Germans had held their prisoners. In the end, almost 50,000 individuals were convicted, of whom two-thirds temporarily lost their citizenship rights, in most cases for a period of ten years.

A third trajectory of the purge was the prosecution of civil servants who had collaborated with the German occupying regime. The Purge Ruling (Zuiveringsbesluit) of January 1944 initially authorized local purge committees to suspend all civil servants with or without continuation of payment and, after evaluation of their cases, to dismiss them, with or without receiving half of their salaries. Later, other measures were added: official reprimand, demotion, or honorable discharge. In the end, about 10 percent of the 380,000 civil servants were purged. The purge of the civil administration also offered the model for the purge of other sectors of society: the universities, the arts, the press, and industry and commerce. In these sectors bodies of peers were established, which constituted examples of a self-purge. However, these bodies had an official statute, acknowledged and in some cases also administered by the state. On this basis, they were able to impose sanctions, varying from a public reprimand to temporary or lifelong suspension. Moreover, the officially acknowledged purge bodies were obliged to hand over to the general prosecutor information collected during their investigations that might indicate criminal behavior.

As a result, in the summer of 1945 purge committees at the different universities but also national bodies, such as the Commission for the Purge of the Press, the Central Council for the Purge of Industry and Commerce, and the Honor Court for the Arts, emerged. No such official courts were established for the liberal professions of doctors and lawyers. Yet because these sectors had a long tradition of setting up their own disciplinary boards, they organized purge committees that could impose disciplinary sanctions.[5]

All in all, postwar Dutch society's purge was comprehensive. Between 120,000 and 150,000 people were arrested and, while awaiting trial, imprisoned for various lengths of time; 100,000 people were subject to punishment of some sort. Moreover, investigative files were opened on 300,000 individuals, and because some people were investigated in several cases, the purge in the Netherlands produced an archive of 800,000 files. Given that the total population of the Netherlands did not exceed 10 million, the purge had a vast impact on Dutch society, as people were confronted with the prosecution or purge of collaborators in families, workplaces, and neighborhoods. In that light, the establishment of the Jewish Honor Court seems to have merely followed a well-known overall pattern; yet it is also clear that its establishment at the beginning of 1946 was rather late compared to most other purge bodies, indicating a certain reluctance of the Jewish community to enter that trajectory.

The existence of tribunals for the judgment of one's peers was not foreign to the Jewish community, though. The establishment of the Jewish Honor Court also fits into a long-term tradition of bodies for self-rule in the Jewish community. Despite the emancipation of Dutch Jews in 1796, the Jewish community was to a large extent left to its own devices. When the Nazis invaded the Netherlands in May 1940, they found a community of 140,000 "full" and 20,000 "partial" Jews. Also, on the basis of Jewish law (Halakha), the Dutch Jewish community before the Holocaust was one of the larger communities in Western Europe, consisting of more than 100,000 Jews at the beginning of the twentieth century. About 60 percent of the Dutch Jews lived in Amsterdam, with the remainder in other parts of the country. Most were extremely poor and came from an Ashkenazic background; the upper-class Jews consisted initially mainly of Sephardic Jews. During the Dutch Republic (1581–1795), the Ashkenazic and Sephardic communities formed a separate Jewish nation, with its own laws and jurisdiction, speaking its own Yiddish language (except for the 2,000–3,000 Sephardim), and governed by the *parnasim* (community elders), who were the only ones who interacted with the non-Jewish authorities. Eager to observe the demands of the city councils and not to disturb the peace of their Gentile neighbors, the *parnasim* maintained strict discipline over the members of the community.[6]

When Dutch Jews acquired equal citizenship in 1796, the majority of the community still remained excluded from non-Jewish public life. Only the Jewish elite participated in life outside the Jewish community, and it remained in charge of Jewish organizations, the most important being the Supreme Commission for Israelite Affairs (Hoofdcommissie tot de zaken der Israëlieten), established in 1814. In effect, the Jewish community was subject to the state, to which the

Supreme Commission was answerable. This state of affairs ended with the final separation of church and state in the Netherlands in 1848, which in 1871 led to the establishment of the Netherlands Israelite Church Organization (Nederlands Israëlietisch Kerkgenootschap; NIK).[7]

But even in the late nineteenth century the Jewish community remained isolated from the rest of Dutch society. Dutch Christians often disliked Jews on religious grounds as unrepentant murderers of Christ who stubbornly persisted in their rejection of Jesus. Yet within the pluralistic religious culture of the Netherlands, it was deemed improper to express manifest anti-Semitic sentiments. Most people rejected the rude and aggressive forms of Nazi anti-Semitism, which they defined as German—that is, foreign to Dutch culture. At the same time, many held social and cultural prejudices against Jews and, if asked, would have agreed that the presence of Jews in the Netherlands was a problem.[8]

The isolation of the Jewish community was also the result of heterogeneity and internal divisions. The Jewish community was geographically divided. The community of Amsterdam and the more or less autonomous Jewish communities in the other parts of the country had little contact with each other. Moreover, although the Jewish elite occupied leading positions in the NIK and other Jewish organizations, it had little interest in religious issues, whereas the lower classes had generally no more than a superficial knowledge of Jewish traditions. Many Dutch Jews turned to the new ideologies of liberalism for the upper class and socialism for the lower classes, neither of which had a positive conception of Jewish identity. And this was hardly discouraged by the rabbinic leadership, often from Germany or Poland, which favored doctrinal and ceremonial purity over popularity. These divisions also characterized the support of Zionism. In the mid-1930s about 10 percent of Dutch Jews were members of a Zionist organization, yet this substantial constituency was spread over several Zionist organizations, which were divided between liberal and socialist currents. As a result of these cleavages, the Jewish community as a whole lacked effective political representation of its interests in Dutch society before the war.[9]

The first secular organizations established with the explicit aim to represent Jewish interests came into being in response to the rise of German anti-Semitism and the influx of large groups of German refugees. The Committee for Special Jewish Interests (Comité Bijzondere Joodsche Belangen; CBJB) was established in March 1933 to act as an intermediary between the Jewish community and the Dutch state. In addition to its aim to represent the interests of the community, its bourgeois leadership also wanted to prevent unrest and anti-Semitic reactions that might result from protests against Nazism and the influx of German Jewish refugees. In the same year the CBJB created a subcommittee, the Committee for Jewish Refugees (Comité voor Joodsche Vluchtelingen) to aid the Jews who fled Germany. The leadership of both committees was in the hands of two men: Abraham Asscher (1880–1950) and David Cohen (1882–1967). Asscher was director of an international diamond company and president of the NIK; Cohen was a professor of classics at the University of Amsterdam and president of the Dutch Union of Zionists (Nederlandsche Zionistenbond; NZB). Asscher became chair of the CBJB, and Cohen served as its secretary and headed the Committee for Jewish Refugees. Despite their attempts to gain the support of the Dutch government in aiding German Jews, the government followed a restrictive policy toward refugees, and, more important, it held the Dutch Jewish community responsible for the support of German Jewish refugees. Asscher and Cohen not only obeyed the government policies but even defended them in the Jewish community. They supported the demand of the Dutch government to concentrate all German Jewish émigrés who had crossed the Dutch border in one place and even managed to persuade the Jewish community to collect funds totaling 1.2 million guilders to establish a refugee camp in Westerbork. The camp began to operate in October 1939; on July 1, 1942, it became the transit camp (*Durchgangslager*) where the great majority of Dutch Jews were interned for some time before their deportation to Eastern Europe.[10]

Soon after the Germans invaded the Netherlands on May 10, 1940, Asscher and Cohen met with other prominent Jews, among them Lodewijk E. Visser (1871–1942), former president of the Dutch Supreme Court, and Isaac Kisch (1905–1980), who in 1940 was about to be appointed as professor of law at the University of Amsterdam. They met on the initiative of the lawyer Marinus L. Kan (1891–1945), the last president of the NZB before it was abolished by the Germans, who proposed to establish the Jewish Contact Committee (Joodsche Contact Commissie). It was founded in December 1940 under the leadership of Visser to protect the interests of the Jewish community, yet it never was able to fulfill that role. The German authorities not only denied the Jewish Contact Committee any hearing but also, two months later, in February 1941, forced Asscher and Cohen to establish a body under their direct control, the Joodsche Raad (Jewish Council) of Amsterdam. The two organizations functioned for some time alongside one another, creating a deepening disagreement within the Jewish elite about whether to hold onto an independent yet ineffective Jewish

Contact Committee or to accept the dependent but potentially more influential Jewish Council. The issue was finally decided by the Germans, who banned the Jewish Contact Committee in October 1941.

The Jewish Council was established in a context of public unrest and street fighting in Amsterdam, and one of its first deeds was to call for calm and order so as not to aggravate the German occupation authorities. Yet within a couple of months it developed into a multifaceted organization, providing assistance in housing, education, medical care, food provision, and many other areas of social life. It established branches in five cities (Amsterdam, The Hague, Rotterdam, Groningen, and Enschede) and in the Westerbork transit camp. The Jewish Council maintained up to a hundred departments, commissions, and subcommissions. At its height, in September 1942, the Jewish Council had 17,000 employees—more than 12 percent of the Jewish community—all of whom received a *Sperre*, that is, a status that exempted them from deportation on the basis of their "vital contribution" to the community. At the same time, through a department called Expositur, the Jewish Council administered many of the German decisions related to deportation, and through the weekly *Joodsch Weekblad* it also served as the mouthpiece of the Germans, relaying their orders. In this fashion the Jewish Council played a role in the introduction of many German anti-Jewish measures, such as the distribution of the yellow star that Jews had to wear from May 3, 1942, onward. Through its department Aid to Those Who Depart (Hulp aan vertrekkenden; in popular parlance, the department was called *Hulp aan verrekkenden*, meaning "those who perish"), the Jewish Council also assisted in the deportations. On German orders the council drafted a list in May 1943 containing the names of all 17,000 of its employees; Cohen and Asscher put a checkmark in pencil next to the names of 7,000 people, who were then selected for deportation. In September of that year German authorities abolished the Jewish Council and deported its last members. Asscher was sent to Bergen-Belsen and Cohen to Theresienstadt. Both survived.[11]

After the war, the rifts between different sections of the Jewish community returned, and they were aggravated by the dramatic fact that the community had lost three quarters of its members in the Holocaust. Separate factions of the community held each another accountable for this dismal fate while all tried nevertheless to contribute to the reconstruction of Jewish life in the Netherlands. This is the third context within which the emergence of the Jewish Honor Court needs to be understood. Of the 107,000 people deported, about 5,000 survived in various camps. Some 2,000 perished in the Netherlands itself. A couple hundred Jews were able to find shelter abroad, and about 25,000 survived in hiding.[12]

The size of the disaster became clear only gradually. The Netherlands was initially only partly liberated, after the Allied offensive stalled on the banks of the Rhine in September 1944. In Maastricht, in the southern part of the country, Jewish survivors established the Committee for Israelite Interests (Comité voor Israëlietische Belangen). Another initiative was taken by people connected to the Circle of Dutch Jews (Kring van Nederlandse Joden), established by Dutch Jewish refugees in London in May 1943 to develop plans for the reconstruction of the Jewish community in the Netherlands.[13] In October 1944 they established the Central Registration Bureau, which together with a number of local branches registered 21,700 Jewish survivors by the end of 1945. From January 1945 onward, these activities came to be coordinated by the Jewish Coordination Committee for the Liberated Netherlands (Joodsche Coördinatie Commissie voor het bevrijde Nederland; JCC). The JCC soon developed various local branches and was itself administered by the Contact Commission. The committee was officially acknowledged by the provisional Military Authorities (Militair Gezag), established in January 1943 by the Dutch government-in-exile to administer the liberated parts of the country. Moreover, the JCC received 1 million guilders from the American Jewish Joint Distribution Committee to support the reconstruction of the Jewish community in the Netherlands.[14]

The first prewar organization that was reestablished was the Zionist union NZB. Although Zionism was supported by a minority of Jews before the war, it became almost generally accepted in the immediate aftermath. However, the initial focus of the NZB's leadership was not moving the remainder of the Dutch Jews to Palestine. Rather, it considered the reconstruction of the Jewish community in the Netherlands its first priority and a necessary precondition for emigration. As a result, the NZB played a major role in the JCC, until its leadership emigrated to Israel.

Both the JCC and the NZB coalesced with the NIK, which was reestablished in January 1946. The Zionists wanted to preserve the decentralized structure of the prewar organization, yet they also wanted to integrate all Jewish denominations into one structure, following the example of the Conseil Réprésentatif des Institutions Juives de France. But the rabbis of the NIK claimed a final say in religious matters that the representatives of the Portuguese and Liberal communities were unable to accept. At the same time, the NIK proposed a drastic reduction in the number of official communities from 139 to 58, because only a remnant was sufficiently viable. This reduction was accompanied by a strong centralization of the decision-making process in the main synagogue in Amsterdam, leading many members of Jewish communities in other parts of the country to feel neglected. The result was that even more Jews left the NIK, whose membership dropped from 19,532 in 1947 to 12,133 in 1951.[15]

As a result, the NIK also lost its central position in the Jewish community. Even though membership in the organized Jewish community became small, a much larger number of Jewish survivors still identified as Jews, based on family ties, collective remembrance of suffering and loss, and solidarity with Israel. They felt much more connected to the foundation Jewish Social Work (Joods Maatschappelijk Werk), established in 1946 by people from within the JCC. Initially, the foundation's main focus was on material support for survivors, which was financed by the sale of real estate and other property of the prewar community and through fund-raising. The foundation also played a pivotal role in the discussions about restitution and *Wiedergutmachung* (the reparations paid by the Federal Republic of Germany to survivors of the Holocaust and forced labor).[16]

The Constitution and Working of the Jewish Honor Court

It is within this complex context of the postwar purge, the tradition of self-rule in the Jewish community, and the contested reconstruction of the Jewish community after the Holocaust that the Jewish Honor Court was established. The precise background of this event is difficult to reconstruct, testifying to the improvised and unorganized nature of the Jewish Honor Court in the Netherlands. The first debates about an honor court emerged in the NZB, which on September 2, 1945, established the Adviescommissie inzake de Zuiverheid (Advisory Committee on the Purge). Some of its members argued that a purge of the community was a necessary precondition for its reconstruction. Others were reluctant to judge fellow Jews. According to the lawyer and historian Abel J. Herzberg (1893–1989), an honor court would lead to further divisiveness in the community and even to "Jewish anti-Semitism."[17] Despite this controversy, two Zionist representatives in the JCC, Abraham de Jong (1913–1995) and Salomon Roet (1892–1960), made the first proposal to set up a Jewish honor court, yet the Permanent Committee, the daily governing body of the NIK, and its main congregation in Amsterdam also played a leading role in the founding of the court.

On February 15, 1946, the Jewish journal *Nieuw Israëlietisch Weekblad* announced that an honor court had been established by the "Contact Commission of the Jewish Coordination Committee, with the approval of the main synagogue of the NIK" as well as that of the Portuguese religious organization and the NZB. However, the Central Committee, the official board representing all the communities of the NIK, appeared to be left out of this decision, as became clear from the notes of its meeting of February 17, where it was debated whether the NIK should become involved in a Jewish honor court that "according to a publication in the NIW [*Nieuw Israëlietisch Weekblad*] appears to have been established with the support of the main synagogue in Amsterdam." As was later acknowledged by the Amsterdam-based Permanent Committee of the NIK, the establishment of the Jewish Honor Court was based on "being in touch [*voeling*, a highly informal term in Dutch] with all official institutions available at the time," indicating once again the improvised nature of the court's constitution and its limitation to a small group of Jewish survivors in Amsterdam.[18] As a result, the representative nature of the Jewish Honor Court was questionable, both in principle and, as it turned out, in practice.

At the same time the Jewish Honor Court was an answer to a widespread call to purge the ranks of the Jewish survivors in order to start with a clean slate for the reconstruction of the Jewish community. The establishment of a purge board gathered momentum after a number of individuals called for a purge of some kind. They represented three groups.[19] The first was a group of former deportees, who sometimes ascribed their dismal fate to the working of the Jewish Council. One of them was Herman Milikowski (1909–1989), who survived various camps himself but lost his wife in 1943. He was a student of sociology at the University of Amsterdam, when, in the fall of 1945, he wrote an article in the current affairs journal *Het Oordeel*, published by the W7, informal study group of Amsterdam students who asked for an investigation of Asscher and Cohen.[20]

A second group favoring a purge consisted of former members of the Jewish Council who at some point had resigned or been dismissed from their positions. They read a highly critical report by Gertrud van Tijn-Cohn (1891–1974), who had been the closest collaborator of David Cohen in the Jewish Council. In 1943 she was deported to Westerbork and from there to Bergen-Belsen, from which she was allowed to leave for Palestine as one of the 110 Dutch Jews exchanged for German internees on June 29, 1944. In Palestine she produced a typescript in which she accused David Cohen of selecting the lower-class Jews for deportation instead of Jews from his own social class.²¹ Similar accusations were made by another deportee released to Palestine, Sam de Wolff (1878–1960). Van Tijn-Cohn's typescript soon started to circulate in the Netherlands, and De Wolff's account was published in 1946. Both accounts inspired Jules Gerzon (1889–1950) to take action. In May 1943 he had been taken off the list of Jewish Council employees and had been deported to Bergen-Belsen. In October 1945 he contacted the Political Investigation Service (Politieke Opsporingsdienst; after 1947 Politieke Recherche Afdeling) and the purge board of the University of Amsterdam to file complaints against David Cohen.

Gerzon's action inspired yet another group: students of the University of Amsterdam, organized in the student organization Algemene Studenten Vereniging Amsterdam. One of its members, the history student Ivo Schöffer, who had been active in rescuing Jews during the German occupation, also sent a request to the purge committee to look into the case of David Cohen, who had been reinstated as a professor of classics. When the purge board failed to take action, the student organization asked the minister of education, Jos J. Gielen (1898–1981), to intervene. Gielen refused, arguing that he not only lacked the competence to intervene but also believed that the issue of Jewish collaboration could be adequately evaluated only by Jews.

In response to these calls, Albert Büchenbacher (1902–1952), the former secretary of the NZB and a member of the JCC, drafted a charter for the Jewish Honor Court. The opening article of the charter posited the court's main aim:

> To evaluate the acts of persons who during the time of German oppression have behaved in a way that is irreconcilable with the most elementary principles of solidarity, which, especially in a period in which they stood under so much pressure, could have been expected of all Jews, or with the attitude which in Jewish public life with respect to others needs to be assumed.

In the fourth article the formulation was further specified, including the passing of judgment "on all who had damaged the Jewish community, or groups or individuals within it in through reprehensible behavior." Reprehensible behavior was further specified as "striving after or receiving financial or material gain" in return for issuing a *Sperre* or other exemptions from deportation, or drafting deportation lists; without necessity handing over Jews to the German authorities while knowing that it would bring them harm; or unnecessary and uncalled for mistreatment or abuse of Jews in concentration camps. These formulations demonstrate an awareness of the situational pressure that might have induced people to act in a "reprehensible" (*laakbaar*) way. This awareness was accentuated in the sixth article, which read that the honor court would take into account the position of the accused during the German oppression. But then the charter cast a wide net, holding accountable all those who after August 1942 were still members of the Jewish Council "when it was clear that the German authorities aimed for the complete deportation of the Jews in the Netherlands and to use the Jewish Council as their instrument." This embraced a large group, because all people employed by the Jewish Council were considered members—*lid van de Joodse Raad*. Membership in the Jewish Council as a ground for accountability thus introduced a division between the great majority of Jews under German occupation who had any dealings with the Jewish Council and the few who had not.[22]

This had serious consequences for the composition of the membership of the Jewish Honor Court. Although it was never stated explicitly in the charter, the final report of the Jewish Honor Court made clear that eligibility to sit on it was restricted to someone who "had not accepted a so-called *Sperre*-stamp and who was in the Netherlands until August 1942, while the chair needs to have an academic title in law."[23] The court's chair was the lawyer M. Bosboom, about whom nothing further is known. Its secretary was the accountant Joop Voet (1909–1995), who was also country director for the Netherlands of the American Jewish Joint Distribution Committee. There were initially seven other members, of whom only two came from outside Amsterdam; in the next year another four members were added to the court. It took almost six months to arrive at the initial list; many people who were asked to participate declined, either because they assumed they were not eligible (because of relations with the Jewish Council) or because they disagreed with the establishment of the honor court.[24]

The court announced it would review cases presented before it by anyone who wished to file a complaint, yet it excluded complaints against individuals who were not present in the Netherlands. Included were all those who had been found guilty in any of the civil courts or purge boards. This introduced the topic of the relation between the dealings of the Jewish Honor Court and official forms of prosecution, which proved controversial later on. Some members of the congregation of the Main Synagogue (*Hoofdsynagoge*) belonging to the NIK pushed to apply to the Ministry of Justice for official recognition of the Jewish Honor Court as a purge board. Yet this recognition would also have involved the obligation to make available to the authorities any incriminating information that might turn up in an investigation against individuals called before the honor court. For the founders of the honor court, this was undesirable. The court was meant to deal internally with collaborators from within the Jewish community itself, not to wash its dirty linen in public. However, given that it had no official standing and no legal authority, basically the only sanction the Jewish Honor Court had available to it was the publication of its judgment in the Jewish press. It could recommend exclusion from Jewish organizations, but in the end it was up to those institutions to decide whether or not to follow that advice. As a result, the court became caught between the desire to pillory Jewish collaborators and the wish to keep its judgment out of the sight of the general public.[25]

The Jewish Honor Court dealt with twenty-six cases. It did not do a systematic search for all suspects but concentrated on a few high-profile cases and on those cases stemming from complaints filed with the court. The most important cases were those of Abraham Asscher and David Cohen and five other members of the Jewish Council, but the court also ruled in nineteen other instances, which hardly attracted any attention.[26] Two of these cases involved people who asked the court to evaluate their own case in order to clean the slate of allegations made against them. In one instance this request backfired; the former head of the Department of Social Affairs of the Jewish Council, the lawyer David Barmes (1914–1980), received a negative judgment. According to the Jewish Honor Court, he had demonstrated reprehensible behavior by removing the files of some members of his staff during the selection for deportation, with the result that others had to take their place. Yet given that he had not acted to his own advantage, the court ruled that an exclusion from the Jewish community was unwarranted.[27]

The court received about seventeen other complaints, some of which were filed after an extension of the filing deadline, which initially had been set for April 15, 1946. Six of the cases were dismissed without further debate: three because the accused were not in the Netherlands and the other three at the discretion of the chair, without any information available on his motives. Four cases were dismissed after review on the grounds that the plaintiffs did not submit sufficient supporting evidence. Most of these cases, twelve in total, involved misbehavior in the transit camp Westerbork. One case involved Nathan Speijer, a member of the internal order police in both Westerbork and Bergen-Belsen who was accused of abuse and harassment. In his case the court judged that his behavior had been disgraceful yet not reprehensible, "in the sense meant in the regulations," on the grounds that he was a large man whose acts could easily be misunderstood as violent. Moreover, Speijer had responded nervously to the "demoralizing circumstances" of the camp, as a result of which he became the Germans' favorite Jewish guard.[28]

In three other cases, all ruled on at the end of 1946, the court came to the conclusion that the behavior of the accused had been reprehensible. One case involved a doctor from The Hague, Eliazer Polak (1891–?), who performed medical examinations for the Jewish Council and who, according to the court, "failed to cooperate in the disqualification of patients, which can reasonably be expected from a Jewish doctor in the circumstances of the time." It was advised that he be excluded from a leading position in any Jewish institution until the end of 1947. In the same report two other cases were discussed: those of the director and the administrator of the Central Israelite Hospital in Amsterdam. They had failed to assume the required attitude with regard to attempts by the hospital personnel to escape or hide; no other comments were added.[29] None of these rulings elicited further attention.

Judging the Jewish Council

That attention was altogether different when it came to the leaders of the Jewish Council, Abraham Asscher and David Cohen. The debate in the Jewish Honor Court soon focused solely on Cohen, as he was the only one who responded to the court's summons to appear. The court also called five other individuals to appear before it. These were people who, according to the court, were still members of the Jewish Council after August 15, 1942, and were still alive. Again, this illustrates the arbitrary working of the court, because it is unlikely that there were not many others to whom these criteria applied.[30] Although these five did not appear before the court, the court still debated their cases and then published an extensive account of its deliberation. The court ruled that there was a difference in responsibility between the leaders and the regular members of the Jewish Council in their relation to the German authorities, but by staying on as members, they were as responsible to the Jewish community as their leaders: "As long as they remained members, they sanctioned the attitude, behavior and acts of the chairmen. That is to say, they were responsible for collaboration with the execution of anti-Jewish measures."[31] In more detail, the court accused the council members of aiding in the deportation of Jews and obstructing the escape of Jews detained in the Hollandsche Schouwburg in Amsterdam, the place where many of the 60,000 Amsterdam Jews were held before their deportation to Westerbork, by barring doors and windows (as proven by the cost for boards and nails in the financial reports of the Jewish Council). Despite these severe allegations, the Jewish Honor Court did not issue a verdict in these cases, because the accused had failed to defend themselves before it.[32]

The treatment of Abraham Asscher's case was different. Asscher was accused, discussed, and judged by the court, despite the fact that he had not responded at all to its calls to appear. From Westerbork Asscher had been deported to Bergen-Belsen, where he had suffered severely. He returned to Amsterdam a damaged man, in bad health, and wanted to have nothing to do with the Jewish Honor Court. Its ruling aggrieved him so badly that he withdrew from the Jewish community altogether. In return, the community paid him no respect. When Asscher visited Israel in June 1948, he was received by Israeli president Chaim Weizmann, who immediately received a letter from the NZB protesting the granting of an official audience to someone who had been excommunicated from the Jewish community. Weizmann replied that he had no knowledge of Asscher's ban and that he had not granted him an official hearing but just five minutes of personal time.[33] When Asscher died in 1950, he was not buried in a Jewish cemetery but in a public cemetery.

This meant that the case against the Jewish Council turned into a fight with David Cohen. Cohen had played a pivotal role in the Jewish community and had held leading positions in many Jewish organizations. This was a role he had actively pursued; he appears to have been a domineering yet also somewhat stubborn man. Meanwhile, his reputation as a professor of classics had created an aura of respectability and wisdom, which he was eager to exploit. At the same time, he generally appears to have adopted a subservient attitude toward the authorities, not just German commanders during the war but also the Dutch government before the war. As such, he appears to have assumed a position similar to that of most other leaders of the Jewish community after the emancipation, who out of fear of provoking anti-Semitism forced their community to obey the rules that were imposed on it.[34]

At first, it appeared that Cohen would also refuse to engage with the Jewish Honor Court. When the chair of the court phoned Cohen's house to inform him about the complaint, Cohen's daughter answered and slammed the phone on the hook after stating that "the case did not interest her one damn bit and neither did it her father."[35] To what extent this was proof of Cohen's or his family's attitude toward the Jewish Honor Court is unclear. His behavior as chair of the Jewish Council had been disapproved of by his wife and his two daughters, both of whom had played an important role in the rescue of Jewish children from the Jewish kindergarten opposite the Hollandsche Schouwburg, the *Umschlagplatz* to Westerbork. But it can be safely assumed that they were thoroughly unhappy about the indictment against their father.[36]

Nevertheless, Cohen engaged in a conversation with the chair of the court, questioning its legitimacy. Initially, he refused to appear before the court, yet on December 15, 1946, he showed up together with his lawyer B. P. Gomperts (1883–1963). He might have expected to be cleared of all charges, "with a thank you for services delivered," but he also could have been reacting to the position taken by the minister of education, Gielen, who suggested that Cohen's case should be evaluated by the Jewish community itself. In subsequent meetings in the first months of 1947, Cohen responded extensively to all questions raised by the court. His basic line of defense was that he had acted in the best interests of the Jewish community and that he and Asscher had aimed to prevent worse outcomes by trying to placate the German authorities. Moreover, he argued that their attitude strengthened the sense of agency of the Jewish community: By actively engaging with the Germans, they had given hope to the Jewish community that it could influence the course of events. Finally, and this was perhaps the most problematic line of defense, Cohen argued that in this way he had tried to save those who did crucial work for and made the most valuable contribution to the Jewish community. In the end, Cohen admitted that he had misjudged the unprecedented, murderous intentions of the Nazis.[37]

While defending himself, Cohen kept on doubting the legitimacy of the court and of the right of specific members to judge him. His interventions were successful in the sense that he was able to stir up disagreements among the court's members and even caused the withdrawal of one of them, Joseph Weisz (1893–1976). At his installation on the court Weisz had already raised doubts about his eligibility for membership because he had been Elder of the Jews (*Judenältester*) in Bergen-Belsen. As a result of these internal disagreements and the failure to find a replacement for Weisz, nothing was heard from the court until the end of 1947. Yet in November 1947 the case suddenly moved toward a verdict, denying Cohen the opportunity to appear in court once again or to hear witnesses who might support his case. Despite the protests of Cohen's lawyer and the fact that the court consisted of a group of people whose standing had been questioned, some of whom had not even been properly installed, the court's chairman wrote to Gomperts on December 22, 1947, that the case would soon come to closure. He failed to mention, though, that a verdict had already been reached five days before and that the day before he wrote the letter to Gomperts, it had been sent to the press.[38]

In the verdict, published in the *Nieuw Israëlietisch Weekblad* on December 26, 1947, the Jewish Honor Court ruled that both Asscher and Cohen had behaved reprehensibly. The court judged the assumption of the leadership of the Jewish Council in itself already unacceptable, and it held the chairmen of the Jewish Council also accountable on more specific counts. The first was the publication of the weekly *Het Joodsche Weekblad*, which Cohen and Asscher had presented as a way to represent the interests of the Jewish community. According to the court, this was false, because the weekly served first and foremost German interests and the communication of German orders, which was actually obfuscated by the presentation of these orders as though they had come from the Jewish Council itself. Even more reprehensible was that Asscher and Cohen had reiterated the threats conveyed or implied by the Germans in case of noncompliance, and in this way they had blackmailed the Jewish community into obedience. These orders included the wearing of the yellow star, the confiscation of property, and the notifications to prepare for deportation. Moreover, the collaboration in the drafting of *Sperre* lists had given many Jews an unwarranted sense of security, which prevented many of them from seeking ways to go into hiding. The most reprehensible act in this respect was the list made in May 1943, by which, as Asscher and Cohen stated at the time, they had "arbitrarily and against earlier agreements" selected a large number of people for immediate deportation. Although individual members of the Jewish Council (notably Walter Süskind [1906–1945], who had been able to rescue a large number of people from the Amsterdam kindergarten and the Hollandsche Schouwburg) deserved to be honored, this did not apply to Asscher and Cohen, because they had not stimulated these rescue efforts. The Jewish Honor Court concluded that Asscher and Cohen should be excluded for life from all leading positions in the Jewish community and expressed the hope that as result of its verdict "calm would ensue around these issues."[39]

Judging the Jewish Honor Court

The opposite was the case. The verdict was issued in a tense context and was hastened by a remarkable upheaval caused by the arrest of Asscher and Cohen on November 6, 1947, by the attorney general of the Extraordinary Court in Amsterdam, Nicolaas J. G. Sikkel (1897–1954). This arrest came rather unexpectedly, because earlier calls to prosecute the leaders of the Jewish Council had been rejected by the Political Investigation Service. After the Amsterdam students had leveled their accusations, Cohen had been questioned by the Political Investigation Unit on April 19 and May 19, 1947, but this had not resulted in a formal indictment. This changed after June 6, 1947, when Asscher gave testimony in support of Edward John Voûte (1887–1950), the National Socialist mayor and chief of police of Amsterdam from 1941 to 1945. In the trial against Voûte for collaboration, Asscher fulfilled a promise he seemed to have made to Voûte when he was still in office: to support him in case the tables turned—a promise motivated by the fact that after the fall of Stalingrad, Voûte appeared to do an about-face and reversed policy regarding the collaboration of the Amsterdam police in the persecution of the Jews of Amsterdam.

Asscher's testimony on this apparent change in Voûte's attitude exasperated Sikkel, who saw an opportunity to take revenge after testimony in two other major trials. First was the testimony of defendant Willy Lages (1901–1971), head of the security police and the security service (Befehlshaber der Sicherheitspolizei und des Sicherheitsdienstes) in Amsterdam. At his trial Lages declared that the Jewish Council had not just maintained peace and order in the Jewish community but had, in fact, facilitated the deportation of the Jews to such extent that "ohne diesen Judenrat hätten wir es nie geschafft" (without this Jewish Council we never would have succeeded). Even more devastating perhaps was the testimony of Ferdinand aus der Fünten (1909–1989), leader of the Central Office for Jewish Emigration (Zentralstelle für Jüdische Auswanderung), a section within the Sicherheitspolizei und Sicherheitsdienst. Aus der Fünten declared that on several occasions Asscher had requested personal favors—among them, ordering the arrest of his son's girlfriend, whom he had considered disreputable. When Cohen then protested against the suggestion of Sikkel's colleague, the prosecutor Marinus H. Gelinck (1910–1989), that the section for Jewish affairs of the Amsterdam police had only executed the orders of the Jewish Council, both Asscher and Cohen were asked to come to the police station to clarify these issues, where they were taken into custody and questioned for several weeks.[40]

The arrest of the leaders of the Jewish Council immediately led to public protests, especially because it became clear that Sikkel had been inspired by anti-Semitic motives and had openly declared his anti-Semitism to one of Cohen and Asscher's lawyers, Abel J. Herzberg. On December 3, 1947, when Minister of Justice Johan H. van Maarseveen (1894–1951) had to account for the arrests before the Dutch parliament, it became clear that the case against Asscher and Cohen was weak. Although Sikkel had written to the minister that the Jewish Council was an example of "collaboration of a formidable scope," he admitted that their acquittal could not be ruled out.[41] Two days later, Asscher and Cohen were released.

In the meantime, Sikkel began preparing an official indictment, for which he received help from the lawyer Isaac Kisch, who in 1941 sided with those who objected to a Jewish council. He also received testimony from several survivors who claimed to have been damaged by the Jewish Council. Despite the production of a 3,000-page dossier, whose focus was Cohen, the trial was endlessly postponed. Finally, in early 1950, when the case was handed over to Sikkel's replacement, L. W. M. M. Drabbe, an actual indictment was formulated, in which Asscher and Cohen were accused of helping the enemy by facilitating the deportation of Jews and refusing to accept the advice of those (like Kisch) who warned against collaboration with the Germans. Testimony supporting these allegations came from Lages and Aus der Fünten as well as from Kisch. Another remarkable witness on Asscher and Cohen's manipulation of lists was Friedrich Weinreb, who only two years earlier had been pardoned after his own conviction for collaboration.

Central to the indictment was the way in which Cohen and Asscher had selected people for deportation in May 1943. The indictment adopted the argument of Van Tijn-Cohn and others that Asscher and Cohen had exempted members of the Jewish upper class from deportation while sacrificing lower-class Jews. In support of this proposition, Drabbe envisaged the testimony of Laura C. Mazirel (1907–1974), who declared that in the summer of 1942 she had tried to convince Asscher and Cohen to help Jews hide from deportation but they had refused. She claimed that Asscher stated: "Let's be honest, around the Waterlooplein [the center of the Jewish quarter in Amsterdam], there are quite a number of miserable orange vendors who are no asset to the Jewish people and not a few idle youngsters whom forced labor would do some good."[42]

However, the case against Cohen and Asscher was never brought to court. Asscher died shortly after Drabbe took over the case. Even more important was a change in the general sentiment toward the prosecution of war criminals and the purge of collaborators. Influential representatives of the legal professions protested against the arbitrary nature of the purge. Catholic politicians were inspired by Pope Pius XII's designation of 1950 as a holy year, centered around forgiveness. Many others longed for a return to normality, in which old enmities could be laid to rest. Most cases against collaborators were dropped, and those who were convicted received parole; the death sentences of Lages and Aus der Fünten were converted to life imprisonment. In the summer of 1951 the general prosecutor, Arnold Abraham Louis Felix (Nout) van Dullemen (1892–1974), who had taken over the case, argued that it should be dismissed, as it would only reveal a "shameful period" in which many representatives of the Dutch people, "notably high civil servants and the complete police force," had demonstrated "a sadly weak attitude."[43]

Although the legal prosecution of Asscher and Cohen thereby ended, their case was not put to rest in the Jewish community. The sudden haste with which the Jewish Honor Court reached a verdict in November 1947, prompted by Asscher and Cohen's arrest, raised the suspicion of many in the Jewish community that the Jewish Honor Court was detrimental to the position of Jews in society. Immediately after the publication of the verdict, Asscher and Cohen's lawyers sent out a general press release stating that they accepted neither the verdict nor the authority of the Jewish Honor Court on the grounds that its composition was partisan and that it had not followed proper procedures in the weeks before the verdict, when Asscher and Cohen were sitting in jail. An additional argument was that the judgment of the Jewish Honor Court constituted an unacceptable influence on the case brought against Asscher and Cohen by the general prosecutor.[44]

These objections found immediate support, first of all in the non-Jewish press but also with the influential board of the Dutch law journal *Nederlandsch Juristenblad*.[45] More important was the disagreement in the Jewish community. On December 21, 1947, in a meeting of the Central Committee of the NIK, a number of people objected to the verdict and even more to its timing, and even though a minority argued in favor of the Jewish Honor Court, the Central Committee accepted a motion expressing its regret over the actions of the court.[46] Over the next few months the controversy became worse, first of all because of the continuation of the proceedings in the Jewish Honor Court against the five regular members of the Jewish Council, leading to its ambivalent judgment in May 1948. But another cause for debate was the refusal of the Jewish Honor Court to answer questions from the Permanent Committee of the NIK and the board of the NZB pertaining to its motives to render a verdict against Asscher and Cohen, even though they had been arrested. As a result, on May 18, 1948, the Permanent Committee of the NIK declared that it no longer felt obliged to follow the rulings of the Jewish Honor Court, and it invited other Jewish organizations involved in the founding of the court to convene to discuss the issue, but none accepted the invitation. Indeed, the position of the Permanent Committee of the NIK was questioned by the Main Synagogue of Amsterdam as well as by the national Central Committee. Many feared that the debate would lead to "secession within the Jewish community," as it was stated by the Permanent

Committee of the NIK.⁴⁷ After extended debates, it was decided in the meeting of the Central Committee of June 27, 1948, that the rulings of the Jewish Honor Court were binding but that its regulations needed to be revised to allow for the possibility of appeal.⁴⁸

It took another year before the revised regulations were ready. The Jewish Honor Court had already presented a final report, apparently as closure to its work. Despite the long period it had taken to draft the revised regulations, they still contained divisive elements, notably the clause that only those who had never received a *Sperre* stamp were eligible to sit on the panel that heard appeals, thereby establishing a division between the large majority of survivors who had and a small minority who had not been *gesperrt*.⁴⁹ Cohen's lawyer, Abel Herzberg, immediately wrote an angry response, in which he stated that the composition of the appeals panel was prejudicial: "This is not objective justice, but an insult to it. Maybe it is meant to be political, but it is the opposite; it is resentment. And this resentment—I would allow it for those who by their behavior during the occupation have distinguished themselves as Jews. But why those who went into hiding should now be considered fit for a judicial function, while those with a stamp are labeled as inadequate, is a mystery to me." In his response to Herzberg's attack, the lawyer Albert Büchenbacher, who had been involved in the initial and revised draft of the regulations, stated that all purge boards had been partisan in the sense that they consisted of people who rejected collaboration and that the regulations did not imply an a priori condemnation of people with a *Sperre*. Because the founding of the Jewish Honor Court had been a democratic decision of the Jewish community, Herzberg's protest, wrote Büchenbacher, was unworthy of an attorney.⁵⁰ Herzberg was unconvinced. Indeed, he was actually angered by the appeal to democratic values, because he considered the establishment of the appeals board on the basis of a distinction between "the political *kashruth* of those who had been in hiding and the *tarfuth* of the stamped" a "flagrant violation of democratic principles, thereby undermining the whole structure of the Jewish community."⁵¹

The title of Herzberg's final letter was "The Jewish Honor Court: Null and Void," and this was basically the consensus that formed as a result of all these debates. Despite Büchenbacher's appeal to democratic support, it proved impossible to find people who were both eligible and willing to participate on the appeals board. As a result, the cases of Asscher and Cohen, or for that matter of any of the others who had been convicted by the court, were not appealed. However, the reputation of the Jewish Honor Court had become tainted beyond repair. Few people in the Jewish community still supported it. This became clear in the first week of 1950, when the Permanent Committee decided that, pending the composition of a board of appeal, those who had appealed the decision of the Jewish Honor Court—there were three such people, including Cohen—would be reinstated as respectable members of the community. This meant de facto the abolishment of the Jewish Honor Court. The decision of the Permanent Committee was confirmed on January 8, 1950, by the Central Committee. The decision to "end the working of the rulings of the Jewish Honor Court," as it was awkwardly phrased, was supported by a vote of 10 to 8 among those present. Because the meeting had run late and some of the members of the Central Committee had already left, a motion to exclude Asscher and Cohen from this general amnesty was not put to a vote. In the next meeting of the Central Committee, some objected that this decision was invalid, but even Büchenbacher acknowledged that once granted, amnesty could not be retracted.[52]

The Afterlife of the Jewish Honor Court

In this way the Jewish Honor Court and the cases against Asscher and Cohen came to an end. When the general prosecutor Van Dullemen argued for the dismissal of the criminal complaint against Cohen, he concluded his argument with a call to "put this whole sad period of our history to rest!" This proved an elusive goal. In the 1960s the issue of Jewish collaboration once again became a central point of public debate in the Netherlands. Yet this time it spilled over to a more general audience as a result of two interconnected events. The first event was the publication in 1965 of Jacques Presser's study of the Holocaust in the Netherlands, *Ondergang* (translated into English as *Ashes in the Wind*). In this two-volume work Presser presented himself as the spokesperson for the Jewish victims in whose name he formulated a moral indictment against all who had been instrumental in the demise of Dutch Jewry. Although he targeted many Dutch institutions, such as the public administration and the police, he reserved his fiercest criticism for the leaders of the Jewish Council. He accused them of having sacrificed the poor "orange vendors of the Waterlooplein," quoting the very terms Laura Mazirel had used in her statement to the general prosecutor. Presser also quoted directly from the indictment formulated by Drabbe and from the verdict of the Jewish Honor Court. Invoking the voice of the deceased, he solemnly condemned collaborators: "Thou hast been the instruments of our moral enemies. Thou hast collaborated in our deportation. Thou hast survived due to these unethical activities."[53]

Presser's work reached a wide audience, selling more than 100,000 copies within a couple of weeks of publication. His moral tone chimed with a general sentiment of resistance against authorities and the appeal to critical reflection and independence from any unthinking and slavish obedience to immoral leaders. Presser's admirers approved his juxtaposition of the unscrupulous subservience of the Jewish Council with the almost picaresque resistance of Friedrich Weinreb. According to Presser, Weinreb had been victimized after the war because he reminded Dutch society and its authorities of their own moral failure. Instead, Weinreb had been a hero who had tried to save as many Jews as possible through cunning and deception. After Presser's glorification of Weinreb, the latter became a champion of part of the radical left, the living example that resistance in the face of severe oppression was actually possible. After some critics objected to the praise Weinreb garnered, he became a cause célèbre and even the object of an official government investigation, which concluded that Weinreb was a pathological liar who had been rightfully convicted.[54]

In a historical study of the Weinreb affair, the historian Ivo Schöffer concluded that the debate about Presser and Weinreb should be understood in the context of the social protest of the 1960s. Schöffer seemed to have forgotten his own role as a student in 1945, when he brought the issue of Cohen's role in the Jewish Council to the attention of the purge board of the University of Amsterdam. In the same way, Presser forgot to mention not only that he, as a teacher at the Jewish high school, had depended on the Jewish Council but also that he had debated the issue of Jewish collaboration with David Cohen in the summer of 1942, when he had acquiesced on the advice of Cohen not to protest the deportation of his pupils.[55] The converse was also the case: one of the strongest defenders of Cohen and the Jewish Council remained Abel Herzberg, who as a historian published the first full-scale chronicle of the persecution of the Dutch Jews. He acknowledged the devilish dilemma that the leaders of the Jewish Council faced, yet he praised them for resisting the position of victimhood, and even in the direst of circumstances for trying to hold onto a sense of agency—thereby echoing Cohen's defense of his role as leader of the Jewish Council.[56]

Also in later years, the issue of Jewish collaboration and the role of the Jewish Council returned to the agenda of public debate. As always, the same issues were debated: Would it have made a difference if the Jewish Council had acted differently? Were there more possibilities of resistance or evasion that a less obedient Jewish Council and the Jewish community at large should have explored? Again in 1982, long after David Cohen had died, his memoirs from the period of the Jewish Council were published in a special issue of the *Nieuw Israëlietisch Weekblad*, evoking once more the division in the Jewish community between those who read in it "from A to Z the spirit of the collaborator," who out of class prejudice had sacrificed the Jewish proletariat, and those who observed an understandable yet tragic loss of moral direction in a deeply unethical situation.[57] In all these debates the crucial point was often lost: that the fatal demise of the Jews in Europe was first and foremost the responsibility of a murderous German regime.

Notes

1. Koos Groen, *Als slachtoffers daders worden: De zaak van joodse verraadster Ans van Dijk* (Baarn, Netherlands: Ambo, 1994).
2. See Regina Grüter, *Een fantast schrijft geschiedenis: De affaires rond Friedrich Weinreb* (Amsterdam: Balans, 1997).
3. For a comparative perspective, see Klaus-Dietmar Henke and Hans Woller, eds., *Politische Säuberung in Europa: Die Abrechnung mit Faschismus und Kollaboration nach dem Zweiten Weltkrieg* (Munich: Deutscher Taschenbuch Verlag, 1991); and István Deák, Jan T. Gross, and Tony Judt, eds., *The Politics of Retribution in Europe: World War II and Its Aftermath* (Princeton, NJ: Princeton University Press, 2000).
4. The remainder of this section is based on Ido de Haan, "Failures and Mistakes: Images of Collaboration in Postwar Dutch Society," in Roni Stauber, ed., *Collaboration with the Nazis: Public Discourse After the Holocaust* (London: Routledge, 2010), 71–90. See also Peter Romijn, *Snel, streng en rechtvaardig: Politiek beleid inzake de bestraffing en reclassering van 'foute' Nederlanders, 1945–1955* (Houten, Netherlands: De Haan, 1989).
5. Nanno K. C. A. in 't Veld, *De ereraden voor de kunst en de zuivering van de kunstenaars* (The Hague: SDU, 1981); Nanno K. C. A. in 't Veld, *De zuivering van artsen en advocaten* (The Hague: SDU, 1983); Jan Brauer and Jan Driever, *Perszuivering: De Nederlandse Pers 1944–1951* (Weesp, Netherlands: Fibula van Dishoeck, 1984); Joggli Meihuizen, *Noodzakelijk kwaad: De bestraffing van economische collaboratie in Nederland na de Tweede Wereldoorlog* (Amsterdam: Boom, 2003).
6. See the contributions to Hans C. H. Blom, Renate G. Fuks-Mansfeld, and Ivo Schöffer, eds., *The History of the Jews in the Netherlands* (Oxford, UK: Littman Library of Jewish Civilization, 2002).
7. See Bart Wallet, *Nieuwe Nederlanders: De integratie van de joden in Nederland (1814–1851)* (Amsterdam: Bert Bakker, 2007).
8. See Hans Blom and Joel J. Cahen, "Jewish Netherlanders, Netherlands Jews, and Jews in the Netherlands, 1870–1940," in Blom et al., eds., *History of the Jews in the Netherlands*, 230–95.
9. Ido de Haan, "Dutch-Jewish Political Representation Before and After the Holocaust," *Perush: An Online Journal of Jewish Scholarship and Interpretation* 1 (2009), http://perush.cjs.ucla.edu/index.php/volume-1-2009-working-papers-series-jewish-politics-and-political-behavior-editors-introduction/ido-de-haan-dutch-jewish-political-representation-before-and-after-the-holocaust (accessed July 26, 2014).

10. Dan Michman, "The Committee for Jewish Refugees in Holland, 1933–1940," *Yad Vashem Studies* 14 (1981): 205–32; Ido de Haan, "The Netherlands and the November-pogrom," *Jahrbuch für Antisemitismusforschung* 8 (1999): 155–76; Ido de Haan, "Vivre sur le seuil: Le camp de Westerbork dans l'histoire et la mémoire des Pays-Bas," *Revue d'histoire de la Shoah* 181 (July–December 2004): 37–59.

11. The literature on the Jewish Council in the Netherlands is generally rather partisan. Very critical is Hans Knoop, *De Joodsche Raad: Het drama van Abraham Asscher en David Cohen* (Amsterdam: Elsevier, 1983). Equally critical is Joseph Michman, "The Controversy Surrounding the Jewish Council of Amsterdam: From Its Inception to the Present Day," in Michael Marrus, ed., *The Nazi Holocaust: Historical Articles on the Destruction of European Jews* (Westport, CT: Greenwood, 1989), 6/2: 821–43. A comparative perspective is offered by Dan Michman, "De oprichting van de 'Joodsche Raad voor Amsterdam' vanuit een vergelijkend perspectief," in David Barnouw, ed., *Oorlogsdocumentatie '40–'45: Derde jaarboek van het Rijksinstituut voor Oorlogsdocumentatie* (Zutphen, Netherlands: Walburg Pers, 1992), 75–100; see also the more wide-ranging comparative study of Dan Michman, "'Judenräte' und 'Judenvereinigungen' unter nationalsozialistischer Herrschaft: Aufbau und Anwendung eines verwaltungsmässigen Konzepts," *Zeitschrift für Geschichtswissenschaft* 46.4 (1998): 293–304. A controversial contextualization of the Jewish Council in the political context of the strike of February 1941 is Friso Roest and Jos Scheren, *Oorlog in de stad: Amsterdam 1939–1941* (Amsterdam: Van Gennep, 1998); an overview of the debate can be found in Hans C. H. Blom, "In de ban van de Joodse Raad," *Bijdragen en Mededelingen betreffende de Geschiedenis der Nederlanden* 116 (2001): 198–203.

12. For the most accurate quantitative account, see Pim Griffioen and Ron Zeller, *Jodenvervolging in Nederland, Frankrijk en België, 1940–1945: Overeenkomsten, verschillen, oorzaken* (Amsterdam: Uitgeverij Boom, 2011).

13. See Chaya Brasz, *Removing the Yellow Badge: The Struggle for a Jewish Community in the Postwar Netherlands, 1944–1955* (Jerusalem: Hebrew University Press, 1995).

14. Chaya Brasz, "After the Second World War: From 'Jewish Church' to Cultural Minority," in Blom et al., eds., *History of the Jews in the Netherlands*, 336–91; Conny Kristel, "De moeizame terugkeer: De repatriëring van de Nederlandse overlevenden uit de Duitse concentratiekampen," in David Barnouw, ed., *Oorlogsdocumentatie '40–'45*, 77–100.

15. J. Sanders, "Opbouw en continuïteit na 1945," in Joseph Michman, Hartog Beem, and Dan Michman, eds., *Pinkas: Geschiedenis van de joodse gemeenschap in Nederland* (Ede/Antwerpen/Amsterdam: Kluwer/NIK/JHM, 1992), 228–68; Mireille Berman, "Herstel en verlies: De reconstructie van het Nederlands Israëlietisch Kerkgenootschap," Doctoral thesis, University of Amsterdam, 1995.

16. Isaac Lipschits, *Tsedaka: Een halve eeuw Joods Maatschappelijk Werk in Nederland* (Zutphen, Netherlands: Waanders, 1997).

17. Evelien Gans, *De kleine verschillen die het leven uitmaken: Een historische studie naar joodse sociaal-democraten en socialistisch-zionisten in Nederland* (Amsterdam: Vassallucci, 1999), 608.

18. Quoted in Nanno C. K. A. In't Veld, *De Joodse Ereraad* (The Hague: SDU, 1989), 38–39.
19. Here I follow Johannes Houwink ten Cate, "De justitie en de Joodse Raad," in Ed Jonker and Maarten van Rossem, eds., *Geschiedenis en Cultuur: Achttien opstellen* (The Hague: SDU, 1990), 151.
20. Milikowski appears to have argued his case on the basis of an early defensive account of the Jewish Council by its former member K. P. L. Berkley, *Overzicht van het ontstaan, de werkzaamheden en het streven van de Joodsche Raad van Amsterdam* (Amsterdam: Publiciteits- en Uitgeversbedrijf Plastica, 1945).
21. Lou de Jong, *Het Koninkrijk der Nederlanden in de Tweede Wereldoorlog*, vol. 8, *Gevangenen en gedeporteerden* (The Hague: SDU, 1978), 783; Bernard Wasserstein, *Gertrude van Tijn en het lot van de Nederlandse Joden* (Amsterdam: Nieuw Amsterdam, 2013); Gertrude van Tijn-Cohen, "Bijdrage tot de geschiedenis der Joden in Nederland van 10 mei 1940 tot juni 1944," Netherland Institute of War Documentation, Amsterdam (hereafter NIOD), Doc II-1720B; Sam de Wolff, *Geschiedenis der Joden in Nederland: Laatste bedrijf* (Amsterdam: De Arbeiderspers, 1946).
22. All quotations are from the regulations of the Jewish Honor Court, as published in *Nieuw Israëlietisch Weekblad* (February 15, 1946).
23. "Verslag van de werkzaamheden van de Joodse Ereraad," *Nieuw Israëlietisch Weekblad* (May 21, 1949).
24. See In 't Veld, *De Joodse Ereraad*, 45–46.
25. See In 't Veld, *De Joodse Ereraad*, 40–43.
26. There is some confusion about the numbers. In the final report of the Jewish Honor Court of May 21, 1949, nineteen cases (excluding the board and members of the Jewish Council) are mentioned, but on the basis of research of the fragmented archive of the Jewish Honor Court, In 't Veld finds twenty-one cases, some of which lack any documentation. Because In 't Veld does not give a full list of names, I follow the numbers of the final report. Moreover, In 't Veld gives only initials of the accused, even when their names were published in the *Nieuw Israëlietisch Weekblad*. I give full names when their names have already been mentioned publicly.
27. "Publicatie Joodse Ereraad," *Nieuw Israëlietisch Weekblad* (February 14, 1947). See also Gans, *De kleine verschillen*, 611–14.
28. "Publicatie Joodse Ereraad," *Nieuw Israëlietisch Weekblad* (June 4, 1948).
29. "Bekendmaking van de Joodse Ereraad," *Nieuw Israëlietisch Weekblad* (December 20, 1946).
30. The five regular members called before the Jewish Honor Court were the notary Arnold van den Bergh (1886–1950), the lawyer (and defense lawyer of David Cohen) Albert Berend Gomperts (1883–1963), the Jewish council director of finance Abraham Krouwer (1883–?), the lawyer Siegfried Jacob van Lier (1877–1976), and the diamond trader Abraham Soep (1982–1953).
31. "Publicatie Joodse Ereraad," *Nieuw Israëlietisch Weekblad* (May 21, 1948).
32. "Publicatie Joodse Ereraad" (May 21, 1948).

33. "Nederl. Zionisten Bond," *Nieuw Israëlietisch Weekblad* (July 2, 1948). At the time, Weizmann was in fact chairman of the provisional state council, but this was a subtlety that the NZB or the *Nieuw Israëlietisch Weekblad* apparently overlooked.

34. See Erik Somers, "David Cohen: Een biografische schets," in Erik Somers, ed., *Voorzitter van de Joodse Raad: De herinneringen van David Cohen* (Zutphen, Netherlands: Walburg Pers, 2010), 11–24; Piet Schrijvers, *Rome, Athene, Jerusalem: Leven en werk van prof. dr. David Cohen* (Groningen, Netherlands: Historische Uitgeveij, 2000); and Blom and Cahen, "Jewish Netherlanders."

35. Note of the chair of the honor court, M. Bosboom, from September 24, 1946; quoted in In 't Veld, *De Joodse Ereraad*, 57.

36. Somers, "David Cohen," 18.

37. For Cohen's defense, see the typescript "Pro domo," written at the end of 1946 and published in Schrijvers, *Rome, Athene, Jerusalem*, 237–64; and Cohen's memories, recorded in 1956 at the request of the director of the Dutch Institute for War Documentation, Lou de Jong, in David Cohen, "Herinneringen van prof. D. Cohen," in Somers, ed., *Voorzitter van de Joodse Raad*, 57–213.

38. In 't Veld, *De Joodse Ereraad*, 57–66.

39. "Uitspraak van de Joodse Ereraad," *Nieuw Israëlietisch Weekblad* (December 26, 1947).

40. See Houwink ten Cate, "De justitie en de Joodse Raad"; Arie Kuiper, *Een wijze ging voorbij: Het leven van Abel J. Herzberg* (Amsterdam: Querido, 1997), 313–40; and In 't Veld, *De Joodse Ereraad*, 60–62.

41. Kuiper, *Een wijze ging voorbij*, 316–17.

42. Houwink ten Cate, "De justitie en de Joodse Raad," 158.

43. Houwink ten Cate, "De justitie en de Joodse Raad," 162; for the changing attitudes toward the purge, see De Haan, "Failures and Mistakes."

44. "De Joodse Ereraad," *Nieuw Israëlietisch Weekblad* (January 2, 1948).

45. *Nederlandsch Juristenblad* (November 29, 1947): 690; see In 't Veld, *De Joodse Ereraad*, 60–61.

46. "Ereraad," *Nieuw Israëlietisch Weekblad* (January 9, 1948).

47. In 't Veld, *De Joodse Ereraad*, 71.

48. "Ereraad," *Nieuw Israëlietisch Weekblad* (July 2, 1948).

49. "Wijziging van het reglement van de Joodse Ereraad: Instelling van een beroepsraad," *Nieuw Israëlietisch Weekblad* (June 24, 1949).

50. "Ingezonden: De Joodse Ereraad ter behartiging" and "Naschrift," *Nieuw Israëlietisch Weekblad* (July 22, 1949).

51. "Ingezonden: De Joodse Ereraad nul en nietig," *Nieuw Israëlietisch Weekblad* (July 29, 1949).

52. "Rondvraag," *Nieuw Israëlietisch Weekblad* (January 8, 1950). It was a decision "een einde te maken aan de werking van de uitspraken van de Joodse Ereraad"; "Ereraad," *Nieuw Israëlietisch Weekblad* (February 10, 1950).

53. Jacques Presser, *Ondergang: De vervolging en verdelging van het Nederlandse jodendom 1940–1945* (The Hague: SDU 1985 [1965]), 514.
54. See Grüter, *Een fantast schrijft geschiedenis*.
55. Ivo Schöffer, "Weinreb, een affaire van lange duur," *Tijdschrift voor geschiedenis* 95 (1982): 196–224; see also Erik Somers, "Over de 'Herinneringen' van David Cohen," in Somers, ed., *Voorzitter van de Joodse Raad*, 41–49, esp. 47; and Dienke Hondius, *Absent: Herinneringen aan het Joods Lyceum Amsterdam, 1941–1943* (Amsterdam: Bert Bakker, 2001).
56. Abel J. Herzberg, *Kroniek der Jodenvervolging, 1940–1945* (Amsterdam: Querido, 1985 [1950]); for the treatment of the Jewish Council in the work of the major historians of the Holocaust in the Netherlands, see Conny Kristel, *Geschiedschrijving als opdracht: Abel Herzberg, Jacques Presser and Lou de Jong over de jodenvervolging* (Amsterdam: Meulenhoff, 1998), 135–74.
57. Erik Somers, "Publicatie in het NIW in 1982 en reacties," in Somers, ed., *Voorzitter van de Joodse Raad*, 51–56.

5

Jurys d'honneur

The Stakes and Limits of Purges Among Jews in France After Liberation

SIMON PEREGO

Building on Peter Novick's 1968 pioneering study *The Resistance Versus Vichy: The Purge of Collaborators in Liberated France*, in 1992 Henry Rousso drew up an initial historical balance of the purges that followed World War II in France and noted different areas in which he believed further research was essential.[1] A decade later a major collection edited by Marc Olivier Baruch provided evidence of the growing dynamism of studies devoted to various facets of this phenomenon.[2] Since the appearance of that volume in 2003, the state of knowledge has expanded even further, as shown by the recent publication of a number of overviews and, more broadly, the lively interest in the history of the "aftermath of the war"—*la sortie de guerre*—and in matters of "transitional justice."[3] But despite this wealth of publications, one sector has hardly attracted the attention of historians of postwar purges in France: the Jews, who, after enduring the brutal anti-Semitic persecutions under the German occupation and the Vichy regime, were not oblivious to the stakes that the purges posed for post-liberation French society as a whole. On the contrary, as several historians who specialize in Jewish history, such as Michel Laffitte and Anne Grynberg, have already demonstrated, whereas on the national scale there was a "settling of scores—between those who had betrayed the nation and those whose national loyalty and combativeness had never faltered,"[4] the confrontation in the Jewish community pitted those considered to have behaved with dignity and altruism during the war against those deemed to have acted dishonorably and to have caused direct or indirect harm to their co-religionists.

Historians of purges have been silent about the specifically Jewish dimension of this phenomenon in France for several reasons. First, it seems logical that they began by studying the measures taken against political circles that were directly involved in collaboration before looking at the wider repercussions of these purges in French society. Second, the relative marginality of purges in the French Jewish community certainly deterred those who specialized in postwar retribution from studying it with regard to French Jews. In fact, they may have been quite unaware of the phenomenon, much as the simplistic image of the postwar Jewish community as a collective of victims worked against a clearer perception of the internal stakes of power and legitimacy at work there. Third, the lack of a comprehensive study of the phenomenon, despite the important contributions made by the previously mentioned historians, is linked to the fact that Jewish history in post-liberation France remains a work in progress. Although certainly the state of our knowledge has expanded considerably over the past decades,[5] many pieces of the reconstruction of Jewish life in France after World War II have yet to be studied in detail. Finally, it seems likely that moral qualms also fed the reticence to call up an undoubtedly sad episode that was part of the history of a bruised and battered group.[6] This reticence seemed especially understandable given that perverse and manipulating elements in French public discourse about the war years, such as the Holocaust denier Robert Faurisson, did not hesitate to exploit this delicate subject for purely ideological ends.[7]

Tackling this subject will lead us to the intersection of two bodies of history that so far have not sufficiently come together: studies of the liberation and purges in France and studies of the revival of Jewish life in the country after the occupation. Although, as a political phenomenon, the purges in France were not limited to the postwar period, the process, which began in the summer of 1944, was the first time that the purges involved both the Jews and French society at large, albeit with different levels of intensity. So when we analyze the full complexity of the internal purges in the Jewish community, we must inscribe them in the general context of the purges in French society and try to understand the roles they may have played in the fabric and reconstruction of the group in question.

To do this, I look first at the strong inclination among French Jews to purge alleged Jewish collaborators with the Nazis and the Vichy regime from their midst. Next, I consider the models and forms of the internal purges. Finally, I evaluate the limits that marked Jewish initiatives to expel those considered to have been guilty of misconduct under the occupation. This allows us to study an important and yet underestimated aspect of the reconstruction of the Jewish community in the specific context of the immediate aftermath of the war in France.

A Strong Desire to Purge the Community
A SOCIETY BEING PURGED

In the immediate aftermath of the war, the Jews of France had to deal with a number of challenges.[8] On the individual level most of them had to find a place to live and resume their professional careers. Many endeavored to attach a meaning to the persecutions they had experienced, but they also, and above all, had to deal with the loss of loved ones. It would have been rare after the war to meet Jewish families in France that did not have relatives who were deported and murdered or who perished in other circumstances.[9] On the collective scale it was necessary to relaunch organizational Jewish life and to handle exceptional tasks: caring for thousands of orphans, assisting the few deportees who had returned from the camps, supporting a population that had largely been broken, and recovering stolen property. The occupation nevertheless left the Jews of France with still another set of aftereffects, perhaps less immediately obvious: the intense feeling harbored by many of a certain distrust or even strong resentment directed against Jewish organizations or individuals whose choices under the occupation were matters of fierce controversy, such as the members of the Union générale des israélites de France (the General Union of Israelites of France; UGIF).[10]

In the broader context the Jews had no choice but to deal with their own ranks. At liberation, French society, ravaged by the defeat of 1940 and four years of state collaboration with Nazi Germany, rang with calls to purify the social body, to stigmatize, exclude, and punish the collaborators. These calls were manifested in various ways, with different cadences and levels of intensity that were a function of the events in question but also of the time and place. Right before, during, and immediately after the liberation of French territory, a series of violent reprisals targeted individuals identified as collaborators or members of the Vichy militia.[11] In this extrajudicial purge, between 8,000 and 9,000 people were executed and about 20,000 women who were accused of, among other things, "horizontal collaboration," had their hair shorn by their compatriots. To channel this violence, the new public authorities swiftly instituted judicial purges, overseen by various courts, which investigated the cases of 350,000 French nationals.[12] If one adds to this number individuals targeted by economic, administrative, and professional purges, we see that the purges in France, even if "inconsistent in time and space, sometimes disjointed," and "in many regards incomplete,"[13] were nevertheless a "massive social phenomenon"[14] that its supporters intended to contribute to the purification of French society, the moral repair of the nation, and the regeneration of the French Republic.

RESENTMENT AND RECOGNITION AMONG THE JEWS

On the Jewish side the need for a purge of the community was felt while the persecution was still under way, running parallel to the threats voiced—and sometimes implemented—by the Résistance against Vichy supporters and collaborators. Under the occupation the underground publications of the Jewish communist resistance repeatedly denounced the heads of the UGIF,[15] considered to be collaborators and dismissed as "little brown Jews" (*broyne yidelekh* in Yiddish). In February 1943 an article in the Jewish communist underground organ *Notre Voix* accused the UGIF of having handed over 100 Jewish children to the Gestapo and warned: "Their crime will be punished without mercy."[16] In June of the same year the threats against the organization were repeated: "The traitors have been unmasked. Their punishment is being prepared."[17] When liberation came, it was in the same spirit that a number of Jewish groups, often under communist influence but not necessarily, called for an internal purge of the Jewish community in order to separate the wheat from the chaff, reconstruct the group on healthy foundations, and launch in Jewish circles the same process of purification that was then beginning to take root in French society as a whole. For example, a text from September 24, 1944, drawn up by a group of Jewish resistance fighters, demanded that "a major purge be effected among the Jews, with the assistance of the local authorities: That is, the Jews should police their ranks with regard to those who did not do their duty, assemble files about the guilty, and forward them to the competent authorities."[18]

Around the same time, the act of incorporation of the Action and Defense Committee of the Jewish Youth of the Alpes-Maritimes (Comité d'action et de défense de la jeunesse juive des Alpes-Maritimes)[19] included the desire "to participate in the struggle for the liberation of France and the final crushing of all the traitors" and accordingly established "a Purge Department to uncover young Jews who collaborated with the enemy in one way or another and to assist the adults' Purge Commission."[20] Not only were Jews accused of collaboration with the persecutors at risk of being handed over to the authorities by their own co-religionists, but they also faced exclusion from Jewish life: Article 6 of the 1945 bylaws of the Organization of Polish Jews in France (Organisation des Juifs polonais en France) stipulated that "no person may be a member of the association who compromised his honor by collaborating with the Hitlerites or their agents."[21]

At the same time, but without going so far as to speak of purges, the Jewish street accused some community figures not of "collaboration" but rather of a failure to demonstrate sufficient solidarity. As renowned a figure as Isaïe Schwartz, chief rabbi of France, was criticized by some members of the Consistoire central for having gone into hiding in January 1944 and not reappearing in public until after the liberation.[22] As for his deputy, Rabbi Jacob Kaplan, who had not done anything unworthy during the occupation in Vichy and Lyons, indeed far from it, he was reproached by the congregation of the Paris synagogue where he had served until 1940 for not returning to Paris after the German invasion to face the persecution alongside them.[23]

In addition to these ad hominem attacks, the Jewish press hosted more general controversies about the manner in which some Jews reacted to the persecutions. The Yiddish press raised the issue of the culpability of the Jewish police in the ghettos of Poland,[24] and Robert Sommer, in the Jewish weekly *Vendredi Soir*, denounced the choices made by certain "French Israelites" during the occupation, who had fled to America or Switzerland or had succumbed to the lure of conversion to Christianity.[25] At the same time as and certainly in association with these debates and calls for a purge, various Jewish figures publicized accounts of their service to the Jewish community during the years of persecution. Although the dominant themes in the narratives of the wartime Jewish experience published in the immediate postwar years in France were the camps and the Warsaw Ghetto Uprising, quite a few books and articles focused on how individual Jews distinguished themselves on French soil by working on behalf of their own people and how the Jewish organizations also had endeavored to assist the persecuted.[26] Along with these publications, public commemorative ceremonies saluted the memory of the Jewish activists who died serving their community and built up the image of heroic and exemplary community figures.

Thus, just as it haunted French society as a whole, the question of who did what during the occupation was part of the agenda of French Jewry in the years that followed the liberation, whether as a basis for distributing honors or for stigmatizing ignoble behavior. And in the latter category, which is the subject of the present chapter, there was more than one answer.

Models and Forms of the Purge in the Community
RECOURSE TO THE JUDICIAL AUTHORITIES

One of these answers is to be found in individual recourse to the French judicial authorities, a frequent practice in postwar France. This procedure could in fact be considered a specific mode of the intracommunity purges, in that those Jews suspected of the most serious acts—notably actual bloodshed—were usually denounced to the public prosecutor by other Jews who saw themselves as their victims and who may have looked for a way to purify their community by expelling the individuals most compromised by collaboration with the persecutors.

Several Jews were indeed tried by French courts for their actions in occupied France. Dezso Leibovits was tried by the court in the Alpes-Maritimes in 1945–1946 for having served in the Sicherheitsdienst (the intelligence agency of the SS) under a false identity in 1944.[27] Ely Shtern was tried in Marseilles in 1946 for having denounced Jews to the Gestapo.[28] The Austrian Jew Oskar Reich was brought before the Paris military tribunal in 1949. As the chief of the camp police in Drancy, Reich had directed the squad that was responsible for arresting Jews who were living under false identities or living underground and bringing them to the camp. Deported to Auschwitz with the last convoy in August 1944, he was originally presumed dead, only to be discovered alive and brought back to France in 1946, as the Jewish press reported with evident satisfaction.[29] After his trial along with two junior SS officers that began on February 8, 1949, he was sentenced to death and shot.[30] According to the Jewish Telegraphic Agency, another inmate of Drancy named Silvain Baur was also sentenced to death by a special court in Paris on April 26, 1945, for having helped the Gestapo and the Vichy militia apprehend and rob Jews.[31] But the most celebrated judicial affair involving a Jew indicted for his behavior under the occupation was without a doubt that of the extremely controversial metal-dealer Joseph Joinovici, who was tried in Paris in July 1949 for his connections with the German authorities, although he, unlike the other individuals just mentioned, was not charged with personal involvement in the anti-Jewish persecutions.

Other Jews were accused of brutality and violence when they served as kapos in the labor, concentration, and death camps in German-occupied Eastern Europe. Pinkus Chmielnicki, arrested in 1945, was convicted in 1950 of theft, assault, and the murder of prisoners under his authority in Auschwitz-Birkenau and sentenced to death.[32] In Paris in 1948 the police arrested Reuven Fayner, suspected of having served as a kapo in the Blechhammer camp.[33] A number of individuals accused of similar crimes were not convicted. Alter Fogel, a block supervisor (*Blockältester*) in the Jaworzno camp, was tried in November 1948 but acquitted.[34] Eliezer Gruenbaum, a communist activist known in France under the pseudonym of Leon Berger, who had been a kapo in Birkenau, managed to escape being tried.[35]

As noted previously, although these cases were tried by French courts, the proceedings were initiated by Jews who denounced the putative criminals, sometimes handed them over to the police, filed complaints, and testified at their trials. They did so because they recognized the French courts as the competent authority, capable of ruling on the extremely serious complaints they had against some of their co-religionists. Reuven Fayner was arrested on the complaint of two former fellow prisoners; the report of his arrest in the communist daily *Naye Prese* invited potential witnesses to contact the Association of Former Jewish Deportees (Association des anciens déportés juifs).[36] Similarly, it was a number of Jewish survivors who identified Pinkus Chmielnicki in June 1945; the publication of his photograph in the Jewish press, accompanied by an urgent appeal for witnesses to come forward,[37] helped the prosecution gather thirty-five affidavits and locate four Jewish survivors who later testified at the trial.[38] Alter Fogel and Eliezer Gruenbaum were also indicted in the wake of complaints filed by former fellow prisoners.[39]

THE DECISION TO STAY IN THE COMMUNITY

Parallel to these trials—into whose details I will not go—a number of actors in the French Jewish community took it upon themselves to evaluate the conduct of other Jews under the occupation in the context of various proceedings that had no official status whatsoever. These proceedings were for the most part conducted by committees that various Jewish bodies created specifically for this purpose, with various names: jury of honor (*jury d'honneur*), honor tribunal (*tribunal de l'honneur*), purge commission (*commission d'épuration*), purge committee (*comité d'épuration*), commission of inquiry (*commission d'enquête*). They addressed difficult cases in which it was thought that, although the individuals implicated might have acted dishonorably, the gravity of their offense did not justify their automatic referral to the legal authorities. I begin by reviewing the five cases that are at the core of the present chapter,[40] which is devoted, it must be emphasized, only to the most formal methods of the intracommunity purge.[41]

The first case concerns the initiatives taken by the Committee for the Unity and Defense of the Jews of France (Comité d'unité et de défense des Juifs de

France; CUDJF)⁴² against the UGIF. During the uprising of Paris, which began on August 19, 1944, members of this resistance organization seized the offices of the UGIF, arrested its president, Georges Edinger, and set up a purge commission that gave itself the task of screening the activities of the employees of the UGIF by means of a questionnaire.⁴³

In the second case (which also concerns the UGIF and has become a fairly well-known affair studied by Jacques Fredj, Michel Laffitte, and Anne Grynberg) five officials of the UGIF were investigated. In the autumn of 1944 the Representative Council of Israelites of France (Conseil représentatif des israélites de France; CRIF)⁴⁴ created a jury of honor to investigate their culpability in the arrest by the Germans, on July 25, 1944, of Jewish children who had been living in Neuilly in one of the organization's facilities. Although this jury concluded that mistakes had indeed been made, the president of CRIF, Léon Meiss,⁴⁵ launched a protracted follow-up inquiry and in January 1947 was able to obtain a reversal of the verdict, exculpating those charged and keeping the inquiry from being expanded to examine the conduct of the UGIF in general.⁴⁶

A member of the Consistoire central was the subject of the third case. Between 1944 and 1947 the Consistoire central, also under the direction of Léon Meiss, conducted an internal investigation of Raymond Ducas, whose escape from the Drancy camp in July 1943 and flight to Switzerland ostensibly led to the reprisal arrest of his cousin by marriage, André Baur, then the vice-president of the UGIF. Baur was deported several months later to Auschwitz, where he was murdered along with his wife and four children.⁴⁷ An initial inquiry, launched by the standing committee of the Consistoire in March 1945, concluded in July of that year that Ducas was not culpable in the matter. But the affair resurfaced in January 1946, after Ducas was reelected to his position as representative of the community of Épinal, a reelection contested by relatives of the deportees. At their insistence a new commission was convened. Without formally recognizing Ducas's guilt, the commission nevertheless considered it appropriate that he not remain a member of the Consistoire. A compromise was finally reached, with some difficulty. On January 19, 1947, the Consistoire confirmed the first verdict, which exonerated Ducas, in exchange for his resignation.

The fourth case involves a man named Sztern.⁴⁸ In 1946 the central office of the Union of Jewish Intellectuals of France (Union des intellectuels juifs de France), in cooperation with leading members of the Federation of Jewish Organizations of France (Fédération des sociétés juives de France; FSJF),⁴⁹ convened a jury to examine the case of its secretary general Sztern, who was charged for having worked for the UGIF newsletter under the occupation. He was ultimately acquitted.

Finally, the last case involves Élie Krouker. In 1947 and again in 1950, two juries returned verdicts in the cases brought against Krouker,[50] who was accused by Jules Jacoubovitch[51] of having implemented German directives with excessive zeal when he headed the Coordinating Committee of Jewish Welfare Organizations (Comité de coordination des oeuvres juives de bienfaisance).[52] The first jury ruled that Krouker had acted improperly; the second jury absolved him of guilt.[53]

The recourse to such tribunals, appointed to determine whether a certain person had acted dishonorably, was not exclusive to the Jews, as shown by various forms of proceedings instituted in France immediately after the war, all of which focused on questions of honor and its corollary, dishonor. The immediate postwar period in France was effectively traversed by these twin ideas. They were essential for the former Résistance fighters, who wanted to "clean up the notion of honor," which had been instrumentalized by the Vichy regime, in order to "disgrace the Vichyites and their henchmen" and, more generally, to "elevate honor to the first rank of the reconstituted republican public order."[54] These were the objectives that motivated the invention of the concept of national unworthiness (*indignité nationale*), a new crime punishable by the equally novel penalty of deprivation of civil rights (*dégradation nationale*), and the convening of a jury of honor—created by an ordinance of the Provisional Government of the French Republic, dated April 6, 1945—to pronounce on the disqualification of the parliamentarians who had voted to grant full powers to Marshal Philippe Pétain on July 10, 1940.[55] The question of dishonorable conduct was also addressed independently by various civil society actors, as attested, for example, by the policy followed by the National Federation of Prisoners of War (Fédération nationale des prisonniers de guerre).[56] Representing a group that was associated with the military defeat of 1940 and subsequently isolated from the developments in occupied France and whose patriotism was called into question after liberation, this organization wanted to demonstrate "that although some prisoners acted dishonorably, it was only in individual and isolated cases," in the hope that "the self-purification and exclusion of the black sheep from their ranks [would permit] the former prisoners to hold their heads high."[57] In order to do so, in 1946 the National Federation of Prisoners of War established juries of honor to judge the behavior of its members in the POW camps.

The influence of this non-Jewish environment can be detected at two levels in the intracommunity proceedings. The first level was implicit, in that the instigators never openly based their approach or methods on Jewish tradition. For all practical purposes, these internal tribunals had nothing in common with the traditional institution of the *beit din* (Jewish rabbinic court); in their deliberations and verdicts, the jurors never made any clear reference to the sanction of excommunication used by traditional Judaism to eject from the community an individual found to have violated the religious precepts or rabbinic rulings. On the other hand, while having no legal basis, the internal Jewish tribunals made explicit use of French judicial instruments and methods, as shown by the concern of André Baur's brother in the Ducas case that the decisions taken rested on "serious foundations, conforming to the most elementary rules of the law."[58] The terminology used provided unambiguous confirmation of this constant concern with conformity to official procedures: "inquest," "juror," "deposition," "witness," "letters rogatory," "further investigation," "preliminary investigation," "oral argument," "confrontation of witnesses," "sentence," "grounds" (of a ruling), "preamble," "purview" (of a statute), "verdict," "discharge for lack of evidence," "force of res judicata"—all technical terms and formulas that reveal the influence of the judicial model, which also left its mark on the actual conduct of these proceedings, whose origins we must now determine.

FROM INVESTIGATION TO VERDICT

Some of the intracommunity investigations were launched at the initiative of Jewish organizations that were anxious to examine the case of one or more of their own members, as we have seen with the National Federation of Prisoners of War.¹ Thus the Consistoire central took it upon itself to investigate the charges levied against Raymond Ducas, who represented the Jewish community of Épinal in this body. Other organizations deemed themselves authorized to pursue nonmembers. The CUDJF undertook to purge the employees of the UGIF, just as CRIF, starting in October 1944, investigated the responsibility of five former UGIF officials in the deportation of the Neuilly children. When a Jewish organization took up a case, it was frequently responding to the demands of individuals who felt that they were victims; the family of André Baur, in particular, exerted strong pressure on the Consistoire to hold a first and then a second inquiry into Raymond Ducas's escape and flight. Sometimes, though, the initiative for an inquiry came from the person incriminated. Implicated by his duties at the UGIF, the secretary general of the Union of Jewish Intellectuals of France, Mr. Sztern, asked to be allowed to defend himself before a tribunal of honor; similarly, Élie Krouker responded to Jules Jacoubovitch's public attack on him in a series of articles in the Yiddish press[59] by calling for the convening of a jury to clear his name. The diversity of those who instigated the convening of tribunals to clear themselves provides an initial indicator of the great variety of purges in the community.

Once an organization had taken up a case, the next and crucial step was to decide who would sit on the jury convened to investigate the matter and issue a ruling. The profile of the individuals selected to carry out this delicate task satisfied various criteria. To start with, all of them, whatever the case, were men, most of them middle-aged, because in those years leadership positions were not open to women, whose community activity was more or less restricted to women's organizations such as the Women's International Zionist Organization. What is more, they were all well-known figures on the Jewish street. A good example is provided by the jury assembled for the Sztern case, which included, in addition to the president and members of the Central Committee of the Union of Jewish Intellectuals of France, other prominent individuals, such as the president of ORT, Abraham Alpérine; the director of the Jewish National Fund in France, Joseph Fisher; and the president and secretary general of the FSJF, Marc Jarblum and Claude Kelman.[60] The jurors' moral caliber was also guaranteed by the respectable professions they practiced and the prestigious citations they had received during World War I and especially World War II.

These criteria were sometimes supplemented by another criterion of a professional nature: Some members were chosen for their legal qualifications, such as the magistrate Léon Lyon-Caen, who presided over the second commission that investigated Raymond Ducas; Raymond Lindon, who was a member of the CRIF jury in the UGIF case and the prosecutor in a number of sensational purge trials; and Lucien Frank, a lawyer for the civil tribunal of the Seine and the foreman of this same CRIF jury. Note also that efforts were sometimes made to ensure that juries represented the diversity of the French Jewish community as a way to increase their legitimacy and ward off possible charges of partiality. For example, the CRIF jury included representatives of the main groups that constituted CRIF's council: Marc Jarblum, one of the leading spokesmen of the Zionist immigrants; Haim Slovès, a lawyer and writer who was active among the communist immigrants; André Weil, a member of the Consistoire central; and Vidal Modiano, a leader of the Sephardic immigrants from the former Ottoman Empire.

The motives of those who accepted an appointment to serve on a jury of honor, for which they were not paid,[61] seem to have been many. In addition to the sincere desire to take on a burden that was certainly difficult but that was considered essential for the reconstruction of the Jewish community, there was also most likely a desire to solidify one's legitimacy in the community, inasmuch as membership on a tribunal deemed competent to judge the behavior of others under the occupation was implicit testimony that one was considered above all suspicion himself.

The investigations were conducted by the jurors as a group. Even if the results were sometimes fiercely debated, there were no hasty or perfunctory proceedings among the cases I studied. The file produced during the preliminary investigation consisted of written documents and newspaper articles but mainly of depositions, elicited directly by the jurors or submitted in writing. In practice, personal testimonies were the most important element for the investigators. The CRIF jury of honor heard twelve witnesses in November and December 1944. The jurors also took pains to authenticate the items in the file they assembled: Testimony was sometimes taken under oath, and documents written in a foreign language were translated into French by certified translators. What is more, the accused were given ample opportunity to defend themselves. They were called to testify in person as a matter of course—no proceeding was conducted in absentia—and often more than once. The two people most directly targeted by the CRIF inquiry, Georges Edinger and Kurt Schendel, testified no fewer than three times between December 1944 and November 1946. The defendants could also submit legal briefs and call their own witnesses. For example, Raymond Ducas submitted various affidavits to support his position.[62] Nor was legal counsel unknown in these cases. Although most of those charged defended themselves, Élie Krouker was accompanied by an attorney named Rosenzweig-Gajac at his second trial.

After completing its inquiry, the jury voted on its verdict. A majority was deemed sufficient, although unanimity was often sought to give the maximum weight to the decision. The penalties considered or meted out in these different cases varied. One possibility was to forward the file to the competent French authorities, thereby establishing a link between the community-based purges and the "official" purges. CRIF conducted fierce debates about this option. Although it was supported by the communist delegate, there was no unanimity and ultimately it was not implemented in the cases studied here.[63]

Less drastic than referring the matter to the judicial authorities was the person's expulsion from Jewish public life, another sanction frequently mooted—notably in the case of the Neuilly children. Obviously well versed in the tradition of the *herem*, or ban, Rabbi Maurice Liber, a member of CRIF and the dean of the Séminaire israélite de France, which trained French rabbis, maintained that individuals found guilty "could be excluded from the Jewish community, temporarily or for their entire lives."[64] Without going so far as a ban from all forms of community life, when an organization investigated one of its members, the sanction envisioned was often stripping that person of his membership, both to punish him and to preserve the organization's good name. In the deliberations about Mr. Sztern, for example, one of the jurors held that it would be "prejudicial to the Union [of Jewish Intellectuals of France] if its secretary general [might] one day incur public blame for his work on the UGIF newsletter."[65] Simpler still, sometimes—once again in the case of the Neuilly children—it might be decided to make do with a reprimand of those charged. But the scope of this penalty differed depending on whether or not the reprimand was made public. In practice, the jury might believe that the decision to publicize a guilty verdict constituted harsh punishment in itself. In the Neuilly children's case, the representative of the Bund, Fayvel Schrager, recommended that "the commission of inquiry's conclusion be given the widest possible publicity in the Jewish community, which would lead to a sort of excommunication from Jewish life."[66] On the other hand, publicity could also be considered positive and useful by those who thought that they had been absolved of blame, inasmuch as the damage to their good name could be fully restored only in the public arena. This was certainly the position that led the editors of the Zionist newspaper *La Terre retrouvée* to publish the verdict returned by the second jury of honor that assessed the conduct of their friend Élie Krouker.[67]

Thus the very existence and history of these cases requires that we revisit the idea that "there was no purge among the Jews"[68] in France, a judgment that may reflect a reality of sorts, but only on condition that we carry it to two levels of analysis: considering the intrinsic limitations of the informal proceedings described previously; and asking about the limited desire for a purge, as illustrated by the way in which some community leaders approached the highly controversial case of the UGIF.

The Limits of the Purge Process in the French Jewish Community
CONTROVERSIAL AND OFTEN CONTESTED PROCEEDINGS

Lacking any powers of enforcement or legal status, the juries of honor and other inquiry commissions created in the French Jewish community could operate only if all the parties involved recognized their legitimacy to deal with a particular case. As Robert Kieffé, CRIF's legal adviser, reminded the organization in the case of the Neuilly children, CRIF "must not lose sight of the fact that a contractual bond was formed between the members of the commission of inquiry and the interested parties who voluntarily agreed to be questioned by it"[69]—an observation that holds for all the internal Jewish tribunals. Even though the individuals implicated recognized this contractual bond, notably by agreeing to the hearing, they nevertheless had no hesitations about criticizing its procedures and disputing the verdict when they considered it to be unfounded.

The parties frequently challenged the legality of the proceedings. André Baur's brother shared with Léon Meiss his doubts about the manner in which the treasurer of the Consistoire, René Worms, conducted the investigation of the Ducas case, noting that he had taken a deposition from a woman "by telephone, without even verifying her identity," and that as a result of the way he questioned her, he had received from this witness only "a limited and incomplete answer that can be interpreted in a sense as totally opposed to what would have been elicited by a complete and detailed deposition."[70] Reacting to the verdict that the CRIF jury of honor had rendered in his case, Kurt Schendel denounced the procedure that had led to his being found guilty of complicity in the Neuilly affair, holding that he had been questioned as a witness rather than as the accused.[71] Edmond Kahn, a defendant in the same case, reacted angrily and accused CRIF of having assumed "power unduly" and of having acted "with no legal right, but in violation of the laws that regulate all jurisdictional or investigative authority."[72] The social and professional affiliations of those implicated in the cases studied here provide a partial explanation of the format of these elaborate challenges. The players—the accused, the accusers, and the jurors—were members of the Parisian and provincial "Israelite" bourgeoisie or drawn from the ranks of the immigrants who were best integrated culturally, socially, and professionally. Thus many of them were capable of putting a lot of time and effort into procedural exchanges that made the cases drag out for a long time; for example, the investigations of Raymond Ducas's escape and of the roundup of the Neuilly children lasted nearly three years.

Another way to dispute a jury's initiative was to attack the legitimacy of the sponsoring organization or of the jurors themselves. The CUDJF was violently challenged by some of those to whom it sent questionnaires; these individuals stated that they were not familiar with the organization and consequently did not recognize its legitimacy to interrogate them: "By virtue of what authority do you act and who are you? What is your nationality? What are your qualifications?" demanded one of them.[73] This attack implicitly reflected the need to assign the conduct of an unofficial purge to an organization recognized by all factions of Jewish society. In the case of CRIF, it was not the organization but the jurors whose legitimacy was disputed. In February 1946, for example, Edmond Kahn notified the president of CRIF that, had he been aware of the composition of its jury in advance, he would not have appeared before a "jury of honor, the majority of whose members had not been in the Occupied Zone."[74] Élie Krouker's attorney was even more outspoken against the members of the first jury, which pronounced his client guilty: "Not a single authorized voice of French Judaism. Not a single veteran of the war of 1914–1918 or of 1939–1944. No

Résistance fighter. All of them are people who ran away from danger and the enemy. Fugitives with neither a past nor glory."[75]

Even more extreme procedures were enlisted. The Épinal community—represented by Raymond Ducas—went so far as to threaten the Consistoire central with secession if its delegate's honor was not fully restored.[76] So although the investigation of Ducas was intended to restore harmony within the Consistoire by resolving the severe conflict between him and André Baur's family, it in fact triggered much more serious problems that ultimately justified a compromise settlement. A stronger counterattack might also involve the convening of a counterjury: Élie Krouker rejected the verdict returned by the first jury and, with the intention of "being judged by his peers,"[77] submitted his case to a second tribunal, this one composed exclusively of Jewish war veterans. Raymond Ducas did the same thing in 1946 in reaction to the commission appointed by the Consistoire, which had recommended his expulsion; he obtained a favorable judgment from the screening committee of the General Confederation of Former Internee and Deportee Victims of Oppression and Racism (Confédération générale des anciens internés et déportés victimes de l'oppression et du racisme),[78] the National Federation of Deported and Interned Resistance Fighters (Fédération nationale des déportés et internés de la Résistance),[79] and a jury set up by the Épinal community.[80] Such a strategy, though, dealt a double blow to the French Jewish community's efforts to purge itself. On the one hand, it sapped the legitimacy of the tribunals whose ruling they contested; on the other hand, it undermined the credibility of any unofficial purge by leading to the formation of counterjuries that were suspected of partiality. It is interesting here to draw a parallel between this strategy and the limits evident in the purges of economic entities: Henry Rousso recalled that in France "the CNIE [Commission nationale interprofessionnelle d'épuration, National Interprofessional Purge Committee] was such a minor threat that it was often the company directors themselves who asked to appear before it in order to be officially cleared," which leads one to suppose that "in many cases, far from playing a role of repressing or renewing the managerial elites, the economic purges (or non-purge) instead played the function of restoring some reputations."[81]

A last strategy implemented by those who rejected a verdict about them was the possibility of recourse to the French courts. A number of letters in which former employees of the UGIF stated their refusal to fill out the CUDJF questionnaire mentioned the possibility of legal action to counter the threats made in the questionnaire.[82] Similarly, after learning the tenor of the verdict returned against him by the CRIF jury of honor, Edmond Kahn immediately threatened "to notify the competent jurisdiction of the usurpation of power . . . effected and of the crime of defamation resulting from the actions of the Commission of Inquiry."[83] The risk of being sued for defamation also hovered over CRIF's deliberations in June 1947 about the possibility of a global inquiry into the activities of the UGIF and its directors. Although attorney Robert Kieffé thought it plausible for CRIF "to set up a study commission or a commission of inquiry," he nevertheless warned that if it published its conclusions, "CRIF would be exposed to a series of suits for defamation."[84]

A PURGE THAT NO ONE WANTED?
THE ARGUMENTS AROUND THE UGIF

Beyond the inherent weakness of informal tribunals that operated outside any legal framework and could be easily contested, we must also look into the limited desire for a purge demonstrated by some community leaders. More precisely, we need to study what CRIF did in the case of the UGIF and its leaders, because it was indeed the UGIF that attracted the essence of the tension in the community associated with the recent persecutions. In fact, some leaders of CRIF—notably its president, Léon Meiss, assisted by secretary general Joseph Fisher—wanted to make sure that the purge of the UGIF did not go too far, as Jacques Fredj, Michel Laffitte, and Anne Grynberg have demonstrated.

The first sign of Meiss's aversion to an internal purge can be found in his systematic "moderating intervention"[85] in the case of the five people accused in the Neuilly children affair.[86] Throughout the debates about ratifying the tribunal's verdict, Meiss kept calling for understanding. On October 10, 1945, he invited his colleagues "to reflect deeply before judging not only an institution but also human beings."[87] On October 15 he proposed "to considerably soften the inquiry commission's decision."[88] And when CRIF renewed its deliberations in the fall of 1946, he declared that "aside from an imprudence that only a person can be blamed for, there is not too much left"[89] in this affair, a position that he managed to make prevail. On January 21, 1947, Meiss brought to a vote a motion that modified the jury of honor's original decision and declared that those incriminated "did not commit any real offense of a nature that would sully their honor."[90]

The concern to contain the scope of the purges can also be read in the desire to limit the inquiry to the case of the Neuilly children and no other matters. As Anne Grynberg notes, CRIF's passion to conduct a purge diminished considerably during the months that followed liberation.[91] On October 2, 1944, the commission of inquiry created by CRIF several days earlier was charged with "judging on the political and moral plane the actions of the UGIF and its directors as well as of the Jewish functionaries in Drancy and the other cases that may be referred to it."[92] On October 8, 1944, the commission was given another assignment: assessing the conduct of certain UGIF officials who wanted to continue their social welfare activities in Jewish organizations.[93] Two months later, the Jewish officials from Drancy were removed from the scope of the inquiry, as were ex-UGIF workers willing to keep up their communal work. CRIF limited its commission "to pronouncing on the activity of members of the UGIF during the occupation, and more specifically the UGIF's responsibility for the children housed in the orphanages under its control and deported by the Germans."[94] Given this task, the commission—which in the meantime had assumed the designation "jury of honor"—also adopted a restrictive approach. It decided to deal exclusively with the UGIF's culpability in the specific case of the arrests of children in July 1944 and, even more so, of the roundup at the Neuilly Children's Home on July 25, 1944, several days after the initial wave of arrests at other UGIF children's homes in the Paris region on the night of July 21–22, 1944.

Nevertheless, in the course of CRIF's numerous discussions in 1945–1947 about the verdict returned by the jury of honor and whether it should be ratified, many voices demanded a general evaluation of UGIF policies that would not be limited to the Neuilly children. On October 15, 1945, the representative of the Consistoire central, André Weil, "believe[d] that the CRIF should refer the file to a jury composed of lawyers, which would examine the UGIF case in its entirety";[95] similarly, the Bundist delegate Fayvel Schrager demanded that "the entire affair of the UGIF be discussed and an overall verdict be rendered."[96] The same desire for a comprehensive purge was expressed by the Association of Former Jewish Deportees, which in May 1947 categorically rejected the final verdict returned by CRIF and demanded "that a jury of honor be set up quickly and charged with investigating and judging the UGIF as a whole."[97]

But Léon Meiss systematically blocked this idea. On October 14, 1946, he stated his position clearly: "We do not have to judge the UGIF as an institution."[98] If the advocates of reopening and expanding the UGIF case thought they had prevailed on June 17, 1947, when the principles of a study commission and a new jury of honor were approved,[99] they finally had to beat a retreat some weeks later when Meiss pointed out that several members had since made known their opposition to pursuing the investigation of the UGIF.[100] The decision not to reopen the file was reaffirmed on November 4, 1947, in the presence of representatives of the Jewish deportees,[101] whom Meiss had already informed several months earlier that "reasons of a largely technical nature seem to prevent the Jewish organizations from undertaking such a difficult and long inquiry three years after the liberation."[102] It is important to note, however, that this reluctance to judge the UGIF as a whole went beyond CRIF. It can also be found among the members of the jury of honor established by the Union of Jewish Intellectuals of France: "If the grievance against Mr. Sztern is upheld, the full problem of involvement in the UGIF would be reopened."[103]

Finally, the decision taken on January 21, 1947, after the final verdict favorable to the defendants, that "CRIF will not take any initiative to make this judgment public,"[104] seems to indicate that the leaders of CRIF were themselves aware that their decision might anger the Jewish street, which had already been stirred up by an article published on February 22, 1946, in the newspaper of Left Poale Tsiyon.[105] It was the same fury that prodded the Association of Jewish Former Deportees into action, starting in the fall of 1946. On November 29 one of its members warned Léon Meiss that in the absence of clarifications about how the inquiry was progressing, his organization would see itself "obliged to raise the question in public opinion by all possible means."[106] After several warnings of the same type,[107] the Association put its threats into practice. On May 17, 1947, it published an open letter in which it formally rejected the CRIF verdict;[108] and on June 16, 1947, it convened a public meeting to demand "that CRIF undertake proceedings that extend to all aspects of the affair of the UGIF, whose activities during the occupation were harmful to the Jewish population."[109]

Although the former deportees' strategy of going public proved insufficient to propel the CRIF to reopen the case of the UGIF, the controversy it sparked in the Jewish street did not die away quickly. Former members of the UGIF set up a new organization, the "Friends of André Baur, Raymond-Raoul Lambert, and their deported colleagues," whom they honored in various ways,[110] but the Jewish immigrant circles remained steadfast in their unfavorable view of the UGIF, expressed notably in an impressive series of thirty-four articles on the UGIF that appeared in *Naye Prese* between October 1950 and March 1951.[111] These articles show the decisive role played by the Jewish press in these conflicts. Starting with the denunciation of an individual or an institution and concluding with the restoration of the good name of those incriminated, while frequently expressing opposition to the verdicts returned, the press constituted a parallel stage where the debates about the internal purges raged and sometimes refused to die away. Thus Léon Meiss's moderating action did not alleviate tensions; at most, it altered where they manifested themselves.[112]

Conclusion

French Jewry's desire to purge the community after World War II was a direct continuation of the war years, as shown by the Jewish communists' urge to purge the community during the occupation itself and after the war. It also fits into the larger context of the purges carried out by French society as a whole. The rhetoric and practices as well as some of the social functions, notably their undeniable role as an "outlet for anger,"[113] are similar. It certainly seems that the goal sought by at least part of the French Jewish community, in the attempt to expel those who had been part of the UGIF, was to restore internal cohesion, which had been seriously dented by the wartime experiences. Although we cannot deny that there was a rapprochement between native-born French Jews and immigrants at the end of the war, it remains the case, as noted by Bernard Wasserstein, that "the wartime experience . . . heightened the antagonism between Jews of Russo-Polish origin and the old French Jewish establishment"[114] that had run the UGIF. What is more, and as Wasserstein implies here, this cleavage predated World War II. From this point of view, one can also see the bitter disputes triggered by the UGIF affair as a replay of old tensions; indeed, the more recent research has strongly underlined the fact that the purge in France made it possible "to replay old conflicts, exacerbated by the years of occupation."[115] Moreover, given that the purge on the national scale was a political enterprise of substantial power, it is not at all insignificant that the most determined partisans of a purge of the community included the Jewish communists, who were eager to denounce the "bourgeois" "traitors" and "collaborators" as a way to consolidate the prestige that their resistance to the German occupier and Vichy had given them in the eyes of many Jews. A final common point between the Jewish community and the French nation as a whole can be found in the dissatisfaction that the purges created both in French society[116] and on the Jewish street, where the UGIF affair triggered genuine bitterness.

The purge in the Jewish community nevertheless had its own unique characteristics. First, and contrary to the fantastic history imagined by author Léo Malet in his detective novel *Du Rebecca rue des Rosiers*, published in 1958,[117] I am unaware of any significant incident of extrajudicial physical violence committed by Jews against other Jews in France after the war. (The exception is in January 1947, when the chief of the Jewish police in the ghetto of Buczacz in eastern Galicia was recognized in Paris by one of his victims, who beat him severely before handing him over to the authorities.)[118] Second, the Jews who pursued the intracommunity cases studied here often gave primacy to certain values over others, as in the Ducas affair. Whereas postwar France viewed escape from the enemy as a magnificent deed, lauded for the courage it required, the principles of family solidarity and self-sacrifice (in the tradition of *Kiddush ha-shem*) seem to have been more important for those who castigated Ducas. Third, the Jews' strong and specific desire for reintegration into the national community, from which they had been excluded for four long years, certainly offers a partial explanation of how their leaders envisioned and conducted "their" purge, modeled on the purges in the non-Jewish environment. Finally, the internal Jewish purge never assumed massive proportions, whereas "entire groups were targeted" in French society as a whole.[119] It is clear—need it be repeated?—that the Jews, having been victimized without mercy by the German and Vichy persecution, could hardly lay themselves open to charges of collaboration, except in a few individual and marginal cases. Nevertheless, the resentment that many felt against the UGIF—an institution that employed quite a few Jews under the occupation all over France[120]—could certainly have spawned a much broader internal purge, as suggested by the ambitions of the short-lived purge commission set up by the CUDJF.

There are explanations for this situation, beginning with the intrinsic weakness of the internal purges, a weakness that the main actors were well aware of. Next comes the intolerable nature of these clashes for those who held that the Jews had to close ranks to confront the massive challenges they faced at the end of the worst persecution in their history. This is the persuasive hypothesis offered by Anne Grynberg to explain the attitude of Léon Meiss, who was perhaps trying "to preserve the recent and still fragile reunion of the diverse components of the Jewish group in France, even if it meant stirring up incomprehension and bitterness on the part of those who demanded that the officials of the UGIF be punished."[121] From this perspective, one can establish yet another parallel with French society as a whole: The French political authorities themselves soon opted for reconciliation, passing general amnesty laws in 1951 and 1953.[122] Here the Jews had certainly been out in front. What is more, as Grynberg also correctly notes, many of the Jewish organizations, having tacked back and forth between legality and clandestine action under the occupation, were at risk of suffering from too strong an indictment of the UGIF, and the community leaders may also have feared that anti-Semites would seize on these "affairs" to cast aspersions on a Jewish community that had already been terribly battered. Finally, we must remember that although the Jews of France made efforts to purge their own ranks, they aspired above all to see those truly responsible for their agony—German and French—brought to justice, as shown by the massive coverage in the Jewish press in the years after the war of the trials of the instigators and implementers of the anti-Jewish persecution.

We may still wonder about the consequences of the ultimately limited character of this internal community purge. Albert Camus wrote in *Combat* in January 1945 that "a country that fails to purge itself is setting itself up to fail in its renewal."[123] To paraphrase Camus, can we perhaps say that a community that fails to purge itself is laying the groundwork to fail in its reconstruction? For the Jews of France the tentative nature of the internal purge does not really seem to have blocked the renewal of community life. Moreover, although the limited dimensions of the purges in the Jewish community were a cause of bitterness, other quarrels soon overtook them, beginning with the continental divide between communists and non- or anti-communists, a split that ultimately had a much greater impact on postwar Jewish life in France than the debates about the behavior of a few people under the occupation.

Notes

Translated from French by Lenn Schramm.

I would like to thank Claire Andrieu and Renée Poznanski as well as the anonymous peer reviewers for their close reading of this article. I would also like to thank the members of the seminar on current research in Jewish studies at l'École des Hautes Études en Sciences Sociales (EHESS), directed by Sylvie Anne Goldberg, where this study was first presented in April 2013, for their helpful comments.

1. Peter Novick, *The Resistance Versus Vichy: The Purge of Collaborators in Liberated France* (London: Chatto & Windus, 1968); Henry Rousso, "L'épuration en France: Une histoire inachevée," *Vingtième Siècle: Revue d'histoire* 33 (1992): 78–105.

2. Marc Olivier Baruch, ed., *Une poignée de misérables: L'épuration au sein de la société française après la Seconde Guerre mondiale* (Paris: Fayard, 2003).

3. For examples of overviews, see Jean-Paul Cointet, *Expier Vichy: L'épuration en France, 1943–1958* (Paris: Perrin, 2008); and Bénédicte Vergez-Chaignon, *Histoire de l'épuration* (Paris: Larousse, 2010). For an idea of what is available in French on the notion of "sortie de guerre," see Guillaume Piketty and Bruno Cabanes, eds., *Retour à l'intime: Au sortir de la guerre* (Paris: Tallandier, 2009).

4. Pieter Lagrou, *The Legacy of Nazi Occupation: Patriotic Memory and National Recovery in Western Europe, 1945–1965* (Cambridge, UK: Cambridge University Press, 2000), 25.

5. See, for example, Maud S. Mandel, *In the Aftermath of Genocide: Armenians and Jews in Twentieth-Century France* (Durham, NC: Duke University Press, 2003).

6. While having studied several aspects of what Primo Levi labeled "the gray zone," Annette Wieviorka has written on this subject: "I know that history is tragic. I do not like to bring up situations that might bring opprobrium on the Jews." See Annette Wieviorka, *L'heure d'exactitude: Histoire, mémoire, témoignage (Entretiens avec Séverine Nikel)* (Paris: Albin Michel, 2011), 173.

7. Robert Faurisson, "À propos de l'arrêt Touvier: L'affaire des 'Juifs bruns,'" *Revue d'histoire révisionniste* 6 (1992): 69–82.

8. On the situation of the Jews in France after liberation, see Anne Grynberg, "Après la tourmente," in Jean-Jacques Becker and Annette Wieviorka, eds., *Les Juifs de France: De la Révolution française à nos jours* (Paris: Liana Levi, 1998), 249–86; David Weinberg,

"The Reconstruction of the French Jewish Community After World War II," in Yisrael Gutman and Avital Saf, eds., *She'erit Hapletah, 1944–1948: Rehabilitation and Political Struggle—Proceedings of the Sixth Yad Vashem International Historical Conference, Jerusalem 1985* (Jerusalem: Yad Vashem, 1990), 168–86; and Annette Wieviorka, "Les Juifs en France au lendemain de la guerre: état des lieux," *Archives Juives: Revue d'histoire des Juifs de France* 28.1 (1995): 4–22.

9. In 1939 there were 300,000–330,000 Jews living in France; 75,721 were deported to death camps, and only 2,500 came back. In addition, about 3,000 Jews died in French internment camps and 1,000 were executed.

10. The UGIF was established on November 29, 1941, by a Vichy law enacted at the order of the German occupiers. The UGIF, which all Jews living in France were required to join, absorbed all existing Jewish organizations (except for the Consistoire central, an institution established by Napoleon in 1808 that supervised Jewish religious activity in France) and was officially charged with taking over the provision of social services and welfare to a Jewish community that had been severely weakened by the exclusion and expropriation measures. Most of its leaders were "French Israelites" who were close to the Consistoire. See Michel Laffitte, *Juif dans la France allemande: Institutions, dirigeants et communautés au temps de la Shoah* (Paris: Tallandier, 2006); and Michel Laffitte, *Un engrenage fatal: L'UGIF face aux réalités de la Shoah* (Paris: Liana Levi, 2003).

11. France's liberation began on June 6, 1944, with the Normandy landings, followed by the Allied invasion of southern France on August 15, 1944, and the liberation of Paris on August 25, 1944. Alsace was not completely freed until March 1945, and a few limited zones such as Dunkirk or the islands of Brittany were not liberated until the German capitulation on May 8, 1945.

12. This is the figure provided by Rousso, "L'épuration en France," 93.

13. Rousso, "L'épuration en France," 101.

14. Baruch, *Une poignée de misérables*, 532.

15. Jewish resistance movements, which benefited from the legal and official cover of the UGIF (e.g., the Éclaireurs israélites de France or the Œuvre de secours aux Enfants), were of course far less vindictive than those that did not ask for its help, such as the communist Jewish resistance groups.

16. "Redoublons d'efforts pour les enfants juifs traqués!" *Notre Voix* (February 15, 1943), reprinted in Union des Juifs pour la résistance et l'entraide (UJRE), ed., *La presse antiraciste sous l'occupation hitlérienne* (Paris: Centre de documentation de l'UJRE, 1950), 67.

17. "L'U.G.I.F. filiale de la Gestapo," *Notre Voix* (June 1, 1943), reprinted in UJRE, ed., *La presse antiraciste sous l'occupation hitlérienne*, 89.

18. "Programme," September 24, 1944, Musée de la Résistance nationale (Champigny-sur-Marne), David Diamant/UJRE Collection, box 108, file 15. The actual identity of those involved is not known.

19. This group comprised the Union of Jewish Youth (Union de la jeunesse juive), the French Jewish scouts (Éclaireurs israélites de France), the Young Zionist Movement

(Mouvement de la jeunesse sioniste), and the Communist Jewish Youth of the Alpes-Maritimes (Jeunesse communiste juive des Alpes-Maritimes).

20. "Charte d'unité du Comité d'Action et de Défense de la Jeunesse Juive," October 13, 1944, David Diamant/UJRE Collection, box 108, file 15.
21. Bylaws of the Organisation des Juifs polonais en France, n.d. [1945], Seine-Saint-Denis Departmental Archives, David Diamant Collection, 335J 107.
22. Simon Schwarzfuchs, "Les Consistoires: La reconstruction dans l'immédiat après-guerre (1945–1949)," *Le Monde Juif* 158 (1996): 96.
23. Schwarzfuchs, "Les Consistoires," 96–97.
24. "Iz di yidishe geto-politsey shuldik?" [Are the Jewish Ghetto Police Guilty?], *Naye Prese* (January 4, 1947).
25. Robert Sommer, "Les trois aventures," *Vendredi Soir: La Semaine israélite* (April 25, 1947).
26. Among individuals who distinguished themselves and were celebrated after the war, I note the memorial volume for David Rapoport, *L'un des trente-six* (Paris: Kiyoum, 1946). Rapoport, who was born in the Ukraine in 1883, played a crucial role during the occupation as a leader of the Comité Amelot, a forum of a number of Jewish immigrant organizations that provided assistance to indigent and interned Jews, produced false papers, and hid children. He was deported to Auschwitz in 1943 and died there in 1944. For an example of a publication praising the action of Jewish organizations that helped persecuted Jews, see Centre de documentation juive contemporaine, ed., *L'activité des organisations juives en France sous l'occupation* (Paris: Éditions du Centre, 1947).
27. Riadh Ben Khalifa, "Sur la corde raide, entre résistance et collaboration: Un Juif hongrois en France occupée," *Archives Juives: Revue d'histoire des Juifs de France* 44 (2011): 102–20.
28. "A yidishe geshtapo-agentin vert fraygelozt fun gerikht" [A Jewish Female Gestapo Agent Is Released by the Court], *Naye Prese* (September 10, 1946).
29. "A yid, a merder fun Dransy" [A Jewish Killer from Drancy], *Naye Prese* (March 5, 1946).
30. On the prewar career of Oskar Reich, the work by his squad in Drancy, and his trial, see Michel Laffitte and Annette Wieviorka, *À l'intérieur du camp de Drancy* (Paris: Perrin, 2012), 296–300 and 323–24.
31. "Paris Court Sentences Jew to Death for Helping Arrest and Rob Jewish Internees," *Jewish Telegraphic Agency* (April 27, 1945). This wire is available for consultation online at www.jta.org/1945/04/27/archive/paris-court-sentences-jew-to-death-for-helping-arrest-and-rob-jewish-internees (accessed October 4, 2013).
32. Memo by Maurice Moch for the Consistoire central, titled "Pinkus Chmielnicki, le kapo tortionnaire, est condamné à mort," March 30, 1950, Centre de documentation du Mémorial de la Shoah (Paris), CRIF Collection, MDI-328.
33. "Arestirt a yidishn kapo" [A Jewish Kapo Has Been Arrested], *Naye Prese* (February 17, 1948).

34. Acquittal order, Permanent Military Tribunal of Paris, November 9, 1948, Israel National Archives, Record Group/32/LAW/115/58. I would like to thank Dan Porat for bringing this document to my attention.
35. Eliezer Gruenbaum's father was Itzhak Gruenbaum, a well-known Jewish political leader in Poland, Mandatory Palestine, and Israel, where he served as interior minister in the provisional government established in 1948. On Eliezer Gruenbaum, see Tuvia Friling, *A Jewish Kapo in Auschwitz: History, Memory, and the Politics of Survival*, trans. Haim Watzman (Waltham, MA: Brandeis University Press, 2014).
36. The Association of Former Jewish Deportees also asked survivors of the Piotrkow ghetto to testify against a former Jewish policeman. "Komunikat fun farband fun di gevezene yidishe deportirte" [Communiqué of the Association of Former Jewish Deportees], *Unzer Vort* (June 24, 1947).
37. "Eyner fun di groyse lagern-merder Pinkus, vart oyf zayn mishpet" [Pinkus, One of the Worst Murderers in the Camps, Awaits Trial], *Naye Prese* (July 11, 1947). The Zionist-oriented daily *Unzer Vort* published a similar appeal: "Gekhapt dem moser fun Birkenau 'Pinkus'" [The Birkenau's Informer "Pinkus" Has Been Caught], *Unzer Vort* (August 7, 1947).
38. Memo by Maurice Moch, CRIF Collection, MDI-328.
39. A survivor wrote about the testimony he gave to the French police against Eliezer Gruenbaum. See Charles Liblau, *Les kapos d'Auschwitz* (Paris: Syllepse, 2005), 45.
40. The Association of Jewish Former Deportees also had its own honor court (*ern-gerikht* in Yiddish), but we know only that in 1947 the court dismissed the accusations of a former deportee regarding a case whose details remain blurred. "Fun yidishn lebn in Pariz" [Jewish Life in Paris], *Unzer Vort* (May 18, 1947). Therefore, aside from a number of personal conflicts in which the possibility of convening a jury of honor was mentioned but never realized, these five cases are the only documented purges in the French Jewish community of which I am aware. We cannot, however, exclude the possibility that there were other cases that have left no traces in the documents I consulted.
41. I do not deal with more informal modes of stigmatization that may have developed in various Jewish circles, in more limited and closed social networks.
42. The CUDJF was a Jewish underground organization established in Paris in late 1943. Its membership was drawn largely from the ranks of immigrant Jews.
43. Renée Poznanski, *Les Juifs en France pendant la Seconde Guerre mondiale* (Paris: Hachette, 2005), 549. Although we do not know how many people the questionnaire was sent to, about 160 filled-in copies are in the David Diamant/UJRE Collection, box 30, file 3.
44. CRIF was founded in January 1944 in the wake of secret talks between the leaders of the Consistoire central and the General Defense Committee of Jews (Comité général de défense des Juifs), an underground organization created in Grenoble in July 1943 by the representatives of three Jewish immigrant groups: the Communists, the Zionists, and the Bundists. On CRIF, see Samuel Ghiles-Meilhac, *Le CRIF: De la Résistance juive à la tentation du lobby* (Paris: Robert Laffont, 2011).

45. A professional magistrate, born in Sarrebourg (Moselle), Léon Meiss was dismissed by the Vichy government. During the occupation he held a senior position with the Consistoire central, eventually replacing its president, Jacques Helbronner, when Helbronner was deported in 1943. After the war Meiss was one of the most important figures in organized Jewish life in France.
46. See Jacques Fredj, "La création du CRIF, 1943–1966," Master's thesis, University Paris–IV, 1988, 27–34; Laffitte, *Juif dans la France allemande*, 323–27; and Anne Grynberg, "Juger l'UGIF (1944–1950)?" in Hélène Arter, Antoine Marès, and Pierre Mélandri, eds., *Terres promises: Mélanges offerts à André Kaspi* (Paris: Publications de la Sorbonne, 2008), 507–25.
47. On the Ducases' escape, which served as a pretext for Baur's arrest, see Laffitte and Wieviorka, *À l'intérieur du camp de Drancy*, 268–69.
48. His first name has been lost to history.
49. The FSJF was an important umbrella organization with a Zionist outlook founded in the 1920s. It included many organizations of Jewish immigrants from Eastern Europe.
50. Krouker was a cofounder, secretary, and later president of the Association of Foreign-Born Jewish Veterans of the French Army (Association des anciens combattants juifs étrangers dans l'armée française). He was also one of the founders of the FSJF.
51. Jacoubovitch was one of the founders (in 1926) of the Colonie scolaire, a Jewish welfare organization that helps the children of poor immigrant families. Under the occupation he served as the secretary of the Comité Amelot.
52. This committee, established at German initiative in January 1941, prefigured the UGIF.
53. Grynberg discusses this incident briefly in "Juger l'UGIF," 523.
54. Anne Simonin, *Le déshonneur dans la République: Une histoire de l'indignité 1791–1958* (Paris: Bernard Grasset, 2008), 11.
55. Simonin, *Le déshonneur dans la République*, ch. 6.
56. Christophe Lewin, *Le retour des prisonniers de guerre français: Naissance et développement de la FNPGD 1944–1952* (Paris: Publications de la Sorbonne, 1986), 143–57.
57. Lewin, *Le retour des prisonniers*, 143.
58. Marcel Baur to Léon Meiss, May 22, 1945, CRIF Collection, MDI-315.
59. I. Yakubovitsh [Jules Jacoubovitch], "Hinter di kulisn fun daytsher yidn-politik in Frankraykh" [Behind the Scenes of the Germans' Jewish Policy in France], *Unzer Shtime* (December 30, 1944, and January 6, 1945).
60. Minutes of a meeting of the Union des intellectuels juifs de France, n.d. [1946], Archives of the Alliance israélite universelle (AIU), Henri Hertz Collection, AP5-102.
61. Except for Lucien Frank, the president of the CRIF jury.
62. Handwritten list, n.d. [1945], CRIF Collection, MDI-315.
63. Minutes of the meeting of CRIF, October 15, 1945, CRIF Collection, MDI-2.
64. Minutes of the meeting of CRIF, October 24, 1945, CRIF Collection, MDI-2.

65. Minutes of a meeting of the Union des intellectuels juifs de France, n.d. [1946], Henri Hertz collection.
66. Minutes of the meeting of CRIF, October 15, 1945, CRIF Collection, MDI-2.
67. "Accusations injustifiées: Élie Krouker n'a jamais failli à l'honneur," *La Terre retrouvée* (May 1, 1950).
68. Schwarzfuchs, "Les Consistoires," 100.
69. Minutes of the meeting of CRIF, October 24, 1945, CRIF Collection, MDI-2.
70. Marcel Baur to Léon Meiss, May 22, 1945, CRIF Collection, MDI-315.
71. Kurt Schendel to Léon Meiss, December 21, 1945, CRIF Collection, MDI-311.
72. Edmond Kahn to Lucien Frank, November 24, 1945, CRIF Collection, MDI-310.
73. Pierre Alcan to the CUDJF, September 24, 1944, David Diamant/UJRE Collection, box 30, file 3.
74. Edmond Kahn to Léon Meiss, February 15, 1946, CRIF Collection, MDI-311.
75. "Conclusion de Me Rosenzweig-Gajac," January 1949, Archives of the Consistoire central, series F, 47-c.
76. Arthur Dreyfus to Léon Meiss, January 10, 1947, CRIF Collection, MDI-315.
77. "Accusations injustifiées: Élie Krouker n'a jamais failli à l'honneur," *La Terre retrouvée* (May 1, 1950).
78. Jacques Darville to Raymond Ducas, June 6, 1946, CRIF Collection, MDI-315.
79. Francis Beltrami to Léon Meiss, June 8, 1946, CRIF Collection, MDI-315.
80. Arthur Dreyfus to Léon Meiss, November 26, 1946, CRIF Collection, MDI-315.
81. Rousso, "L'épuration en France," 101.
82. See, for example, Jean Vilenski to the CUDJF, September 25, 1944, David Diamant/UJRE Collection, box 30, file 3.
83. Edmond Kahn to Lucien Frank, November 24, 1945, CRIF Collection, MDI-310.
84. Minutes of the meeting of CRIF, June 17, 1947, CRIF Collection, MDI-4.
85. Grynberg, "Juger l'UGIF," 516.
86. Meiss had already demonstrated his moderation and pragmatism during the deliberations, in July 1944, about the liquidation of the UGIF, which the Communists wanted to implement without delay. On these discussions, see Poznanski, *Les Juifs en France*, 544–46.
87. Minutes of the meeting of CRIF, October 10, 1945, CRIF Collection, MDI-2.
88. Minutes of the meeting of CRIF, October 15, 1945, CRIF Collection, MDI-2.
89. Minutes of the meeting of CRIF, October 14, 1946, CRIF Collection, MDI-3.
90. CRIF verdict, December 3, 1946, CRIF Collection, MDI-313.
91. Grynberg, "Juger l'UGIF," 512.
92. Minutes of the meeting of CRIF, October 2, 1944, CRIF Collection, MDI-1.

93. Minutes of the meeting of CRIF, October 9, 1944, CRIF Collection, MDI-1.
94. Unsigned letter to Lucien Frank, December 14, 1944 (copy), CRIF Collection, MDI-310.
95. Minutes of the meeting of CRIF, October 15, 1945, CRIF Collection, MDI-2.
96. Minutes of the meeting of CRIF, October 15, 1945, CRIF Collection, MDI-2.
97. Naum Fansten to CRIF, May 13, 1947, CRIF Collection, MDI-312.
98. Minutes of the meeting of CRIF, October 14, 1946, CRIF Collection, MDI-3.
99. Minutes of the meeting of CRIF, June 17, 1947, CRIF Collection, MDI-4.
100. Minutes of the meeting of CRIF, July 8, 1947, CRIF Collection, MDI-4.
101. Minutes of the meeting of CRIF, November 4, 1947, CRIF Collection, MDI-4.
102. Léon Meiss to the Association des anciens déportés juifs, June 3, 1947 (copy), CRIF Collection, MDI-312.
103. Minutes of a meeting of the Union des intellectuels juifs de France, n.d. [1946], Henri Hertz collection.
104. Minutes of the meeting of CRIF, January 21, 1947, CRIF Collection, MDI-4.
105. This article denounced "the silence about the crimes committed against our children by Jews themselves, by those whom the enemy imposed as the leaders of the Jews, despoiled, humiliated, and deprived of their rights during the Occupation" (quoted in Grynberg, "Juger l'UGIF," 518).
106. J. Frydman to Léon Meiss, November 29, 1946, CRIF Collection, MDI-312.
107. Minutes of the meeting of CRIF, December 16, 1946, CRIF Collection, MDI-3; Committee of the Association des anciens déportés juifs to CRIF, March 20, 1947, CRIF Collection, MDI-313.
108. "Farband fun deportirte kegn an urteyl vos vasht rayn 'UGIF'-tuer" [The Association of Deportees Against a Verdict That Clears the UGIF Activists], *Naye Prese* (May 17, 1947).
109. Naum Fansten to Léon Meiss, June 17, 1947, CRIF Collection, MDI-312. See also H. Bulavko [Henry Bulawko], "'Uzhif' a flek vos mir muzn bazaytikn" [UGIF a Blot We Have to Eliminate], *Unzer Vort* (June 24, 1947).
110. See Laffitte, *Juif dans la France allemande*, 331–35. It is worth noting that Léon Meiss took part in a commemoration held by the Friends organization in November 1949 and dedicated to André Baur and Raymond-Raoul Lambert, the president of the UGIF in the Southern Zone. "À la mémoire d'André Baur et R.-R. Lambert," *La Terre retrouvée* (December 1, 1949).
111. The overall title of the series written by David Diamant is "Di shendlekhe rol un tetikeyt fun yudenrat in Frankraykh beys der natsisher okupatsye" [The Scandalous Role and Activity of the Jewish Council in France During the Nazi Occupation].
112. The debate about the UGIF resurfaced from time to time later, notably in the 1980s. See Laffitte, *Juif dans la France allemande*, ch. 10.

113. Rousso, "L'épuration en France," 104.
114. Bernard Wasserstein, *Vanishing Diaspora: The Jews in Europe Since 1945* (London: Penguin, 1997), 61. It is worth noting that 55,000 of the 80,000 Jewish victims in France were foreigners (mostly of Polish and Romanian origin) and that among the 25,000 French Jews deported, 8,000 were children of foreign origin and 8,000 were foreigners who had obtained French citizenship before the war.
115. Baruch, *Une poignée de misérables*, 537.
116. See Novick, *Resistance* ("Conclusion").
117. In this novel, part of his "New Mysteries of Paris" series, Malet's famous detective, Nestor Burma, investigates a certain Bramovici, a Jewish gangster who had business dealings with the Germans during the occupation and handed Jews over to them. Also hunted by an Israeli veteran of the pre-State Irgun underground intent on revenge, Bramovici is found stoned to death by Jews in front of the Tomb of the Unknown Jewish Martyr. See Lucette Le Van-Lemesle, "Léo Malet et ses 'Nouveaux Mystères,'" *Sociétés & Représentations* 17.1 (2004): 171–82. (The novel has appeared in an English translation by P. Hudson, under the title *Mayhem in the Marais*.) It is interesting to note that the 1992 French television adaptation of the novel replaced the Jewish collaborator with a non-Jewish character who had served in the Vichy militia and as a Gestapo auxiliary.
118. Yisrael Cohen, ed., *Book of Buczacz: In Memory of a Martyred Community* (Tel Aviv: Am Oved, 1956), 297–98 (Hebrew). English translation by Jessica Cohen online at www.jewishgen.org/yizkor/buchach/buc284.html#Page297 (accessed June 23, 2013).
119. Baruch, *Une poignée de misérables*, 532.
120. For instance, in July 1944 the administrative services of the UGIF in the Northern Zone employed 915 people. See Laffitte, *Juif dans la France allemande*, 85.
121. Grynberg, "Juger l'UGIF," 524.
122. See Henry Rousso, *The Vichy Syndrome: History and Memory in France Since 1944*, trans. Arthur Goldhammer (Cambridge, MA: Harvard University Press, 1991), 49–54.
123. Albert Camus, quoted in Christian Delporte, "L'épuration des journalistes: polémiques, mythes, réalités," *Matériaux pour l'histoire de notre temps* 39–40 (1995): 29.

6

Viennese Jewish Functionaries on Trial

Accusations, Defense Strategies, and Hidden Agendas

HELGA EMBACHER

Before the so-called *Anschluss*, the German annexation of Austria in March 1938, the Viennese Jewish community was one of the largest and wealthiest in Europe. Of the 200,000 Austrian Jews, 175,000 lived in Vienna, which amounted to 9.4 percent of the city's population. Approximately two-thirds of Austrian Jews survived the Holocaust in various countries of exile.[1] It was in Vienna that Adolf Eichmann first set up the SS's Central Office for Jewish Emigration (*Zentralstelle für Jüdische Auswanderung*) in the fall of 1938 to guarantee the systematic expulsion, deportation, and ultimate annihilation of European Jewry.[2] After the *Anschluss* the leadership of the Viennese Jewish Community (Israelitische Kultusgemeinde; IKG) became the prototype of a Jewish administration under Nazi control and a precursor of the later Jewish councils, or Judenräte, in other German-occupied countries. Jewish functionaries were forced to communicate with the SS, and this communication was asymmetric with respect to power, which means that the Nazis could insidiously and consciously design situations in which Jewish leaders had no choice between good and evil. In the months following the *Anschluss* it seemed necessary and even useful for Jewish interests to cooperate with the National Socialist oppressors in order to secure Jewish welfare and emigration, but with the beginning of mass deportations of Jews from Vienna in November 1941, the IKG turned into an instrument that assisted the Nazi regime in its deportations. With the growing number of tasks the IKG had to manage, the size of its workforce increased from 537 in March 1938 to 1,518 in June 1940.[3] IKG employees issued instructions to the deportees; Jewish doctors and nurses were present at the final registration and at the station from which the trains departed. Under massive pressure from the Nazi regime, the IKG ordered Jewish functionaries to assist as marshals (*Ausheber*), who, hoping to ensure their own survival, supported the SS in removing Jews from their apartments, escorting them to the collection points, and standing guard to prevent their escape.[4] The last Jew many victims saw before being deported was Robert Prochnik, *Gruppenführer* (section commander) of the marshals. Leonard Ehrlich, a professor of philosophy and Judaic studies at the University of Massachusetts who had himself been expelled from Austria, described the situation in Vienna in these terms: "It was a time for corruption within the unprecedentedly huge staff that now sprang up, including many volunteers, and it was a time for accusing the leadership of corruption when one's frustrated hope for help was juxtaposed with a neighbor's good luck in attaining help."[5]

In April 1945 the IKG had only 5,512 members.[6] Viennese Jews vented their emotions, displayed their hatred for Jewish functionaries, and issued denunciations. Some functionaries were interrogated and imprisoned by the Red Army. Beginning in the summer of 1945 the Vienna State Police filed charges against Jewish functionaries, including Dr. Emil Tuchmann, Wilhelm Reisz, Jewish marshal Leo Balaban, and Jewish policeman Oskar Münzer.[7] The arrests and criminal proceedings were based on the Austrian War Crimes Law (Kriegsverbrechergesetz). Promulgated in June 1945, this law applied to a variety of crimes, such as violence against individuals and degrading human treatment in connection with the pogrom of November 1938, involvement in the deportation of Jews, violence and murder in concentration camps and euthanasia institutions, and criminal material enrichment, so-called Aryanization. Until 1955 the Austrian People's Courts, composed of three lay and three professional judges with one of the professional judges presiding, were responsible for trying Nazi crimes.[8] The Vienna State Police equated forced cooperation with collaboration and made no distinction between perpetrators and victims. This view was also shared by many Viennese Jews. There were also complaints that Jewish functionaries used the same excuses as non-Jewish Austrian war criminals.

Nevertheless, the Jewish community in Vienna never established an honor court. However, such an internal Jewish court was formed among Austrian Jewish émigrés in London. In Austria honor courts were held in some Jewish displaced persons (DP) camps, because Austria was an important country for the Jewish exodus from Eastern Europe; between 1945 and 1948, 300,000 Jewish refugees came through the country.[9] Immediately after the liberation some former concentration camp prisoners took the law into their own hands and murdered a dozen kapos. Soon thereafter honor courts were established in DP camps, and each court was controlled by the respective Zentralkomitee (camp administration).[10]

Using the case studies of Dr. Josef Löwenherz, Dr. Emil Tuchmann, and Dr. Ernst Feldsberg, each of whom held different positions in wartime Vienna, I analyze the assertions of Jewish witnesses and the allegations of the Vienna State Police that were used to accuse Jewish functionaries of collaboration. I further demonstrate how Löwenherz defended himself and was defended by other Jews and Jewish organizations in a tribunal held by Austrian Jewish exile organizations in London. Furthermore, I show that the fiercely emotional debates about Jewish functionaries were used by Jewish organizations to advance their respective agendas. It is interesting that non-Jews and Jews alike used the term *collaboration* without defining it and without differentiating between, on the one hand, the various forms of collaboration by non-Jews and, on the other hand, forced cooperation by Jews, which is, in my opinion, the role Jewish functionaries were forced to play. The focus of this chapter is on the minute room for maneuver and agency that Jewish functionaries were given and that confronted them with a moral dilemma. Thus I deal with the problem of the deportation lists. Although the Jewish leadership did not draw up the initial lists of deportees and had no influence on the transports and the number of Jews the Nazis required, they could negotiate for the exemption of certain groups, for example, war veterans, sick people, and the staff of Jewish institutions and their immediate family members. Thus many Jews assumed that the selection had been made by the Jewish leadership and that Jewish functionaries were much more powerful than they actually had been. It was this assumed power that opened the door to rumors and denunciations after the liberation. Likewise, during and after the war it was also this agency that gave some Jewish functionaries the feeling that they held a powerful position.

Whereas the role played by the IKG during the Nazi period is well researched, little research has been done until now on retribution in the postwar Jewish community. This chapter is based on my own previous work[11] and has also profited from several chapters in Evelyn Adunka's *Die vierte Gemeinde* and, most of all, from Doron Rabinovici's *Eichmann's Jews*.[12] In his important study Rabinovici shows how the Viennese IKG became the prototype for the subsequent Jewish councils convened under circumstances that offered little room for maneuver.

He also touches on the problem of how Jewish functionaries were treated after the war in the Jewish community and criticizes how Jewish functionaries were treated in their court trials, in which some received much harsher sentences than their Nazi superiors. Whereas Rabinovici focuses on the line that has to be drawn between National Socialist perpetrators and Jewish victims, I analyze the debate about Austrian Jewish functionaries in the context of reestablishing the postwar Viennese Jewish community and the competition among various Austrian exile organizations. I also focus on the IKG after the end of the mass deportations and on the case of Dr. Emil Tuchmann. I elaborate on how he portrayed what he was trying to accomplish and juxtapose this description with descriptions given by some of his former co-workers in the Jewish hospital.

Trapped: From Independent Jewish Community to the Nazis' Council of Elders

During the "Austro-fascist period"—the authoritarian rule by the Patriotic Front (Vaterländische Front), which was supported by the Catholic Church and lasted from 1933 to the *Anschluss* in March 1938—the IKG was already cooperating with an authoritarian government as a means of protecting its interests. Not only left-wing political parties, such as the Social Democrats and the Communists, but also left-wing Jewish organizations and left-wing Zionist groups were dissolved in 1934.[13] Immediately after the *Anschluss* prominent leaders of the IKG were arrested and the organization was dissolved. Many Austrian Jews were also among the first to be deported to Dachau. The IKG was reestablished in May 1938, reorganized by Adolf Eichmann to serve the Nazi regime's goal of rapid mass emigration. Instead of elected community representatives, Jewish functionaries of the IKG were Nazi appointees. To guarantee a certain degree of continuity, Dr. Josef Löwenherz, IKG vice-president from 1924 to 1937 and thereafter its administrative director, was installed as director. In this position he had to inform the Jews of the countless discriminatory laws and interact with the Central Office for Jewish Emigration and the Gestapo headquarters in Vienna. Although many former Jewish functionaries and rabbis had left the country as quickly as possible, Löwenherz, though he had obtained a visa for the United States, still felt responsible for the community and stayed. As director of the IKG, he was assisted by Wilhelm Bienenfeld, who served as head of the IKG's bureaucracy, and Benjamin Murmelstein, a young rabbi who headed the emigration department and thus later also had to assist in deportations. Murmelstein was loathed by Viennese Jews because of his overzealousness and cruelty, but it is extremely difficult to arrive at a sober, balanced scholarly judgment of this man.[14]

By September 1942 the mass deportations had been completed for the most part; more than 50,000 Austrian Jews had been deported from Vienna to ghettos in Eastern Europe and to Theresienstadt; thousands had been sent to concentration camps in Germany. It was only at this point that the Jewish administration in Vienna learned about the systematic extermination of European Jewry.[15] On October 31, 1942, the IKG's legal status under public law was annulled, and its work was carried on by the Council of Elders of the Jews in Vienna (Ältestenrat der Juden in Wien). Löwenherz was officially appointed head of this council, and, at his suggestion, Murmelstein, Bienenfeld, and Heinrich Dessauer were also appointed to it. Only a few weeks later, Murmelstein and Dessauer were deported to Theresienstadt, where in 1944 Murmelstein was appointed Eldest Among the Jews by the SS. In July 1945 he was arrested by the Czech government for possible collaboration, but he was released in December 1946 for lack of evidence. In 1947 Murmelstein testified at the trial of Karl Rahm, the last commandant of Theresienstadt, who, after having been convicted of crimes against humanity, was executed.[16] In 1949 Murmelstein was investigated in absentia by the Provincial Criminal Court of Vienna; his case ultimately got bogged down and was finally dropped in 1955 because of a lack of evidence.[17]

Back in Vienna the Jewish population was reduced to a few thousand, most of them individuals with non-Jewish spouses and employees of the Council of Elders, the Jewish hospital, or the Jewish old-age home. In the summer of 1944 the Council of Elders also had to care for 15,000 Hungarian Jews (8,000 in Vienna and 7,000 in Lower Austria), slave laborers who were interned in camps. They had been diverted to Austria to alleviate a labor shortage.[18]

After the liberation most of the Jewish functionaries did not expect to be arrested. Wilhelm Stern, who as a young man had worked for the Central Office for Jewish Emigration, could not believe that he was summoned to the Vienna State Police. As he put it, "That would have been the ultimate irony—if I had survived seven years of Hitler, and the State Police had ordered that I be arrested for collaboration."[19] But he also confessed that some employees of the IKG misjudged their situation and behaved arrogantly: "There were also colleagues at the IKG who forgot that they are the same as the rest of us. They sat at their desk and thought they were something special. They ended up in trouble. After 1945, some of them were arrested."[20]

Altogether, our knowledge is vague about how Jewish functionaries could live with their burden and how, after the Holocaust, they justified what they had done to survive. Although some stylized themselves as saviors of as many Jews as possible, others had a hard time continuing to live, even if they were not publicly accused.²¹ Dr. Paul Klaar served as head physician at the collection point, where he had to examine Jews who were going to be deported to the camps. His nephew, George Clare, later described how his uncle had functioned like a robot. Although no survivor accused Klaar of collaboration, he attempted suicide three times. In 1948 he died after being run over by a streetcar on Ringstraße.²² Dr. Julius Donath was a physician at the Jewish hospital and the husband of a non-Jewish woman. When he died in 1951, one of his colleagues wrote in an obituary: "Until his end he could not get rid of the sadness that had overcome him during the Nazi regime."²³ Hermann Wenkart, on the other hand, openly justified his position as Jewish kapo in a forced labor camp in Częstochowa in occupied Poland. Interestingly, he pointed out that he was proud of the fact that this position even permitted him to give orders to Germans. In 1945 he returned to Vienna. Later, he spent some time in Frankfurt, where he announced his candidacy for office in Jewish community elections. Ignaz Bubis, the former chair of the Central Council of Jews in Germany (Zentralrat der Juden in Deutschland), who had himself been an inmate in Częstochowa, vehemently opposed Wenkart's candidacy, recalling him as the "king of the Jews."²⁴ But Bubis also confessed that his uncle had nothing bad to say about Wenkart.²⁵ In 1969 Wenkart published his memoirs, not least of all to justify his position during the war.²⁶

In any case, it was not easy for the Jewish postwar leadership to face the problem of how to deal with Jewish collaboration and how to integrate or exclude Jewish functionaries after the war. Many survivors opposed those Jews who, in their opinion, had had a close relationship with the SS. But, as I show in the following examples, there were many gray zones and various forms of collaboration, most of which entailed communication with the SS.

A Jewish Honor Court in Exile: The Trial of Josef Löwenherz

On April 21, 1945, Dr. Josef Löwenherz was arrested by the Russian military administration. A month later, his wife, Sofie Löwenherz, head of the Viennese branch of the Zionist women's charity organization WIZO (Women's International Zionist Organization) and thus a central figure in Zionist circles, still did not know her husband's whereabouts. In a letter to their son Sigmund, who was about to get married in the United States, she expressed her extreme concern and despair.

> Russian soldiers came to his office at about 12:30 in the afternoon and took him away, apparently to answer a few questions. They said he'd be released that same afternoon, but he's still not back. All efforts to find out where he is have been fruitless. The gentlemen of Vienna's

municipal administration tried to help, but that too was in vain.... It's presumed that the Russian authorities want to try to pin some of the blame on Father as head of the Viennese Jewish Community for the horrible, tragic crimes the Nazis committed on Vienna's Jews.[27]

With the help of the Red Cross, Sofie Löwenherz learned that her husband was imprisoned by the Red Army in Czechoslovakia. On July 31, 1945, the Austrian government and the Jewish community in Prague brought about his release. Löwenherz was then admitted to the Jewish hospital in Prague, where physicians cared for his broken arm and ruined health.[28] A day after his release from captivity, Sofie and Josef were reunited. After several Jews spoke out in his defense, the charges of collaboration were dropped by the Soviets.[29] On October 10, 1945, the couple left Prague with the help of the International Red Cross and went to Switzerland, where they waited for a visa to enter the United States and to be reunited with their children.[30] Before their reunion, Erna Patak, former president of WIZO and longtime friend of the Löwenherz family, wanted to prove that the rumors of Löwenherz's collaboration were totally unfounded. In her touching letter to Sigmund Löwenherz, she described the heroic behavior of his parents.

> They were giants of fortitude and angels of kindness, and of a moral strength without equal. There was no rest for them, neither by day nor night—forever ready to serve, to help—always in danger—under consequent pressure—their composure and dignity compelled everyone's respect. Thus they gave their service to people who, without them, were forlorn and helplessly delivered to destruction. In this way, everything that was possible under those terrible circumstances was done for us.[31]

Back in Vienna, Ernst Fischer, the communist minister of popular enlightenment, education, and religious affairs, appointed Prof. Heinrich Schur as temporary head of the IKG. During the Nazi period, Schur, who was protected by a mixed marriage, was offered the position of chair of the Department of Internal Medicine in the Jewish Hospital on Malzgasse. In his position as temporary head of the IKG, he was assisted by Benzion Lazar, a retired high school teacher who was a member of the religious Zionist Misrachi organization and still an admirer of the Austro-Hungarian monarchy. Also protected by a mixed marriage, Lazar survived as a forced laborer in Vienna. Under the Nazi regime he was president of the Association to Aid Jewish War Victims, Invalids, Widows, and Orphans (Hilfsverband jüdischer Kriegsopfer, Invaliden, Witwen und Waisen) and successfully negotiated the release of disabled Jewish veterans of World War I from assembly and concentration camps. In 1941 he was replaced by the Central Office for Jewish Emigration and a rumor (proof of which never surfaced) spread that he had lost his position for embezzling funds from the Association to Aid Jewish War Victims, Invalids, Widows, and Orphans. Neither Schur nor Lazar was popular in Vienna. Although IKG social worker Franzi Löw characterized the 78-year-old Schur as an "egoistic, senile man," she portrayed Lazar as a weak character.[32]

Soon it became obvious that these two elderly men were unable to lead the Jewish community in this difficult time of the immediate aftermath of the war. Thus, not unexpectedly, employees of the IKG, led by Wilhelm Bienenfeld, former head of the IKG's bureaucracy and deputy leader of the Council of Elders, submitted a petition to Minister Fischer asking him to support the release and return of Löwenherz. Bienenfeld also remarked that there was still no working relationship with the American Jewish Joint Distribution Committee (known as the Joint), whereas Löwenherz, because of his excellent connections, would be able to raise financial aid for the needy Viennese Jewish community.[33] Indeed, Löwenherz had been the Viennese representative to the Joint since 1920 and had also worked with various international Jewish organizations to support emigration.[34] The IKG also needed Löwenherz's comprehensive knowledge about the Aryanization of its property and of the property of more than 600 Jewish associations and 300 foundations, only a few of which were reestablished after the Holocaust.[35] Representatives of the IKG were also aware that Austrian Jewish exile organizations in Great Britain, the United States, and Palestine and later Israel were in the process of developing plans for restitution demands; they regarded themselves as legitimate representatives of Viennese Jews and thus demanded heirless property for the support of Austrian Jewish émigrés.[36] The Jakob Ehrlich Society, named after a Viennese Zionist who was murdered in Dachau, was founded in London in 1941. Led by Franz Rudolph Bienenfeld, a well-known Viennese lawyer, Zionist, and leading member of the British branch of the World Jewish Congress, the Ehrlich Society aimed to represent *all* Austrian Jews and during the war had already started to prepare for restitution negotiations.[37]

Nevertheless, not everybody in Vienna was longing for the return of Josef Löwenherz. In August 1945, shortly after his release in Prague, the New York–based *Aufbau*, the most important German Jewish exile periodical, published an interview that Lazar had given to the *Daily Bulletin*, the publication of the Jewish Telegraphic Agency,[38] in which he claimed that Löwenherz and Wilhelm Bienenfeld had collaborated with the Gestapo on the deportation and extermination of Austrian Jews to save their own lives. He further accused them of having frequently shared the confiscated property of the Jewish victims with the Gestapo.

The editorial board of *Aufbau* was suspicious of Lazar's accusations and explained the arrest of Löwenherz as the result of the many conflicts in the Austrian Jewish community.[39] After the paper was inundated with letters to the editor either defending Löwenherz or showing sympathy with Lazar, the editors decided not to publish anything further on the subject until the matter was clarified.[40]

But representatives of major international Jewish organizations were eager to defend Löwenherz. On August 28, 1945, the *Daily Bulletin* published an interview with Löwenherz in which he defended himself against the charge of collaboration. He emphasized that he was proud of having supported the emigration of 136,000 Austrian Jews, although this resulted in his arrest several times.[41] The World Jewish Congress sent Alfred Weishut, a former Austrian and, like Löwenherz, a member of the Zionistischer Landesverband (Austrian Zionist Association) to Vienna to investigate the matter. His report stressed Löwenherz's integrity and his merits for having saved the lives of a great number of persecuted Austrian Jews. Lazar, on the other hand, was characterized as an "individual of ill repute."[42] Weishut also brought up the rumor that Lazar had stolen money from the Association to Aid Jewish War Victims, Invalids, Widows, and Orphans.[43] Because Lazar's interview with the Jewish Telegraphic Agency was also published in the *Berner Tagwacht* and because Josef and Sofie Löwenherz had already moved to Switzerland, a summary of Weishut's report was published in the *Israelitisches Wochenblatt* in Zürich. For its part the Swiss Union of Jewish Communities issued a statement describing as "baseless" the charge that Löwenherz had collaborated with the Nazis during the occupation.[44]

Nevertheless, the accusations of collaboration seemed never-ending. There were various reasons for this. In Vienna, returning concentration camp survivors spoke out publicly against Jewish functionaries, some of whom were still working for the IKG or in Jewish social welfare institutions. Beginning in the summer of 1945, the Vienna State Police filed charges against several Jewish functionaries. Thus it was inevitable that Löwenherz's position during the Holocaust would come under scrutiny. Some Viennese Jews presumed that collaboration explained the fact that he had not been deported to Theresienstadt when most of the other Jewish functionaries not married to non-Jews were deported from Vienna. They rejected Löwenherz's version that he had pleaded with tears in his eyes to be permitted to follow them to Theresienstadt.[45]

At the same time, left-wing Jewish representatives who had not served as members of the Council of Elders and who also had not had any connections to the prewar Jewish community took charge of the IKG. On September 24, 1945, Minister Fischer appointed his comrade David Brill as the new leader of the IKG.

Brill had survived in Vienna in a mixed marriage and worked as the private secretary of Johann Koplenig, who was briefly vice chancellor and leader of the Austrian Communist Party (KPÖ), a member of the Austrian coalition government. In its first report the newly elected IKG leadership criticized its predecessors for having hushed up the problem of the wartime behavior of Jewish functionaries.[46] It even briefly considered initiating disciplinary proceedings against Jewish functionaries such as Wilhelm Bienenfeld, Dr. Emil Tuchmann, Wilhelm Reisz, Rabbi Murmelstein, and Josef Löwenherz. In October 1945 the IKG dismissed Wilhelm Bienenfeld and accused him of collaboration with the Gestapo.[47]

In Great Britain, where approximately 30,000 Austrian Jews found refuge, *Zeitspiegel*, the most important Austrian exile publication and the official organ of the Free Austrian Movement with a circulation of 3,000 copies in forty countries, accused Löwenherz of collaboration. Founded in London in December 1941, the Free Austrian Movement was the most active Austrian exile organization. Although dominated by Austrian communists, most of whom had Jewish roots, it attracted many refugees by offering popular social and cultural programs. Contrary to Zionist exile organizations, the Free Austrian Movement wanted its members to return to Austria after the war and to participate in the building of a new—if possible, socialist—country.[48]

On April 19, 1946, the Association of Jewish Refugees organized a meeting to offer Löwenherz an opportunity to answer the charges leveled against him. Löwenherz defended himself by emphasizing his meritorious service helping the majority of Austrian Jews to emigrate. He also made it clear that Eichmann's Central Office for Jewish Emigration was solely responsible for compiling lists of people to be deported and for arranging the deportations. He further stated that the Central Office for Jewish Emigration did not collaborate with or consult the IKG in these matters. At the end of the meeting, which can be regarded as the prelude to an honor court proceeding, Bienenfeld emphasized that Löwenherz had saved the lives of tens of thousands of Jews while risking his own life.[49] The next day, Löwenherz and his wife Sofie left London for the United States to finally meet their children, whom they had not seen for years.[50] In New York Löwenherz received financial support from the American Jewish Joint Distribution Committee.[51]

In London the *Zeitspiegel* was not satisfied with Löwenherz' explanation and criticized him for having talked too much about his courage, ordeal, and efficiency while almost totally ignoring the deportations and mass murder of the Jews, thereby not addressing the most sensitive issue of Jewish cooperation with the Nazi regime.[52] Enraged by the report, Bienenfeld wrote to Löwenherz:

May I add that a thorough investigation is the more necessary, as one day after your departure an article was published in the *Zeitspiegel* under the heading "Dr. Löwenherz Again," which attacks in its first paragraph myself and then continues to call you a collaborator as the interviews in the [Jewish Telegraphic Agency] were never denied. I sent a letter to the Austrian Center [meeting point of the Free Austrian Movement] under whose auspices the *Zeitspiegel* is published, through a solicitor, in which I stated that the remarks quoted are a distortion of the truth and told them that I would make a writ of libel if they would not publish a withdrawal and pay a certain sum for Jewish purposes. As to the attacks against you, I cannot do anything, as a writ of libel is very difficult here if the Plaintiff is absent and cannot be called as a witness.[53]

To try to clear Löwenherz's name, Bienenfeld set up a sort of honor court.[54] Under his leadership, the Austrian Section of the Association of Jewish Refugees in Great Britain, the Jacob Ehrlich Society, and the London-based IGUL (an alumni association of Zionist fraternities at Austrian universities) formed a committee to investigate Löwenherz's activities in connection with the Nazi regime. Each organization appointed two representatives to read the report of the investigative committee before the final meeting.[55] Although the Association of Jewish Refugees suggested setting up a commission to work in New York in order to be able to invite Löwenherz to a meeting if necessary, Bienenfeld preferred London because the charges against Löwenherz were leveled there. Löwenherz, who was integrated in the discussion, supported Bienenfeld's position, adding that there was no appropriate network in New York. Thus it seems that Austrian Zionists were much more influential in London than in New York, where most of the Austrian émigrés lived. Finally, the commission was installed in London and Löwenherz was tried in absentia.[56]

Unfortunately, sources to document the concrete work of the investigative committee as well as its final report are missing. We also know nothing about the criteria according to which witnesses were selected and interviewed or who the interviewers were. From the correspondence between Bienenfeld and Löwenherz, at least we get the information that members of the committee made copies of source material in the possession of the IKG in Vienna, presumably from the *Tätigkeitsbericht* of the IKG (activity reports by Löwenherz to the SS). We also know that the commission was supported by European representatives of the World Jewish Congress, presumably friends of Bienenfeld, who had been a Congress member since 1937. As Bienenfeld informed Löwenherz, Alfred Weishut, the Congress's representative in Geneva, who had already defended Löwenherz against Lazar's accusations, had received reports from Vienna according to which all Jews and Jewish organizations expressed great appreciation for his activities during the Holocaust.[57] Bienenfeld further told Löwenherz that Dr. Charles Kapralik was invited as a witness. Because Kapralik had been in charge of the finances of the Jewish community in Austria between 1938 and 1939, he was no stranger to Löwenherz.[58] After Löwenherz was released in Prague, Kapralik expressed his loyalty to him: "We all know that Viennese Jewry is indebted to you. It is only due to your foresight, your energy and your purposefulness that it was possible for two-thirds of the Viennese Jewish population to emigrate before the outbreak of the war.... All these Viennese Jews now in Great Britain and the U.S. owe their lives to your work. God bless you."[59]

Thus it seemed that Löwenherz had little to fear. In September 1946, a year after its installation, the investigative committee published its results in *AJR Information*, the weekly publication of the Association of Jewish Refugees.

> The committee, acting on reliable information received, unanimously found Dr. Löwenherz's activities not only to be beyond reproach but rendering at the risk of his own life outstanding services to Viennese Jewry, saving the lives of tens of thousands and alleviating the tragic fate of many more. The committee feels bound by justice and honor to express on behalf of the Austrian Jewish immigrants in this country its confidence in and gratitude to Dr. Löwenherz and its appreciation of his heroic and unselfish struggle against the cruel treatment of Austrian Jews by the Nazis.[60]

On the whole, the outcome of the investigative committee in London seems to have been of little importance among Austrian émigrés or in the Austrian Jewish community; *AJR Information* published the findings of the commission only on page 71. In any case, the debate about Löwenherz demonstrates that the sensitive issue of Jewish functionaries was used in the power struggle between the various Jewish organizations. Obviously, Bienenfeld installed the investigative committee not only to clear Löwenherz's name and to silence *Zeitspiegel* but also to demonstrate the leading position of the Association of Jewish Refugees among the Austrian Jewish immigrants in Great Britain. In a letter to Löwenherz, Bienenfeld emphasized the importance of the result, arguing that *AJR Information* was "the paper of all Jewish refugees in Great Britain" and that the societies constituting the committee represent all Jewish-minded refugees from Austria in Great Britain." He also stressed that the Association of Jewish Refugees in

Great Britain represented two-thirds of Austrian Jewry.[61] But because the Free Austrian Movement, the most influential Austrian exile organization and the one behind *Zeitspiegel*, was not included, in fact the committee represented only a small number of Austrian Jewish refugees in Great Britain. This can be explained by the competition between the Free Austrian Movement and Zionist exile organizations, bad feelings that had been going on for years. As early as 1942, Bienenfeld had published *Die Aufgabe der Jacob Ehrlich Society* (The Mission of the Jacob Ehrlich Society), a brochure in which he vehemently denied the Free Austrian Movement any legitimate right to represent Austrian Jews as a whole.[62]

The endeavor to portray the Association of Jewish Refugees and the Jacob Ehrlich Society as the leading exile organizations of Austrian Jews also has to be analyzed in the context of the anticipated restitution negotiations and the power struggle that had already commenced among the various Austrian exile organizations and in which Bienenfeld had already taken a prominent position. One of the primary areas of contention was advancing their respective claims to heirless Jewish property in Austria, assets that were much needed by the IKG and Austrian Jewish organizations abroad.[63] At the time, no exact numbers with respect to the heirless property existed; at the beginning of the restitution negotiations, Jewish organizations demanded 1 billion Austrian schillings.[64]

How did Löwenherz react to the accusations against him? According to Sofie Löwenherz, he was never "crushed and disappointed, not even bitter because of the ingratitude and injustice of the people."[65] Some Austrian emigrants, however, remembered Löwenherz as a man who could never find peace of mind. Whenever he met a Viennese Jew in New York, he felt obliged to justify his behavior during the Nazi period.[66] In a letter to Wilhelm Bienenfeld in November 1946, he bitterly complained about the many ingrates for whom he had risked his life.

> I went out on a limb for everyone, and I rescued what could be rescued. I was in constant danger and what I received in the way of thanks was that I was forced to hear the basest slanders about me. They [the slanderers] caused me many a sleepless night, ruined my health, dragged my name through the dirt and, despite knowing better, spread lies about me.[67]

When, in 1947, an Austrian People's Court sentenced Johann Rixinger, head of the Gestapo's Jewish Department, to ten years' imprisonment, Löwenherz voiced the criticism that former employees of the Council of Elders had given one-sided testimony as witnesses. In a letter to Wilhelm Bienenfeld, he further expressed his contempt for them.

> The system during the Hitler era was damnable, and the methods of the Gestapo must be condemned. Nevertheless, a decent respect for the truth makes it incumbent upon me to mention the decency Rix [Rixinger] displayed in his dealings with the Jews.... The testimony by Gottesmann[68] and Kolisch[69] was wrong, personally biased, and it confirms my judgment of that whole group of men who groveled on their bellies before every SS man they encountered and now want to play the role of hero or martyr.[70]

Löwenherz himself had testified in the form of an affidavit on behalf of Rixinger. He felt compelled to differentiate among Gestapo men with respect to their character and behavior. He emphasized that Rixinger, along with Karl Ebner, former deputy head of the Viennese State Police, was "more humane" than Eichmann.[71] Rixinger, on the other hand, admitted at his trial that Löwenherz himself could not have sent anyone anywhere.[72] Löwenherz's judgment might also have been influenced by the fact that Rixinger, with Wilhelm Bienenfeld's support, made it possible for Löwenherz to stay in Vienna after most of the Jewish functionaries who were not married to non-Jewish spouses had been deported to Theresienstadt.[73]

But this did not come without a price. In 1952, when Rixinger was released from prison, he contacted Löwenherz. Portraying himself as a victim of false testimony by witnesses and "after seven years full of suffering, affliction, and defamation of all kinds," Rixinger pleaded for Löwenherz to send him a written declaration made under oath, confirming that he had never appeared in SS uniform and had always treated Jews in a humane way. He also asked Löwenherz to testify that he had not been responsible for the deportation lists.[74] There are no accounts of Löwenherz's reaction. Interestingly, in 1950 Margarete Ebner asked Löwenherz to provide a similar affidavit for her husband, Karl Ebner, former deputy head of the Viennese State Police and thus Rixinger's superior. In 1948 Ebner had been sentenced to twenty years in prison and was preparing an appeal. Having already spoken out on behalf of Rixinger, Löwenherz was regarded as the perfect character witness. "My husband sends his fondest regards" was how Margarete Ebner ended her letter.[75] In 1953 Ebner was pardoned by the president of Austria. Obviously, after the Holocaust Ebner was not bashful about using the long-lasting forced relationship between him and Jewish functionaries to stylize himself as a victim just like his Jewish counterparts.

Josef Löwenherz died shortly before the Eichmann trial was held in Jerusalem in 1961. He had already been hospitalized when the Israeli consul in New York sent him a questionnaire to be used in preparation for the trial.[76] Indeed, Löwenherz would have been an important witness. Nevertheless, he was spared the critical appraisal by Hannah Arendt, who, in her controversial book *Eichmann in Jerusalem*, accused Löwenherz and other Jewish functionaries of having collaborated with the Nazis. In her opinion, Löwenherz, hoping to facilitate his own emigration, had organized the IKG in such a way as to make it easy for the Nazis to deport the Jews. Without the support of Jewish functionaries, there would have been chaos and, in Arendt's scenario, more Jews would have been able to escape.[77] Charles Kapralik again vigorously defended Löwenherz at a forum held by the British section of the World Jewish Congress in response to Hannah Arendt's *Eichmann in Jerusalem*. In his opinion the picture given by Arendt was misleading, and he emphasized that "Dr. Löwenherz had displayed incredible courage in returning to Austria after he had been out of the country because he thought this was his duty."[78]

A Jewish Physician on Trial: Dr. Emil Tuchmann

Dr. Emil Tuchmann was one of the most prominent Jewish functionaries in Vienna. In 1938 he was appointed medical director of the IKG's social welfare service, and in 1942 he became head of the entire Jewish health service. In this position he had to submit monthly reports to the Gestapo and was responsible for handling complaints about the Jewish health facilities and their employees.[79] Despite all the difficulties he faced, he managed to maintain the medical infrastructure and to obtain necessary supplies for the Jewish community.[80] When 8,000 Hungarian Jews arrived in Vienna in the summer of 1944, Tuchmann also had to take responsibility for their medical care. He managed to set up a postnatal department and made arrangements with the Jewish employment office for exemptions from work for sick Hungarian forced laborers.[81] Nevertheless, Tuchmann was a controversial figure, and there were many complaints about his quick temper and the arrogant and authoritarian way he dealt with the staff of the Jewish hospital.[82] In a postwar act of vigilante justice, some camp survivors even went to his apartment and tried to beat him up.[83]

After liberation Tuchmann was briefly arrested by the Soviet authorities on April 19, 1945. Nevertheless, in August 1945 he was officially appointed Austrian representative of the American Jewish Joint Distribution Committee, which he interpreted as the ultimate reward for his successful work for the Jewish community during trying times. Presumably with the support of the Austrian Social Democratic Party (SPÖ), which after the first elections in 1945 formed a coalition with the conservative Austrian People's Party (ÖVP) and (until 1947) the small Communist Party (KPÖ), he also started his career as head physician of the Wiener Gebietskrankenkasse, an important health insurance provider.[84] Thus Tuchmann was shocked when, in the early morning of September 11, 1945, he was summoned to Vienna State Police headquarters. From there he was transferred to the police detention center. He would later recall:

> The officer did not even give me the opportunity to get urgently needed articles from my apartment. I was brought to the police lock-up like a pickpocket, without my overcoat and hat, without clean underwear or a toiletries kit, and without being permitted to leave behind even the most vital instructions for the *Hilfswerk* [Charitable Association] and the *Krankenkasse* [Health Insurance Provider].[85]

The Vienna State Police justified Tuchmann's arrest with the argument that Löwenherz was treated similarly by the Soviet occupation powers.[86] Obviously, the Vienna State Police used Tuchmann as a prime example of the many Viennese Jewish functionaries who kept their positions in the IKG and Jewish social institutions even after the war. In the summary of its criminal proceedings against Tuchmann, the Vienna State Police stated that many Jewish survivors reported Jewish collaborators and those who aided the Gestapo to the police and called for purging all Jewish institutions of former Jewish functionaries. As these survivors put it, Jewish functionaries had treated them "in many ways even worse than the SS did."[87] In the criminal proceedings against Tuchmann, a group of former employees of the Jewish hospital, among them physicians, nurses, and two janitors, filed charges against their former boss.

After Tuchmann spent ten days in custody, the examining magistrate informed him that his arrest was based on the Austrian War Crimes Law and that criminal proceedings had been initiated. The charges by the Vienna State Police against Tuchmann were based on the testimony of thirty-three witnesses and can be summarized succinctly: The IKG and Jewish doctors had executed the orders of the Gestapo and SS more than 100 percent. To make deportations as effective as possible, victims were never warned in advance and thus never had a chance to go into hiding. Tuchmann was regarded as the person with the closest relationship to Eichmann's Central Office for Jewish Emigration. The worst offenses he was personally blamed for included designating sick people for deportation in place of healthy ones and threatening rebellious employees with deportation to the camps.[88] The ultimate assessment of Tuchmann by the Vienna State Police was harsh.

Dr. T. must have been fully aware of the purpose to which he was lending his support and of his complicity. His active participation in the organized annihilation of the Jews was attributable solely to political motives, since the Gestapo offered him and his ilk the prospect of being permitted to emigrate once the other Jews had been transported to the extermination camps. The result of this active involvement was to condemn thousands of Jews to death or to agonizing oppression in the concentration camps.[89]

The Vienna State Police equated forced cooperation with collaboration. Despite the asymmetry of power, which meant that the Nazis could insidiously and consciously design situations in which Jewish leaders had no choice between good and bad, the Vienna State Police—headed by Heinrich Dürmayer, a communist anti-Fascist who had rigorously implemented the de-Nazification process in his organization—made no distinction between Nazi perpetrators and their Jewish victims. During the preliminary investigation conducted before Tuchmann's trial, it became obvious that there had indeed been certain gray zones and that Jewish functionaries had had a certain amount of decision-making latitude. But rather than indicating a symmetric relationship between Nazi officials and Jewish functionaries, this relationship should be characterized by what Lawrence Langer refers to as a "choiceless choice."[90]

Whereas the committee investigating Löwenherz concentrated on the problem of collaboration during emigration and mass deportation, the Tuchmann trial focused, moreover, on the period after mass deportations had come to an end in 1942. By this time, only a few thousand Jews remained in Vienna. After the Central Office for Jewish Emigration was dissolved in March 1943, smaller-scale deportations were sporadically carried out by the Gestapo, which also ordered that a certain number of IKG employees had to be included among those deported. As head of the Council of Elders, Löwenherz had to report to that body the number required by the Gestapo and how many from each department were to go. In this excruciating task he was assisted by Wilhelm Bienenfeld; Dr. Arnold Raschke, director of the Jewish hospital; Max Birnstein, director of the old-age home; and Dr. Emil Tuchmann.[91] At these meetings Tuchmann vehemently fought for his employees. In his report to the Vienna State Police he emphasized: "As a physician, I always protested against the evacuation of hospital staff members, often with great success, and I rescued a few in the nick of time from the claws of the Gestapo. These protests were often the cause of major disputes."[92] Bienenfeld confirmed Tuchmann's successful advocacy for employees he regarded as indispensable, but he also mentioned that this success sometimes left a bitter aftertaste: Hospital employees saved by Tuchmann had to be replaced by employees of the Council of Elders. In his testimony Bienenfeld stated that Tuchmann—to the disadvantage of the IKG—was quite successful in removing his co-workers from the deportation list.

> The names were determined by the Gestapo. Tuchmann had the names of employees he deemed essential removed from the list—members of the staff of the hospital and the old-age home. He made very extensive use of this right of appeal and in doing so he often worked at cross-purposes to us. He never provided substitutes for those who were spared due to his appeals. When such a substitute had to be named, then the IKG had to do it.[93]

It was this slight room for maneuver that Jewish functionaries were sometimes given that raised the crucial question of what criteria they used to select who would be deported and who would survive by continuing to work at the hospital. Did existing interpersonal networks have an impact on these selections? Tuchmann regarded his work as dangerous, a deadly form of self-sacrifice. In his testimony at the trial he pointed out that he had risked his life by sending sick people on a transport in place of healthy ones, justifying this decision on the basis of the greater chance of the healthy to survive than those who were seriously ill. He also recalled that he kept Jews at the hospital who, after the death of their "Aryan" spouse, were at risk of being deported.[94]

But Jews who had been deported refused to accept Tuchmann's narrative. They questioned the selflessness and heroism of his deeds and instead labeled him a detestable collaborator. Some witnesses came forth with the accusation that he deported people he disliked, whereas he tried to save those to whom he was close.[95] Members of his staff also reported that they felt intimidated and were even threatened with deportation to the camps.[96] In the words of Isak Rubinger, Tuchman was the most feared person in the hospital, though he too was "only a Jew."[97] Another witness remembered that Tuchmann was called a "Jewish Hitler."[98] But most of those accusations were based on rumors and have to be interpreted as acts of revenge and the culmination of years of people's struggle for their own survival.

However, this testimony also leads to the conclusion that it was Tuchmann's authoritarian leadership style that gave the impression that he was a much more powerful Jewish functionary than he actually was. Living in permanent fear of deportation, employees could not understand that threatening employees and shouting at them was, according to Tuchmann's testimony, the only instrument

The honor court at the Jewish displaced persons camp in Leipheim, Germany, 1946–47. Yad Vashem, photograph 1486/1267.

Survivors attack an unidentified former guard at Bergen-Belsen immediately after the liberation of the camp on April 15, 1945. United States Holocaust Memorial Museum, photograph 30428; courtesy of Lev Sviridov.

Jewish DP police detain a former kapo who was recognized on the street at the Zeilsheim Jewish displaced persons camp, 1945–48. United States Holocaust Memorial Museum, photograph 89566; courtesy of Alice Lev.

The honor court of the Jewish displaced persons camp in Hofgeismar, Germany; no date. Yad Vashem, photograph 3883/2614.

An investigation of a suspected former kapo by the Jewish honor court at the Jewish displaced persons camp in Ulm, Germany, July 7, 1947. *Left to right*: Meir Greenshpan, director of the camp's Judicial Department; Yerachmiel Yaakobovitz, commander of the camp police; and Yaacov Shazar, the accused. Yad Vashem, photograph 5020/230; courtesy of Eli Sagi.

Judges seated on the honor court of the Central Committee of Polish Jews presiding over the trial of Shepsl Rotholc, November 23–28, 1946, in Warsaw. In the middle sits Róża Koniecpolska, one of two female judges on the court. United States Holocaust Memorial, photograph 97033; courtesy of Żydowski Instytut Historyczny imienia Emanuela Ringelbluma.

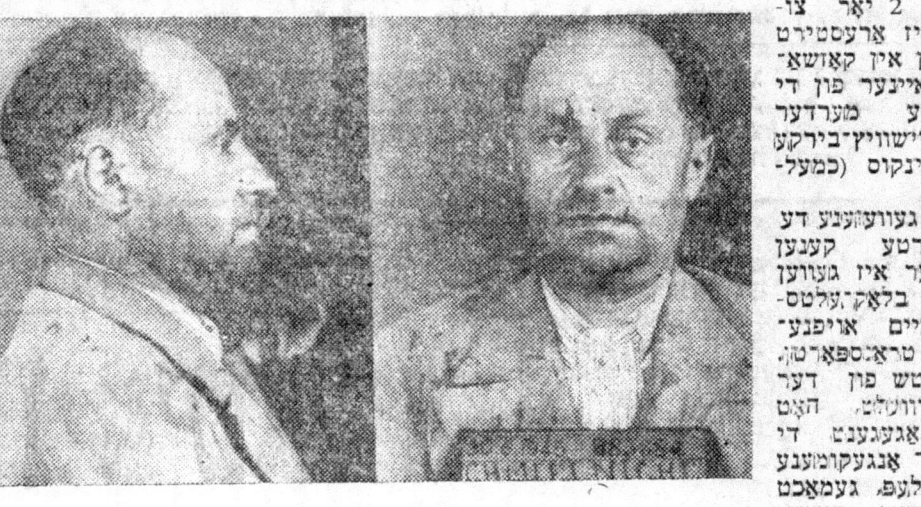

An appeal for witnesses to testify against Pinkus Chmielnicki, a Jewish prisoner at Auschwitz-Birkenau who was accused by fellow survivors of having tortured and even murdered other Jews; the call for witnesses was published in *Naye Prese* on July 11, 1947. It resulted in thirty-five affidavits and four witnesses who later testified at Chmielnicki's trial before a French military court in April 1950; the trial ended with Chmielnicki's death sentence. Courtesy of Simon Perego.

חקירה מוקדמת של משה פוצ'יץ הנאשם בהשמדת יהודים במחנות

אתמול הובא לבית משפט השלום בתל אביב לחקירה מוקדמת משה פוצ'יץ מתל-אביב, הנאשם בעבירות בניגוד לחוק לעשיית דין בנאצים ועוזריהם.

כעד ראשון מטעם התביעה הופיע צבי רואר כ"ץ, בן 29, מת"א.

לשאלת הקטיגור, סגן פרקליט מחוז א. דינרי סיפר העד, כי פוצ'יץ הת־נהג כרוצח במחנה אוסטרוביצה, שם שימש כסגן מפקד המשטרה היהודית, ולא־חר שמפקד המשטרה, בלומנפלד, הוצא להורג ע"י הנאצים בגלל יחסו הטוב אל היהודים, נתמנה פוצ'יץ למפקד המשטרה.

להלן סיפר העד על כמה וכמה מקרים בהם היה נוכח וראה כיצד פוצ'יץ הכה ופצע קשות יהודים במחנות.

העד עצמו הוכה אף הוא קשה ונקרע לו קרום האוזן הימנית, ורק כאן בארץ התרפא.

ב־1944 ניסו רבים מהעצורים במחנה אוסטרוביץ' לברוח ממעצרם, כיוון שנודע כי עומדים להעבירם למחנה ההשמדה. אך פוצ'יץ וזייפמן סגרו את שערי המחנה ומנעו את הבריחה.

לנאשם טוענים עו"ד י. בנימיני, ד"ר י. וירקליך. הסניגוריה ויתרה על חקירה נגדית של העד הזה, והמשך החקירה נדחה ע"י השופט צ. וולדמן ל־17 בפברואר.

ת"א תנוח מזמר "יו־יו"

רוכל הצעצועים הידוע, יוסף בכר, הידוע בתל אביב בשם "יו־יו", הובא לדין ביום א' באשמת תקיפת אנשים שסירבו לקנות אצלו, סחורה, הקמת רעש, תקיפת שוטרים בבתי קפה שונים בתל אביב. על חמש האשמות אלה נדון בכר למאסר 4 חדשים.

רופא ממשלתי שבדק את בכר, קבע שהלה. אינו סובל ממחלת הנפילה, כפי שהאמינו רבים מתושבי העיר, אלא מהתקפת היסטריה בלבד. צחי"ם

Headline from January 3, 1951, in the Israeli newspaper *Herut* for a report on the trial of Moshe (Marian) Puczyc, who was accused of being a kapo. Courtesy of Rivka Brot.

he had to maintain the exacting order and discipline demanded by the Gestapo. But Tuchmann vehemently denied dismissing anybody from employment on the grounds that he was aware that this would have meant deportation and death.[99] He also did not accept the claim that his harsh style and strict way of doing things were useful to the Gestapo. He also did not want to understand that once one participates in the decision of who shall not die, one also participates in choosing who shall die. Thus he could not accept the accusations leveled against him and described the trial as a smear campaign against him, assuming that some of the agitators had the "right connections to important people." Those who testified against him were accused of dragging his "very hard, self-sacrificing, and life-threatening work for the Jewish hospital, his employees, and patients through the dirt."[100] Most of all, he believed that some influential Jewish functionaries were exploiting the trial in order to take over his position as the Austrian representative of the Joint, the most important Jewish aid organization at the time.[101] He informed Saly Mayer, the Joint's representative in Geneva, that his arrest was the result of spiteful, irresponsible denunciations. In Tuchmann's opinion the IKG was run by elderly bureaucrats who were disgustingly deploying denunciations and intrigues to wrest control over the shabby remnants of a once proud and rich community.[102] Indeed, many fights were raging over the question of who was entitled to receive support from the Joint.[103]

Emil Tuchmann was released from prison in October 1945, and on April 19, 1946, the case against him was dropped because of a lack of incriminating evidence. As already mentioned, many accusations were based mostly on rumors and were difficult to prove. Tuchmann once again attracted the attention of the IKG when he gave testimony at the Rixinger trial in 1947. Like Löwenherz and Bienenfeld, he characterized Rixinger as the "only humane Gestapo official."[104] *Der Neue Weg*, the publication of the now communist-dominated IKG, reacted with scorn and demanded the exclusion from public life of all Jewish functionaries during the Nazi period. *Der Neue Weg* commented:

> But now this dirty laundry has been washed in public, exposed to Jews and non-Jews alike, so that hushing this up is no longer an option. We have already kept silent too long. Millions of Jews were gassed, and Jews acted as accomplices in sending these unfortunates to their death. We wanted to forgive and would have only too gladly forgiven. But one thing could have been expected of these people—that they, those who were the henchmen of our bloodiest oppressors, would disappear from Jewish public life and submerge into the darkness or . . . sit *shiva* [mourn] for the

rest of their life. But instead, they go about business as usual and stand side-by-side before the eyes of the world with Rixinger and his consorts. ... This festering wound must be cauterized. We should have nothing to do with them. They are not members of our community.[105]

Der Neue Weg also expressed its disappointment that most of the proceedings against Jewish functionaries had been dropped. Indeed, Wilhelm Reisz, *Gruppenführer* of the Jewish marshals under SS-Scharführer Herbert Gerbing, was the only Austrian Jew sentenced by an Austrian People's Court. The verdict was extremely harsh: fifteen years of imprisonment, including three months of hard labor. Reisz regarded himself as a victim and not as a perpetrator, and in no way had he expected to be convicted. He hanged himself in his cell.[106]

This raises the question of why no honor court was established in Vienna. I have identified several factors to explain this phenomenon. First, there was the continuity of personnel in the IKG. Furthermore, Löwenherz and Murmelstein, the most prominent Jewish functionaries, were investigated in Czechoslovakia and did not return to Austria. By autumn 1945, after concentration camp survivors and some emigrants had returned to Vienna, a new IKG leadership had been installed and feelings of rage might have already subsided. In addition, in the summer of 1945 the Vienna State Police filed charges against Jewish functionaries and thus took over the role of an honor court. And at this time Jewish survivors and the IKG did not expect that most of the cases would ultimately be dropped. We also have to take into consideration that in 1946 the IKG was confronted with restitution questions and had to compete with Austrian exile organizations and international Jewish organizations to assert its position as representative of Austrian Jewry and thus as legal administrator of the heirless property. It might also be relevant that in the same year a cold war had started in the IKG, whereby delegates of the World Jewish Congress supported by Austrian Zionists tried to influence the IKG elections to eliminate the communist leaders.[107]

In any case, Tuchmann no longer played a role in the Jewish community. He continued his career as head physician at the Wiener Gebietskrankenkasse and became medical adviser to the Austrian social security program, a member of the Supreme Health Advisory Board (Oberster Sanitätsrat) in Austria, and the head of the Viennese youth clinic.[108]

Dr. Ernst Feldsberg: A Tool in an Internal Jewish Power Struggle?

In 1952 *Die Stimme*, the official publication of the General Zionist party (Allgemeine Zionisten), warned that Ernst Feldsberg was "playing into the hands of the

Communists, who have threatened to publish embarrassing information about him." The article went on to say: "We only need to say one word: Nisko! Can't he remember that he once threatened that everyone who refuses to go to Nisko will end up in a concentration camp?"[109] Thus *Die Stimme* made reference to a meeting in the internally ruined city temple in Vienna in 1939. The IKG had invited all the men eligible for transport, and Feldsberg was asked—solely owing to his stentorian voice—to provide information about the Nisko project and to encourage people to volunteer. The reason for this was to avoid forcing the IKG to make a selection. At this time Jewish functionaries had no idea about what would happen to these people in Nisko. Feldberg, head of the cemetery department until his deportation to Theresienstadt in 1942, did not have the power to threaten anybody with deportation.[110]

The Nisko transport was the first mass deportation that the IKG was forced to organize. On October 10, 1939, six weeks after the outbreak of World War II, the IKG was instructed by SS-Obersturmführer Rolf Günther to send approximately 1,600 Jews from Vienna to this "autonomous Jewish settlement" in the vicinity of Lublin, in the newly founded General Government in German-occupied Poland. There the deportees were mostly left to fend for themselves, moving around lost for days and finally finding accommodation in small villages; some escaped across the border to the Soviet-occupied parts of eastern Poland and farther into the Soviet Union; those who remained in Soviet-occupied Poland fell into the hands of the German Wehrmacht after June 1941. When Nisko was closed in April 1940, because local Nazi authorities refused to handle the humanitarian catastrophe that befell the deportees, the 198 Viennese Jews who remained were allowed to return to Vienna.[111] But even though they were living under devastating conditions at Nisko, many of the deportees wrote letters to the Jewish community of Vienna in which they asked for help and also leveled accusations at Jewish officials. Some even charged them with responsibility for the deportations. Because of his role at the synagogue, Feldsberg's responsibility for this tragedy was established in the collective memory of Austrian Jews.[112]

In 1952 *Die Stimme* exploited this terrible situation that Jewish functionaries had been placed in by the Nazis as an election campaign tactic. The Zionists were disappointed that in the 1952 Jewish community elections, Feldsberg was a candidate of the Bund Werktätiger Juden (Association of Gainfully Employed Jews), which was closely affiliated with the SPÖ and, in the wake of those elections, had dominated the IKG, whereas it was hard for Zionist parties to gain a foothold in the Jewish community in Vienna.[113] Despite all accusations, Feldsberg was elected member of the IKG in 1952 and succeeded in gaining wide acceptance in the Jewish community. In 1963 he even became president of the IKG. Even political opponents appreciated his profound knowledge of Jewish tradition and religion and his meritorious service to the Jewish burial society Chewra Kadisha.[114] Thus it was unexpected that Simon Wiesenthal revived the charges against him in the 1960s.

At this time, Wiesenthal had already moved from Linz to Vienna and set up a new organization, the Association of Jewish Victims of the Nazi Regime (Bund Jüdischer Verfolgter des Naziregimes), to function as a public voice on behalf of former Jewish displaced persons who had stayed in Austria after the war. In the 1959 IKG election, his party won six out of twenty-four mandates. Most of his voters, like Wiesenthal himself, came to Austria from Eastern Europe as displaced persons after 1945. Wiesenthal repeatedly complained that "Viennese Jews" treated them arrogantly and tried to exclude them from the IKG. Thus in the 1964 election Wiesenthal wanted to break the majority of the Bund Werktätiger Juden and finally become president himself. In his opinion the IKG was "a prisoner of the Social Democratic Party,"[115] by which he meant that its leaders were primarily serving the interest of the SPÖ and thus neglecting Jewish interests.

During the election campaign, Wiesenthal tried to gain supporters by invoking Nisko. He circulated a document signed by an Eichmann aide from which it emerged that in 1939 Ernst Feldsberg took part in the selection of the Jews who were transferred from Vienna to Nisko. "The Vienna community seems to be the only Jewish community in the world headed by a person who also held a position during the period of the Nazi regime," Wiesenthal wrote.[116] Tom Segev shows that Wiesenthal also tried to mobilize the support of journalists and members of the Israeli parliament, the Knesset, as well as the World Jewish Congress. Nahum Goldmann, president of the World Jewish Congress, refused to get involved in this Austrian matter. In 1964 Wiesenthal broke with the IKG after the community's leadership fired him and took over his Documentation Center. This is the basis of Segev's assumption that almost everything concerning the conflict with the IKG was personal, a matter of ego battling ego.[117]

In 1966 *Der Ausweg*, the publication of Wiesenthal's Association of Jewish Victims of the Nazi Regime, which was dominated by Wiesenthal, demanded that "the Jewish Novaks have to be brought to justice."[118] SS-Hauptsturmführer Franz Novak, who had been one of Eichmann's aides and had organized transports of tens of thousands of European Jews to the gas chambers, was tried by an Austrian court in 1964 and sentenced to eight years in prison. Two years later a new trial led to Novak's acquittal, as he argued successfully that he had acted on the orders of a superior officer. It was not until 1972 that Novak was found guilty and sentenced to seven years in prison.[119] Wiesenthal used Novak as a drastic example to force the IKG to pass a resolution excluding all Jewish functionaries and Jewish kapos from any function in Jewish life. As Doron Rabinovici suggests, he calculated that his efforts to have former Nazis and war criminals prosecuted would be hindered if any current representatives in the Jewish community were suspected of having cooperated with the perpetrators.[120] The Bund Werktätiger Juden rejected Wiesenthal's demand because it became apparent that Feldsberg was again the intended target. Because Feldsberg had also been appointed Austrian representative of the World Jewish Congress, Wiesenthal again tried to convince Nahum Goldmann to support his fight against the former Jewish functionary. In his letter to Goldmann he wrote: "We cannot get worked up over the fact that there is a Nazi in office in Austria or Germany and at the same time ignore the fact that people like Dr. Feldsberg hold leading positions in Jewish institutions."[121] Goldmann again ignored Wiesenthal's request, and in the 1970s the two finally broke for good and Goldmann expressed how little he thought of the contribution Wiesenthal had made as a Nazi hunter.

How can we explain Wiesenthal's accusations against Feldsberg? One reason for them was the debate about the many former Austrian Nazis and war criminals who had gone unpunished. It was shortly after Wiesenthal attacked Feldsberg that he handed over the *Schuld und Sühne* (crime and punishment) memorandum to Austrian Chancellor Josef Klaus, member of the conservative ÖVP, emphasizing that a disproportionate number of Austrians took part in the destruction of European Jewry.[122] Wiesenthal had already criticized the fact that war criminals had been found not guilty by Austrian courts: war criminals such as Franz Murer, an Austrian SS officer who had set up, organized, and ruled the Vilna ghetto and was also known as the "butcher of Vilnius" (in 1963); the two Maurer brothers, SS members who committed atrocities and murdered the Jews of Stanisławów, Poland, now in Ukraine (in 1966); and Franz Novak (also in 1966). Wiesenthal had always been convinced that every manifestation of cooperation with the Nazis should be condemned. In this fashion he was still following the strategy he developed after the war, when he started publicly exposing the deeds of Jewish functionaries of the Viennese IKG[123] and collaborators in the Bindermichl DP camp. Tom Segev emphasizes that the hunt for Jewish collaborators was no less important to Wiesenthal than the search for Nazi war criminals. Like Hannah Arendt, Wiesenthal tended to believe that if no Jews had cooperated with the Nazis, more Jews would have remained alive. He also rejected a distinction between "good" and "bad" Jewish functionaries. Accordingly, he demanded the application of the "Wiesenthal law": Whoever cooperated with the Nazis in any way was to be excluded from any role in the Jewish community.[124] Only after Feldsberg had been dead for almost twenty years did Wiesenthal admit that "he was basically a good Jew. I can say this with a clear conscience though he was my opponent, a major opponent."[125]

But all these interpretations seem insufficient. Wiesenthal's attacks against Feldsberg, as Segev suggests, have to be seen as a fight against the IKG, especially against the Bund Werktätiger Juden. Dominated by the Bund Werktätiger Juden, the IKG ignored the *Schuld und Sühne* memorandum and also refused to support Wiesenthal in his fight with Bruno Kreisky, who had survived in Sweden and became the first Social Democratic Austrian chancellor in 1970. When Wiesenthal revealed that four ministers appointed by Kreisky had been members of the Nazi Party, the SPÖ threatened to close the Documentation Center of the Association of Jewish Victims of the Nazi Regime. Shortly after Kreisky was reelected in 1975, Wiesenthal proved that Friedrich Peter, chair of the Austrian Freedom Party (FPÖ), had been a member of the 1st SS Infantry Brigade, which had functioned as a killing unit. In his defense of Peter, Kreisky argued that nobody had yet been able to prove that Peter personally took part in massacres, and he compared Wiesenthal's accusations with "methods of the Mafia."[126] Kreisky, who felt personally attacked, termed Wiesenthal an agent of the ÖVP. Indeed, Wiesenthal had kept silent about the Nazi past of leading ÖVP politicians. It has to be mentioned that secret pre-election negotiations had taken place between Kreisky and Peter to form a coalition in case the SPÖ did not gain an absolute majority of votes in the 1975 elections. Historians have also interpreted the so-called Kreisky-Wiesenthal affair as an internal Jewish dispute, a conflict between Bruno Kreisky, a secular Viennese Jew who felt himself to be first and foremost an Austrian, and Simon Wiesenthal, the *Ostjude*, a pejorative term used by German-speaking Jews for Jews from Eastern Europe. This conflict had dominated the IKG since 1945.[127]

It is ironic that, at the escalation of the conflict, Wiesenthal himself was being confronted with accusations of having collaborated with the Gestapo. After the fight between Kreisky and Wiesenthal subsided, Kreisky, without any proof to back up his charges, accused Wiesenthal of having been a Gestapo collaborator. "Mr. Wiesenthal, I claim, had different relations with the Gestapo than I did," Kreisky announced at the Concordia Press Club during a briefing for foreign correspondents.[128] The conflict between Kreisky and Wiesenthal led to the outbreak of a wave of anti-Semitism. Many people in Austria were eager to believe Kreisky's accusation, and Wiesenthal was in any case quite isolated in Austria. Moreover, many Jews who were allied with the SPÖ and identified first and foremost as Social Democrats regarded Wiesenthal as an agent of the ÖVP. The IKG, run by the Bund Werktätiger Juden until 1981, did not defend Wiesenthal against the attacks by Kreisky; it preferred to keep more or less silent.[129]

Conclusion

In its first report after the Holocaust, the newly elected IKG described the difficulties and embarrassment it was faced with when dealing with the problem of former Jewish functionaries.[130] Or, as expressed by the Jewish periodical *Der Neue Weg*, the way to solve the problem of Jewish collaboration seemed to be the exclusion from the Jewish community of those Jews who were widely suspected of collaboration.[131] This strategy did not allow for a gray area in which ambiguity reigned between the victims and the perpetrators. This radical answer was also much supported by Simon Wiesenthal, a major opponent of the left-wing IKG who, as I have discussed, exploited this sensitive issue in an attempt to become president of the IKG.

The three case studies also demonstrate that the perspective of Jewish functionaries who for many years had worked closely with Nazi officials was quite different from those who had been deported or had been forced to emigrate.[132] It also became clear that witnesses who testified in support of the Jewish functionaries had held similar positions during the time of the Nazi regime or had survived in Vienna with their support.[133] Concerning the way Jewish functionaries defended themselves, it is interesting that Josef Löwenherz, Emil Tuchmann, and Ernst Feldsberg, though they had quite different personalities, portrayed themselves in a similar way: as saviors of as many Jews as possible and sometimes even as martyrs. They all showed their disappointment in those Jews for whom, in their opinion, they had risked their lives but who expressed only ingratitude. Some Jewish functionaries, such as Emil Tuchmann, Wilhelm Bienenfeld, and Leopold Balaban, went so far as to interpret the accusations against them as the result of a political conspiracy within the context of a power struggle in the Jewish community. Even though this defense strategy was used to escape the most painful questions of their cooperation with the Gestapo, there was at least some truth to it. The honor court proceedings in the case of Löwenherz in London and the criminal trial of Tuchmann in Vienna blatantly show that the debate about Jewish functionaries was exploited by various Jewish organizations and that the dispute about the distribution of heirless Jewish property, in which those Jewish organizations were involved, was of great importance.

Notes

1. In 1938 the Jewish population was estimated to be 206,000, according to the Nuremberg Laws. See Jonny Moser, *Demographie der jüdischen Bevölkerung Österreichs 1938–1945* (Vienna: Schriftenreihe des Dokumentationsarchivs des österreichischen Widerstandes zur Geschichte der NS-Verbrechen, 1999), 29.

2. See, for example, Herbert Rosenkranz, *Verfolgung und Selbstbehauptung: Die Juden in Österreich 1938–1945* (Vienna: Herold, 1978); Gabriele Anderl, Dirk Rupnow, and Alexandra-Eileen Wenck, *Die Zentralstelle für Jüdische Auswanderung als Beraubungsinstitution. Veröffentlichungen der Österreichischen Historikerkommission: Vermögensentzug während der NS-Zeit sowie Rückstellungen und Entschädigungen seit 1945 in Österreich* (Vienna: Oldenbourg, 2002), 20: 1; and Hans Safrian, *Eichmann's Men* (New York: Cambridge University Press, in association with the United States Holocaust Museum, 2010).

3. Doron Rabinovici, *Instanzen der Ohnmacht: Wien 1938–1945: Der Weg zum Judenrat* (Frankfurt: Jüdischer Verlag, 2000), 171–74.

4. Dokumentationsarchiv des österreichischen Widerstandes, ed., *Jüdische Schicksale: Berichte von Verfolgten* (Vienna: Österreichischer Bundesverlag, 1992), 286.

5. Leonard H. Ehrlich, "Leadership Under Duress: Some Ethical Problems," paper prepared for the Zachor Faculty Seminar, CUNY Graduate Center, December 9, 1991, Archives of the Leo Baeck Institute New York, Joseph Löwenherz Collection, AR 25055 (hereafter LBI Löwenherz Collection), box 1, folder 7.

6. Moser, *Demographie*.

7. See, for example, criminal proceedings against Leopold Balaban, Provincial Criminal Court of Vienna, as People's Court, Vg 2f Vr 2943/45; criminal proceedings against Wilhelm Reisz, July 8, 1946, Provincial Criminal Court of Vienna, as People's Court, Vg 1b Vr 2911/45; and criminal proceedings against Robert Prochnik, Provincial Criminal Court of Vienna, as People's Court, Vg 8c Vr 3532/48 and Vg 8c Vr 41/542. These documents are held at the Vienna Municipal and Regional Archives (Wiener Stadt- und Landesarchiv) (hereafter VMRA).

8. Winfried R. Garscha and Claudia Kuretsidis-Haider, "War Crime Trials in Austria," paper presented at the 21st Annual Conference of the German Studies Association (GSA) in Washington, DC, September 25–28, 1997; available at www.doew.at (accessed August 9, 2014).

9. See, for example, Thomas Albrich and Ronald W. Zweig, eds., *Escape Through Austria: Jewish Refugees and the Austrian Route to Palestine* (London: Frank Cass, 2002).

10. Susanne Rolinek, *Jüdische Lebenswelten 1945–1955: Flüchtlinge in der amerikanischen Zone Österreichs* (Innsbruck: Studien, 2007), 100–101. In the Ebensee DP camp, a kapo accused of informing on ten prisoners was executed by former prisoners. See *Oberösterreichische Nachrichten* (May 18, 1946): 3.

11. Helga Embacher, *Neubeginn ohne Illusionen: Juden in Österreich nach 1945* (Vienna: Picus, 1995).

12. Evelyn Adunka, *Die vierte Gemeinde: Die Wiener Juden in der Zeit von 1945 bis heute* (Berlin: Philo, 2000); Doron Rabinovici, *Eichmann's Jews: The Jewish Administration of Holocaust Vienna, 1938–1945* (Cambridge, UK: Polity Press, 2011). Also see the much longer German edition, Rabinovici, *Instanzen der Ohnmacht*.

13. Sylvia Maderegger, *Die Juden im österreichischen Ständestaat* (Vienna: Geyer, 1975).

14. See, for example, Rabinovici, *Eichmann's Jews*, 72–77.

15. Rabinovici, *Eichmann's Jews*, 202.

16. Murmelstein then went to Italy, where he failed to get a job as a rabbi. Finally, he became a successful salesman selling Italian furniture. See, for example, Ronny Loewy and Katharina Rauschenberger, eds., *"Der Letzte der Ungerechten": Der Judenälteste Benjamin Murmelstein in Filmen 1942–1975* (Frankfurt: Campus, 2011); Ehrlich, "Leadership Under Duress"; and Lisa Hauff, *Zur politischen Rolle von Judenräten: Benjamin Murmelstein in Wein 1938–1942* (Göttingen: Wallstein Verlag, 2014).

17. Rabinovici, *Eichmann's Jews*, 178.

18. Eleonore Lappin-Eppel, *Ungarisch-Jüdische Zwangsarbeiter und Zwangsarbeiterinnen in Österreich 1944: Arbeitseinsatz, Todesmärsche, Folgen* (Vienna: LIT, 2010); Rosenkranz, *Verfolgung*, 308.

19. Dokumentationsarchiv des österreichischen Widerstandes, *Jüdische Schicksale*, 290.

20. Dokumentationsarchiv des österreichischen Widerstandes, *Jüdische Schicksale*, 290.

21. Embacher, *Neubeginn ohne Illusionen*, 32–33.

22. George Clare, *Letzter Walzer in Wien: Spurensuche einer Familie* (Frankfurt: Ullstein, 1984), 276.

23. Julius Donath, "Nachruf," *Die Stimme* 45 (1951): 1.

24. Ignaz Bubis, *Ich bin ein deutscher Staatsbürger jüdischen Glaubens: Ein autobiographisches Gespräch mit Edith Kohn* (Köln: Kiepenheuer & Witsch, 1993), 77–79.

25. Bubis, *Ich bin ein deutscher Staatsbürger jüdischen Glaubens*, 78.

26. Hermann Wenkart, *Befehlsnorstand anders gesehen: Tatsachenbericht eines Lagerfunktionärs* (Vienna: Eigenverlag, 1969), 2.

27. Sofie Löwenherz to Sigmund Löwenherz, Vienna, May 20, 1945, LBI Löwenherz Collection, box 1, folder 7.

28. Comment by Sofie Löwenherz, n.d., LBI Löwenherz Collection, box 1, folder 7.

29. George E. Berkley, *Vienna and Its Jews: The Tragedy of Success* (Cambridge, UK: Madison Books, 1988), 343.

30. Comment by Sofie Löwenherz, n.d., LBI Löwenherz Collection, box 1, folder 7.

31. Erna Patak to Sigmund Löwenherz, February 16, 1945, LBI Löwenherz Collection, box 1, folder 7.

32. Embacher, *Neubeginn ohne Illusionen*, 36; Adunka, *Die vierte Gemeinde*, 20.

33. Adunka, *Die vierte Gemeinde*, 19–20.

34. With official German authorization, Löwenherz visited Paris in 1939 and Lisbon in 1941 to negotiate with representatives of the World Jewish Congress and to reach an agreement for mass emigration of Jews from Germany. See Löwenherz to his son, Sigmund Levarie, Paris, January 9, 1940; and Löwenherz to Sigmund Levarie, Paris, February 9, 1945, both in LBI Löwenherz Collection, box 1, folder 6.

35. Angelika Shoshana Duizend Jensen, *Jüdische Gemeinden, Vereine, Stiftungen und Fonds: "Arisierung" und Restitution, Veröffentlichungen der Österreichischen*

Historikerkommission—Vermögensentzug während der NS-Zeit sowie Rückstellungen und Entschädigungen seit 1945 in Österreich, vol. 21/2 (Vienna: Oldenbourg, 2002).

36. Helga Embacher, *Restitutionsverhandlungen mit Österreich aus der Sicht jüdischer Organisationen und der Israelitischen Kultusgemeinde: Veröffentlichungen der Österreichischen Historikerkommission: Vermögensentzug während der NS-Zeit sowie Rückstellungen und Entschädigungen seit 1945 in Österreich*, vol. 27 (Vienna: Oldenbourg, 2002).

37. Thomas Albrich, "Jewish Interests and the Austrian State Treaty," *Contemporary Austrian Studies* 1 (1993): 147.

38. The Jewish Telegraphic Agency is an international news agency serving Jewish community newspapers and media around the world. It was founded in 1917 by Jacob Landau as the Jewish Correspondence Bureau in The Hague with the mandate of collecting and disseminating news among and affecting the Jewish communities of the Diaspora. Since 1922, it has been based in New York.

39. "Der Fall Löwenherz," *Aufbau* (August 10, 1945).

40. Oskar Maria Graf, secretary of editor Manfred George, to Victor Ornstein, August 20, 1945, LBI Löwenherz Collection, box 1, folder 7.

41. "Austria," *Daily Bulletin* (August 28, 1945).

42. Adunka, *Die vierte Gemeinde*, 21.

43. Adunka, *Die vierte Gemeinde*, 21.

44. "Zu einer Verdächtigung," *Israelitisches Wochenblatt* (December 28, 1945).

45. Rosenkranz, *Verfolgung*, 360.

46. Embacher, *Neubeginn ohne Illusionen*, 31.

47. Adunka, *Die vierte Gemeinde*, 26.

48. Dokumentationsarchiv des österreichischen Widerstandes, *Österreicher im Exil, Großbritannien 1938 bis 1945* (Vienna: Österreichischer Bundesverlag, 1992), 166–68.

49. "Dr. Josef Loewenherz," *AJR Information* 9 (September 1946): 71.

50. Comment by Sofie Löwenherz, n.d., LBI Löwenherz Collection, box 1, folder 7.

51. Erwin Goldwasser to Löwenherz, August 13, 1946, LBI Löwenherz Collection, box 1, folder 7.

52. *Zeitspiegel* (April 20, 1946).

53. Bienenfeld to Löwenherz, May 2, 1946, LBI Löwenherz Collection, box 1, folder 7.

54. *AJR Information* 9 (September 1946).

55. The representatives were Dr. Robert Schwarz and Dr. Arthur Prager for the Association of Jewish Refugees and Dr. Immerglück and Mr. Lichtman for the Jacob Ehrlich Society; the delegates from IGUL were not known yet. See Bienenfeld to Löwenherz, May 2, 1946, LBI Löwenherz Collection, box 1, folder 7.

56. Löwenherz to Bienenfeld, May 24, 1946, LBI Löwenherz Collection, box 1, folder 7.

57. See Bienenfeld to Löwenherz, May 2, 1946, LBI Löwenherz Collection, box 1, folder 7.

58. Charles J. Kapralik, "Erinnerungen eines Beamten der Wiener Israelitischen Kultusgemeinde 1938–1939," *Bulletin des Leo Baeck Instituts* 58 (1981): 52–78.
59. Kapralik to Löwenherz, London, September 12, 1945, LBI Löwenherz Collection, box 1, folder 7.
60. "Dr. Josef Loewenherz," *AJR Information* 9 (September 1946): 71.
61. Bienenfeld to Löwenherz, September 10, 1946, LBI Löwenherz Collection, box 1, folder 7.
62. Franz Rudolf Bienenfeld, *Die Aufgabe der Jacob Ehrlich Society* (London: Jacob Ehrlich Society, 1942). See also Evelyn Adunka, "Franz Rudolf Bienenfeld: Ein Pionier der Menschenrechtgesetze," *David: Jüdische Kulturzeitschrift* 45 (2000), http://david.juden.at/kulturzeitschrift/44-49/menschenrecht-45.htm (accessed May 11, 2013).
63. Embacher, *Restitutionsverhandlungen*, 23–28.
64. Embacher, *Restitutionsverhandlungen*, 20.
65. Comments by Sophie Löwenherz, n.d., LBI Löwenherz Collection, box 1, folder 7.
66. Berkley, *Vienna and Its Jews*, 343.
67. Löwenherz to Bienenfeld, November 10, 1946, LBI Löwenherz Collection, box 1, folder 7.
68. Emil Gottesmann worked for the Aktion Gildemeester. In November 1943 he was deported to Theresienstadt. He survived Auschwitz and was liberated in Dachau. See Dokumentationsarchiv des österreichischen Widerstandes, *Jüdische Schicksale*, 211–15.
69. Sigfried Kolisch was head of the Association of Jewish War Victims. In 1943 he was deported to Theresienstadt. See Rabinovici, *Eichmann's Jews*, 120.
70. Löwenherz to Bienenfeld, November 10, 1947, LBI Löwenherz Collection, box 1, folder 7.
71. Löwenherz to Bienenfeld, October 17, 1946, and Löwenherz to Bienenfeld, November 15, 1947, LBI Löwenherz Collection, box 1, folder 7.
72. Testimony of Rixinger before the Provincial Criminal Court of Vienna, as People's Court, April 5, 1945, Vg 11g Visitor 4866/46/HV 1319/46; 63–65, VMRA.
73. Rosenkranz, *Verfolgung*, 360.
74. Rixinger to Löwenherz, Hinterbrühl, July 20, 1952, LBI Löwenherz Collection, box 1, folder 7.
75. M. Ebner to Löwenherz, Vienna, March 16, 1950, LBI Löwenherz Collection, box 1, folder 7.
76. Consul of Israel in New York to S. Löwenherz, LBI Löwenherz Collection, box 1, folder 7.
77. Hannah Arendt, *Eichmann in Jerusalem: Ein Bericht von der Banalität des Bösen* (Munich: Serie Piper, 1991), 93.
78. *Daily News Bulletin* 27 (October 31, 1963): 5–6.

79. Emil Tuchmann, "Report of My Activities in the Vienna IKG During the Nazi Regime from 1938 to 1945," criminal proceedings against Dr. Emil Tuchmann before the Provincial Criminal Court of Vienna, as People's Court, October 18, 1945, Vg 3c 1955/45, VMRA.
80. Rabinovici, *Eichmann's Jews*, 78–79.
81. Rosenkranz, *Verfolgung*, 308.
82. See, for example, Elisabeth Fraller and George Landnas, ed., *Mignon: Tagebücher und Briefe einer jüdischen Krankenschwester in Wien 1938–1949* (Innsbruck: Studien, 2010).
83. Tuchmann, "Report of My Activities."
84. Tuchmann, "Report of My Activities."
85. Tuchmann, "Report of My Activities."
86. Polizeidirektion Wien to Staatsanwaltsschaft Wien, September 1, 1945, criminal proceedings against Dr. Emil Tuchmann before the Provincial Criminal Court of Vienna, as People's Court, Vg 3c 1955/45, VMRA.
87. Schlußbericht der Polizeidirektion Wien, Staatspolizei, Ref. III, Herreng. 13, criminal proceedings against Dr. Emil Tuchmann before the Provincial Criminal Court of Vienna, as People's Court, September 13, 1945, Vg 3c 1955/45, VMRA.
88. Schlußbericht der Polizeidirektion Wien, Staatspolizei, Ref. III, Herreng. 13, criminal proceedings against Dr. Emil Tuchmann.
89. Polizeidirektion Wien to Staatsanwaltsschaft Wien, September 1, 1945, criminal proceedings against Dr. Emil Tuchmann.
90. Lawrence L. Langer, *Versions of Survival: The Holocaust and the Human Spirit* (Albany: State University of New York Press, 1982), 74.
91. Rabinovici, *Eichmann's Jews*, 125.
92. Tuchmann, "Report of My Activities."
93. Testimony of Wilhelm Bienenfeld, October 23, 1945, criminal proceedings against Dr. Emil Tuchmann.
94. Tuchmann, "Report of My Activities."
95. Testimonies of Isak Rubinger, Vienna, September 10, 1945, and Siegfried Kolisch, August 30, 1945, criminal proceedings against Dr. Emil Tuchmann.
96. Testimonies of D. Schulhof, August 8, 1945, Emil Gottesmann, August 8, 1945, Adolf Bienenstock, August 8, 1945, and Dr. Siegfried Seidl, August 8, 1945, criminal proceedings against Dr. Emil Tuchmann.
97. Testimony of Isak Rubinger, Vienna, September 10, 1945, criminal proceedings against Dr. Emil Tuchmann.
98. Testimony of Franzi Löw, August 1, 1945, criminal proceedings against Dr. Emil Tuchmann.
99. Report by Emil Tuchmann, September 27, 1945, criminal proceedings against Dr. Emil Tuchmann.

100. Report by Emil Tuchmann, September 27, 1945.
101. Report by Emil Tuchmann, September 27, 1945.
102. Adunka, *Die vierte Gemeinde*, 23.
103. Embacher, *Neubeginn ohne Illusionen*, 49; Adunka, *Die vierte Gemeinde*, 27.
104. Criminal proceedings against Johann Rixinger before the Provincial Criminal Court of Vienna, as People's Court, April 5, 1946, Vg 11 g Vr 1866/46/HV 1319/47; 49, VMRA.
105. *Der Neue Weg* 19 (mid-October 1947).
106. Rosenkranz, *Verfolgung*, 299–300.
107. Embacher, *Restitutionsverhandlungen*, 28–32; Embacher, *Neubeginn ohne Illusionen*, 150–67.
108. Embacher, *Neubeginn ohne Illusionen*, 36–37; Adunka, *Die vierte Gemeinde*, 22.
109. "Das Schicksal der Kultusgemeinde," *Die Stimme* 58 (1952): 2
110. Rabinovici, *Eichmann's Jews*, 186.
111. Hans Safrian, *Eichmann und seine Gehilfen* (Frankfurt: Fischer Taschenbuch, 1995), 68–81.
112. Andrea Löw, "Hilferufe aus dem besetzten Polen: Briefe deportierter Wiener Juden vom Herbst 1939 bis zum Frühjahr 1940," *Vierteljahrshefte für Zeitgeschichte* 60 (2012): 603–33.
113. Embacher, *Neubeginn ohne Illusionen*, 169.
114. Embacher, *Neubeginn ohne Illusionen*, 34–35.
115. Embacher, *Neubeginn ohne Illusionen*, 34–35.
116. Tom Segev, *Simon Wiesenthal: The Life and Legends* (New York: Schocken, 2010), 178.
117. Segev, *Simon Wiesenthal*, 179.
118. "Die jüdischen Novaks müssen gestellt werden," *Der Ausweg* 6 (December 1966).
119. Berndt Rieger, *Der Fahrdienstleiter des Todes: Franz Novak, der Transportexperte Eichmanns—Eine Biographie* (Norderstedt, Germany: Books on Demand, 2001).
120. Rabinovici, *Eichmann's Jews*, 187.
121. Simon Wiesenthal to Nachum Goldmann, June 28, 1966, Central Zionist Archives, Jerusalem, Z6, frame 1175.
122. "Schwere Schuld ohne Sühne? Memorandum über die Beteiligung von österreichischen NS-Verbrechen," *Der Ausweg* 5 (November 1966): 1–7.
123. See, for example, Rabinovici, *Instanzen der Ohnmacht*, 384.
124. Segev, *Simon Wiesenthal*, 130–34.
125. "Nachruf auf Dr. Feldsberg," *Heruth* (March 1989): 4.
126. Ingrid Böhler, "'Wenn die Juden ein Volk sind, so ist es ein mieses Volk': Die Kreisky-Peter-Wiesenthal-Affäre 1975," in Michael Gehler and Hubert Sickinger, eds.,

Politische Affären und Skandale in Österreich vom Ende der Monarchie bis zur Zweiten Republik (Thaur, Germany: Kulturverlag, 1995), 505.

127. Böhler, "Wenn die Juden ein Volk sind,'" 505.
128. Segev, *Simon Wiesenthal*, 82–83.
129. Helga Embacher, "Die innenpolitische Partizipation der Israelitische Kultusgemeinde in Österreich," in Werner Bergmann, Rainer Erb, and Albert Lichtblau, eds., *Schwieriges Erbe: Der Umgang mit Nationalsozialismus und Antisemitismus in Österreich, der DDR und der Bundesrepublik Deutschland* (Frankfurt: Campus, 1995), 321–38.
130. *Bericht des Präsidiums der Israelitischen Kultusgemeinde Wien über die Tätigkeit während der Jahre 1945–1948* (Vienna: Israelitische Kultusgemeinde, 1948), 5.
131. *Der Neue Weg* 19 (mid-October 1947).
132. See also Rabinovici, *Eichmann's Jews*, 184.
133. Embacher, *Neubeginn ohne Illusionen*, 35–36.

7

"The Lesser Evil" of Jewish Collaboration?

The Absence of a Jewish Honor Court in Postwar Belgium

VEERLE VANDEN DAELEN AND NICO WOUTERS

On September 1, 1942, after the assassination of Robert Holzinger, a prominent member of the Association of Jews in Belgium (Vereinigung der Juden in Belgien; Association des Juifs en Belgique; Vereeniging der Joden in België; AJB), the German-appointed Jewish council, Salomon Van den Berg, another AJB leader, responded in his diary to the accusation of collaborating with the German authorities: "God knows that I and the others among us have done our utmost to avoid deportations."[1] As Van den Berg's diary entry shows, he had no inkling that he lived in a world in which he was regarded as a collaborator. He did not understand his fellow Jews' hostility toward the AJB, because he was convinced that the organization had done nothing blameworthy. Clearly, Van den Berg suffered from delusions.

As a matter of fact, during the German occupation of Belgium during World War II, there was a strong sentiment in the Belgian Jewish community, expressed, for example, in the clandestine Jewish press, that Jewish traitors and collaborators, including the AJB, had to be dealt with. For example, historian Maxime Steinberg illustrates how *Unzer Vort*, the periodical of the Marxist-Zionist party Linke Poale Zion, became one of the most important voices of the

Jewish resistance. In its fourth issue in June 1942 the editors wrote: "The Jewish community is fully aware of the role this mandatory community has played in Jewish life and considers it, rightly so, as an instrument of our most bloody enemy.... [These men] may have the best intentions to serve Jewish interests—we highly doubt this and their brief activity proves otherwise. This community, imposed and controlled by the enemy, must be fought."[2] Jewish resistance fighters considered the AJB's leaders traitors to the Belgian Jewish community and threatened them with retaliation. In this spirit, Robert Holzinger, who was responsible for satisfying German demands for the recruitment of Jewish forced labor, was assassinated on August 29, 1942, and AJB president Marcel Blum was threatened with death and his home was plundered.[3]

After the liberation of Belgium in the fall of 1944, however, criticism of Jewish collaboration from within the Jewish community itself remained surprisingly muted. Only a few isolated retaliatory measures taken against Jewish collaborators by the resistance are documented.[4] And a Jewish honor court was mentioned or planned at one stage, but until now, apart from an isolated reference in an interview conducted many years later and a local Liège initiative that did not seem to have had any effects, concrete evidence of its existence has not been found.[5] The daunting challenges of material reconstruction, not to mention coming face to face with the harsh reality of the community's destruction in the gas chambers of Auschwitz-Birkenau, left the community with few resources to dedicate itself to matters of justice from within its own ranks.[6] In the aftermath of the Holocaust only a few surviving Jews in Belgium sought to bring members of the AJB to justice. Lazare Liebmann, for example, did not wait for the liberation of the camps or the hoped-for return of the deportees; rather, he filed a formal complaint against the AJB in a Belgian military court in October 1944, almost immediately after the liberation of Brussels on September 3, 1944, but the complaint was dismissed without punitive repercussion in 1947. Liebmann's complaint may have been an exception to the rule, but the complaint's dismissal by the court was indicative of the Belgian legal system's reluctance to touch the sensitive issue of Jewish collaboration. In this chapter we seek to explain why the Jewish community and the Belgian judiciary alike were hesitant to pursue justice against putative Jewish collaborators.

Jewish Life in Belgium on the Eve of World War II

When trying to illuminate the postwar reactions to Jewish cooperation with German authorities in occupied Belgium, one should first take into consideration the composition of the Jewish population in Belgium before, during, and immediately after World War II. Most Jews in Belgium did not have Belgian citizenship. In contrast with the neighboring countries of France and the Netherlands, where 56 percent and 80 percent of the Jewish populations were French and Dutch citizens, respectively, in Belgium in 1940 only about 6.6 percent of the registered Jewish population held Belgian citizenship.[7] This was partly because the number of Jews in Belgium grew considerably, from 5,000 in the last quarter of the nineteenth century to 65,000–75,000 on the eve of World War II, as a result of immigration from Eastern and Central Europe.[8] Another reason for the low number of Belgian citizens among the country's Jewish population was that Belgium, even though it had a liberal immigration policy, did not easily grant citizenship. Even being born in the country did not automatically confer citizenship, and the procedure for acquiring it was lengthy and expensive.[9] Thus, in general, when speaking of Belgian Jewish life around the time of World War II, we are speaking of a society of immigrants (*société d'immigration*),[10] with more than 90 percent of the total Jewish population in Antwerp and Brussels, with a far lesser amount in Liège, Charleroi, Ghent, Ostend, and elsewhere.[11]

Most Jews with Belgian citizenship were among those who had settled in Belgium before the major waves of immigration at the end of the nineteenth century; theirs a well-integrated, mostly bourgeois milieu.[12] However, Belgium's Jewish population included a vast range of outlooks characteristic of prewar Jewish life: from non-Zionist to Zionist; from Bundist to communist; from Conservative to modern Orthodox, including Agudat Yisrael and even Hasidic. Although most Jews in Belgium were of Eastern European Ashkenazic origins, there were also Sephardic Jews in the community. The Jewish Central Consistory of Belgium (Centraal Israëlitisch Consistorie van België; Consistoire Central Israélite de Belgique), the main umbrella organization of Belgian Jewry, dating from the Napoleonic era, embraced representatives of all officially recognized Jewish religious communities and represented the interests of the Jewish communities to the civil authorities.[13]

The survival rate of Jews with Belgian citizenship during the Nazi occupation was considerably higher than that of Jews without it. Shortly after liberation about 10 percent of Jews remaining in Belgium were Belgian nationals, compared to the previously noted 6.6 percent in 1940. Yet until the mid-1950s many of Belgium's Jewish population lived in the country with temporary residence permits or expulsion orders (*uitwijzingsbevelen*) or even illegally. Immediate postwar Jewish life, though changed by the war, was still diverse and defined by divisions between the religious and the nonreligious, the left and the right, and the Zionist and the non- and even anti-Zionist. Cohesion was hard to find. Uncertainty about residence permits plagued most members of the community, who remembered how Jewish refugees and communists were expelled from the country in the 1930s, and made them fearful of attracting attention from government officials and the police. As a result, they adopted caution and prudence when it came to publicly expressing political and social opinions.[14]

Nazi Occupation and the Association of Jews in Belgium

The invasion by the German army on May 10, 1940, was quickly followed by Belgium's surrender on May 28, after which the Germans installed a military occupation regime (Militärverwaltung), led by Alexander von Falkenhausen. This regime was replaced by a civil administration (Zivilverwaltung) in July 1944, which remained in place until Belgium's liberation in September–October 1944. In theory, this relatively moderate German occupation regime (compared with those in other countries) had no political mandate. Its priority was the economic exploitation of Belgium, and so its basic objectives were political pacification, social stability, and public order. The SS structures—the security police (Sicherheitspolizei, or Sipo) and security service (Sicherheitsdienst, SD)—had to fight for their influence in occupied Belgium and only gradually gained a foothold.

In general, anti-Jewish policies were not a top priority. However, the Brussels Militärverwaltung followed Berlin's orders and developed anti-Jewish legislation that generally followed the standard pattern used elsewhere: from identifying and registering Jews and their assets, to exclusion and isolation, to marking, and finally to deportation. Between October 1940 and May 1942 the Militärverwaltung issued eighteen anti-Jewish decrees. The last decree was the implementation of the yellow Star of David. This decree marked the end of the first phase of anti-Jewish measures. The Sipo and the SD—by this time firmly installed in occupied Belgium—assumed responsibility for anti-Jewish policy from the Militärverwaltung after May 1942. The Sipo and the SD managed the phase of mandatory labor, roundups, arrests, and deportations. Anti-Jewish policy in Belgium was therefore exclusively implemented through German legislation and German initiative. Nevertheless, Belgian authorities played an important role in implementing the German measures. Belgian involvement ranged from the registration of Jews, to police controls, economic and social exclusion, and physical concentration of Jews in larger cities (Brussels, Antwerp, and Liège), to, in some cases, active collaboration by the Belgian police and *gendarmerie* in searches and arrests.[15] The German Militärverwaltung exercised only relatively soft pressure when it came to anti-Jewish policy, and in this vein mediated between Belgian authorities and the radical German Sipo and SD.

THE ABSENCE OF A JEWISH HONOR COURT IN POSTWAR BELGIUM

This was the general context in which the AJB was founded by the German decree of November 25, 1941 (published in the *Verordnungsblatt* on December 2, 1941).[16] In other words, the Germans created this organization. It had its seat in Brussels, with local committees for Antwerp, Brussels, Liège, and Charleroi, all of which were represented in the central office—the umbrella committee—in Brussels.[17] Membership was mandatory for all individuals in Belgium who had registered as Jews following the decree of October 28, 1940.

The board of the AJB counted seven members: a president, a vice-president, and five regular members. The board was appointed by the German military command; resignations were possible only if approved by von Falkenhausen. Most of the board's members belonged to the Belgian Jewish bourgeoisie and were active in Jewish community life, such as Jewish religious congregations and welfare organizations. The chief rabbi of Belgium, Salomon Ullmann (born in Budapest in 1882), became the AJB's first president. Before his appointment as chief rabbi in October 1940, he had been the head rabbi of the Orthodox community Machsike Hadas in Antwerp and a military chaplain in the Belgian army.[18] He survived to see the end of the war and was eventually liberated by Allied troops at Kazerne Dossin in August 1944.[19] The board's vice-president was Niko David Workum (born in Amsterdam in 1907), who also served as the head of the local AJB committee in Antwerp. Originally Dutch, Workum had become a Belgian national in the 1930s. He was deported during Operation Iltis, the major roundup and deportation of Jews in Belgium during the night of September 3–4, 1943, and never returned.

The other representatives of the AJB board from Antwerp were Joseph Teichmann and Maurice Benedictus (born in Antwerp in 1907). Little is known about Teichmann. He did not attend any AJBs meetings. Benedictus, an Antwerp-based cigar manufacturer, was from a Dutch family that had settled in Antwerp a century earlier, but he did not hold any positions in Jewish organizational life before being assigned to the AJB. He was head of the AJB administration until he fled to Lisbon in December 1942.[20] Salomon Van den Berg (born in Leiden in 1890) became head of the local Brussels AJB committee and the representative for Brussels in the central office, where he took up the function of treasurer, and, after Benedictus's flight, from April 1943 onward he served as head of the administration.[21] Van den Berg, who was originally Dutch but had become Belgian in 1930, was a furniture wholesaler; from the outset of the occupation, he was the vice-president of the Israelite Community of Brussels. Van den Berg's diaries, together with reports written by Benedictus in Lisbon, offer an exceptionally rich source on the internal workings of the AJB. For Charleroi, Juda (alias Jules)

Mehlwurm (born in the Lublin area of the Russian Empire in 1899) received a seat in the central office. Mehlwurm, who in 1934 had settled as a merchant in Charleroi, not only became an AJB representative during the war but also, along with the rest of the local AJB in Charleroi, was active in the resistance. The Liège community was represented by Noé Nozice (or Nozyce), a furrier of Polish origins. On April 13, 1943, Nozice was arrested with his wife and their two daughters and deported to Auschwitz. He would be the only survivor from his family.[22]

The board of the central office underwent several changes during the occupation. Teichmann was replaced by David Lazare (also known as Lazer or Lazar, born in Poland in 1885).[23] Lazare was the vice-president of the Brussels Orthodox community and since 1940 the head of the Central Jewish Relief Work (Oeuvre Centrale Israélite de Secours); he was also the father-in-law of Noé Nozice, the Liège representative. Mehlwurm went into hiding around the time that the local committee of Charleroi ceased its activities on September 23, 1942, and he was replaced in the central office by Louis Rosenfeld, an industrialist from Berlin who had moved to Belgium in January 1939.[24]

The next person to be replaced on the committee was Ullmann, the president, who, after his incarceration (together with Benedictus, Van den Berg, Alfred Blum, and Eugène Hellendall) in the Breendonk concentration camp on September 24, 1942, tendered his resignation letter on October 8, 1942, to von Falkenhausen.[25] Ullmann was replaced by Marcel Blum (born in Hirsingen, Alsace, in 1883), whose son, Alfred Blum, had been the treasurer of the local Brussels AJB committee. Marcel Blum was an industrialist in the textile sector; he had moved to Brussels in 1900 and become a member of the Consistory and of the board of directors of the Israelite Community of Brussels, of which he became president at the beginning of the occupation.[26]

The last two changes resulted from a compromise: Judenreferent SS-Obersturmführer Kurt Asche wanted a German Jew to head the AJB, perhaps because he expected a German to be more loyal. The AJB wanted to appoint someone else. After negotiations, Asche accepted Blum, even though he was non-German. The appointment of Rosenfeld to the AJB did bring a German into the central office.[27] This indicates the difficult internal relations between German and non-German Jews in Belgium during the occupation, a point that would also briefly surface during the judicial investigation of the AJB leadership after the war.

After Operation Iltis, all local AJB committees ceased to exist, except the one in Brussels. Between April and October 1943 the Jewish communities in Antwerp, Charleroi, Ghent, Mons, Arlon, and Liège were liquidated. The few members of the local AJB committees who had been able to save themselves were incorporated into the central office, which merged with the local Brussels AJB committee.[28] In this way Chaïm Perelman (born in Warsaw in 1912) became more involved on the central level. Perelman had moved from Poland to Belgium in 1925, acquiring Belgian citizenship in 1936. He taught philosophy of law at the Université Libre de Bruxelles; during the war he became one of the founding members of the Jewish Defense Committee (Comité de Défense des Juifs), a Jewish resistance group.[29] Perelman was involved with the local Brussels AJB committee from its inception, but, owing to personal reservations, he joined the AJB as a full member only in November 1942. Next to him, David Ferdman was also active both in the AJB central office and in clandestine resistance activities. It was not until August 20, 1944—two weeks before liberation—that the remaining members of the AJB decided to go into hiding.[30]

The AJB committees, both central and local, assumed responsibility for a wide range of communal and welfare activities, which the Germans restricted to the purview of the AJB.[31] The AJB was also responsible for aid to Jewish forced laborers and prisoners and, later, also deportees. All this was basically implied in Paragraph 3 of the German decree that installed the AJB.[32] The funding of the AJB's activities came from obligatory membership fees, from incorporating Jewish organizations (or their assets in case of obligatory dissolution) into the association, and, in case of insufficient funding, from the Belgian state. Apart from being the Jewish community's official liaison with the German occupying authorities, the AJB was responsible for registering the country's Jewish population;[33] because membership in the AJB was obligatory, the organization compiled detailed demographic and occupational data on each Jewish family.[34] After the nineteen mayors of the Brussels urban agglomeration refused, the Germans delegated to the AJB the task of distributing Star of David patches that all Jews were required to wear. Summonses for "forced labor in the East" were also communicated by the AJB, with the following guarantee: "According to assurances given by the occupying authorities, it [the appeal] is indeed about performing labor and not a measure of deportation."[35] It should come as no surprise, then, that members of the Jewish community increasingly resented the AJB.

The history of the AJB in Belgium is complex. On the one hand, its members assisted the harassed Jewish community; on the other hand, they became an instrument of persecution in the hands of the German occupier. Within certain limits the AJB's leaders resisted German anti-Jewish policies. According to historian Insa Meinen's study of the minutes of the Executive Committee, the Executive Committee actively sought contact with the Germans to defend Jewish interests and intervened often sharply to achieve this.[36] But the AJB was beset by regional differences between the central office and the local departments. To further complicate the AJB's image, some of its leaders were highly active in the resistance movement, for example, Perelman and Hellendall in Brussels and the whole local AJB committee in Charleroi.[37] An overall assessment could be that the AJB leadership had begun with good intentions but became ensnared in entanglements detrimental to Belgian Jewry, entanglements from which it was unable to withdraw.[38]

The Investigation of Anti-Jewish Persecution in Belgian Courts, 1944–1951

With liberation, all German legislation in Belgium was nullified.[39] In September 1944 Belgium reverted to the legal status quo before May 1940. Because all Nazi legislation disappeared overnight, the German-constructed Jewish "problem" likewise ceased to exist in the Belgian state.

Like all other European countries, Belgium faced immense political and material challenges after liberation. Punishment for the commission of war crimes and collaboration was one of those challenges, yet it was not the government's highest priority. The responsibility for postwar trials in Belgium was given to the military courts, as had been the case after World War I. For obvious reasons the German occupation of Belgium left these military courts with an enormous amount of work in 1944. The number of military courts (*Krijgsraad* in Dutch) grew from four in September 1944 to twenty-one by mid-1946, and the various chambers of the military court of appeal (*Krijgshof* in Dutch) grew from a handful of chambers to a court with twenty-four chambers. The military courts were organized by judicial district, with courts seated in most larger cities, whereas the military courts of appeal were located in the four major cities of Belgium. The number of military magistrates, many of them young and inexperienced, grew exponentially. In 1944 and 1945 these courts were understaffed and inexperienced and to a large extent had to invent a judicial strategy and adapt the classic Belgian penal framework to the massive scale of war crimes and collaboration executed on Belgian soil.

The persecution of Jews in occupied Belgium was highlighted in trials against German war criminals, trials against members of the Belgian elite who had followed a policy of cooperation with the German occupier, and trials against other Belgian Nazi collaborators. The Belgian political and legal establishment adhered to a strict interpretation of the universal principle of nonretroactivity. Therefore war crimes and collaboration were to be tried based on the existing prewar penal framework. Belgian penal law was not adapted in any way to take into account the specificity of the wartime persecution of the Jews.

In general terms, by 1947 the Belgian military prosecutors were aware of the specific nature and the scale of the genocide that had been perpetrated against the Jews during the war years. A 1947 report by the Belgian War Crimes Commission on the persecution of Jews was a remarkably accurate document for the period.[40] It addressed the systematic and exceptional nature of the Nazi mass murder of the Jews, although the report limited itself to the specific Belgian situation. But this awareness about the exceptional nature of the Holocaust did not translate into practical legal solutions. In this vein the report failed to offer any legal analysis or legal strategy for prosecuting these crimes within the Belgian legal framework. Therefore the prosecution of anti-Jewish persecution in Belgian military courts ended up being legally fragmented over several lesser crimes (e.g., theft, maltreatment, and arbitrary incarceration), and the general context and systematic nature of the specific persecution and genocide of the Jews were completely lost in the proceedings.

Over the course of several years and myriad judicial investigations, a massive amount of relevant information was gathered on the crimes committed against Jews on Belgian soil between May 1940 and September 1944. Many military prosecutors attempted to use such evidence to indict and convict certain German and Belgian perpetrators. This was generally the case in the investigations and trials of German war criminals; these proceedings were undertaken in Belgium and were based on the Belgian war crimes law of June 20, 1947. Based on this law, thirty-seven trials were held in Belgium between 1947 and 1951, involving 106 defendants, of whom 13 were Belgians and the rest were mostly Germans and Austrians.[41] In some of these cases the persecution of Jews in Belgium played a significant role. However, with a few exceptions, the issue of Jewish complicity or Jewish perpetrators was entirely absent. When it did emerge, this issue did not elicit special attention. Most Jewish defendants accused of complicity with the German occupying forces did not hold Belgian citizenship and were thus considered only minor and unimportant foreign helpers. The 1946 Breendonk trial, which we discuss later, was the only notable exception. No specific legal strategy was ever developed to address the issue of Jewish complicity, and we have found no legal correspondence between judicial actors that dealt with the issue. Likewise, the extensive archives of the so-called General Instruction Service of the Chief Military Prosecutor's Office include no files or correspondence relating to Jewish perpetrators.[42] In short, it appears that after the war the Belgian judiciary never paid systematic attention to the problem of alleged Jewish collaboration.

The Cases Against the Leadership of the Association of Jews in Belgium

The AJB did not appear on any lists of collaborationist organizations or in the hundreds of judicial instructions and decrees issued by the Chief Military Prosecutor's Office. The AJB was hardly a priority in the immediate postwar context for a military court system working under poor conditions and overwhelmed with cases. However, the Belgian courts were forced to deal with the issue of the AJB in October 1944, when Lazare Liebmann filed an elaborate complaint with the Brussels Military Court against the council's leadership.[43] The judicial investigation against the AJB became the only postwar case in which putative Jewish collaboration was the central issue.[44]

Who was Liebmann and why did he file this complaint?[45] Liebmann (born in Warsaw in 1892) had been rejected for a seat on the AJB's board of directors. He was president of the Association of Former Civilian Prisoners of 1914–1918 (Amicale des anciens Prisonniers civils de 1914–1918) and considered himself a Belgian patriot.[46] The complaint itself was elaborate and well prepared. Liebmann accused the AJB leadership of executing German anti-Jewish measures with regard to mandatory membership (and collecting mandatory fees for it), establishing and transferring lists of names, distributing the yellow star and labor summonses, selling "protection cards," and protecting themselves and their relatives to the prejudice of others. Liebmann made a distinction between the "bad" AJB leadership by Jews of German and Austrian origins and the "good" non-German AJB leaders. He weakened his complaint in successive testimonies during interrogations in 1945 by stressing that despite the "mistakes" the AJB leadership had made, they had never intended to betray the Belgian state.[47] This essentially neutralized the central legal grounds for conviction, as discussed below.

A second complaint against the AJB was filed in November 1946 by another survivor, Roger Van Praag of the Jewish Defense Committee. Van Praag's main points of complaint about the central AJB leadership were establishing registration files, including list of names, propagating the creation of local AJB sections, and distributing summonses for mandatory labor. In particular, he mentioned letters from the occupation in which the AJB leadership called for strict obedience to the German calls for mandatory labor.[48] Van Praag stressed that the option of the underground organization would have been much better but that Ullmann and the other AJB leaders had always resisted this option, also, as Van Praag suggested, to ensure their own personal safety. After offering a critical assessment of the AJB's strategy and policies, Van Praag strongly undermined his own complaint from a legal perspective by concluding: "However, I believe I can say that they [the council's leaders] did not have the intention to serve the enemy."[49]

By making arguments like these, both Liebmann and Van Praag undermined their elaborate complaints from the outset. The most important legal bases for the entire case were both Penal Article 118-bis (which dealt with political collaboration) and Penal Article 115 (pertaining to economic collaboration). Penal Article 121-bis, regarding denunciation, also surfaced in the indictments during the investigations, but it never played a significant role. The entire legal logic and usefulness of both "political collaboration" and "economic collaboration" was founded on the assessment of whether the defendant had tried to act against Belgian state interests ("internal and external threats to Belgian state security"). Jurisprudence on different forms of collaboration after the liberation would develop along the lines of this national (patriotic) paradigm. The underlying key question was whether the defendant had, willingly and/or with malicious intent, betrayed the Belgian state. In the case of the AJB leadership, when the two most important accusers (Liebmann and Van Praag) stressed from the beginning that betrayal was certainly *not* the case, they basically said that in legal terms the AJB had never been a collaborating organization. Indeed, this made things difficult for Belgian judicial authorities. They had to open official investigations. But the legal basis was weak from the beginning, despite the elaborate nature of the complaints.

The judicial investigation quickly focused on seven members of the AJB's central office leadership: Salomon Ullmann, Maurice Benedictus, Alfred Blum, Salomon Van den Berg, David Lazare, Nico David Workum, and Juda (Jules) Mehlwurm, paying particular attention to the first four men. It is important to note that all the accused were part of the initial board and that none of those who had been assigned in 1942 or later were included in the investigation.

It seemed clear already in 1945 that the Brussels military prosecutors had many other priorities and in general did not know how to handle the AJB case.[50] As was often the case with judicial investigations pertaining to collaboration, the Belgian State Security was in charge of the investigation. For more than two years, however, there was hardly any actual investigation. The Belgian judiciary police[51] confiscated the remaining AJB documents from what had formerly been the organization's head office, where in the meantime Jewish social welfare was being organized. However, the search of the building at Kazernestraat 33 in Brussels was not carried out until February 13, 1946, and this was how the judicial file at the Military Prosecutor's Office came to contain the minutes of the national and Brussels AJB meetings from 1942 and 1943. Other documents had already been confiscated on December 20, 1944.[52]

The separate investigations against Salomon Van den Berg and David Lazare concerning economic collaboration (files opened in 1945 and 1946, respectively, and subsequently closed without further action) were added to the AJB case on September 10, 1946, and August 12, 1946, respectively, but were never used.[53] However, despite investigative material and fragmentary evidence having been collected in response to the two complaints by Liebmann and Van Praag, a great deal of relevant evidence remained unused or unexamined. David Lazare, for example, was never even interrogated by the Belgian investigators during the entire case.[54] The attitude of the Belgian military prosecutors in this case can be described as being somewhere between doubtful and passive. Even when the association Aid to Jewish War Victims (Hulp aan Israëlieten Slachtoffers van de Oorlog/Aide aux Israélites Victimes de la Guerre) filed a complaint with the Brussels military court against the AJB in June 1945, in which it cited many new names, facts, and sources, the Brussels military court offered no response and undertook no investigative action.

Several parallel satellite investigations were conducted in other military courts. The Liège military court opened an investigation into two leading members, Noé Nozice and David Ackerman of the AJB's Liège office, following complaints from the Jewish Defense Committee.[55] However, it seems that this local investigation remained dormant and that the Liège court was waiting for a decision in the central Brussels case. The Charleroi military court also opened an investigation into the Charleroi branch of the AJB. The indictment was based on Article 118-bis, but after an unfruitful investigation, the case was closed in April 1946.

Apart from these investigations, several other local leading AJB members were investigated. The Liège military court opened an investigation against Grégoire Garfinkels after a complaint from the Jewish Defense Committee. This complaint primarily concerned Garfinkels's handing over of lists of Jews to the German occupying forces. However, because the Belgian military courts generally used a highly restrictive judicial interpretation of Penal Article 121-bis, pertaining to denunciations, it was clear from the beginning that the basis of the case was weak; the case was closed in April 1947.[56] The Brussels military court opened separate investigations into Hans Berlin, Hans Blum, and Félix Meyer on the basis of Articles 118-bis and 115, all of which were eventually closed. Berlin and Meyer were members of the Aid Society of Jews from Germany (Hilfswerk der Arbeitsgemeinschaft von Juden aus Deutschland), of which also German

AJB members Louis Rosenfeld and Robert Holzinger were part.[57] No judicial investigations were initiated against members of the AJB in Antwerp. This was perhaps because most of the AJB members in Antwerp were deported and killed.

The Belgian military courts never made any serious attempt to make a proper judicial analysis of the AJB's wartime policy and actions. Not only were these issues never systematically investigated and analyzed, but there were also no attempts to connect these actions to possible infractions of the Belgian penal law. Finally, no cooperation was ever attempted between the central Brussels judicial investigation and the parallel local investigations undertaken by the other military courts.

In the meantime, however, the defense teams for those indicted had ample time to collect supporting testimonies. Pivotal in this regard were Chaïm Perelman's official declarations he made during the judicial AJB investigation in August and September 1946; his statements would ultimately lead the Brussels military prosecutor responsible for the investigation to close the case. Perelman was an expert in law and philosophy.[58] His dual affiliation with the AJB and the Jewish Defense Committee made him a key witness and an important voice in the postwar Belgian Jewish community. His declarations were strategic in two respects. First, he condoned the council's policy after September 1942, which was perfectly in line with certain changes implemented by Belgian authorities in the penal law.[59] Second, Perelman kept the focal point of his declarations on the parallels between the AJB's policy and the Belgian "policy of the lesser evil," as discussed below. At one time he explicitly compared the Jewish leadership's policy with that of Belgium's leading administrators and civil authorities during the occupation. Benedictus had made the same points in his reports from Lisbon in 1943, and, according to testimony by Henri Carton de Wiart to the investigators,[60] Ullmann had accepted his wartime functions only in consultation with prominent Belgians, such as Cardinal Jozef-Ernest Van Roey and Carton de Wiart himself.[61] In so doing, Perelman attributed to the AJB the same patriotic policy of cooperation as undertaken by members of the Belgian establishment during the occupation.[62] The patriotic nature and intentions of the AJB leadership, Ullmann in particular, were confirmed by the testimonies of many leading members of the Belgian establishment, and these testimonies were explicitly used by the AJB's legal defense.

Perelman simply used the opportunities already present at the beginning, with the original complaints of Liebmann and Van Praag. By 1946 the Belgian military judiciary had already encountered the difficulties of applying the existing legal instruments (such as Penal Article 118-bis on political collaboration and Article 115 on economic collaboration) to the complex occupation reality and especially the so-called "policy of the lesser evil" by Belgian authorities. The policy of the lesser evil was the commonly known concept used to indicate the general policies of cooperation of Belgian authorities with German policies during the occupation in order to defend the interests of Belgium and its population.[63] In 1940 the focal point of this policy was economic cooperation. Indeed, the protection of Belgium's economic interests remained the ruling elite's main goal; this meant maintaining a high employment rate in Belgium and thus avoiding the deportation of laborers to the Reich, safeguarding the industrial apparatus, and increasing employers' powers over workers. This policy quickly escalated into ever increasing concessions to the German occupiers, also in domains such as public order and policing, food supply organization, and a general authoritarian reform of Belgian institutions. This way, several members of the Belgian elite who remained in office during the occupation unavoidably compromised themselves.

One of the most prominent examples is certainly Leo Delwaide, the mayor of Antwerp, who remained in office until February 1944. As mayor, Delwaide played an active role in several illegal reforms in Antwerp's municipality and police, and under his leadership the Antwerp police persecuted Jews and Belgian laborers in hiding. Although Delwaide was subjected to a judicial investigation after the war, the investigation was quickly closed in 1945. A prominent member of the Belgian Catholic Party, Delwaide remained highly popular in Antwerp after the occupation. It was politically and legally unthinkable to convict members of the Belgian patriotic establishment such as Delwaide for the same "political collaboration" committed by, for example, pro-German members of the Flemish SS. In general terms the policy of the lesser evil was condoned after the war by the Belgian judicial elite and accepted as an unavoidable part of occupation. In concrete and strongly simplified terms, this meant that when collaborationist mayors affiliated with the extreme right Rexist Party or the Flemish National Union (Vlaams Nationaal Verbond) transferred lists of laborers in hiding to the Germans, this was considered after the war as an integral part of their political-ideological collaboration, whereas when Catholic or socialist mayors did the same thing, their actions were condoned. These mayors were considered to have made some mistakes but always with the intention to serve the general interest, never with any malicious intent to betray the Belgian state. In other words, they had collaborated with the enemy as a patriotic duty. The mistakes and compromises they made were considered the lesser evil, and the greater evil would have been to resign and let pro-German collaborators take over.

The strategy of the AJB defense from the beginning was to point to the parallels between the AJB policy on the one hand and this Belgian policy of the lesser evil on the other, and it was a smart strategy indeed. Benedictus himself made good use of it. He declared during a key interrogation that "the Association of Jews of Belgium conducted a policy of the lesser evil in Belgium during the occupation."[64] Using this term was basically Benedictus's way of sending a message to the Belgian judiciary in terms they understood quite well. Benedictus simply said that the AJB was exactly like all the other Belgian institutions created during the occupation that had perhaps "cooperated" with the German occupier but had done so to protect the interest of the Belgian or Jewish people, never with "malicious intent" to betray the interests of the Belgian state.

Perelman also understood this concept well and followed the exact same arguments. He essentially offered the Brussels military prosecutors an excuse to shelve cases involving Jewish collaboration. Already in August 1945 Perelman had said in an official statement during the investigation that he thought that the AJB leaders had "disqualified" themselves from any future positions as leaders of the Jewish community.[65] This statement would be used by the substitute military prosecutor in March 1946, when he suggested to the general military prosecutor's office to drop the case. On that occasion this Belgian military magistrate wrote that after December 1942 the activity of the AJB leadership "does not seem to lead to any criticisms on the part of the members of the Jewish community."[66] The substitute military prosecutor then continued by using exactly the same phrase Perelman had uttered during his testimony in August 1945, saying that the AJB leaders had "disqualified" themselves as representatives of the Jewish community. On November 19, 1946, Perelman added another important official statement: "On the other hand, I don't want to pass judgment on the appropriateness of this policy of the lesser evil. Personally, I would not have wanted to assume the responsibilities touched upon by the AJB's interventions, but I also don't want to pass a categorical judgment on the appropriateness of this policy."[67] Most notably, Perelman concluded his statement by emphasizing again that the AJB leaders should be excluded from adopting any future leadership positions in the Jewish community. Perelman therefore hinted at the possibility that some kind of informal internal purge might be conducted in the Jewish community.

The Belgian military prosecutor responsible for the case seemed to pick this up. Thus shortly after Perelman's intervention, the Brussels main military prosecutor decided to drop the charges and permanently closed the cases against the less prominent defendants in January 1947 and closed the cases against Ullmann, Blum, Benedictus, and Van den Berg six months later. The prosecutor's argument for terminating these cases was that the leadership of the AJB had basically followed the Belgian policy of the lesser evil and therefore the defendants could not be convicted under Article 118-bis pertaining to political collaboration, of betrayal to the Belgian state.[68]

How can this course of events be explained? From the side of the Jewish community the lack of initiative is noteworthy. Only two major complaints were filed in the Brussels AJB case, both of which were motivated by personal grievances. There was no mobilization by Jewish parties to file complaints between 1944 and 1947, not even from the left-leaning circles of Zionists and communists, who during the occupation had vehemently condemned the AJB. Historian and jurist André Donnet attributes this to the internal divisions within these former resistance networks.[69] But there was also complete silence from the victims, the deportees, or their surviving relatives. All this was probably also due to an unspoken policy on the part of Jews in Belgium who did not want to draw attention to themselves. This was especially true of Jews without Belgian citizenship and even more so of Zionists and communists, all of whom feared that unwanted attention would lead to their expulsion because of a lack of citizenship or permanent residence permits. (In addition, the Belgian State Security did follow up on communist and Zionist activities as potentially dangerous to the Belgian state.)[70] Similarly, in other major court cases, notably the Breendonk trial, the Sipo and SD cases, and the many trials of Belgian non-Jews accused of collaboration with the Nazis, in which Jews, the Nazis' primary victims, had a stake, the aggrieved parties remained silent for fear of drawing attention to themselves. In this sense the intervention by Perelman had all the bearings of an orchestrated and strategic decision to end the continuing judicial predicament, although until this day, it remains unclear whether Perelman's intervention was an individual decision or whether he acted on the advice of others or was supported by a broader circle. In any case, the intervention itself was well prepared and thought-out.

But perhaps an even more essential cause was the attitude of the Belgian judiciary. From the outset the Brussels military court seemed disinclined to pursue AJB-related cases. On the one hand, the courts were already overwhelmed with work in 1944–1945 and were not eager to add cases to their workload. But this does not explain the minimum amount of investigative actions or the complete lack of judicial analysis and certainly not the final decision to close the cases.[71] The approach to the AJB cases was indicative of a politically motivated Belgian judicial attitude that did not want to draw attention to complicity of certain members of the Belgian elite with Nazism in general. The AJB case was

THE ABSENCE OF A JEWISH HONOR COURT IN POSTWAR BELGIUM

closely linked to the legal strategy that the Belgian military courts developed toward the cooperative attitude of members of the wartime Belgian political establishment at the state level. In any event, the notion of political collaboration (Article 118-bis) was applied to Nazi collaborators who had betrayed the Belgian state, but it was not used against, for example, the Catholic mayor of Antwerp or the socialist mayor of Liège, although each had played an important role in the registration and persecution of the Jews. Closing the cases against representatives of the AJB, who, like the mayors, were not part of the state establishment, was the only logical legal decision. However, we believe that more was at stake than just this politically motivated judicial logic. We would argue that the military courts had many other priorities in 1944–1947—dealing with large-scale Belgian collaboration in its many shapes and forms—and simply did not know how to handle this specific Jewish case.

Perelman suggested to the Belgian judiciary that the Jewish community should deal with its own perpetrators. This idea was not entirely illogical. One segment of the general postwar purges in Belgium was in fact internal purges conducted by political parties, trade unions, professional interest groups, and even private businesses; these bodies took on the responsibility of cleaning their own houses. Perhaps because of the sensitivity of the Jewish case, the Belgian judiciary was more than willing to delegate its responsibility to the Jewish community.[72] We can only hypothesize that Perelman's suggestion—namely, that it should fall to the Jewish community *itself* to organize its own purges and trials—was in line with what the Belgian military prosecutors had been privately considering all along.[73]

If Perelman did indeed make an implicit suggestion, it was, however, ignored by the Jewish community. Apart from a reference in an oral interview in 1995, there are no indications that the Jewish community in Belgium considered establishing an honor court to pass judgment on the AJB's surviving members. Rather than adopting this form of internal communal justice—which could have led in the most egregious examples to the excommunication of those found guilty—Belgian Jewry left it to reluctant state courts to adjudicate these cases. Essentially no one was eager to try putative Jewish collaborators. The unwillingness of the Belgian legal system to pass judgment on the AJB's leadership foreclosed debate on Jewish cooperation with the Germans in the postwar Jewish community.[74]

As mentioned, in general, the issue of Jewish complicity surfaced only as a minor aspect in trials of German war criminals and Belgian collaborators in Belgian courts. The most important and notorious court case in which it nevertheless played a considerable role was the trial against the so-called executioners of Breendonk.

The Breendonk Trial: The Jewish Dimension

In Belgium, after their postwar trials, 242 Belgians were executed for collaboration. However, the Belgian judicial system did not limit its trials to Belgian nationals; foreign nationals, mostly Austrians and Germans, were tried in Belgian courts. The Breendonk trial was the only trial in Belgium in which putative Jewish collaborators, former Jewish guards in the camp, played a major role and were also convicted. It even resulted in the implementation of the death sentence for two of these Jewish perpetrators, who all hailed from outside Belgium.

The Breendonk concentration camp was the only concentration camp erected on Belgian soil. (Dossin Mechelen, in contrast, was a transit camp and detention facility from which Jews were deported.) Between September 1940 and September 1944, about 3,500 prisoners passed through Breendonk.[75] The camp was governed by a notoriously brutal and violent regime. As in other camps, the Germans sought to install a regime of complicity, in particular by employing a coercive, psychological stick-and-carrot approach, whereby prisoners were inducted into the tasks and responsibilities of the camp's daily organization.[76] Although Breendonk was small compared to other German concentration camps, it gave rise to the same types of social dynamics and hierarchies between prisoners as obtained in other camps. As they did elsewhere, these dynamics functioned along political, racial, national, and ethnic lines and accentuated blunt distinctions between the strong and the weak.

The Breendonk trial was held in 1946 before the Military Court of Mechelen.[77] Twenty-three individuals were accused in this trial, most of them members of the Flemish SS but also some barrack supervisors and civil laborers. Sixteen of the accused received the death penalty (of which twelve would be actually implemented in April 1947) based partly on penal articles defining forms of collaboration (political and military collaboration in particular) but mostly on "classic" penal articles such as maltreatment, involuntary manslaughter, or homicide.

The perpetrators who surfaced in the investigation leading up to this trial included some foreigners: Germans and Austrians but also Hungarians and Romanian guards, most of whom fled after 1945 and were thereby difficult to identify, let alone trace.[78] Some of these foreigners were Jewish and had originally been prisoners in the camp; during their incarceration they had developed a collaborationist attitude in accepting certain responsibilities, mainly as "supervisor" of a barrack (*kameroverste* in Dutch) or foreman (*Arbeitsführer*). Although it can

THE ABSENCE OF A JEWISH HONOR COURT IN POSTWAR BELGIUM

be assumed that such tasks were tantamount to survival mechanisms for most of the people in question, some of them engaged in excessive and escalating violence.

The three most notorious Jewish guards were Walter Obler, Sally Lewin, and Leo Schmandt, all of whom were indicted and convicted in the Breendonk trial. All three had been born in the German Empire before World War I. Obler arrived first in Breendonk and was the most prominent figure there of the three. Born in 1906, Obler had moved from Berlin to Vienna and received Austrian citizenship.[79] Knowledge of his life remains generally vague, although he may have been involved in socialist revolutionary activities in the 1930s. After the German annexation of Austria in 1938 (*Anschluss*), he fled to Belgium, quickly followed by his non-Jewish wife. In May 1940 the Belgian authorities expelled him to France; when he made his way back to German-occupied Belgium, the Germans sent him to Breendonk. Apparently, his impressive physique was noticed by an SS officer, Arthur Prauss, who quickly offered him a position within the camp system. Obler accepted and immediately became one of the camp's most violent perpetrators. He and Prauss were among the first to use systematic violence, such as beatings, during the first phase of the camp's operations.[80] Obler also used systematic extortion to rob prisoners of jewels, money, and other valuables. He was eventually promoted to the rank of *Oberarbeitsführer*, supervising the work of the prisoners. The motivations for his actions at the camp remain unclear, although he claimed that he had been broken by brutal pressure from the Germans. Obler was himself deported, in either August or September 1943, ending up in Sachsenhausen, where he survived by enlisting in the so-called Fälscherkommando. After a brief internment at Mauthausen, he was liberated and returned to Vienna after May 1945.

Obler was quickly identified and actively sought by the Belgian authorities, who considered him one of the main Breendonk perpetrators. He was found in Vienna by Belgian representatives in Austria, arrested, and brought back to Belgium in 1945 to face justice there.[81] The Belgian War Crimes Commission report on Breendonk identified Obler as a notorious perpetrator of the camp. In preparation for the Breendonk trial, he was interviewed by Belgian investigators, but he failed to give many details about his background or motivations. His name also briefly surfaced in the massive collective trial of the Brussels Sipo and SD, in which Ernst Landau, an Austrian Jewish journalist who served time as a political prisoner in Breendonk, testified at length about the treatment of Jews in that camp, mentioning Obler as one of the perpetrators.

Somewhat less notorious was Sally Lewin. He was a German Jew, born in 1899, in Wongrotwitz (at that time in the Prussian province of Posen; after World War I the town became part of the Polish Republic); during World War I he was injured, leaving him a partial invalid. After the 1938 November pogrom, he migrated to Schaarbeek in Belgium. Like Obler, he was first deported by the Belgians to France, in May 1940; and after his return to Belgium, the Germans incarcerated him at Breendonk. He arrived at the camp one month after Obler, and Obler soon set an example for him. Following Obler, Lewin inclined toward collaboration and violence against other Jewish prisoners.[82] Remarkably, Lewin was released in June 1942 and apparently lived out the rest of the occupation with his wife in freedom and even material well-being, but the source for this financial security and the exact nature of his arrangement with the Germans remain unknown.

The third accused Jewish guard, Leo Schmandt, followed a path similar to that of Obler and Lewin. A Berlin Jew, Schmandt arrived in Belgium in 1938. Like Obler, he was married to a non-Jewish wife and was also deported to France in May 1940; after his return to Belgium he was sent to Breendonk in November 1940. He was in Lewin's barracks, and after Lewin's release Schmandt followed in his footsteps, exhibiting violent behavior against fellow Jewish prisoners.

At the Breendonk trial Lewin was found guilty of being an accessory to the murder of eight prisoners, including the murder of the young Polish Jew Hirsz Swirsky (committed together with Obler). Obler and Lewin were sentenced to death and, together with eight other non-Jewish Breendonk perpetrators (mostly Flemish SS men), executed on April 12, 1947.[83] Apparently, Lewin, who was attended by a rabbi the night before his execution, attempted to shout "Deutschland über alles" while the final shots were being fired.[84] Schmandt's case was more ambiguous. The scale of his violence was much less excessive, and there had been many positive testimonies on his behalf about his offering help to several prisoners. At trial, Schmandt argued that it was impossible for a Jewish barrack supervisor to remain uncompromised in the camp system and retain moral integrity. The Belgian military tribunal accepted the claim that Schmandt's behavior had been a survival strategy. He was sentenced to fifteen years in prison but, as with many German war criminals convicted in Belgium, he received an early release, concluding his sentence in June 1951.

In his book on Breendonk, historian Patrick Nefors cites the testimony of Belgian Jewish journalist Paul Lévy from 1944, who remarked that the Jewish camp guards in Breendonk were former Germans and Austrians who strongly identified with German and Austrian nationalism and even sympathized with National Socialism. Among those guards Lévy identified Obler and Schmandt.

Their victims originated primarily from Eastern Europe, mainly Poland and Hungary. Merely as a hypotheses, we might speculate that for these German Jews—German patriots who never considered themselves Jews until the Nazis forced them to do so—the confrontation with their, in their eyes, inferior Jewish brethren from Eastern Europe motivated their violent behavior. This is supported by the many testimonies of victims (and by Patrick Nefors's extensive study), who point to "compensating behavior" by these Jewish barrack supervisors who wanted to confirm their German or Austrian backgrounds and saw severe and even violent behavior toward non-German Jews as a means to do so. It should be noted that the Jewish backgrounds of the three perpetrators never received any specific attention, either from the judges, prosecutors, and defense counsel at the trial or from the Belgian media, which closely followed the proceedings. This also means that the defense counsel did not use the Jewish background of his clients as a mitigating factor.

Conclusion

In explaining the absence of internal Jewish purges and trials of putative Jewish collaborators in postwar Belgium, one should be mindful of the perspectives of both the Belgian judicial system and the Jewish community.

The Belgian military magistrates never explicitly outlined their strategy in the AJB case. Consequently, in assessing their approach during the investigation, we can only hypothesize about their underlying stance. The AJB case was the only major judicial proceeding that focused on Jewish complicity. Because it did not involve instances of direct physical violence, the form of collaboration at the heart of the case was deemed ultimately excusable. In contrast, the Breendonk trial held at the Military Court in Mechelen between March and December 1946 was concerned with the use of direct physical violence, mostly by Flemish SS camp guards but also by several Jewish barrack supervisors. Certainly, the AJB case, or to be more specific, the investigations of individual AJB members by the Brussels Military Court, paled in comparison with the investigations of Jewish guards in the Breendonk case. It is clear, therefore, that the AJB case was not a priority for the military courts after 1944. The participation of certain AJB figures in the resistance or in social aid to fellow Jews both during and after the war also complicated matters at a time when the patriotic paradigm dominated occupation assessment.

For years the AJB-related investigations languished, with the investigators remaining passive. During this period, there were no interventions from any leading Belgian officials. Belgian authorities clearly had no intentions of delving into the many complexities and nuances of the AJB and the Jewish community in general. The military prosecutors gladly accepted the escape route offered by Chaïm Perelman, which seems to indicate that Belgian authorities were eager to be relieved of the responsibility. It took the Belgian military courts several years of inactivity to finally reach an acquittal in this case. Perelman hinted at the permanent exclusion of the AJB leaders as representatives of the Jewish community in the future, and the Belgian military prosecutor responsible for the case clearly heard this message. The Belgian authorities appeared to regard the matter of Jewish complicity as an internal Jewish issue, to be addressed by the community itself.

One could consider this passivity part of an overall judicial strategy that was not specific to the Jewish community or the issue of Jewish complicity. Internally organized purges by political parties, professional associations, trade unions, and the like—that is, the essential agents of a rebuilding civil society—were an integral part of transitional justice policies in postwar Belgium. Moreover, this scheme fitted within a larger tradition of the highly decentralized Belgian state to delegate parts of its powers and responsibilities to certain representative bodies. It should be further noted that Belgian courts condoned the so-called policy of the lesser evil by Belgian elites. Legal strategy with regard to the AJB was partly determined by the fact that the AJB could be subsumed under the overall postwar excuse for the Belgian policy of cooperation with the German occupier.

We also need to consider another body of explanations, one that lies in the Jewish community in Belgium. Most Jews were not Belgian citizens; only an estimated 10 percent of the Belgian Jewish population were Belgian citizens. Lest they jeopardize the extension of temporary residence permits or risk eviction from the country, Jews generally tried to avoid drawing attention to themselves. This meant that they generally refrained from filing formal complaints with Belgian authorities against Belgian or German perpetrators, let alone against the AJB and its leaders. Indeed, the general context was one of organized silence, from Belgian Jews and foreign Jews alike.

One might think that this would have been a perfect argument for the establishment of an internal Jewish honor court, on either a national or a local level. But material reconstruction of the Jewish community and the securing of residence permits took priority over internal purges. The blurring of boundaries between the AJB and the Jewish resistance (because a few men such as Perelman were active in both) and the prominence of key former AJB members in the postwar Jewish community (such as Ullmann, who remained chief rabbi of Belgium, and Van den Berg, who remained active on the board of the Jewish religious community of Brussels) may have impeded the construction of an honor court. It is clear that Jews in Belgium after the war—heterogeneous as the community may have been—were able to reach a consensus that its future-oriented reconstruction held priority over confronting the past.

Notes

We would like to thank Rudi Van Doorslaer (director of the Center for Historical Research and Documentation on War and Contemporary Society in Brussels) and Robby Van Eetvelde (junior research fellow with the Vienna Wiesenthal Institute for Holocaust Studies) for the additional information they provided.

1. Rudi Van Doorslaer, "Salomon Van den Berg of de ondraaglijke mislukking van een joodse politiek van het minste kwaad," in Rudi Van Doorslaer and Jean-Philippe Schreiber, eds., *De curatoren van het getto: De Vereniging van de joden in België tijdens de nazibezitting* (Tielt, Belgium: Lannoo, 2004), 111, 125–26.

2. Maxime Steinberg, *L'Etoile et le fusil, 1942: Les cent jours de la déportation des Juifs de Belgique* (Brussels: Vie Ouvrière, 1984), 111–13 (original Yiddish quotation from *Unzer Vort* 4 [June 1942], taken from Steinberg's French translation, 113).

3. Jean-Philippe Schreiber, "Tussen traditionele en verplichte gemeenschap," in Van Doorslaer and Schreiber, *De curatoren van het getto*, 56; Van Doorslaer, "Salomon Van den Berg," 111, 125, 136.

4. Jean-Philippe Schreiber and Rudi Van Doorslaer, "Inleiding," in Van Doorslaer and Schreiber, *De curatoren van het getto*, 10.

5. André Donnet, "Het onderzoek door het militaire gerecht: Het geheugen buitenspel gezet," in Van Doorslaer and Schreiber, *De curatoren van het getto*, 316–17; Rudi Van Doorslaer and Jean-Philippe Schreiber, "Besluit: Duitse perversie, joodse accommodatie," in Van Doorslaer and Schreiber, *De curatoren van het getto*, 352.

6. Schreiber and Van Doorslaer, "Inleiding," 18, 21.

7. Studiecommissie betreffende het lot van de bezittingen van de leden van de joodse gemeenschap van België, geplunderd of achtergelaten tijdens de oorlog 1940–1945, *De bezittingen van de slachtoffers van de jodenvervolging in België: Spoliatie, Rechtsherstel, Bevindingen van de Studiecommissie—Eindverslag* (Brussels: Diensten van de Eerste Minister, 2001), 35–36. According to Patrick Weil, out of an estimated 330,000 Jews in France, 58 percent held French citizenship. See Patrick Weil, "The Return of Jews in the Nationality or in the Territory of France," in David Bankier, ed., *The Jews Are Coming Back: The Return of the Jews to Their Countries of Origin after WWII* (Jerusalem: Yad Vashem, 2005), 58.

8. Lieven Saerens, *Vreemdelingen in een wereldstad: Een geschiedenis van Antwerpen en zijn joodse bevolking (1880–1944)* (Tielt, Belgium: Lannoo, 2000), 10, 201–2, 547; Rudi Van Doorslaer, "Jewish Immigration and Communism in Belgium, 1925–1939," in Dan Michman, ed., *Belgium and the Holocaust: Jews, Belgians, Germans* (Jerusalem: Yad Vashem, 1998), 65.

9. Frank Caestecker, "The Reintegration of Jewish Survivors into Belgian Society, 1943–1947," in Bankier, *The Jews Are Coming Back*, 74.

10. Dan Michman, "Les mouvements de jeunesse sionistes en Belgique durant l'occupation allemande: Etude d'un point de vue comparatif," in Rudi Van Doorslaer, ed., *Les Juifs de Belgique: De l'immigration au génocide, 1925–1945* (Brussels: Centre de Recherches et d'études historiques de la Seconde Guerre Mondiale, 1994), 176.

11. For example, in 1936 the division was 53 percent in Antwerp, 38 percent in Brussels, with the remaining 9 percent spread over smaller Jewish centers such as Charleroi, Liège, Ghent, and Ostend (Saerens, *Vreemdelingen in een wereldstad*, xvi).

12. Van Doorslaer, "Jewish Immigration," 65.

13. The number of officially recognized communities rose from five in 1870 to seventeen in 2013 (see www.jewishcom.be; accessed September 6, 2013).

14. Veerle Vanden Daelen, *Laten we hun lied verder zingen: De heropbouw van de joodse gemeenschap in Antwerpen na de Tweede Wereldoorlog (1944–1960)* (Amsterdam: Uitgeverij Aksant, 2008), 264–66.

15. The Belgian police was a decentralized force that fell under the Ministry of the Interior and local governments (mayors); the Belgian *gendarmerie* was a centralized force that fell under the Ministry of War (during the occupation, the Ministry of Justice).

16. "Verordnung über die Errichtung einer Vereinigung der Juden in Belgien vom 25. November 1941," *Verordnungsblatt des Militärbefehlshabers in Belgien und Nordfrankreich für die besetzten Gebiete Belgiens und Nordfrankreichs, herausgegeben vom Militärbefehlshaber (Militärverwaltungschef)* 63 (December 2, 1941): 798–800.

17. Antwerp, Brussels, Charleroi, and Liège were the four cities with the most important Jewish communities. The cities of Ghent, Ostend, and Arlon had "added agencies" (*toegevoegde bureaus*) but no local committee and no representative in the central office. See Dan Michman, "De oprichting van de VJG in international perspectief," in Van Doorslaer and Schreiber, *De curatoren van het getto*, 36; and Insa Meinen, "De Duitse bezettingsautoriteiten en de VJB," in Van Doorslaer and Schreiber, *De curatoren van het getto*, 51.

18. Jean-Philippe Schreiber, "Ullmann, Salomon," in Jean-Philippe Schreiber, ed., *Dictionnaire biographique des Juifs de Belgique* (Brussels: Editions De Boeck, 2002), 343–44.

19. See Schreiber, "Tussen traditionele," 108.

20. Jean-Philippe Schreiber, "Benedictus, Maurice," in Schreiber, *Dictionnaire biographique des Juifs de Belgique*, 48.

21. Van Doorslaer, "Salomon Van den Berg," 111.

22. Schreiber and Van Doorslaer, "Inleiding," 8–9; Michman, "De oprichting van de VJB," 44; Meinen, "De Duitse bezettingsautoriteiten," 46–47, Schreiber, "Tussen traditionele," 104; Van Doorslaer, "Salomon Van den Berg," 114, 134–35.

23. Van Doorslaer, "Salomon Van den Berg," 117–18.

24. Frank Caestecker, "Rosenfeld, Louis," in Schreiber, *Dictionnaire biographique des Juifs de Belgique*, 295.

25. Van Doorslaer, "Salomon Van den Berg," 126–29.

26. Elisabeth Wulliger and Jean-Philippe Schreiber, "Blum, Alfred dit Freddy," in Schreiber, *Dictionnaire biographique des Juifs de Belgique*, 62–63.

27. Schreiber and Van Doorslaer, "Inleiding," 8–9; Michman, "De oprichting van de VJB," 44; Meinen, "De Duitse bezettingsautoriteiten," 52, 54–55, 66; Schreiber, "Tussen traditionele," 77, 81, 99; Van Doorslaer, "Salomon Van den Berg," 126–27.

28. Schreiber, "Tussen traditionele," 104–5.

29. Lucien Steinberg, *Le Comité de défense des juifs en Belgique* (Brussels: Ed. de l'Université de Bruxelles, 1973). Other founding members included Hertz Jospa, Abush Verber, and Perelman's wife, Fela Perelman.

30. Schreiber and Van Doorslaer, "Inleiding," 10; Van Doorslaer, "Salomon Van den Berg," 118, 136–37, 139; Sophie Vandepontseele, "De verplichte tewerkstelling van joden in België en Noord-Frankrijk," in Van Doorslaer and Schreiber, *De curatoren van het getto*, 174; "Life and Work of Chaïm Perelman," on the website of the Centre Perelman de Philosophie du Droit, Université Libre de Bruxelles (www.philodroit.be/spip.php?page=rubrique&id_rubrique=30&lang=fr#b343; accessed April 10, 2013).

31. For a detailed overview of the activities and working of the AJB, see the following chapters in Van Doorslaer and Schreiber, *De curatoren van het getto*: Vandepontseele, "De verplichte tewerkstelling," 149–81; Barbara Dickschen, "De VJB en het onderwijs," 182–203; Laurence Schram, "De distributie van de davidster," 204–14; and Catherine Massange, "De sociale politiek," 215–44.

32. "Verordnung über die Errichtung einer Vereinigung der Juden in Belgien," 798–800.

33. "Verordnung über die Errichtung einer Vereinigung der Juden in Belgien," 798–800; Michman, "De oprichting van de VJB," 41–43; Meinen, "De Duitse bezettingsautoriteiten," 50–54.

34. Laurence Schram, "De oproepen voor 'tewerkstelling' in het Oosten," in Van Doorslaer and Schreiber, *De curatoren van het getto*, 247–51.

35. Van Doorslaer, "Salomon Van den Berg," 122; Schram, "De oproepen," 251–66.

36. Meinen, "De Duitse bezettingsautoriteiten," 55–56, 61–67, 363.

37. Van Doorslaer, "Salomon Van den Berg," 118, 129.

38. Van Doorslaer and Schreiber, "Besluit," 335–57.

39. This section is largely based on Nico Wouters, "The Belgian Trials (1944–1951)," in David Bankier and Dan Michman, eds., *Holocaust and Justice: Representation and Historiography of the Holocaust in Post-War Trials* (Jerusalem: Yad Vashem, 2010), 219–45.

40. Commission des Crimes de Guerre, *Les crimes de guerre commis sous l'occupation de la Belgique 1940–1945: La persécution antisémitique en Belgique* (Liège: Thone, 1947).

41. Wouters, "Belgian Trials," 236.

42. Archives of the Service de Instructions Générales / Dienst voor Algemene Richtlijnen, of the Chief Military Prosecutor's Office, CEGESOMA, Brussels.

43. Nico Wouters, "De Jodenvervolging voor de Belgische rechters, 1944–1951," in Rudi Van Doorslaer, Emmanuel Debruyne, Frank Seberechts, and Nico Wouters, eds.,

Gewillig België (Amsterdam: Meulenhoff & Manteau, 2008), 801–1029, esp. 915–22 for the Jewish council in Belgium.

44. The dossier of the AJB is registered under number 8036/44 in the "Incivisme" Archives of the Chief Military Prosecutor's Office. For two different takes on this court case, see Donnet, "Het onderzoek door het militaire gerecht," 291–319; and Wouters, "De Jodenvervolging," 916.
45. André Donnet ("Het onderzoek door het militaire gerecht") provides detailed information on the protagonists of the court case, the chronological proceedings of the investigation, and the different testimonies by the defendants.
46. Van Doorslaer, "Salomon Van den Berg," 123; Jean-Philippe Schreiber, "Liebmann, Lazare Maurice," in Schreiber, *Dictionnaire biographique des Juifs de Belgique*, 226–27.
47. Written complaint by Lazare-Maurice Liebmann, n.d., Archives of the Chief Military Prosecutor's Office, Judicial File AJB (8036/44). See also the testimony of Liebmann, July 24, 1945. Liebmann's written complaint probably dates from a few days before October 17, 1944. On this day the military prosecutor gave the order to start the official investigation following Liebmann's complaint. The judicial file also contains a note, dated October 13, 1944, from the military prosecutor that refers to an oral contact with Liebmann a short time before. So apparently, Liebmann contacted the Brussels military prosecutor's office around the beginning of October 1944, probably asking for information on how to file a complaint.
48. Statement by Roger Van Praag on November 26, 1946, Archives of the Chief Military Prosecutor's Office, Penal File AJB (8036/44).
49. Quoted in Wouters, "De Jodenvervolging," 916.
50. Wouters, "De Jodenvervolging," 917.
51. The Judicial Police (*Gerechtelijke Politie* or *Police Judiciaire*) was a small police force that was directly added to the various judicial Public Prosecutors Offices in Belgium (in Dutch, *Openbaar Ministerie* or *Parket*). It was mainly charged with purely investigative tasks.
52. All these materials are today stored and digitized at Kazerne Dossin: Memorial, Museum and Documentation Center on Holocaust and Human Rights. Other materials were kept by partisans (because they, the Front de l'Indépendance, used the former AJB buildings at the Zuidlaan shortly after the liberation and most probably found some archives of the AJB there) and deposited at the National Museum of the Resistance in Anderlecht (see Schreiber and Van Doorslaer, "Inleiding," 16–18). The materials kept by the partisans were not known or used during the trials.
53. Archives of the Chief Military Prosecutor's Office, Penal Files 54 199/45 and NNSE 24291/46, respectively. According to Donnet, both investigations were added to the general AJB case at the moment when the general investigation was on the verge of being closed. See Donnet, "Het onderzoek door het militaire gerecht," 301.
54. André Donnet calls this fact "remarkable." See Donnet, "Het onderzoek door het militaire gerecht," 309.
55. Nozice was accused of economic collaboration and of denouncing Jews to the enemy (Articles 115 and 121-bis of the penal code, respectively), but his case was closed without

consequence on June 17, 1947. Ackerman was accused of having denounced Jewish people to the enemy (Article 121-bis) but the case was closed without consequence on January 11, 1952. Letter of the military prosecutor of Liège to the general military prosecutor's office, March 1, 1966, Archives of the Chief Military Prosecutor's Office, Administrative File AJB. See also Wouters, "De Jodenvervolging," 919.

56. Handing over lists of people to the Germans in an administrative context was generally not penalized or used for indictments during postwar trials. For elaboration of this issue, see Nico Wouters, *De Führerstaat: Overheid en collaboratie in België (1940–1944)* (Tielt, Belgium: Lannoo, 2006), 181–98.

57. Schreiber, "Tussen traditionele," 77–78.

58. See Perelman's *Traité de l'argumentation: La nouvelle rhétorique*, written with Lucie Olbrechts-Tyteca and published in 1958 by Presses Universitaires de France (Paris). The book was translated into English by John Wilkinson and Purcell Weaver and published under the title *The New Rhetoric: A Treatise on Argumentation* (Notre Dame, IN: University of Notre Dame Press, 1969). The book has also been translated into eight other languages.

59. These changes had nothing to do with anti-Jewish persecution or the deportations but more with the implementation of mandatory labor (October 1942) and the gradual hardening of occupation conditions after this date. The Belgian government in London publicly condemned cooperation or collaboration with the German occupiers by the end of 1942, and a certain chronological caesura was inscribed in Belgian penal legislation to reflect this.

60. Henri Carton de Wiart was a former prime minister and, during World War II, part of the Belgian government in exile in London.

61. Wouters, "De Jodenvervolging," 919; Schreiber, "Tussen traditionele," 80.

62. In general, representatives of this patriotic policy of the lesser evil were never convicted after the war; see Wouters, *De Führerstaat*, 181–98.

63. Wouters, *De Führerstaat*.

64. Quoted in Wouters, "De Jodenvervolging," 918.

65. Official statement by Chaïm Perelman, August 17, 1945, Archives of the Chief Military Prosecutor's Office, Penal File AJB (8036/44).

66. "L'activité après cette date ne semble pas donner lieu à critique de la part des membres de la communauté juive." Letter of the substitute military prosecutor to the general military prosecutor's office, March 29, 1946, Archives of the Chief Military Prosecutor's Office, Penal File AJB (8036/44).

67. "Je ne désire pas, d'autre part, porter un jugement sur l'opportunité de cette politique du moindre mal. Personnellement je n'aurais pas voulu assumer les responsabilités que comportent ces différentes interventions de l'AJB mais je ne désirerais pas non plus porter un jugement catégorique sur l'opportunité de cette politique." Official statement by Chaïm Perelman, November 19, 1946, Archives of the Chief Military Prosecutor's Office, Penal File AJB (8036/44).

68. Van Doorslaer, "Salomon Van den Berg," 143.
69. Donnet, "Het onderzoek door het militaire gerecht," 316.
70. Vanden Daelen, *Laten we hun lied verder zingen*, 264–66.
71. As jurist and historian Donnet confirms, the actual investigation was far from over at the time of Perelman's interventions. See Donnet, "Het onderzoek door het militaire gerecht," 313.
72. Donnet writes that the "way out" offered by Perelman was received extremely warmly by the Belgian judiciary ("een uitermate warm onthaal"). See Donnet, "Het onderzoek door het militaire gerecht," 317.
73. Wouters, "De Jodenvervolging," 921.
74. Schreiber and Van Doorslaer, "Inleiding," 21. Only after the publication of Betty Garfinkels's book *Les Belges face à la persecution raciale 1940–1945* (Belgians Under Racial Persecution, 1940–1945) was there considerable controversy on the image of the AJB in the Jewish community. As a result, the AJB archives remained closed for research until the late 1990s. The AJB was mentioned in a few publications in between but without really causing any public debate in or outside the Jewish community (Schreiber and Van Doorslaer, "Inleiding," 10–17, 357).
75. Breendonk Memorial website (www.breendonk.be/EN; accessed April 15, 2013).
76. Karin Orth, *Das System der nationalsozialistischer Konzentrationslager: Eine politische Organisationsgeschichte* (Hamburg: Hamburger Edition, 1999); and Karin Orth, *Die Konzentrationslager-SS: sozialstrukturelle Analysen und biografische Studien* (Göttingen: Wallstein, 2000).
77. The trial started in March 1946. The first judgment was issued on May 7, 1946; an appeal judgment was issued on November 14, 1946; and the final appeal was rejected on December 23, 1946, effectively closing the trial.
78. "Incivisme" Archives of the Chief Military Prosecutor's Office, Penal File Sipo-SD Bruxelles.
79. Patrick Nefors, *Breendonk 1940–1945: De geschiedenis* (Antwerp: Standaard, 2004), 256–58.
80. Nefors, *Breendonk*, 135.
81. Nefors, *Breendonk*, 259.
82. Nefors, *Breendonk*, 260. There are even indications that Lewin's son performed uniformed service for the Germans.
83. Nefors, *Breendonk*, 245.
84. Nefors, *Breendonk*, 248.

8

Jews Accusing Jews

Denunciations of Alleged Collaborators in Jewish Honor Courts

KATARZYNA PERSON

"I am not a denouncer, nor have I ever been one," wrote Samuel Silberstein from Vienna in 1946 to the Provincial Jewish Committee in Lodz. He had just heard that Stanisław Rowiński, manager of the Braun and Rowiński knitwear workshop in the Warsaw ghetto, had survived World War II and was participating actively in postwar Jewish communal life in Poland. Of course, in his letter Silberstein did exactly what he purported not to do: He denounced a fellow Jew. "I cannot come to Poland to personally settle my scores," he explained, "but my conscience does not allow me not to write to you. . . . I believe this to be my sacred duty."[1] Silberstein's letter became part of Rowiński's case file in the honor court of the Central Committee of Polish Jews. The postwar quest by Jewish survivors of the Holocaust to seek justice from—and wreak revenge on—suspected Jewish collaborators with Nazi rule is refracted in large measure through the prism of such denunciatory letters. Addressed to Jewish communal bodies, political parties, or newspapers, they describe chance meetings with former kapos on the streets or in communal kitchens, rumors of the return of a former Jewish policeman to his prewar hometown, or, most alarmingly, publication of a putative Jewish collaborator's face in the newspaper among leaders of the postwar Jewish community.

The denunciations discussed in this chapter were composed with the objective not only to shame or ostracize alleged Jewish collaborators but also explicitly to bring them to justice, however the concept of justice may have been understood by their Jewish authors, who believed strongly that justice had to be served and that only the surviving Jewish community could administer it properly, acting through the honor courts that had been newly created for this purpose. When survivors turned to Jewish honor courts for redress, they were mutatis mutandis signaling their personal investment in the Jewish community's postwar self-renewal—self-renewal in two senses: The honor courts allowed Jews not only to clean house and rid the community of traitors but also to take charge of internal Jewish affairs and overcome feelings of victimhood, indeed to reestablish Jewish autonomy. For Eastern European Jews both in Poland and in the Jewish displaced persons (DP) camps in Germany, Austria, and Italy, the existence of independent Jewish courts, which is what honor courts were, represented unprecedented and unimaginable legal sovereignty in the modern period.

In this chapter I examine the defining features of denunciations and of the corresponding reactions to them in the practices of two honor court systems: the honor court in Warsaw and the Jewish DP honor courts in Germany, Austria, and Italy. The Warsaw honor court was established by the Central Committee of Polish Jews in October 1946 solely for the purpose of dealing with assumed collaborators, in particular, barring them from occupying influential posts in the Jewish community. Between its establishment in 1946 and its dismantling in 1950, the court opened some 140 files on suspected Jewish collaborators and eventually prosecuted 28 of them.[2] On the other hand, the primary aim of Jewish DP honor courts, which were established by survivors following liberation and generally operated until 1950 in all large DP camps (and in many small ones), was to deal with the running of the DP camps on a daily basis. The courts played a crucial role in establishing normalcy among the inhabitants of DP camps and in rebuilding a sense of Jewish community. They allowed Jewish communities to sit in judgment of their own without having to resort to intermediaries between the occupation army administration and international relief organizations, and the German judicial system. In Germany, Jewish honor courts in all large camps and many smaller camps tried suspected collaborators beginning in 1946. For instance, in the first trial held on October 2, 1946, before the Landsberg camp court in the American zone of Germany, Majer Rubin, a former policeman in the Skarżysko-Kamienna forced labor camp who was accused of beating his fellow prisoners, was sentenced to four months' imprisonment and lifelong banishment from the Jewish community, the harshest punishment envisaged by such a court.[3]

Starting in the same year, the most important collaboration cases in the British zone of occupied Germany were referred directly to the briefly operational Court of Honor in Belsen[4] and in the American zone of occupation to the Court of Honor and Rehabilitation Commission of the Central Committee of Liberated Jews in the American Zone of Occupied Germany, located in Munich. This was mainly due to the camp courts' limited powers to penalize offenders. Similarly, in Italy cases of suspected collaborators were first tried by camp and regional courts and then, starting in the summer of 1946, directed to the Court of Honor of the Central Organization of Survivors in Italy.[5] In Austria DP camp courts had more limited capabilities, surrendering greater power to the camp police in many localities.[6] However, starting in 1947, the Court of Honor established by the Central Jewish Committee in Austria served as the court of appeal for those who thought they had been wrongly judged by camp courts; this court also dealt with rehabilitation requests.[7] The key element in prosecuting reputed collaborators, both in Poland and in the DP camps, was gathering information from the public. Given the urgency of the situation and with a population in constant flux, the courts actively sought such information and were prepared to act swiftly on it.

Denunciations in the Postwar Jewish Community

Sheila Fitzpatrick and Robert Gellately define denunciations as "spontaneous communications from individual citizens to the state containing accusations of wrongdoing by other citizens or officials and implicitly or explicitly calling for punishment."[8] Written statements that fit this definition (though directed to the Jewish leadership rather than the state per se) can be found in the archives of Polish and DP courts, ranging from spur-of-the-moment notes scribbled on scraps of paper to multipage typed letters that elaborately describe the wartime behavior of the alleged collaborator and provide extensive lists of witnesses or even quotes from academic works. Most of these denounce the wartime behavior of former members of the Judenrat, the Jewish Order Service (Jüdischer Ordnungsdienst, i.e., the Jewish police), or prisoner functionaries in forced labor and concentration camps. These behaviors ranged from profiting economically from the Germans, bribery, and violence toward fellow camp prisoners or ghetto inhabitants, to direct participation in killing operations, that is, handing Jews over to the Germans to be killed. Such denunciations came mainly from direct witnesses of the crimes, from victims who "survived it, and saw it, and felt the blows on my own back,"[9] or from their family members who sought justice for their suffering.

Not all of those who desired to denounce an alleged collaborator thought that their voice would be heard, and thus some addressed the court through an intermediary with higher authority, such as a rabbi or a representative of a local Jewish organization who could write letters on their behalf.[10] Others felt a moral obligation to write a denunciation from their positions of achievement during wartime or the postwar period or, on the other hand, saw themselves as the voice of the street, that is, as representatives for Jews more socially or politically powerless than they who could not bear to see crimes go unpunished. Therefore, whereas one author of a denunciation introduced himself as "the father of a soldier of the Haganah who fought in the Old Town in Jerusalem [and] a brave worker at [the] Givat Zaid [kibbutz in northern Israel]"[11] in an effort to establish credibility, another author with the same aim wrote, "My name means nothing, I am not a member of a party but a regular Jew."[12] Regardless of the means chosen, almost all writers of denunciations signed them clearly with their name and address, generally also providing contact information of individuals who could corroborate their stories.

Although denunciations focused primarily on shedding light on the wartime role of a suspected collaborator and urging the court to take a stance regarding alleged crimes, in many cases they took the form of elaborate descriptions of the criminals and their resort to cruelty. Such narratives often used emotionally charged language, with alleged collaborators usually referred to as "gangsters" or "thugs." They were "outcasts,"[13] "traitors,"[14] or, in case of one former policeman in Ostrów, one of "Hitler's dogs" who bathed in "Jewish sufferings and torments."[15] To strengthen their accusations, the denouncers emphasized particular aspects of the alleged collaborators' crimes, such as instances of sexual violence or cruelty toward children. Those denounced often had evidently acted of their own volition. Additional details seen as incriminating by the denouncers ranged from physical attributes, such as a "murderous face,"[16] to earlier inclinations to criminal behavior, with one Jewish policeman in Płaszów camp described as "having the opinion of a quarrelsome boy"[17] since childhood. Others mentioned collaborators' postwar criminal activity, such as involvement in the black market,[18] as proof of their bad character. Authors of denunciations often asserted that an alleged collaborator was hated or feared by the whole Jewish local community or camp population to buttress their claim.

Most denunciations from direct victims or their relatives appear to have been submitted as a result of an unexpected encounter with a wartime collaborator. A denouncer who came upon a former kapo while visiting friends described one such chance meeting: "When I entered the building, my blood froze, as among three people there, I recognized a Jewish henchman. Not sure who this man with a murderous face was, I listened for a few moments to his boasting about his time spent in different camps and what his name really is.... I ran to find my friend from Koło, who was at those camps at the same time and told him that today, by coincidence, I met a murderer of the Jews."[19] Still, not all denunciations were driven by actual physical encounters. Many of them were in fact written without the denouncers' ever setting eyes on the putative collaborators but rather after learning of their survival through the media or by word of mouth.

Denunciations and the Postwar Sense of Justice: Motives for Denunciations

One of the main objectives of denunciations was undoubtedly revenge. Denouncers often saw the aim of courts as "serving justice and punishing rascals" and called for alleged collaborators "to be placed at the whipping post and handed over to the court."[20] This pursuit of revenge was most evident in the cases pressed by relatives and friends of victims who perished. A woman denouncing an alleged collaborator whose presence in Belsen she heard about from her sister-in-law wrote:

> It has been a few days as I was attempting to address you with this matter, but memories of this horrible tragedy lead me to despair. I am not able to speak about it. I would never rest in peace if I would not take revenge on this man, the perpetrator of my young husband's death, the father of my unfortunate son. Please forgive me the excited state in which I am writing this letter.... The blood of my husband calls for revenge. Maybe this, at least in some way, will give me calm.[21]

Another denouncer requested revenge for a suspected collaborator "in the name of Jews who were harmed by his murderous hands."[22] In accordance with the sentiments prevalent in many such letters, one author wrote, "Providence saved us not only to remain alive but also to take revenge for our own torment and suffering and for that of those who no longer can take revenge."[23]

Both the honor courts and the rehabilitation commissions were limited in the punishments they could issue. Still, these punishments held poignant symbolic meanings. In DP camp courts these varied from exclusion from the Jewish community and prohibition from holding any position in the organizations and institutions serving displaced persons to loss of entitlement to material assistance by any Jewish relief organization or the right to emigrate with the help of the Jewish Agency for Palestine, as well as being labeled a traitor to the Jewish people. The punishments outlined in the Polish Jewish honor court's charter list a formal rebuke, a three-year suspension of communal rights, including rights to financial aid, with exclusion from the Jewish community as the harshest measure. In most cases denouncers appeared to lack familiarity with the practices of the courts and consequently rarely gave indications of which form of punishment they saw as appropriate; conversely, some denouncers demanded punishments that were outside the scope of the courts' authority. For example, some denouncers described "gallows as the only fitting punishment for those human animals."[24]

This call for revenge can be seen as reflecting the general attitude in the postwar Jewish community rather than being limited to those likely to write denunciations. Both in Poland and in the DP camps, rulings of the honor courts often stimulated ferocious discussion, mainly because they were considered too lenient. Individuals who gathered in the courtrooms raised such protests, as did the Jewish press, demanding punishment proportional to the crimes committed by those sentenced.[25] The courts' proceedings were seen as unjust in general, but they were particularly at odds with the moral vision of Judaism, at least insofar as the survivors perceived it.[26] Many of the sentences even bitterly referred to the limited punitive powers of the courts. Considering the magnitude of the crimes they dealt with, it is unsurprising that in numerous cases courts simultaneously issued the supreme penalties at their disposal and lamented their inadequacy in relation to the crimes committed. In one case, for example, the sentence explained, "Spilled Jewish blood must be avenged, even if only to the extent allowed by the statute of the rehabilitation committee."[27]

A large proportion of the authors of denunciations were individuals who opposed allowing alleged collaborators to continue as part of the postwar community, particularly if they held a position of influence. Even though the DP honor courts did not expect those who held a position of power in the camps to automatically undergo rehabilitation trials, they nonetheless stated, "It is the stance of the community that its leaders should not be recruited from among those who lent a hand to the destruction of this people."[28] In Poland the Jewish press strongly encouraged and occasionally reminded former policemen and kapos to submit requests for rehabilitation to the honor court. Still, not all complied. Some members of the Central Committee of Polish Jews even became subjects of denunciations because they were seen as "desecrating by their presence the leadership of the remnants of surviving Jews."[29] In both Poland and the DP camps, there was a strong consensus on wartime collaborators not taking positions of privilege in the postwar Jewish community, and this topic was passionately discussed in the Jewish press and in personal conversations, especially during elections for various Jewish representative bodies.[30]

One of the victims of such a denunciation was the first secretary of the Central Committee of Liberated Jews in the American Zone of Occupied Germany, Beinisz Tkacz, who faced the Rehabilitation Commission in March 1948 following accusations that he had abused his position as a secretary of the Jewish police in the Kovno ghetto. These accusations were presented to the election commission as he put forward his name for the 1948 Congress of the Central Committee of the Liberated Jews, the official representative body of displaced Jews in the American zone of Germany.[31] In the last sentence of his statement presented to the Rehabilitation Commission in Munich, Tkacz urged that the issue be resolved for the sake of both his image and the commission's.[32] The commission agreed and treated the case as particularly important.[33] Its final decision was that neither membership in the Jewish police nor being a kapo alone was reason enough to remove someone from postwar Jewish communal life. Only in cases of particular brutality was an individual suspended from holding a position of leadership in the community. Such was the case of Juliusz Zeigel (Julius Siegel), director of the Padua DP camp in Italy and a former councilman in the Będzin ghetto and head of its labor department during the occupation. The case was tried before the Court of Honor in Milan, and the verdict was announced on July 19, 1946. Despite the fact that Zeigel had not benefited from his wartime actions and "expressed severe remorse," he was nonetheless condemned for displaying particular cruelty and thus forbidden to hold any position in Jewish public life.[34]

In many such cases denunciations or accusatory testimonies made at trial came from people who had not necessarily been personally affected by the actions of the suspected collaborators. For instance, in the Munich trial of Beinisz Tkacz, the court decided, in his favor, that witnesses testifying in his case "did not show particular bitterness caused by his behavior [in the ghetto] but saw it as inappropriate that a former policeman would hold an eminent position in Jewish society."[35] Similarly, in the trial of Ludwik Jaffe, a former Lvov Judenrat member, undoubtedly the best-known collaboration case adjudicated at the Central Court of Honor in Italy, one of the witnesses, who based his testimony only on hearsay of Jaffe's behavior and on personal experience, justified his statement as a "duty toward society, because a man so discredited as Dr. Jaffe, due to his cooperation with the Germans, should not participate in public life."[36] It should be noted that the denouncers' definitions of "leadership" and "position of power" were broad. For instance, members of the Polish Jewish community protested numerous times against allowing alleged collaborators to work with children,[37] and patients in the Jewish sanatorium in Jar, near Wałbrzych, denounced the director of that institution, a former head of the building department in the Lodz ghetto, claiming that his presence was detrimental to their health.[38]

In some cases, when the alleged collaborator held a position of prominence, the denunciation and subsequent trial were perceived to be a result of political dynamics in the camp. For example, in Ludwik Jaffe's case the defendant believed that he had been accused as a combined result of his affiliations with the Bund and his position as the director of ORT in Italy.[39] Jaffe was accused of acting as a go-between for the Gestapo and the Judenrat and of participating in organizing deportations from the Sobieski school (the March action) in the Lvov ghetto, when between March 16 and April 1, 1942, 15,000 Jews were deported to the Belzec extermination camp. Despite a lack of direct witnesses to his actions, Jaffe was nevertheless forbidden from holding a public position in the Jewish community and from benefiting from aid from Jewish organizations.[40] In another case a former policeman requested that his case be tried in the Central Jewish Honor Court in Munich rather than in the appropriate camp court because he thought that the camp court was ruled by party interests and would look unfavorably on those of different political viewpoints.[41] In Poland a former policeman accused by a member of the Central Committee of Polish Jews, in a letter to that body, attributed the accusation leveled against him to partisan politics: "It is fitting that on the presidium should sit an individual Jews are running away from and are more afraid of than of professional denouncers."[42]

In some cases that involved alleged collaborators who held high-level communal posts, denouncers expressed skepticism, often probably grounded in reality, that colleagues of the accused would be capable of delivering a just sentence. For instance, an anonymous letter sent to the president of the honor court in Warsaw after the court discontinued proceedings in a case asked "if it is also in your interest that collaborator Rosen remains a member of the Central Committee of Jews in Poland" and warned of an "impending fight against all those who hide such a villain."[43] Although most denunciations were clearly signed and often provided the authors' contact details, in these cases the authors occasionally chose to remain anonymous or explicitly requested that their names not be passed on to the alleged collaborator. For example, in one case tried in Warsaw the author of a denunciation asked that the investigation be carried out in a strictly confidential way, because the accused, a former policeman from the Płaszów concentration camp, was a "cunning, rich, and influential man."[44]

It should also be noted that, in the self-contained DP communities, not every outburst of "kapo" directed at a member of the camp leadership could of course be considered an act of denunciation. The discourse of collaboration was commonly used, for example, against camp law enforcement. One such instance took place in Bad Ischl camp in Austria, where the head of the local table tennis club accused the head of the DP camp police of purposefully knocking over a game table and damaging it. He wrote, "I am under the impression that we do not deserve such behavior and treatment by an *OD-man* [Jewish police man] and I assume that we are no longer in concentration camps or ghettos. If we can arrange every matter formally, through the committee, also the police commandant can adhere to human and democratic rules and not barbarian ones."[45] Within a month an inhabitant of the same camp was tried for referring to the chief of the camp police as a "concentration camp murderer," while the head of the camp's Jewish committee was tried for accusing his fellow committee members of collaboration.[46] Although the courts were quick to punish those who resorted to such language, such instances rarely led to collaboration trials.

The potential flight of an alleged collaborator served as another strong declared motivation for submitting a denunciation in the postwar Jewish community. The best-known case of an individual caught on his way out of Germany was that of David Gertler, former head of the Special Department (Sonderabteilung) in the Lodz ghetto Jewish Order Service and, following the September 1942 deportations, the most powerful man in the ghetto. It seems that despite numerous denunciations of him that reached the Central Committee of Liberated Jews, Gertler was residing unperturbed in Munich and even participating in the activities of the Lodz *landsmanshaft* (hometown mutual aid society).[47] Gertler's fate changed when he began looking into immigrating to the United States to join his family. In November 1948 the Central Committee of Liberated Jews received a letter from a World Jewish Congress employee, Kurt R. Grossmann, who had been alerted to Gertler's presence in Munich by former displaced persons sailing from Germany to South America. The letter stated quite explicitly that the World Jewish Congress expected the Jewish leadership in Munich to undertake decisive steps in this matter.[48] Upon Gertler's arrest, the court was barraged with testimonies in his defense. On the basis of overwhelmingly positive evidence, including a number of testimonies from the United States that appeared to be part of an organized defense attempt, and after consulting with the Jewish Historical Institute in Warsaw, the Central Court of Honor dismissed the case against Gertler.[49] His accusers, however, managed to prevent Gertler from emigrating; rather, he remained in Munich until the end of his life. Nevertheless, his case, and others, undoubtedly served as evidence of the extraordinary exchange of information between Jewish communities around the world, whether news or gossip, following the migration paths of Eastern European Jews.

The best-known such case is probably that of Michał Weichert, one of the central figures of interwar Polish Jewish social and cultural life and the most famous person to ever be tried by the Polish Jewish Honor Court. Weichert, a lawyer and illustrious theater director, was accused of accepting in October 1942 the appointment to head the JUS (Jüdische Unterstutzungstelle für das Generalgouvernement), an organization set up by the Germans to distribute relief from abroad among the Jews in the Generalgouvernement in Nazi-occupied Poland. However, it was seen by the Jewish underground as an attempt by the SS to take charge of relief supplies intended for the Jews and to conceal the mass murder of Jews in Poland. Despite warnings from the underground, it was only in July 1944 that Weichert liquidated the JUS and went into hiding. He was arrested by the Public Security Office in March 1945 but was acquitted by a Polish appellate court in January 1946 because of a lack of criminal intent on his part. Following the court's decision, Weichert returned to the public sphere, being engaged by Polish state prosecutors as an investigator and expert witness in a number of trials of senior Nazi officials held in Poland. Yet the Jewish press campaign led to his being retried in December 1949, this time in the honor court of the Central Committee of Polish Jews, which found him guilty of "having committed the crime of collaboration with the Hitlerite authorities" and ordered his "severe stigmatization" as a collaborator.[50] Weichert never again held any public role in Poland. Unable to find a place in either the research institutions or theater, he found work only as a clerk in a construction company. He immigrated to Israel in 1957, but there too he encountered accusations and never found work in communal life.[51]

Defense Strategies

Those who stood accused of collaboration before DP honor courts ranged from former kapos in small camps, who struggled to compose a short defense statement, to educated members of the Judenrat, who presented the presidium with files overflowing with letters of support from the highest echelons of society. Some of them had, by that point, already attempted to prove their innocence to other courts and tribunals, constantly facing denunciations, rumors, and finger-pointing. Some alleged collaborators eventually found themselves in Germany precisely in an effort to escape justice.[52] For others a court order brought them back to events they had presumed buried and forgotten among the ruins of Jewish life in postwar Poland. What all shared was that in the absence of documentation, their only method of defense was to pit their word against that of their accusers. In communities created by memory, one's word could become the toughest weapon in the fight for justice and revenge. For the defendants the ability to recall not only what had happened during the war but also the individuals with whom they had been in contact and the circumstances under which said contact had occurred became their greatest and only asset when facing the tribunal. Even though the courts sought out as many witnesses as possible, this process was facilitated by the fact that both the defendant and the prosecution were equally eager to find numerous voices that would offer favorable testimony. Both the court files and the personal collections of defendants contain evidence to indicate that in many cases individuals had preemptively gathered such testimonies because they feared that their wartime activities might put them at risk for being accused later on.

Just as Jewish survivors were determined to chase down kapos, those who felt falsely accused were determined to clear their name. The Warsaw honor court received correspondence from as far away as Buenos Aires and La Paz requesting that it resolve community tensions that had arisen from gossip about collaboration.[53] In some cases these rehabilitation requests took the shape of counterdenunciations against those who had spread false accusations. These were not always filed by alleged collaborators. In one case a group of Jews from Lodz and Silesia, identifying itself as "former citizens of Vilna," drew the attention of the Warsaw court to an article published in September 1946 in *Dos Naye Lebn*, the official press organ of the Central Committee of Polish Jews, claiming that it disseminated a false accusation and that "it is in the interest of the Jewish community to call to account the person who launched such a shameless accusation toward a fellow citizen who went through the tortures of German henchmen in the concentration camps and [to compel him] to compensate the victim."[54]

Individuals seeking to refute what they considered to be a false accusation of collaboration before a tribunal first had to establish who they were and prove that they shared the identity and values of the community. To prove their "Jewishness" in the DP camp courts, defendants often composed their court statements in Yiddish, even if flawed, rather than in Polish.[55] In these statements, as in those presented by witnesses for the defense, the individuals identified themselves as "sons of decent middle-class Jewish families"[56] or even from "old Zionist families."[57] Defendants presented, almost uniformly, evidence of strong connections to the Jewish national cause from an early age, with one former policeman invoking his brother who had been killed in Eretz Yisrael in 1938.[58] Such links played a part during the occupation, with the defendants extending help to Zionist activists in ghettos and camps, thus proving their "loyalty toward Jewish interests."[59] At least two defendants claimed that they had been delegated to work in the Jewish police by the Zionist underground; in one of these cases the court accepted it as a valid argument.⁶⁰

In other instances, emphasizing involvement in prewar Jewish life could prove detrimental. Judges were often prone to deal more harshly with alleged collaborators who had been involved in the prewar Jewish community than with those who had no prior links to it on the assumption that prewar activists should have known better and had a more developed social conscience. For example, in the Munich trial of Józef Hoch, a former member of the Lvov Judenrat, the facts that he was found to have played a key part in the organization of deportations from the ghetto and that "as a long-term social activist he did not behave honestly during the occupation"⁶¹ proved important in determining his sentence, which forbade him from taking up positions of prominence in the Jewish community.

In the Jewish honor court in Poland, proving one's place in the postwar Polish Jewish community as a good, hard-working citizen was a stronger method of defense than evidence of a strong commitment to Zionism. Similarly, to improve their standing before the court or maybe also to show that the new government was behind them, accused individuals often cited their wartime connections with the clandestine socialist or communist movements or their extended assistance to Poles in need rather than their links to the Zionist underground.⁶² Some of the accused in the Polish Jewish honor court, however, made no secret of their desires to emigrate and saw their trials as an opportunity to clear their names before beginning a new life abroad; in fact, some delayed emigration to ensure that they left Poland with an untarnished name.⁶³ In such cases they did not refrain from using highly emotionally charged Zionist rhetoric and often attempted to reinforce their narratives by mentioning names of people of high social standing, including underground leaders, social activists, or rabbis who could vouch for past behavior.

Stories of Zionist or communist affiliations frequently proved to be the only detailed accounts that pertained to the defendants' wartime experiences. Defendants usually denied all wrongdoing, or admitted to it to only a limited degree; they rarely divulged their duties as a kapo or policeman. However, the same people often discussed in great detail their fate in hiding or immediately after liberation. Although these individuals may have been in better positions in the ghetto than their peers, as these testimonies seem to suggest, they experienced equal suffering when hiding in the countryside or in the forests. After all, they too belonged to the persecuted group, the community of sufferers.⁶⁴ Thus those who did speak of their wartime experiences often focused their narratives on their suffering to further affirm their innocence. As one of those accused asked, "Should a heart broken so badly, suffer even more? ... I am writing this with tears and open wounds. Please heal them."[65] Many defendants endeavored to show that they had been wrongly classified as perpetrators and should instead have been viewed as victims, who were then further victimized by groundless accusations.

The next step for defendants was disputing the charges as personal in intent and motivated by malice, "ill will, hatred, jealousy, and personal accounts."[66] The defense also cited wartime conflict resulting from the privileged position of the defendant during the occupation as a factor in groundless postwar accusations for the sake of revenge. For example, Ludwik Jaffe, while serving as head of the housing department in the Lvov ghetto, found enemies in those for whom he had not been able to arrange dwellings. As one of his supporters wrote in a statement provided to Jaffe, "It is clear that he was not able to fulfill the requests and demands of thousands of people gathered at that time in the Jewish center in Lvov; it is also clear that helping thousands was not possible."[67] Jaffe himself stated in his defense that even though he was saving some people, "others muttered: why not us."[68] A similar issue was brought up in the case of David Gertler. When Gertler became responsible for provisions in the ghetto, living standards did indeed improve and, despite his contacts with the Gestapo, numerous survivors hailed him as a savior who had managed to prolong the lives of many. His supporters argued that "if some suffered needlessly in those years, it was because of the impossible situation rather than through the intent or neglect of Gertler's direction."[69]

The second, and probably more important, reason for the desire of their accusers to seek revenge was defendants' privileged position after liberation.[70] As was the case with wartime conflicts, such denunciations often came from individuals whose requests to the defendants for assistance had gone unanswered. One defendant attributed the denunciation of his accuser to a grievance that arose from the fact that "after his [accuser's] return [to Poland] from the Soviet Union, acting in the capacity of a member of the commission of social aid for the local Jewish committee, I refused his request for rations, as the warehouse was empty. While still in the building of the committee, he threatened that he will 'teach me.'"[71]

Still, for many defendants, activity in the postwar community, including holding a public role, served as their main defense and sign of moral authority. Someone who had "vanished after liberation" was understood to have done so for the purpose of escaping revenge,[72] whereas remaining visible among the community signified a clear conscience. One of those who successfully used this argument was Władysław Friedheim, the chairman of the Association of Jews from Poland and a member of the presidium of the Central Committee of Liberated Jews in the American Zone, who was accused in 1948 of brutal behavior as a kapo in the Budzyń concentration camp. In the statement he presented to the Central Jewish Honor Court in Munich, Friedheim wrote:

> All conferences took place under my leadership. Hundreds, and maybe thousands of Jews participated in them, among them a great number of those who were in camps with me and were liberated with me. None of them accused me of anything.
>
> From the first day after liberation until today I live in Munich. During my work I visited many camps where I met people who were with me in camps, none of them accused me of anything. . . . If I felt guilty of anything, I would not have held the above mentioned offices and under no circumstances would I take the lead in social work.[73]

Similarly, in Poland, where it was common practice to change names after the war, an accused individual might emphasize that he had not changed his name in an attempt to prove that he was undeserving of ostracism.[74]

Aside from discrediting the authors of denunciations, defendants attempted to question the credibility of witnesses for the prosecution by revealing reasons that might have influenced them to testify at trial. For example, one alleged collaborator before the honor court in Warsaw uncovered a network of family links between those who had accused him. He wrote: "The persecutors, with a large dose of ill will, attempt to create an impression as if there were more of them. In reality this whole scandal takes place strictly within one family. . . . My own sense of justice does not allow me to present witnesses of whom there would be even the slightest suspicion that they are driven by factors other than the truth."[75] Others claimed that denouncers had gotten carried away with the communal rush to prosecute and, "excited to the brink with the proceedings taking place, also wanted to take part in them."[76] A former Lodz ghetto official denounced by a group of sanatorium patients evocatively described his accusers' supporters as "sick people, seeking any sensation, who rarely have any visits from the outside, spending months or even years in an empty town, located 5 km from the nearest railway station, and for whom the only spiritual nourishments are conversations conducted during long hours of rest, creating an air where even the wildest gossips strike a chord."[77]

In many cases those at risk of standing trial attempted to discredit their accusers by resorting to rhetoric that portrayed Holocaust survivors as ridden with mental disorders and incapable of functioning in an ordered society in the absence of outside control and guidance. For example, the attorney for Regina Kupiec, who was later sentenced for crimes as a prisoner functionary in Birkenau, stated, "There is no doubt that difficult experiences and the horror of sufferings in the camp led to changes in the psyche of the witnesses, making them unable to organize events according to time, place, person, etc."[78] Although official court statements do not question the reliability of witnesses, leading social activists from among the Jewish displaced persons also discussed the effect of Holocaust trauma on early testimonies.[79] One organizer of the Stuttgart DP camp court wrote in a letter that was used in the Polish trial of an alleged collaborator: "The experiences of people were so awful, tragedies so horrible, that often unintentionally the unfortunates, those hurt, search for culprits among people who according to their subjective belief are the perpetrators. We reached the opinion that judgment of crimes linked to one's behavior in those times can be made only on the basis of concrete, objective proof."[80] This rhetoric was often linked to the portrayal of a denunciation as residual of wartime demoralization. One witness for a defense elaborated, "I was wondering what motives there are for those various denunciations. This is not only the urge to immediately find those guilty of their misfortune, the will to achieve satisfaction in finding the scapegoat, but very often also jealousy, that someone else survived. These are the results of general moral demoralization. Unfortunately the best ones perished."[81] In a similar manner it was suggested during the trials that those who denounced others after the war were already known denouncers or had even been collaborators themselves during the occupation.[82]

This need to question the credibility of witnesses may have been partly a result of the court carefully scrutinizing those who were called as defense witnesses. It was clear from the choice of witnesses for the defense that they came from the same prewar and postwar social circles as the defendants and that they had profited from the work of the defendants during the war, rather than being chosen as witnesses so that they could testify to the defendants' actual conduct during the occupation. Moreover, many of the testimonies came from those who used the trial as a means to clear their own name. In many cases, for example, people who themselves had been tried for collaboration would volunteer to testify in favor of or against former fellow policemen from the same ghetto or camp. As a result, the tribunal sometimes rejected testimony from certain witnesses automatically, including "prisoners who thanks to their work had a privileged position in the camp."[83] During the trial of Regina Kupiec, for example, the honor court rejected statements in her favor as unreliable, because these were presented by prisoners who had been employed in "Kanada," a large warehouse where the belongings of those brought to Auschwitz-Birkenau were sorted, a position that was considered privileged.[84] Similarly, during the trial of Henryk Frydman, head of the Ordnungsdienst in the Mielec concentration camp, the court did not outwardly reject the positive statements of his former co-workers, but it did not take them into consideration in determining his sentence, stating that, "Even if individual prisoners chosen by the accused benefited from his actions, this does not make him less guilty."[85] Typically, the court also rejected statements from witnesses who were called by the defense only to state that they had not heard of or seen any criminal actions by the accused.[86]

As a last resort, defendants both in Poland and in the DP camps questioned the right of the courts to judge them and proceeded to seek justice outside the courts.[87] In both communities honor courts were only one part of the tapestry of formal and informal methods of dealing with suspected collaborators. Some involved in trials also turned to other methods, such as social ostracism and beatings of defendants, to make their point outside court and ultimately prevail in court.[88] During the rehabilitation proceedings of one former policeman in Poland, his denouncer, accompanied by Public Security Office functionaries (the Polish communist secret police), paid him a visit and beat him up. The denouncer may have used similar methods to force some witnesses to testify in the case.[89] In other cases those who felt wrongly accused carried out independent investigations into the source of the denunciation, including seeking out authors of anonymous letters.[90] Others chose to forward their cases to non-Jewish courts, with known cases of false denouncers being tried by either Polish courts or the U.S. Army Counter Intelligence Corps in Germany and Austria.[91]

Conclusion

Debate on the practices, functions, and discourses of denunciation usually focuses on the negative aspects of this practice. Indeed, in many cases denunciation used as a weapon in the quest for personal revenge turned victims into victimizers. Justice in postwar honor courts was undoubtedly buried deep beneath piles of fraudulent testimonies and the settling of personal scores. Some of those who should have been sentenced were set free, whereas others received sentences they did not deserve. For many the fact that they had stood before a tribunal marked them for the rest of their lives. Irrespective of the sentence, the label of kapo or Jewish policeman stuck for years, whether the individual stayed in Poland or left for Israel, the Americas, or Western Europe. Some were tried again by other bodies and had to present their previous testimonies anew. In addition, the trials in the honor courts failed to resonate after 1950. The open, public, and unprecedented discussion in Jewish circles of collaboration, presented in newspapers read only by displaced persons or Jews living in Poland, dissipated after the displaced persons resettled in their new homes in Israel or in countries in the Jewish

Diaspora and after Stalinist suppression of Jewish institutions in Poland. The topic of collaboration, if broached at all, was again relegated to hushed exchanges and meaningful looks behind someone's back.

Denunciations did, however, play an important part in rebuilding the postwar Jewish community. With the establishment of honor courts, for example, Jews who encountered their former tormentors on the street found themselves, for the first time, in the presence of a body that would listen to them, irrespective of their social or political standing. Honor courts served as a symbol of approachable leadership that was prepared to act on the information received. The act of writing a denunciation was also empowering; it elevated the author from a position of victimhood to one in which he or she could shape and decide the fate of the community. The fact that those who sought justice did not shy away from putting their names on their letters, even when they referred to those in positions of power, indicates that they viewed courts as just bodies, truly representative of the Jewish community, rather than fearing that courts were ruled by those in the position of privilege.

Denunciations should not be studied, as is typically done, only in terms of the postwar quest for revenge or as a sign of fragmentation of the Jewish society, but just as much so as a symptom of its trust in the newly created Jewish community. In the process of coming forward and presenting denunciations, individuals allowed their voices to be heard and expressed their trust in their courts, a first step in rebuilding communities that had suffered so significantly.

Notes

1. Samuel Silberstein, "Do Wojewódziego Komitetu Żydowskiego w Łodzi," December 24, 1946, Achiwum Żydoskiego Instytutu Historycznego, Warsaw (hereafter AŻIH), 313/106, p. 4.
2. On the Polish Jewish honor court, see David Engel, "Who Is a Collaborator? The Trials of Michał Weichert," in Sławomir Kapralski, ed., *The Jews in Poland* (Kraków: Judaica Foundation Center for Jewish Culture, 1999), 2: 339–70; Gabriel N. Finder, "The Trial of Shepsl Rotholc and the Politics of Retribution in the Aftermath of the Holocaust," *Gal-Ed: On the History and Culture of Polish Jewry* 20 (2006): 63–89 (English section); and Gabriel N. Finder and Alexander V. Prusin, "Jewish Collaborators on Trial in Poland, 1944–1956," *Polin: Studies in Polish Jewry* 20 (2008): 122–48.
3. "Fun gerichts-zal," *Landsberger Lager Cajtung* (April 15, 1946): 2.
4. On the Court of Honor in Belsen, see Yad Vashem Archive (hereafter YVA), O-70/30, and documents in the YIVO Archive, RG 294.2, MK 483, Microfilm reel 114, folder 1583.
5. For the July 1946 honor court case of Juliusz Zeigel, former member of the Judenrat in Będzin, see "Urteil," July 19, 1946, YIVO Archive, RG 294.3, MK 489, Microfilm reel 16, folder 175. On the discussion over the honor court in Italy, see A. Beker, "A por veter

vegn plitim-gerikht," *Il Cammino* 30.39 (July 26, 1946): 5; and W. Sh., "Plitim-gerikht vert tetik," *Il Cammino* 27.33 (June 11, 1946): 3.

6. On the power of camp police in a DP camp in Austria, see, for example, "Instruction to the Police," February 4, 1947, YIVO Archive, RG 294.3, MK 489, Microfilm reel 14, folder 353.

7. See, for example, the honor court's sentence in the trial of Shlomo Zimmerman, former kapo in the Bełżec, Budzyń, and Wieliczka camps in "Urtayl vegn a yidishn krigsfarbrekher," *Il Cammino* 9.197 (January 23, 1948): 2.

8. Sheila Fitzpatrick and Robert Gellately, "Introduction to the Practices of Denunciation in Modern European History," *Journal of Modern History* 68.4 (1996): 747.

9. Statement of Eliahu Weinberg, n.d., AŻIH, 313/ 29, p. 5.

10. For example, for a letter written by the Jewish Committee in Olsztyn on behalf of the survivors from Święciany and Vilna passing through the city, see for example "Wojewódzki Komitet Żydowski w Olsztynie to the honor court in Warsaw," January 21, 1947, AŻIH, 313/97, p. 4.

11. "Maurycy Rubin do Prezydium Sądu Społecznego," January 26, 1949, AŻIH, 313/128, p. 286.

12. "Do Wydziału Prawnego przy CKŻP," July 14, 1948, AŻIH, 313/53, p. 6.

13. Henryk Mandel, "Do Sądu Obywatelskiego przy Centralnym Kom. Żydów w Polsce," July 3, 1948, AŻIH, 313/1, p. 10.

14. Statement of Abram Rymarz, July 22, 1942, AŻIH, 313/ 118, p. 7.

15. Majer Goldberg, "Nieczyści," *Unzer Veg*, n.d., AŻIH, 313/107, p. 7.

16. Letter to the Central Jewish Committee in Warsaw, July 26, 1948, AŻIH, 313/50, p. 4.

17. "Protokół," January 14, 1948, AŻIH, 313/1, p. 9.

18. Decision of the Prosecution, August 26, 1949, AŻIH, 313/98, p. 5.

19. Letter to the Central Jewish Committee in Warsaw, July 26, 1948, AŻIH, 313/50, p. 4.

20. "Do Sądu Społecznego przy C.K.Ż.P.," n.d., AŻIH, 313/43, p. 4.

21. "Drodzy Przyjaciele," n.d., AŻIH, 313/82, p. 11.

22. Letter to the Central Jewish Committee in Warsaw, July 26, 1948, AŻIH, 313/50, p. 4.

23. "Nieczyści," *Unzer Veg*, n.d., AŻIH, 313/107, p. 8.

24. "Nieczyści," 7.

25. For a protest in a courtroom, see "Harbere sztrofn far kapos!" *Landsberg Lager Cajtung* (November 12, 1945): 6.

26. See Ben Ami, "Vi zet oys bay undz der gerikhtikayts-organ," *A Heim* (June 4, 1946): 11. The author of the article lamented the "lack of discipline of our masses, truly laughable actions of our security and legal bodies [and] ... a cowardly behavior of our judges" and complained about the leniency of the sentences: "According to what codex do those gentlemen work? Maybe according to the Jewish Torah? But there are points there such as 'an eye for an eye' guaranteeing that everyone will get a deserved sentence."

27. See "Baschluss in Angelegenheit nr. R. 65/48 c.," August 2, 1949, YVA, M 21.2, folder 77.
28. "Baricht wegn di arbet fun Rehabilitacje Komisje, Minchen, dem 25.8.1948," YIVO Archive, RG 294.2, MK 483, Microfilm reel 21, folder 223.
29. "Nieczyści," 7; Hilary Sztrowajs, "Do Wojewódzkiego Komitetu Żydowskiego w Łodzi," July 4, 1947, AŻIH, 313/126, p. 9.
30. See B. Orenstein, "Wos iz azojns kapo?" *Jidysze Cajtung* (December 6, 1946): 6. For personal communication, see, for example, the letter to Szpigler regarding Berysz Mandelbaum, September 18, 1947, YIVO Archive, RG 294.2, MK 483, Microfilm reel 47, folder 639.
31. Beinisz Tkacz, "Dringende wendung," March 19, 1948, YIVO Archive, RG 294.2, MK 483, Microfilm reel 20, folder 221.
32. Tkacz, "Dringende wendung."
33. "Rehabilitacje komisje cu der Centraler Wal-Komisje," March 21, 1948, YIVO Archive, RG 294.2, MK 483, Microfilm reel 20, folder 221.
34. "2-ter kolaboratsye-protses in gez. Gerikht," *Il Cammino* 95.283 (September 3, 1948): 3. On the Juliusz Zeigel (Julius Siegel) case, see also Rivka Brot, "Julius Siegel: A 'Kapo' in Four (Judicial) Acts," *Dapim: Studies on the Shoah* 25 (2011): 65–127.
35. Tkacz, "Dringende wendung."
36. "Erklärung von Dr. Moises Landau," YIVO Archive, Bund Collection, ME 17–240.
37. See, for example, "Protokół," March 3, 1949, AŻIH, 313/120, p. 21.
38. "Do Wojewódzkiego Komitetu Żydowskiego we Wrocławiu," n.d., AŻIH, 313/39, p. 6.
39. On the Zionist critique of Bundism in DP camps, see Ze'ev Mankowitz, *Life Between Memory and Hope: The Survivors of the Holocaust in Occupied Germany* (Cambridge, UK: Cambridge University Press, 2002), 73–76. Ludwik Jaffe's case was widely reported in the displaced persons press in Italy. See, for example, "Protses kegn Dir. L. Yafe in gezelschaftl. gerikht," *Il Cammino* 92.280 (August 27, 1948): 4.
40. "Urtayl in Protses fun Dr. L. Yafe," *Il Cammino* 112.303 (November 15, 1948): 2.
41. For an accusation of one of the members of the Boelcke Kaserne committee of collaboration and a request that the case be forwarded to the Munich honor court to guarantee an objective ruling, see also "M. Nochhauser do sądu honorowego w Boelcke Kaserne," April 19, 1948, YIVO Archive, RG 294.2, MK 483, Microfilm reel 18, folder 202.
42. Meyer Pinchas, "Do Sądu Społecznego w Warszawie," May 26, 1949, AŻIH, 313/71, p. 62.
43. "Do rzecznika Sądu Obywatelskiego," January 24, 1948, AŻIH, 313/107, p. 98.
44. "Protokół," June 24, 1947, AŻIH, 313/76, p. 3.
45. "Do Komitetu Ośrodka w Goldenes Kreuz," September 19, 1946, YIVO Archive, RG 294.4, MK 492, Microfilm reel 14, folder 346.
46. Komenda Policji Żydowskiej Bad Ischl, "Akt Oskarżenia," no. 13/46 (August 3, 1946), 14/46 (September 20, 1946), and 15/46 (September 30, 1946), YIVO Archive, RG 294.4, MK 492, Microfilm reel 14, folder 345. For other cases, see "Protokol" for Berek Aved,

a policeman in Feldafing accused of "being a ghetto policeman and killing people with his own hands," YIVO Archive, RG 294.2, MK 483, Microfilm reel 53, folder 714; and "Urteil," n.d., for a Föhrenwald camp inhabitant sentenced to a 400-mark fine for claiming that a DP camp policeman "threw living people into the oven." YIVO Archive, RG 294.2, MK 483, Microfilm reel 51, folder 694.

47. See IPN Archive, GK 164/60, vols. 1 and 2. Investigation into the case of David Gertler was initiated in Poland in 1947, following a denunciation to the Main Commission for the Investigation of German Crimes in Poland. The case was dropped because of a lack of incriminating evidence, and no extradition request was filed. See also AŻIH, 313/64 (case file of David Gertler); and an interview with David Gertler in YIVO, RG 697, Isaiah Kuperstein Collection.

48. Kurt R. Grossman to Mr. Shlomowitz, October 29, 1948, YVA, M.21.2, folder 111.

49. For another case, see the correspondence between the Jewish Historical Institute in Warsaw and Jewish Historical Documentation in Linz regarding Józef Pilawski, a putative collaborator in Sobowice, March 27, 1947, AŻIH, 313/96, p. 4.

50. Quoted in Engel, "Who Is a Collaborator?" 343.

51. See Engel, "Who Is a Collaborator?" 367–68.

52. See AŻIH, 313/48, for the case of Józef Hoch, a former member of the Judenrat in Lvov accused of forcing Judenrat employees to participate in deportation actions. Following the request of the prosecutor, the honor court transferred the case to the Polish criminal court. Hoch most likely left Poland before it took place, as he was tried again in Germany. Similarly, in the case of Hersz Goldsztajn (AŻIH, 313/33), a former policeman from Międzyrzec Podlaski, the investigation in Poland was suspended because Goldsztajn was already in Germany. The honor court of the Central Committee of Polish Jews later cooperated with the Central Committee of Liberated Jews in the American Zone in his trial, which took place in Munich. Numerous others, whose cases were brought in front of the honor court in Warsaw, managed to disappear in Germany more successfully because there is no documentation referring to their subsequent trials.

53. For a Jewish committee in La Paz asking for an opinion on an alleged collaborator living in La Paz, see Moises Rosenbach to the Central Jewish Committee in Warsaw, December 8, 1946, AŻIH, 313/20, p. 6; and for an agency asking for assistance in a case of an alleged collaborator living in Buenos Aires, see HIAS (Jewish Agency of Palestine) of America, Warsaw, to the Jewish Committee, January 25, 1947, AŻIH, 313/73, p. 3.

54. W. Chelem, M. Vogelbaum, and M. Pruzan, "Do CKŻP w Warszawie," September 9, 1946, AŻIH, 313/14, p. 4.

55. Hermann Altbauer composed his defense statement in faulty Yiddish, although he conducted his personal correspondence in Polish, which was the language in which he was educated. See Testimony of Hermann Altbauer, February 10, 1942, YIVO Archive, RG 294.3, MK 489, Microfilm reel 17, folder 189.

56. "Abraham Sterczer do Sądu Honorowego Żydów w Milano," March 10, 1948, YIVO Archive, RG 294.3, MK 489, Microfilm reel 17, folder 189.
57. Testimony of Mordechaj Karnowsky, n.d., YIVO Archive, RG 294.2, MK 483, Microfilm reel 20, folder 221.
58. Testimony of Mordechaj Karnowsky. See also Benisz Tkacz, "Cu der Rehabilitacje Komisje Munchen," March 25, 1948, and, in the same folder, a testimony of Jicchok Batner for Tkacz's links to Zionism in his university years, YIVO Archive, RG 294.2, MK 483, Microfilm reel 20, folder 221.
59. Testimony of Zelmar Finkel, March 23, 1948, YIVO Archive, RG 294.2, MK 483, Microfilm reel 20, folder 221.
60. See YVA, M.21.2, folder 32 (case file of Chaim Aleksandrowicz). In the case of Henryk Gliksman, former policeman from Częstochowa, the court believed that he was working on orders from the Zionist underground. YVA, M.21.2, folder 51 (case file of Henryk Gliksman).
61. "Baszlus," October 29, 1947, YIVO Archive, RG 294.2, MK 483, Microfilm reel 14, folder 180.
62. "Przesłuchanie Marii Urbanowicz," January 26, 1948, AŻIH, 313/116, p. 78.
63. See "Wyjaśnienie M. Rozenmana," October 24, 1947, in which the accused claimed to have returned from his journey to South America to defend himself in Europe. AŻIH, 313/107, p. 15.
64. See, for example, testimony of Hermann Altbauer, February 10, 1942, YIVO Archive, RG 294.3, MK 489, Microfilm reel 17, folder 189.
65. Masza Engel, "Życiorys," January 21, 1947, AŻIH, 313/18, p. 7.
66. "Nieczyści," *Unzer Veg*, n.d., AŻIH, 313/107, p. 9.
67. Stefania Milwiw, "Zaświadczenie," YIVO Archive, Bund Collection, ME 17–240.
68. Ludwik Jaffe, "Derklerung," YIVO Archive, Bund Collection, ME 17–240.
69. Testimony of Gustawa Beckerman, April 30, 1946, YVA, M 21.2, folder 111.
70. On survivors in privileged positions after liberation, see Mankowitz, *Life Between Memory and Hope*, 204–5.
71. Pinchas, "Do Sądu Społecznego w Warszawie," 59.
72. "Baschluss in Angelegenheit nr. R. 65/48 c.," August 2, 1949, YVA, M 21.2, folder 77.
73. Władysław Friedheim, "Cum Presidentum fun Central Komitet fun di befrajde idn in Us-Zone Dajczland," August 7, 1947, YIVO Archive, RG 294.2, MK 483, Microfilm reel 18, folder 195.
74. Aleksander Eintracht, "Do Plenum Sądu Społecznego przy CKŻ w Polsce," n.d., AŻIH, 313/1, p. 48.
75. M. Rozenman, "Wyjaśnienie," January 17, 1948, AŻIH, 313/107, p. 94.
76. Aleksander Eintracht, "Odwołanie," June 24, 1949, AŻIH, 313/1, p. 57.

77. "Wyjaśnienie do zeznań złożonych w dniu 21 marca 1947," March 31, 1947, AŻIH, 313/39, p. 30.
78. "Adw. Dawid-Julian Holcman do Komisji Rehabilitacyjnej przy Centralnym Komitecie Żydowskim w Monachium, June 17, 1948," YIVO Archive, RG 294.2, MK 483, Microfilm reel 20, folder 222.
79. See Samuel Gringauz, "Some Methodological Problems in the Study of the Ghetto," *Jewish Social Studies* 12.1 (1950): 65.
80. Henry Griffel, letter to Gutmacher, February 18, 1947, AŻIH, 313/121, p. 99.
81. Letter by N. Szenderowicz, April 18, 1946, AŻIH, 313/121, p. 12.
82. "Zeznanie w sprawie Runy Kornblich," December 15, 1948, AŻIH, 313/20, p. 109.
83. Dawid Honigman, "Baszlus," November 25, 1948, YIVO Archive, RG 294.2, MK 483, Microfilm reel 21, folder 244.
84. Dawid Julian Holcman, "Skarga o rewizję procesu," June 17, 1948, "YIVO Archive, RG 294.2, MK 483, Microfilm reel 20, folder 222.
85. Henryk Frydman, "Baszlus," January 16, 1949, YIVO Archive, RG 294.2, MK 483, Microfilm reel 21, folder 224.
86. Frydman, "Baszlus."
87. See "Adw. Dawid-Julian Holcman." See also "Baszlus" in Hoch's case.
88. On "clearing out the kapos" in the Wildflecken DP camp, see the memoir of Kathryn Hulme, a deputy director of the United Nations Relief and Rehabilitation Administration (UNRRA): Kathryn Hulme, *The Wild Place* (Boston: Little, Brown, 1953), 14. Even though there are no data on how many suspected collaborators were killed in the camps following the liberation, beatings were undoubtedly widespread. In November 1945 the *Landsberg Lager Cajtung* described "many instances of Center residents attacking people designated as kapos by individuals and seriously injuring them." See "Appeal to Residents of the Landsberg Center," *Landsberg Lager Cajtung* (November 12, 1945): 6. For assaults on former Jewish policemen after the war in Poland, see, for example, Aleksander Berger (Zamieński), "Protokół," January 29, 1947, AŻIH, 313/7, p. 7.
89. Meyer Pinchas, "Do Szefa Wojewódzkiego Urzędu Bezpieczeństwa Publicznego w Lublinie," March 25, 1949, AŻIH, 313/71, p. 43.
90. Pinchas, "Do Sądu Społecznego w Warszawie," 59. See also "Gutachten," for the accused in a displaced persons court in Austria ordering a forensic analysis of handwriting in a denunciation, March 4, 1947, YIVO Archive, RG 294.4, MK 492, Microfilm reel 14, folder 346.
91. Dr. J. Bardach, "Do Sądu Obywatelskiego przy Centralnym Komitecie Ż.P.," November 2, 1947, AŻIH, 313/128, p. 193.

9

"I'm Going to the Oven Because I Wouldn't Give Myself to Him"

The Role of Gender in the Polish Jewish Civic Court

EWA KOŹMIŃSKA-FREJLAK

On December 8, 1946, Mojżesz Rosenbach, writing on behalf of the Jewish community in Bolivia, demanded in a rather laconic letter sent from La Paz to the Central Committee of Polish Jews (Centralny Komitet Żydów w Polsce; CKŻP) in Warsaw that it "settle" the case of Runa Fakler.[1] Details of the case were provided in an enclosed transcript of an arranged confrontation between Mojżesz Aftergut and Runa Fakler, née Lewinger, that was held on December 4, 1946, on the premises of the Polish Democratic Association (Polski Związek Demokratyczny) in La Paz.[2] Their face-to-face encounter was presided over by activists from Jewish organizations in Bolivia: a Dr. Allerhand, a member of the Jewish community board; Emma Krumholtz, president of the local branch of WIZO (Women's International Zionist Organization); and A. Kaswiner, former vice-president of Circulo Israelita, the first Jewish organization founded in Bolivia by Jewish immigrants from Eastern Europe in 1935. According to the transcript, Aftergut, a former Jewish inmate of the Płaszów labor camp, located outside Kraków, saw Runa Fakler in La Paz and recognized her as the wife of a kapo, Dawid Fakler, known in the camp as Maciek Fakler, who had died in the meantime. During the confrontation, Aftergut, speaking first, accused

Dawid Fakler of openly collaborating with the Germans, which included beating and harassing Jews. According to Aftergut, Dawid Fakler used to kick him for no apparent reason and threatened to take him to the execution site. Fakler's wife, Runa, in turn, was supposedly "collaborating with her husband" and "enjoying the benefits of a kapo's wife"—that is, "She did no physical work, lived with her husband in a separate room, and incited him to commit excesses." Moreover, according to Aftergut, Runa Fakler was the beneficiary of services rendered to her husband by prisoners under him, which she should have known were involuntary. In fact, Aftergut—not acting, of course, on his own volition—was forced to haul water for the Faklers and clean and deliver their shoes, which Runa Fakler often collected from him.[3]

It is not clear whose idea it was to conduct the confrontation on December 4. In a letter sent from Bolivia to the "Historical Committee" in Kraków, Runa Fakler insisted that she herself had "initiated the confrontation" in the belief that she would succeed in exonerating herself.[4] In any case, judging by the statements of those who took part, it was the proponents of a tough stand on Holocaust survivors with questionable wartime pasts who played a decisive part in the preparations of the confrontation and in the proceedings. In this case these were people in Mojżesz Aftergut's camp. From about twenty participants in the confrontation—the Faklers' main opponents and a dozen other "private" individuals (including "a few senior members of the Jewish community")[5]—the transcript contains statements by five survivors from Europe who reached Bolivia after the war, not including Aftergut. Of those five only one was in Płaszow for sure, and he had not known Fakler personally. Nevertheless, all five unanimously deemed Runa Fakler guilty.[6] If her husband had been a kapo who collaborated with the Germans and if he had harassed his fellow prisoners in numerous ways, his actions, they reasoned, rendered his wife guilty too. A male witness whose name was Szapiro claimed that "she tolerated what he was doing, helping him and enjoying the privileges of his position."[7] A female witness by the name of Szpirsztajn, a "former partisan," insisted that "not only was Fakler the guilty one, but his wife [was guilty] too, and so was everyone who was living with him and making use of his services."[8] If one is to trust the transcript, Runa Fakler's conduct was indeed questionable and she deserved punishment. The question is whether one should trust the witness statements. It was Aftergut's cousin, Mojżesz Rosenbach, who called for a "boycott" of Runa Fakler on the grounds that she had promised him that she would produce evidence to rebut Aftergut's version of events but had failed to do so. Indeed, in Rosenbach's opinion the confrontation tended to prove that Aftergut's accusations against Dawid and Runa Fakler were accurate. Another female witness by the name of Tuerk sided with Rosenbach. Runa Fakler had also promised her that she would explain why Aftergut was beaten and kicked but then said nothing.

Runa Fakler, branded as the defendant from the outset of the meeting, sought to prove her innocence in numerous ways. She rose to speak twice, for the first time to reply to Aftergut's charges. She stressed that at the camp, Aftergut, 17 years old at the time, was widely regarded as a liar and that his revelations should therefore be taken with a grain of salt. However, she did not convince the gathering. In the same breath she insisted that her husband had beaten only traitors. Still, she admitted that he had been a kapo and that during the last phase of her internment in the camp she indeed had not worked on account of, in her own words, a "mental breakdown." (It is a fact that before she reached Płaszów she had lost a 5-year-old son.)[9] She then spoke again after all the other witnesses had finished. In support of her innocence she said that after she had been rescued from Bergen-Belsen and transferred to a provisional encampment in Sweden for Holocaust survivors, her 350 female companions appointed her as "camp leader." This argument did not change any minds either. As Lusia Hufnagel, a former Bergen-Belsen prisoner explained, "Precisely such individuals, whose role in the German camps had been rather dubious, jumped at the opportunity to assume the position of leader." Exhausted by hard work and their ordeals in the camps, "other" (implying "honest") ex-prisoners, she emphasized, did not have enough strength to apply for high-ranking positions.[10]

The confrontation was highly emotional. During Aftergut's preliminary presentation of the charges, Runa Fakler shouted, "Silence, you're lying!" several times.[11] Aftergut, for his part, reacted strongly throughout the entire meeting, refuting Runa Fakler's claims. He further preempted her defense by casting doubt in advance on the credibility of her potential witnesses. Any list of such people, he claimed, would contain only Fakler's favorites. "Such favoritism," he asserted, "was not uncommon, even among these notorious criminals, kapos."[12] Other participants echoed and backed Aftergut's words with continuous comments, replies, and disputes. They spontaneously cross-examined Runa Fakler and refuted her arguments. No one spoke in her defense.

It was Aftergut who had the last word as well as the first. He demanded that Christine Finkerlpel, another former prisoner at Płaszów, residing at that time (1946) in Italy, be contacted. Aftergut recommended her as the perfect source of information on "the cruelties of [Dawid] Fakler and [Runa] Fakler."[13] The transcript concludes with a request by Allerhand, Krumholz, and Kaswiner that the Jewish committee in Kraków clarify whether Dawid Fakler, or Maciek as he was known at Płaszów, was on its blacklist, and, if not, that it gather pertinent details about him. Moreover, in the event that Runa Fakler was implicated by her husband's actions, they asked for the Kraków committee's opinion on how the Bolivian Jewish community should respond in "the case of Runa Fakler." Thus, even though Aftergut admitted that he "[could] not prove anything against her, as she did not take any action in public,"[14] his words sufficed to institute legal proceedings against Runa Fakler in the Polish Jewish civic court or honor court. As far as the Jewish community in Bolivia was concerned, Aftergut's incriminating assertions against her husband at least partly supported her own guilt. Nevertheless, in his letter to the Jewish committee in Kraków, Mojżesz Rosenbach felt compelled to admit that "the local community has *insufficient evidence* to exclude Runa Fakler from our nation."[15] In other words, the community wanted to put Runa Fakler on trial at all costs, however attenuated the evidence of her own alleged misdeeds was, because she was the wife of a kapo. As it was written in the transcript, "She herself eventually *admitted* that her husband was a kapo and wore an armband."[16] By the same token, the bias against Runa Fakler in the Jewish community of La Paz is palpable from Rosenbach's letter to the Central Committee of Polish Jews in Warsaw, because he fails to acknowledge the fact that she adamantly stood her ground and claimed her innocence.

The investigation of Runa Fakler went on for more than two years. While the Jewish Historical Commission in Kraków gathered evidence, the small Jewish community in Bolivia boycotted her. At least once, in August 1947, she was attacked on the street. The perpetrator was Mojżesz Aftergut. Today it is impossible to determine whether he planned his assault beforehand or acted spontaneously on meeting her by chance. His motives remain unknown. Was he only seeking revenge for the maltreatment he had suffered at the hands of Dawid Fakler in the camp? Was he really convinced of the wife's equal guilt? Or was he simply experiencing frustrations of his own and venting them? Was he irascible by nature and prone to violence? What can be said for certain is that he acted with complete impunity. Even the fact that Runa Fakler was visibly pregnant (in her fifth month) did not deter him. "When crossing the street, I was suddenly attacked by this boy, Mojsie Aftergut, and knocked to the ground with a strong blow in the chest. He disappeared, calling me the filthiest of names," she recounted in a letter addressed to the "Historical Committee."[17] After this incident and following the advice of "indignant Jewry," in her own words, she herself turned to the Jewish Historical Commission in Kraków, remonstrating that it devote its attention to people who "truly did something" in the Płaszów camp rather than occupying itself with her and asking it to write an official note to the Federación Israelita that would exonerate her from all blame.[18]

From the documents in her file, prepared for the Polish Jewish honor court, one can assume that no such note ever reached Bolivia. Presumably instead, on

January 21, 1948, the Jewish Voivodeship Committee in Kraków (Wojewódzki Komitet Żydowski w Krakowie; WKŻK) wired a conciliatory telegram to the Federación Israelita in Oruro, instructing it to "wait for verdict, avert disgraceful persecution."[19] Meanwhile, tensions surrounding Runa Fakler were rising. Five months after Aftergut's attack, representatives of the Federación Israelita in Oruro informed the Jewish Historical Commission in Kraków that "our organization has taken a wait-and-see approach to the case of Mrs. Fakler. To avoid any unpleasant incidents, we let Mrs. Fakler know that she should not visit our club."[20] Again, at the end of April 1948, representatives of the Federación Israelita urged the Jewish Voivodeship Committee to proceed with haste.[21] Three months later, in yet another letter, the Federación Israelita addressed its concerns directly to the Polish Jewish "civic court" or honor court: "The accused Runa Fakler-Kornblüh lives in our city and we are interested in settling this case once and for all. We ask you to give us a final verdict, which would be authoritative and useful in our midst."[22] Toward the end of December 1948, Runa Fakler herself was complaining to the Jewish honor court in Poland: "I've been suffering innocently for two years. I'm being boycotted by the local Jews. They treat me like a black sheep."[23] Sanctions taken against Runa Fakler were being applied as well to one of her relatives, who, upon arriving in Bolivia, intimated in a letter to an acquaintance in Poland that "now I too suffer as the brother-in-law of a person boycotted by local Jewry."[24]

During the investigation testimonies were collected from more than thirty-five people, including fifteen women and twenty men. From among the men, six are known to have testified outside Poland: one in Rome, one in Brussels, and the rest in South America (Bolivia, Brazil, and Argentina).[25] Runa Fakler was accused of misdeeds by eight of them, mostly former prisoners from Płaszów; three of them were women, the rest men. Alongside the various accusations leveled against her were assertions in favor of her innocence. The accusations encompassed charges scrutinized by the CKŻP's civic court in other cases of women accused of collaboration with German occupying forces and their allies. These charges raised several issues: whether the woman under investigation occupied a privileged position among camp prisoners, whether she mistreated other prisoners, whether she had sexual relations with camp personnel, and whether she had a close relationship with an obvious collaborator and should be held responsible for *his* actions.

The civic court finally announced its decision on January 10, 1949. The court held that the "judicial investigation did not find evidence in support of the allegations that Runa Fakler, ... specifically during her stay at the camp in Płaszów, acted to the detriment of her fellow prisoners and served the occupier."[26] The verdict, formulated in legalese, was not entirely favorable to the defendant. To be sure, the court noted the lack of evidence of Runa Fakler's guilt, but by the same token it did not formally acquit her either. Formally, it neither discontinued the case nor questioned the viability of the main charges, even though in a previously drafted document the prosecutor not only distanced himself from the charges but also moved the court to drop the case.

Why the decision was not relayed to the relevant Jewish organizations in Bolivia immediately after it had been pronounced remains subject to speculation. Reasons for this neglect are probably not attributable to the diminishing latitude of Jewish organizations in Poland after 1948. The civic court operated until 1950, and throughout 1949 it had a full docket of cases. Moreover, by this time the Polish government was taking pains to isolate Polish Jews from Jews in other countries, but correspondence between Polish Jewish organizations, including officials of the civic court, and their counterparts abroad was still robust. Perhaps it was just a matter of mere negligence. It is, however, conceivable that the decision was not relayed to Jewish organizations in Bolivia because it might cause consternation among them. It is known that for the first ten months after pronouncement of the court's decision, no official document containing the decision reached Bolivia. In a letter dated October 17, 1949, Karolina Natanek, a resident of Kraków who claimed to be Runa Fakler's relative, admonished the civic court for its tardiness in announcing its decision, emphasizing, "It is about a human life."[27] News of the court's decision actually reached Jewish organizations in Bolivia earlier through Runa Fakler's relatives.[28] Representatives of the community of Polish Jews in Bolivia did not find it entirely believable, though. On June 24, 1949, they wrote the CKŻP to make sure that the court took into account the statements of those accusing Runa Fakler: "We know nothing of the circumstances in which the verdict was passed, and particularly whether the court that pronounced [the decision] was aware of the witnesses who were summoned and their testimonies."[29]

It does not seem likely that the civic court's decision would appease the Jewish community's enmity toward and ostracism of Runa Fakler, especially after such long a time had passed since the commencement of the investigation. In the same vein, presumably not too many people became convinced of her innocence as a result of the decision. In the second half of the 1940s even a shadow of suspicion of collaboration with the Germans and their allies during the war could cause vehement and long-term reactions, especially in communities deeply affected by the war. In addition, in communities of Jews who survived the war outside occupied Europe, the very fact that some people survived the Holocaust raised suspicions about them. Most important, however, in the case of Runa Fakler and in many other cases brought to the civic court, especially those against women, as I will show, the charges essentially resisted efforts to rebut them. In the course of the investigation it was proven that Dawid Fakler did in fact serve as a kapo and, according to the camp survivors, had his moments of cruelty. It is hard to imagine that Runa Fakler would have been able to prove that she had had no influence whatsoever on her husband's actions. In turn, the allegation that she was a mistress of a member of the camp's staff was merely conjecture, yet there was nothing other than her own words, which, after all, did not convince the unconvinced, to change her opponents' opinion on the matter.

I base this chapter on an analysis of files collected in the CKŻP's civic court or honor court and found in the Archives of the Jewish Historical Institute (AŻIH) in Warsaw. Apart from correspondence and organizational documents, the AŻIH includes files of cases examined by the civic court. Each case begins with a short note, written presumably ex post by an archivist. This note contains the most significant, though sometimes misleading, information about the subject of the investigation and its course. Sometimes it also includes a list of summoned witnesses and the final verdict. The preserved documentation of the cases is not always complete, and it also remains unknown whether all the cases brought to the civic court were recorded and archived.

The civic court operated under the auspices of the CKŻP between 1946 and 1950.[30] The CKŻP's legal department, which prepared cases for the court, investigated some 150 cases.[31] Pursuant to Article 2 of the court's charter, it was created to pass judgment "(a) In cases of misconduct by a member of the Jewish community during the Hitlerite occupation unbefitting a Jewish citizen, through his participation and harmful activity on 'Jewish councils,' in the [ghetto police], in the administration of concentration camps or any other type of collaboration with the occupier to the detriment of society; [and] (b) In cases of a violation by CKŻP members of this organization's charter or of actions in contravention of their duties and good customs."[32] Only 17 of the 147 preserved files[33] of the investigated cases refer to women (11 percent), one of which is registered under the names of two non-Jewish Poles, a man and a woman.[34] The Polish Jewish honor court ruled in only four, or one-quarter, of these cases: those of Runa Fakler, Masza Engel, Rita Knyszyńska, and Wiera Gran.[35] Two of the investigated cases of women (12 percent)[36] do not pertain to their conduct during the war; on the surface, they refer to violations allegedly committed by CKŻP members. (However, in their testimonies the witnesses did refer to the behavior of the women in question under the German occupation.) The first of these investigations was motivated by a complaint filed against a CKŻP office worker, who in the presence of others questioned the truthfulness of a plaintiff's testimony.[37] The second grew out of an argument between two neighboring families in Otwock. One of the parties purportedly said, "What a pity that so many Jews remained, what a pity that Hitler killed so few of them."[38] In her own defense, she merely said, when provoked: "What a pity that he wasn't in Poland at that time and didn't go through this hell; otherwise he would judge those who survived the occupation in a different manner."[39] In contrast, in 130 cases involving men,[40] only 8 (6 percent)[41] were not directly connected to the conduct of the defendants during the war (among them was a complaint filed against a husband,[42] an inheritance feud,[43] and, twice, a conflict over property[44]). Three files pertain to non-Jewish Poles.[45]

The ratio of women suspected of collaboration with the Germans is even lower in four extant lists of names of Jews suspected of "collaborating with the Germans." These lists are preserved in the files of the civic court. They were prepared in 1947 by members of the Central Jewish Historical Commission (Centralna Żydowska Komisja Historyczna, CŻKH), on the basis of a written request of the civic court, dated December 7, 1946.[46] (It is unknown, however, what the lists were based on). These lists were gradually submitted to the court: on February 20, 1947,[47] March 10, 1947,[48] March 14, 1947,[49] and April 14, 1947.[50] One list, comprising about 950[51] names of Lodz Jews, contained as few as 4 women.[52] Among the names in the second list, 7 belonged to women.[53] The third list contained 141 names, 3 of whom were women.[54] Among the 822 people on the fourth list, 18 were women.[55]

When it comes to men accused of failing to act in a manner befitting a Jewish citizen during the Nazi occupation, it was mostly members of collaborating organizations whose cases were considered by the civic court. Cases of former ghetto police functionaries formed 50 percent of all the investigations (71 people), former Jewish council (Judenrat) members or those associated with Jewish councils 17 percent (24 people), and prisoner functionaries in German camps 14 percent (20 people). Charges were also brought against two workers of the Arbeitsamt in Drohobycz and in Sosnowiec,[56] a workshop manager in the Będzin ghetto,[57] two factory overseers from the Warsaw ghetto,[58] and the head of Jewish Social Self-Help (Żydowska Samopomoc Społeczna), Michał Weichert.[59]

Four women—one-fourth of the total number of women with case files—who had been prisoner functionaries in concentration camps during the war petitioned the Polish Jewish court for rehabilitation. Masza Engel, an overseer[60] and kapo at Auschwitz (Oświęcim), submitted a petition for rehabilitation to the court on January 21, 1947. She wrote: "It is with deepest pain and a clear conscience that I would like to redeem myself in the eyes of Jewish society."[61] Another application for rehabilitation was filed by Rita Knyszyńska, who, in her own words, was delegated by a Białystok Judenrat commissioner to administer the Volkovysk camp's property and manage the kitchens.⁶² According to a fellow prisoner, she was an *Aufseherin*, an overseer of women.⁶³ Chawa Sznit was a block overseer at Elbląg, a division of the Stutthof camp. On February 4, 1949, her name was mentioned in the Yiddish periodical *Folksztime*. As a result, she appealed to the civic court to investigate her case and rehabilitate her. "I feel slighted by this [notice in the newspaper]. As I don't feel guilty of any transgression against Jewish honor, I respectfully ask the civic court to investigate the case of my conduct during the German occupation."⁶⁴ On February 8, 1949, Augusta Weber, a block overseer in the Płaszów camp during the war, filed a rehabilitation request with the civic court. The prosecuting attorney rejected her request, however, because the application was filed too late.⁶⁵

Not all defendants in the honor court filed petitions to clear their names; some like Wiera Gran and Michał Weichert eventually succumbed to pressure to stand trial. (The civic court had no power to compel putative collaborators to stand trial before it.) But the number of women who submitted petitions for rehabilitation is worth emphasizing here. Among the five who did (the fifth was a woman by the name of Linde who was allegedly an agent for the Gestapo),⁶⁶ two of the four women who stood trial before the civic court initiated the proceedings themselves. This ratio was much smaller for men. Of the twenty-five or so men who were tried by the civic court, only six initiated their proceedings with petitions for rehabilitation.

The four women who wished to have their names cleared by the civic court—Engel, Knyszyńska, Sznit, and Weber—had been camp functionaries. But were any Jewish women investigated because they sat on a Jewish council or exercised administrative or managerial authority? In short, the answer is no. This is not surprising because with rare exceptions Jewish women in Europe did not sit on Jewish councils or occupy administrative positions in labor camps. Gisi Fleishman (Judenrat member in Slovakia), Olga Goldfein (Judenrat member in the Prużany ghetto), and Olga Markowicz (commandant of the Werk "C" camp in Skarżysko-Kamienna) were, according to historians Dalia Ofer and Leonore J. Weitzman, utter exceptions.⁶⁷

In fact, most investigations of putative Jewish female collaborators—69 percent—conducted by the lawyers attached to the civic court entailed various types of open-ended "collaboration with the occupier to the detriment of society." The women allegedly acted "in a manner unbefitting a Jewish citizen." Meanwhile, this open-ended charge of collaboration led prosecutors to open a file in a mere 12 of the total 140 Polish Jewish men under investigation. Charges underpinning such investigations, in the cases of men and women alike, were formulated in a variety of manners. The most general ones were simple accusations of collaboration. In the case of Rena Majzel, the charge was not specified at all. Such charges served first and foremost to discredit the accused; there is no doubt that they were often instigated by those who used them to settle everyday arguments. Majzel was accused simply of "collaborating with the Germans" in the Lodz ghetto.[68] Eventually, the investigation was discontinued for lack of incriminating evidence.[69] Eugenia Mirel, in turn, asked the court to bring to justice Chaim Nisebaum, her lodger, who was not paying his rent, because he made "slanderous" and "derogatory" statements, accusing her of "consorting with SS-men" (who remained unidentified), "leading people to perdition," and "insulting the medals" he had received during the war.[70] In Mirel's case the court did not start proceedings. (As this case clearly shows, shortly after the war denunciations involving collaboration were common.) An anonymous letter sent to the legal department of the CKŻP led the lawyers to open a file on Samuel Kac. The author of an anonymous letter intimated only that "during the German occupation, Kac had many crimes on his conscience."[71] The case was later discontinued. Men were therefore not immune from general, unspecified accusations, but they were much less vulnerable to them than women.

With regard to men, investigations in part were prompted by specific deeds purportedly committed by the accused: Abram Rosenman, chairman of a workers' unit in the Ostrowiec ghetto, apparently beat the workers he was overseeing;[72] Abram Icek Kierbel (or Kerbel) was accused of extorting "money, jewelry, anything that held any value;"[73] Chaim Chajet was accused of speculations and scheming;[74] Ferdynand Unholz was a masseur of the Płaszów camp commandant, Amon Goeth;[75] and Marian Frauenglas, among other charges, supposedly beat the person he shared a room with in the Zbaraż ghetto.[76] Accusations of collaboration against women were worded in a much more general way. To initiate an investigation of a woman, it often sufficed to accuse her of consorting with a "dubious character," for example, a man whose function in the German-organized apparatus of violence made him suspicious by default. The case of Runa Fakler was hardly a solitary one. In her case the community was holding her responsible for the deeds of her husband.

In contrast, some women wondered whether they themselves might be implicated by their husbands' questionable behavior. Franciszka Brzezińska, widow of Mieczysław Brzeziński, wrote first to the CKŻP's legal department, to ask whether "wives of former Jewish police functionaries are required to be verified."[77] In her apparently next letter, addressed directly to the civic court, she asserted that during the ghetto evacuation she was "remonstrating" with her husband and "insisting" that he not take any part in it. In this period, she claimed, she was not taking advantage of the privileges afforded to a policeman's relative. After her efforts proved fruitless, she left her husband, taking their child with her.⁷⁸ Whereas Brzezińska's sense of duty to her husband is hardly surprising, what gives one pause was her deep conviction that to some extent she was guilty of his participation in the operation because she was unable to dissuade him. It is quite evident that her own accountability, independent of her husband's, was highly unclear to her. If she took pains to explain herself and prove her own innocence by pointing out that, despite their relationship, her standpoint was different from her husband's and that she disagreed with his actions, it was because she thought there was a real possibility that she would have to answer for his—not her—crimes. In the end, the case was not opened, because, according to the court, "Everyone is accountable for his own guilt and his own actions."⁷⁹

The case of Ida Szenderowicz, wife of Naum Szenderowicz, chairman of the Radom Judenrat, is similar. However, the charges against Ida—that she collaborated on the preparation of the so-called Palestinian lists, which were supposed to protect Jews from being evacuated from the ghetto, and that she accepted bribes—pertained directly to her own actions.⁸⁰ One could come to the conclusion that the case against Szenderowicz confirms an unspoken assumption that the spouse of a man accused of collaboration was deemed inevitably guilty or at least morally suspect. However, an analysis of the Szenderowiczes' file leaves no room for doubt that the case was opened because, as one witness put it, "In his harmful actions he [Szenderowicz] was aided and abetted by his wife."⁸¹ What was meant by "aiding and abetting" (*pomoc i współdziałanie*), a legal phrase applying by default to a partner and wife, was initially unspecified.⁸² But the accusation was sufficient to prompt the CKŻP's lawyers to look further into the case.

However, joint responsibility for her spouse's conduct during the war did not entirely define a woman's role in the relationship. It is impossible to ascertain to what extent one applied the notion of joint responsibility to the female spouse when judging the wartime conduct of Polish Jewish men. The negligible number of investigations in this regard was dictated, no doubt, by an extremely limited number of possibilities for Jewish women to collaborate with the German occupier, as I have already mentioned.⁸³ This issue arose only once in the civic court in the case of Lipa (Leon) Czarny-Gidy. Czarny-Gidy submitted an application for rehabilitation to the honor court in January 1947. (He had also been investigated earlier by Polish state prosecutors.) As he himself admitted, his wife, Fani Czarna, was Moniek Merin's deputy; Merin was chairman of the Central Office of Jewish Councils of Elders in East Upper Silesia.⁸⁴ A handwritten note in Leon Czarny-Gidy's case file instructs prosecutors to pursue the following line of investigation: "What was the role of Czarny's wife in carrying out jobs for the

Gestapo, what was Czarny's relationship with his wife, how did Czarny actually react to his wife's actions?"[85] There is no doubt that the investigators took these instructions into account when they questioned witnesses. "About the relationship of Czarny Gidy with his wife, I know nothing," testified Rózia Kozak.[86] Bernard Jegier (Jeger) claimed that "Czarny-Gidy had good relations with his wife."[87] Szyja Monowicz was of a different opinion: "According to rumors circulating in Sosnowiec at that time, relations between Czarny-Gidy and his wife were strained because of her apparently close involvement with Moniek Merin. I know for a fact that during the evacuation of the ghetto Fani Czarna acted in an utterly bestial way toward the Jews. However, how Czarny-Gidy reacted to his wife's actions is unknown to me."[88] Although Czarny-Gidy's relations with his wife were treated seriously during the pretrial investigation, they were not even mentioned once formal charges were brought. The CKŻP's lawyers indicted him on charges of cooperation with the Central Office of Jewish Communities in Sosnowiec and its board and thus of participation in "collecting forced tributes" from the Jewish inhabitants of Sosnowiec, taking part in their evacuation, and "taking" and forcing ransom from them "in exchange for exemption from deportation." Other charges included "cavorting with the Gestapo," "living a life of dissipation," and "trying to gain monetary profits from fraternizing with the Germans."[89] Eventually, Czarny-Gidy was convicted and received a rebuke from the civic court.

Putative Jewish collaborators were frequently accused of close connections to German authorities. Both men and women were accused of relations with the Gestapo and its minions. Adam Żurawin was accused of intelligence activities for the Gestapo.[90] Zygmunt Berland[91] and Feliks Dobrowolski[92] were accused of collaboration with the Department for the Struggle Against Usury and Speculation, the so-called Thirteen, a semi-official German agency in the Warsaw ghetto. The case of Ziuta Frank, a Jewish woman, was initiated by Beniamin Mordowurka. "As far as I know," he wrote in a letter to the civic court, "[she] was in the service of the Gestapo and collaborated, among others, with Lolek Skosowski[93] and Bela Kranz. I used to see her in the company of men from the German Gestapo."[94] Another alleged Gestapo agent was the aforementioned Mrs. Linde from Lublin. Sylwia Schapiro, according to a complaint filed with the civic court, was supposedly not only a Gestapo confidante but also chief assistant of the Lvov Arbeitsamt chairman, German Heinz Weber.[95] Wiera Gran was accused of "having social relations with persons who were conspicuous Gestapo agents" in the Warsaw ghetto from 1941 to August 1942 and after August 1942 on the so-called Aryan side of Warsaw.[96]

THE ROLE OF GENDER IN THE POLISH JEWISH CIVIC COURT

In the catalog of types of "misconduct by a member of the Jewish community during the Hitlerite occupation, unbefitting a Jewish citizen," charges pertaining to what historians have called "collaboration through the body" occupy a special place.[97] To be sure, accusations of collaborating with one's body were filed, though worded in a variety of ways, in civic court cases against Polish Jewish men as well as women. That said, the charges always implicated the female body. They served to buttress evidence adduced of the collaboration of the accused, but they never constituted a main charge. In the cases of women they referred directly to the issue of their sexuality; in the cases of men they evoked the problem of domination and violence.

Charges of having sexual contacts with "suspicious characters"—German officials or those who openly collaborated with them—were filed in as many as four investigations of women or one-fourth of the investigations related to women's conduct during the war. There is no conspicuous correlation between the main charge and these women's sexuality. Accusations were usually formulated in a literal way. In the case of Wiera Gran, Dawid Szwajer testified: "In the ghetto they were saying that [she] was the mistress of a certain Szternfeld from the Thirteen."[98] About Sylwia Schapiro, who "was always accompanying him [Weber, chairman of the Lvov Arbeitsamt], also outside working hours," Zygmunt Tune said, "As I've heard from many people, Schapiro was also Weber's lover."[99] Testifying against Runa Fakler, Henryk Tigner said, among other things, "I know that she was the lover of SS Rottenführer Hans Sold. This case was quite famous in the camp."[100] Representatives of the Jewish Voivodeship Committee in Kraków took Tigner's word for fact.[101] Only in the case of Masza Engel, a senior room overseer in Auschwitz, were the charges formulated in a more euphemistic manner. During Engel's trial, she was accused of "having a French friend, who was helping her."[102] The insinuation that she had sexual contacts with the "French friend" was clear to all in attendance at the trial.

The concept of collaboration through the body, which in these cases was considered obvious, derives from far-reaching social control over woman's sexuality: Her body belongs to a woman, but the limits of its "ownership" are set by the society. In periods of instability, social power over women grows stronger, restricting their freedom to exercise control over their own bodies, which is not too impressive to begin with even in more stable times. In contrast, as one can see in the documents from the CKŻP's civic court, such restrictions did not apply to the male body, even in cases of relations between Jewish men and non-Jewish women. The only exception is the case of Jerzy Rejtman, a kapo in a camp near Drohobycz. One of the accusations leveled against him was worded similarly to those leveled against women: He was accused of "consorting with an ethnic German woman."[103] Transgression of standing cultural norms is evident not only from the uniqueness of this accusation, compared to the rest of the cases against men tried before the civic court, but also from the euphemistic, though fully understandable, wording of the accusation. What is noteworthy is that the author of the complaint filed with the civic court was most probably a female activist, head of a women's work retreat in Janowce, and the information comes from another woman, Rejtman's fellow prisoner, "wife of an engineer."[104]

For men the concept of collaboration through the body was strictly connected with their attitude toward Jewish women. Violation of a Jewish female fellow prisoner was treated as an instance of "misconduct, unbefitting a Jewish citizen" and a manifestation of collaboration with the German occupier. It was a recurring problem. In as many as thirteen cases, twelve of which concern men, there were accusations of sexual abuse,[105] rape and extortion, procurement (one case),[106] and violence (usually beating and harassing), often with sexual undertones. One often finds references to various sexual crimes in one accusation. Violence against women was strictly connected with authority, because its use was sanctioned by prisoner functionaries and members of organizations collaborating with the Germans. The relative universality of such crimes—they were referred to in almost every tenth case of men whose wartime conduct was investigated—is testament to the fact that there was no special taboo that would protect women, especially their carnal integrity and inviolability.

Let us remember that we are talking about norms regulating social interactions in a closed group. (All possible reservations aside, it seems that the Jewish community, even under Nazi occupation, could be regarded as one.) Thus according to Dawid Zycher, "In Sosnowiec it was a widely known fact that members of the Jewish ghetto police [Ordnungsdienst; OD] were treating the Jewish population very badly; in particular they used to beat Jewish men and rape Jewish women."[107] Mieczysław Garde, manager of a paper plant in Płaszów, "abusing his power, used to assault women and give vent to his sick instincts. [Fear of his reaction] should they be late for work, stay too long in the latrine, or commit some other minor 'infractions' was enough to strike fear into the hearts of women and drive them into the arms of the OD. Meanwhile, however, they were led by colleagues to the laundry room, where orgies took place."[108] "[Garde] was behaving boorishly, looking down on his fellow prisoners, especially women, in a manner unbefitting a Jewish inmate," testified another witness.[109] Poldek Piekarski "personally murdered over one hundred people—Jews, of whom he raped many women."[110] According to the testimony of Jachet Enzel, Mendel Helesiewicz, a kapo from the Krzepice camp, "was a master of life and death over all those women who wouldn't succumb to him. He literally robbed us of our possessions, paying no heed to our needs.... Women who didn't want to have anything with him, he would cruelly beat and lock them in a cellar with no food."[111] Frania Szpering, in turn, testified that Helesiewicz "was treating badly especially those women who wouldn't give themselves to him."[112] About Aleksander Eintracht, a member of Płaszów's Ordungsdienst who "was harassing especially women," it was said that "it gives [him] pleasure of a certain sexual nature."[113]

In their statements on crimes against women, the witnesses spoke of not only rape but also sexual extortion. As one can see from the files, sexual extortion ensued from unequal power relations, in this case among the victims themselves. In an environment of overwhelming oppression, women's bodies were treated as currency by the victims and by their oppressors. According to one witness in the trial of Mieczysław Garde, "Eighty percent of women in this *Gemeinschaft* [paper mill in the Płaszów camp] used to sell themselves for soup, white bread, etc."[114] However, the women exercised no control over this currency. In the cases under analysis women were resigned to sexual contacts because they were aware of the dreadful consequences should they refuse, as some of the witnesses found out themselves. Dawid Zycher recounted a story that two women from Sosnowiec told about Chaskiel Szpigelman: "They were saying that they gave Szpigelman dollars, gold, and themselves, and he in return was going to try to send them to Hungary."[115] In Fela Zycher's opinion it was her refusal "to give herself" to Szpigelman that made him select her child for the death camp.[116] Maria Nadel testified in the case of the Judenrat chairman in Radom, Naum Szenderowicz: "I heard . . . that he was behaving very boorishly toward young women and trying to use his position so that when one of them requested something of him, he would promise that he would do it, under the condition that she went to bed with him."[117] Bela Fridman, who during the war worked as a hospital nurse, was threatened by Szenderowicz with the words "You'll regret it, Bela," after she rejected him. Thus, when the evacuation ensued, Szenderowicz sent her "mother and sister away, even though an SS officer was ready to save them."[118] Rita Knyszyńska was apparently sent to the Volkovysk camp because she rejected the advances of a deputy chair of the Białystok Judenrat.[119] About Hersz Zameczkowski, a Judenrat official in Radom, Hersz London wrote to the civic court: "He was obliging to women who succumbed to him, and vengeful toward those who refused his offers. This is exactly what happened with my wife. When she offered him a diamond or money to be on a certain list, Zameczkowski announced that from women he is not taking payment in money, but in kind. During the operation he didn't read her name and so my wife with a seven-year-old son and distant relatives were evacuated. . . . Her words still ring in my ears, 'I'm going to the oven because I wouldn't give myself to him.'"[120]

Witnesses in the civic court, during both the pretrial investigations and trial proceedings in open court, depicted violence directed at Polish Jewish women, including sexual violence, openly and freely, often in detail, even divulging the names of other victims and describing what they endured.[121] To take but three examples: Frania Szpering recounted: "While in the Krzepice camp, I got a boil on my leg, making my work extremely difficult. Helesiewicz, seeing that I couldn't work, told me to go to the barrack and rest. After a short while he turned up and started shouting that I can't just keep lying around, that I need to get medication. So he had me go with him to the room where the clinic was. There he locked the door from the inside with a key, gagged and raped me. I was fifteen at the time."[122] About Chaskiel Szpigelman, Fela Zycher said in one of her pretrial statements: "Once, when I entered my sister's room, where militiaman Chaskiel Szpigelman with his family lived, too, I found him alone. He locked the door, threw me onto the bed, and demanded that I put myself at his disposal. I struggled with him as much as I could so as not to give him what he wanted, and prayed silently that someone would knock on the door and free me from his vile intentions."[123] She recounted the same event at Szpigelman's trial: "At first [upon entering the room, where she saw Szpigelman], he embraced me, but I didn't know it would take such a turn, then he pushed me so hard that I fell and then he jumped on me, I was with my legs on the floor and he was trying to reach with his hands. . . . He didn't tear anything on me. The struggle lasted for about two minutes."[124] Bela Frydman's reluctance to testify against Naum Szenderowicz, because she was initially "too ashamed to tell" what she suffered at his hands, was rare.[125] Nevertheless, she eventually overcame her disinclination and decided to testify—in such a manner that there could be no doubt about the veracity of the incidents she described. As it appears in her witness statement, "She often fell prey to his wild instincts, of course defending herself."[126] What is more, not only the victims but also those close to them and eyewitnesses unrelated to them, including men, recounted these victims' ordeals to prosecutors attached to the civic court and to its judges.

It is also noteworthy that the victims' statements were not hindered by the fact that they were given before a predominantly male judicial panel. Among the eighteen people who served on the civic court, only two were women: attorney Róża Koniecpolska, secretary of the court's three-person presidium or executive committee; and one member of the fifteen-person plenum, Genia Lewi, a representative of the Poalei Tsion Left, a liberal party in the Jewish political spectrum, a teacher, and head of the Warsaw Jewish Committee.[127] No woman served in the capacity of a prosecutor. Nor did any woman exercise the function of ombudsman.[128]

Arguments made in their own defense by those men accused of collaboration through the body tell a lot about attitudes toward female sexuality that were buried deep in the mass subconscious of Polish Jewish men and women alike. At least some of the men accused of sexual abuse seemed to have no idea that they had violated normative standards of any kind. They reasoned that their female victims "had agreed" to contacts with them. If they failed to mention that this "agreement" stemmed mostly from their victims' fear of consequences should they refuse, it was partly because some of the attributes of power they possessed during the war, even as victims themselves, were considered obvious and unquestionable. One of these obvious attributes was apparently domination over women, which was further augmented by these men's position in the ghetto or camp hierarchy. (Presumably they did not consider it open to doubt before the war either.) Mieczysław Garde, accused of extreme cruelty and violence toward women by both male and female witnesses[129] explained: "I was having closer relations with some women on account of mutual feelings. I would never abuse my position in the OD to this end."[130] Chaskiel Szpigelman, in turn, discredited his victim, describing her simply as "easy." Using this argument, which is classic in sexual violence discourse, he not only denied her the right of authority over her own body but also indirectly pointed out that the norm protecting the sovereignty of a woman's body is easily relativized. He testified: "There was nothing between us. At that time Zycher was known as 'Miss Fela'—and by this title of 'Miss Fela' I mean nothing honorable. To 'rape her' you didn't have to try very hard, but let's leave that aside."[131]

The only case of a woman who defended herself against collaboration through the body that is preserved in the civic court files is that of Runa Fakler. In a letter to the Jewish Historical Commission in Kraków, she reasoned: "At the camp I was already thirty-five. I am no beauty. I was with my husband and I loved him more than anything.... The 'fashionable' life was always foreign to me, what with my downright Spartan outlook on life I would never be capable of any marital infractions, especially seeing as I was simply crazy in love with my husband."[132]

A socially and culturally limited sphere of potential collaboration with the German occupier and concurrently the very activities deemed collaboration—different for men and women—dictated the differences in charges pressed against Polish Jewish men and women before the civic court. In most of the cases against men the judicial panel tried to ascertain whether, in the course of performing their functions, the accused abused their power against their fellow inmates. In a large proportion of cases against women, however, those participating in the investigation resorted to reasoning that can hardly be found in the cases against men. Namely, they pointed to an accused's supposedly privileged position during the war, considering it a sign of authority and therefore simultaneously one of the major proofs of her collaboration with the Germans. Sonia Surażko remembered Rita Knyszyńska's "luxurious" situation in the camp: "She herself didn't work; every day, together with the Germans, she would send us out to work; she had a separate room, visited daily by Germans. When we were at work, she entertained herself with them pleasantly."[133] One supposed proof of Wiera Gran's guilt (referred to also in the verdict, which acquitted her)[134] was that in the ghetto she did not wear the required armband and that after 1941 she was seen wearing a fur, despite an order, issued at that time, that Jews relinquish their furs.[135] As Henryk Tigner intimated, "[Runa Fakler's] way of life was dramatically different from that of other inmates; the difference lay in the comfort, better food, well-being, reading books. Her life stood apart from the life of others. She had her work done by a certain young lady, who was her servant."[136] "During the greatest torment of her fellow prisoners," Runa Fakler was allegedly "keeping a Jewish hairdresser, who did her hair three times a day, . . . [and] she ran a sumptuous kitchen."[137]

Only 18 of the 131 (14 percent) investigations of Jewish misconduct during the war, conducted under the auspices of the civic court, ended in convictions.[138] (According to my calculations, in the files of twelve cases, including one of a Polish Jewish woman, documentation of the court's final decision is missing. Presumably, if the accused had been convicted, it would have been noted in the file. Nevertheless, this number should be considered approximate.) In most of the cases the court discontinued the proceedings, on rarer occasions suspended them, and, according to its own inventory of cases from October 1949, heard at least twenty-eight cases, issuing an acquittal in at least nine of them.[139] The only woman convicted of "misconduct during the Hitlerite occupation unbefitting a Jewish citizen" was Masza Engel. The civic court found her guilty of "the fact that in 1944, while at the Auschwitz (Oświęcim) camp, . . . she exercised the function of a kapo, and there were cases in which she beat her fellow prisoners."[140] According to the verdict, witness testimony did not prove, however, that Engel mistreated her fellow prisoners. Therefore, taking into account "the level of the social development of the accused," which was "not too high," and the fact that she was the mother of two children and expecting her third child, the court deemed it sufficient to impose a reprimand.[141]

Verdicts imposed on men entailed a rebuke (one convicted defendant), a reprimand (three), ostracism (four), suspension of the rights of a Jewish community member (five), and exclusion from the Jewish community (four). Five of the convicted Polish Jews[142] were accused of violence toward women. In an additional case the final verdict of the court is missing in one of the files.[143] In this group it was Aleksander Eintracht who received the most severe sentence: exclusion from the Jewish community. However, neither the decision nor its rationale contains any direct reference to the accusation made by witnesses of Eintracht's special cruelty toward women. Perhaps it is conveyed between the lines of the verdict, according to which Eintracht "was acting to the detriment of the society by most eagerly, voluntarily, and constantly beating and flogging [the prisoners] and, moreover, harassing and humiliating them as a block overseer."[144] In any case, only in his appeal of the verdict, questioning the punishment, did Eintracht's attorney return to the originally pressed charges. In the appeal the attorney disputed the charges of sexual violence against women, arguing that they were exemplary of the low credibility of the other charges leveled against Eintracht, which, according to the attorney, suffered from a lack of specificity. That "it was being said [that Eintracht derived pleasure from sexual abuse]" were "words of no account," as nowhere was it specified who said it and where the alleged abuse took place.[145] The civic court rejected the appeal.[146] Only in 1957, long after the dismantlement of the civic court, did a special commission established by the board of the Towarzystwo Społeczno-Kuturalne Żydowskie (TSKŻ), the successor to the CKŻP, decide that the punishment had already been served.[147]

The verdict in the case of Abraham Kon, a camp kapo, does not even mention assaulting women, of which he was accused in the course of the proceedings. The punishment of suspension from the Jewish community for three years, the maximum period of time for this penalty,[148] was meted out because, as we read in the decision, "As a manager of a tailoring department in the Lodz ghetto ... he indulged in severe physical assaults on workers of the department, beating them and calling them names," whereas as a kapo in the Görlitz camp, "He exhibited excessive eagerness and brutalized his fellow prisoners, often beating them and humiliating their human dignity."[149] (In February 1950 the civic court commuted his sentence of suspension to one year.)[150]

The verdict in the case of Mieczysław Garde was formulated in a similar, universalizing way. He was sentenced to a reprimand for "beating and humiliating" undisciplined prisoners when he worked for the Ordnungsdienst in the Kraków ghetto and Płaszów camp.[151] The verdict did not make any reference to the indictment, in which the prosecutor reasoned that women constituted a separate category of Garde's victims, at least in theory, because "the last names of the aggrieved persons cannot be determined."[152] The indictment indicates the prosecutor's sensitivity to assaults on women. Thus we read: "[Garde] could not rein in his inhuman instincts and, in order to enforce the camp's regime, he would beat his fellow prisoners and insult their personal dignity. And if the accused committed such deeds against helpless women, his behavior should be deemed unbecoming for a human being."[153]

Only in the verdict against Chaskiel Szpigelman did the civic court refer directly to the charges of crimes committed against women. Szpigelman, a former policeman, was sentenced to three years' suspension from the Jewish community for, among other things, "extortion of money, valuables, and 'services in kind,' committed at the camp in Sosnowiec."[154] The court's stance was clarified in its reasoning: "The court does not indulge in inquiries—actually not being in the position to verify them—into whether the 'favors' from women [Szpigelman] received were obtained by means of rape, that is, physical force, but the court deemed the testimony of the witness Mrs. Warman that he used his position to make women pliable and in return promised to rescue them from the catastrophe [i.e., the Holocaust] probable."[155] The sentence proved highly controversial. Some observers at the trial, professing to be the "public eye" of the Śląsko-Dąbrowskie Voivodeship, were overcome by outrage at so lenient a sentence for his crimes, which they announced in a petition (sent most probably to the civic court).[156] Stanisław Temczyn and Róża Koniecpolska submitted a votum separatum. In their opinion the only sentence appropriate for Szpigelman was "his complete elimination from the community."[157] The prosecutor was of a similar opinion. He argued that, taking into account the findings of the court—among them that the defendant "was physically assaulting women who were helpless in the face of his violence"[158]—the sentence "does not fit the crime whatsoever."[159]

Only the defense counsel, attorney Bolesław Listopadzki, was of a different opinion about the extent of the sentence imposed on Szpigelman. It could be assumed that Listopadzki was simply fulfilling his duty, but his arguments are worth scrutinizing. Not only did he apply for an annulment of the verdict, but he also stipulated that the court had heard the witnesses for the defense but had not questioned them for lack of time. In his appeal Listopadzki argued that Szpigelman's role was exaggerated and that he should, in fact, be considered a victim of the Judenrat's policy: "Szpigelman can be blamed only for the deeds that were proven against him.... Everyone is accountable only for the crime he committed, that is, *his own crime*, and in the world of law there is no such thing as 'participation in crime of a third party.'"[160] Moreover, Szpigelman was apparently "a primitive, semi-intelligent person," a tool in the hands of not only his superiors but also the German occupier, and the unprecedented wartime events required a "cautious, understanding judgment."[161] In conclusion, the defense counsel demanded that Szpigelman's case be reexamined by a different set of judges so that the "judges *in this case* are people who at the time of the occupation were in Poland and are well-acquainted with all these issues because of their own personal experiences."[162]

It is unknown why in this specific case the court decided to consider the charges of sexual abuse as one of the main points of the indictment. In all probability it was indeed the composition of the judicial panel that tipped the scale. It did include people who spent the Holocaust outside Poland, which allowed them, even though they themselves were Jewish, to consider what Jews experienced in wartime Poland with a certain acuity born of detachment. Certainly, it was not the only factor: Róża Koniecpolska, who had spent the war in the Soviet Union and was the only woman on the panel, took part also in the case of Abraham Kon, as well as the prosecutor Marek Marian Lasota. Why the civic court referred directly to the charges of crimes committed against women in Szpigelman's case but not in others defies a facile explanation and, like all other cases of male violence committed against women considered by the Jewish honor court not only in Poland but also in other countries, deserves further research.

Under the influence of German rule in Poland, gender roles and social rules of coexistence between Jewish men and women, previously taken for granted, were changing. Emanuel Ringelblum, chronicler of the Shoah, creator of the underground archive Oyneg Shabes, and catalyst of the study of Jews during the war, wrote on June 10, 1942: "Future historians will have to devote a separate page to the Jewish woman during the war. She will have a prominent role in the history of the Jews."[163] This conviction—that the changes in traditional women's roles that were taking shape under the influence of wartime conditions were significant—was probably what prompted Ringelblum and his associates to commence studies of "the Jewish woman during the war" in the second half of 1941, following the example of prewar studies conducted by YIVO, the institute for the study of Eastern European Jewry.[164] Cecylia Słapakowa, the lead coauthor of the project, which survives only in fragments, based her reflections on at least seventeen interviews (at least this is how many have survived to the present day) with women from various professions and environments. The material gathered by Słapakowa is an invaluable source of information on the metamorphosis of Jewish women's social roles under Nazi occupation. However, it is impossible to say whether this change was permanent—a consequence of other changes, initiated as early as before 1939—or whether it should be treated as an ad hoc consequence of the special wartime conditions. Słapakowa herself was aware of the fragmentary nature of her evidence: "Today, while it's happening, it is difficult to give a thorough and objective analysis of the role of the Jewish woman in shaping our wartime reality. Such an analysis requires a historical perspective."[165]

The documentation gathered right after the war in the files of the CKŻP's civic court provides us with just this historical perspective, as suggested by Słapakowa. It helps to unravel the still insufficiently explored areas of how Jewish women experienced the Shoah, their experiences limited by female physicality and social roles attributed to women, though not always directly linked to them. As my study shows, even in the period of most dramatic changes, the scope of possible revisions to culturally encoded scripts had its limits. An astonishingly large increase in women's activities, as noted by the chroniclers of that time, did not translate into more radical shifts in the social status quo. It was still uncommon for women to hold high-ranking positions; yet it was common for them to fall victim to those who wielded power—men. This state of affairs finds its reflection in the files of the women investigated by the civic court. The percentage of cases of women suspected of holding "privileged" positions during the war was three times lower (26 percent) than those of men (81 percent). Sexual violence toward women, in turn, was an everyday and thus socially familiarized occurrence, best evidenced by the fact that there was indeed a language to describe it after the war as well.

The Shoah did not revolutionize the way Polish Jews thought about a woman's role in the society. In the aftermath of the war the Jewish community in Poland, busy rebuilding its existence in its most rudimentary forms, still perceived a woman's identity as a shadow, a mere extension of her male partner (as, for example, in the cases of Runa Fakler and Franciszka Brzezińska). The scope of social control over women was also incomparably higher. In the opinions of pretrial investigators, almost 31 percent of cases of women pertaining to their wartime conduct required a trial. One could call this social verification. In men's cases the percentage was half that (15.5 percent). In other words, the civic court, built on highly codified legal rules (all the prosecuting attorneys and most of the judges were lawyers by profession), functioned in large part to reconstruct the prewar moral order. This institution, taking seriously its part in painstakingly rebuilding the postwar existence of Polish Jews, inevitably reflected the sentiments and norms of the community in whose name it acted.

Notes

Translated from Polish by Katarzyna Maciejczyk.

1. Mojżesz Rosenbach to Central Komitet Żydów w Polsce (Central Committee of Jews in Poland; CKŻP), December 8, 1946, file of Runa Fakler-Kornblüh, Sąd Społeczny przy CKŻP, Archiwum Żydowskiego Instytutu Historycznego, Warsaw (hereafter AŻIH),

313/20, p. 1. (This archival collection is available also at the Archives of the United States Holocaust Memorial Museum, Washington, DC, under RG 15.189M.) In the files of the Polish Jewish civic court (Sąd Społeczny przy CKŻP), which was established by the Central Committee of Polish Jews, the case was registered under the name Runa Fakler-Kornblüh (Kornblüh after her second husband, whom she married in Bolivia in November 1946), but in most of the documents she is still referred to by her first husband's name only. Therefore in this text I simply call her Runa Fakler.

2. In the legal context meant here, "confrontation" refers to a face-to-face meeting between Aftergut and Fakler along with their respective supporters and detractors for the purpose of determining who was telling the truth and who was lying.

3. Transcript of the confrontation between Mojżesz Aftergut and Runa Fakler, née Lewinger, signed by E. Krumholtz, Dr. Allerhand, A. Kaswiner, and M. Rosenbach, AŻIH, 313/20, p. 2.

4. Runa Fakler-Kornblüh to the "Historical Committee" in Kraków, August 23, 1947, AŻIH, 313/20, p. 12. The actual recipient of her letter was the Kraków branch of the Central Jewish Historical Commission.

5. Transcript of the confrontation between Aftergut and Fakler, 2.

6. Transcript of the confrontation between Aftergut and Fakler, 2–3.

7. Transcript of the confrontation between Aftergut and Fakler, 3.

8. Transcript of the confrontation between Aftergut and Fakler, 3.

9. Runa Fakler-Kornblüh to the "Historical Committee," p. 12.

10. Transcript of the confrontation between Aftergut and Fakler, 3.

11. Transcript of the confrontation between Aftergut and Fakler, 2.

12. Transcript of the confrontation between Aftergut and Fakler, 2.

13. Transcript of the confrontation between Aftergut and Fakler, 3.

14. Transcript of the confrontation between Aftergut and Fakler, 2.

15. Moises Rosenbach to CKŻP, December 8, 1946, AŻIH, 313/20, p. 1 (my emphasis).

16. Transcript of the confrontation between Aftergut and Fakler, 2 (my emphasis).

17. Runa Fakler-Kornblüh to the "Historical Committee," p. 12.

18. Runa Fakler-Kornblüh to the "Historical Committee," p. 14.

19. WKŻK to Federación Israelita, January 21, 1948, AŻIH, 313/20, p. 57.

20. Federación Israelita to the Jewish Voivodeship Historical Commission in Kraków, January 26, 1948, with two illegible signatures, AŻIH, 313/20, p. 60.

21. Federación Israelita to the Jewish Voivodeship Historical Commission in Kraków, April 30, 1948, signed by the secretary and president of the organization (signatures illegible), AŻIH, 313/20, p. 73.

22. Federación Israelita to the CKŻP's civic court, signed by the president of the federation, Dynes, and the secretary, Adelson, Oruro, Bolivia, July 25, 1948 (translation from Yiddish), AŻIH, 313/20, p. 79.

23. Runa Kornblüh to the CKŻP civic court, December 28, 1948, AŻIH, 313/20, p. 106.
24. Józef Zawoźnik (Runa Fakler's brother-in-law) to a female addressee in Poland, possibly Karolina Natanek, February 17, 1949, AŻIH, 313/20, p. 109.
25. See the unpaginated list of witnesses in AŻIH, 313/20.
26. Decision of the CKŻP civic court, January 10, 1949, AŻIH, 313/20, p. 108.
27. Karolina Natanek to the CKŻP "civic court division," written in Kraków on October 17, 1949, AŻIH, 313/20, p. 113. The files contain one more similar undated note from Natanek, addressed to the CKŻP. She wrote, among other things, "My relative Runa Fakler cannot walk the streets, being thus ostracized by the local Jews." See AŻIH, 313/20, p. 114.
28. See Józef Zawoźnik's letter from Oruro to an acquaintance in Kraków, probably Karolina Natanek, February 17, 1949, AŻIH, 313/20, p. 109; and the letter from the Community of Polish Jews in Bolivia to the CKŻP, June 24, 1949, AŻIH, 313/20, p. 112.
29. Representatives of the Community of Polish Jews in Bolivia to the CKŻP, June 24, 1949, signed by the secretary and president of the organization (signatures illegible), AŻIH, 313/20, p. 112.
30. The CKŻP civic court (Sąd Obywatelski przy CKŻP) was established in September 1946 by the CKŻP presidium. It commenced its activity only toward the end of that year and operated formally until 1950. The archives also contain documents dated later. Most cases were investigated between 1947 and 1949. In 1948, following the example of similar institutions in contemporary Poland, the court was renamed Sąd Społeczny przy CKŻP. On the civic court, see David Engel, "Who Is a Collaborator? The Trials of Michał Weichert," in Sławomir Kapralski, ed., *The Jews in Poland* (Kraków: Judaica Foundation Center for Jewish Culture, 1999), 2: 339–70; Gabriel N. Finder, "The Trial of Shepsl Rotholc and the Politics of Retribution in the Aftermath of the Holocaust," *Gal-Ed: On the History and Culture of Polish Jewry* 20 (2006): 63–89 (English section); Gabriel N. Finder and Alexander V. Prusin, "Jewish Collaborators on Trial in Poland, 1944–1956," *Polin: Studies in Polish Jewry* 20 (2008): 122–48; and Agnieszka Jarzębowska, ed., *Inwentarz Zespołu Sąd Obywatelski przy CKŻP 1946–1950, Sygn. 313* (Warsaw: Żydowski Instytut Historyczny im. Emanuela Ringelbluma, 2006), 2–5.
31. According to the docket of cases on October 1, 1949, the legal department had 155 cases. See AŻIH, 313/147, pp. 3–6; the AŻIH's Record Group 313 contains 147 case files.
32. Charter of the CKŻP's civic court, AŻIH, 313/150, p. 4.
33. The personal files of suspected collaborators in Record Group 313 number from 1 to 146 and then from 155 to 156, but file 4 is empty.
34. The case of Aleksandra Kurowska and Zbigniew Jasiński. The author of an anonymous letter from February 3, 1947, accused the Poles, Kurowska and Jasiński, of tricking Jews whom they were hiding into parting with their valuables and later denouncing them to the Germans. See AŻIH, 313/62.
35. See the files of Runa Fakler, AŻIH 313/20; Masza Engel, AŻIH, 313/18; Rita Knyszyńska, AŻIH 313/59; and Wiera Gran, AŻIH 313/36.

36. The basis for the calculation of percentages in this and all other instances is the total number of Polish Jewish women investigated by the court: sixteen.
37. The case was instigated by Zofia Goldkrant's complaint, addressed to the civic court on November 18, 1946. See AŻIH, 313/31.
38. The case of Róża Konstantynowska, note from Ira Wurman and Masha Groman, addressed most probably to the CKŻP with a request to refer it further to the civic court, July 29, 1947, AŻIH, 313/61, p. 1.
39. Undated note from Róża Konstantynowska to the civic court, AŻIH, 313/61, p. 5.
40. At least eight cases against men pertain to more than one person. In total, the court investigated the conduct of at least 140 Polish Jewish men.
41. The basis for the calculation of percentages in this and all other instances involving men is the total number of Polish Jewish men investigated by the court.
42. File of Marian Piekarski, AŻIH, 313/94.
43. File of Szymon Goldcwajg, AŻIH, 313/32.
44. File of Szymon Jentes, AŻIH, 313/49; and file of Pochlebnik (first name missing), AŻIH, 313/98.
45. File of "Rudy" Cymerman and Jek (first name missing), AŻIH, 313/16; file of Józef Pilawski, AŻIH, 313/96; and file of Aleksandra Kurowska and Zbigniew Jasiński, AŻIH, 313/62.
46. In the files of the civic court there is a note from the CŻKH to the civic court, written on February 20, 1947, in which the co-signors, Józef Kermisz and Nachman Blumental, inform the court that they are preparing lists of Jews suspected of collaborating with the Germans, including a separate list of putative Jewish collaborators from Lodz. See AŻIH, 313/149, p. 9.
47. Note from the CŻKH to the civic court, February 20, 1947, signed by Józef Kermisz and Nachman Blumental, 9. The list was supposed to contain 816 names.
48. Note from the CŻKH to the civic court, March 10, 1947, signed by Kermisz and Blumental, AŻIH, 313/149, p. 11.
49. Note from the CŻKH to the civic court, March 14, 1947, signed by Kermisz and Blumental, AŻIH, 313/149, p. 12.
50. Note from the CŻKH to the civic court, April 14, 1947, signed by Kermisz and Blumental, AŻIH, 313/149, p. 13 (with an enclosed list of Lodz Jews, which was supposed to include 936 people).
51. This is an estimate, because some of the names on the list appeared more than once.
52. List 1 of Jews collaborating with the Germans, Lodz, AŻIH, 313/152, pp. 12–52. All the numbers in this paragraph are based on my own calculations; the number of women was calculated on the basis of first names. The numbers are approximate, because in some cases only last names were given. Some of the names appeared more than once.
53. List 2 (no title), AŻIH, 313/152, pp. 53–57.
54. List 3 (no title), AŻIH, 313/152, pp. 58–63.

55. List 4 (no title), AŻIH, 313/152, pp. 64–114.
56. File of Zachariasz Hercyg, AŻIH, 313/45; and file of, among others, Julek Fajner, AŻIH, 313/83.
57. File of Julek Siegel, AŻIH, 313/113.
58. File of Marmur N., AŻIH, 313/74; file of Sioma (Stanisław) Rowiński, AŻIH, 313/106.
59. File of Michał Weichert, AŻIH, 313/137. On the trials of Weichert in both the Polish legal system and the civic court, see Engel, "Who Is a Collaborator?"
60. In Polish *Sztubowa*, in German *Stubendienst*, a camp functionary responsible for one room or part of a barrack.
61. Masza Engel to the CKŻP's civic court, January 21, 1947, AŻIH, 313/18, p. 2.
62. Rita Knyszyńska to the legal division of the CKŻP, n.d., AŻIH, 313/59, p. 1.
63. Testimony of Sonia Surażko, July 20, 1947, WKŻ (Voivodeship Committee of Jews in Poland) in Białystok, AŻIH, 313/59, p. 5.
64. Letter from Sara Sznit to the head of the civic court of the CKŻP, February 8, 1949, AŻIH, 313/120, p. 6.
65. Civic court decision signed by the prosecutor M. Lasota, September 30, 1949, AŻIH, 313/136, p. 2.
66. File of Linde, AŻIH, 313/68.
67. See Dalia Ofer and Leonore J. Weitzman, eds., *Women in the Holocaust* (New Haven, CT: Yale University Press, 1998).
68. Hebrew Immigrant Aid Society (HIAS) in Warsaw to attorney Gutmacher, January 25, 1947, signature illegible, AŻIH, 313/80, p. 3.
69. Undated decision of the civic court, signed by prosecutor P. Kowalski, AŻIH, 313/73, p. 10.
70. Eugenia Mirel to the civic court, July 10, 1947, AŻIH, 313/80, p. 3.
71. Anonymous letter from July 14, 1948, to the legal department of CKŻP, translation from Yiddish, AŻIH, 313/56, p. 6.
72. Note titled "In the Case Against Rosenman," translation from Yiddish of an article titled "Impurities," published in *Unzer veg* (no. 48), AŻIH, 313/107, p. 3.
73. Self-Help Landsmanschaft Association of Ostrowiec and Surroundings in Buenos Aires to "Union" in Paris, March 13, 1947, AŻIH, 313/55, p. 8.
74. Prosecutor's petition to drop the case against Chaim Chajet, May 9, 1949, AŻIH, 313/14, p. 37.
75. Ferdynand Unholz's witness interview report, branch department of the CKŻP's civic court in Kraków, February 8, 1949, AŻIH, 313/133, p. 1.
76. Undated letter from Marian Frauenglas to the CKŻP, which reached the civic court on June, 9, 1948, according to a note in the margin, AŻIH, 313/23, p. 1.
77. Franciszka Brzezińska to attorney Aleksander Ołomucki, legal department of the CKŻP, n.d., AŻIH, 313/149, p. 108.
78. Franciszka Brzezińska to the CKŻP's civic court, May 7, 1948, AŻIH, 313/13, p. 1.

79. Motion of the prosecutor of the civic court to dismiss the case, August 16, 1949, signed by the chairman and clerk of the court, ratified on September 29, 1949, AŻIH, 313/13, p. 4.
80. See the witness statement of Józef Tempelhof, made in the presence of the deputy prosecutor of the civic court, July 8, 1947, AŻIH, 313/119, p. 1; see also the interrogation of Maurycy Bojman by the deputy prosecutor, July 26, 1947, AŻIH, 313/119, p. 4.
81. Witness statement of Józef Tempelhof, 1.
82. This train of thought, whereby a woman is considered an incomplete, dependent person, can be identified in the case of Dr. Linde's wife as well. Although it was she who faced charges, she is not even identified by her first name. Indeed, it is missing from the files altogether, but sometimes the first name is missing also from men's files. However, unlike the men, Mrs. Linde is defined not by her own social role or function but rather by her husband's, for she is referred to as the wife of Dr. Linde from Lublin. See AŻIH, 313/68.
83. In 1944 *Biuletyn Informacyjny*, an underground newspaper issued by the Polish Home Army Headquarters, published a note about a reprimand for a Pole "for passive tolerance of his wife's crimes" (who was sentenced by the Polish underground for crimes against Polish society, among them consorting with the Germans). See *Biuletyn Informacyjny* (April 6, 1944). I am indebted to Agnieszka Haska for this reference.
84. Witness statement of [Leon] Czarny-Gidy, questioned by the prosecutor, December 20, 1946, AŻIH, 313/28, p. 19.
85. Unsigned handwritten note, January 15, 1947, WKŻ in Katowice, file of Czarny-Gidy, AŻIH, 313/28, p. 24.
86. Witness statement of Rózia Kozak in the offices of the WKŻ in Katowice, January 24, 1947, AŻIH, 313/28, p. 29.
87. Witness statement of Bernard Jegier (Jeger) before attorney Piotr Kowalski, June 28, 1947, AŻIH, 313/28, p. 58.
88. Witness statement of Szyja Monowicz in the offices of the WKŻ in Katowice, January 24, 1946, AŻIH, 313/28, p. 30.
89. Wyrok Sądu Społecznego przy CKŻP in the case of Gidy vel Leon Czarny, August 6, 1947, AŻIH, 313/28, p. 84.
90. See AŻIH, 313/146.
91. See AŻIH, 313/9.
92. See AŻIH, 313/30.
93. Leon Skosowski was an employee of the Department for the Struggle Against Usury and Speculation. He was later co-organizer of a scheme associated with the Polski Hotel in Warsaw. Beginning in June 1943, the Polski Hotel became a refuge for Jews who possessed documents from neutral countries, usually bought for top dollar with the help of Skosowski and Adam Żurawin, a Gestapo agent in the Warsaw ghetto. From among 2,500 people who went through the Polski Hotel, only 300 survived the war. In postwar accounts the operation is usually considered a German trap, but it is still a topic for debate. See, for example, Agnieszka Haska, *Jestem Żydem, chcę wejść: Hotel Polski w Warszawie 1943* (Warsaw: Wydawnictwo IFiS PAN, Centrum Badań nad Zagładą, 2006).

94. Beniamin Mordowurka to the civic court, n.d., AŻIH, 313/24, p. 1.
95. Dawid Kahane, Chief Rabbi of Poland, to the civic court, February 24, 1947, AŻIH, 131/117, p. 7.
96. Verdict of the CKŻP civic court, January 15, 1949, file of Wiera Gran, AŻIH, 313/36, p. 308. For Wiera Gran's account of her life, see her self-published book *Sztafeta oszczerców* (Paris: n.p., 1980).
97. The concept of collaboration through the body is described by Joanna Ostrowska in a text on the still largely taboo topic of prostitution in the ghettos. See Joanna Ostrowska, "Prostytucja w gettach," www.krytykapolityczna.pl/Teksty-poza-KP/Ostrowska-Prostytucja-w-gettach/manu-id-129.html (accessed September 2013).
98. Witness statement of Dawid Szwajer, February 20, 1947, file of Wiera Gran, AŻIH, 313/36, p. 46.
99. Witness statement of Zygmunt Tune, September 5, 1947, file of Sylwia Schapiro, AŻIH, 313/117, p. 21.
100. Witness statement of Henryk Tigner, who testified in front of the Jewish Historical Commission on January 13, 1947, file of Runa Fakler, AŻIH, 313/20, p. 26.
101. WKŻ in Kraków to Asociación Democratica Polaca en Bolivia, January 15, 1947, signed by the secretary Dr. Reichman, AŻIH, 313/20, p. 55.
102. Testimony of Dora Grynszpan, transcript of the session from June 25, 1948, file of Masza Engel, AŻIH, 313/18, p. 95.
103. Copy of a complaint to the civic court via the Ministry of Work and Social Service, lodged by Maria Wąsowska, head of the women's work retreat in Janowce, file of Jerzy Rejtman, AŻIH, 313/102, p. 2.
104. Complaint to the civic court lodged by Maria Wąsowska, 2.
105. Some of the files contain information about sexual abuse perpetrated by individuals other than the accused. For instance, in the case of Aleksander Eintracht, one former Płaszów prisoner testified: "I know for a fact that in Szopienice resides a former member of the Płaszów OD [Ordnungsdienst, security personnel], Gross. I know of one particular case. At Płaszów Gross raped a woman who was ill, and as a result she became pregnant and was chosen for deportation by one SS woman, who knew of it." See witness statement of Wiktor Traubman, August 4, 1948, file of Aleksander Eintracht, AŻIH, 313/1, p. 9. In fact, Leon Gross was a physician at Płaszów who was sentenced to death in a Polish state court for his part in selections and his administration of lethal injections to fellow Jews. He was executed in December 1946. See Finder and Prusin, "Jewish Collaborators," 134–35.
106. Accusations of "abusing helpless victims, young girls," "forced into prostitution with the Germans," were filed in the case of Abram and Lejbuś Zajfman. These deeds were purportedly committed by their sisters, who, testifying in defense of the defendants, made it even worse for them, because, according to a note of a commission investigating the case in Rio de Janeiro, they were closely cooperating with the brothers during the war. See the copy of the note to the Polish Minister

in Rio de Janeiro, January 18, 1947, signed by representatives of the commission appointed to investigate the charges against Abram and Lejbuś Zajfman, AŻIH, 313/143, p. 5.

107. Testimony of Dawid Zycher, given on September 3, 1947, before the legal officer of the WKŻ in Katowice, file of Zygmunt Mitelman, Julek Fajner, Sigel (first name missing), and Abram Wygnański, AŻIH, 313/83, p. 4.

108. Witness statement of Samuel Grobler before the civic court prosecutor, January 31, 1949, file of Mieczysław Garde, AŻIH, 313/26, p. 19.

109. Witness statement of Wiktor Traubman before the civic court, January 31, 1949, file of Mieczysław Garde, AŻIH, 313/26, p. 18.

110. Witness statement of Bernard Jegier (Jeger), WKŻ in Katowice, September 3, 1947, file of Poldek Piekarski, AŻIH, 313/93, p. 3.

111. Witness statement of Jachet Enzel, May 9, 1949, file of Mendel Helesiewicz, AŻIH, 313/43, p. 6.

112. Witness statement of Frania Szpering, May 11, 1949, file of Mendel Helesiewicz, AŻIH, 313/43, p. 7.

113. Testimony of Samuel Grobler, transcript of the civic court session on June 24, 1949, file of Aleksander Eintracht, AŻIH, 313/1, p. 30.

114. Testimony of Ozjasz Horowitz, transcript of the civic court session on June 22 and 23, 1949, file of Mieczysław Garde, AŻIH, 313/26, p. 42.

115. Testimony of Dawid Zycher, transcript of the civic court session, January 23, 1949, file of Chaskiel Szpigelman, AŻIH, 313/122, p. 158.

116. Testimony of Fela Zycher, transcript of the civic court session, January 23, 1949, file of Chaskiel Szpigelman, AŻIH, 313/122, p. 164. In a statement attached to the files, Zycher wrote, "Afterwards, he was constantly threatening that he would not allow me to take my child to work with me, which was equivalent to evacuation, because almost every second day a car would come, onto which they would pack anyone they saw in the labor camp, except the functionaries." See statement of Fela Zycher, written by her and attached to her letter to the security office in Wałbrzych, March 26, 1947, file of Chaskiel Szpigelman, AŻIH, 313/122, p. 45.

117. Testimony of Maria Nadel, November 26, 1946, before the secretary of the civic court, file of Naum Szenderowicz, AŻIH, 313/121, pp. 46–47.

118. M. Gutharc to O. Marbach, October 30, 1946, file of Naum Szenderowicz, AŻIH, 313/121, p. 22. Marbach was a member of the Jewish committee in Wrocław, who after the autumn of 1948 became acting chief prosecutor attached to the civic court; Gutharc must have known Marbach and provided him with information about Szenderowicz.

119. Rita Knyszyńska to the legal department of the CKŻP, n.d., file of Rita Knyszyńska, AŻIH, 313/59, p. 1.

120. Hersz London to the civic court, date illegible, received on September 7, 1948, file of Hersz Zameczkowski, AŻIH, 313/144, p. 115.

121. For example, Frania Szpering testified: "I also witnessed a situation when Mendel Helesiewicz was trying to rape Lis Fele." Witness statement of Frania Szpering, May 11, 1949, file of Mendel Helesiewicz, AŻIH, 313/43, p. 7.
122. Witness statement of Frania Szpering, 7.
123. Witness statement of Fela Zycher, written by her and attached to a letter to the security office in Wałbrzych, March 26, 1947, file of Chaskiel Szpigelman, AŻIH, 313/122, pp. 48 and 45 (the pages in the file are out of order).
124. Testimony of Fela Zycher, transcript of the civic court session, January 23, 1949, file of Chaskiel Szpigelman, AŻIH, 313/122, p. 164.
125. Melech Gutharc to Marbach, file of Naum Szenderowicz, AŻIH, 313/121, p. 22.
126. Witness statement of Bela Frydman, November 3, 1946, file of Naum Szenderowicz, AŻIH, 313/121, p. 30.
127. See Jarzębowska, *Inwentarz*, 3.
128. Jarzębowska, *Inwentarz*, 3.
129. Witness statement of Wiktor Traubman before the civic court prosecutor on January 31, 1949, file of Mieczysław Garde, AŻIH, 313/26, p. 18; witness statement of Samuel Grobler before the civic court prosecutor, file of Mieczysław Garde, AŻIH, 313/26, p. 19.
130. Statement of Mieczysław Garde before a representative of the civic court in Kraków, February 22, 1949, file of Mieczysław Garde, AŻIH, 313/26, p. 25.
131. Transcript of the civic court session, January 23, 1949, testimony of the accused Chaskiel Szpigelman, AŻIH, 313/122, p. 164.
132. Runa Fakler-Kornblüh's letter from Bolivia to the "Historical Committee" in Kraków, August 23, 1947, AŻIH, 313/20, p. 13.
133. Statement of Sonia Surażko about an *Aufseherin* in the Volkovysk camp, July 20, 1947, WKŻ in Białystok, file of Rita Knyszyńska, AŻIH, 313/59, p. 5.
134. Wyrok Sądu Społecznego przy CKŻP in the case of Wiera Gran, pronounced on January 15, 1949, signed by A. Ołomucki, AŻIH, 313/36, p. 309.
135. Witness statement of Dawid Sznajer, given before the CKŻP's civic court secretary, November 6, 1946, AŻIH, 313/36, p. 8. On December 25, 1941, the ghetto governor Heinz Auerswald issued an order that Jews hand over all furs and fur coats, collars, and other garments by December 28 under pain of death.
136. Testimony of Henryk Tigner, transcript of an open session before the CKŻP civic court, file of Runa Fakler, December 20, 1948, AŻIH, 313/20, p. 98.
137. Motion of the prosecutor to the CKŻP civic court in the case of Runa Fakler's petition for rehabilitation, December 10, 1948, AŻIH, 313/20, p. 86.
138. In the number of cases that concluded with a verdict, I have also included the case of the brothers Lejbuś and Abram Zajfman, residents of Argentina after the war. Pursuant to a decision of the local Jewish officials, they were excluded from the community, of which the CKŻP's civic court was informed through the Polish Legation in Rio de Janeiro. See letter to the Polish Minister in Rio de Janeiro, January 18, 1947, AŻIH, 313/143, pp. 5–6. The

file also contains a motion by the CKŻP's prosecutor to the civic court to create a blacklist and put the Zajfmans on it, indicating acceptance of the verdict issued in Argentina. See an unsigned note of the prosecutor, July 13, 1949, AŻIH, 313/143, p. 7.

139. According to civic court's inventory of its docket, prepared on October 1, 1949, out of 155 investigated cases, 27 proceeded to trial. This document does not specify whether the case of Michał Weichert, who was tried in December 1949, went to trial; I include it in my count. Moreover, neither this document nor the case files make it possible to tell whether the indictment of Henryk Barenblatt led to a trial. According to the court's inventory, it acquitted seven of the defendants who stood trial before it. Two out of four people listed in the inventory but without a corresponding verdict were also acquitted, as we can infer from the files (Eliasz Tabaksblatt and Karol Herc). The verdict in the case of Rita Knyszyńska remains unknown. See Wykaz spraw Sądu Społecznego CKŻP na dzień 1 X 1949, AŻIH, 313/147, pp. 4–6.

140. Wyrok Sądu Społecznego przy CKŻP in the case of Masza Engel, June 24, 1948, signed by Szaja Szechatow, Leon Lew, and Szymon Kirszenberg, AŻIH, 313/18, p. 101.

141. Wyrok Sądu Społecznego przy CKŻP in the case of Masza Engel, AŻIH, 313/18, pp. 102–3.

142. In this group of cases I include the case of the Zajfman brothers as well.

143. The case of Kuba Haubenstock, investigated together with the case of Mieczysław Garde. See AŻIH, 313/26. Six other suspects, excluding Haubenstock, who were accused of violence against women did not stand trial before the civic court.

144. Wyrok Sądu Społecznego przy CKŻP in the case of Aleksander Eintracht, June 24, 1949, signed by Samuel Szarf (chairman) and two other people (illegible), AŻIH, 313/1, p. 36.

145. Appeal submitted by attorney Leopold Lisocki to the plenum of the CKŻP's civic court, July 7, 1949, AŻIH, 313/1, p. 46.

146. Undated verdict of the civic court, after a closed-door examination of Aleksander Eintracht's appeal, AŻIH, 313/1, p. 62.

147. The minutes of the deliberation in Eintracht's case are attached to a note from TSKŻ's board to the Jewish Historical Institute (Żydowski Instytut Historyczny), directed to the attention of [Adam] Rutkowski, April 29, 1957, signed by Sz. Hurwicz, A. Rutkowski, and J. Wilf, AŻIH, 313/1, pp. 72–73.

148. According to Paragraph 7 of the civic court's charter, it was authorized to pronounce sentences ranging from rebuke, reprimand, ostracism, and suspension of communal rights from one to three years to permanent exclusion from the Jewish community. The court could decide to publish the sentence on the CKŻP's message board, on the message board of the local Jewish committee in the locale where the convicted defendant resided, or in the press. See the civic court's charter, AŻIH, 313/150, pp. 4–5.

149. Wyrok Sądu Społecznego przy CKŻP in the trial of Mieczysław Jakobson, Abraham Kon, and Zygmunt Widawski, February 7, 1949, AŻIH, 313/51, pp. 154–55.

150. Wyrok Sądu Społecznego przy CKŻP, February 7, 1950 [unsigned], AŻIH, 313/51, p. 160. In fact, a Polish state court acquitted Kon in May 1949 of essentially the same

charges. After his acquittal in the Polish state court, Kon petitioned the civic court to reconsider his conviction there. Although it offered no reason for its decision to commute his sentence, the civic court seems to have been swayed by Kon's acquittal in state court. See Finder and Prusin, "Jewish Collaborators," 142–44.

151. Wyrok Sądu Społecznego przy CKŻP in the case of Mieczysław Garde, June 24, 1949, AŻIH, 313/26, p. 50.

152. Indictment against Mieczysław Garde, March 5, 1949, signed by the prosecuting attorney Henryk Sniedziński, AŻIH, 313/26, p. 30.

153. Indictment against Mieczysław Garde, 31.

154. Wyrok Sądu Społecznego przy CKŻP in the case of Chaskiel Szpigelman, January 27, 1949, signed by the secretary of the Court [signature illegible], AŻIH, 313/122, p. 179.

155. Wyrok Sądu Społecznego przy CKŻP in the case of Chaskiel Szpigelman, January 27, 1949, signed by S. Temczyn, AŻIH, 313/122, p. 181.

156. Letter from "the audience at the trial of Chaskiel Szpigelman," signed by nineteen people (no heading with the names of the addressee or date when the letter was written), AŻIH, 313/122, p. 183.

157. Votum separatum in the civic court's verdict against Chaskiel Szpigelman, January 27, 1949, signed by R. Koniecpolska and S. Temczyn, AŻIH, 313/122, p. 182.

158. Appeal of the sentence in the case of Chaskiel Szpigelman, passed to the plenum of the CKŻP's civic court, March 4, 1949, signed by the author [signature illegible], AŻIH, 313/122, p. 191.

159. Appeal of the sentence in the case of Chaskiel Szpigelman, 192.

160. Appeal of the sentence in the case of Chaskiel Szpigelman, 187 (emphasis in original).

161. Appeal of the sentence in the case of Chaskiel Szpigelman, 187.

162. Undated appeal by attorney Bolesław Listopadzki to the plenum of the civic court of the verdict against Chaskiel Szpigelman, AŻIH, 313/122, pp. 185–86 (emphasis in original).

163. Emanuel Ringelblum, *Kronika getta warszawskiego, wrzesień 1939–styczeń 1943*, ed. Artur Eisenbach, trans. Adam Rutkowski (Warsaw: Czytelnik, 1983), 394.

164. See the draft of this project prepared by Emanuel Ringelblum, Ringelblum Archives, AŻIH, ARG I, 11, Ring. I/507/4.

165. See NN [Cecylia Słapakowa], *Kobieta żydowska w Warszawie od września 1939 do chwili bieżącej [1942]*, AŻIH, Ring. I/49, quoted in Katarzyna Person, ed., *Archiwum Ringelbluma: Konspiracyjne Archiwum Getta Warszawy* [Ringelblum's Archive: A Conspiratory Archive of the Warsaw Ghetto], vol. 5, *Getto warszawskie: Życie codzienne* [Warsaw Ghetto: Daily Life] (Warsaw: ŻIH Wydawnictwo DiG, 2011), 195.

10

Revenge and Reconciliation

Early Israeli Literature and the Dilemma of Jewish Collaborators with the Nazis

GALI DRUCKER BAR-AM

Collaboration with a foreign regime has been a prevalent theme in Jewish culture from its beginnings. One of the principal and most widespread manifestations of this engagement is the prayer Shemoneh-Esreh (in Hebrew, "eighteen"), known also as the Amidah ("standing"). This is the major prayer in the weekday service and is traditionally recited three times a day.[1] Despite its name, the prayer actually comprises nineteen benedictions. One of these, which was added at a later date and is thus not referred to in the prayer's title, is the Birkat ha-minim (literally, "benediction of types" or "benediction of species"). When reciting this prayer, the worshipper requests that Israel's enemies be punished by discontinuing their lineage (*karet*). The group of foes includes internal enemies, or collaborators with external foes, who in the prayer are called *malshinim* (informers).[2] The term *minot* (derived from the Hebrew word for species or type) denotes heretical Jews who strayed from the community and accepted other orthodoxies and became the first Christians and followers of Gnostic cults and subsequently Sabbateans, Frankists, and atheists. The Birkat ha-minim was added to the Shemoneh-Esreh by the rabbinic leadership in an attempt to unify and bolster the community in the face of the threat presented by its division.³ This benediction was amended by Rabbi Gamliel of Yavne and was appended to the Shemoneh-Esreh in the late first century in response to the crisis that beset Judaism when members of foreign cults began to behave like certain Jewish communities and even attended services in synagogues. This invocation was intended to expose these "types"; they would be deterred from enunciating it when serving as prayer leaders or cantors and could thus be separated from the community until they repented. Contrary to other benedictions in the Shemoneh-Esreh, including those that refer to the wish that the people of Israel regain their independent existence, such as Birkat ha-mishpat (which expresses hope in the restoration of proper judges and leaders), Birkat kibbutz galuyot (ingathering of the exiles), Birkat yerushalayim (rebuilding of Jerusalem), and Birkat matsmiah qeren yeshu'ah (restoration of the Davidic line), the Birkat ha-minim is in fact a curse that is euphemistically presented as a blessing. These prayers were part of the core material taught in the earliest stage of Jewish education in Ashkenaz (Germany) and Poland.⁴ This major prayer was (and still is) recited in public, enabling the community to identify those who betrayed it and expel them. Through it the community applied the heaviest penalty it possessed, namely, ostracism. The individual punishment of collaborators (the *karet*) is not meted out by the community but by God himself.

Since the late eighteenth century, processes of modernization and secularization have gathered momentum among the Jewish communities of Eastern Europe, dividing traditional societies into subgroups that have vied with one another to shape the character of the Jewish people. The modern era brought with it new challenges for the communities and their leadership. Among the most significant of these was the rise of modern nationalism. In the countries in which they resided in Eastern Europe, Jewish communities were compelled to resolve this tension by defining the boundaries of their loyalty to the community and to the nation-state in which they lived. Attempts to maintain the communities' inner cohesion meanwhile generated further significant tension. At this time the common identity that emerged among the Jewish communities was far more varied and far less stable and controlled than that which had characterized the traditional, premodern communities. According to Ernest Gellner, culture rather than religion is the most precious resource of the individual in modern national societies and in the nation-states that these societies create. Culture defines their external social and political boundaries and renders them homogeneous. This contrasts with the old, traditional society (in which the Shemoneh-Esreh prayer was created), in which cultural and political differences were emphasized, both with regard to the strata that formed the communities and among the various communities.⁵

The judicial approach to collaborators with Nazism predominates in modern scholarship. This is unsurprising in light of the central role played by the legal system in the modern nation-state. In the immediate aftermath of World War II, Europeans sought legal punishment of collaborators from within their societies. Jewish survivors of the Holocaust desired no less to bring collaborators to justice. But they had an additional ax to grind. In their quest to rebuild their lives, Jewish survivors in Europe sought redress in state judicial systems or in quasi-judicial Jewish-run honor courts for the collaboration of fellow Jews with the Nazis.[6] Jewish collaborators with the Nazis were put on trial by Jewish survivors in honor courts established in the displaced persons (DP) camps[7] and in Poland,[8] the Netherlands,[9] and elsewhere. In Israel putative Jewish collaborators stood trial in Israeli state courts on the basis of the 1950 Nazis and Nazi Collaborators (Punishment) Law.[10] The notorious libel trial of Rudolf Kasztner (1954–1958) elevated the issue of Jewish collaboration to a cause célèbre.[11] The practice of labeling an "internal enemy," denouncing him, ostracizing him for being "unclean," and removing him from society was sometimes portrayed by the survivors who implemented it in terms of "purifying" the community.[12]

This was true to a lesser degree also for Israeli literature. Literature is a prism, apart from yet interacting with the judicial system, through which the national conversation on collaborators was refracted. In this chapter I seek to examine the way in which early Israeli literature, written in Hebrew and in Yiddish, tackled the challenge presented by Jewish collaborators with the Nazis and addressed the appropriate manner of dealing with them. In particular, I seek to explain this mechanism whereby a national society—in this case, the nascent State of Israel—was crystallized by rejecting elements within it. Who was entitled to apply this sanction? What benefit was derived by applying it in the circumstances of Israel in the 1950s? And what differences can one discern in the approach of Hebrew literature on the one hand and Yiddish literature on the other to this sensitive and vexing topic?

The theme of collaborators with the Nazis and their appropriate treatment by the new society was discussed in Israeli Hebrew and Yiddish literature of the 1950s, albeit not extensively. The survivor immigrants (*olei she'erit ha-pleta*)[13] who arrived in Israel differed from their counterparts in all other countries because they had come to a new Jewish nation-state and were taking part in its construction. The trauma of the war led many of them to view the founding of a national home as a mission, a moral imperative, and a consolation for the losses they had endured.[14] Unlike other groups of Holocaust survivors who migrated to different locations around the world, the half a million survivors who came to Israel transformed the social fabric of the absorbing society.[15] Between 1946 and 1956 two-thirds of the Holocaust survivors who had assembled in the DP camps in Germany arrived in Israel in three waves.[16] They were joined by thousands of Jewish refugees from all across Europe. Various studies have estimated their numbers at between 383,000 and 500,000.[17] In the first two years after Israel's establishment, this group constituted about 70 percent of all immigrants.[18] In the early 1960s one of every four Jews in Israel was a Holocaust survivor.

In this chapter I address literary representations of the topic of collaboration with the Nazis and attitudes toward the collaborators from two complementary perspectives: that of the absorbing, hegemonic culture written in Hebrew and that of a Yiddish author, an *oleh she'erit ha-pleta* who continued to write in his language after arriving in Israel because he perceived Yiddish and its culture as "major" ones. The reading of these literary works allows us to appreciate some of the complexity that characterized Israeli society and its culture during its first decade. Israeli literature did not of course begin in 1948. This literature is part of Jewish culture that evolved worldwide over hundreds and even thousands of years. Against the backdrop of this protracted period (*la longue durée*), I focus on the literary representations written in Israel. This type of reading enables us to trace the similarities and the differences between a modern, national literature, written in both Hebrew and Yiddish, and its ancient cultural tradition.

"Heroic Community Leaders and Lobbyists": The Judenrat as Portrayed in Nathan Alterman's Political Poetry

Nathan Alterman[19] was one of the most well-known and influential writers of Hebrew literature in Israel's early decades, partly by virtue of his regular column, titled "Ha-tur Ha-shvi'i" (The Seventh Column), in the daily *Davar*, the newspaper of the ruling party, Mapai.[20] In 1954 and 1955 Alterman devoted six columns to the topic of collaboration with the Nazis, and in particular to the Jewish councils (Judenräte): "Memorial Day and the Fighters," "The Shape of the Uprising and the Shape of Its Time," "On the Two Paths," "More on the Two Paths," "The Fate of a Principle," and "On the Matter of the 'Lesson for the Generation.'" When the columns were collected in a book, Alterman titled them collectively "Measures of Justice."[21] Israeli literary scholar Dan Laor maintains that Alterman's literary engagement with the Judenräte should be observed against the backdrop of his prolonged engagement with the topic of the Holocaust, which generated "impressive and widely read poems that relate to the tragic fate of European Jews and which were written in the midst of the Holocaust or shortly after World War II."[22] In these poems Alterman constructed the myth of heroism and rebellion in the ghettos, which took hold in the public's consciousness in the Yishuv (the Jewish community in Palestine) and later in Israel. The poems appeared in the Hebrew mainstream press (in *Davar*) and in school textbooks and became part of the permanent repertoire of Holocaust commemorative ceremonies.

At the time that the "Measures of Justice" columns were written, the Holocaust was still an integral part of Israeli society's public agenda, which included the reparations agreement and relations with West Germany (1952), the Gruenwald and Kasztner trials (which extended from January 1954 to January 1958), and the Remembrance Day Law (1959).[23] Nevertheless, the cultural atmosphere that prevailed in the Yishuv and subsequently in the State of Israel was largely shaped by the concept of "negation of the Diaspora" and the myth of heroism and armed revolt. The prevalent attitude toward Holocaust survivors boiled down to what Alterman termed "the two paths": The first path is armed resistance and uprising, and the second path is that of surrender. And indeed, Holocaust survivors, as individuals and as a collective, were blamed for their own catastrophe by having "gone like lambs to the slaughter" or were suspected of having survived by devious means. Forms of collective survival other than armed resistance, such as those organized by the leadership of Diaspora communities, were perceived as tantamount to surrender, and their initiators were accused of "deviousness." This cultural atmosphere was characterized by the need to affirm one group within the Jewish people by scorning another.[24] Laor notes that

> the provocative element in the debate—all along the line—were the members of the fighting Jewish underground, who, in their various publications that began to appear in the early 1950s … bluntly accused the Jewish leadership during the Holocaust of choosing to maintain contacts with the Germans rather than supporting preparations for engaging in resistance to the Nazis, and even of placing obstacles in the way of the fighters.[25]

The political struggle for acceptance into the new Israeli society was thus manifested in a struggle between two different groups. In the "Measures of Justice" columns Alterman took issue with this split between the echelon of fighters and the Jewish leadership in the Diaspora. In the first poem, "Memorial Day and the Rebels," Alterman speaks on behalf of the fighters.

> On Memorial Day the ghetto fighters said:
> Don't shine a spotlight on us apart from the [Diaspora in a bright light].

> At this time of remembrance we come down from the pedestal
> To mingle [once again] in the shadows with masses of [the house of] Israel[26]

Alterman here engages with the "victors," namely, the sole group among the survivors that won respect and prestige in Israeli society. Their heroism is demonstrated in this stanza by their daring "to mingle once again" with that ostensibly dark history of the people of Israel, as Zionist thought understood and portrayed it and from which it sought to distance itself. Alterman proposes here a model of leadership that would allow the fighters and partisans to express their social and political advantage and even to reaffirm it: Once Israel had been established and the Diaspora obliterated, these people could allow themselves to embrace the broad community of survivors rather than seeking to dissociate themselves from it and continuing to label them as "others" and "diasporic." By so doing, they would be able to broaden the consensus on their leadership.

The circumstances under which the poem was written and published, the marking of Holocaust Memorial Day eleven years after the Warsaw Ghetto Uprising, underscored the need for this new model of leadership. It is fitting and interesting to note that Israeli society contained various groups of survivors that contested the nature of the ethos of Holocaust memory that would come to be assimilated therein. This struggle was waged not merely over the Holocaust Memorial Day Law, the date on which the memorial was to be marked, and the form the memorial would take;[27] it also protested government's non-involvement the previous year, on the tenth anniversary of the uprising.[28] These groups had likewise lived the reality of life "there," during the war, and did not invariably agree with the ghetto fighters about how it should be perceived or on the model of heroism to be derived from it.[29] These groups failed to gain the same status and prestige in Israeli society as the groups of fighters. The lowest status and prestige was reserved for the group of members of the Judenräte. And, indeed, in his poem Alterman refers not only to "the masses of the House of Israel" but also to this group, which came to symbolize the old Jewish leadership:[30] "Those who fell gun in hand might not accept the barrier between / the communities, the heroes [the community leaders and lobbyists] who negotiated or complied—and them." In a different column Alterman notes that "community leaders and lobbyists" is a euphemism for the Judenräte.[31] The accolade of heroism that Alterman conferred on the Judenräte is blatantly anomalous against the backdrop of contemporary norms. In this poem Alterman thus suggests to the echelon of fighters that it use the prestige it has gained in Israeli society to unify its ranks, including even the most despised among them: the Judenräte, collaborators with the Nazis.

The task of unifying all the strata of the new Israeli society entailed bridging the chasm between the well-established population and the *olei she'erit ha-pleta*, whom the absorbing society perceived as diasporic and therefore as enjoying lower prestige than the native (often allegedly native) sabras. Dan Laor has made the interesting point that Alterman did not hesitate to renounce the sabras' ethos of heroism, manifested in the image of the "boy and the girl" that he himself created in his canonical poem "Magash ha-kesef" (The Silver Platter), published during the War of Independence in December 1947.[32] He did so in order to stress the need to update and modify this ethos of heroism.

> Said those who fought and rebelled: the major and true
> symbol of this day is not a glorious barricade on fire
> nor a youth and a girl leaping to break free or die,
> like the eternal images of world rebellions alight.
>
> Not from this was time hewn. Let's not deck it with battle flags
> and in them see its essence, its honor redeemed.
> Said those who fought and rebelled: we are part of the many,
> part of its honor, heroism and deep weeping,
>
> part of an unparalleled time that rejects standard slogans
> and standard symbols that do not reveal its true face. . . .
>
> Said the partisans and the fighters: heroism and honor belong as well
> to Jewish elders who said: "Resistance will destroy us all,"
> to the boy and the girl who walked till they are lost somewhere
> leaving behind, on a stone, just a small white sock as memorial.[33]

In these stanzas Alterman asserts that the act of testimony is the paramount need of Israel's new society. He contrasts it with the frozen, static picture into which the image of the girl and the boy and the War of Independence in which they fought has transformed. The speech of the fighters, which recurs in these verses (and in fact in all the poem's four sections), is portrayed as suggesting a new form of heroism, befitting the present social and poetical times. The gist of this new form of heroism is the courage to expand the prevalent national ethos—which identified valor with giving one's life for one's country during battle—by including such acts of more subtle self-sacrifice, such as that of "those who fought and rebelled" and that of the "Jewish elders" during the Holocaust.

The ghetto fighters and their supporters, who occupied a position of power and prestige in the young Israeli society, refused to accept Alterman's new model of heroism, and this prompted him to elucidate his thesis once again in writing. In his response, which on this occasion was offered in prose and titled "Pnei hamered u-fnei dvaro" (The Nature of the Rebellion and the Nature of Its Message), he listed the reasons that should deter the ghetto fighters from setting themselves apart from the leaders of the Jewish communities in Europe during the Holocaust: "When we observe the uprising against the background of its period and its entanglements, it acquires many complexions and many voices; unfamiliar deliberations and contradictions emerge, and thus something of the sphere beyond it naturally becomes valid and open to discussion and to claims."[34] In other words, in judging the wartime period, says Alterman, we should consider the chaos that characterized it rather than regard it from the perspective of a citizen living in an orderly and autonomous nation-state. In light of this chaos, the sharp boundaries between the group of the rebels and the group of the Judenräte tend to blur: Both operated under extreme and exceptional circumstances; both were victims of the Nazis' policy of disinformation, which deliberately generated uncertainty and nurtured illusions of life within a reality of murder; and both exhibited mutual solidarity and collective responsibility, although they had no way of knowing whether their attempts at rescue would succeed or would merely put their lives in danger. Also, we must remember that not all the Judenräte became morally corrupt, and some sacrificed themselves for the sake of their community. Others managed to secure brief periods of respite and a modicum of decent conditions for their communities by virtue of the negotiations they held with the Nazis. The Judenräte should therefore be judged individually, according to the conditions under which each operated. One should thus not turn the Judenräte and the fighters into symbols and should not discuss them in terms of two paths.

Alterman articulated this explicitly in his poem "On the Two Paths": "'There were two paths,'—we became accustomed to say—two opposing and divergent paths— / Is that so? When and where? Where is the partition between one path and the other?"[35] He attributes the split between the two paths to the need of one group to empower itself by censuring the other.

> As we prepare to address and to write, prepare to glorify
> the bravery of fighters and emissaries, let us not always oblige
>   it [the bravery]
> To stand on a heap of rocks made for stoning, in order to
>   raise itself high,
> Rocks that speech and text hurl at *everything that is different to it*!
>   (emphasis in original)

In his "Measures of Justice" columns Alterman thus articulated a forgiving and empathetic attitude toward the Judenräte. This approach contrasted starkly with the myth of heroism and uprising that he himself had created only a few years before, in poems such as "Simhat Ani'im" (Joy of the Poor) and "Tefilat Nakam" (Prayer of Revenge). This myth, articulated on the eve of the founding of the state during the war waged against it, asserts that heroism is measured exclusively on the battlefield, in warfare, which is the only appropriate mode of action of the new Jew. Yet, following the establishment of Israel, Alterman expanded the concept of heroism to include the "community leaders and lobbyists" who attempted to gain life or time for their communities. How, then, can this dramatic transformation in his attitude toward heroism be explained? Scholarship has pointed to a major theme that runs through Alterman's work, namely, the distinction between Jewish behavior in the Diaspora (which should be accepted in light of the exceptional circumstances that prevailed there) and the desirable mode of Jewish behavior in Israel at a time of war.[36]

I wish to offer an additional interpretative dimension concerning the poet's perception of himself and the "other" in light of his existence (or nonexistence) in a nation-state. This interpretation rests on Dominick LaCapra's terms *identification* and *empathic unsettlement* on the part of a "secondary witness to the trauma of the Holocaust": During the Holocaust, Alterman represented the ghetto fighters by identifying himself with them. In other words, he exhibited an unmediated union between himself and the "other." During the course of identification, aspects of the "other" were incorporated into the self and encoded accordingly. The poet perceived the ghetto insurgents as a projection of the model familiar to him, namely, that of the combatants in Israel's War of Independence, and thus presented them with the same heroic pathos that he used in "The Silver Platter." In "Measures of Justice," however, some distance began to emerge between Alterman and the object of his identification, the ghetto fighters. Although he still spoke with their voice, he began to develop an empathic attitude toward the Diaspora from which the fighters had come, toward the "masses of Jews" and their leadership. This may have been a consequence of his intensive study of the singular attributes of the life of Jewish communities under Nazi occupation. "Empathy may be contrasted with identification (as fusion with the other)," asserts LaCapra, "insofar as empathy marks the point at which the other is indeed recognized and respected as other, and one does not feel compelled or authorized to speak in the other's voice or take the other's place, for example, as surrogate victim or perpetrator."[37] Owing to this empathic sentiment, the national poet no longer needed to perceive the lives of Jews during the Holocaust in the stable, dichotomous terms of combat versus collaboration: "Empathic unsettlement poses a barrier to closure in discourse and places in jeopardy harmonizing or spiritually uplifting accounts of extreme events from which we attempt to derive reassurance or a benefit."[38]

An example of such an attempt to avoid closure of definitions and judgment can be found in one of Alterman's workbooks, in which he recounts a debate he held with Abba Kovner during Kovner's visit to Alterman's home on May 5, 1954, following publication of the column.

> I asked him whether all those who had said "the underground will bring a catastrophe upon us" were all villains and cowards and had merely sought to save themselves. He responded by offering the example of Kalmanowicz of the YIVO Institute, who had implacably and consistently opposed the underground's preparations, actions, and slogans and was a noble and courageous figure whom Kovner admires to this day. I asked him whether deep within himself, in times of deliberation and wavering, there had not been something of Kalmanowicz that had argued his arguments and claimed his claims, and he replied with the utmost vigor and clarity—indeed.[39]

Although Selig Kalmanowicz had not served on the Vilna Judenrat, this passage is an indication of the "empathic unsettlement" that Alterman felt toward those who "had been there" and that he sought to inculcate in the stratum of ghetto fighters who bore a grudge against those who had opposed their wartime activity.

Alterman's stature as a major national poet who was close to the leadership of the nation-state is manifest in his attempt to unify Israeli society and in his call to the echelon of leaders of the survivors, insofar as this was perceived by the young state's hegemonic culture, namely, the ghetto insurgents. Leora Bilsky has examined Alterman's writing during the Gruenwald and Kasztner trials as a test case of the intellectual's involvement in political trials. She maintains that "the real contribution of the intellectual in such trials lies in transforming them into political occasions in the original sense of politics, that is, occasions for the public to subject the most fundamental values of the common consensus to critical reflection."[40]

Thus in his works Alterman did not address specific individuals, including those now in Israel, who had collaborated with the Nazis; rather, he sought to engage with a matter of principle: How should Israeli society, and in particular the leadership echelon of the ghetto fighters, judge the Diaspora and the former Jewish leadership that functioned within it during the years of Nazi occupation, once it had been privileged to live in an autonomous state of the Jewish nation? Engagement with this question in the poetry of a national poet that appeared in one of Israeli society's leading newspapers provides evidence of the contribution made by literature in its role, as transmitter of (high) culture, to shape public attitudes in the nation-state.

Fiery Vengeance in a Cold Winter: The Yearning for Israeli Identity in the Work of Yitskhok Perlov

The many topics relating to the Holocaust were also frequently and extensively addressed in the Yiddish press and literature that appeared in Israel since the eve of its establishment. These included depictions of the figures, life, and culture destroyed in the Holocaust, descriptions of survival and combat during wartime, and reports, discussions, and literary accounts of social, cultural, and political efforts made in Israel and of course around the world to rehabilitate the survivors' life and culture. The Yiddish press in Israel carried reports of trials of Jewish collaborators in Europe, covered the Gruenwald and Kasztner trials, and naturally reported the murder of Kasztner in March 1957. Yet compared to the coverage of other aspects of the Holocaust, engagement with the topic of collaboration with the Nazis was remarkably limited, particularly in the works of literature that frequently appeared in newspapers. The fact that Yiddish authors continued to write in their own language after arriving in Israel meant that they occupied only a marginal and at times apologetic position in the local culture, because Yiddish language and culture became a symbol of the Diaspora shunned by the Zionist ethos. Collaboration with the Nazis was perceived as a reprehensible "Diaspora trait," and Yiddish writers were thus far from eager to address this issue. The writer Yitskhok Perlov was among the few who chose to deal with this charged theme in the short story "Nekome" (Vengeance) and the novel *Dzshebeliya* (Jebeliya). These works were published between 1953 and 1955, virtually contemporaneous with Alterman's columns.

"Nekome" appeared in serial form during 1953 in the most widely read daily newspaper among the survivors in Israel, *Letste nayes*,[41] primarily because it was an independent publication, unaffiliated with any political party. The paper was founded in 1949 by Mordkhe Tsanin (1906–2009), a Holocaust refugee who dedicated the paper to the survivors.[42] Perlov was a popular author among broad sections of the people; his work was thus not regarded as "elevated" or canonic.[43] Precisely because he did not belong to the ranks of the great Yiddish authors, such as Avrom Sutzkever, who represented (willingly or unwillingly) Yiddish language and culture in Israeli society, he could afford to address a topic so charged as collaboration and even the extreme attitude adopted toward collaborators, namely, vengeance.[44] Unlike Alterman's writing, which addressed the topic in response to the Gruenwald and Kasztner trials, Perlov's work arguably expressed an interest and sentiment that were apparently prevalent among *olei she'erit ha-pleta*, because it was written and published before the trials. Whereas Alterman addressed the leadership echelon among the survivors, Perlov's interest lay in the "simple Jew" who lived among the "common people of Israel." This is a typical focus in modern Yiddish literature.

Because of their large numbers in a fledgling state that was absorbing tens of thousands of immigrants, the inadequate supply of housing in Israel at the time of its founding, and the difficulties that the young state encountered in absorbing the newcomers, the *olei she'erit ha-pleta* were initially housed in empty Palestinian towns and villages, then in absorption and transit camps, and finally in immigrant housing rapidly built on the periphery of the cities. This crowded environment generated unexpected and at times dramatic encounters between survivors who had lost contact with one another before the war, during its course, or upon its conclusion. These chance meetings were not always congenial in nature, as was the case when collaborators with the Nazis unexpectedly came across their victims.[45] Such a situation is portrayed in the story "Nekome." Its protagonist, Gedalye, stumbles upon a *landsman* (a Jew who hails from the same town in Eastern Europe) as he waits in line for a bus at Tel Aviv's central bus station. The acquaintance tells him about a woman named Khinke Melnitser from their town, Częstochowa, in Poland, who had also survived; she had come to Israel and was living in a transit camp (*ma'abara*) on the outskirts of Tel Aviv. The reader learns that Khinke was the daughter of a Judenrat official who had been involved in the death of Gedalye's relative. Upon hearing the news, the protagonist forgets that he should be hurrying home from work (because he had arranged to go out to a movie with his girlfriend). Instead, he boards a different bus that takes him toward the *ma'abara*. He is consumed by a deep anger and a desire to wreak revenge on the daughter for the deeds of her father. It is a rainy and harsh winter's day,[46] and the bus journey to the *ma'abara* is arduous and protracted.

Yet these hardships seem negligible compared to the scene that meets the protagonist when he finally arrives at the camp: Many of the tents had been torn apart and were floating in the valley, which was entirely flooded by the rains. Gedalye encounters an extensive rescue operation undertaken by a large contingent of rescuers who are attempting to extract the camp's residents from the flooded tents, the mud, and the water. Nevertheless, amid the chaos, the protagonist is still bent on exacting his revenge. During the course of his search for Khinke, Gedalye learns that her young son had died of pneumonia only a few days before, and that she, consumed by despair, has asked to be allowed to drown, as her child was the only family member she had left. When Gedalye finally locates Khinke, he barely recognizes the woman, who was in a psychotic-like condition and was struggling with a fireman who had come to rescue her. Gedalye approaches her, identifies himself as her *landsman*, and helps to evacuate her. The women who attend to her persuade him to take her into his home in Tel Aviv so long as the rains continue, because she has no one and, after all, they are from the same town.

Gedalye thus finds himself in an impossible predicament. He had come to the *maʻabara* to take revenge on the daughter of the hated Judenrat member and now had not merely helped to save her life but was even assisting in her rehabilitation by taking her into his home. He was apprehensive about his neighbors' gossip, because he was unmarried, and was particularly concerned about the reactions of his fellow townsmen who were his friends. As the story's plot moves to Gedalye's home, the reader learns through his thoughts that even before the war he had loathed Khinke and her family. His own family lacked social standing in the community, as his father was a butcher, and the Melnitser family had looked down on them and scorned them. The wartime actions of Melnitser the father naturally exacerbated Gedalye's repulsion. The hostility and anger he feels toward Khinke and her family is manifested in the formal language he uses in communicating with her (which is lost in the Hebrew translation, as this form of address hardly exists in it). The sense of distance is enhanced by the borrowing of German words (such as *Sie* instead of the Yiddish *ir* and *bitte* instead of *zayt azoy gut*). The choice of German words reflects, on the one hand, the inferiority that the protagonist senses in the presence of the daughter of the Judenrat official, which drives him to use a "Germanized" and ostensibly "high" and "proper" form of Yiddish, and, on the other hand, expresses the scorn and disdain associated with the "return of the suppressed," namely, Gedalye's anger toward Khinke's father, who had collaborated with the Nazis, and toward her family, which had behaved arrogantly toward the Yiddish-speaking "ordinary Jews." The formal and alienating language that the story's protagonist uses when addressing Khinke contrasts starkly with his polite invitation that she "feel at home"—"filn zi zikh heymish." Nonetheless, through his hostility and anger the protagonist is aware of her immense deterioration and her poor condition and even feels some responsibility for her.

The tension between these conflicting emotions reaches a climax when Gedalye offers Khinke his bed and goes to sleep on the floor below her. On the one hand he is polite and caring toward her, but on the other hand he senses acute humiliation. He regards this situation as a symbol of the class difference between them and as a manifestation of the feeling of superiority on the part of the Melnitser family, which enabled the father to collaborate with the enemy during the war. Gedalye attempts to reconcile these conflicting emotions by creating a mechanism of separation: between the father and the daughter and between the treatment that each deserves. He thus says to Khinke, "I would not have done this for your father! With him I would have now settled a completely different score!"[47] Yet Khinke's presence in his life, in his home, and even in his own bed threatens to erode these boundaries. Speaking about herself, Khinke explains that the painful losses she has suffered have destroyed her ability and will to maintain boundaries and distinctions through what she terms "scores": "I don't know what gossip you have heard about my father. I know but this, that one shouldn't settle scores with the dead. I am done with settling my scores. Both with the living and the dead. I lost my family in Poland, my husband in Russia, and my child—here in Israel. I'm through with all scores."[48]

The losses she experienced have led Khinke to erase the distinctions between the dead and the living, between geographic regions (Poland, Russia, Israel), and between the concrete historical circumstances that gave rise to her terrible loss. Dominick LaCapra defines trauma as "a disruptive experience that disarticulates the self and creates holes in experience."[49] Indecisiveness and a tendency to erase all distinctions are characteristics of trauma and of posttraumatic acting out.[50] Khinke's behavior indeed indicates that she is in a state of trauma: "Khinke resisted no longer and allowed herself to be cared for without a word. This was an act of surrender through resignation, of total apathy toward her fate and whatever may happen to her. She pressed herself into a corner of the taxi, curled up like a beggar woman beside a church, withdrawn, desperately exhausted, silent. She no longer wept, and only rolled her eyes in strange glances."[51]

Neither Gedalye nor the reader understands why he set out on this "quest for vengeance." Why did he search for Khinke in the first place? The story begins with a description of a bachelor who combines work with evening leisure activity with his girlfriend. Their relationship symbolizes a new beginning, because she is of Yemenite origin. A chance encounter with an acquaintance then triggers deep emotions that lead Gedalye to undertake extreme and unpredictable actions that ostensibly turn his orderly life upside down. Yet one may in fact read this quest as an attempt to bring order and stability into his life. The fact that the protagonist is now at a stage of his life at which he must build a home of his own—or fail to do so and disintegrate—has reawakened the traumas linked to his own family and its status in the community. The relative calm he enjoys in his current life has allowed him to reopen past wounds and to cope with them.

In contrast to Alterman's poems, the theme of collaboration with the Nazis is not presented in this story as an exceptional phenomenon that emerged only during the Holocaust but rather as part of the history of Jewish community life: The protagonist, as mentioned, already felt enmity toward the Judenrat family before the war, which was generated by the economic, social, and cultural class differences between the families. Israel, the new nation-state, facilitated his mobility, and Gedalye has indeed tried to become a "new Jew," who fell in love with a girl of origins different from his own. To this end he is compelled to internalize the characteristics of that "new Jew." One way of doing so is by establishing differences and delineating the boundaries between himself and the "old Jew," the Diaspora Jew that he once was, whose traits he has projected onto Khinke, namely, passivity, failure, humiliation, foreignness, femininity, and even treachery, because her father collaborated with the Nazis.

In Perlov's story Khinke symbolizes the "reappearance of the suppressed," with which the protagonist is compelled to contend in order to be reincarnated as an "Israeli." Khinke appears in a *ma'abara*, a liminal sphere populated by uprooted refugees, located between the Jewish communities of the Diaspora and the new Israeli society. The camp is portrayed in the story as covered in mud, or "contaminated." Khinke's very appearance in Israel has in fact turned her into something "impure," according to Mary Douglas's well-known definition, namely, material that is not located in its rightful place. Khinke and the culture she symbolizes "rightfully" belong to the Diaspora. Indeed, when she and Gedalye arrive at his Tel Aviv apartment, Gedalye suggests that she take a shower and then showers himself lest he become "infected" by her "impurity." The boundaries between the "unclean" woman and the "pure" man are erased when they wash themselves in the shower (the modern equivalent of the Jewish ritual bath); and even the final partition between them is breached when, toward the end of the story, Khinke invites Gedalye to share the bed with her upon noticing his discomfort as he lies beneath her on the floor.

In her renowned book *Purity and Danger*, Mary Douglas maintains that a group defines its boundaries by formulating opposites that underpin its identity.[52] One of the fundamental distinctions is that between pollution and purity. The rules governing purity constitute an attempt to regulate pollution, which represents anomaly and disorder. Their application expresses an aspiration to establish political and social unity, thereby creating a complete, unified, and pure civil body. Thus a story that apparently revolves around two individual survivors manifests the concepts of pollution and purity through which the emerging Israeli society defines itself and the manner in which the protagonist internalizes and seeks to apply them. Gedalye examines Khinke and her family according to dichotomous yardsticks—good versus evil, pure versus impure, high versus low—clearly aware of the boundaries between them. Yet he finds it difficult to act according to them. He goes to the *ma'abara* intending to take revenge on Khinke and finds himself rescuing her. LaCapra would consider this a sign of successful processing of trauma,[53] through which awareness is gained of the limitations of consolation and the individual refrains from adopting absolute values as a compensation for this incompleteness. Successful working through of trauma enables the individual to return to society while meeting its demands and accepting the responsibility that it places upon him. The individual recognizes the concrete historical circumstances that generated the trauma and relinquishes belief in a utopian or redeeming future or identity.

Khinke, the story's female protagonist, constitutes a symbol of the Eastern European Jewish Holocaust survivors who migrated to Israel. This harks back to the biblical image of the people of Israel as a woman ("daughter of Zion," who appears as a virgin, a bride, or a widow).[54] Perlov's ploy of confronting the protagonist with the Judenrat member's daughter rather than with the man himself or even his son allows readers of the story to sense empathy toward Khinke and to accept her into the young Israeli society. In the novel *Dzshebeliya* (Jebeliya), which appeared two years after "Nekome," Perlov enhances the tension encompassed in this image: The women there are described as collaborators who succeed in entering Israel, the "holy place" (unlike Khinke's father, who died in exile).[55]

In *Dzshebeliya* Perlov portrays a group of women concentration camp survivors who were sexually promiscuous with Nazi men (and following their liberation, with German men in the DP camps). This is a further type of collaboration, which became a sore point in the history of many European peoples in the wake of the liberation, namely, the treatment of women suspected of having had relations with the Nazis. The women in Perlov's novel claim that their behavior was a response to the collapse of previous moral values, which they had imbibed with their tradition, and the murder of those who believed in them.

> Sin? If wanton hatred is not a sin, then why should wanton love be a sin? And the God who serenely observed the shame of the beating of naked women, the shame of the gas chambers and the incinerators, let him now observe the shame of the women of the liberated concentration camps, who no longer know what "sin" is. . . . Ah, morality? . . . Morality has been consumed in the flames of the incinerators, together with fathers and mothers, brothers and sisters. Together with teachers and *melamdim* [traditional Jewish teachers], with rabbis and Hasidic sages, together with all the righteous, the educators and leaders of the people. Morality is no more after this universal decline.[56]

Amid their efforts to rebuild families and communities, the Jewish refugees who gathered in the DP camp ostracized this group of women. They came to Israel with the waves of *olei she'erit ha-pleta* and settled in Jebeliya, a suburb of Jaffa.[57] Here too the immigrants remembered them and attached the "mark of Cain" to them.

The pejorative name given to these women by their fellows survivors—"Lot's daughters"—indicates Perlov's ambivalent attitude toward them. In the biblical story found in Genesis 19, Lot's daughters are the victims of violence—their father offered them to the evil people of Sodom, who sought to rape them—who themselves commit one of the most abhorrent sins in the Hebrew Bible, incest. They slept with their father because they believed that the world had been destroyed and thus sought to ensure its continued existence. On the one hand, this name, Lot's daughters, indicates that Perlov recognized that these women were themselves victims and that he was aware of the dire circumstances that had led them into sin. Thus the survivors' identity as traitors was not permanently cast; some chose to take leave of the group of Lot's daughters, learn a trade, and marry. On the other hand, these figures are presented in a negative light as seductresses; the novel's protagonist, Zekharye Karlsbakh, is obliged to resist the sexual temptation that they offer him as well as their violence before he can succeed in rebuilding a kosher home in Israel.

In both "Nekome" and *Dzshebeliya* Perlov chose female figures to represent the "other" in relation to whom the male protagonists defined their identity. In both works the female protagonists are not redeemed. The losses she suffered divested Khinke of her traditional roles as daughter, wife, and mother, and none of these are restored to her at the end of the story. In the novel several of Lot's daughters, who could not summon up the strength to rehabilitate themselves, became prostitutes and worked in the liminal area between Jaffa and Tel Aviv. Perlov's use of female figures in engaging with the sensitive issue of collaboration with the Nazis enables him to generate empathy toward them on the part of his readers and a willingness to readopt them into the new Israeli community. These female figures are in fact a new version of a cultural tradition that refers to the people of Israel as "the daughter of Zion" and that is defined in terms of God's attitude toward her—as a bride, a faithful or unfaithful wife, or a widow. In Perlov's stories, as in the modern, secular nation-state, men replace God and take center stage (and indeed the names of both the male protagonists refer to God: *Gedal-ya*, that is, "mighty God," and *Zekhar-ya*, "remember God"). Yet these are simple, beaten men, Holocaust survivors who seek to rebuild a home in the new Jewish nation-state.

Between Alterman's Hebrew and Perlov's Yiddish writings one sees numerous and interesting differences in 1950s Israeli society's approach to the subject of Nazi-collaborators. Alterman addresses the topic from the top down in the wake of political trials, focusing on the leadership echelon among the survivors, on the ethical and political tension between the group of fighters and the group of community leaders. This engagement is conducted from "without," because Alterman himself had "not been there" (as the well-known Yiddish poet H. Leivick terms the experience of those who were not Holocaust survivors). His poems portray public spheres, such as the stages for Memorial Day ceremonies. Perlov, on the other hand, addresses an issue that appears to have occupied the masses of *olei she'erit ha-pleta* during the course of their day-to-day lives from the bottom up as well as from within: Not only was he a survivor and a newcomer himself, but he also engaged directly, eschewing immediate recourse in favor of sublimation, with the desire to wreak revenge on the collaborators, including personal vengeance on them and their families. His stories deal with the most intimate of spheres, with the home and the family, from which the community grows upward. Grand ideologies, such as pronouncements on vengeance, disintegrate in the face of complex reality, and the struggles for power and control between groups and classes are minimized to fit the intimate space between a man and a woman.

It is interesting to note that both Alterman and Perlov express in their works a forgiving and reconciliatory position toward the collaborators and a willingness on the part of the new society to accept them into its fold. This contrasts with the position expressed in the Shemoneh-Esreh prayer addressed at the beginning of this chapter, which calls for the ostracism of Israel's enemies and wishes upon them the punishment of discontinuity. This approach represents a traditional society founded on religious identity. By contrast, the later, modern literary engagements with the issue, written in Hebrew and in Yiddish, reflect the way in which literature, integral to the culture of the nation-state, defines the ethical boundaries of the national community and the manner in which it contributes to their expansion.

Notes

Translated from Hebrew by Avner Greenberg.

1. "No prayer in the liturgical cycle appears more often than the Amidah. As the most widely prayed statutory service it was denominated *ha-tefillah*, 'the prayer.'" Reuven Kimelman, "The Daily 'Amidah' and the Rhetoric of Redemption," *Jewish Quarterly Review* 79 (1988–1989): 165. I thank Hillel Ben Sasson for his valuable references and insightful suggestions regarding the Amidah prayer.

2. The Ashkenazic version of the benediction is as follows: "Let there be no hope for informers, and may all the wicked instantly perish; may all the enemies of Your people be speedily extirpated; and may You swiftly uproot, break, crush, and subdue the reign of wickedness speedily in our days. Blessed are you, Lord, who crushes enemies and subdues the wicked."

3. Talmud Bavli, *Berakhot* 28:72.

4. Chava Turniansky, "Ha-limud be-heder ba-et ha-hadasha ha-muqdemet" [Study in the Heder in the Early Modern Period], in Emanuel Etkes and David Assaf, eds., *Ha-heder: Mehqarim, te'udot, pirqei sifrut ve-zikhronot* [The Heder: Studies, Documents, Literature, and Memoirs] (Tel Aviv: Tel Aviv University, 2010), 9–10.

5. Ernest Gellner, *Nations and Nationalism* (Malden, MA: Blackwell, 2006), 8–18.

6. See Isaiah Trunk, "Postwar Trials of Councilmen and Ghetto Police," in his *Judenrat: The Jewish Councils in Eastern Europe Under Nazi Occupation* (Lincoln: University of Nebraska Press, 1996), 548–69.

7. See Rivka Brot, "Julius Siegel: A Kapo in Four (Judicial) Acts," *Dapim: Studies on the Shoah* 25 (2011): 65–127. I thank Rivka Brot for sharing this article with me. See also Chapters 2 and 8 in the present volume.

8. See David Engel, "'U-ve'arta ha-ra mi-qirbekha': le-virur ha-musag 'shituf pe'ula' be-tequfat ha-shoah be-aspaqlaria shel mishpetei micha'el weichert" ["Root Out the Evil Within Your Midst": On the Concept of Collaboration During the Holocaust Period as Reflected in the Trials of Michael Weichert], in Shmuel Almog, David Bankier, Daniel Blatman, and Dalia Ofer, eds., *Ha-Shoah: Historia ve-zikaron* [The Shoah: History and Memory] (Jerusalem: Yad Vashem, 2001), 1–24. See also Chapter 3 in the present volume.

9. See Chapter 4 in the present volume.

10. See Hanna Yablonka, "Ha-hoq le-asiyat din ba-natsim ve-ozreihem: hebet nosaf le-she'elat ha-yisra'elim, ha-nitsolim veha-shoah" [The Nazis and Nazi Collaborators (Punishment) Law: An Additional Aspect of the Question of Israelis, Survivors, and the Holocaust], *Qatedra* 82 (1997): 135–52. See also Chapters 11 and 12 in the present volume.

11. In 1954 the attorney-general of the government of Israel sued the journalist Malkiel Gruenwald for slander. A year earlier Gruenwald had published a pamphlet in which he accused Mapai member Rudolf Israel (Rezső) Kasztner, a government official, of active collaboration with the Nazis during World War II. Kasztner, a member of the Hungarian Aid and Rescue Committee, had negotiated with Adolf Eichmann and Kurt Becher over the escape of 1,685 Hungarian Jews to Switzerland in exchange for money and other goods. Gruenwald's attorney, however, succeeded in turning the trial into a broader examination of Mapai's conduct during the Holocaust. Kasztner was found complicit in assisting in the murder of Jews and collaboration with the Nazis. Judge Benjamin Halevi concluded that "Kasztner had sold his soul to the devil." The verdict shocked the Israeli public. In 1957 Kasztner was assassinated in what was the first political murder in the history of Israel. In the following year he was cleared of the charges against him by the Israeli Supreme Court. See Yechiam Weitz, *The Man Who Was Murdered Twice: The Life, Trial, and Death of Israel Kasztner* (Jerusalem: Yad Vashem, 2011).

12. See the testimonies in Engel, "U-ve'arta ha-ra," 1; Brot, "Julius Siegel," 73–76; Weitz, *Man Who Was Murdered Twice*, 102; and Yablonka, "Ha-hoq," 145.
13. The term *olei she'erit ha-pleta* is used in this chapter to refer to Jewish refugees born in Eastern Europe who arrived in Israel on the eve of its founding and during its first decade. It differs from the more prevalent terms *immigrants* and *migrants*. It was chosen to underscore their singular cultural-national identity, as manifested in the newspapers, periodicals, and literature that they produced almost as soon as they arrived in Israel. Many of them sensed a deep cultural responsibility to preserve and to revive the last remnants of their Yiddish culture, which but a decade or two previously had reached the zenith of its creative flowering, its golden age. Yet the Holocaust also induced many of them to support Zionism. For a detailed discussion of the definitions of *migrants*, *refugees*, and *immigrants* and their inadequacy in the context of *she'erit ha-pleta*, see Gali Drucker Bar-Am, "Be-kolam uvi-sfatam: Yisrael bire'i siporet yidish she-nikhteva be-yisrael be-yedei olei she'erit ha-pleita" [In Their Voice and in Their Language: Israel as Reflected in Yiddish Prose Written in Israel by Survivor Immigrants], in Dalia Ofer, ed., *Yisrael be-einei sordei ha-shoah ve-nitsoleha* [Israel in the Eyes of Survivors of the Holocaust] (Jerusalem: Yad Vashem, 2014 [in press]).
14. Hagit Lavsky termed this ideological stance, which was peculiar to the survivors, "spontaneous" Zionism. See Hagit Lavsky, *New Beginnings: Holocaust Survivors in Bergen-Belsen and the British Zone in Germany, 1945–1950* (Detroit: Wayne State University Press, 2002), 216.
15. The Yishuv (prestate Jewish society), which numbered 670,000 individuals on the eve of independence, absorbed 717,923 immigrants by the end of 1952 (compared to the 82,000 immigrants of the fourth wave of immigration in the mid-1920s and the 217,000 immigrants of the fifth wave in the early 1930s). See Dvora Hacohen, *Olim be-se'ara: ha-aliya ha-gedola ve-qlitata be-yisrael 1948–1953* [Stormy Immigration: The Great Immigration and Its Absorption in Israel, 1948–1953] (Jerusalem: Yad Ben Zvi, 1994), 6.
16. Israel Gutmann, *Sugiot be-heqer ha-shoah: Biqoret ve-truma* [Issues in Holocaust Studies: Criticism and Contribution] (Jerusalem: Merkaz Zalman Shazar, 2008), 21.
17. Zeev Mankowitz, *Life Between Memory and Hope: The Survivors of the Holocaust in Occupied Germany* (Cambridge, UK: Cambridge University Press, 2002), 12; David Sha'ari, "'Yihuda shel She'erit ha-pleita,' berihim shel shtiqa: she'erit ha-pleita ve-erets—yisra'el" ["The Singularity of the Survivors," Bars of Silence: The Survivors and the Land of Israel], *Masua* 28 (2000): 30. According to Yablonka, 70,000 survivors immigrated to Palestine/Israel between 1945 and 1947, 280,000 between 1948 and 1951, and a further 100,000 during the latter half of the 1950s. See Hanna Yablonka, "Tsayarim nitsolei shoah be-yisra'el: Hebet nosaf la-shetiqa she-lo haita" [Holocaust Survivor Painters in Israel: A Further Aspect of the Silence That Never Was], in Almog et al., eds., *Ha-Shoah*, 207.
18. Hanna Yablonka, *Ahim zarim: Nitsolei shoah be-medinat yisra'el 1948–1952* [Foreign Brothers: Holocaust Survivors in the State of Israel, 1948–1952] (Jerusalem: Yad Ben Zvi, 1994), 9–17.
19. Nathan Alterman was born in Warsaw in 1910. Partly thanks to his father, among the pioneers of the Hebrew kindergarten, he received a Jewish education. In 1925 he

immigrated to Palestine with his family and studied at the Gymnasia Herzlia high school. He began to publish his poetry in the Hebrew press in 1931 and engaged also in journalism, playwriting, and writing for children. His first book of poetry, *Kokhavim Ba-hutz* (Stars Outside) was published in 1938 by Yahdav (literally, "together"), a group of poets to which he belonged. Alterman was close to David Ben Gurion and to the Mapai party. Following the Six Day War he was among the founding members of the Movement for Greater Israel. He was awarded many literary prizes, including the Israel Prize for his entire literary opus in 1968. Alterman died in Tel Aviv in 1970.

20. On Alterman's political poetry, which included *The Seventh Column*, see Dan Miron, "Darko shel Natan Alterman el ha-shira ha-le'umit" [Nathan Alterman's Path to National Poetry], in Dan Miron, *Mi-prat el iqar: Mivneh, janer ve-hagut be-yetsirato shel Natan Alterman* [From Detail to Essence: Structure, Genre, and Thought in the Work of Nathan Alterman] (Tel Aviv: Ha-kibutz ha-meuhad, 1981), 211–31; Dan Laor, *Ha-shofar veha-herev: Masot al Natan Alterman* [The Shofar and the Sword: Essays on Nathan Alterman] (Tel Aviv: Tel Aviv University, 1983), 9–74; and Ziva Shamir, "'Meshorer hatser' o 'meshorer le'umi'" ["Court Poet" or "National Poet"], in Ziva Shamir, *Al et ve-al atar: Poetiqa ve-politiqa be-yetsirato shel Natan Alterman* [On Time and on Place: Poeticism and Politics in the Work of Nathan Alterman] (Tel Aviv: Ha-kibutz ha-meuhad, 1999), 7–58.

21. Nathan Alterman, "Midot ha-din" [Measures of Justice], in Nathan Alterman, *Ha-tur ha-shevi'i* (Tel Aviv: Ha-kibutz ha-meuhad, 1975), 2: 405–40.

22. Dan Laor, "Od al shtei ha-drakhim: aharit davar" [More on the Two Paths: An Epilogue], in Natan Alterman, *Al shtei ha-drakhim: Dapim min ha-pinqas* [On the Two Paths: Pages from the Notebook] (Tel Aviv: Ha-kibutz ha-meuhad, 1989), 141. This essay was included in Laor's book *Ha-ma'avaq al ha-zikaron* [The Contest over Memory] (Tel Aviv: Am oved, 2009), 142–79. In these essays Laor traces the complex political circumstances in Israel within which Alterman operated and which he influenced. For an examination of Alterman's writings during the Gruenwald and Kasztner trials as a political act within Israel's judicial reality, see Leora Bilsky, "The Poet's Countertrial," in Leora Bilsky, *Transformative Justice: Israeli Identity on Trial* (Ann Arbor: University of Michigan Press, 2004), 67–82.

23. See Dina Porat, *Qafeh ha-boqer be-reiah ashan: Mifgasham shel ha-yishuv veha-hevra ha-yisra'elit im ha-shoah ve-nitsoleha* [Morning Coffee with a Smoky Aroma: The Encounter of the Yishuv and Israeli Society with the Holocaust and Its Survivors] (Tel Aviv: Am oved, 2011).

24. For a comprehensive and rigorous description of the "two paths debate" in the "Measures of Justice" poems, its analysis against the backdrop of the contemporary literary and cultural climate and current circumstances, and its assessment from the perspective of time, see Avner Holtzman, "Nathan Alterman u-fulmus 'shtei ha-drakhim'" [Nathan Alterman and the "Two Paths" Debate], in Avnar Holtzman, *Ahavot tsiyon: Panim be-sifrut ha-ivrit ha-hadasha* [Loves of Zion: Aspects of Modern Hebrew Literature] (Jerusalem: Carmel, 2006), 306–15.

25. Laor, "Od al shtei ha-drakhim," 117.

26. Alterman, "Midot ha-din," 407. The English translation is based on that of Vivian Eden, "Memorial Day and the Fighters," *Jerusalem Post* (July 28, 1989): 7. I thank Prof. Dan Laor for referring me to this translation, and I thank Ms. Eden for providing the precise reference. Deviations from Ms. Eden's translation are marked by brackets.

27. On the part played by survivor organizations in shaping the Holocaust Memorial Day Law, see Hanna Yablonka, "Ma lizkor ve-keitsad? Nitsolei ha-shoah ve-itsuv yediata" [What Should We Remember and How? Holocaust Survivors and the Shaping of Holocaust Awareness], in Anita Shapira, Yehuda Reinhartz, and Ya'akov Haris, eds., *Idan ha-tsionut* [The Age of Zionism] (Jerusalem: Merkaz Zalman Shazar, 2000), 303. On the process whereby the form that Holocaust Memorial Day would take was determined by Israel's political establishment, see Dalia Ofer, "Ma ve-ad kama lizkor mehashoah? Zikaron ha-shoah be-medinat yisra'el be-asor ha-rishon le-kiuma" [What and How Much of the Holocaust Should We Remember? Holocaust Memory in the State of Israel During the First Decade of its Existence], in Anita Shapira, ed., *Atsma'ut: 50 ha-shanim ha-rishonot* [Independence: The First 50 Years] (Jerusalem: Merkaz Zalman Shazar, 1998), 171–93; Yablonka, "Ma lizkor ve-keitsad," 306–14; and Roni Stauber, "Holocaust Remembrance Day: 1945–1951," in Roni Stauber, *The Holocaust in Israeli Public Debate in the 1950s: Ideology and Memory* (London: Vallentine Mitchell, 2007), 30–46.

28. See, for example, the editorial column in *Letste nayes*, the most popular newspaper among Yiddish-speaking *olei she'erit ha-pleta*: "The Israeli government has proclaimed itself to be the heir to the six million murdered Jews, and in return for their blood has concluded a reparations agreement with Hitler's heirs. Yet this same government did not even see fit to hold a national memorial [evening] for the six million Jews who have just now been sold. The memorial was left to political parties and groups, each of which individually turned the ghetto uprising into an uprising of a party or an uprising of a group." Mordkhe Tsanin, "10ter yortog nokhn geto ufshtand" [The Tenth Anniversary of the Ghetto Uprising], *Letste nayes* (April 17, 1953): 1.

29. Thus, in the same year that Alterman published his poem in the daily *Davar*, *Letste nayes* chose to highlight the exploits of other groups that fought in the Warsaw Ghetto Uprising by carrying an article by Marek Edelman on the part played by the Bund fighters in the uprising (the paper marked Memorial Day on April 19 rather than on the Israeli calendar date of Nissan 27). See Marek Edelman, "Azoy hobn mir gekemft kegn di daytshn" [Thus Did We Fight the Germans], *Letste nayes* (April 19, 1954): 3.

30. Addressing the question of whether the Judenräte should be regarded as an example of Jewish leadership, Israel Gutman asserted that "the very use of the concept of leadership to characterize bodies and figures that headed the institutions responsible for the sphere of internal Jewish life during the Holocaust engenders reservations and on occasion also uncompromising resistance. The question often arises whether it is fitting to view the Jewish councils that the Nazis forced on the Jews in the occupied countries and the Judenräte in Eastern Europe, which were established according to the instructions of the Nazi authorities and operated under their supervision, as a phenomenon of Jewish leadership." See Israel Gutman, "Ha-yudenrat ke-hanhaga" [The Judenräte as Leadership], in Israel Bartal, ed., *Kahal yisra'el: Ha-shilton ha-atsmi*

ha-yehudi le-dorotav [The Jewish Congregation: Jewish Self-Government Through the Ages] (Jerusalem: Merkaz Zalman Shazar, 2004), 3: 373.

31. Alterman, "Midot ha-din," 416.
32. See Laor, "Od al shtei ha-drakhim," 133–34n20.
33. Alterman, "Midot ha-din," 407.
34. Alterman, "Midot ha-din," 412.
35. Alterman, "Midot ha-din," 422.
36. Laor, "Od al shtei ha-drakhim," 133; Dina Porat, "'Lo hayu shtei drakhim': Nathan Alterman, al shtei ha-drakhim" ["There Were Not Two Paths": Nathan Alterman, On the Two Paths], in Porat, *Qafeh ha-boqer be-reiah ashan*, 385.
37. Dominick LaCapra, *Writing History, Writing Trauma* (Baltimore: Johns Hopkins University Press, 2001), 27n31.
38. LaCapra, *Writing History*, 41–42.
39. Laor, "Od al shtei ha-drakhim," 21.
40. Bilsky, "Poet's Countertrial," 67.
41. Yitskhok Perlov, "Nekome" [Vengeance], *Letste nayes* (February 20, 1953): 3; *Letste nayes* (February 27, 1953): 5; *Letste nayes* (March 6, 1953): 4. The story was included in Perlov's collection of stories titled *Matilda lebt*, published in Buenos Aires in 1954 (pp. 92–102). For a Hebrew translation of the story, see Yitzkhak Perlov, "Nekama," in Yitzkhak Perlov, *Ahava u-nedudim: Kitvei Yitzkhak Perlov* [Love and Wanderings: The Writings of Yitzkhak Perlov], trans. Barukh Kro (Tel Aviv: Carmi et Naor, 1954), 202–10.
42. On the founding of *Letste nayes* and its characteristics, see Gali Drucker Bar-Am, "'Ani afarekh?' Yitsug ha-havaya ha-yisraelit be-siporet yidish be-yisrael 1948–1968" ["Am I Your Dust?" Representations of the Israeli Experience in Yiddish Prose in Israel, 1948–1968], Ph.D. diss., The Hebrew University of Jerusalem, 2013, 59–76.
43. Yitskhok Perlov was born in Biała Podlaska in 1911. He received a traditional education and subsequently attended high school in Warsaw, where he lived in the interwar period. He began writing poetry in his teens, publishing his work in the Yiddish press. Upon the outbreak of World War II he fled to the Soviet Union. After the war he was repatriated to Lodz, from where he made his way to displaced persons camps in Germany. In 1947 he attempted to enter Israel illegally on the refugee ship *Exodus*, which was seized by the British and returned to Germany. In 1949 he immigrated to Israel and was housed in an abandoned quarter of Jaffa named Jebeliya (renamed Giv'at Aliya), from where he moved to Tel Aviv. In 1954 he was awarded the Mexican Zvi Kessle Prize for his literary work. In 1961 he left Israel to settle in New York, where he died in 1980.
44. On calls made by survivors for vengeance against the Nazis at the time of the Eichmann trial, see Gali Drucker Bar-Am, "The Holy Tongue and the Tongue of the Martyrs: The Eichmann Trial as Reflected in *Letste nayes*," *Dapim: Studies on the Shoah* 28.1 (2014): 17–37.
45. For a description of this phenomenon in the Yiddish press, see Mordkhe Tsanin, "Geratevete yidn in yisroel gefinen zeyere payninker fun di lagern" [Jewish Survivors

in Israel Find Their Tormentors from the Camps], *Forverts* (November 19, 1950), Genazim Institute, Tel Aviv, Tsanin Archive, 504.

46. The winters in the initial years of statehood were indeed described as harsh in the contemporary Israeli press. This was particularly true of the winter of 1951, when *ma'abarot* were flooded by the heavy rains, to the extent that several people drowned. Israeli society came to the assistance of the *ma'abarot* residents. Citizens took children and women into their homes. At the time this was not a simple operation, because under the austerity regime then in place, people received food vouchers that were valid only for specific stores in their place of residence.

47. Yitskhok Perlov, "Nekome" [Vengeance], in Yitskhok Perlov, *Matilda Lebt* (Buenos Aires: Farband fun brisk d'lite un umgegnt in argentine, 1954), 100.

48. Perlov, "Nekome," in *Matilda Lebt*, 100.

49. LaCapra, *Writing History*, 41.

50. LaCapra, *Writing History*, 22.

51. Perlov, "Nekome," in *Matilda Lebt*, 96–97.

52. Mary Douglas, *Purity and Danger: An Analysis of the Concepts of Pollution and Taboo* (London: Routledge, 2002).

53. See LaCapra, *Writing History*, 21–22: "Working through is an articulatory practice: to the extent one works through trauma ... one is able to distinguish between past and present and to recall in memory that something has happened to one (or one's people) back then while realizing that one is living here and now with openings to the future. This does not imply either that there is a pure opposition between past and present or that acting out ... can be fully transcended towards a state of closure or full ego identity. But it does mean that processes of working through may counteract the force of acting out and the repetition compulsion. These processes of working through ... involve the possibility of making distinctions or developing articulations that are recognized as problematic but still function as limits and as possibly desirable resistance to undecidability, particularly when the latter is tantamount to confusion and the obliteration or blurring of all distinctions."

54. For example, "It was the beginning of sin to the daughter of Zion, for in you were found the transgressions of Israel" (Micah 1:13); "With what could I equate you? How can I comfort you, young woman Daughter Zion? Your hurt is as vast as the sea. Who can heal you?" (Lamentations 2:13); "Your offenses, daughter of Zion, are atoned for; he will keep you in exile no longer" (Lamentations 4:22); "It is the sound of the daughter of Zion gasping for breath as she spreads her hands: Woe to me! Everything in me is so weary before the killers" (Jeremiah 4:31).

55. Yitskhok Perlov, *Dzshebeliya* (Buenos Aires: Yidbukh, 1955). Before its publication in novel form, this work appeared in serial form in the New York daily *Forverts* under the title *Tsu a nayem lebn* (Toward a New Life).

56. Perlov, *Dzshebeliya*, 77.

57. For an account of the capture of Jaffa (December 1947–May 1948) on the eve of Israel's War of Independence, see Benny Morris, *The Birth of the Palestinian Refugee Problem Revisited* (New York: Cambridge University Press, 2004), 109–16, 211–21.

11

Changing Legal Perceptions of "Nazi Collaborators" in Israel, 1950–1972

DAN PORAT

It was a hot summer day in July 1949 when a group of young Israel Defense Forces soldiers stopped for refreshments at a small coffee shop in Ein-Karem, a neighborhood on the outskirts of Jerusalem. The group sat down at one of the tables, and the shop owner, Joseph Paal, approached them to take their order. At the sight of the one-eyed Paal, one of the soldiers, Yerachmiel Y.,[1] became visibly agitated. He recognized the owner. He was "Blind Max" who had served as his *Blockältester* (block elder) in Block 10 of the Jaworzno concentration camp, an auxiliary camp of Auschwitz, a man who had beaten and tortured Yerachmiel and his fellow prisoners. Yerachmiel confronted Blind Max, but Paal categorically denied the accusation, insisting that he had never in his life heard of Jaworzno and that he was not Blind Max. Paal's wife of three years, whom he had married after the Nazis had murdered his first wife and children, turned to the soldiers and commented that it was time to forget the past now that they were in their new land.[2]

But the Holocaust survivor Yerachmiel Y. could not and did not want to forget his tormentor. Four months later, in October 1949, he met with a friend from Block 10, David L., and shared that he had seen Blind Max. The two approached the Israeli police and filed a complaint with the Jerusalem station. In February 1950 the police ordered Paal in for questioning. In the investigation room Paal was adamant that he had never served as a *Blockältester* in Jaworzno. The policeman called Yerachmiel into the investigation room and brought the two men face to face. Hearing Paal's denial, Yerachmiel lost his cool and screamed in Yiddish, "You don't know me? You didn't hit me? You don't know that I was one of the inmates in Block 10 in Jaworzno? You dare tell me that you are not Blind Max?" Paal paled and answered, "Yes, I was in Jaworzno, and if I was there, does that make me a criminal?"[3]

Holocaust survivors did not want to forget their tormentors. Likewise, Israeli authorities felt an obligation to confront the culprits. The Paal incident was just one of dozens of such incidents that took place in Israel in the two decades following the Holocaust, confrontations in which surviving Jews accused other Jews of tormenting them. The police investigated the cases and in some instances arrested suspects. As in Paal's case, all the accusations addressed events that had occurred before the establishment of the State of Israel and were outside its territory and jurisdiction. The police and judicial system could not act on these matters, and this lack of response angered and distressed many survivors. In one instance, in February 1949, the morning newspaper *Ha-boker* published an open letter from a reader named Dov to Minister of Justice Pinchas Rosen in which he described encountering an individual named Julius Siegel, whom he accused of collaboration with the Nazis. Dov had filed a complaint with the police, who investigated and arrested the suspect. At the moment of his arrest, the letter continued, Siegel brandished a document signed by Yerachmiel (Yaron) Lustig, head of the Israel Police Criminal Investigation Unit, which indicated, "One cannot prosecute a person in Israel for crimes conducted outside the State of Israel." Seeing Siegel walk away scot-free, Dov's only recourse was to turn to the Polish consulate in Tel Aviv and demand that Poland submit an extradition request to the State of Israel to have Siegel sent back to stand trial there.[4]

The police investigations in all these cases had no legal basis. Still, the police continued to investigate. On July 6, 1949, Police Inspector Joseph Gorski wrote to Lustig and to Israel police commissioner Sahar Yechezkel about those whom he defined as "war criminals."

> Due to the lack of sufficient laws on the books in Israel, [criminals] are not being penalized here for crimes they committed in Europe. On the contrary, the paradoxical situation is that many war criminals . . . find a calm shelter in Israel. There are a large number of Jewish "kapos" and other "privileged" individuals who are already in Israel and the heads of security forces and the courts cannot penalize them. I will ask you, Sir, to take the steps needed . . . so as to create appropriate laws that will allow bringing these criminals to court.[5]

Lustig in turn wrote to Ram Salomon, the director general and legal adviser of the Police Ministry, with a request to initiate legislation on the issue. Salomon replied in October 1949: "I wish to inform you that the Ministry of Justice is preparing a proposal for a law related to war criminals and collaborators.[6] It is anticipated that the bill will be brought to the Knesset [the Israeli legislature] in its next session."[7]

As these interactions demonstrate, the initiative for prosecuting Jews deemed putative Nazi collaborators came from two directions: Holocaust survivors on the one hand, and the State of Israel on the other. Survivors who identified their own tormenters or individuals who had harmed members of their family, friends, and acquaintances demanded justice. Similarly, the State of Israel, which saw itself as the heir of the Nazis' innocent victims, demanded justice from those whom it viewed as betrayers of the nation by having colluded with the Germans. Still, it took the state—both its executive and judicial branches—years before it changed its approach to those Holocaust survivors it considered "war criminals" and "collaborators."

In this chapter I discuss the dramatic paradigm shift in the view of Israel's legal system toward Jews who allegedly collaborated with the Nazis. First, I focus on the Knesset's deliberation of the legislation of the Nazis and Nazi Collaborators (Punishment) Law of 1950, and then I examine some of the trials that resulted from it.[8] Initially, in the early 1950s the prosecutors aimed to apply the harshest components of the law, such as "war crimes" and "crimes against humanity," in cases of Jewish collaborators, in a manner that corresponded with the Knesset members' original intentions in legislating this law. Yet from the beginning and contrary to the legislators' intention, the courts expressed concern regarding the limited applicability of these components of the law to Jewish defendants. Following these initial verdicts, prosecutors throughout the remaining years of the 1950s treated defendants only under sections of the law that were less harsh in nature.

Only after the Eichmann trial did these trials come to an end, culminating in the exceptional 1964 Supreme Court decision in the case of Hirsch Barenblat, when it concluded that Jewish collaborators could be judged only in the court of history and not in the court of law. The justices interpreted the law in a way that made it almost inapplicable to Jewish victims, even if they had played a privileged role in the concentration camp system or in the ghetto police, a stance that contradicted the original view that Jews who had assisted the Nazis were their collaborators.

The 1950 Nazis and Nazi Collaborators (Punishment) Law

In March 1950 Minister of Justice Rosen presented the Israeli Knesset with a proposed piece of legislation, the Nazis and Nazi Collaborators (Punishment) Law.

This was the first Holocaust-related law considered by the Knesset. In its first clause the bill focused on "crimes against humanity" that had taken place in the Nazi era, crimes including "murder, extermination, enslavement, starvation, or deportation and other inhumane acts committed against any civilian population, and persecution on national, racial, religious, or political grounds." The following clause focused on "war crimes," which constituted "murder, ill-treatment, or deportation to forced labor or for any other purpose, of civilian population of or in occupied territory; murder or ill-treatment of prisoners of war or persons on the seas; killing of hostages; plunder of public or private property; wanton destruction of cities, towns or villages; and devastation not justified by military necessity." As the explanatory notes to the bill indicated, the formulation of these two sections emanated from the wording of the sixth principle of the "Principles of International Law Recognized in the Charter of the Nuremberg Tribunal and in the Judgment of the Tribunal," which defined war crimes and crimes against humanity.[9]

In presenting the law, Rosen explained its target: "Nazi criminals who are guilty of the crimes presented in this law will not dare come to Israel." "In reality," he stated later, "the law will apply less to Nazis than to Jews who collaborated with the Nazis and are here in the State of Israel."[10] Because the bill had to be presented in neutral language, it did not use the word *Jew*, not even once, in either its definition of "perpetrator" or its definition of relevant crimes. The Ministry of Justice, which had drafted the proposed law, used completely neutral language that made no distinction between, for example, a Jewish policeman, a Latvian collaborator, and a German SS man who had served the Nazis.

None of the Knesset members seated that day in the chamber disputed Rosen's assertion that the law aimed to punish those from within the Jewish people whom it defined as collaborators. In their deliberation of the bill, Knesset members accepted the neutral language suggested by the Ministry of Justice when it came to perpetrators, whether Jewish or German. However, they criticized it when it came to victims. According to some, the lack of any distinction in the proposed law between crimes committed against members of the Jewish nation and those committed against members of other groups was unacceptable. In an op-ed piece that reflected the criticisms he and others had leveled against the proposed law from the podium of the Knesset, Knesset member Yaakov Gil of the centrist party General Zionists (Ha-tsiyonim ha-kelali'im), wrote:

> It is surprising that the government of Israel did not mention in this law, which primarily affects us, even once the "Jewish people," as if it were the Nuremberg court which spoke about the slaughter of millions

of people, at the same time that it was the Jewish people who were the greatest victims of this crime.... After two thousand years without a state, the government of the State of Israel needs to appear and assert: "[a crime] committed against Israel and humanity."[11]

In Gil's view the Israeli government's failure to explicitly make a distinction between crimes against the Jewish people and crimes against humanity indicated the mentality of Diaspora Jews and hesitations, he believed, the State of Israel had to rid itself of. On the contrary, the government of Israel owed it to Israelis and Jews in the Diaspora alike to define the crime for which Nazis and their collaborators deserved to be punished under Israeli law as a crime against the Jewish people.

The Knesset decided to refer the law for consideration to the Constitution, Law, and Justice Committee, a committee that in turn established a subcommittee to deliberate the law's details. The subcommittee heeded the criticism expressed by Knesset members when it added a new clause titled "Crimes Against the Jewish People" to Section 1 of the law, which already sanctioned war crimes and crimes against humanity. This clause included crimes such as "killing Jews," "placing Jews in living conditions calculated to bring about their physical destruction," and "inciting hatred of Jews." Like the two other clauses included in Section 1 of the law—crimes against humanity and war crimes—this one also carried mandatory capital punishment.[12]

Disagreement among Knesset members emerged surrounding the clause that focused on sentencing (Section 10), a debate that reflected diverging views on the purpose of trying and punishing Jewish collaborators. The argument focused on the question of whether or not the court should consider leniency for a Jew, "a persecuted person," when it sentenced him or her. According to the proposed law, the sentence of a persecuted person would be reduced if he or she had acted under duress or had attempted to prevent, through said action or lack of action, worse consequences.[13] One group, which included Knesset members Yaakov Klibanov of the General Zionists and Moshe Ben-Ami of the Sephardim and Oriental Communities Party (Sefaradim ve'edot ha-mizrah), argued that the courts should not only reduce the sentence but even "release [the individual] from criminal responsibility" entirely. Knesset member Nahum Nir, the chair of the committee who sided with this group, explained, "In the bill it is written that [a persecuted person found guilty of violating the law] will not bear criminal responsibility; it does not say that he did not commit a crime."[14]

Knesset member Joseph Lam also sided with this group in the committee. In a speech to the Knesset's general assembly, he recounted his own experience of being arrested by Nazis in 1938 and interned at Dachau before he immigrated to Mandatory Palestine in 1939.

> I myself was a prisoner in a camp, and I know how many crimes the people who were responsible committed—not only the Nazis, but also their collaborators, who were prisoners themselves in the camps. But I know many instances in which these people, who themselves were persecuted, did everything possible to prevent crimes. There were different instances in which a kapo had to take an action that in our view was an act that helped the Nazis, all this in order to prevent the people under his authority from harsh wounds that might cause their death. If, for example, in a room of one hundred people, two did not keep order—and this happened frequently—there was the danger that the Nazi responsible would find the disorderly cabinet of so-and-so and would take out hundreds of people and make them stand barefoot for many hours outside in temperatures of minus seventeen or eighteen Celsius or that he would punish the entire block with harsh punishments, and all of this since two of the prisoners did not keep order.... And thus, in this kind of case there was no other choice but to impose on the disorderly one a specific punishment so as to prevent the danger of death to the entire group.[15]

The opposing group of Knesset members, who strongly identified with the Jewish resistance movement in German-occupied Eastern Europe and who were influenced by the Soviet Union, was not swayed by this personal account. These members argued that the court should not be obliged to release a defendant from criminal responsibility because of his or her acting under duress. On the contrary, the group, which included Yisrael Bar-Yehudah and Hannan Rubin, both members of the United Workers Party (Mapam), argued that the extreme circumstances of the Holocaust demanded that each and every Jew act in an extraordinary fashion and place the good of the nation above his own personal and selfish interests. "I refuse to release this person [from criminal responsibility]," asserted Knesset member Bar-Yehudah, "because he did what he did out of cowardice."[16] This group of Knesset members saw the law as a means of achieving historical justice with Jewish collaborators—first and foremost with the members of the Judenräte, whom they saw as traitors. In the words of Knesset member Yaakov Gil, the intention of the law was "first and foremost revenge, although only a symbolic revenge for the blood of Israel."[17] Furthermore, the law served as a means of educating the nation, as it "will tell the Jews [worldwide] how they need to act if it [a Holocaust] were to happen again."[18] Whereas the first group of Knesset members aimed, by way of the law, to achieve calm in the survivor community, the opposing group saw the law as a means of revenge and education to prevent a future genocide of the Jews.

On July 12, 1950, the Constitution, Law, and Justice Committee convened. Haim Cohn, the attorney general who, according to his own account, took part in initiating the law, expressed his opposition to the suggestion that the defendant be released "from legal responsibility."[19] Contrary to Cohn's advice, the committee formulated a compromise, wording Section 10 in a manner that allowed the court to release the defendant from criminal responsibility, but only under specific and limited circumstances, which were much stricter than the original wording. The new formulation allowed release from criminal responsibility in two cases:

> (a) if the defendants did or omitted to do the act in order to save themselves from the danger of immediate death and the court is satisfied that they did their best to avert the consequences of the act or omission; or
>
> (b) if the defendants did or omitted to do the act with intent to avert consequences more serious than those which resulted from the act or omission, and actually averted them; however, these provisions shall not apply to an act or omission constituting an offence under Sections 1 and 2(f).[20]

The compromise between the two groups resulted in the final line of this paragraph, which permitted the court to consider leniency in lesser crimes mentioned in the law, such as common assault or unlawful compulsory labor, but not in those related to the first paragraph of war crimes, crimes against humanity, and crimes against the Jewish people, as well as the case of murder.

The Knesset approved the newly worded Nazis and Nazi Collaborators (Punishment) Law on August 1, 1950. In Section 2 the law focused on "crimes against persecuted persons," which it defined as "an act by which had he committed in Israeli territory, he would have become guilty of an offence under one of the following sections of the Criminal Code." These offenses included "rape," "grievous harm," and "robbing." In Section 4 the law repeated many of these crimes but this time in relation to "offences at places of confinement," that is, ghettos and concentration camps and the like. Section 5 focused on the case of "a person who, during the period of the Nazi regime, in an enemy country, was instrumental in delivering up a persecuted person to an enemy administration." Finally, Section 6 focused on instances of blackmailing persecuted individuals.[21]

War Crimes, Crimes Against the Jewish People, and Crimes Against Humanity in the Courthouse

The police conducted hundreds of investigations in the years preceding passage of the Nazis and Nazi Collaborators (Punishment) Law.[22] As a result, within weeks of the passage of the legislation, the Office of the Attorney of the State of Israel had ample investigation material immediately at its disposal and was able to file charges against more than ten alleged Jewish collaborators.

Upon the addition of the category of crimes against the Jewish people, Section 1 of the law consisted of three provisions: war crimes, crimes against the Jewish people, and crimes against humanity. Only one case involved a charge of crimes against the Jewish people as part of the indictment. Although the police leveled this charge against a few suspects, prosecutors did not use it against any Jews, because a member of the Jewish nation cannot be a member of the nation and at the same time have "intent to destroy the Jewish people in whole or in part."[23] They did, however, apply it to the sole case of a non-Jew who was indicted, Andrej Banik. He was accused of the following: "As a member of the Hlinka Guard in Slovakia and with the intention of destroying the Jewish people, he caused on the Hungarian-Slovakian border . . . dire physical damage to Jews, among others, he trampled the belly of a child approximately three years old . . . [and] beat a Jew named Liush Louis Grossman and knocked out his teeth." At trial the witnesses turned out to be unreliable, and in June 1951 the court acquitted Banik of all charges; he then immigrated to Canada.[24]

Although the prosecution did not indict Jews of crimes against the Jewish people, it did indict them of war crimes. In the September 1951 case of *Attorney General v. Hezekiel Jungster*, the state attorney accused Jungster of committing war crimes when, as a kapo in charge of Jewish prisoners at a labor camp in Germany, he abused "a civilian population in an occupied territory, causing [its members] grave injury, pain and suffering."[25] The district court, however, dismissed the charges, explaining, "We have no hesitation to determine that the actions of the accused . . . constitute cases of ill-treatment as defined in the definition of war crimes [in the law]. Yet we accept the argument of the defendant's attorney that one should not convict the defendant of war crimes if he and his victims belong to the same persecuted nation."[26]

Of the three clauses included in Section 1 of the law (war crimes, crimes against the Jewish people, and crimes against humanity), the prosecution used the last one most frequently. In *Attorney General v. Elsa Trunk* the indictment asserted that the defendant committed four such crimes against humanity. These included accusations that Trunk had "tortured T. R., of an age of about 45, when she forced her to kneel for two hours in a puddle of water with her hands raised with blocks in each of her hands."[27] In her October 1950 decision, Judge Mina Shamir implicitly criticized the legislators for their formulation of the law in general and specifically for their formulation of what constituted crimes against humanity, stating, "Within the defined terms, the legislator used flowery words of a very broad meaning." She then went on to define crimes against humanity as crimes conducted against "a group of people as a group and not against individuals as such—there being numerous individual cases does not matter.... Whenever there is no connection between one case and another and it is not committed against a body, a group, a population . . . it is not a crime against humanity as it is intended in the law." She therefore ordered the removal of three of the four charges of crimes against humanity from the indictment against Trunk. In contrast, she approved presenting the charge of crimes against humanity in one instance in which Trunk was accused of forcing an entire block of women prisoners to kneel on their knees for hours.[28]

The courts, however, convicted a defendant of crimes against humanity only once, a conviction that carried with it mandatory capital punishment. This was the aforementioned case of *Attorney General v. Hezekiel Jungster*, which was brought before the Tel Aviv District Court on November 28, 1951. Jungster was accused of torturing prisoners by beating them repeatedly with a rubber stick. The court majority rejected the defense argument that it was necessary to prove intent of "persecution on national, racial, religious, or political grounds" in order to obtain a conviction for crimes against humanity.[29] However, the judges construed the law as requiring proof of intent only in a case in which a defendant was accused of persecution but *not* in the other cases mentioned later in same section of the law, including murder and "inhuman actions," which also fell under crimes against humanity. The judges defined Jungster's repeated hitting of prisoners with a rubber stick as an inhuman action that did not demand proof of intention. The court convicted Jungster of crimes against humanity and sentenced him to death.

Judge Joseph Lam, the Knesset member who had been an inmate in Dachau and advocated defining the law in more lenient terms, dissented from this ruling. Lam held that for a conviction of crimes against humanity, two conditions needed to be present: first, that the actions were inhuman, as they indeed were in this case; and second, that the actions were "aimed at the destruction of a population in its entirety or partially." In this case, Lam stated, it was clear that the accused did not intend to destroy a human population in part or as a whole. All three components of Section 1 of the law, he determined, demanded identification of the accused with the Nazis' motivation to destroy a group. He held that all other sections of the law, such as Section 2, covering "crimes against persecuted persons," or Section 5, "delivering up a persecuted person to enemy administration," did not demand such a common motivation and thus applied to Jewish collaborators.[30]

The court sentenced Jungster to death. Nevertheless, it was clear that the majority found this verdict inappropriate.

> Since we found the defendant guilty of a crime against humanity, the law does not leave us any choice but to sentence him to death. This result is against our better judgment, as we believe that it was better for the legislator to leave to the court the authority to sentence a defendant to a lighter sentence.... It is quite clear that it is not the same [to impose the death sentence] in the case of a Nazi criminal who identified himself as a Nazi or identified with the barbaric Nazi regime and [in the case] of this defendant who himself was a persecuted person and lived in inhuman conditions like his victims.[31]

In April 1952 the Supreme Court overturned Jungster's conviction for crimes against humanity and let his crimes based on Section 6, Paragraph 4 ("assault causing actual bodily harm" of four individuals), stand. The court reduced his sentence to two years of imprisonment. The Supreme Court ruling, which seems to have adopted the dissenting view of the district court, reduced the reach of the law. Although no explanation of the ruling seems to have ever been published, it did indicate that Section 1, which carried with it capital punishment, should not be applied to Jewish collaborators.[32] From 1953 onward, with only a few insignificant exceptions, the state attorney avoided charging defendants under the clause of crimes against humanity or any of the other clauses from Section 1 of the law, that is, crimes against the Jewish people and war crimes.

The prosecution avoided Section 1 and mostly used Sections 2, 4, and 5 of the law. These sections focused on a person who "committed certain offenses against a persecuted person because of [or in connection with] his being a persecuted person" under the Nazi regime (Section 2) or a person who "during the period of the Nazi regime, in an enemy country, was instrumental in delivering up a persecuted person to an enemy administration" (Section 5) or on actions performed "in a place of confinement on behalf of an enemy administration or of the person in charge of that place of confinement" (Section 4). For conviction on the basis of these sections there was no need to prove identification with and motivation similar to that of the Nazis. The courts continuously convicted defendants on these lesser counts of the law.[33]

The Barenblat Case

The approximately forty trials at the district court level against collaborators continued uninterrupted until the early 1960s. It was the case of *Attorney General v. Hirsch Barenblat*, which began as a typical case against a collaborator, that would mark, with one exception, the end of the collaborator trials and the end of the implementation of the Nazis and Nazi Collaborators (Punishment) Law as it pertained to putative Jewish collaborators.[34]

On February 5, 1964, the Tel Aviv District Court convicted the assistant conductor of the Israeli Opera House, Hirsch Barenblat, on five counts of serving as a Nazi collaborator in occupied Europe. The court found that between 1941 and 1943 Barenblat served first as deputy commander and then as commander of the Jewish police in the ghetto of Będzin in the Zagłębie region in Upper Silesia, where he surrendered dozens of orphaned Jewish children to the Nazis, prevented Jews from escaping during a Nazi selection for deportation to Auschwitz, beat Jewish residents in two instances, and in a different event turned Jews over to the Nazis for shipment to forced labor camps.

Defense attorney Aryeh Rosenblum argued that in accordance with the interpretation of Section 1 of the law by the courts, it was also necessary, in the case of turning Jews over to the Nazis for forced labor, to prove that the defendant shared the Nazis' motivations. The court rejected this claim: "It is not a fundamental part of the offense that the defendant have the same malicious motivation with regard to the persecuted person as the hostile regime had with regard to the handing over, but it is enough that his action assist that handing over."[35] In this instance the court upheld the precedent that outside Section 1 all other offenses included in the Nazis and Nazi Collaborators (Punishment) Law did not require parallel motivation. The verdict continued in the same vein.

> Indeed, what is astonishing and typical of this historical period is that in this time of extraordinary pressure all moral judgments and values had changed and small people, educated and likable people, did not refuse a saving anchor even if it meant taking part in the handing over of their brethren Jews to the murderous Nazis. . . . The Israeli legislator who spoke in 1950 in the name of the people did not want to forgive these pleasant people, normal in normal times, who sinned towards the nation for selfish reasons in abnormal times.[36]

The Tel Aviv District Court sentenced Barenblat to five years in prison.

Between the lines of the verdict one can also read a condemnation of another offender: the Judenrat as an institution. In the twelfth count of the original indictment, the prosecution charged Barenblat with having "held a position in a hostile organization 'on behalf of the Judenrat and the Nazi administration,'" an offense based on Section 3 of the law.[37] For the first time in the collaborator trials, a prosecutor attempted to have the Judenrat categorized as a hostile organization, but after presenting his case, and in all likelihood because of political pressure, David Libai, the prosecutor in this case, informed the court that he would remove this charge. However, in its verdict the district court indicated that it viewed the Judenrat of Będzin in negative terms and would have pronounced it a hostile organization had it been given the opportunity to do so. Indeed, in the eyes of the judges, the Jewish councils represented the epitome of the Nazis' deployment of "human weaknesses" for their own purposes. According to the district court:

> Those Jewish councils, Judenräte in their language . . . as if they were the continuation of previous Jewish communities—[the Germans] forcibly enslaved them to do their will and gradually turned them, through threats, great pressure, extortion, and punishment, on the one hand, and false promises, acts of treachery, and promotion of false hopes, on the other hand, into tools in their hands, which eased their despised business. [The Germans] gave them [the Jewish councils] the sort of internal autonomy granted to submissive serfs and turned them into persecutors of their brothers. And the power they placed in their hands was the Jewish police.[38]

The district court saw in Jewish councils in general and Jewish policemen like Barenblat in particular "submissive serfs" of the Germans, who out of "human weakness" served the Nazis and assisted them in their murderous task.[39]

The Supreme Court's *Barenblat* Opinion: An End to the Collaborator Trials

Upon hearing the pronouncement of the verdict of the Tel Aviv District Court, which sentenced him to five years in prison, Barenblat immediately appealed to the Israeli Supreme Court in Jerusalem. In all previous appeals of Nazi collaborators, the Supreme Court had not once overturned a conviction in its entirety; it had only overturned one count or commuted sentences. The Barenblat case, however, would change this.[40]

CHANGING LEGAL PERCEPTIONS OF "NAZI COLLABORATORS"

In refuting the decision of the District Court, the Supreme Court justices cited the twelfth count of the original indictment, which asserted that as the deputy commander and commander of the Jewish police the defendant had "held a position in an enemy organization 'on behalf of the *Judenrat and the administration one of whose aims was to assist in carrying out the activities* of an enemy administration against persecuted persons,'" a count that, as mentioned earlier, had been removed from the indictment by the prosecution.[41] In his concurring opinion to the lead opinion that was written by Justice Cohn, Justice Yitzhak Olshan, the president of the Supreme Court, lashed out at the prosecution for the wording of this charge: "For all the criticisms leveled against the methods of the Judenrat, or the Jewish police, I have yet to hear an opinion that their existence resulted 'from the aim' they set themselves of 'assisting in the carrying out of the activities of an enemy administration against persecuted persons.'"[42] Although the Judenrat did "assist" the Nazis by fulfilling their commands, the Supreme Court asserted, the Judenrat had never shared the "aims" or intentions of the Nazis. Justice Moshe Landau wrote in his concurring opinion that "the prosecution committed a mistake in dealing with this particularly sensitive issue when it inserted in the indictment filed in the district court a charge which sought to declare the Jewish militia of Będzin a 'hostile organization.'"[43] The Supreme Court took this uncommon move of criticizing a count that the prosecution had dropped, probably because it reflected in the justices' minds the zeal of the prosecution to convict a Jewish collaborator, a viewpoint the court aimed to change in this ruling.

Ultimately, the Supreme Court reversed Barenblat's conviction on all counts, an acquittal that in my opinion emanated more from the court's goal of putting an end to the trials against Nazi collaborators than from a strict reading of the law. Some of the reasoning, especially that of the lead opinion by Justice Cohn (who, as mentioned earlier, was one of the initiators of the law but appeared to have changed his mind), rested on splitting hairs between the wording and the structure of the law. The strongest example of this fine reading is reflected in the Supreme Court's criticism of the lower court's conviction of Barenblat for "delivering up" (*mesira* in Hebrew) to the Nazis a "persecuted person" during an *Aktion* that took place at the Będzin sport field on August 12, 1942. The district court found that Barenblat had prevented a group of Jews selected by the Nazis for a transport to Auschwitz from escaping to a group destined for release or to one destined for forced labor. At the end of the selection, the Nazis deported those thousands of Jews who were in the first group to Auschwitz.

In explaining the reasoning for the court's reversal of Barenblat's conviction for "delivering up" a "persecuted person" (Section 5 of the law), Cohn did not dispute any of the testimonies or facts established by the district court. Rather, he drew two distinctions to support the acquittal. First, wrote Justice Cohn, when Barenblat prevented Jews from escaping from one group to another at the sports field, Nazi soldiers had already surrounded them. Thus the Jews were already in the hands of the Germans, and even by preventing them from escaping from one group to another, Barenblat did not hand them over. Cohn chose to ignore the fact established by the lower court that in keeping the two groups separate from one another, Barenblat had determined which individuals would be turned over to the Germans and which would be saved.[44]

A second distinction that Cohn drew was that the notion of "delivering up" as stated in the law was unlike the "prevention of escape" (*meniat-berichah* in Hebrew): "May we say that the prevention of escape from an enemy administration is equivalent to delivering up to that administration? I am afraid that in so doing we exceed by far the widest meaning which the term 'delivering up' bears."[45] Yet Cohn never explicated what qualitative distinction he saw between the two terms. After all, in every handing over there is also a component of prevention of escape, and because Cohn drew a distinction between the two, it would have been reasonable to expect that he would have explained the distinction between them, but he did not.

The Supreme Court also justified overturning the lower court's verdict on the grounds that Barenblat had been convicted of surrendering orphaned children to the Nazis on the basis of a single testimony. Yet the district courts had previously convicted defendants based on a single testimony and the Supreme Court had upheld those convictions. For example, in the 1952 case of *Jacob Honigman v. Attorney General* the Supreme Court upheld Honigman's conviction on various counts, most of these convictions supported by the testimony of a single witness. In Honigman's case the Supreme Court justified reliance on sole testimonies given years after the event by distinguishing these testimonies from regular testimonies. "No, these kinds of acts do not easily erode from the mind of a person, and if the [district] Court says it believes the [single] witnesses who described this, we shall not come and contradict its view," wrote the justices.

Furthermore, Section 15 of the Nazis and Nazi Collaborators (Punishment) Law explicitly allowed, "in an action for an offence under this law, [that] the court may deviate from the rules of evidence if it is satisfied that this will promote the ascertainment of the truth and the just handling of the case."[46] In scores of Nazi collaborator trials the courts accepted evidence based on hearsay and rumors.

Given that the courts relied on such testimonies, it seems that the district court had a basis for its legal conviction of Barenblat for surrendering dozens of orphaned children to the Nazis, a guilty verdict based on the single testimony of Abraham F., a witness whom the lower court had found to be reliable; however, the Supreme Court's justices chose to overturn the conviction of Barenblat because it was based on a single testimony.

In his verdict Chief Justice Olshan articulated a new and unprecedented argument not heard in any of the previous trials. The justice asserted that in the case of a defendant who was a persecuted person himself, as were all defendants in these trials (save Andrej Banik), such a single testimony could not stand alone. He explained that unlike the case of a member in a hostile organization, such as the SS, where the testimony of one witness would suffice for conviction because the accused has "a blot" on him, in the Barenblat case, "belonging to the camp of the persecuted is certainly no blot; when the alleged offense is proved against such an accused by only one witness, manifold caution is required in the nature of things ... and sometimes it will be dangerous to convict on the evidence of one witness, however credible."[47]

As Hemda Gur-Arie points out, contrary to the basic legal principle that the court should weigh the quality of the testimonies on their own merit, in the Barenblat case the Supreme Court based its overturning of Barenblat's conviction in the lower court on its impressions of the defendant and his social context. The court's verdict came in part from Barenblat's membership in the group of persecuted individuals, a status that had no direct bearing on his surrendering of orphaned children to the Germans.[48]

In the same spirit of the "blot on him" argument, Chief Justice Olshan gave a novel interpretation of the Nazis and Nazi Collaborators (Punishment) Law, a law that, according to one scholar, Olshan viewed as "a bad law."[49] This new interpretation, which had no clear grounding in the law itself (except for the sentencing phase alone), distinguished between two types of criminals: (1) the persecutor who was a member of an enemy organization; and (2) "'persecuted people'—the victims of the 'persecutors,' who committed offenses against other persecuted people."[50] By way of this new distinction in the law, the court demanded a greater burden of evidence from the prosecution when it brought Jews to justice who were accused of collaboration with the Nazis than in cases of any other type of other offender.

After describing different contemporary views related to the role of the Judenräte in the Holocaust, Justice Olshan concluded that the appropriateness of the actions of Jewish collaborators should not be determined in court. "It is clear that the question ... which line the leader [of a Judenrat] should have followed, is one for history and not for a court before which a persecuted person is brought to face criminal charges under the law."⁵¹

Although no documentation exists, it is difficult to escape the impression that the Supreme Court had first determined its goal of clearing Barenblat as a means of ending the collaborator trials and only then searched for ways to achieve the goal of overturning the defendant's conviction in the district court. In effect, the Supreme Court deemed the prosecution of people like Barenblat unfair. Referring to the district court's verdict, Justice Moshe Landau wrote:

> And it is also the bitter truth that "in the atmosphere of [the] extraordinary pressure of those days, moral concepts and values changed." But it would be hypocritical and arrogant on our part—on the part of those who never stood in their place ... to make this truth a cause for criticizing those "little men" who did not rise to the heights of moral supremacy, when mercilessly oppressed by a regime whose first aim was to remove the image of man from off their faces. And we are not permitted to interpret the elements of the special offenses defined in the Nazis and Nazi Collaborators (Punishment) Law, 1950, by some standard of moral conduct which only few are capable of reaching. One cannot impute to the legislator an intention to demand a level of conduct that the community cannot sustain.⁵²

Here Landau expressed an opinion that essentially foreclosed the possibility of sitting in judgment of putative Jewish collaborators with the Nazis, an opinion that questioned the feasibility and wisdom of trying them in Israeli courts. Landau, who had headed the panel of the Eichmann trial and had heard hours upon hours of testimonies about life and death under Nazi rule, indicated that judgment of those "extraordinary" circumstances was suited to the realm of history but not to a court of law.⁵³

The court's reversal of the view of trying collaborators in Israel came within the context of a larger social change of their treatment in Israel's public sphere. One expression of this change of perspective came in the responses to an argument put forth by Hannah Arendt in *Eichmann in Jerusalem*, where she wrote that the leadership of the Jewish communities was "responsible" for the devastating results of the Holocaust. In her view:

> Wherever Jews lived, there were recognized Jewish leaders, and this leadership, almost without exception, cooperated in one way or another, for one reason or another, with the Nazis. The whole truth was that if the Jewish people had really been unorganized and leaderless, there would

have been chaos and plenty of misery but the total number of victims would hardly have been between four and a half and six million people."[54]

Responding to Arendt, the renowned Jewish scholar Gershom Scholem wrote, "There were among them [the Jewish leadership] also many people in no way different from ourselves, who were compelled to make terrible decisions in circumstances that we cannot even begin to reproduce or reconstruct. I do not know whether they were right or wrong. Nor do I presume to judge. I was not there."[55]

Scholem takes an ahistorical viewpoint here, placing the actions of the Judenräte as standing outside history, beyond comprehension. For Scholem the events of the Holocaust stand in a unique historical time. When it comes to the victims (although not necessarily so to the perpetrators), "We cannot even begin to reproduce or reconstruct." The argument of "I was not there" would come to dominate and stifle any debate about the position of the victims.

In a 1963 publication Ernst Simon wrote: "One should completely deny the formulation that creates a parallel between 'the Nazi authorities' and 'the Jewish authorities,' as it comes to blur the basic distinction between those commanding the murder in light-headedness and the situation of those who in all probability in most instances attempted with bad conscience to minimize and slow down the pace of killings."[56] To the members of the Jewish councils Simon attributed a role of subversion against the incentives of the Nazis, of aiming to minimize as much as possible the result of their murderous goals. This was a view new to the period, one that placed the Judenräte on a different moral ground from that previously seen and portrayed its members as individuals who implicitly sabotaged the German plan and thus as resisters to the Nazis.

In an article from the same year titled "Eichmann in New York," Marion Mushkat, a professor of international law at the Hebrew University of Jerusalem who hailed from Poland, expressed a similar opinion, viewing the Judenräte as an institution whose motivations and actions focused on the good of the wider Jewish populace. How had Arendt come to the conclusion of Jewish cooperation with the Nazis, asked Mushkat. "These arguments ... have no basis.... Any harm that arose from these quisling-like governments came not out of bad intention in the first place; even in the cases of treason and attempts to save individuals at the cost of the masses—everything was done out of true dedication, so as to lighten the burden and allow the saving of the persecuted, to act against the hunger and sickness and to give a [supportive] hand to the underground," he wrote.[57] Beyond Scholem's "I was not there" argument, Simon and Mushkat present here a new image of the Judenräte and of the Jewish police under their control. Unlike earlier times, by the 1960s these groups were seen, first and foremost, as victims and as those who acted against the motivation and intentions of the Nazis. In instances in which Jewish policemen had turned Jews over to the Nazis, the critics argued, they acted to counter the Nazis' goals.[58]

In this newly expressed view the critics defined true collaborators as those individuals with motivations equal to those of the perpetrator, which clearly was not the case with the Judenräte. This view went beyond the outcome of the Jungster trial, which demanded identification with the perpetrators only for crimes against humanity. In the view of the critics all actions taken by Jews during World War II, including assault, abduction, murder, or any other acts against individuals, demanded a motivation equal to that of the Nazis in order to qualify as collaboration. For the first time a view held by key figures in Israel's intellectual elite portrayed all these actions as outside the responsibility of Jewish collaborators and thus as actions that were not criminal and not morally dubious.

As David Engel points out, this view is quite surprising given the harsh criticism and hatred that surfaced in the 1950s toward the Judenräte in the public sphere in Israel.[59] However, the trial and conviction of Adolf Eichmann presented the Israeli public, as well as the world public, with an image of a "total villain," one who epitomized true evil in the eyes of many. This image of Eichmann replaced the previous image of the archetypical villain, that of the Jewish Nazi collaborator. Following the Eichmann trial, an image of "pure victims" took shape, which saw *all* Jews under Nazi rule as heroic and morally superior, as victims who, in their efforts to survive, had not acted in ways that jeopardized other victims, even if they had served as Jewish policemen or *Blockälteste*. The victims' image stood in clear and direct contrast to that of the total villain, Adolf Eichmann. Within this framework the view of Judenrat members and kapos as collaborators could not be upheld.[60]

In the legal arena the reversal of Barenblat's conviction brought an almost complete end to trials against accused Jewish collaborators with the Nazis. In May 1964 the Office of the Attorney General received an anonymous letter that alleged collaboration of a certain R. G. with the Romanian fascist regime. In the internal correspondence of the Ministry of Justice, an official in Israel's Office of the Attorney General wrote that "in light of the result of the Barenblat appeal, I do not believe that there is room to open an investigation in a complaint like this that addresses the actions of surrendering Jews by a Jewish policeman as part of his job in the years 1942–1944."[61] In June of that year the Ministry of Justice sent a letter to all district attorneys, according to which, "One should not submit a criminal indictment based on the Nazis and Nazi Collaborators (Punishment)

Law 1950 without prior consent from the attorney general."⁶² With this, the collaborator trials in Israel for all intents and purposes came to an end.

Epilogue

On the evening of August 5, 1971, Sonia P., who had immigrated to Israel from the Soviet Union just a few years earlier, finished watching a TV program and went into her kitchen in her Rishon LeZion apartment. She stood by the kitchen window and looked out. A car stopped in front of her neighbor's home. Two teenage boys emerged, followed by a red-haired woman, all evidently tourists. "That moment I fainted," she said a day later at the police station. The red-haired woman who stepped out the car was Loba Meschkup (Gricmacher), Sonia's *Lagerälteste*—camp senior—in the Landsberg concentration camp in Germany.⁶³

On that day Sonia not only phoned the police but also informed her sister. The word about the arrival in Israel from Germany of "Red-Haired Loba," as she was known by former inmates, spread to several survivors. Some of these survivors showed interest in Red-Haired Loba not only for who she was but also for who her husband was, Isaac Gricmacher, a notorious former kapo. The police arrested her, and the prosecution deliberated whether to present another case of a collaborator after it had decided to stop these cases following the Barenblat trial. Probably because she lived in Germany and because influential people pursued her, among others, District Court Judge Aryeh Sagalson and Dov Shilansky, who would later become a Knesset member and its speaker, the Attorney General's office decided to make an exception in this case and filed charges against Loba Gricmacher at the Tel Aviv District Court.⁶⁴

At the culmination of Gricmacher's trial in September 1972, the court convicted her on two counts, one of assault and the other of breaking the finger of an inmate. The judge sentenced her to three months of imprisonment. With this case the trials in Israel of Jewish collaborators with the Nazis concluded.

Notes

I wish to thank and acknowledge the support of the Gerda Henkel Stiftung, the Aharon Barak Center for Interdisciplinary Legal Research at the Hebrew University, the National Endowment for the Humanities (NEH), and the Memorial Foundation for Jewish Culture. I would also like to thank the following individuals for reading and commenting on this chapter: Raanan Forshner, Joshua Schoffman, and Douglas Morris. The opinions and views expressed in this chapter are strictly mine.

1. Because of privacy issues, I am prohibited from giving the full names of the witnesses in the trials, and therefore I use their first names only.

2. Testimony of Yerachmiel Y., March 18, 1951, *Attorney General v. Joseph Paal*, Magistrate Court Judicial Inquiry, located in the District Court file, Tel Aviv District Court, Israel National Archives (hereafter ISA)/Record Group (hereafter RG)/32/LAW/48/51, p. 7.
3. Testimony of Yerachmiel Y., 10.
4. Dov, "Question to Minister of Justice," *Ha-boker* (February 28, 1949). For more about Siegel and his trial, see *Attorney General v. Julius Siegel*, Tel Aviv District Court, September 29, 1951, ISA/RG/32/475/52; for a detailed analysis of this case, see Rivka Brot, "Julius Siegel: A 'Kapo' in Four (Judicial) Acts," *Dapim: Studies on the Shoah* 25 (2011): 65–127. To the best of my knowledge, in no instance did the State of Israel extradite to any country anyone accused of committing crimes during World War II.
5. July 6, 1949, ISA/RG/74/Israel Police (hereafter IP)/2162/45.
6. The title of the Israeli law uses literarily the term "The Nazis and Their Helpers" to describe the collaborators. However, I use the term "collaborators" throughout this article because this is the word used in different documents translated into English and because it reflects the common view held among legislators, prosecutors, and others at the time.
7. October 21, 1949, ISA/RG/74/IP/2162/45.
8. This set of trials, in which between 1950 and 1972 Israel prosecuted alleged collaborators with the Nazis, are discussed as a general historical episode by Hanna Yablonka, "Ha-hok le-asiyat din be-natsim uve-ozreihem: Hebet nosaf li-she'alt ha-yisra'elim, ha-nitsolim veha-sho'ah" [The Nazis and Nazi Collaborators (Punishment) Law: An Further Aspect of the Question of Israelis, Survivors, and the Holocaust], *Cathedra* 82 (December 1996): 135–52; Yechiam Weitz, "Ha-hok le-asiyat din be-natsim uve-ozreihem ve-yahasah shel ha-hevra ha-yisra'elit bi-shenot ha-hamishim la-sho'ah ule-nitsoleihah" [The Nazis and Nazi Collaborators (Punishment) Law and the Attitude of Israeli Society in the 1950s toward the Holocaust and the Survivors], *Cathedra* 82 (December 1996): 153–64; and Orna Ben-Naftali and Yogev Tuval, "Punishing International Crimes Committed by the Persecuted: The Kapo Trials in Israel (1950s–1960s)," *Journal of International Criminal Justice* 4 (2006): 128–78. Other articles (which I refer to later) center on specific trials and examine them mostly from a perspective of legal history. In this chapter I focus on the development of the trials as a whole from a cultural and social perspective.
9. *Hatsa'ot hok* 36 (February 28, 1950). See also "Principles of International Law Recognized in the Charter of the Nuremberg Tribunal and in the Judgment of the Tribunal," *Yearbook of the International Law Commission* 2 (1950): par. 97.
10. *Devrei ha-Knesset* (March 27, 1950): 1148, 1161.
11. Yaakov Gil, "The Law for Punishing the Nazis," *Ha-boker* (April 13, 1950).
12. For the wording of the law, see www.mfa.gov.il/MFA/MFAArchive/1950_1959/Nazis%20and%20Nazi%20Collaborators%20-Punishment-%20Law-%20571 (accessed August 18, 2014).
13. *Hatsa'ot hok* 36 (February 28, 1950): sec. 10.

14. Knesset Archives, Jerusalem, Protocols of the Knesset Constitution, Law, and Justice Committee, protocol 29/2, July 12, 1950, p. 16.
15. *Devrei ha-Knesset* (August 1, 1950): 2394–95.
16. Protocols of the Knesset Constitution, Law, and Justice Committee, protocol, 29/2, 6.
17. Gil, "Law for Punishing the Nazis."
18. Protocols of the Knesset Constitution, Law, and Justice Committee, protocol 29/2, 18.
19. Protocols of the Knesset Constitution, Law, and Justice Committee, protocol 29/2, 18–21. In years to come, Cohn would attempt to minimize his role in promoting and defining this law aimed at Jewish collaborators. In his autobiography, he wrote that he aimed the law against Nazi criminals; he portrays himself as the defender of Jewish collaborators who were put on trial, pointing to his acquittal of Hirsch Barenblat. See Haim Cohen, *Mavo ishi: Otobiyografiyah* (Or-Yehudah, Israel: Kinneret, Zmorah-Bitan, Devir, 2005), 336.
20. www.mfa.gov.il/MFA/MFAArchive/1950_1959/Nazis%20and%20Nazi%20Collaborators%20-Punishment-%20Law-%20571 (accessed August 14, 2014).
21. English version of the law, in Attorney General, War Crimes 7/1949–11/1950, ISA/RG/130/MFA/1884/6.
22. The exact number of investigations remains unknown because the police files in the Israel National Archives remain sealed. However, in November 1951 one police officer, Josef Singer, testified in court that he himself had been in charge of 350 investigations. See *Attorney General v. Elsa Trunk*, Tel Aviv District Court, November 29, 1951, ISA/RG/32/2/51, p. 56.
23. English version of the law, in Attorney General, War Crimes 7/1949–11/1950, ISA/RG/130/MFA/1884/6.
24. *Attorney General v. Andrej Banik*, Haifa District Court, April 17, 1951, Indictment, ISA/RG/33/LAW/121/51, p. 1.
25. *Attorney General v. Hezekiel Jungster*, Tel Aviv District Court, September 9, 1951, Indictment, ISA/RG/32/9/51, p. 1.
26. *Attorney General vs. Hezekiel Jungster*, in *Peskaim* 9/51 (1951), vol. 5, p. 163.
27. *Attorney General v. Elsa Trunk*, Tel Aviv District Court, September 1950, Judiciary Inquiry, ISA/RG/32/2/51, p. 1.
28. *Attorney General v. Elsa Trunk*, Tel Aviv District Court, October 16, 1950, Verdict of Judiciary Inquiry, ISA/RG/32/2/51, p. 35.
29. *Sefer ha-Hukim* 57 (August 9, 1950): 282.
30. *Attorney General v. Hezekiel Jungster*, Tel Aviv District Court, April 1, 1952, ISA/RG/32/LAW/9/51, pp. 176–77.
31. *Attorney General v. Jungster*, in *Pesakim* 9/51 (1951), vol. 5, p. 178.
32. The Supreme Court ruled in Jungster's case on the same day that the hearing took place and promised to publish its opinion later; however, it seems that the justices

never did so. Two and a half months after the ruling, Hebrew University professor Benjamin Akzin requested a copy of the opinion, but the court secretary informed him that it had not yet been written. Furthermore, in no other court proceedings did I find any reference to the full Supreme Court opinion from this case. See *Hezekiel Jungster v. Attorney General*, April 4, 1952, ISA/RG/30/LAW/7/52. Because of Jungster's health condition, Israel's police minister pardoned him from his two-year sentence in early July 1952. He died a natural death a few days later in his home. See Kibel hanina u-met [Received Pardon and Died], *Herut* (July 18, 1952).

33. One exception in which the state attorney charged the defendant with crimes against humanity was the 1959 case of Abraham Tikochinsky; however, he was acquitted. It remains unclear why in this case the state attorney did charge the defendant with crimes against humanity. See Tel Aviv District Court, January 30, 1959, ISA/RG/32/LAW/3/59. In two other cases, those of Alter Fogel and Hanokh Baiski, the indictments included crimes from Section 1 of the law; however, because in both cases a plea bargain was reached, an uncommon practice at the time, this seems to be part of a negotiation practice. For the case against Fogel, see Tel Aviv District Court, March 13, 1956, ISA/RG/32/LAW/159/56; and for the case against Baiski, see Tel Aviv District Court, September 10, 1959, ISA/RG/32/LAW/59/137.

34. As pointed out by Hemda Gur-Arie, the Supreme Court did not draw a distinction between the Judenrat and the Jewish police and saw them as one and the same entity (the Judenrat was the Jewish council established by the Nazis, and the Jewish police was under its jurisdiction to enact and implement Nazi decisions). Hemda Gur-Arie, "'Sham've-'Kan': Mishpato shel Hirsh Barenblat" ["There" and "Here": The Trial of Hirsh Barenblat], *Iyunei Mishpat* 34 (2011): 256n64. For a close analysis of the Barenblat trial, see Avihu Ronen, Hadas Agmon, and Asaf Danziger, "Collaborator or Would-Be Rescuer? The Barenblat Trial and the Image of a Judenrat Member in 1960s Israel," *Yad Vashem Studies* 39.1 (2011): 117–67. Avihu Ronen has also published an important book about the events in Będzin as seen through the diaries of his mother, Haykah Klinger: Avihu Ronen, *Nidonah le-hayim: Yomanah ve-hayeha shel Haikeh Klinger* (Haifa: University of Haifa; and Tel Aviv: Yediot aharonot and Sifre hemed, 2011). Also see Idit Zertal, *Ha-umah veha-mavet: Historyah, zikaron, politikah* (Or Yehuda, Israel: Devir, 2002). For the historical context in which Barenblat acted and a discussion of the history of civilian Nazi administrators and their actions in Będzin, see Mary Fullbrook, *A Small Town Near Auschwitz: Ordinary Nazis and the Holocaust* (Oxford, UK: Oxford University Press, 2012).

35. *Attorney General v. Hirsch Barenblat*, Tel Aviv District Court, February 5, 1964, ISA/RG/32/15/63, pp. 4–5.

36. Verdict of Tel Aviv District Court, *Attorney General v. Hirsch Barenblat*, Tel Aviv District Court, February 5, 1964, ISA/RG/32/15/63, p. 11.

37. *Barenblat v. Attorney General*, Supreme Court Decision, [May 22, 1964], DP: ISA/RG/30/77/64. English translation available at elyon1.court.gov.il/files_eng/64/770/000/Z01/64000770.z01.pdf (accessed August 18, 2014), p. 39 (emphasis in original).

38. *Attorney General v. Hirsch Barenblat*, Tel Aviv District Court, February 5, 1964, ISA/RG/32/15/63, p. 3. This negative view of the Judenräte by the district court was also sensed by Justice Olshan. See *Barenblat v. Attorney General*, Supreme Court Decision, p. 40.
39. *Attorney General v. Hirsch Barenblat*, Tel Aviv District Court, February 5, 1964, ISA/RG/32/15/63, p. 3.
40. For previous cases in which the Supreme Court commuted the sentence, see, for example, *Jacob Honigman v. Attorney General*, 22/52 Piskei Din, vol. 7, pp. 296–305; and *Paal v. Attorney General*, 119/51 Piskei Din, vol. 6, pp. 498–510.
41. *Barenblat v. Attorney General*, Supreme Court Decision, 39 (emphasis in original).
42. *Barenblat v. Attorney General*, Supreme Court Decision, 39.
43. *Barenblat v. Attorney General*, Supreme Court Decision, 41.
44. The translation of the term "delivering up" into English is based on an English translation of the law. See www.mfa.gov.il/MFA/MFAArchive/1950_1959/Nazis%20and%20Nazi%20Collaborators%20-Punishment-%20Law-%20571 (accessed August 18, 2014).
45. *Barenblat v. Attorney General*, Supreme Court Decision, 11–12.
46. *Sefer ha-Hukim* 57 (August 9, 1950): 284, par. 15.
47. *Sefer ha-Hukim* 57 (August 9, 1950): 26.
48. Gur-Arie, "'Sham' ve-'Kan,'" 273–74.
49. Gur-Arie, "'Sham' ve-'Kan,'" 263.
50. *Barenblat v. Attorney General*, Supreme Court Decision, 26. The law made this type of distinction between persecutor and persecuted persons, which Olshan addresses *only* in the sentencing clause but *not* in determining the guilt of a defendant. In fact, Olshan's interpretation stands in stark contrast to the intention of the Knesset members who would not allow for such a distinction and in contrast to his own initial response to the appeal in the Paal case.
51. *Barenblat v. Attorney General*, Supreme Court Decision, 34.
52. *Barenblat v. Attorney General*, Supreme Court Decision, 42.
53. Also, Cohn came to change his initial opinion about the wisdom of trying the Jewish collaborators of the Nazis. See *Barenblat v. Attorney General*, Supreme Court Decision, 9–10.
54. Hannah Arendt, *Eichmann in Jerusalem: A Report on the Banality of Evil* (Middlesex, UK: Penguin Books, 1964), 111.
55. Gershom Scholem to Hannah Arendt, June 23, 1963, in Ron H. Feldman, ed., *The Jews as Pariah: Jewish Identity and Politics in the Modern Age* (New York: Grove Press, 1978), 242–43. On the sources of Scholem's view on the Holocaust as one that emanates in a mystical view of Jewish history, see Moshe Halbertal, "Banality, Mystification, Radicalism: An Examination of the Problem of Evil in the Wake of the Eichmann Trial," *Legacy* 4 (2011): 38–47.

56. Ernst Akiva Simon, "Diokna shel Hannah Arendt" [A Portrait of Hannah Arendt], *Molad* 21.179–180 (July–August 1963): 242–43.
57. Marion Muskhat, "Eichmann in New York," *Yediot Yad Vashem* 31 (December 1963): 10. In the same spirit, see Jacob Robinson, *And the Crooked Shall Be Made Straight: The Eichmann Trial, the Jewish Catastrophe, and Hannah Arendt's Narrative* (New York: Macmillan, 1965), 171, 223.
58. Robinson, *And the Crooked Shall Be Made Straight*, 205.
59. David Engel, *Historians of the Jews and the Holocaust* (Stanford, CA: Stanford University Press, 2010), 178.
60. Ben-Naftali and Tuval, "Punishing International Crimes," 177.
61. June 5, 1964, ISA/RG/74/G/5274/11.
62. June 15, 1964, ISA/RG/74/G/5274/11.
63. *The State of Israel v. Loba Gricmacher (Meschkup)*, August 20, 1971, ISA/RG/32/LAW/1116/71. See also Ahron Priel, "Tayeret yehudiya mi-germaniya to'amad le-din be-yisra'el al heyota 'kapo' be-mahane rikuz" [A Jewish Tourist Will Face Trial in Israel for Being a 'Kapo' in a Concentration Camp], *Maariv* (August 20, 1971).
64. For the prejudice against Jews who lived in Germany, see Anthony D. Kauders, *Unmögliche Heimat* (Munich: Deutsche Verlags-Anstalt, 2007), 33–36, 133–38.

12

The Gray Zone of Collaboration and the Israeli Courtroom

RIVKA BROT

The principal pitfall, in my opinion, that lies in wait for anyone who would conduct an objective trial concerning the behavior of those who took part in past actions—and even those in the recent past—stems from the fact that he [the judge] will not always strive to put himself in the shoes of the participants themselves; evaluate the problems they faced as they might have done; take into consideration sufficiently the needs of time and place, where they lived their lives; and understand life as they understood it.[1]

Prologue: Historical Reality in Juridical Language

Moshe (Marian) Puczyc and Mordechai Goldstein, Jewish residents of the Polish city of Ostrowiec,[2] were ordinary people whose lives were transformed by the tumult of war. They both served in the Jewish police force of the Ostrowiec ghetto and in the labor camp set up outside the city after the liquidation of the ghetto. In this chapter I focus on the legal proceedings conducted against them in an Israeli court: the trial of Puczyc, deputy commander of the ghetto police force and later the commander of the camp police force; and the trial of Goldstein, an "ordinary" policeman.[3] The tension between the historical sphere, namely, the attempt to comprehend the complex reality of the ghetto and the camp, and the legal domain, which sought to reduce this reality to unequivocal juridical categories, lies at the center of my discussion. As I show, both cases represent the difficulties of the criminal law in struggling with the Holocaust in general and in the gray zone of collaboration in particular. Notwithstanding the common denominator, each of these cases found its own way to deal with the complicated phenomenon of Jewish collaboration within the narrow framework of legal categories.

During Israel's early years, the survivors posed a palpable threat to the myth of the heroic "new Jew," and they were subjected to critical judgment and blame.[4] The Italian philosopher Giorgio Agamben suggests that "according to the law that what man despises is also what he fears resembles him, the *Muselmann* is universally avoided because everyone in the camp recognizes himself in his disfigured face."[5] The "new Israelis" likewise looked into the faces of the survivors and saw themselves, because they had, after all, come from the same Diaspora whose attributes they sought to erase, and it had only been by virtue of chance circumstances that they had been spared the fate of the survivors. Moreover, individual survival that was bereft of physical courage was not an eventuality that public discourse could entertain, all the more so if this was a matter of collaboration with the Germans as a means of survival, which was incompatible with the national ethos of the time.[6]

This is an appropriate place to mention that the Hebrew term *shituf pe'ula*, generally translated as "cooperation," by no means expresses the singularly negative connotation associated with the term *collaboration* in other languages, which denotes specifically cooperation with the enemy and implies perforce treason.[7] Quite ironically, these negative attitudes were actually reinforced by the survivors themselves through complaints that they lodged with the British Mandate police and later the Israeli police against other survivors whom they identified as former policemen, Judenrat members, or camp functionaries. This formed the social, cultural, and political backdrop to the Nazis and Nazi Collaborators (Punishment) Law of 1950 (5710 in the Jewish calendar), which was passed in August 1950 as a means of adjudicating mainly Jews suspected of collaboration with the Nazis rather than Nazi war criminals, because at that time it seemed inconceivable that a Nazi would be brought to trial in an Israeli court. Enacted only two years after Israel became an independent state, the law arrived too early to facilitate a historical perspective or an understanding of the lives of Jews during the Holocaust. Several dozen Jews were indicted under this law from the end of 1950 up to at least the early 1970s.[8] The press reported cases of people identified as former functionaries, generally through chance encounters in the streets, restaurants, parties, and elsewhere. The papers portrayed the commotion that occurred on these occasions and reported on subsequent arrests. After August 1950 many of these complaints turned into indictments in Israeli courts of law. The audience that attended the trials generally included survivors from the town, ghetto, or camp in which the accused had served.[9] Hanna Yablonka writes that in the Israeli context at the time, these trials were primarily "an internal affair in the life of the survivors."[10]

The Nazis and Nazi Collaborators (Punishment) Law was an attempt to conceptualize the destructive reality of the ghetto and the camp through categories derived from a sphere that seeks to impose a normative order that clearly distinguishes between right and wrong. The artificial transplantation of modern criminal law to a location in which the normal order had been overturned inevitably led to a clash between the modern state and "l'univers concentrationnaire."[11] Analysis of the testimonies and the judgments in the legal proceedings of both Puczyc and Goldstein also raises the question of whether it is possible to make value judgments about human situations in which the protagonists cannot be readily and clearly categorized as evil or good or as guilty or innocent within a judicial framework. The testimonies reveal a "gray zone," the expression coined by Primo Levi that denotes a sphere that is "poorly defined, where the two camps of masters and servants both diverge and converge. This gray zone possesses an incredibly complicated internal structure and contains within itself enough to confuse our need to judge."[12] The principal attributes of the gray zone are a restricted sphere of choice, difficulty in distinguishing between good and evil, collapse of the common values and morality, and the establishment of a moral code that fits the extreme circumstances in which preservation of life is the ultimate imperative. Puczyc and Goldstein operated within the gray zone of Ostrowiec until the dissolution of the ghetto and the labor camp. It was their gray zone as well as the gray zone of the entire Jewish population that was put on trial.

The narrative of the legal proceedings comprises not merely the stories of individual defendants but also the story of the Jewish police force, a body formed by order of the Nazis as the operational arm of the Judenrat. An official police force that possessed powers of enforcement had never been part of the Diaspora Jewish community's inner structure, because the Jews were subservient to the central regime regarding all matters pertaining to the enforcement of law and order. In this respect the Jewish ghetto police was an exceptional phenomenon and thus was perceived as a foreign element. Before the period of deportations, the policemen engaged in activities associated with the administration of life in the ghetto, such as combating crime, maintaining order, and levying taxes, but they also engaged in activities that were directly linked to the German occupation, such as rounding up Jews for the purpose of forced labor or collecting, quite frequently by force, various valuable objects from Jewish houses on orders from the Germans. The period that rendered the Jewish ghetto police force notorious was that of the mass deportations, when Jewish policemen were actively involved in locating the Jews' hiding places and transferring them to assembly points, accompanying people to the trains, and loading them into the boxcars.[13] The police force, which represented the Nazis for all practical purposes and was even identified with them, was generally the most hated body in most ghettos.[14] In the complicated and fraught reality in which Jews performed functions in the service of the Nazis, the Jewish police force, or the Jüdischer Ordnungsdienst (Jewish Order Service) as it was known in German, occupied a singular position. In this respect the Jewish police force in Ostrowiec, which was formed in spring 1941, was unexceptional, other than the fact that, contrary to most ghettos, it possessed greater authority and exerted more influence than the Judenrat.[15]

My proposed reading of the testimonies and judgments does not restrict itself to just the legal narrative, which addresses the determination of guilt or innocence. My reading seeks to add a further historical and cultural narrative to the self-explanatory legal narrative, a reading that derives from the realization that the testimonies are not merely a means of establishing guilt or innocence. The proposed reading also perceives the testimonies as a means of conveying the reality of life in the ghetto and the camp, a story that does not necessarily involve the forbidden acts ascribed to the defendants.[16] This historical and cultural reading seeks to comprehend the total collapse of all that was familiar in the world to Ostrowiec's Jews, a reality that defies criminal categories and therefore can hardly be "heard" by the law. Through this historical and cultural reading I seek to reveal the tension between the gray zone of everyday life and the legal discourse that seeks to paint the reality of the ghetto and the camp in black (the prosecution) and white (the defense). I have no intention of resolving this tension but merely seek to expose it and to understand its origins.

The defendants themselves realized that in order to explain the unique connotations of "injury" or "assault" in the ghetto in relation to the meaning of these terms as they appear in the Nazis and Nazi Collaborators (Punishment) Law,[17] they would have to expand the boundaries of the legal narrative. This was the only way to explain how "injury" or "assault" lost their "criminal" meaning and became an act of everyday life in the ghetto or an act of survival. Thus the testimonies enable us to begin to comprehend how acts committed by the policemen that are punishable from the perspective of Israeli law could be considered normative actions on the part of the policemen-defendants when one observes them from the perspective of the ghetto or the camp.[18] The narrative that emerges reveals that human life, even at the lowest rung of existence, is an intricate web of relationships, ties, and individual stories that are not contained in the uniform mold into which both contemporary public discourse in Israel and the legal process sought to place them. The legal files, crumbling with age in the Israel State Archive, bear witness to a painful and tormented human world that broke free of the boundaries of juridical language and was related in an archaic form of Hebrew, for the most part translated from the Yiddish.

This chapter is broken into two main sections. The first presents an analysis of the testimonies and judgment in the Puczyc trial, and the second analyzes the testimonies and judgment in the Goldstein trial. Both cases manifest the tension between the historical and the judicial spheres, between the reality of the gray zone and the binary nature of legal thought.

The Commander: Moshe Puczyc

Moshe (Marian) Puczyc was born in Warsaw in 1910. He received a broad education, spoke Hebrew already as a youngster, and came from a Zionist background. As he related in his testimony, he completed his studies at a Warsaw high school, continued to study at a Polish college in the Department of Administrative Law, and took a course in political science.[19] In 1936 he began to work as secretary to Dr. Emil Sommerstein, head of the Jewish delegation to the Polish Sejm, and he subsequently became the director of this delegation's archive until the outbreak of war. After the war began, he moved to Ostrowiec, where he was appointed head of the Judenrat's sanitation department in 1941. In his testimony he recounts that the head of the Judenrat, Yitshak Rubinstein, asked the Zionists to volunteer to perform various functions under the auspices of the Judenrat. Some time later, on the initiative of the head of the Judenrat, Puczyc was appointed deputy commander of the Jewish police force. The historian Aharon Weiss notes that the appointment was apparently made by virtue of family connections, because Puczyc was the son-in-law of Judenrat member Ya'akov Mintzberg.[20]

From the outset Puczyc came to prominence as a strong individual who overshadowed the police commander and forged ties with Judenrat functionaries and with the Nazis. When the police force commander was murdered by the Nazis early in the summer of 1944, just before the dissolution of the labor camp, Puczyc was chosen to replace him and was, as he himself remarked, "omnipotent." Upon the dissolution of the camp, Puczyc was deported to Auschwitz together with the remaining Jews in the camp. When the war ended, Puczyc made his way to Munich, where he was elected to the Central Committee of Liberated Jews in the American Zone of Occupied Germany, on which he served as the first general secretary. In addition, he became a member of the central committee of the United Zionist Organization in Germany.[21] He immigrated to Israel in 1948 and worked at the Interior Ministry before his arrest.

THE PROSECUTION: "THE MASTER OF LIFE AND DEATH"

In September 1950 Puczyc was indicted in the Tel Aviv District Court after an investigating judge in the Magistrate's Court found that there were grounds for putting him on trial.[22] The indictment listed thirteen separate counts, among which were indictments under Article 1 of the law, namely, war crimes and crimes against humanity, which carried a mandatory death penalty.

As is customary in criminal trials, the prosecution portrayed Puczyc as a rational, autonomous person in control of his life, both with regard to his choice to accept his role in the Jewish police and through the choices he made while functioning in his position. From the prosecution's perspective the fact that Puczyc was a Jew living in a ghetto and a camp, subject to the Nazis' authority and, like the rest of Jews, eventually destined for extermination, did not impinge on his freedom of choice. But the prosecution went further, presenting testimonies that cast a dark shadow over Puczyc's personality to reinforce the image of the defendant as someone who chose to abuse his power and authority partly because of his negative personality traits. This created an anomalous situation in the courtroom by applying a liberal line of thought to the extreme circumstances in which people lived during the Holocaust.

Most of the prosecution witnesses focused on the assertion that the defendant possessed the power to decide how to treat the members of the community. One of many examples is provided by a prosecution witness who maintained, "I don't know from whom the defendant received orders. . . . I believe he did whatever he wanted."[23] To underline his evil behavior, the witnesses compared Puczyc to other policemen. For example: "Blumenfeld was head of the police. He treated everyone very well. The defendant treated [people] like a murderer from beginning to end."[24] The witnesses did not make do with this comparison and compared the defendant to the Nazis: "He was the Himmler of the camp";[25] he "was the ruler, the master of life and death."[26] These testimonies present a process of demonization of the defendant, during which he acquired "Nazi" traits.

The witnesses spoke about the defendant's active involvement in the selection conducted during the second *Aktion* in the ghetto in January 1943 and about the power his status afforded him to determine whether people would live or die: "After some time the defendant told me that had he wanted to, he could have passed over my name and I would then have been sent to Treblinka, but that he hadn't wanted to do so."[27] The indictment sheet contains no charge relating to this event, but this testimony nevertheless constitutes part of the body of evidence owing to its great importance to the prosecution. It provides an additional perspective on the defendant's sphere of choice, even when the Nazis were present. Another prosecution witness described how, on the day of the second *Aktion*, a woman designated for deportation approached the defendant and exchanged words with him, which the witness could not hear: "I understood that she was asking for something. *It was well known that the defendant could assist her.* The defendant began to beat her with a whip. And I saw that she spread her arms imploringly. SS men came and took her."[28] This was not direct testimony because the witness did not overhear the conversation between the woman and the defendant, but the details are unimportant. The moment the testimony focused on the general "knowledge" ostensibly shared by all, according to which the defendant could have assisted the woman had he wished to do so, the prosecution achieved its goal, which was to place the defendant at center stage, where he exerted his free will. The perception of the defendant as an autonomous person is likewise manifested in his portrayal as being exceptional among the policemen themselves, because he was "the life and soul of the police force"[29] and "the only educated person among them [the police], since they were all simple people."[30]

The prosecution attempted to establish that the defendant collaborated with the Nazis for his own selfish interests, namely, the pursuit of authority and a desire to curry favor with the Nazis in the hope of saving himself. In legal terms these assertions carried no weight at all, but they were designed to establish the figure of the defendant not only as a person who acted of his own free will but also as someone who would harm others out of egoistic motives. We learn of his special relations with the Nazis from the defendant's response to the question referring to what the prosecution described as his habit of drinking with them. The defendant responded to this by relating that on certain occasions the Jewish policemen were required to serve drinks to the Nazis who came to the ghetto, because they would "force us to drink with them."[31] The direct questions were coupled with indirect insinuations to portray the defendant as a cruel individual who stood on his honor and who sought the company of the Nazis in order to save his life.

THE DEFENSE: "IF I SLAPPED SOMEONE ON THE CHEEK, IT WAS ALWAYS IN THE LINE OF DUTY"

The defense team naturally pursued a different path. The defense testimonies proceeded along two interconnected tracks that sought to enhance the figure of the defendant as a responsible public functionary on the one hand and to minimize his image as a cruel policeman on the other. These two processes went hand in hand.

The personal narrative traced by the defense ran counter to the prosecution's liberal narrative. Whereas the prosecution's narrative emanated from the liberal ethos that rests on the perception of the autonomous individual and his freedom of choice, the defense's narrative responded by presenting a man who was connected to the community and who pursued the general interest. The actions that the defendant *chose* to take and that are portrayed by the prosecution as proscribed acts turned out, according to the defense, to have been performed for the good of the community.

The initial step in constructing the defendant as a responsible public servant was to present his own testimony, in which he described his broad education, his public duties, and in particular his Zionist activity.[32] Puczyc portrayed his appointment to the post of deputy commander of the Jewish police force as having been forced upon him; he had by no means "pursued" honor: "The list I saw was an appointment order. Blumenfeld was appointed commander and I his deputy."[33] Puczyc furthermore stressed his inferior position in the police hierarchy: "Of the two of us, Blumenfeld [the police commander] and I, Blumenfeld was the major and the active [one].... He would give me orders and I gave no order without permission and in some cases he annulled my orders."[34] Puczyc's public responsibility, according to his testimony, was an onerous burden: "Not only did I fail to make an effort to become an officer, I also did not attempt to enter the police force. With my connections I could have become a major actor and things would have been easier for me. I continually tried to resign from the police but . . . they did not agree."[35] He likewise failed to exploit an opportunity to escape from the camp: "I did not escape although I could easily have done so, but I did not do so because of my responsibility."[36]

Seeking to demonstrate that he accepted public responsibility beyond his formal roles, the defendant recalled his involvement in voluntary activity on behalf of the ghetto community, such as the establishment of workshops in the ghetto to provide employment for Jews and thereby forestall their deportation. He stressed that this activity "had nothing to do with the police, I did it voluntarily."[37] This account, related in the first-person singular, underscores the active element in Puczyc's behavior: The defendant initiated, organized, and implemented projects, all for the good of the community.

Puczyc regarded his election to the Central Committee of the Liberated Jews in the American Zone of Occupied Germany following the war, with the support of former residents of Ostrowiec, as conclusive proof of his honorable behavior: "I was liberated together with many people from Ostrowiec who went with me . . . and I was elected to the committee after being proposed by the people of Ostrowiec. There were some forty to fifty former Ostrowiec residents in the camp. . . . I was active on the camp committee and then . . . elected to the Central Committee of Liberated Jews in Bavaria. I was chosen to be the first secretary of the Central Committee."[38] This story had of course nothing to do with the legal indictments, yet it acquired great significance because it presented a different picture from that of the prosecution with regard to the relationship between Puczyc and the people of Ostrowiec. It transpired that although his deeds as recounted by prosecution witnesses were ostensibly still "fresh" in their memory, the people of Ostrowiec supported him and his public activity. In other words, reality was far more complex than the prosecution would have it.

Puczyc recounted his activity among the displaced Jews at length.

> I began my activity as first secretary toward the end of May or the beginning of June 1945. . . . At that time they also founded the United Zionist Organization of Germany and I was elected as a delegate to the central body. My first action was to obtain from the American commander, General Patton, a license for the operation of the Central Committee. Then we organized aliyah [immigration to Palestine] activity in cooperation with the people of the [Jewish] Brigade.[39]

With a view to reinforcing the impression of his elevated public standing among the displaced Jews and in order to counter the assertions of witnesses regarding investigations of him because of his former position as deputy police commander in the ghetto and the camp, the defendant submitted documents that apparently cleared him of all guilt. Chief among these were photographs that showed him sharing a podium with David Ben-Gurion. The defense correctly believed that these photos would reinforce the public aspect of the defendant's persona.

Yet this is but one aspect of the story. We must remember that this was a criminal trial that would determine the defendant's fate, and for this reason Puczyc was obliged to work toward his acquittal rather than merely relating a historical narrative. Thus, alongside his effort to build up his image as a public figure and a Zionist activist, he likewise tried to minimize as much as possible his resemblance to the figure of the cruel and power-seeking policeman constructed by the prosecution. He did this by portraying himself as someone who resorted to beatings only when left with no choice as he performed his duty, not as an end in itself.

Regarding the *Aktion* of October 1942, the prosecution witnesses testified that Puczyc was present and took part in the deportation of Jews to their extermination, but Puczyc maintained: "On the first day of the deportation I coordinated police activities from the office of the Jewish council and I played no role outside. I would send policemen to every location I was ordered to, such as the collection of the dead and so forth."[40] Puczyc did not claim that the prosecution's testimonies were a libel designed to besmirch him and the Jewish police. Rather, he located himself as a clerk who sat by the telephone and obeyed orders. The defendant thereby distanced himself from the procedure whereby the Jews were assembled and deported to Treblinka: "I saw nothing of what happened on that day [the first day of the *Aktion*] adjacent to the labor office and the market, and heard about it from the reports that the policemen would submit to me."[41] Referring to the second operation in January 1943, the defendant stressed that he, alongside other policemen, made an effort to find work for the people in order to prevent their deportation.[42]

Puczyc presented the beatings frequently described by the witnesses as an integral part of his (and his colleagues') role as a policeman: "There was not one case in which I beat someone without a reason. I never beat [anyone] beyond the line of duty. If I slapped someone's cheek it was always in the line of duty."[43] The beatings were thus an integral part of his role, the local "rule" in fact. The manner in which the defense sought to portray the use of beatings reveals the tension between the judicial discourse, namely, the Nazis and Nazi Collaborators (Punishment) Law, which stipulates that beating may constitute an offense ("injury," "assault," and so forth) and the historical discourse, represented through the description of reality, according to which beating was the norm. Therefore the defendant took care to point out that he beat people "only" in the line of duty. Thus was the essence of the beatings transformed from an unacceptable means used by those wielding power into a part of the laws of the ghetto and the camp. In other words, if one considers the nature of the beatings according to the circumstances of the time and the place in which they were administered, one begins to appreciate the perspective of the defendant (and in fact of the police in general), who were obliged to operate within a sphere of choice that was a total inversion of what those who were sitting in judgment of him could conceive.

THE JEWISH GHETTO POLICE

The defendant was not the only "actor." Apart from him, the Jewish ghetto police formed an integral part of the arguments of both the prosecution and the defense, although it played no part in the judicial course of the trial.[44] Both parties understood that, given the unprecedented circumstances, it was necessary to broaden the court's perspective beyond the judicial categories and the indictments. These testimonies were not meant to establish guilt but rather to frame the arena in which the actions attributed to the defendant had been taken.

The prosecution presented the Jewish police, an unknown organ in the annals of the Jewish communities, as a group of people, most of whom were heartless opportunists, who chose to exploit their position to accumulate money and to survive. Witnesses told of policemen who were known to be "experts in beatings."[45] With a view to underscoring the policemen's freedom of choice, the witnesses related that "in Ostrowiec there were good policemen who didn't bother people, but I don't remember their names."[46] The prosecution witnesses' admission that it had been possible to be a "good policeman" underscored the volitional element of the policemen's behavior and the choice to treat the Jews harshly. The picture of the police force that emerged from the prosecution testimonies accorded with that portrayed by external sources: This was the most hated of the Jewish authorities in the ghettos.[47]

In contrast to the general narrative presented by the prosecution, the defense's account of the police force can be distilled into a narrative of "public responsibility." The defense could not construct the Jewish policemen as "classic" victims because it was impossible to ignore the use of force or to deny it completely. Therefore the defense decided to alter the perspective and to present the behavior of the police, including its resort to beatings, not as actions that were either unequivocally good or evil but as actions associated with the exceptional circumstances.[48] For example, in response to claims by prosecution witnesses that Jewish policemen confiscated private property from owners who attempted to salvage it or that policemen demanded and received payments for freeing people from the prison (located in the ghetto) or for removing people from the lists of forced laborers or deportees, the defense maintained that what appeared to be confiscation of money from Jews was in fact part of a general plan to bribe Nazis in order to rescue Jews.

How, then, did the defense contend with a prosecutorial assertion such as this? "The police personnel lived very well. Between the first deportation in October 1942 and the second deportation in January 1943, they took money at every opportunity from the workers in the factory, and anyone who did not give [to them] was removed from the factory."⁴⁹ Puczyc rebutted this accusation.

> First of all, the council would levy a tax, and apart from that, if an order came in for certain objects [from the Nazis], it would be submitted to the same branch for fulfillment, without charge. On one occasion they took their time about fulfilling an order for furniture, and then the SS people went from house to house and beat people severely. The police did not intervene in any way in the collection of these objects, a committee of the council took care of this. If someone refused to hand over [items], the council would employ its own means.⁵⁰

The defendant not only transferred the burden of guilt from the police to the Judenrat but at the same time recalled the context in which the events had occurred: The behavior of the police portrayed by the prosecution witnesses in terms of theft and a lack of solidarity was in fact prompted by the obligation to obey Nazi orders. The defendant thereby sought to legitimize the policemen's behavior: "If I caught someone robbing, I gave him a few slaps on the cheek, took the articles from him and sent him away; the other policemen did likewise. ... We then conveyed these articles to the general store and distributed them among the people."⁵¹

Although the prosecution witnesses expressed no reservations about the acts of looting committed by "ordinary" Jews, they blamed the policemen for doing precisely the same thing. The phenomenon of looting empty apartments represented the upheaval in ghetto life, as people acted in ways they never would have contemplated under normal circumstances. Jews forcibly entered houses whose owners were forced to vacate them and looted whatever they could. Jewish police then stole from the thieves, maintaining that they were exercising their authority as policemen. They failed to consider the moral implications of their action (according to the moral criteria of their former lives) because these were the laws of the place.

By rights, the conduct of the police should have played no part in the proceedings, which were supposed to focus solely on the behavior of the defendant, Puczyc, yet the prosecution and the defense alike placed it on the judicial agenda. Both parties realized that they must, each from its own perspective, refract Puczyc's own story through the prism of police conduct because they sensed that it was all but impossible to convey what had transpired in those days solely by means of the judicial categories of the Nazis and Nazi Collaborators (Punishment) Law. The combined narratives of the prosecution, which portrayed the police as a cruel and self-seeking body, and of the defense, which described the police as a communal body that operated under exceptional circumstances while attempting to cope with reality as it unfolded, displayed before the court a broader canvas than that encompassed in the indictment; thereby it augmented people's capacity to comprehend what had actually occurred and to appreciate that it could not be reduced to a matter of black and white but was, instead, a complex human tale. To this complex portrait we should add a number of prosecution testimonies that did not conform to a one-dimensional portrayal of the police. For example, one prosecution witness expressed an understanding of the need to impose order under the exceptional circumstances that prevailed in the ghetto and the camp but voiced reservations about the means used by the police: "There were things that they had to do, but they could have made things far easier."[52]

Twenty-seven prosecution witnesses and fourteen defense witnesses related the story of the defendant and the story of the Jewish community and the Jewish ghetto police in Ostrowiec. I have sought to present not a tale of guilt or innocence but rather a complex narrative of people who struggled to survive. The judgment, on the other hand, is a tale of extremes, because it represents the juridical imperative to arrive at an unequivocal decision: guilty or innocent.

THE VERDICT

It appears that Moshe Puczyc was not only among the first defendants tried according to the Nazis and Nazi Collaborators (Punishment) Law but also the first Jewish policeman to be indicted in an Israeli court. This was thus the first occasion on which Israeli judges came face to face with a senior functionary in a body that was one of the most hated in public discourse but whose day-to-day activities in the ghetto were unfamiliar to most Israelis. The lengthy judgment suggests that the judges made an effort to decipher the figures who appeared before them and the circumstances of their lives. I focus on the verdict's final section, which displays, to my mind, the most significant line of thought in the decision-making process. In this section the judges not only determined the legal verdict (guilty or innocent) but also revealed their position with regard to the reality they learned of during the course of the trial.

I suggest that we view the judges' path to their verdict as a process at whose base lay the perception of the defendant and the witnesses as victims. Yet these were two quite different types of victim, and the judges adopted diametrically opposite standpoints toward them. On the one hand, they augmented the figure of the defendant as victim as someone who "engaged in public activity already prior to the war and also thereafter, and when he was assigned the unfortunate role of one of those primarily responsible for order and discipline in the life of the ghetto and the camp, he fulfilled his role in a public spirited manner, respecting the general good."[53] On the other hand, they accused the witnesses of being people "without a conscience, who, because of the grudge they bear toward the defendant owing to negligible harm he may have caused them, took the liberty to make false and serious accusations about the defendant that were utterly baseless."[54] On the one hand, the judges pointed to the defendant's prominent position among the general group of victims and underscored his activity on behalf of the community; on the other hand, taking their cue from the public discourse in Israel at the time, which regarded the Holocaust survivors as responsible for their own tragedy, they blamed the witnesses, as a group, for leveling false accusations at the defendant.[55] In choosing between the two types of victim, the judges unequivocally preferred the defendant, as they unreservedly rejected *all* the prosecution evidence and accept the defense's version.

From the outset of the judgment it is clear that the judges found themselves grappling with an awkward dissonance. Before them stood a defendant who differed considerably from the criminal representation to which they were accustomed, because his persona incorporated an unfamiliar hybrid between a public figure concerned with the good of the community and someone who admitted to having beaten Jews. To judges accustomed to binary thought patterns that perceive defendants as either good or evil, this hybrid figure presented a problem in coming to a decision. The difficulty manifested itself in the judges' thought process, as they sought a framework within which to place the defendant and thereby understand him. Unable to comprehend the destructive reality of the ghetto and the camp, they seized on two periods that could be understood more easily, namely, the periods before the war and after it, in the Jewish displaced persons (DP) camps.[56] Public activity was familiar territory to the judges, and they indeed focused on this. They portrayed the defendant as

> an educated man, active in the Zionist movement since his youth, [who] acts with conviction on behalf of the poor and the wretched ... speaks amiably to everyone, strictly maintains the cleanliness in the huts and in times of stress, left with no choice, he occasionally slaps people's faces, he does his best and more to save human life, deports himself simply, without arrogance, wears regular clothes and no hat, apart from official occasions when he would wear the police hat.[57]

THE GRAY ZONE OF COLLABORATION AND THE ISRAELI COURTROOM

Relying on the defense testimonies, the judges created a superficial, one-dimensional figure, shaped according to the familiar mold of a responsible public figure in ordinary places and times. Nothing more. Thus, at a stroke, the descriptions of a defendant who used beatings to instill fear and to facilitate the handing over of Jews to the Gestapo were set aside. His behavior was reduced to one attribute, namely, public responsibility, which the judges placed at the center of the juridical narrative. This was the figure of the defendant that was accorded the seal of objective truth the moment it became a part of the judgment.

The Jewish ghetto police force in general underwent a similar process of exoneration. By adopting the public persona of the defendant, the judges likewise accepted the defense's version of the police force, largely ignoring the police's participation in deportations, beatings, exposure of hiding places, trade in work permits in exchange for money, and avarice. These events, which even the defense witnesses, including the defendant himself, admitted had occurred and which could thus have been used to trace a human image of the police on the scale between good and bad, found no place in the judgment. The judges thus created a "defense manifesto" for the Jewish police, the likes of which cannot be found even among those who experienced the events themselves.

Underlying the failure of the court to comprehend the defendant and to judge his actions in the context of temporal and spatial circumstances was a lack of knowledge on the judges' part and particularly their unwillingness to familiarize themselves with an exceptional reality and to contend with it. The judges did not seek to inquire about the world of the defendant and the witnesses, there and then, but took the opposite path: They drew the defendant and the witnesses toward their own world, here and now. The difference between these two actions has a decisive impact on the process of judgment, because someone who leaves his own sphere broadens his world by "visiting" unfamiliar places. On the other hand, someone who brings an unfamiliar world closer to the world he knows blurs the differences between the two worlds so that the world that was unfamiliar before the judgment process also remains so thereafter.[58]

Because the judges constructed the defendant in the mold of a public servant while differentiating and disconnecting him from the company of survivor witnesses, they turned the prosecution witnesses into a group of people lacking an individual identity, who were a priori defined as constituting a "problem": "In light of all this we are perplexed by the problem of why such a large number of people saw fit to come to court and to level a large number of most serious accusations against the defendant."[59] Yet the judges did not rest here. They proceeded to cast aspersions on the witnesses. As one delves further into the judgment, one becomes aware of the process by which the image of the witnesses was besmirched by castigating their motives in coming to testify against the defendant while the persona of the defendant was meanwhile enhanced.

Upon reading the judgment, one becomes perturbed not only because of the generalized and monolithic manner in which the judges referred to the witnesses but also because of the blunt way they expressed this attitude. For example, as they examined the testimony of one of the prosecution witnesses who referred to the defendant's involvement in turning a Jewish boy over to the Nazis, the judges stated, "We can place no trust whatsoever in the witness . . . [and] he admitted that he was prepared to sell his conscience for a pair of shoes and some other benefit."[60] This statement rested on the witness's declaration during his cross-examination, according to which he had in the past signed documents attesting to the defendant's good behavior. This indeed detracted from the witness's reliability, but the judges were not content to note this and offer their personal opinion of the witness's behavior, determining that he was prepared to sell his conscience for "a pair of shoes and some other benefit." The judges thereby compounded their justified criticism by proceeding to level personal and irrelevant criticism, which echoes the public critique of the survivors for having survived at all and for the ways in which they had managed to survive.[61] The judges noted that a particular female prosecution witness "was prone to exaggeration,"[62] and the story of another witness was described as "a fantastic story. . . . It appears to us that these utterances are a product of imagination or base slander."[63] These are merely examples of the wide range of pejorative descriptions of the prosecution witnesses used by the judges.

Although it is not uncommon to come across blunt utterances addressed by judges to witnesses in criminal trials, it is most unusual to find a judgment that contains a sequence of pejorative references to *all* the prosecution witnesses. It is this sequence that exposes the judges' nonjudicial approach to the prosecution witnesses: They did not stop at rejecting their accounts because of the unreliability of the evidence itself, as befits a legal proceeding, but added their personal perspective, which had no essential bearing on the evidence. This was intimately linked to the image of the survivors in Israeli society. To the judges, the witnesses were hardly distinguishable as individuals and were in the main "a group," whereas they perceived the defendant to have a robust personality of his own. Trapped in their negative conceptual group image of the witnesses, the judges were unable to address the harsh reality laid out before them or to comprehend the reasons that led Jews to, for example, loot one another's possessions. Their lack of understanding led them to portray the prosecution witnesses as people who "are unable to forgive the defendant for having confiscated their prey and attribute purely selfish intentions to people with respect to these actions."[64]

The defendant, by contrast, represented law and order and was, in other words, a man of moral stature. The judges thereby inverted the "reality" of the ghettos and the camps as construed by public discourse, which regarded the Jewish collaborators as morally wanting and the others as "ordinary" victims. The judges, for their part, perceived the ordinary victims to be "beasts of prey" and viewed the collaborating policeman as having acted nobly. This inversion of the role of the policeman, whom the public viewed with contempt, served the defendant as a protective suit, as it were, that preserved his personal and Jewish identity and raised him above the indistinct group of survivor witnesses.

The judges furthermore determined that the witnesses made false accusations against the defendant "through a lack of knowledge of all the details of the matter"[65] and thus erroneously regarded him as being responsible for their own catastrophe. The judges, who were not "there" and whose knowledge of life in the ghettos and the camps was in all likelihood limited (one should remember that the testimonies were heard in 1951–1952), adopted a patronizing attitude toward the witnesses who were not eligible, in their view, to testify about their own lives.[66] By dismissing the accounts of the witnesses, the judges in effect dismissed their lives and experiences and reduced them to envy and vengeance.

Dismissing the voice of the survivor victims was, as I suggest, the outcome of the disparity between historical and judicial narratives. It was likewise the outcome of what one may term the judges' selective hearing, because they listened to the witnesses' accounts through a filter of social background narratives that shaped reality and thus perceived the witnesses as unreliable. The combination of the failure to translate the witnesses' accounts into judicial language and this selective hearing eventually led to the collective conviction of the witnesses and, in turn, to the defendant's absolute exoneration.

The judicial procedure involving Puczyc's subordinate, the policeman Mordechai Goldstein, represents a different aspect of the law's attempt to come to terms with reality.

The Ordinary Policeman: Mordechai Goldstein

Compared to the legal procedure involving Moshe Puczyc, which produced hundreds of pages of transcript, the file of the legal procedure against Mordechai Goldstein is decidedly thin. The two defendants' life stories before the outbreak of war are likewise different. Born in the city of Lodz in Poland in 1911, Goldstein studied at a yeshiva (a traditional Jewish school) up to the age of 18 and worked as a textile merchant until war broke out. In December 1939 he escaped from Lodz and arrived in Ostrowiec together with his wife and son, who were both subsequently killed while attempting to escape the ghetto. Goldstein remained in the ghetto and was appointed as a policeman shortly after the *Aktion* of October 1942. The testimonies tell us nothing about how he was liberated or what happened to him following the war.[67]

Goldstein was indicted in September 1951 in the Tel Aviv District Court.[68] The original indictment was amended by erasing the offense according to Article 1 of the Nazis and Nazi Collaborators (Punishment) Law, namely, a crime against humanity. This released Goldstein from the threat of having the death penalty imposed on him.[69] The accusations detail physical acts of varying severity committed against Jews as well as one count of delivering a group of people to a "hostile regime."

Unlike Puczyc, Goldstein was unable to present a narrative with any redeeming qualities to counter the prosecution's harsh portrayal of him as a policeman whose role boiled down to administering cruel and gratuitous beatings. Goldstein lacked all the attributes that had provided ammunition for the defense in the Puczyc trial. He lacked a broad education, and he had been neither a public figure nor a Zionist activist before the war or after it. He himself stressed that he had been a simple policeman. In this respect his attorney, Asher Levitsky, who served as Puczyc's defense attorney as well, was faced with a tougher task, because the case of Goldstein represented the "exposed" Jewish policeman, without redeeming qualities (such as education, a history of public or Zionist activity, and fluent Hebrew), which had helped to blur the aggressive elements presented by the prosecution in Puczyc's trial. Thus the Jewish ghetto police force, represented by Goldstein, the simple policeman, presented the defense attorney and the judge with a far more difficult and complex task than the court had confronted with regard to Puczyc, whose image as a Jewish policeman had been replaced with an image of a public servant.

The judicial narrative that emerges from the accusations against Goldstein is a uniform and superficial one, with a focus on beatings. As in the case of Puczyc, the prosecution testimonies were framed in liberal thought, which portrayed an autonomous individual who exercised freedom of choice. In these circumstances the defense sought to minimize the damage done by the prosecution testimonies by portraying the use of beatings as something of positive value. It claimed that these were no ordinary beatings but were, in fact, intended to prevent the collective punishment of Jews by the Nazis.

The day-to-day life of the camp and Goldstein's life as a Jewish policeman were located between the poles presented by the prosecution and the defense. To "take into consideration sufficiently the needs of time and place, where *they* lived their lives; and understand life as *they* understood it,"[70] in the words of Justice Simon Agranat referring to the Kasztner affair, I propose a historical and cultural reading that plants the testimonies in the time and the place in which the events took place.

THE PROSECUTION: "SINCE BECOMING A POLICEMAN HE BEGAN TO BEAT"

According to the prosecution, Goldstein was a prime example of a policeman who chose to be evil. As one prosecution witness testified, "Since becoming a policeman he began to beat."[71] Goldstein's image was accordingly structured to portray a cruel and merciless policeman who committed the deeds attributed to him in order to survive. All the prosecution witnesses, at the preliminary examination and during the course of the District Court hearings alike, referred to Goldstein's gratuitous cruelty, although the law required no reference to the manner in which the deed was performed. Alongside the personal narrative of the defendant as a policeman who chose to be evil, the prosecution likewise transmitted the narrative of the Jewish police force, as it did in the Puczyc trial.

For example, in the preliminary examination a prosecution witness described the cruel manner of the defendant: "The defendant used to walk around with a stick. . . . I saw him beating the people of the camp in Ostrowiec . . . everyone feared him. They feared him more than the German. When a German would enter the hut, he would not beat [us]. The defendant beat [us]. The Germans were not present when he beat [people]."[72] One of the witnesses described an event during which the defendant had beaten a prisoner for no reason (so the witness believed): "I asked the defendant why he was beating him, and then the defendant ran toward me like a menacing beast; I took hold of him with both my arms and he then began to call for policemen to be brought to help."[73] The defendant's cruelty, according to the prosecution, did not stop at beatings: "The defendant would chase people out of the hut at night in winter by beating [them] with a stick and with shoes. He didn't give the people time to get dressed. They went out into the cold undressed."[74] A different prosecution witness underscored the volitional element of the defendant's behavior: "When we asked him why he beat [us], he replied that he wished to do so."[75] These descriptions were not required to convict the defendant, because they did not contain elements of the offenses with which he was charged, yet the prosecution nevertheless prompted the witnesses to recount these details because they highlighted the defendant's choices.[76]

In fact, it was one of the prosecution witnesses who, perhaps inadvertently, modified the dark portrait painted by the prosecution when he attempted to explain Goldstein's behavior: "After several weeks I approached the defendant and said to him: 'Motel, we know each other after all; why did you beat me? We were on our own.' He replied and said to me that since they deported his wife, he had become completely wild."[77] This testimony deviated from the line taken by the prosecution and presented the camp as a whirlpool that swept up people, who lost their former lives in an instant. Although this testimony was superfluous as far as the prosecution was concerned, it in fact portrayed actual reality and reinforces my assertion that it was precisely those who had been there, those who had experienced the catastrophic reality firsthand, who were able to represent reality rather than making do with one-sided descriptions designed to reinforce judicial arguments.

THE DEFENSE: "IN SOME CASES IT WAS ABSOLUTELY NECESSARY TO BEAT"

As I have noted, defending Goldstein proved a complex task, far more exacting than defending Puczyc. How, then, did the defense attorney choose to portray Goldstein in a way that would enable the judge to understand him? This is how Goldstein explained the accusations that the prosecution witnesses leveled at him: "It is not true that I regularly beat [people], but I do not say that I never beat a Jew. In some cases it was absolutely necessary to beat in order to head off vengeance on the part of the Gentiles."[78] The beatings were thus dictated by reality; they were a part of the concern for the general good and the maintenance of order in the camp: "They didn't beat people gratuitously. They occasionally beat [people] to maintain order or because people evaded work."[79] Goldstein did not deny the accusations made against him but located them within a certain context: He had no choice, and he acted in good faith. It was necessary to beat people in order to expose cases of theft from the plant where some of the camp's prisoners were employed (because of the Germans' threat of collective punishment should the thefts fail to cease) or to motivate the shirkers (because the Polish plant managers threatened to submit the names of shirkers and lingerers to the Nazis).

This is, in fact, the crux of the defense argument: If Goldstein did beat people, he did so in the line of his duty to impose order and to preempt Nazi actions that harmed Jews. When, during the course of the cross-examination, the prosecutor sought to substantiate the prosecution argument that Goldstein had beaten Jewish prisoners because he chose to do so, Goldstein responded as follows: "It was prohibited to beat [people] for no reason; the injured party could lodge a complaint with the commander of the Jewish police, and the policeman would be punished. No one complained about me."[80] Goldstein's evidence illuminates the difference between a modern police force and the police in the ghetto and the camp: Resorting to beating was not exceptional but was rather the rule, an integral part of the policemen's authority. The beatings, so Goldstein maintained, were not an end in themselves but a means to survival, designed to keep the Nazis away from the camp area. It is therefore no surprise that the judges in both Goldstein's and Puczyc's cases found it difficult to comprehend this reality and to incorporate it into their familiar thought patterns.

Other defense witnesses similarly portrayed the police as having the general interest in mind: "Someone who fell into line had nothing to fear. If shirkers and so forth collected a slap from a policeman, that was for the general good."[81] From the defense testimonies the police in general, along with Goldstein, did not appear to be a body that pursued authority or that was intent on gaining personal benefits. The following observation by a defense witness can be understood in the same vein: "The Ostrowiec camp was far better. There were no sadistic beatings; one was not required to doff one's hat and to stand at attention before the Jewish policemen. The policemen did not prevent us from contacting Poles on the outside and returning with products we had bought. We did not suffer hunger."[82]

The prosecution narrative of the cruel policeman and the defense narrative of the responsible policeman were laid before the judge. He, for his part, was obliged to come to a clear-cut decision, to determine innocence or guilt, to decide between black and white.

THE VERDICT

In mid-July 1953, exactly two months after the trial began, Judge Benjamin Cohen read out the verdict in the case of the policeman Mordechai Goldstein. This is a fascinating document. It is structured differently from conventional criminal judgments and thereby indicates that the judge realized that he was treading in unknown territory. The verdict includes, as usual, the decision finding Goldstein guilty of some charges and the sentence meted out to him. However, contrary to usual practice, instead of merely determining the defendant's innocence or guilt, the judge added a section to the verdict titled "I Shall End with a General Comment," in which he expressed his feelings about the gray reality that had been revealed to him.

The first section of the verdict contains a judicial analysis that is utterly detached from the historical context of the events. Not only did the Ostrowiec labor camp, where the events attributed to Goldstein took place, hardly feature here, but it also appears that the destructive circumstances under which the Jews lived evaporated. The judge analyzed events related by the witnesses by using what he termed "common sense." This was a most unusual means of analysis of historical events that were so far removed from common sense. The legal discourse contained not a hint of comprehension of the exceptional circumstances of the reality of that time and place, nor was there any indication of empathy. The thought process revealed in the first section of the verdict reflects the fraught encounter between the historical and the judicial spheres and the difficulty on the part of legal discourse to broaden its scope when faced with a reality unfamiliar and incomprehensible to the legal discourse, even though the facts were clearly evident. The judge analyzed the charges, although one cannot understand from the analysis what actually occurred in each case. The result was that in a judgment that addressed a Jewish policeman and Jews living in a camp, their presence was hardly felt.

In the first section of the judgment in the Puczyc case one can almost physically sense the ghetto and the camp and the horror of daily life there. Conversely, in the Goldstein verdict the testimonies are hardly mentioned. Reality is absent. One senses that the judge found an escape from unfamiliar reality in a judicial analysis devoid of context. This spare report indeed meets the normative expectations of a legal decision, yet the fact that the survivors' testimonies are absent precisely at a point at which they should be the focus of the discussion is congruent, I suggest, with the public approach prevalent at the time, which deprived the survivors of their status as witnesses authorized to retell their personal stories.[83]

Upon concluding the purely legal analysis but before proceeding to announce the defendant's sentence, the judge began a fresh section, surprisingly frank it must be said, with the words "I shall end with a general remark." This is the most significant part of the judgment. It is an unusual passage devoid of judicial rulings, in which the judge collects his personal thoughts. In the first part of the verdict the judge speaks in the binary language of legal proceedings, guilty or innocent. In the second part he broadens his perspective beyond that of criminal law as he addresses the persona of the defendant and the nature of the place where he operated alongside the other Jewish policemen. This is ostensibly a superfluous section. The judge could have concluded the verdict upon determining on which counts to convict Goldstein and on which he would be exonerated. But he did not do so.

The historical and cultural reading I offer of this section of the judgment reveals that the judge senses that, although it contains "correct" answers to "correct" legal questions, the judicial analysis misses the crux of the matter. This feeling led the judge to take the unusual step of adding a personal, critical point of view, which constitutes a form of admission of judging Goldstein according to the mandatory tools that the Nazis and Nazi Collaborators (Punishment) Law placed at his disposal. It manifests the tension between the judicial sphere (delivering a verdict according to rigid legal categories) and the historical sphere (the gray zone in which the policemen and the other Jews existed, all of whom were ordinary people who perpetrated deeds that they never would have contemplated under regular circumstances). The judge acutely senses this tension. In the first judicial section he manifests the "judge" in him, who accepts a priori the constraints of legal discourse and judges Goldstein according to the law. Yet it is the sense of unease that arises precisely because of his acceptance of the yoke of the law and his respect for its constraints that leads him to this "general remark." Here he is able to some extent to loosen the legal harness and voice criticism of the Nazis and Nazi Collaborators (Punishment) Law. This is an attempt to adhere to the boundaries of the restricted categorical legal discourse while refusing to relinquish the critical personal view.

When the judge casts off the limitations of the law and the obligation to come to a decision—guilty or innocent—he is able to understand Goldstein as he was: "a decent man of average temperament and a good Jew throughout the year."[84] In other words, the terrible reality did not change him, and, having been an ordinary man before the Holocaust, he remained thus during its course, even if the extreme circumstances led him to exhibit attributes or to take actions that would never have emerged in regular times. This conclusion, which was in fact unnecessary for the sake of coming to a decision about the defendant's guilt or innocence, is vitally important because it reflects a more balanced view than what is required and facilitated by legal discourse. Goldstein is here not merely a Jewish policeman who beat other Jews in the line of duty but a "decent Jew" like most of the policemen and the camp prisoners, and the judge states this explicitly: "I am convinced that the defendant did not behave differently from any other average person of average temperament who saw the links of society dismantling around him and who was placed in a position of authority."[85] These reflections represent the historical rather than the legal sphere, the reality experienced by living people that was revealed to the judge by the witnesses and by Goldstein himself, and not as the law perceived it. In this "actual" reality in which, on the one hand, "the links of society were dismantling," in the judge's words, and in which, on the other hand, authority was placed in the hands of people who were unaccustomed to it, someone who had previously been a decent Jew could continue to be a decent Jew and fulfill the role of a policeman. A man could remain decent even when performing his duties; it was the fraught circumstances in which these duties were performed that manifested other aspects of the same person. In his general remark the judge views Goldstein as "everyman": not as an angel, because he "possessed an average temperament," but neither as a sadist, because "I found no stain of sadism in the defendant's behavior."[86]

The general remark shows that the judge was able to comprehend the gray zone of the life of the ghetto and the camp, the life that drove people to a state in which the difference between right and wrong, between what was prohibited and what was permitted, became utterly blurred. It was only when the gray zone revealed itself that the judge could state that "the defendant too, to some extent, came to think lightly of employing beatings. Rather than serving him as a last resort when there was no alternative, beatings served him sometimes as his first resort."[87] This statement reflects a realistic view of the role of a Jewish policeman rather than a judicial view. It is only when the judge comprehended reality and not merely the legal rule that he was able to determine that "the general routine of the Jewish police force in the aforementioned places of detention did not exceed what it considered at the time to be reasonable for the purpose of maintaining good order."[88] These comments exceeded what was legally called for because, as I have previously mentioned, the Jewish police force was not on trial. All this turned the general remark into a singular legal document that represents the complexity and the difficulty encountered by the judicial system in grappling with the gray zone of collaboration: On the one hand, there is the legal narrative that relies on the facts listed in the indictment, whereas on the other hand, there is the historical narrative, which rests on the actual reality, the gray zone of the labor camp in the city of Ostrowiec.

After all this, the judge remarks that "the law obliges me to judge the defendant." Finding Goldstein guilty on four counts of the indictment, he sentenced him to one month in prison. This light sentence reflects the sentiment that the judge expressed before the verdict: "I am indeed unable to dismiss the thought that, had the attorney general's representative been aware of my decisions beforehand, he would not have set the machinery of the law in process against the defendant in the first place."[89]

Epilogue: The Gray Zone in Court

Their different outcomes notwithstanding—Puczyc's full acquittal and Goldstein's partial conviction and light sentence—the two judgments display a similar pattern of thought. They both expose both the difficulty and the challenge presented by the encounter between legal discourse and the historical gray zone. From this perspective one should distinguish between the personal outcome—both defendants won "favorable" judgments as far as they were concerned—and the general outcome, which signified that both judgments erased the historical confrontation "from there," namely, the individual and communal confrontation between the survivors and the defendants, by focusing on the other confrontation, which took place "here," in the judicial arena between the state and the defendants. The voice of the victims was erased in both proceedings. In Puczyc's case the judges exposed the confrontation between the witnesses and the defendant, only to reduce it to a matter of the scheming on the part of the witnesses at the expense of the defendant, explained by their being "bitter and unscrupulous" people.[90] In Goldstein's case the confrontation between the witnesses and the defendant was not manifested in the judgment at all. Thus neither judgment enabled the survivor witnesses to make their voices heard, to gain the opportunity to turn themselves and their stories into a part of the historical narrative of the Holocaust.

In this respect these legal proceedings represent the obverse of the Eichmann trial: Gideon Hausner, the prosecutor at the Eichmann trial, created a clear-cut distinction between perpetrator and victim by aligning the survivors unequivocally with the prosecution against the actual perpetrator, Adolf Eichmann. In doing so, Hausner deviated from the narrow criminal perception that put the defendant and proof of his guilt at the center of the legal proceeding. From Hausner's point of view, it was a necessary step in order to take advantage of the proceedings to divert blame from the victims to those who bore the brunt of the guilt—in this case one defendant who stood in for the system he served. Hausner chose to represent the witnesses as a homogeneous group of survivors, with no distinction between "ordinary" Jews and Jews who had been functionaries; they all represented the absolute good with which the Israelis could easily identify.[91] None of this happened at the trials of Puczyc and Goldstein, or in fact at any of the trials involving Jews indicted under the Nazis and Nazi Collaborators (Punishment) Law, especially because the defendants, like the witnesses, were, after all, victims themselves. The difference between the Eichmann trial and the trials of Jews under the Nazis and Nazi Collaborators (Punishment) Law is the difficulty encountered by the law in coming to terms with the gray zone of collaboration.

It is thus worth noting that the Eichmann trial, held in 1961, was not the first occasion that Holocaust survivors were offered an official legal platform to make their voices heard. The trials of Jewish collaborators, the earliest of which were held at the end of 1950, in fact constituted the first opportunity for the public to hear the voices of Holocaust survivors other than "heroes," such as ghetto fighters and partisans, and to listen to their stories. Yet the public failed to take advantage of this opportunity. As a result, despite the legal platform offered them, the stories of the witnesses remained locked within the confines of the courtroom and failed to be incorporated into Israeli collective memory.

Examination of Israel's historical and social context in the early 1950s suggests that the times were perhaps not ripe for focusing on the victims. This was a period of recovery in the wake of the War of Independence and the establishment of routine life in the new nation—and of a process of recuperation and integration of the survivors. Moreover, contemporary social discourse perceived the Holocaust survivors, apart from the "heroes," as "tainted" victims who were morally compromised by their very survival. Their very capacity to recount the Holocaust was thus held against them. This discourse was manifested in the Nazis and Nazi Collaborators (Punishment) Law and the indictments submitted on the strength of it. All these factors worked against acceptance of the witnesses in the trials of alleged Jewish collaborators as recognized narrators. The cases of both Puczyc and Goldstein show us that the encounter between actual reality and binary legal categories is a problematic one, yet it is not an impossible one. The fact that some of the witnesses for the prosecution expressed, as I have attempted to demonstrate, an understanding of the complicated role of the Jewish ghetto police in light of the extreme circumstances that obtained in the ghetto shows us the advantage of a historical and cultural reading of these trials as a means of comprehending a unique reality within the legal framework.

Notes

Translated from Hebrew by Avner Greenberg.

1. Justice Simon Agranat, in Criminal Appeal (CrA)232/55, *Attorney General v. Gruenwald*, 12 Piskey Din. 2017, 2058 (Hebrew). Agranat's ruling represents the culmination of the well-known Kasztner affair.
2. The city's full name is Ostrowiec Świętokrzyski, but it was called Ostrowce (in Yiddish) by the Jews. It is located in south-central Poland, formerly in the province of Kielce and nowadays in the province of Świętokrzyski. The city was captured by the Germans on September 7, 1939, and liberated by the Red Army on January 16, 1945. The city's Jewish community dates back to the sixteenth century. Throughout its existence the Jewish community in Ostrowiec lived a vibrant religious and social life. The interwar period witnessed a flowering of cultural life alongside burgeoning Zionist activity and the growth of the Bund association. Ten thousand Jews lived in Ostrowiec on the eve of World War II. Toward the end of September 1939 the German authorities ordered the Jews to form a Jewish council, or Judenrat, headed initially by an attorney by the name of Zeitel, whom the Germans soon replaced with Yitshak Rubinstein, the former chairman of the city's Zionist organization and a member of the city council. Many of the city's Jews were employed in local industrial plants. The ghetto in Ostrowiec was established in April 1941, and a Jewish police force was formed on the

THE GRAY ZONE OF COLLABORATION AND THE ISRAELI COURTROOM

order of the German mayor. The Judenrat appointed Ber Blumenfeld, deputy chairman of the city's Maccabi association and a soldier in the Polish army, to command the force. The ghetto housed approximately 15,000 individuals, among whom were many refugees. Moshe Puczyc was appointed head of the sanitation department and subsequently deputy commander of the Jewish police force. After the roundup of Jews by German forces or *Aktion* of January 1942, the Jewish police took over the Judenrat, which practically ceased functioning. On October 10, the ghetto was surrounded by SS and Gestapo officers, Polish policemen, and others, and 2,000 of the city's Jews were deported to Treblinka. Several hundred other Jews were murdered in the ghetto. Upon conclusion of this *Aktion* the "small ghetto" was established. On January 10, 1943, the Germans conducted another *Aktion* in the "small ghetto" and another 2,000 Jews were deported to Treblinka. At this point about 1,000 Jews remained in the small ghetto, and they were moved to a labor camp outside the city two months later. Puczyc was put in charge of the Jewish camp police. The ghetto was entirely liquidated in April 1943, and Ostrowiec was declared *judenrein* (cleansed of Jews). In July 1944, as the Red Army approached the area, the labor camp was likewise liquidated and its inmates were deported to Auschwitz. Few of them survived. This account is based on Avraham Wein, ed., *Pinkas hakehilot: Entsiklopedya shel ha-yeshuvim ha-yehudi'im* [Register of the Communities: Encyclopedia of the Jewish Settlements] (Jerusalem: Yad Vashem, 1999), 7: 52–58. See also Gershon Silberberg, ed., *Sefer Ostrowiec: Le-zikaron ule-eidut* [The Ostrowiec Book: Memory and Testimony], published by the Organization of Ostrowiec Immigrants in Israel (year and place of publication unspecified). The book is accessible on the website of the New York Public Library at http://yizkor.nypl.org/index.php?id=1958 (accessed July 29, 2014). In addition, see Aharon Weiss, "Ha-mishtarah ha-yehudit be-general gouvernement uve-shlezia ilit be-tekufat ha-shoah" [The Jewish Police Force in the General Government and in Upper Silesia During the Holocaust Period], Ph.D. diss., The Hebrew University at Jerusalem, 1973, 335–40.

3. Criminal Case (CrC) (Tel Aviv) 10/51, *Attorney General v. Moshe Puczyc*, State Archives 3354-bet; CrC (Tel Aviv) 93/52, *Attorney General v. Mordechai Goldstein*, State Archives 2314/93-bet.

4. As the author and journalist Ruth Bondi wrote in her autobiography: "Yet here, in Israel, the Jews also asked me: how come you remained alive? What did you have to do in order to survive? And in their eyes a glint of suspicion: Kapo? Whore? ... And how come was it precisely I who remained alive when these [others] were murdered?" See Ruth Bondi, *Shevarim Shleimim* [Whole Fragments] (Tel Aviv: Gevanim, 2002). It was commonly believed that the kapos, a general term denoting functionaries, managed to survive by virtue of their role; their very survival was thus perceived as immoral.

5. Giorgio Agamben, *Remnants of Auschwitz: The Witness and the Archive*, trans. Daniel Heller Roazen (New York: Zone Books, 1999), 52.

6. Anita Shapira, *Ha-halikhah al kav ha-ofek* [Walking on the Horizon] (Tel Aviv: Am Oved, 1988), 325–54; Roni Stauber, *The Holocaust in Israeli Public Debate in the 1950s: Ideology and Memory*, trans. Elizabeth Yuval (London: Vallentine Mitchell, 2007).

7. The etymological origin of the word *collaboration* is Latin, in which it had a neutral connotation of joint action or cooperation. The historian Timothy Brook writes that following Marshal Petain's declaration on French radio on October 30, 1942, six days after meeting Hitler, to the effect that there was "collaboration" between France and Germany, the term acquired a negative connotation and became synonymous with political cooperation with an occupying force. See Timothy Brook, *Collaboration, Japanese Agents, and Local Elites* (Cambridge, MA: Harvard University Press, 2005), 1.

8. The precise number of such trials is not known. See also chapter 11 of this volume.

9. For example, a report on the preliminary examination of Puczyc in the Tel Aviv Magistrate's Court stated that "the investigation of Moshe Puczyc ... continued yesterday ... marked by considerable tension, as the testimony of the witnesses was disturbed from time to time by interruptions from the audience of ex-Ostrowiecians that completely filled the hall." "Eiduyot meza'aza'ot be-mishpat Puczyc" [Shocking Testimonies at the Puczyc Trial], *Ha'aretz* (January 24, 1951).

10. Hannah Yablonka, "Ha-hok le-asiyat din be-natsim uve-ozreihem: hebet nosaf lishe'elat ha-yisra'elim, ha-nitsolim veha-sho'ah" [The Nazis and Nazi Collaborators (Punishment Law): A Further Aspect of the Question of the Israelis, the Survivors, and the Holocaust], *Cathedra* 82 (1997): 147.

11. See the memoirs of David Rousset, *L'univers Concentrationnaire* (1946), which were translated into English under the title *The Other Kingdom*, trans. Ramon Guthrie (New York: H. Fertig, 1982 [1947]).

12. Primo Levi, *The Drowned and the Saved*, trans. Raymond Rosenthal (London: Sphere Books, 1989), 42.

13. On the relations between the community and the ghetto police, see Isaiah Trunk, *Judenrat: The Jewish Councils in Eastern Europe Under Nazi Occupation* (Lincoln: University of Nebraska Press, 1996), 172–85; and Weiss, "Ha-mishtara ha-yehudit," 335–40. For a report by an individual Jewish policeman in the Warsaw ghetto, see the memoir by Stanislaw Adler, *In the Warsaw Ghetto, 1940–1943: An Account of a Witness* (Jerusalem: Yad Vashem, 1984).

14. Many diaries and memoirs have noted the cruelty of the Jewish ghetto police force. For example, Emanuel Ringelblum writes about the Warsaw ghetto following the large deportation to Treblinka in the summer of 1942: "The cruelty of the Jewish police force at times surpassed that of the Germans, the Ukrainians, and the Latvians. A good number of hiding places were uncovered by the Jewish police force, which sought to be holier than the Pope, to find favor with the occupier. [On more than one occasion] victims who evaded the Germans fell into the hands of a Jewish policeman. . . . In general, the Jewish police force displayed really wild, incomprehensible brutality. From whence did our Jews find such murderousness? When did we raise these hundreds of murderers, all those who seized children in the streets, threw them into carts, and dragged them to the *Umschlagplatz*." Emanuel Ringelblum, *Yoman ve-reshimot mi-tekufat ha-milhamah, getto varsha, September 1939–December 1942* [A Diary and Notes from the Period of War, Warsaw Ghetto, September 1939–December 1942] (Jerusalem: Yad Vashem, 992), 429. For more on

THE GRAY ZONE OF COLLABORATION AND THE ISRAELI COURTROOM

this topic, see Yosef Zelkowicz, *Be-yamim ha-nora'im ha-hem: Reshimot mi-getto Lodz* [In Those Terrible Days: Notes from Lodz Ghetto], trans. Arieh Ben Menahem and Yosef Rav (Jerusalem: Yad Vashem, 1994), 306; David Liver, *Ir Ha-meitim: hashmadat ha-yehudim be-aizor Zagłębie* [City of the Dead: The Extermination of the Jews in the Zagłębie Region], trans. A. S. Stein (Tel Aviv: Twersky, 1946), 34; and Moshe Maltz, *Years of Horror, Glimpse of Hope: The Diary of a Family in Hiding*, trans. Gertrude Hirschler (New York: Shengold, 1993), 52.

15. Regarding the relations between the Judenrat and the Jewish police force, the historian Aharon Weiss classifies Ostrowiec as belonging to the ghettos in which the Judenrat deferred to the police force. He maintains that the Germans encouraged such processes and exploited these circumstances to punish "disobedient" Judenräte. See Aharon Weiss, "Ha-yahasim bein ha-yudenrat, ha-mishtara ha-yehudit, veha-mahteret ha-yehudit halohemet be-Krakow" [The Relations Between the Judenrat, the Jewish Police Force, and the Fighting Jewish Underground in Kraków], *Masu'ah* 5.III (1977): 177.

16. Robert Cover, "Nomos and Narrative," in Martha Minow, Michael Ryan, and Austin Sara, eds., *Narrative, Violence, and the Law: The Essays of Robert Cover* (Ann Arbor: University of Michigan Press, 1993), 95; Austin Sarat and Thomas R. Kearns, "Writing History and Registering Memory in Legal Decisions and Legal Practices: An Introduction," in Austin Sarat and Thomas R. Kearns, eds., *History, Memory, and the Law* (Ann Arbor: University of Michigan Press, 1999), 1–24.

17. The various offenses are listed in Articles 2 and 4 of the Nazis and Nazi Collaborators (Punishment) Law by means of reference to the Israeli criminal law in force at the time, the Criminal Law Ordinance of 1936.

18. Dan Diner, "Historical Understanding and Counterrationality: The Judenrat as Epistemological Vantage," in Saul Friedlander, ed., *Probing the Limits of Representation, Nazism, and the Final Solution* (Cambridge, MA: Harvard University Press, 1992), 128–42.

19. According to his own testimony, Puczyc was not a lawyer, although on occasion he is referred to as such. See Zeev W. Mankowitz, *Life Between Memory and Hope: The Survivors of the Holocaust in Occupied Germany* (Cambridge, UK: Cambridge University Press, 2002), 102; and Yehuda Bauer, "The Initial Organization of the Holocaust Survivors in Bavaria," *Yad Vashem Studies* 8 (1970): 127–57.

20. Weiss, "Ha-mishtarah ha-yehudit," 195–98. These biographical details are derived from the following sources: the prosecutor's introductory remarks in *Attorney General v. Moshe Puczyc*, p. 3; the defendant's main testimony in the same case, pp. 123–71; and Weiss, "Ha-mishtara ha-yehudit." Weiss notes that he provides details about Puczyc on account of the important role he played in the life of the community. See Weiss, "Ha-mishtara ha-yehudit," 196.

21. Mankowitz, *Between Memory and Hope*, 101n21.

22. The trial began on December 12, 1951. Three judges presided over the proceedings, because this was a serious criminal indictment, as Puczyc was accused, among other matters, of offenses that carried the death penalty (a crime against humanity and a war crime). The presiding judge was Justice Pinhas Avisar, and sitting alongside him

were Justice Israel Levine and Justice Joseph Lam. The prosecutor was an attorney by the name of Tomkowicz, and Puczyc was represented by attorneys Asher Levitsky and Yitzhak Tunik. The verdict was announced on March 10, 1952.

23. Prosecution witness Moshe Bamberg, cross-examination, *Attorney General v. Moshe Puczyc*, p. 16.
24. Prosecution witness Zvi Katz, direct examination, *Attorney General v. Moshe Puczyc*, p. 86.
25. Prosecution witness Yitshak Birnzweig, direct examination, *Attorney General v. Moshe Puczyc*, p. 39.
26. Prosecution witness Moshe Bamberg, direct examination, *Attorney General v. Moshe Puczyc*, p. 15. The witness provides examples that demonstrate Puczyc's control over the fate of others: "[He] would not allow people to go out to work since he suspected they may escape. He would take money from people and thereby prevented them from making contact with Poles and obtaining help."
27. Prosecution witness Aharon Friedental, direct examination, *Attorney General v. Moshe Puczyc*, p. 49. Those whose names were called were selected to work; those whose names were not called were sent to Treblinka.
28. Prosecution witness Pinhas Steinhart, direct examination, *Attorney General v. Moshe Puczyc*, pp. 92–93 (emphasis mine).
29. Prosecution witness Aharon Friedental, direct examination, *Attorney General v. Moshe Puczyc*, p. 47.
30. Prosecution witness Aharon Friedental, direct examination, *Attorney General v. Moshe Puczyc*, p. 47.
31. Moshe Puczyc, cross-examination, *Attorney General v. Moshe Puczyc*, p. 174. The defendant denied the accusation that he had fraternized with the Germans, apart from the occasions when it was necessary to bribe them. On this matter his evidence accords with descriptions found in external sources regarding the need to bribe the Germans with money and alcohol. See also Trunk, *Judenrat*, 349–58.
32. Moshe Puczyc, direct examination, *Attorney General v. Moshe Puczyc*, p. 124.
33. Moshe Puczyc, direct examination, *Attorney General v. Moshe Puczyc*, p. 125.
34. Moshe Puczyc, direct examination, *Attorney General v. Moshe Puczyc*, p. 140. It should be noted that this account contradicts the descriptions of the prosecution and defense witnesses, according to which the figure of Puczyc, the deputy, overshadowed that of Blumenfeld, the commander.
35. Moshe Puczyc, cross-examination, *Attorney General v. Moshe Puczyc*, p. 173.
36. Moshe Puczyc, direct examination, *Attorney General v. Moshe Puczyc*, p. 164.
37. Moshe Puczyc, direct examination, *Attorney General v. Moshe Puczyc*, p. 128 (emphasis mine).
38. Moshe Puczyc, direct examination, *Attorney General v. Moshe Puczyc*, pp. 167–69. On Puczyc's election to the first central committee, see prosecution witness Moshe Bamberg, cross-examination, *Attorney General v. Moshe Puczyc*, p. 16.

39. Moshe Puczyc, direct examination, *Attorney General v. Moshe Puczyc*, p. 169. I have reservations regarding the historical reliability of Puczyc's factual account. But historical reliability and accuracy are not the primary issue here. What is important is the manner in which Puczyc attempts to construct his image in the eyes of the judges, in direct contrast to the image created by the prosecution.
40. Moshe Puczyc, direct examination, *Attorney General v. Moshe Puczyc*, p. 131.
41. Moshe Puczyc, direct examination, *Attorney General v. Moshe Puczyc*, p. 130.
42. Moshe Puczyc, direct examination, *Attorney General v. Moshe Puczyc*, p. 137.
43. Moshe Puczyc, direct examination, *Attorney General v. Moshe Puczyc*, p. 167.
44. The mere fact that a person served in the ghetto police force did not constitute an offense under the Nazis and Nazi Collaborators (Punishment) Law. Those who were indicted were tried solely for their behavior while performing their duties.
45. Prosecution witness Yisrael Loewental, direct examination, *Attorney General v. Moshe Puczyc*, p. 62.
46. Prosecution witness Yisrael Sherman, cross-examination, *Attorney General v. Moshe Puczyc*, p. 81.
47. For accounts of various Jewish police forces, see note 14 above, and Sarat and Kearns, "Writing History."
48. On the topic of rationality and counterrationality, see Diner, "Historical Understanding."
49. Isthak Birnzweig, direct examination, *Attorney General v. Moshe Puczyc*, p. 44.
50. Moshe Puczyc, direct examination, *Attorney General v. Moshe Puczyc*, p. 127.
51. Moshe Puczyc, direct examination, *Attorney General v. Moshe Puczyc*, p. 158.
52. Prosecution witness Hanania Malakhi (Sherman), cross-examination, *Attorney General v. Moshe Puczyc*, p. 61.
53. Verdict, *Attorney General v. Moshe Puczyc*, p. 50.
54. Verdict, *Attorney General v. Moshe Puczyc*, p. 52. It is difficult to ignore the contradictions in the words of the judges themselves regarding the defendant's status in the ghetto and the camp. On occasion they refer to him as "merely" the deputy police commander, who thus cannot be held responsible for the behavior of the police; and on other occasions he is "the most prominent among the heads of the ghetto and the camp." These inconsistencies lend weight to the assertion that the judges found it difficult to comprehend Puczyc's persona and therefore constructed an imagined figure.
55. See, for example, Bondi, *Shevarim Shleimim*.
56. Verdict, *Attorney General v. Moshe Puczyc*, pp. 12–13.
57. Verdict, *Attorney General v. Moshe Puczyc*, p. 14.
58. "To think with an enlarged mentality means that one trains one's imagination to go visiting." See Hannah Arendt, *Lectures on Kant's Political Philosophy*, ed. Ronald Beiner (Chicago: University of Chicago Press, 1982), 42–43.

59. Verdict, *Attorney General v. Moshe Puczyc*, p. 51.
60. Verdict, *Attorney General v. Moshe Puczyc*, p. 16.
61. On the prevalent images of the survivors among the Israeli public and among themselves, see Hanna Yablonka, *Survivors of the Holocaust: Israel After the War* (London: Macmillan, 1999), 9–78.
62. Verdict, *Attorney General v. Moshe Puczyc*, p. 24.
63. Verdict, *Attorney General v. Moshe Puczyc*, p. 32.
64. Verdict, *Attorney General v. Moshe Puczyc*, p. 51.
65. Verdict, *Attorney General v. Moshe Puczyc*, p. 52.
66. The approach of the judges in general is indicative of a prevalent attitude at the time, which regarded survivors as unreliable witnesses, primarily owing to the suspicion that their traumatic experiences had affected their memory. On this issue, see Gideon Hausner, *Justice in Jerusalem* (New York: Harper & Row, 1966), 294–97, esp. 297. Of Puczyc's three judges, Justice Lam was the only one who had experienced the Holocaust, although he had in effect escaped it. He was arrested in 1938 while in Vienna and sent to the Dachau concentration camp, where he remained for about one year. He arrived in Palestine in 1939. Justice Lam served as a member of parliament (Knesset) when the Nazis and Nazi Collaborators (Punishment) Law was passed, and he indeed adopted a view different from that of the majority opinion during the debates over the new law, which placed sweeping blame on the collaborators. In the trial of the kapo Yehezkel Jungster, over which the same three judges who tried Puczyc presided, the defendant was convicted and sentenced to death (a conviction subsequently annulled upon appeal to the Supreme Court). Judge Lam believed that the two other judges at the District Court convicted Jungster of a "crime against humanity" on the strength of a sequence of actions rather than of one single deed. Thus, because he believed that some of these actions met the stipulation of the defense provided by the Nazis and Nazi Collaborators (Punishment) Law, he deemed it correct to commute the death penalty and to impose a sentence of ten years' imprisonment. See CrC (Tel Aviv) 9/51, *Attorney General v. Yehezkel Jungster*, Psakim Mekhozim (District Court Judgments) 5753(2) 267. Because the verdict in Puczyc's trial was unanimous, we cannot identify differences of opinion among the three judges.
67. These details are derived from Goldstein's statement to the police and from his direct evidence. See *Attorney General v. Mordechai Goldstein*, pp. 21–22. Goldstein maintained that he had been active on various Zionist committees and had engaged in philanthropic matters. The testimonies in the police file reveal that Goldstein escaped from the camp shortly before it was dissolved. See *Attorney General v. Mordechai Goldstein*, preliminary examination, p. 8. I have found no additional biographical details in external sources.
68. The first indictment submitted to the district court is not found in the file. The trial was conducted before a single judge, Benjamin Cohen, rather than before a panel of three judges, as in Puczyc's trial because, following the amended indictment, Goldstein was not accused of committing a crime against humanity or a war crime. The first hearing took place on May 18, 1953, and continued until July 7, 1953. The judgment

was delivered on July 15, 1953, about eighteen months after the judgment in the Puczyc trial. The state was represented by an attorney by the name of Tal, and Goldstein was represented by attorney Asher Levitsky, the same lawyer who represented Puczyc. Although both trials revolved around the same ghetto and camp and the same police force, the judgment in the Goldstein case makes no mention of Puczyc's trial. During his direct examination Goldstein relates that he was invited by the prosecution to testify in the Puczyc trial, to which he responded, "I said that I knew of nothing bad against Puczyc" (*Attorney General v. Mordechai Goldstein*, p. 24). Ultimately, Goldstein was not summoned to testify.

69. The annulment of the accusations according to Article 1 of the Nazis and Nazi Collaborators (Punishment) Law led to Goldstein's release on bail following a prolonged detention.
70. Justice Simon Agranat, Criminal Appeal (CrA) 232/55, *Attorney General v. Gruenwald*, 12 Piskey Din. 2017, 2058 (Hebrew) (emphasis mine).
71. Prosecution witness Ephraim (Fishel) Pipek, direct examination, *Attorney General v. Mordechai Goldstein*, p. 19. Pipek appeared as a prosecution witness in Puczyc's trial as well.
72. Prosecution witness Yokheved Schiff, preliminary examination, *Attorney General v. Mordechai Goldstein*, p. 1.
73. Prosecution witness Ya'akov Schneider, direct examination, *Attorney General v. Mordechai Goldstein*, p. 4.
74. Prosecution witness Ya'akov Fuchs, preliminary examination, *Attorney General v. Mordechai Goldstein*, p. 8.
75. Prosecution witness Ephraim Pipek, direct examination, *Attorney General v. Mordechai Goldstein*, p. 4.
76. The witnesses were perhaps coached to testify in this manner to preclude the defendant's possible reliance on Article 10 (exemption from criminal responsibility) or Article 11 (circumstances indicating a mitigation of sentence), although the transcript provides no indication of such reliance.
77. Prosecution witness Ephraim Pipek, *Attorney General v. Mordechai Goldstein*, p. 19.
78. Mordechai Goldstein, direct examination, *Attorney General v. Mordechai Goldstein*, p. 22.
79. Defense witness Yosef Schneider, direct examination, *Attorney General v. Mordechai Goldstein*, p. 31.
80. Mordechai Goldstein, cross-examination, *Attorney General v. Mordechai Goldstein*, p. 30.
81. Defense witness Yosef Schneider, direct examination, *Attorney General v. Mordechai Goldstein*, p. 31.
82. Defense witness Yosef Schneider, direct examination, *Attorney General v. Mordechai Goldstein*, p. 31.
83. An exceptional incident that occurred during the cross-examination of a prosecution witness perhaps indicates the judge's personal attitude toward survivor witnesses. Fearing self-incrimination by the witness, the judge disallowed the question "Did

you kill a Jew following the liberation?" He explained as follows: "This is a *primitive* witness, who does not understand the fine distinctions of the law" (*Attorney General v. Mordechai Goldstein*, p. 31n3). The judge could have selected a different word to describe a witness as a layman unfamiliar with the mysteries of the law, yet he chose to describe him as a "primitive witness." This choice, I suggest, indicates the judge's mental process, which regarded survivors as "primitive witnesses," who, because of their traumatic experiences, were not competent to report on events in which they participated.

84. Verdict, *Attorney General v. Mordechai Goldstein*, p. 38.
85. Verdict, *Attorney General v. Mordechai Goldstein*, p. 39.
86. In this respect the judge's approach resembled that of one of the prosecution witnesses, who said, "There were also cases in which the police were in the right, since not everyone always behaved properly." Prosecution witness Ya'akov Teomim, cross-examination, *Attorney General v. Mordechai Goldstein*, p. 11.
87. Verdict, *Attorney General v. Mordechai Goldstein*, p. 39.
88. Verdict, *Attorney General v. Mordechai Goldstein*, p. 39.
89. Verdict, *Attorney General v. Mordechai Goldstein*, p. 39.
90. For a discussion of the manner in which Puczyc's judges tarnished the witnesses' characters, see "The Verdict" subsection of "The Commander: Moshe Puczyc" main section. The judges did not regard Puczyc as a "classic" victim. They divested him of the traits of "victim" by constructing him as a public and Zionist activist.
91. On the Eichmann trial and the role of the witnesses, see Leora Bilsky, *Transformative Justice: Israeli Identity on Trial* (Ann Arbor: University of Michigan Press, 2004), 85–115; and Lawrence Douglas, *The Memory of Judgment: Making Law and the History of Trials of the Holocaust* (New Haven, CT: Yale University Press, 2001), 97–182.

Contributors

RIVKA BROT received her B.A. in political science and sociology from the University of Haifa, and her LLB and LLM from Tel Aviv University. After having practiced law for several years, she is now a Ph.D. candidate at the Zvi Meitar Center for Advanced Legal Studies at Tel Aviv University. Her dissertation project explores the use of law in two different transitional time periods in Jewish history by analyzing the legal discourses about Jewish collaborators with the Germans during the Holocaust in both the displaced persons camps in postwar Germany and the State of Israel. In 2011–12 she held a Matthew Family Fellowship at what is now The Jack, Joseph and Morton Mandel Center for Advanced Holocaust Studies at the United States Holocaust Memorial Museum. Her publications include "Tzivia Lubetkin: Between Private and Public—Body and Symbol," in *Dapim: Studies of the Holocaust* (2009) (Hebrew); "Benjamin Wilkomirski: 'Fragments' of Identity," in *Zmanim: A Historical Quarterly* (2010) (Hebrew); "Julius Siegel: A Kapo in Four (Judicial) Acts," in *Dapim: Studies on the Holocaust* (2011) (Hebrew and English); and "The Gray Zone of Collaboration in Court," in *Theory and Criticism* (2012) (Hebrew).

GALI DRUCKER BAR-AM received her Ph.D. in Yiddish literature from the Hebrew University of Jerusalem. Her doctoral thesis is a study of Yiddish literature written in Israel during its first two decades of independence. She teaches modern Yiddish literature at Tel Aviv University. Among her publications are "In Their Own Voice and in Their Mother Tongue: Newborn Israel in Israeli Yiddish Prose," in Dalia Ofer, ed., *Israel in the Eyes of Survivors of the Holocaust* (Jerusalem: Yad Vashem, 2014); "The Holy Tongue and the Tongue of the Martyrs: The Eichmann Trial as Reflected in *LetsteNayes*," in *Dapim: Studies on the Holocaust* (2014); and "'May the Makom Comfort You': Place, Holocaust Remembrance, and the Creation of a National Identity in the Israeli Yiddish Press, 1948–1961," in *Yad Vashem Studies* 42:2 (2014).

CONTRIBUTORS

HELGA EMBACHER is professor of history in the Department of History at the University of Salzburg. Her research focuses on the history of National Socialism and anti-Semitism, Jewish history in Austria, and the history of Islam in Europe. In the past she has taught at the University of Pennsylvania, the University of Minnesota, and the University of Innsbruck. Her publications include *Restitutionsverhandlungen mit Österreich aus der Sicht jüdischer Organisationen und der Israelitischen Kultusgemeinde* (Vienna: Oldenburg, 2003); *Neubeginn ohne Illusionen: Juden in Österreich nach 1945* (Vienna: Picus, 1995); and *Gratwanderungen: Die Beziehungen zwischen Österreich und Israel im Schatten der NS-Vergangenheit* (Vienna: Picus 1998), coauthored with Margit Reiter. She also edited *Jews in Salzburg: History, Cultures, Fates* (Salzburg: Anton Pustet, 2003) and coedited with Margit Reiter *Europa und der 11. September* (Vienna: Böhlau, 2011).

DAVID ENGEL is the Greenberg Professor of Holocaust Studies, professor and chair of Hebrew and Judaic studies, and professor of history at New York University and a fellow of the Goldstein-Goren Diaspora Research Center at Tel Aviv University. A member of the Academic Committee of the United States Holocaust Memorial Museum, his books include *Historians of the Jews and the Holocaust* (Stanford, CA: Stanford University Press, 2010); *Between Liberation and Flight: Holocaust Survivors in Poland and the Struggle for Leadership, 1944–1946* (Tel Aviv: Am Oved, 1996) (Hebrew); *Facing a Holocaust: The Polish Government-in-Exile and the Jews, 1943–1945* (Chapel Hill: University of North Carolina Press, 1993); and *In the Shadow of Auschwitz: The Polish Government-in-Exile and the Jews, 1939–1942* (Chapel Hill: University of North Carolina Press, 1987).

GABRIEL N. FINDER is an associate professor in the Department of Germanic Languages and Literatures and director of the Jewish Studies Program at the University of Virginia. He has a Ph.D. in modern European history from the University of Chicago and a law degree from the University of Pennsylvania. His research interests lie in the Holocaust, the rebuilding of Jewish life in Europe after the Holocaust, including the establishment of honor courts, relations between Jews and non-Jews in postwar Europe, Holocaust-related trials, and Holocaust memory with an emphasis on Poland. In 2000–2001 he held a fellowship at what is now The Jack, Joseph and Morton Mandel Center for Advanced Holocaust Studies at the United States Holocaust Memorial Museum. His publications in these areas have appeared in several edited books and scholarly journals. He is contributing guest coeditor of volume 20 of *Polin: Studies in Polish Jewry* (2008), which is devoted to the construction of Holocaust memory in Poland.

CONTRIBUTORS

IDO DE HAAN is a professor of modern political history and director of the Humanities Honors Program at the University of Utrecht. He taught as a visiting professor at the University of California, Los Angeles, and served as a member of the Committee for the Study of History and Culture of Jews of the Royal Dutch Academy of Sciences and is editor of *The Low Countries Historical Review*. His fields of interest are the history of modern democracy, citizenship, and the state; the history and memory of large-scale violence; the comparative study of political transitions; the history of political thought; and contemporary Jewish history. Among his publications are *Border and Boundaries In and Around Dutch Jewish History* (coedited with Joel Cahen, Judith Frishman, and David Wertheim) (Amsterdam: Aksant, 2011); "Failures and Mistakes: Images of Collaboration in Postwar Dutch Society," in Roni Stauber, ed., *Collaboration with the Nazis: Public Discourse After the Holocaust* (London: Routledge, 2010); "Imperialism, Colonialism, Genocide: The Dutch Case for an International History of the Holocaust," in Klaas van Berkel and Leonie de Goei, eds., *The International Relevance of Dutch History* (Den Haag: KNHG, 2010); and *Na de ondergang: De herinnering aan de Jodenvervolging in Nederland 1945-1995* (Den Haag: Sdu Uitgeverij, 1997).

LAURA JOCKUSCH is a postdoctoral fellow in Jewish history at the Martin Buber Society of Fellows at the Hebrew University of Jerusalem. She received her Ph.D. in modern European Jewish history from New York University with a thesis on the beginnings of Holocaust research from a Jewish perspective in the immediate aftermath of World War II. The dissertation was published as *Collect and Record! Jewish Holocaust Documentation in Early Postwar Europe* (New York: Oxford University Press, 2012), and it received the 2012 National Jewish Book Award and the 2013 Sybil Halpern Milton Book Prize. In 2012–13 she held the Ben and Zelda Cohen Fellowship at what is now The Jack, Joseph and Morton Mandel Center for Advanced Holocaust Studies at the United States Holocaust Memorial Museum. Her research and teaching interests include twentieth-century European Jewish history, history and historiography of the Holocaust, and the history of Holocaust survivors in the postwar era. Her current research project explores Jewish conceptions of retributive justice in postwar Germany. She also teaches in the International M.A. Program in Holocaust Studies at the University of Haifa.

EWA KOŹMIŃSKA-FREJLAK is a sociologist, a research fellow at the Jewish Historical Institute in Warsaw, and a contributor to *Midrasz*, a Jewish periodical published in Warsaw. She is currently writing her Ph.D. dissertation on the adaptation strategies of Polish Jews in the immediate postwar period. She has edited several books, including two collections of family letters from the Holocaust: *Adresat nieznany* (Warsaw: Baobab, 2009); and *Tęsknota nachodzi nas jak ciężka choroba: Korespondencja wojenna rodziny Finkelsztejnów 1939–1941* (Warsaw: Stowarzyszenie Centrum Badań nad Zagładą Żydów, 2013). She is also the author of several book chapters and articles on Jewish life during and after the Holocaust.

SIMON PEREGO is a graduate of Sciences Po Paris and holds the *agrégation d'histoire*, the highest state teaching qualification in France. He was a fellow of the Fondation pour la Mémoire de la Shoah and now holds a grant to conduct research on anti-Semitism and xenophobia awarded by the City of Paris. He is completing his Ph.D. thesis at Sciences Po Paris on Holocaust remembrance among Parisian Jews between France's liberation and the Six Day War. In 2013 he was the co-curator, with Renée Poznanski, of the exhibition *Le Centre de documentation juive contemporaine, 1943-2013: Documenter la Shoah* at the Mémorial de la Shoah in Paris. His publications include several contributions to the *Dictionnaire du judaïsme français depuis 1944* (Paris: Éditions Le Bord de l'Eau, 2013); and "Les commémorations de la destruction des Juifs d'Europe au Mémorial du martyr juif inconnu du milieu des années cinquante à la fin des années soixante," *Revue d'histoire de la Shoah* (2010).

KATARZYNA PERSON is a historian of Eastern European Jewish history working in the Jewish Historical Institute in Warsaw. After completing her Ph.D. at the University of London in 2010, she held postdoctoral fellowships from the International Institute for Holocaust Research in Yad Vashem, the Center for Jewish History in New York City, and La Fondation pour la Mémoire de la Shoah. She has written a number of articles on the Holocaust and its aftermath in occupied Europe, and she has edited three volumes of documents from Emanuel Ringelblum's underground archive in the Warsaw ghetto. Her most recent book is *Assimilated Jews in the Warsaw Ghetto, 1940–1943* (Syracuse, NY: Syracuse University Press, 2014), which is based on her Ph.D. thesis and deals with assimilated, acculturated, and baptized Jews in the Warsaw ghetto.

DAN PORAT is a historian in the School of Education at the Hebrew University of Jerusalem. In 2010 he published the book *The Boy: Story of an Image* (New York: Hill & Wang) that focuses on the story behind the iconic photograph of a little boy raising his hand in the Warsaw ghetto. He has also published several articles in the field of history and education.

CONTRIBUTORS

VEERLE VANDEN DAELEN holds a Ph.D. in history from the University of Antwerp. Her dissertation examined the return and reconstruction of Jewish life in Antwerp after World War II. She has held fellowships at the Frankel Institute for Advanced Judaic Studies (University of Michigan) and the Herbert D. Katz Center for Advanced Judaic Studies (University of Pennsylvania). Besides numerous articles, she has written two books: *Vrouwbeelden in het Vlaams Blok* (Ghent: RUG-Centrum voor Genderstudies, 2002) and *Laten we hun lied verder zingen: De heropbouw van de joodse gemeenschap in Antwerpen na de Tweede Wereldoorlog (1944–1960)* (Amsterdam: Uitgeverij Aksant, 2008). Currently, she is a project coordinator for the European Holocaust Research Infrastructure (EHRI) at the Center for Historical Research and Documentation on War and Contemporary Society (CEGESOMA) in Brussels. She is also affiliated with the University of Antwerp, where she has taught courses on migration history, Jewish history, and other topics.

NICO WOUTERS holds a Ph.D. in contemporary history from Ghent University. He is coordinator of the Academic Activities Section of the Center for Historical Research and Documentation on War and Contemporary Society (CEGESOMA) and a guest lecturer in the Department of History, University of Ghent and The Brussels School of International Relations (Kent University). His main scholarly interests include administrative and political collaboration during World War II, local government (1930–1950), transitional justice, oral history, and war memory and remembrance. He is co-editor-in-chief of the *Journal of Belgian History* and an editorial board member of the *Low Countries Historical Review*. His publications include *Oorlogsburgemeesters: Lokaal bestuur en collaboratie in België* (Tielt: Lannoo, 2004); *De Führerstaat: Overheid en Collaboratie in België (1940–1944)* (Tielt: Lannoo, 2006); *La Belgique Docile: Les Autorités Belges et la Persécution des Juifs en Belgique durant la Seconde Guerre Mondiale* (Brussels: CEGES/Luc Pire, 2007) (co-authored with Rudi Van Doorslaer, Frank Seberechts, and Emmanuel Debruyne); and (as editor) *Transitional Justice and Memory in Europe (1945–2013)* (2014). He is preparing an English book on mayors under Nazi occupation in Belgium, the Netherlands, and France.

Index

Fictional characters alphabetized by first name.

Abraham F. (a reliable witness in the Barenblat trial), 317
Ackerman, David, 208
Action and Defense Committee of the Jewish Youth of the Alpes-Maritimes, 140
Adunka, Evelyn, 167; *Die vierte Gemeinde*, 167
Advisory Committee on the Purge (Netherlands), 117
Aftergut, Mojżesz, 247–48, 249, 250–51
Agamben, Giorgio, 328
Agranat, Simon, 345
Agudat Yisrael, 199
Aharon Barak Center for Interdisciplinary Legal Research at the Hebrew University, 321
Aid Society of Jews from Germany, 208
Aid to Jewish War Victims (Belgium), 208
Aid to Those Who Depart (Netherlands), 115
AJB, Association of Jews in Belgium, 18, 197–98, 200–204, 206–9, 211–13, 217–18
AJR Information, 176
Aleksandrowicz, Chaim, 66
Alexander, Vera, 13
Allerhand (member of the Jewish Community Board in Bolivia), 247, 249
Allied Control Council Law No. 10, 51
Allied-Occupied Germany, Jewish Honor Courts in, 49–82
Alpérine, Abraham, 147
Alpes-Maritimes, 142

Alterman, Nathan, 20, 282–90, 296; debate with Abba Kovner, 288; empathic attitude, 287–88; "Magash ha-kesef" (The Silver Platter) (poem), 285, 287; "Measures of Justice," 282–83, 287; "Memorial Day and the Rebels" (poem), 283–84; "On the Two Paths" (poem), 286; political poetry of, 282–89, 292; regular column, "Ha-tur Ha-shvi'i" (The Seventh Column), 282; "Simhat Ani'im" (Joy of the Poor) (poem), 287; "Tefilat Nakam" (Prayer of Revenge) (poem), 287; "the two paths," 283; writings from "without," 296
American Displaced Persons Acts of 1948 and 1950, 52
American Jewish Joint Distribution Committee (known as the Joint), 69, 73, 116, 120, 172, 174, 179
American Labor Zionist, Baruch Zuckerman, 1, 2, 3, 11, 22
American Occupation Zone in Germany, 42, 54–56, 60; Central Committee of Liberated Jews in, 54, 60
Amidah (prayer), 279. *See also* prayer.
Amsterdam, 112, 113, 114, 115, 117–18, 120, 122–23
Amsterdam Jewish council, 17
Amsterdam kindergarten and the Hollandsche Schouwburg, 125
Andrieu, Claire, 157
Anschluss, 50, 165, 168, 215
Antek (Yitzhak Zuckerman), 88. *See also*

INDEX

Cukierman, Icchak.
anti-Semitism, 52, 85, 108, 113, 114, 123, 126, 137, 156, 188
Antwerp, 199, 200, 201, 202, 209, 210, 213
Arbeitsamt in Drohobycz and in Sosnowiec, 254
Archives of the Jewish Historical Institute (AŻIH), 253
Arendt, Hannah, 8, 9, 75, 108, 179, 187, 318, 319; *Eichmann in Jerusalem: A Report on the Banality of Evil*, 8, 13, 108, 179, 318; "right to have rights," 75
Argentina, 251
Arlon, Belgium, 202
armband, required in the ghetto, 250, 264
arranged confrontation, 247–49
Aryan, 70, 71
Aryanization, 166, 172
Aryan side of Warsaw, 258
"Aryan" spouse, 182
Asche, Kurt, 202
assassination, 2, 5, 33, 35, 38, 87, 88, 90, 99, 102, 197, 198
Asscher, Abraham, 17, 109, 110, 114, 115, 118, 121, 122–30; verdict and arrest of, 125–28
Association of Former Civilian Prisoners (Belgium), 206
Association of Former Jewish Deportees (France), 143, 153–54
Association of Gainfully Employed Jews (Austria), 185–88
Association of Jewish Refugees in Great Britain, 174–77
Association of Jewish Victims of the Nazi Regime (Austria), 186
Association of Jews in Belgium (AJB), 18, 197–98, 200–204, 206–9, 211–13, 217–18
Association to Aid Jewish War Victims, Invalids, Widows, and Orphans (Austria), 171–73
atheists, 279
attacks: at a soccer match, Regina Szenberg, 72–73; on the street, Runa Fakler, 250–51
Aufbau, 172–73
Auschwitz, 13, 50, 51, 142, 144, 202, 259, 264, 303, 313, 315, 331
Auschwitz-Birkenau, 50–51, 72–73, 142, 143, 198, 239
Auschwitz-Monowitz, 50
Austria, 4, 18, 50, 56, 165–67, 176, 179, 186
Austrian: Center, 175; citizenship, 215; internal Jewish court, 166; Jewry, 177, 184; Jews, 165, 168–69, 173, 174, 176, 184; People's Court, 166, 177, 184; universities, 175; Zionists, 175, 184
Austrian Communist Party (KPÖ), 174
Austrian Freedom Party (FPÖ), 188
Austrian People's Party (ÖVP), 179, 187
Austrians, 188, 205, 206, 214
Austrian Section of the Association of Jewish Refugees in Great Britain, 175
Austrian Social Democratic Party (SPÖ), 179, 185
Austrian War Crimes Law, 166, 180
Austrian Zionist Association, 173
Austro-Hungarian monarchy, 171
AŻIH (Archives of the Jewish Historical Institute, Warsaw), 253

Baer, Emil, 70
Baer, Marie, 70
Balaban, Leo, 166, 189
Banik, Andrej, 310, 317
Barenblat, Hirsch, 305, 313–21; Supreme Court decision in the case of, 305, 315–18, 320
Barmes, David, 121
Baruch, Marc Olivier, 137
Bar-Yehudah, Yisrael, 308
Bauminger, Leon (Arieh), 88
Baur, André, 144, 146, 150, 151, 154
Baur, Silvain, 142
Bavaria, 54; Burgau concentration camp in, 64; DP camp Landsberg in, 54
Będzin ghetto, 90, 231, 254, 313

368

INDEX

Belgian: Catholic Party, 210; citizenship, 199, 205, 212; Jewry, 199, 204, 213; Jews, 218; media, 217; military courts, 198, 209, 213, 218; "policy of the lesser evil," 209; State Security, 207, 212; War Crimes Commission, 205, 215
Belgium, 4, 18, 39, 197–224
Belgium's Jewish population, 199
Bełżec extermination camp, 94
Ben-Ami, Moshe, 307
benediction, 279–80; a curse, euphemistically presented as a blessing, 280
Benedictus, Maurice, 201–2, 207, 209, 211
Ben-Gurion, David, 335
Berger, Alter, 60
Berger, Leon (Eliezer Gruenbaum), 143
Berland, Zygmunt, 258
Berlin, 16, 51, 53, 54, 55, 57, 67, 69, 202, 215; Jewish honor courts in, 16, 53, 57–59, 62, 64–68, 70, 71; Jewish Hospital at Schulstrasse, 67; Mitte neighborhood, 70; Nazi war crimes trials held in, 77; Office of Religious Affairs, 55; Schulstrasse camp, 63; Senate, 55; Soviet sector, 54–55; Wedding neighborhood, 74; Weissensee neighborhood, 61
Berlin, Hans, 208
Berner Tagwacht, 173
Białystok, 41, 102
Białystok Judenrat, 254, 261
Bienenfeld, Franz Rudolph, 172
Bienenfeld, Wilhelm, 168–69, 172, 174–78, 181–83, 189
Bier, Selma, 71, 72
Bilsky, Leora, 288
Bindermichl DP camp, 187
Birnstein, Max, 181
blacklist, 249
Blechhammer camp, 143
Blind Max (Joseph Paal), 303–4
Blond, Rosa, 74
Blum, Alfred, 202, 207, 211
Blum, Hans, 208
Blumenfeld, 332, 334

Blum, Marcel, 198, 202
Bolivia, 247, 248, 251, 252; Jewish community in, 247, 250; Jewish organizations in, 252
Bosboom, M. (The Netherlands Jewish Honor Court's chair), 120
boycott: of German products, 23; of Richard Wagner's music, 23; of Runa Fakler, 248, 250–51
Brand, Hansi, 13
Brazil, 251
Breendonk concentration camp, 202, 214, 216
Breendonk trial, 205, 212, 214–17
Brill, David, 173–74
Brot, Rivka, 20, 21, 327–60, 361
Browning, Christopher, 10, 14; *New York Review of Books*, 14
Brucks (workshop employer on Rosenthalerstrasse in Mitte), 70
Brussels, 198, 199, 200, 201, 203, 204, 209, 251; Military Court, 206, 208, 212, 217; military prosecutors, 207, 209, 211; Orthodox community, 202
Brzezińska, Franciszka, 256–57, 268
Brzeziński, Mieczysław, 256
Bubis, Ignaz, 170
Büchenbacher, Albert, 119, 129, 130
Budapest, 13, 201
Bund, 100, 149
Bundist, 153, 199
Burgau concentration camp in Bavaria, 64
Bursztajn, Ruchela, 75
butcher of Vilnius (Franz Murer), 187

camps, 5, 19, 21, 36, 53, 66, 85, 86, 88, 116, 139, 141, 142, 169–70, 180, 198, 263, 331, 339–40; Blechhammer, 143; death, 3, 49, 85, 142, 261; Drancy, 142, 144, 153; extermination, 94, 110; German camp system, 50; Grosse Hamburger Strasse, 61, 62, 67–68; Jaworzno, 143; POW, 145; predeportation assembly camps, 58, 171; refugee,

INDEX

114; Schulstrasse, 63, 74; Skarżysko-Kamienna, 255; Zentralkomitee (camp administration), 167. *See also* concentration camps; displaced persons camps; labor camps; transit camps.
Camus, Albert, 156; *Combat*, 156–57
Canada, 310
Carton de Wiart, Henri, 209
Catholic Church, 168
Catholic or socialist mayors (Belgium), 210, 213
CBJB, Committee for Special Jewish Interests (Netherlands), 113–14
Center for Historical Research and Documentation on War and Contemporary Society in Brussels, 219
Central Committee in Munich, 72
Central Committee of Liberated Jews in Bavaria, 54, 55–56, 60, 227, 231, 335
Central Committee of Polish Jews (also known as the Central Committee of Jews in Poland, CKŻP), 36–37, 83–85, 88–91, 95, 100–102, 247, 251, 252, 253–54, 256, 257, 258, 259, 265, 268
Central Committee of the Union of Jewish Intellectuals of France, 147
Central Council for the Purge of Industry and Commerce (Netherlands), 111
Central Council of Jews in Germany, 170
Central Israelite Hospital in Amsterdam, 122
Central Jewish Historical Commission (CŻKH), 90, 91, 97, 254
Central Jewish Honor Court in Munich, 55–57, 60
Central Jewish Relief Work (Belgium), 202
Central Office for Jewish Emigration (Vienna), 126, 168, 169, 172, 174, 181
Central Office of Jewish Communities in Sosnowiec, 258
Central Office of Jewish Councils of Elders in East Upper Silesia, 257
Central Office of the Jewish Communities in Eastern Upper Silesia (the region's Jewish council), 91, 92, 97
Central Registration Bureau (Netherlands), 116
Chajet, Chaim, 256
chance encounters and meetings, 225, 290, 303, 321, 329
Charleroi, 199, 201–2, 204
Charleroi military court, 208
children, 140, 144, 231, 313, 342; deportation of the Neuilly, 144, 146, 149, 150, 152, 153; deported, 153; housed in orphanages, 85, 153; Mischling, 67, 71; orphaned Jewish, 313, 316, 317; orphans, 139
Chmielnicki, Pinkus, 142, 143
choiceless choice(s), 59, 63–68, 76, 181
Christianity, 141
Christians, the first, 279
Cincinnatus, 83–84, 90; "Traitors to the Nation—to the People's Court," 83–84
Circle of Dutch Jews, 116
Circulo Israelita, 247
Civic Tribunal for Former Collaborators with the Germans (Poland), 36–40, 42
CKŻP, Central Committee of Polish Jews, 83–85, 88–91, 95, 100–102, 247, 251, 252, 253–54, 256, 257, 258, 259, 265, 268
Clare, George, 170
CNIE, National Interprofessional Purge Committee (France), 151
Cohen, David, 17, 109, 110, 114, 115, 118, 119, 121, 122–32; verdict and arrest of, 125–28
Cohen, Benjamin, 347
Cohn, Haim, 309, 315–16
collaboration: through the body, 259–60, 263; economic, 207, 208, 210; gray zone of, 328, 329, 331, 351; individual, 107; the lesser evil of, 197–24; as a means of survival, 328
"Collaboration Among Jews" (Szechatow), 100
Collaboration with Tyranny in Rabbinic Law (Daube), 22n2

collaborators, 29–48; denunciations of alleged, 225–46; in prayer, *malshinim* (informers), 279; and release from criminal responsibility, 308–9; trials, 314, 318, 321; who were prisoners themselves, 308
Combat (Camus), 156–57
Commission for the Purge of the Press (Netherlands), 111
Committee for Israelite Interests (Netherlands), 116
Committee for Jewish Refugees (Netherlands), 114
Committee for Special Jewish Interests, CBJB (Netherlands), 113–14
Committee for the Unity and Defense of the Jews of France (CUDJF), 143
"common sense," and the Mordechai Goldstein verdict, 348
Communist Party (KPÖ), 180
communist underground, 16, 36
concentration camps: Bergen-Belsen, 50, 51, 115, 118–19, 121–22, 123, 124, 249; Breendonk, 202, 214–16; Budzyń, 238; Burgau, in Bavaria, 64; Dachau-Kaufering, 65, 66; Hessental, 73; Jaworzno, 143, 303–4; Landsberg, 321; Mielec, 239; Płaszów, 232; Reichenbach, 65; Sachsenhausen, 51, 72, 215; Stutthof, 75; Volkovysk, 254, 261. *See also* Auschwitz.
Concordia Press Club, 188
confrontations, 3, 20, 72, 248–49, 303–4; arranged, 247–49; with "Blind Max," 303–4; Szapiro (male witness in Runa Fakler's arranged confrontation), 248; Szpirsztajn (female witness in Runa Fakler's arranged confrontation), 248; Tuerk (female witness in Runa Fakler's arranged confrontation), 248
connotation of, in the ghetto: "assault," 330; "injury," 330
Consistoire central (France), 141, 144, 146, 147, 150, 151, 153

Constitution, Law, and Justice Committee (Israel), 307, 309
Contact Commission of the Jewish Coordination Committee (Netherlands), 118
Coordinating Committee of Jewish Welfare Organizations (France), 145
Council of Elders of the Jews in Vienna, 169, 172, 173, 177, 181–82
CRIF, Representative Council of Israelites of France, 144, 146–54
crimes against humanity, 51, 307, 309–12, 320, 332, 344
criminals, two types of: persecutor who was a member of an enemy organization, 317; victims of the persecutors, 317
Crystal Night pogrom, 51, 166
CUDJF, Committee for the Unity and Defense of the Jews of France, 143–44, 146, 150, 156
Cukierman, Icchak, 33–34. *See also* Antek; Zuckerman, Yitzhak.
Czarna, Fani, 91–92, 257–58
Czarny-Gidy, Leon (Lipa), 91–93, 257–58; former Jewish council member convicted by the honor court, 91; a member of the Central Office of the Jewish Communities in Eastern Upper Silesia (the region's Jewish council), 91
Czech government, 169
Czechoslovakia, 4, 39, 171, 184
Czerniaków, Adam, 90–91, 99–100
Częstochowa, 170
Częstochowa-Raków labor camp, 67
CŻKH, Central Jewish Historical Commission, 97, 254

Dachau, 77, 168, 172, 308, 311
Dachau-Kaufering concentration camp, 65, 66
Daily Bulletin, 172–73
Datner, Szymon, 102
Daube, David, 22; *Collaboration with Tyranny in Rabbinic Law*, 22n2
Davar, 282–83

David L. (friend from Block 10), 303
Dawidowicz, Lucy, 10; *The War Against the Jews*, 10
death marches, 52
de Jong, Abraham, 117
Delwaide, Leo, 210
Denmark, 39
denunciations: of alleged collaborators, 225–46; in the postwar Jewish community, 227–29
Department for the Struggle Against Usury and Speculation, 258; the so-called Thirteen, a semi-official German agency in the Warsaw ghetto, 258
Department of Internal Medicine (Vienna), 171
Department of Social Affairs of the Jewish Council (Netherlands), 121
deportation: exempt from, 108–9; of laborers to the Reich, 210; lists, 167, 178, 182; of the Neuilly children, 146
deprivation of civil rights, 145
Der Ausweg, 186
Der Neue Weg, 183–84, 189
Dessauer, Heinrich, 169
Destruction of the European Jews, The (Hilberg), 8
de Wolff, Sam, 119
Diaspora, 6, 14–15, 192, 241, 283–84, 287–88, 289, 328, 329; Jewish leadership in the, 283; Jews, 307; negation of the, 283
Die Aufgabe der Jacob Ehrlich Society (The Mission of the Jacob Ehrlich Society), 177
Die Stimme, 184–85
Die vierte Gemeinde (Adunka), 167
disabled Jewish veterans of World War I, 171
displaced persons (DP) camps, 16, 20, 30, 40, 41–42, 52, 56, 58, 69, 167, 227, 230, 231, 240, 281, 282, 340; Bindermichl, 187; Deggendorf, 55; Föhrenwald, 55; Landsberg in Bavaria, 54, 55; Neu-Freimann, 72
displaced persons, Jewish, 52–55, 57, 59, 72, 186, 335; courts, 19, 59, 77, 167
Dobberke, Walter, 51
Dobrowolski, Feliks, 258
Documentation Center of the Association of Jewish Victims of the Nazi Regime (Austria), 186, 188
dog attack of women, 75
Donath, Julius, 170
Donnet, André, 212
Dos naje lebn, 84, 89, 90, 235
Dossin Mechelen transit camp and detention facility, 214
Douglas, Mary, 293; *Purity and Danger*, 293
Dov (a reader of *Ha-boker*), 304
Drabbe, L. W. M. M., 127, 130
Drancy camp, 142, 144, 153
Drohobycz, 259
Drowned and the Saved, The (Levi), 13
Drucker Bar-Am, Gali, 20, 279–302, 361
Ducas, Raymond, 144, 146, 147, 148, 150, 151, 155
Du Rebecca rue des Rosiers (Malet), 155
Dürmayer, Heinrich, 181
Dutch: Christians, 113; government-in-exile, 110, 116; Jewish refugees in London, 116; Jewry, 17, 130; Jews, 17, 112–13, 131; parliament, 126; Supreme Court, 114
Dutch Union of Zionists (NZB), 114
Dzshebeliya (Perlov), 289, 294–96

Ebner, Karl, 178
Ebner, Margarete, 178
economic collaboration, 207, 208, 210
Edinger, Georges, 144, 148
Ehrlich, Leonard, 166
Eichmann, Adolf, 12, 13, 165, 168, 178, 320, 351; trial, 8, 12, 13, 20, 178, 305, 318, 351
Eichmann in Jerusalem: A Report on the Banality of Evil (Arendt), 8, 13, 108,

INDEX

179, 318
"Eichmann in New York" (Mushkat), 319
Eichmann's Central Office for Jewish Emigration, 174, 180
Eichmann's Jews (Rabinovici), 14, 167–68
Ein-Karem neighborhood, 303
Einsatzgruppen, 9
Eintracht, Aleksander, 261, 265
Eisenmann, Samuel, 68
Embacher, Helga, 18, 165–96, 362
empathic unsettlement, 287–88
Engel, David, 15, 16, 29–48, 89, 320, 362
Engel, Masza, 253, 254, 255, 259, 264
Engelking, Barbara, 91
Enschede, 115
Enzel, Jachet, 260
Épinal, Jewish community, 144, 146, 151
Eretz Israel, 2
euphemism for the Judenräte, "community leaders and lobbyists," 284
European Jewish Diaspora, 15
European Jewry, 42, 49, 50, 53, 60, 165, 169, 187
European Jews, 29, 282
euthanasia institutions, 166
exclusion from the Jewish community, 264–65
excommunication from Jewish life, 57, 123, 146, 149
excommunication from the Jewish community, 72
exemption from deportation, 115, 119, 127, 167; *Sperre*, 115, 119
exile, 165
exile organizations, 168
Expositur, 115
extermination, 172, 336
extermination camps, 94, 110
Extraordinary Court in Amsterdam, 125
Extraordinary Criminal Law Ruling, 110

face to face, 304
Fakler, Dawid (pseud. Maciek Fakler), 247–50, 253

Fakler, Runa, 247–53, 256, 259, 263–64, 268; attacked on the street, 250–51; "boycott" of, 248, 250–51; "enjoying the benefits of a kapo's wife," 248; implicated by her husband's actions, 249; née Lewinger, 247; Runa Fakler-Kornblüh, 251
Falkenhausen, Alexander von, 200, 201, 202
Fälscherkommando, 215
Faurisson, Robert, 138
Fayner, Reuven, 142–43
Federación Israelita, 250–51
Federation of Jewish Organizations of France (FSJF), 144
Feldsberg, Ernst, 18, 167, 184–89
Ferdman, David, 203
Finder, Gabriel N., 1–27, 83–106, 362
Finkerlpel, Christine, 249
firing squad, 108
First, Izrael, (also, Fürst, Izrael) 34, 88, 99
Fischer, Ernst, 171–73
Fisher, Joseph, 147, 152
Fitzpatrick, Sheila, 227
Fleishman, Gisi, 255
Flemish National Union, 210
Fogel, Alter, 143
Folksztime, 255
forced labor, 68, 93, 198, 306
Forshner, Raana, 321
FPÖ (Austrian Freedom Party), 188
France, 39, 137–64, 199, 215, 216
Frankfurt, 170
Frankists, 279
Frank, Lucien, 147
Frank, Ziuta, 258
Frauenglas, Marian, 256
Fredj, Jacques, 144, 152
Free Austrian Movement, 174–75, 177
freedom of choice, 334, 337, 344
free will, 333
French: courts, 151; Jewish scouts, 158n19; Jewry, 141, 154; Jews, 138–39; Judaism, 150; judicial authorities, 142
Freudinger, Pinchas, 13

INDEX

Fridman, Bela, 261
Friedheim, Władysław, 237–38
Friedländer, Saul, 86
Friedman, Philip, 7, 10
"Friends of André Baur, Raymond-Raoul Lambert, and their deported colleagues," 154
Frydman, Bela, 262
Frydman, Henryk, 239–40
FSJF, Federation of Jewish Organizations of France, 144, 147
Fünten, Ferdinand aus der, 126–27

Galicia, 93, 155
Gallas, Elisabeth, 77
Garde, Mieczysław, 260–61, 263, 265–66
Garfinkels, Grégoire, 208
gas chambers, 186, 198
Gedalye ("Nekome"), 290–93, 295
Gelinck, Marinus H., 126
Gellately, Robert, 227
Gellner, Ernest, 280
gender roles, 19–20, 247–78
General Confederation of Former Internee and Deportee Victims of Oppression and Racism (France), 151
General Instruction Service of the Chief Military Prosecutor's Office (Belgium), 205
General Zionist party, 184
General Zionists, 306–7
Geneva, 176, 183
genocide, 6, 55, 76, 86, 205, 309
Gens, Jacob, 90
Gerbing, Herbert, 184
German: internees, 118; Jewish refugees, 113–14; Jews, 53–54, 57, 58, 69, 72; occupation, 110, 120, 137, 330; occupation of Belgium, 197; speaking Jews, 188; war criminals, 205; Wehrmacht, 185
Gertler, David, 233, 237
Gerzon, Jules, 119
Gestapo: camp Grosse Hamburger Strasse 26, 51; camp at Schulstrasse in the Wedding neighborhood, 74; confidante, 258; headquarters, 168; informants, 32, 51, 90; Jewish Department (Austria), 177
Ghent, 199, 202
ghetto: Będzin, 90, 231, 254, 313; Buczacz, in eastern Galicia, 155; evacuation, 256, 258; fighters, 41, 284–88; heroism and rebellion in, 283; hierarchy, 263; Kovno (also, Kaunas), 40, 60, 66, 88; Kraków, 265; liquidation of, 86, 90, 94–95; Lodz, 68, 100, 232, 233, 238, 256, 265; Ostrowiec, 74, 256, 327, 329, 330, 335, 337, 339, 344, 345; Prużany, 255; Środula, 92; Świętokrzyski, 74; Tłuste, 94; underground, 67; Vilna, 187; Warsaw, 32, 37, 84, 88, 102, 225, 254, 258; Zbaraż, 256
Gielen, Jos J., 119, 124
Gil, Yaakov, 306–8
Gliksman, Henryk, 67
Goeth, Amon, 256
Goldberg, Sylvie Anne, 157
Goldfein, Olga, 255
Goldmann, Nahum, 186, 187
Goldschlag, Stella, (also Kübler, Stella, or Isaaksohn, Stella), 51, 58, 62
snatcher of Jews in hiding, 51
Goldstein, Mordechai, 20–21, 327, 329, 331, 343–52; and "common sense," 348; defense witnesses, 21, 347; and the gray zone of collaboration, 328–29, 347; and "I Shall End with a General Comment," 347–50; prosecution testimonies, 344, 346; verdict, 347–50
Goldstein, Siegfried, 64
Gomperts, B. P., 124–25
good and evil, 165, 293, 329, 337, 340
Görlitz camp, 265
Gorski, Joseph, 304
Gottesmann, 178
Gran, Wiera, (also, Vera), 14, 37, 90, 253, 255, 258, 259, 264; succumbed to pressure to stand trial, 255

INDEX

gray zone, 21, 170, 329, 349–52; of everyday life, 330; expression coined by Primo Levi, 329; "The Gray Zone of Collaboration and the Israeli Courtroom," 327–60
"Gray Zone, The" (Levi), 13
Great Britain, 172, 174, 176, 177
Greece, 4
Greenberg, Avner, 296, 352
Gricmacher, Isaac, 321
Gricmacher, Loba Meschkup (pseud. Red-Haired Loba), 321
Groningen, 115
Grosse Hamburger Strasse 26, 51, 58, 61, 62, 67
Gross, Jan T., 53
Grossman, Kurt R., 233
Grossman, Liush Louis, 310
Gross-Rosen, 50
Gruenbaum, Eliezer (pseud. Leon Berger), 143
Grynberg, Anne, 137, 144, 152, 156
Günther, Rolf, 185
Gur-Arie, Hemda, 317
Gutmacher, Ludwik, 92

Haan, Ido de, 17, 107–36, 363
Ha-boker, 304
Hackett, Amy, 77
Hague, The, 115, 122, 192
Halevi, Benjamin, 13
Harrison Report of August 1945, 56
Hausner, Gideon, 12, 351
Hebrew, 15, 296, 316, 331, 344, 352; literature, 20, 281–82, 296; mainstream press, 283
Hebrew Immigrant Aid Society, 73
Hebrew University of Jerusalem, 319
heirless Jewish property, 177, 184, 189
Helesiewicz, Mendel, 260–61, 262
Hellendall, Eugène, 202, 204
heroes, 3, 351–52
heroic, 38, 141, 171, 282–89, 320
heroic "new Jew," 328

heroism, 2, 283–87
Herzberg, Abel J., 117, 126, 129, 131; "The Jewish Honor Court: Null and Void," 129
Hessental concentration camp, 73
Het Joodsche Weekblad, 125
Het Oordeel, 118
Heymont, Irving, 54
hiding, 51, 86, 210, 330, 341
Hilberg, Raul, 8, 9, 10; *Destruction of the European Jews, The*, 8, 10; *Perpetrators, Victims, Bystanders*, 10
Hirsingen, Alsace, 202
"Historical Committee" in Kraków (Jewish Voivodeship Committee in Krakow, WKŻK), 248, 251, 259
Hitler (Adolf), 169, 178, 254
Hitlerism, 2
Hitlerite, 96, 141, 253, 259, 264
Hoch, Józef, 236
Hoheneck prison camp, 51
Holland, 39, 50
Holocaust: commemorative ceremonies, 283; denier, 138; Memorial Day, 284; Memorial Day Law, 284
Holzinger, Robert, 197–98, 209
Honigman, Jacob, 316
Honor Court for the Arts, 111
honor courts, 3–5, 7, 225; absence of in Postwar Belgium, 197–98, 204–5; of the Central Committee of Polish Jews, 225; decisions not binding, 3; judging accusations and offenses, 59–63. *See also* Jewish honor courts.
Horodenka Jewish council, 17, 93–98
Hufnagel, Lusia, 249
Hungarian army, 93
Hungarian Jews, 13, 169, 179
Hungarians, 214
Hungarian-Slovakian border, 310
Hungary, 4, 13, 217, 261

Ichud Party (General Zionists), 100
IG Farben factory, 50

375

INDEX

IGUL (an alumni association of Zionist fraternities at Austrian universities), 175
IKG, Viennese Jewish Community, 165–89
internal: Jewish courts, 53, 54–59, 166, 218; Jewish issue, 218; purges, 156–57, 211, 213, 218; Jewish tribunals, 145–46, 149
International Military Tribunal (IMT), 49, 59
International Red Cross, 171
Isaaksohn, Rolf, 58
Isaaksohn, Stella, (also, Kübler, Stella), 51
Israel: Defense Forces soldiers, 303; enemies, 279; a new Jewish nation-state, 281–82, 289–90; Office of the Attorney General, 320; Police Criminal Investigation Unit, 304; State Archive, 331; War of Independence, 287
Israeli: collaborator trials, 14, 22; consul, 179; courts, 5, 12–13, 16, 21, 41, 281, 318, 328–29, 339; government, 307; law, 331; literature, 281–82; parliament, 186; Remembrance Day Law, 283; reparations agreement and relations with West Germany, 283; society's public agenda, 283; Supreme Court, 314
Israeli Opera House, 313
Israeli Philharmonic Orchestra's boycott of Richard Wagner's music, 23
Israelite Community of Brussels, 201, 202
Israelitisches Wochenblatt, 173
Italy, 30, 231, 249

Jacob Ehrlich Society, 172, 175, 177
Jacoubovitch, Jules, 145, 146
Jaffee, Ludwik, 231–32, 237
Janowce, 260
Jarblum, Marc, 147
Jaworzno concentration camp, 143, 303–4
JCC, Jewish Coordination Committee for the Liberated Netherlands, 116, 119
Jedwabne, 86
Jegier (Jeger), Bernard, 258

Jerusalem, 178, 303, 314
Jewish: exodus from Eastern Europe, 167; hospital, 168, 169, 170, 171, 179, 180, 181; kindergarten, 124; law (Halakha), 22, 112; old-age home, 169; police force, a body formed by order of the Nazis, 87, 329; press, 154, 156, 197; resistance movement in German-occupied Eastern Europe 308
Jewish Agency, 73
Jewish Central Committee (Poland), 101
Jewish Central Consistory of Belgium, 199
Jewish community: in Bolivia, 247, 250; defined the terms of belonging for its members, 77; excommunication from, 72; public life, expulsion from, 148; heaviest penalty, ostracism, 280; levels of punishment, 69; suspension from, for three years, 265–66
Jewish Contact Committee, 114, 115
Jewish Coordination Committee for the Liberated Netherlands (JCC), 116, 119
Jewish Correspondence Bureau, 192
Jewish council(s). *See* Judenrat; Judenräte.
Jewish Defense Committee, 203, 206, 208, 209
Jewish Fighting Organization (ŻOB), 16, 32–38, 41, 84, 87, 88, 90, 99, 100, 102
Jewish Historical Commission in Kraków, 250–51, 263
Jewish Historical Institute, 97, 101–2
"Jewish Hitler," 182. *See also* Tuchmann, Emil.
Jewish honor courts: in Allied-Occupied Germany, 49–82; charter for, 119–20; and effects of age and immaturity, 64; in the Netherlands, 107–36; in postwar Poland, 16, 83–106; scale of offenses, 69–71; unorganized and arbitrary, 109
Jewish Hospital at Schulstrasse 78, 58, 67
Jewish Military Union (ŻŻW), 87
Jewish National Fund in France, 147
Jewish Novaks, 186
Jewish Palestine, 3

INDEX

Jewish Social Assistance Society, JSS (Poland), 88
Jewish Social Self-Help (Poland), 254
Jewish Social Work (Netherlands), 117
Jewish Telegraphic Agency, 142, 172, 173, 175, 192
Jewish Voivodeship Committee in Kraków (WKŻK), 251, 259
Jews with Belgian citizenship, 199
Jews in Belgium without Belgian citizenship, 212, 218
Jockusch, Laura, 1–27, 49–82, 363
Joinovici, Joseph, 142
Joint, the (American Jewish Joint Distribution Committee), 172, 183
Joodsche Raad (Jewish Council) of Amsterdam, 114
Joodsch Weekblad, 115
Joodse Ereraad (Jewish Honor Court), 108
Judaism, 70–71, 146, 230, 280
Judenrat (Jewish council): of Będzin, 314; categorized as a hostile organization, 314; judgment of, by Polish Jewry, 83–106
Judenrat: The Jewish Councils in Eastern Europe Under Nazi Occupation (Trunk), 9
Judenräte (Jewish councils): "community leaders and lobbyists" is a euphemism for the, 284; forgiving and empathetic attitude toward, 287
judgment: of the Jewish Council in the Netherlands, 122–25; of the Jewish Honor Court in the Netherlands, 125–30; in the Puczyc trial, 339–43
Jungster, Hezekiel, 310–12, 320
jurors: fugitives, 151; legitimacy disputed, 150; moral caliber of, 147
jury of honor (*jury d'honneur*), 137–64; appointment to serve on, 147; composed exclusively of Jewish war veterans, 151; counterjury, 151
Jutrznia (Dawn), 87

Kac, Samuel, 256

Kahn, Edmond, 150, 151
Kalmanowicz, Selig, 288
Kan, Marinus L., 114
Kantian: judicial retribution, 42; retributive justice, 34, 36; sense, 33, 39
Kant, Immanuel, 31, 32
Kaplan, Jacob, 141
Kapralik, Charles, 176, 179
Kaswiner, A., 247, 249
Kasztner, Rudolf, (also, Rezső; Rudolph) 12–13, 43n4, 281, 283, 288–90, 345
Kaunas. *See* Kovno.
Kazerne Dossin, 201
Kazernestraat 33 in Brussels, 207
Kelman, Claude, 147
Khinke Melnitser ("Nekome"), 290–94, 295
Kieffé, Robert, 149, 152
Kierbel (or Kerbel), Abram Icek, 256
kindergarten, 125
Kisch, Isaac, 114, 127
Klaar, Dr. Paul, 170
Klaus, Josef, 187
Klibanov, Yaakov, 307
Knesset (Israeli legislature), 186, 305–9, 311, 321
Knyszyńska, Rita, 253, 254, 255, 261, 264
Kolisch, Sigfried, 178, 193n69
Kołomyja, 94
Kon, Abraham, 265, 267
Koniecpolska, Róża, 262, 266–67
Koplenig, Johann, 174
Kovner, Abba, 288
Kovno ghetto, 40, 60, 88
Kozak, Rózia, 258
Koźmińska-Frejlak, Ewa, 19, 20, 91, 247–78, 363–64
Kraków, 37, 88, 247, 248, 249, 250, 251, 259
Kraków ghetto, 265
Kramer, Josef, 50
Kranefeld, Ferdinand Abraham, 70, 71
Kranefeld, Werner, 70
Krankenkasse (Health Insurance Provider), 180
Kranz, Bela, 258

Kreisky, Bruno, 188
Kreisky-Wiesenthal affair, 188
Krouker, Élie, 145, 146, 148, 149, 150, 151
Krumholtz, Emma, 247, 249
Krzepice camp, 261, 262
Kübler, Manfred, 51
Kübler, Stella, (also, Isaaksohn, Stella), 51
Kupiec, Regina, 238–39
Kweczer, Julian, 95, 97, 98

labor camps, 3, 38, 42, 49, 59, 85, 92, 94, 142, 170, 327, 329, 331; Częstochowa-Raków, 67; Janowska Road, 94; Ostrowiec, 347, 350; Płaszów, 228, 247, 248, 249, 250, 251, 253, 255, 256, 260, 261, 265; Radom, 73; Skarzysko-Kamienna, 226
LaCapra, Dominick, 287, 292; empathic unsettlement, 287; and successful processing of trauma, 294
Lachmuth, Felix, 61–62
Laffitte, Michel, 137, 144, 152
Lages, Willy, 126, 127
Lambert, Raymond-Raoul, 154
Lam, Joseph, 307–8, 311–12
Landau, Ernst, 215
Landau, Justice Moshe, 315, 318
Landsberg concentration camp, 321
Landsberg DP camp, 54
Langer, Lawrence, 59, 181; and "choiceless choice," 59, 181
language, 328, 331; judicial, 343; juridical, 327–31; of legal proceedings, 348; neutral, 306; negative connotation of the term collaboration, 328; Yiddish authors continued to write in their own, 289
Lanzmann, Claude, 13–14; *The Last of the Unjust*, 13–14
Laor, Dan, 282–83, 285
La Paz, 235, 247, 250
Lasota, Marek Marian, 95, 267
Last of the Unjust, The (Lanzmann), 13–14
La Terre retrouvée, 149
Latvian collaborator, 306

Laurahütte, 50
Lazar, Benzion, 171–73, 176
Lazare (also known as Lazer or Lazar), David, 202, 207, 208
Left Poale Tsiyon, 154
Leibovits, Dezso, 142
Leivick, H. (Yiddish poet), 296
Lejkin, Jakób, 33, 34
Lemberg, 108. *See also* Lvov.
"lesser evil" of Jewish collaboration, 197–224
Letste nayes, 289; published "Nekome" by Yitskhok Perlov, in serial form, 289
Letts (Latvians), 34
Levi, Primo, 13, 21, 157, 329; coined the expression, "gray zone," 329; *The Drowned and the Saved*, 13
Levitsky, Asher, 344
Lévy, Paul, 216
Lewi, Genia, 262–63
Lewin, Sally, 215, 216
Lewkowicz, Szlama, 92, 93
Libai, David, 314
Liber, Maurice, 148
Liebmann, Lazare, 198, 206–9
Liège, 198, 199, 200, 201, 202, 213
Liège initiative, 198
Liège military court, 208
Linde (allegedly an agent for the Gestapo), 255, 258
Lindon, Raymond, 147
Linke Poale Zion, 197
Linz, 186
Lipstadt, Deborah E., 9, 13
Lisbon, 201, 209
Listopadzki, Bolesław, 266
literature, 281; Hebrew, 281, 296; Israeli, 281; morality theme in, 290–96; the "simple Jew," typical focus in modern, 290; Yiddish, 281, 289, 296
Lodz ghetto, 93, 232, 233, 238, 256, 265
Lodz Jews, 254
Lodz, Poland, 41, 90, 225, 343, 344
London, 18, 33, 110, 116, 167, 172, 174,

175, 176, 189
London, Hersz, 261–62
Löwenherz, Josef, 18, 167, 168, 169, 170–79, 180, 181, 183, 184, 189
Löwenherz, Sigmund, 170, 171
Löwenherz, Sofie, 170–71, 173–74, 177
Löw, Franzi, 172
Lubański, Marian, 97
Lubetkin, Cywia, 33, 35
Lublin, 36, 185, 202, 258
Lüneburg, 50, 77
Lustig, Yerachmiel (Yaron), 304–5
"luxurious" situation in the camp, 264
Lvov, 94. *See also* Lemberg.
Lyon-Caen, Léon, 147
Lyons, 141

Maastricht, 116
"machinery of destruction," 8
Main Committee for the Victims of Fascism (Germany), 55
Majzel, Rena, 255, 256
Malet, Léo, 155; *Du Rebecca rue des Rosiers*, 155
Mandatory Palestine, 308. *See also* Palestine.
Mapai, 282
Markowicz, Olga, 255
Marseilles, 142
Maurer brothers, 187
Mauthausen, 50, 215
Mayer, Saly, 183
Mazirel, Laura C., 127, 130
McBride, Horace L., 56
"Measures of Justice" (Alterman), 282–83, 287
Mechelen, Military Court of, 214, 217
Mehlwurm, Juda (alias Jules), 201–2, 207
Meinen, Insa, 203
Meiss, Léon, 144, 150, 152–54, 156
Memorial Day ceremonies, 296
Memorial Foundation for Jewish Culture, 321
men accused, 254, 256, 259; of domination and violence, often with sexual undertones, 259–60; of procurement, 260; of rape and extortion, 260; of sexual abuse, 260, 263
Merbaum, Alfred, 17, 93, 95–101
Merin, Chaim, 90
Merin, Moshe (also, Moniek), 90–92, 97, 257, 258
Meschkup (Gricmacher), Loba (pseud. Red-Haired Loba), 321
Mexico City, 100
Meyer, Félix, 208
Milikowski, Herman, 118
Ministry of Justice (Netherlands; Israel), 120, 305, 306, 320
Mintzberg, Ya'akov, 331
Mirel, Eugenia, 256
Mischling children, 67, 71
mixed marriage, 170, 171, 174, 215, 216
Moabit District Court, 51
Modiano, Vidal, 147
Monowicz, Szyja, 258
Mons, 202
moral: accounting, 32; balance, 31, 33, 40, 60; collapse, 8, 9; regeneration, 2; rehabilitation, 16, 53, 76; reprimand, 69; restoration, 33; wrongdoing, 62
morality theme in "Nekome" and *Dzshebeliya*, 290–96
Mordowurka, Beniamin, 258
Morris, Douglas, 77, 321
Moscow Declaration, 49
motivation, 87, 313, 346; for denunciations, 229–34
Munich, 16, 53, 54, 58, 74, 227, 236, 332; Central Committee in, 72; Jewish honor courts in, 16, 53, 55, 56, 58, 59, 60, 66, 73; Rehabilitation Commission of the Central Jewish Honor Court in, 60, 64, 65, 66, 72, 73, 74
Münzer, Oskar, 166
Murer, Franz (pseud. butcher of Vilnius), 187
Murmelstein, Benjamin, 14, 168–69, 174, 184

INDEX

Mushkat, Marion, 319; "Eichmann in New York," 319

Nadel, Maria, 261
Najman, Dawid, 74–75
Natanek, Karolina, 252
National Endowment for the Humanities (NEH), 321
National Federation of Deported and Interned Resistance Fighters (France), 151
National Federation of Prisoners of War, 145, 146
National Socialism, 216
National Socialist, 71, 165, 168
National Socialist Movement, 111
Naumann, Curt, 61, 62
Naye Prese, 143, 154
Nazi: administration, 314; anti-Semitism, 113; policy of disinformation, 286
Nazis and Nazi Collaborators (Punishment) Law of 1950, 4, 5, 12, 16, 20, 30, 40, 41, 281, 305–9, 310, 313, 317, 318, 320, 321, 328, 329, 330, 336, 338, 339, 349, 351, 352; as a means of adjudicating mainly Jews suspected of collaboration with the Nazis rather than Nazi war criminals, 328; neutral language in, 306; and release from criminal responsibility, 308, 309; Section 1 (or Article 1), war crimes, crimes against the Jewish people, and crimes against humanity, 306, 307, 310, 312, 313, 332, 344; Section 2, crimes against persecuted persons, 309, 312; Section 3, 314; Section 4, concentration camps, 309; Section 4, ghettos, 309, 312, 316; Section 5, delivering up a persecuted person to an enemy administration, 309, 312, 316; Section 6, instances of blackmailing persecuted individuals, 309; Section 6, Paragraph 4, assault causing actual bodily harm, 312; Section 10, 309; Section 15, the court may deviate from the rules of evidence, 316; two types of criminals, 317

Nederlandsch Juristenblad, 128
Nefors, Patrick, 216, 217
"Nekome" (Perlov), 289–96; appeared in serial form in *Letste nayes*, 289
Netherlands, 4, 17, 108, 109, 113, 114, 115, 116, 117, 119, 120, 121, 130, 199, 281; Jewish Honor Court in, 107–36. *See also* Holland.
Netherlands Israelite Church Organization (NIK), 113
Neu-Freimann DP Camp, 72
Neuilly children, 144, 146, 148, 149, 150, 152, 153
Neuilly Children's Home, 153
Neumann, Selmar, 67
New York, 172, 174, 175, 177, 179
New York Review of Books, 14
Nieuw Israëlietisch Weekblad (NIW), 118, 131–32; verdict on David Cohen published in, 125
NIK, Netherlands Israelite Church Organization, 113, 114, 116, 117, 118, 120; Central Committee of the, 128, 129, 130; Permanent Committee of the, 117, 118, 128, 129, 130
Nir, Nahum, 307
Nisebaum, Chaim, 256
Nisko, first mass deportation, 185, 186
Norway, 39
Novak, Franz, 186, 187
Novick, Peter, 137; *The Resistance Versus Vichy: The Purge of Collaborators in Liberated France* (study), 137
Nozice (or Nozyce), Noé, 202, 208
Nuremberg, 49; court, 306; International Military Tribunal (IMT) at, 49; trials, 12, 59, 77; Tribunal, 306
NZB, Dutch Union of Zionists, 114, 116–19, 123, 128

Obler, Walter, 215–16
Ofer, Dalia, 255
old-age home, 181
Olshan, Yitzhak, 315, 317

ombudsman, 263
Operation Iltis, 201, 202
Oranienburg, 50
Oranienburgerstrasse, 54–55
Organization of Polish Jews in France, 141
orphanages, 85, 153
orphans, 139
Oruro, 251
Ostend, 199
Ostrowiec ghetto, 256, 327, 329, 330, 335, 337, 339, 344, 345
Ostrowiec labor camp, 347, 350
Ostrowiec, Poland, 20, 327, 331
Oświęcim (Auschwitz) camp, 264
Ottoman Empire, 147
Otwock, Poland, 254
ÖVP (Austrian People's Party), 187, 188

Paal, Joseph (pseud. Blind Max), 303–4
Palestine, 85, 116, 118, 119, 172, 308, 335; Jewish Agency for, 229–30
Palestinian, 290
Palestinian lists, 257
paper plant in Płaszów, 260, 261
Paris, 141, 142, 144, 153, 155
Parisian bourgeoisie, 150
Paris military tribunal, 142
Patak, Erna, 171
Patton, General George S., 335
Penal Article 115 (pertaining to economic collaboration), 207, 208, 210
Penal Article 118-bis (which dealt with political collaboration), 207, 208, 209, 212, 213
Penal Article 121-bis, regarding denunciation, 207, 208
Perego, Simon, 18, 137–64, 364
Perelman, Chaïm, 203, 204, 209, 211–13, 218
Perlov, Yitskhok, 20, 289–90, 296; *Dzshebeliya* (Jebeliya), 289, 294–96; "Nekome" (Vengeance), 289–96
permanent exclusion, 218
permanent residence permits, 212

perpetrators: surrogate, 287; and victim, clear-cut distinction between, 351
Perpetrators, Victims, Bystanders (Hilberg), 10
Person, Katarzyna, 19, 225–46, 364
Pétain, Marshal Philippe, 145
Peter, Friedrich, 188
petition for rehabilitation, 254, 255
Piekarski, Poldek, 260
Płaszów labor camp, 228, 247, 248, 249, 250, 251, 253, 255, 256, 260, 261, 265
Płaszów's Ordungsdienst, 261
Poalei Tsion Left, a liberal party in the Jewish political spectrum, 262
pogrom, Crystal Night, 51, 166
Polak, Eliazer, 122
Poland, 4, 10, 16, 17, 19, 36, 38, 39, 40, 41, 42, 85, 96, 102, 113, 170, 185, 202, 203, 217, 225, 251, 252, 254, 267, 280, 281, 304, 319, 343
Polish: consulate in Tel Aviv, 304; criminal court, 39; Jewish honor court, 11, 14, 16, 17, 19, 20, 86, 89, 250, 251, 253, 254; Jewry, 39, 83–106; Jews, 83, 93, 100, 102, 252, 265; legal system, 89
Polish Democratic Association, 247
Polish Republic, 216
Polish Security Office militiamen, 88
political collaboration, 207, 209, 210, 212, 213, 214
Political Investigation Service, 119, 126
Pope Pius XII, 127
Porat, Dan, 20, 303–26, 364
Portuguese, 116, 118
"potato commando" at the Stutthof concentration camp, 75
Poznanski, Renée, 157
Prague, 171, 172, 176
Prauss, Arthur, 215
prayer, 279–80; Amidah, 279; nineteen benedictions, 279
Presser, Jacques, 130; study of the Holocaust in the Netherlands, *Ondergang (Ashes in the Wind)*, 130–31
press, Hebrew mainstream, 283

INDEX

press, Yiddish, 289
prison camps: Hoheneck, 51; Sachsenhausen, 51, 72, 215; Torgau, 51; Waldheim, 51
privileged role in the concentration camp system, 251, 264, 304, 305
Prochnik, Robert, 166
"protection cards," 206
Provincial Criminal Court of Vienna, 169
provincial "Israelite" bourgeoisie, 150
Provincial Jewish Committee (Poland), 225
Provisional Government of the French Republic, 145
Prussian province of Posen, 216
Puczyc, Moshe (Marian), 20, 21, 327, 329, 331–43, 344, 346, 347, 348, 350–52; defense witnesses testimonies, 334, 337, 338, 339, 341; freedom of choice, 337; and the gray zone of collaboration, 328, 329, 336; prosecution witnesses testimonies, 21, 332, 333, 336, 337, 338, 339, 342, 352; verdict, 339–43, 350
punishment: of collaborators, 29–48; handed down by honor courts, 68–75
purge: Advisory Committee on the Purge (Netherlands), 117; economic, 151; in France, postwar, 137–64; internal, of the Jewish community, 140, 151, 152, 154, 155, 218; intracommunity (France), 142, 143; judicial (France), 140; in the Netherlands, 110–12; trials, 147; of the UGIF, 146, 152
Purge Commission, 4, 141, 143, 144, 156
Purge Department, 140
Purge Ruling, 111
Purity and Danger (Douglas), 293

questionnaire, 150, 151, 179

Rabinovici, Doron, 11, 14, 167–87; *Eichmann's Jews*, 14, 167–68
Radom, 261
Radom Judenrat, 257
Radom labor camp, 73
rape, 260, 261, 262, 263, 266, 309
Raphael, Martha, 62, 63
Rapoport, David, 159
Raschke, Dr. Arnold, 181
reconciliation, 22, 156
reconstruction, 157, 198; future-oriented, 219; of the Jewish community, 117, 118, 139, 147; of Jewish life in France, 138; of Jewish life in the Netherlands, 115–16
Red Army, 93, 94, 166, 171
Red Cross, 171
Red-Haired Loba (Gricmacher, Loba, also Meschkup, Loba), 321
rehabilitation, 4, 41, 49–82, 92, 95, 254, 255, 289; commissions, 4, 40, 59, 60, 61
Rehabilitation Commission of the Central Committee of Liberated Jews in the American Zone of Occupied in Germany, 40, 41
Rehabilitation Commission of the Central Jewish Honor Court in Munich, 64, 65, 66, 72, 73, 74
Reich Association of Jews in Germany, 67
Reichenbach concentration camp, 65
Reich, Oskar, 142
Reisz, Wilhelm, 166, 174, 184
Rejtman, Jerzy, 259–60
Remembrance Day Law, 283
Representative Council of Israelites of France (CRIF), 144
residence permits, 200
resistance, 39, 108, 145, 151, 202, 283
Résistance fighters, 145, 151
Resistance Versus Vichy: The Purge of Collaborators in Liberated France, The, (Novick), 137
restitution, 172, 184
retribution, 6, 12, 15, 16, 31, 32, 34, 35, 36, 39, 41, 42, 138, 167
retributive justice, 21, 33, 41
revenge, 296, 308
Rexist Party, 210
Rhine, 116

Ringelblum, Emmanuel, (also, Emanuel), 32, 33, 35–36, 38, 267
Rixinger, Johann, 177–78, 183–84
Roet, Salomon, 117
Romanian guards, 214
Rome, 251
Rosen, Pinchas, 304, 305–6
Rosenbach, Mojżesz, 247–50
Rosenberg, Arnold, 63, 64
Rosenblum, Aryeh, 313
Rosenfeld, Louis, 202, 209
Rosenman, Abram, 256
Rosenzweig-Gajac, 148
Rosenzweig, Ruth, 64–65
Rotholc, Shepsl, 11, 37, 39, 89
Rothschild, Hermann, 67–68
Rotterdam, 115
Rousso, Henry, 137, 151
Rowiński, Stanisław, 225
Rubin, Hannan, 308
Rubin, Majer, 226
Rubinger, Isak, 182
Rubinstein, Yitshak, 331
Rumkowski, Chaim (pseud. King Chaim), 93
Russian Empire, 202
Russian military administration, 170

Sabbateans, 279
sabotage, 67, 87
Sachsenhausen prison camp, 51, 72, 215
Sagalson, Aryeh, 321
Salomon, Ram, 305
Schaarbeek, 216
Schapiro, Sylwia, 258, 259
Schendel, Kurt, 148, 150
Schlomowicz, Ignatz, 50–51
Schmandt, Leo, 215, 216
Schöffer, Ivo, 119, 131
Schoffman, Joshua, 321
Scholem, Gershom, 319
and the argument of "I was not there," 319–20
Schrager, Fayvel, 149, 153

Schulstrasse camp in Berlin, 63, 74
Schur, Heinrich, 171–72
Schwartz, Isaïe, 141
SD, Sicherheitsdienst, security service of the SS, 126, 142, 200
Segev, Tom, 186–88
Seine, civil tribunal of the, 147
Séminaire israélite de France, 148
Sephardic immigrants, 147
Sephardic Jews, 112, 199
Sephardim and Oriental Communities Party, 307
sexual: abuse, 19, 33, 91, 260, 262, 263, 265, 267; contacts, 259, 261; extortion, 261; harassment, 91; relations, 251, 253; violence, 262, 263, 265, 268
sexuality, female, 263
Shamir, Mina, 311
Shilansky, Dov, 321
Shoah (Lanzmann), 14, 267, 268
Shtern, Ely, 142
Siegel, Julius, 304
Sikkel, Nicolaas J. G., 125–27
Silberstein, Samuel, 225
Simon, Ernst, 319
Sipo, or Sicherheitspolizei, security police of the SS, 200, 212, 215
Skarzysko-Kamienna labor camp, 226
Skosowski, Lolek, 258
Słapakowa, Cecylia, 267–68
Śląsko-Dąbrowskie Voivodeship, 266
Slovakia, 255
Slovès, Haim, 147
Smolensk camp, 36
snatcher of Jews in hiding, 51, 61, 62. See also Isaaksohn, Stella; Kübler, Stella.
Social Democrats, 168, 188
Sold, Hans, 259
solidarity, 141, 155, 286, 338
Sommer, Robert, 141
Sommerstein, Emil, 331
Sonia P. (recognized "Red-Haired Loba"), 321. *See also* Gricmacher, Loba; Meschkup, Loba.

INDEX

Sosnowiec, 91, 92, 258, 260, 261, 266
South America, 251
Soviet: authorities, 179; liberation of Warsaw, 88; military court, 51; occupied, 185; zonal trials, 50
Soviets, 95, 171
Soviet Union, 4, 9, 85, 93, 185, 267, 308, 321
Speijer, Nathan, 121, 122
Sperre, 115, 119; lists, 125; stamp, 120, 129
SPÖ (Austrian Social Democratic Party), 185, 186, 188
spouse: "Aryan," 182; beneficiary of services rendered to, by prisoners, 248; converted to Judaism upon marriage, 70; and "luxurious" situation in camp, 264; non-Jewish, 216; responsibility for conduct of, 248, 250, 256, 257
SS: Central Office for Jewish Emigration, 165; security police (Sipo), 200; security service (SD), 108, 200
Stalingrad, 126
Stanisławów, 187
Star of David, 94, 115, 125, 200, 203. *See also* yellow star.
State of Israel, 3, 4, 12, 14, 20, 40, 41, 42, 52, 85, 281, 283, 304, 305, 306, 307; heir of the Nazis' innocent victims, 305
Steinberg, Maxime, 197
Stern, Wilhelm, 169
Stiftung, Gerda Henkel, 321
Stutthof concentration camp, 75, 255; Elbląg, a division of the, 255
Supreme Commission for Israelite Affairs, 112, 113
Supreme Court (of Israel), 305, 312, 314, 215, 315, 316, 318
Supreme Health Advisory Board (Austria), 184
Surażko, Sonia, 264
survival mechanisms, 215
survivors: communities, 52; Harrison Report of August 1945, 56; moral and ethical rehabilitation, 16, 53, 57; witnesses, 341, 343

Süskind, Walter, 125
Sutzkever, Avrom, 289
Sweden, 188, 249
Swirsky, Hirsz, 216
Swiss Union of Jewish Communities, 173
Switzerland, 141, 144, 171, 173
Szapiro (male witness in Runa Fakler's arranged confrontation), 248
Szechatow, Szaje, 100–101; "Kolaboratsye bay yidn" (Collaboration Among Jews), 100–101
Szenberg (Kupiec), Regina, 72–73
Szenderowicz, Ida, 257
Szenderowicz, Naum, 91, 257, 261–62
Szeryński, Józef, 33–34, 99
Sznit, Chawa, 255
Szpering, Frania, 261–62
Szpigelman, Chaskiel, 261–63, 266–67
Szpirsztajn (female witness in Runa Fakler's arranged confrontation), 248
Szternfeld from the Thirteen, 259
Sztern (secretary general of the Union of Jewish Intellectuals of France), 144, 146–49, 154
Szwajer, Dawid, 259

Tabaksblatt, Eliasz, 93
Tablet Magazine, 14
Tarnów, 95
Tätigkeitsbericht of the IKG, 175
Teichmann, Joseph, 201, 202
Tel Aviv, 304
Tel Aviv District Court, 311, 313, 314, 321, 332, 344
telephone deposition for Ducas case, 150
Temczyn, Stanisław, 266
temporary residence permits, 199, 218
Theresienstadt, 115, 169, 173, 178, 185
Third Reich, 30, 49
Thirteen, a semi-official German agency in the Warsaw ghetto 258, 259
Tigner, Henryk, 259, 264
Tkacz, Beinisz, 40, 60, 231
Tobias, Wilhelm, 69

INDEX

Torgau prison camp, 51
traitors, 87, 88, 140, 155, 198, 249, 308
"Traitors to the Nation—to the People's Court" (Cincinnatus) 83–84
Transcarpathian Ukraine, 93
transit camps, 114, 115, 290; Dossin Mechelen, 214; Westerbork, 114–15, 118, 121, 122, 124
trauma, 292, 294
treason, 328
Treblinka, 32, 36, 75, 333, 336
Tribunal Ruling, 110
Truman, Harry S., 56
Trunk, Elsa, 310–11
Trunk, Isaiah, 9–10; *Judenrat: The Jewish Councils in Eastern Europe Under Nazi Occupation*, 9–10
Tsanin, Mordkhe, 289
TSKŻ (Towarzystwo Społeczno-Kuturalne Żydowskie), 265
Tuchmann, Emil, 18, 166, 167, 168, 174, 179–84, 189; "Jewish Hitler," 182
Tuerk (female witness in Runa Fakler's arranged confrontation), 248
Tune, Zygmunt, 259
Tuszyńska, Agata, 14

UGIF, the General Union of Israelites of France, 139, 140, 144, 146, 147, 149, 151, 152, 153, 154, 155, 156
Ukraine, 187
Ukrainian Insurgent Army, 94
Ukrainian police, 94, 97
Ukrainians, 34, 93
Ullmann, Salomon, 201, 202, 206, 207, 209, 211, 218
Umschlagplatz, 35
underground, 16, 58, 61, 84, 87, 140, 206, 288, 319; archive Oyneg Shabes, 267; courts, 41; ghetto, 67; Jewish, 9, 84, 96, 283; *Jutrznia* (Dawn), 87; *Notre Voix*, 140; political parties, 38; press, 99; Zionist, 66
Unholz, Ferdynand, 256

Union of Jewish Intellectuals of France, 144, 146, 154
Union of Jewish Youth, 158
United States, 73, 168, 170, 171, 172, 174, 176
United Workers Party (Mapam), 308
United Zionist Organization of Germany, 332, 335
Université Libre de Bruxelles, 203
University of Amsterdam, 114, 118–19, 131
University of Massachusetts, 166
unofficial tribunals, 52
Unzer Vort, 197–98
Upper Silesia, 97
Urynowicz, Marcin, 99
U.S. military government, 56
U.S. zone, of Germany, 54, 56
U.S. zonewide congress of liberated Jews, 55
U.S. zonewide survivor congresses, 56

vaccinations, 94
van den Berg, Salomon, 197, 201, 202, 207, 208, 211, 218
vanden Daelen, Veerle, 18, 197–224, 365
van Dijk, Ans, 108–9, 110
van Doorslaer, Rudi, 219
van Dullemen, Arnold Abraham Louis Felix (Nout), 127–28, 130
van Eetvelde, Robby, 219
van Maarseveen, Johan H., 126
van Praag, Roger, 206–9
van Roey, Cardinal Jozef-Ernest, 209
van Tijn-Cohn, Gertrud, 118–19, 127
Vendredi Soir, Jewish weekly, 141
vengeance, 290, 296
Verordnungsblatt, 201
Vichy, 141, 155
Vichy militia, 139, 142
Vichy persecution, 156
Vichy regime, 137, 139, 145
Vichy supporters and collaborators, 140
Victim of Fascism, 51
victims: commemoration of, 86; surrogate, 287; witnesses as, 339

INDEX

Victims of the Nuremberg Laws, 55
Vienna State Police, 166, 167, 169, 173, 180, 181, 184
Vienna Wiesenthal Institute for Holocaust Studies, 219
Viennese: Jewish Community (IKG), 165, 168, 171, 172, 187; Jewish council, 14; Jewish functionaries, 165–96; Jewry, 176; Jews, 166, 168, 173, 185, 186, 188
vigilante justice, 2, 5, 15, 21, 22, 57, 75, 88, 89, 179
Vilna: ghetto, 187; Judenrat, 288. *See also* Vilnius; Wilno.
Vilnius, butcher of (Franz Murer), 187
Visser, Lodewijk E., 114
Voet, Joop, 120
Volkovysk concentration camp, 254, 261
Voûte, Edward John, 126

Waldheim prison camp, 51
Walewski (stated opinion in academic discussion in Warsaw), 102
War Against the Jews, The (Dawidowicz), 10
war crimes, 306, 307, 309, 310–12, 332
war criminals, 304, 305
War of Independence (Israel), 285, 287, 352
Warman (witness in the Chaskiel Szpigelman trial), 266
Warsaw, 32, 87, 90, 99, 101, 203, 206, 247, 250, 253, 331; ghetto, 11, 14, 16, 32, 38, 84, 88, 89, 102, 225, 254, 258; Ghetto Uprising, 88, 100, 141, 284; Jewish council, 91, 99, 100; Jewry, 34; Jews, 33, 35
Warsaw Jewish Committee, 263
Wasserstein, Bernard, 155
Waterlooplein, center of the Jewish quarter in Amsterdam, 127
Weber, Augusta, 255
Weber, Heinz, 258–59
Wehrmacht, 70
Weichert, Michał, 37–39, 88, 89, 234, 254, 255
Weil, André, 147, 153
Weinreb, Friedrich, 108–9, 127, 131
Weishut, Alfred, 173, 175
Weiss, Aharon, 331
Weissensee neighborhood, in Berlin, 61
Weisz, Joseph, 124
Weitzman, Leonore J., 255
Weizmann, Chaim, 123
Wenkart, Hermann, 170
Wenzel (a Gestapo officer), 68
West Berlin, 51
Westerbork transit camp, 114, 115, 118, 121, 122, 124
Western Europe, 2, 86, 112
"Wiesenthal law," 187
Wiesenthal, Simon, 186–89
Wieviorka, Annette, 15, 157
Wilno, 41, 90. *See also* Vilna; Vilnius.
witnesses, 143, 148, 150, 167; in the Eichmann trial, 351, 352; in the Goldstein trial, 348, 351; in the Puczyc trial, 342, 343, 351; as victims, 339
WIZO, Zionist women's charity organization (Women's International Zionist Organization), 147, 170, 171, 247
WKŻK, Jewish Voivodeship Committee in Kraków, 251, 259
Wlodawski, Josef, 73–74
women, 19, 139, 147, 251, 252, 253, 254, 255, 257, 261, 267; changes in traditional women's roles under the influence of wartime conditions, 267; and collaboration through the body, 259, 261, 263; dog attack of, 75; held responsible for the actions of their husbands, 19; "horizontal collaboration," 139; and "ownership" of their bodies, 259; prewar Jewish views of, 19; prewar studies conducted by YIVO, 267, 268; and privileged position among camp prisoners, 251, 256, 268; role of gender, 247–78; sexual abuse of, 19; violence against, 260, 261, 262–68
Women's International Zionist Organization (WIZO), 147, 170, 171, 247

INDEX

Wongrotwitz, 216
Workum, Niko David, 201, 207
World Jewish Congress, 2, 172, 173, 175, 179, 184, 186, 187
World War I, 147, 171, 204, 216
World War II, 30, 83, 93, 137, 138, 147, 154, 155, 185, 197, 198, 199, 225, 281, 282, 320
Worms, René, 150
Wouters, Nico, 18, 197–224, 365; "The Belgian Trials (1944–1951)," 221n39
Wrocław, 96

Yablonka, Hanna, 329
Yavne, Rabbi Gamliel of, 280
Yechezkel, Sahar, 304
yellow Star of David, 115, 125, 200, 206
Yerachmiel Y. (recognized "Blind Max"), 303–4. *See also* Paal, Joseph.
Yiddish, 15, 84, 282, 296, 304, 331; authors, continued to write in, 289; language, 112; press, 289
Yiddish literature, 20, 281, 282, 289, 296; coverage of collaboration with the Nazis limited, 289; morality theme in, 290–96; typical focus in modern, 290
Yishuv (the Jewish community in Palestine), 283
YIVO, the institute for the study of Eastern European Jewry, 267, 288
Yugoslavia, 39

Zagłębie region in Upper Silesia, 313
Zameczkowski, Hersz, 261, 262
Zawierz, 92
Zbaraż ghetto, 256
Zbik, Szmul, 65
Zeitspiegel, 174–75, 176–77
Zekharye Karlsbakh (*Dzshebeliya*), 295
Zentralkomitee (administration in respective camps), 167
Zionism, 113, 116, 236
Zionist: Congress, 43n4; exile organizations, 174; Gordonia, 87; *La Terre retrouvée*, 149; Misrachi organization, 171; underground, 66; union NZB, 116; WIZO (Women's International Zionist Organization), 147, 170, 171, 247; youth movement, 66
ŻOB, Jewish Fighting Organization, 16, 32–38, 41, 84, 87, 88, 90, 99, 100, 102
Zonszajn, Mordechai, 100, 101
Zuckerman, Baruch, 1, 2, 3, 11, 22
Zuckermann, Samuel, 65
Zuckerman, Yitzhak (pseud. Antek), 88–89, 99–100, 102. *See also* Cukierman, Icchak.
Żurawin, Adam, 258
Zürich, 173
Zycher, Dawid, 260–61
Zycher, Fela, 261–63

www.ingramcontent.com/pod-product-compliance
Lightning Source LLC
Chambersburg PA
CBHW051555230426
43668CB00013B/1854